INTRODUCTION TO MANAGEMENT: A CAREER PERSPECTIVE

WILEY SERIES IN MANAGEMENT

INTRODUCTION TO MANAGEMENT: A CAREER PERSPECTIVE

ELMER H. BURACK
University of Illinois, Chicago

NICHOLAS J. MATHYS
DePaul University, Chicago

JOHN WILEY & SONS
NEW YORK · CHICHESTER · BRISBANE · TORONTO · SINGAPORE

Library of Congress Cataloging in Publication Data

Burack, Elmer H.
  Introduction to management.

  (Wiley series in management, ISSN 0271-6046)
  Includes index.
  1. Management—Vocational guidance. I. Mathys,
Nicholas J.   II. Title.   III. Series.
HD38.B7774   1982   658′.0023′73   82-17660
ISBN 0-471-86359-9 (pbk.)

Printed in the United States of America

10 9 8 7 6 5 4 3 2 1

Text design by Sheila Granda. Photo research by Elyse
Rieder. Copy edited by Catherine Caffrey, supervised by
Deborah Herbert. Cover design by Jerry Wilke.
Production supervised by Harold Vaughn.

REFLECTIONS

Much of my life has revolved around the world of management as practitioner, student, and teacher. Learning is a key part of these roles. I've tried to learn well, though not always successfully or fast enough, from family, friends, students, and colleagues.

E. H. B.

My own career has been aided greatly by many friends and colleagues. However, without the loving support of my family, especially Jacqueline, this book might never have been completed.

N. J. M.

ABOUT THE AUTHORS

Elmer H. Burack, Ph.D., A.P.D., is the author of 15 books and numerous articles in the human resource field. He has consulted with many organizations, conducted numerous work-shops in the human resource field, and is a Vice-Chairperson of the Governor's Advisory Council on Employment and Training (Illinois). He also serves on the Board of Personnel Accreditation Institute and has been President or Chairperson of the Human Resource Management Association of Chicago, the Personnel/Human Resource Division and Health Care Administration Division of the Academy of Management, the Illinois Management Training Institute, and the Midwest Human Resource Planning Group. He has consulted with many organizations including Union Pacific Corp.; Banker's Trust (New York); Skidmore, Owens and Merrill; Westinghouse Corp; A.T. & T.; Digital Equipment Corp.; and Evangelical Hospital Association. His books include: *Manpower Planning & Programming* with James Walker, *Personnel Management* with Robert A. Smith, and *Growing: A Woman's Guide for Career Growth* with Maryann Albrecht and Helene Seitler. He is Professor of Management and Management Head of the College of Business Administration, University of Illinois at Chicago Circle.

Nicholas J. Mathys, Ph.D., has established a solid record of client assignments in the human resource field, including studies of job structure, needs analysis, and management development. He has also conducted workshops on human resource planning, supervisory training, career planning, and management development. Dr. Mathys has authored or coauthored many articles on career planning, manpower planning, and career programming. With Dr. Burack, he has written two major books in the human resource management field: *Human Resource Planning* and *Career Management in Organizations*. Dr. Mathys has also consulted with a number of organizations. Active in numerous professional organizations, he is currently Chairman of Management at DePaul University (Chicago).

PREFACE

This book on management has been written especially for students, adult learners, and instructors who are seeking materials that are relevant to the work world and that build useful bridges between learning (school) and work. The distinct career orientation of this book will enable readers to explore the relevance of management to their careers and many of the exciting job possibilities of management. A careful selection of cases, examples, and real-world experiences illustrates management approaches as well as their relation to students' personal and professional lives. A chapter on careers ties together useful ideas on this subject with the various management items discussed throughout the book. More conventional areas of management are covered in such a way as to focus on the essence of task and function, and to illustrate these concepts through the real-life experiences of the writers.

Thus, this writing effort is built around the twin objectives of providing realistic insights into the essentials of the management world in an interesting way, and developing a career theme to assist personal career decisions, professional growth, and everyday living.

What this Book Is Not—Virtually any book must be designed to meet only a modest but useful area of reader needs and "can't be all things to all people." This is very much the case with *Introduction to Management: A Career Perspective*. This is a compact, modest-length book for introductory management courses. It does not provide advanced treatment of the field and, consequently, assumes that the student has had little or no previous contact with the subject area. Extensive footnoting is avoided in favor of developing important ideas in an understandable way. For those interested in related discussions and research, a bibliography is provided at the close of each chapter. Selected subject matter from introductory material in management science, organization behavior, and "introduction to business," is needed to promote the understanding of "management" and is included at appropriate points. However, these topics are themselves major subject areas that can only be treated in a limited way here. In summary, this book focuses on the essential features of management and the areas of knowledge that we view as critical to the understanding of the many roles of management. The chapters emphasize "hands-on" experience in thinking and approach plus an exposure to the many interesting and challenging career opportunities in this field.

Organization of the Book—The organization of this management material represents a resolution of several different philosophies of reader learning. This text *focuses primarily on managers and managing* aside from policymaking and strategic action. We de-emphasize *initially* the very difficult and complex considerations that go along with top management planning. Policy, goals, and planning often are elusive ideas for the management student. Thus, we build toward more complex themes once the basic ideas have been established.

Part One concentrates on the manager's environment. In the first chapter, the lives of well-known historical figures provide a rich mixture of management ideas. In the second and third chapters, respectively, structure and systems are discussed. Structures provide a framework for managerial action and are the key means of fulfilling enterprise policy and strategies. Systems thinking provides an understanding of the interdependence of activities, and the fact that performance is a joint product of human effort *and* technical capabilities.

Part Two presents the basic management functions of planning (Chapter 4), decision making (Chapter 5), organizing (Chapter 6), and controlling (Chapter 7). These chapters emphasize the traditional functions, but in a contemporary framework of models, viewpoints, and approaches.

The behavioral side of management is explored in Part Three. At that point in the discussion, the reader will be able to think meaningfully about topics such as motivation (Chapter 8), leadership (Chapter 9), groups (Chapter 10), and communication (Chapter 11). These concepts have little meaning to the learner (and practitioner as well!) unless the context for utilizing them is understood. Equally important, of course, the concepts themselves must be understood. This result is facilitated if persons can apply them to managerial situations and in their own lives. Numerous application examples and case situations are included.

The thrust of the book's underlying message of creative management and career orientation is found in Part Four. Part Four deals with change (Chapter 12), creativity (Chapter 13), work/work design (Chapter 14), and career planning (Chapter 15). These chapters could start this management book, and some instructors may start off their classes with this subject matter, wishing to emphasize that these topics are really what management is all about. On the other hand, many others may find this organization of material too different from the existing literature.

The Individual in the Organization–The stage on which individual and organization are viewed is reflected in the theme of the book—*career planning*. These elements are found throughout the book, but Chapter 15 presents this theme in a comprehensive way. This discussion is unique for an introductory management book. The book orients the adult learner or class member to the problems and issues he or she will confront at the entry level as well as at more advanced points in his or her career. This textbook is designed to help people take charge of their career by providing the opportunity to think through some important personal and career-related matters. For instance:

1. One should seek compatibility between personal and organizational goals but recognize that if a workable fit cannot be achieved,

alternatives should be actively sought rather than permitting one's life (and career) to stagnate.

2. Many paths are said to exist to the "top" but upward striving is a product of our society. Doing a good job where one is, however, may be equally good or more appropriate at a particular point in one's life.

3. Needed skills can be thought of as highly varied combinations of technical, conceptual, and human relations abilities. Understanding the combinations and expertise needed in a job or occupation relative to one's current skills, abilities, and interests can prove to be a big step forward in individual career planning.

The Life-Space Model—This model is described in detail in the introductory chapter and is used throughout the book. The model provides a way of viewing the world of work and management that emphasizes the central elements with which a manager must contend: the worker as an individual and task group member; the work system/technology; the internal company environment of policy, rewards, staff, and procedures; and the external environment representing legal, social, and technological change. But each of these elements is a dynamic factor in its own right. Thus, the interrelationships and the manner in which the manager coordinates, controls, or mediates these elements is the heart of the managerial function.

Communication plays an essential role in the managerial lifespace, and managers seek to capitalize on its possibilities. It is also the vehicle for integrating the diverse groups, activities, and events comprising the managerial role.

A sketch of the life-space model opens each chapter. The primary thrust of the chapter is reflected in the shading of this life-space model. In addition, every chapter presents a discussion of the relevance of the life-space idea to the chapter's theme.

Acknowledgments—Every book benefits from the contributions, thoughts, ideas, and suggestions of many people, quite aside from the writing of the authors' themselves. We are pleased to acknowledge with thanks the ideas regarding the initial manuscript provided by Professor Thomas Calero, Illinois Institute of Technology. Initial versions of this manuscript also benefited considerably from the work of Charles Burack, Graduate Research Assistant, University of Chicago; Associate Professor William Sukel, DePaul University; Associate Dean F. James Staszak, DePaul University; and Associate Professor Helen LaVan, DePaul University.

Reviewers for the various stages of manuscript development provided numerous and valuable suggestions. We are most grateful for their ideas, presented in a constructive and helpful way. Professors George Otto, Harry S. Truman College, Chicago; David Gray, University of Texas; Ricky Griffin, Texas A & M University; Don Hooper, Jacksonville University; Eugene B. Konecci, University of Texas; Edward Lee, Allegheny County Community College; Mary Lippitt-Nichols, University of Minnesota; Mark. A. McKnew, Clemson University; Richard Randall, Nassau Community College; Charles Strain, Ocean County College; Raymond Vegso, Canisius College; and Fred Weber, Saddleback Community College, served as reviewers. Also, research assistants at the University of Illinois and DePaul University assisted us in compiling the bibliography, glossary, and portions of the instructors manual. We thank Alan Burack, Sveinung Medaas, Lynne Doubleday, Chuck Mathys, and Lynne Sorkin for their efforts.

Rick Leyh of John Wiley performed all of the regular editorial functions and much more. From the beginning, he assumed an active role in guiding manuscript development and also in passing along many useful suggestions. This is a modest "thank you" for his assistance.

Thanks also are due to Pat Balskus, Caren Grillo, and Dianne Cichanski for transforming many scribbled notes into readable form.

Finally, it must be said that although many have helped and contributed in useful ways, as authors, the final responsibility for the book rests with us—and we accept it.

Elmer H. Burack
Nicholas J. Mathys

CONTENTS

INTRODUCTION TO MANAGEMENT: A CAREER PERSPECTIVE

STRUCTURE AND SYSTEMS OF MANAGEMENT

MANAGEMENT: PAST, PRESENT, AND FUTURE

KEY
QUESTIONS
ADDRESSED
IN CHAPTER

1. Why is the study of management necessary?
2. What are the benefits that a grass-roots approach and a top-down approach have when undertaking the study of management?
3. What are the key ideas formulated by different schools of management?
4. What are the current challenges facing modern managers, and the implications for the future?

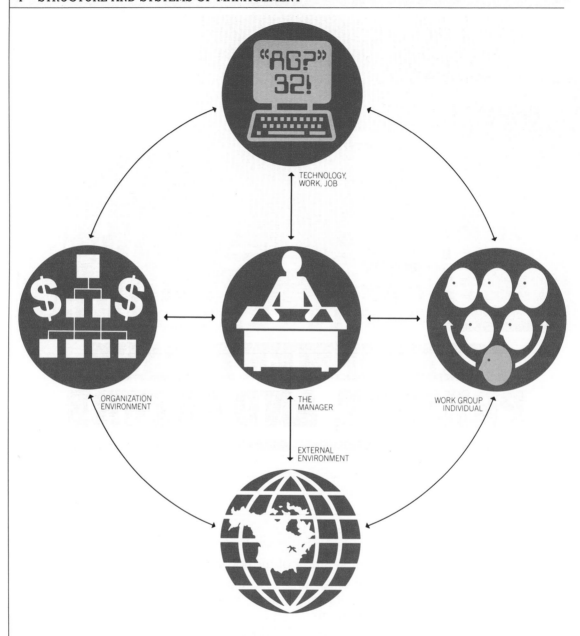

The manager's work-life spaces

The society which scorns excellence in plumbing because it is a humble activity and tolerates shoddiness in philosophy because it is an exalted activity will have neither good plumbing nor good philosophy. Neither its pipes nor its theories will hold water.

John Gardner

THE CHAPTER IN BRIEF

In this introductory chapter we discuss why **managers** are necessary and what they do. We also examine **management** approaches from a historical perspective, look at the lives of a few exemplary "managers" from the past. Finally, we introduce a number of issues and problems facing modern managers. Whenever appropriate, management concepts will be explained to you, the reader, on a personal or career-oriented level. Our hope is that you will gain a solid understanding of management to see its application in your daily life and career. With this in mind we have developed a managerial **life-space model** that will be used as a heading for each chapter.

The Life-Space Model

This book has the purpose of bringing more closely together the *why,* the *what,* and the *how* of managerial processes with the knowledge *and* career requirements of the individual. Managers have a need for systematic thinking and specific approaches to deal with the growing complexity of organization life. This is reflected by a certain managerial style and approach to decision making. Yet what is often neglected is the fact that various managerial concepts and methods may be equally relevant in one's own personal life as well. We have attempted to develop a text that fits many of the day-to-day experiences of the reader—and thus improves your identification with ideas and learning expressed here. The joining of the manager's work space and approaches to that of the individual's **career** and life activities can result in important benefits for both and is one of the central themes of this book.

Another aspect of our philosophy of management expressed in this book has to do with *how* the manager or organization member *views* his or her work space or situation. Of particular interest is how managers deal with and understand the issues or problems that confront them in order to resolve those issues or problems successfully. In our years of teaching and working with managers in consulting assignments and workshops, approaching world-of-work situations in a comprehensive way often proves beneficial. More particularly, what's needed is to view, in a systematic way, many of the key forces, flows, relationships, and elements that make up the manager's envi-

ronment. One approach that helps to bring it all together for purposes of analysis is the use of the life-space model. This model identifies each of the major sectors or components making up the environment (life space) of the manager. Emphasis is placed on the relationships of the manager to those elements in his or her environment that lead to a unified system of managing his or her portion of the work world.

Exhibit 1-1 is a sketch of the life-space model; it features each of the main sectors that the manager must blend artfully. The four sectors shown in the exhibit have the following meaning:

- *Work groups and individuals.* This sector includes the people and groups that the manager must supervise or deal with to fulfill organizational objectives.

- *Work processes, technology, and equipment.* This sector reflects the main work-related purpose(s) of the enterprise (e.g., the assembly line for making automobiles) or those that support the main services (e.g., computers for information processing in an insurance company). This sector largely determines the nature of work within the organization.

- *Organization's (internal) environment.* This sector includes the established objectives, policies, and structural arrangements that have an impact on such things as compensation, career opportunities, degree of responsibility, and other behavioral considerations of concern to organization members.

- *External (to the organization) environment.* This sector includes social, economic, technical, and political forces and trends that can affect the organization and its managers in widely different ways.

The four sectors involved in the life-space model also can (and usually do) affect one another as shown by the arrows in Exhibit 1-1. For example, a change in the external environment such as a worsen-

Exhibit 1-1 The Manager's Work–Life Spaces

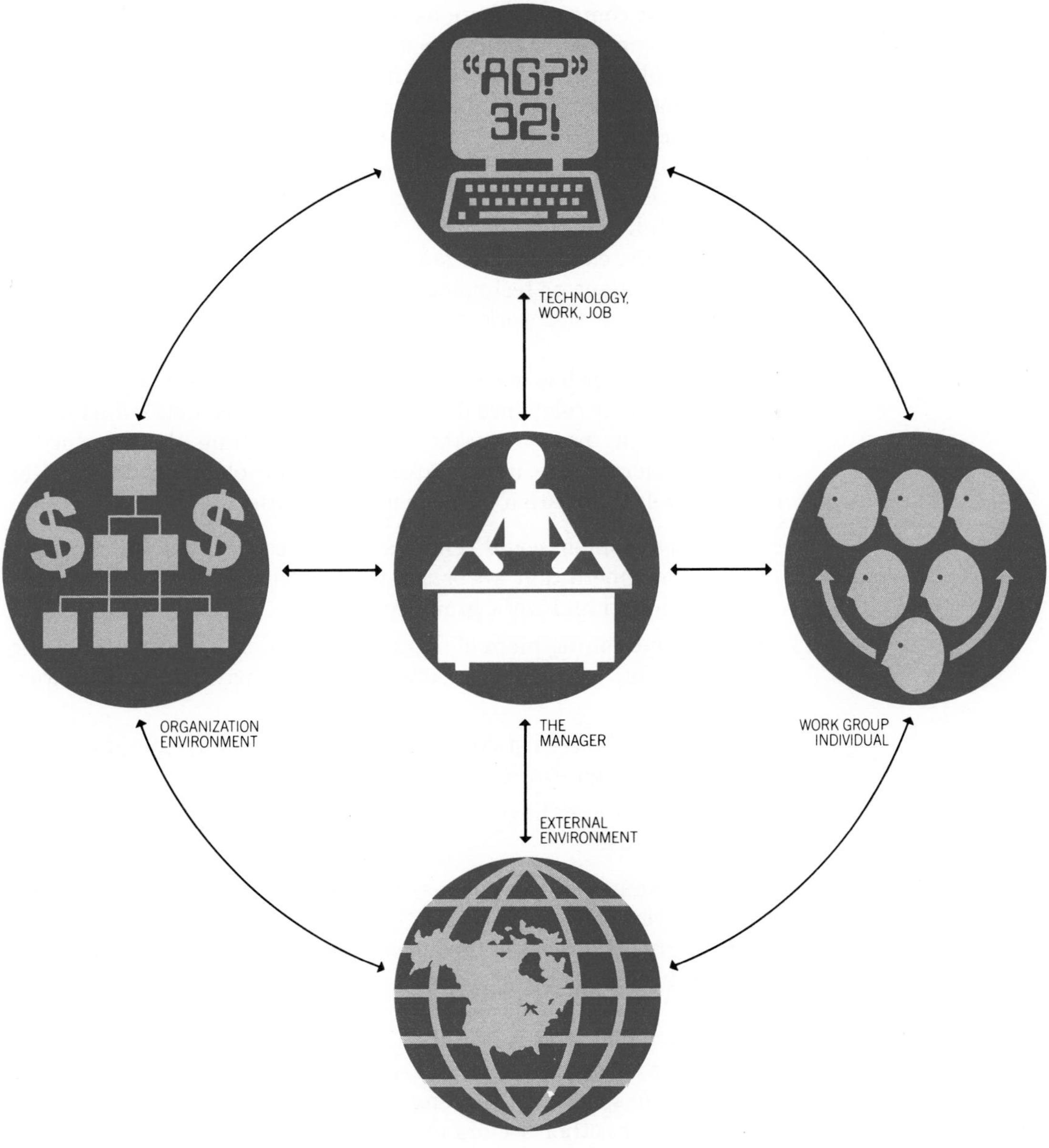
"AG?"
32!
TECHNOLOGY, WORK, JOB
ORGANIZATION ENVIRONMENT
THE MANAGER
WORK GROUP INDIVIDUAL
EXTERNAL ENVIRONMENT

ing economy or competitive pressure on an organization can result in a number of company reactions. Budgets can be tightened, departmental arrangements can be modified, more efficient equipment can be put in place, or employees can be laid off or terminated. All of these impact on individuals and their work groups, who, in turn, might react defensively to planned changes as feelings of uncertainty and insecurity spread among workers. Managers need to realize that these reactions are to be expected and anticipated if approaches are to be successful.

Similarly, changes in organizational policies or the introduction of new equipment or technology can significantly alter the makeup and attitudes of the work groups and individuals whom managers direct.

The manager has to deal with all of these sectors, yet each varies in importance or relevance depending on the situation. For example, a manager may have a worker who is complaining about his or her pay. Considering the interrelatedness of the elements in the life-space model, there are a number of possibilities:

1. The pay problem could reflect a lack of cooperation among work group members that keeps the worker from obtaining his or her quota (individual/work group space).
2. A malfunctioning piece of equipment could be affecting the worker's output, in turn affecting his or her pay (technology/work space).
3. There may be a mistake in wage calculations by the payroll department (organization environment space).
4. Other firms may have increased their wage rates (external environment space).

Of course, managerial problems often are far more complex and may involve several different sectors or life spaces at one time. For the example given, several of the spaces named could easily be involved in the indicated problem.

To help in establishing continuity in the book, each chapter has been headed with a sketch of the life-space model. Various sectors or components of the model have been shaded in to indicate the particular work–life space that is being emphasized. As a situation is dealt with, however, other sectors or components will often become relevant.

Why Is the Study of Management Necessary?

Why is management a necessary component of such activities as constructing a high-rise building, operating a supermarket, running a parking garage, or, as far as that goes, holding church services or

Exhibit 1-2 The Management Hierarchy and Skills Required

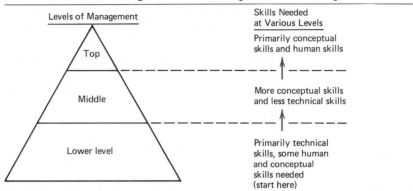

offering health care through a community clinic? One way to pursue an answer to these questions is to observe that in any organization, its employee composition and the circumstances it faces are constantly changing. Organization members come and go. Many may improve and strive to "get ahead," while others lose their desire to advance. Some lose interest in the organization and begin to "coast" or leave. The objectives of the organization are also subject to change. New products or services may be added, and others may be dropped, often in response to changes in the environment such as new government product-safety requirements. All these events require that someone assume the responsibility to monitor the changes and regularly redirect and coordinate the actions of people and other organizational resources. This "someone" is a manager, or, put more generally, management.

Yet managers within an organization vary greatly in the things they do and the skills they need (see Exhibit 1-2). Most readers of this book will be starting at entry-level positions or first-level management positions in organizations. Lower-level managers, in general, need technical and human skills and operate under more constraints than do upper-level managers, who require more conceptual skills and usually rely on their lower-level counterparts to carry out the technical details. Experience and continual life-long learning help to develop the conceptual skills to understand the "big picture" that is essential for managers at the top. The next chapter gives a more detailed discussion of the hierarchical relationships that exist in an organization.

Management in Perspective

Management today is as much a way of thinking about organizational matters as it is a method or process. The central themes have grown from a consideration of two quite different approaches—one considering individual, job, and work elements of an organization and the other dealing with *overall organization* and activities. We have termed these the *grass-roots* and *top-down* approaches, respectively. In about 150 years of study we have come full-circle to the realization that management actions can be understood only if we can appreciate the importance of looking simultaneously in two different directions.

The Grass-Roots Approach   Managers must be able to understand the way in which the use of organizational resources (most especially people) affects the progress of an organization in achieving its goals. The grass-roots approach focuses on the *individual–work group* elements of an organization. Issues such as job satisfaction, work conditions, job efficiency, and employee relations are considered. The **human relations** movement initiated through research at the Hawthorne Works of the Western Electric Company (1925–1933) illustrates the grass-roots approach. This research study at the Western Electric Company is described in later sections.

The Top-Down Approach   Managers must also be able to understand the relationships between organizational activities, as well as how different environmental circumstances affect these activities. The top-down approach provides an organizational focus that deals with the "big picture" of management function, and stresses the *goals, purposes,* and *strategies of the enterprise,* and the organization design required for effective implementation. Work done in the early 1900s by Henri Fayol in France and Max Weber in Germany is representative of the top-down, or big picture, approach. Shortly, we shall discuss these people at length. The major management ideas that emerged from these earlier efforts indicated that superior work performance was achievable only if the individual, job, and job environment were considered jointly. Consequently, designing a job for efficiency in an operational sense requires that the psychological needs of the job holder be given significant weight. Additionally, work performance will be affected by the **"climate"** that a given organization creates through its work rules and the quality of day-to-day relationships. True, both technology and the physical conditions of work, such as lighting and temperature, were always present and even major factors in performance, but the human dimension of work also had to be dealt with to achieve a well-rounded picture.

Effective modern managers integrate the *impersonal* considerations along with the *personal*, within the context of specific situations. As a result, general principles and guidelines about how an organization *should* be managed are further shaped and refined to fit individual and organizational circumstances.

GREAT PERSON PROFILE

Benjamin Franklin (1706–1790)

Benjamin Franklin is known primarily for his accomplishments as a statesman and scientist; however, he was also a successful businessman. Born as the fifteenth child of a Boston candlemaker, he grew up disliking the smell of tallow and chose a career in the printing business. He worked as an apprentice in Boston before, at the age of 17, he went to Philadelphia. Soon, he had his own print shop and became the official printer for the states of Pennsylvania, Delaware, Maryland, and New Jersey—publishing his own periodical. When he sold out at age 42, he was wealthy enough to support his other careers in science, public service, and diplomacy.

Benjamin Franklin epitomizes that successful businesses have positive benefits for society as a whole and that individuals can, and often do, have more than one career. These issues are interspersed throughout this text. He also practiced what he preached—helping many people get started in business. One of his major accomplishments was to explain the nature of management to the American people, communicating in words everyone could understand, such concepts as the relation between time and money, the nature of markets, and the advancement of technology. Franklin's *Poor Richard's Almanack* played an important role in shaping the mind of rural America toward becoming a leader in the world economy.

What Do These Management Ideas Mean in My Life?

All of us are bombarded from infancy about what to expect from parents and other adults, from friends, from school, and from work. Each of us starts to build a picture of what we may want to do for a job or career. We also start to build a set of expectations, or "principles," as to how organizations are put together and run. At times this early picture may be enlarged still further regarding our ideas as to productive ways of making decisions, getting into a line of work, and achieving personal goals. At first we usually think about *only* what *we want* and what we *need*. After some extended period of job seeking or having worked for various employers, the idea grows that an organization's requirements also have to be brought into the picture. This lesson is not learned easily, as some events in the life of Joan Stepanek illustrate.

Joan was born and raised in a suburb of St. Louis. Her father had worked as long as she could remember, and she had the definite impression her family was always struggling financially. True, they bought a new car every few years, and their home was comfortable, but Joan could recall one hassle after another when she asked for things such as new clothing, records, or extra spending money for something special. When she finished high school and enrolled in a community college, her request to have her own car was completely overruled.

After Joan received her certificate of arts degree from school, she began seeking employment and was soon hired as a sales service trainee by the local office of a national insurance company. Her primary goal was to earn enough money, while still living at home, to buy her own car and other things she had always wanted.

Although Joan was usually on time and kept up with her work, her supervisor felt she was taking little or no interest in the business and was not doing the extra things that would make her a successful sales representative. The supervisor had a series of discussions with Joan regarding her performance, the purposes of the training period, and the needs of the organization and its clients. Gradually Joan came to understand that the insurance company was more than a means to her own ends—a car, clothing, and the like. As her supervisor pointed out, "the success of a business today requires far more than the routine approaches of the past, and the efforts of each and every employee counts. . . . Your rewards and ours are very much tied together." Acceptable performance in her current job, as well as her potential for success in the future, clearly will require more than she had been prepared to give when she started to work. Joan had much to think about.

BACKGROUND

Today's management practices have grown out of past trends and events, as well as out of current thought, experience, and research. We examine the development of management practices over three periods of time: (1) the more distant past, (2) the more recent past, and (3) the current scene.

Management in the More Distant Past

Persons acting in managerial capacities are easily found as far back as we have historical records. But the term *manager* itself is of rather recent origin, appearing to gain acceptance in the United States in the middle 1800s. In prior centuries, historical, political, and religious writings made frequent references to "leaders," such as kings, generals, shoguns, holy men, and explorers. These writings often highlighted the leadership qualities and actions of important historical figures. For our purposes, **leading,** taking the initiative in setting objectives, and guiding the efforts of others in their accomplishment are management functions whatever the person may be called. There are other important managerial skills, but four represent an important basic set. They are conceptual, analytical, organizing, and executing. These will be discussed in greater detail shortly.

A word of caution is appropriate here. Although all *successful* leaders must necessarily act as managers, the reverse may not hold true. That is, an individual may gain appointment to a management job but through lack of competence, bad luck, and other circumstances, be unable to exert effective leadership. People who are expected to "follow" refuse to. Leadership ability is of varying degrees of importance in managerial performance, since much depends on the circumstances and the responsibilities assigned to the manager. Great stress may be placed on technical or administrative abilities. (There will be much more to say on this subject in subsequent discussions.)

Great historical events, when closely examined, always reveal the crucial role played by certain individuals acting in managerial (leadership) capacities. The need for managers seems inherent in the nature of momentous events. Thomas Jefferson's role in the Louisiana Purchase and the initiation of the Lewis and Clark expedition illustrates this principle.

Long before he became the third President of the United States, Jefferson had developed a strong need to learn what manner of country and inhabitants were to be found in the vast, uncharted territory that lay West of the Mississippi River, between the Spanish possessions to the South and Southwest, and the British possessions in and near what is now Canada. More particularly, he wanted to learn if there was a "northwest passage," a navigable river or practical overland route, beginning roughly where the city of St. Louis is located today and terminating on the northwest Pacific coast. Jefferson had cast himself in the role of organizer and did not intend actually to go on the expedition.

On three occasions (in 1786, 1792, and 1793) he had tried to organize expeditions, but leaders and plans continually fell through. His chance for success was not to come until he was President, for only then did he have the authority to act on his views.

By early 1803, Jefferson had become convinced that free access to the Mississippi River was crucial in preserving and expanding U.S. water commerce. Later that same year, Jefferson learned that France had forced Spain to cede to the French all Spanish territory from the mouth of the Mississippi all the way to the present state of Montana. Immediately, Jefferson dispatched James Monroe to Paris, where he was to team up with the U.S. ambassador to France, Robert Livingston. Together they were to seek an audience with Napoleon. Unknown to them, Napoleon was planning to go to war with England and was in the proper mood to discuss the purchase of French land by the United States, since he needed a great deal of money to finance the war. Napoleon agreed to a purchase price of $15 million, and, as a result, the geographic area of the United States was approximately doubled.

Jefferson was now in a position to organize the expedition that thus far had eluded him. Early in 1804 he selected Meriwether Lewis, who, in turn, selected his good friend William Clark as co-leader of the expedition. Jefferson was confident that he saw in Lewis all the qualities needed for success in this venture. He put Lewis in charge of planning the details of the mission while Jefferson himself laid out the master plan that was to guide the efforts of all participants and secure the desired results. The plan called for study and record keeping on soil conditions, rivers, mountains, and products and resources of all descriptions. It also called for investigating the nature, number, and customs of inhabitants, and above all, discovering if there was a northwest passage. The expedition succeeded gloriously in every respect *other* than finding such a passage, since none exists.

There are several features of this brief excerpt from Jefferson's life that are of interest from a management standpoint. First was his ability to *conceptualize* or understand an important situation, in this case the economic possibilities for his country's development. Second was his *analysis*, a search for information, as well as the thinking time Jefferson devoted to planning his actions. A third step was *organization*, as Jefferson started to assemble the people and resources needed to develop more information and to carry out specific projects. Finally, there was *execution* of the plan, the arrangement of the land purchase through Monroe and Livingston, and the later expedition of Lewis and Clark. Especially noteworthy in the exploration plan followed by Lewis and Clark was the systematic organization of information regarding all manner of land conditions, natural resources, and native civilizations. It is true that the "bottom line" for the outcome of the expedition and its specific short-term objective was a "loss," but its longer term results have proved of incalculable value.

Management in the More Recent Past

By the late 1800s, systematic application of management functions was due in large part to the **Industrial Revolution,** which was taking place in England, Germany, the United States, and elsewhere.

These actions had the main intent of improving profitability, through increasing efficiency and reducing costs. Consensus was growing as to what management meant, namely, that it denoted both a set of functions as well as the people and other resources needed to carry them out. Most often the functions started to assume certain characteristic activities: setting organizational objectives and incorporating these objectives into specific plans; allocating resources (people, money, land, equipment, etc.) required for execution of plans; monitoring and guiding activities; and redirecting the use of resources whenever necessary. By the late 1800s, management approaches were well established in many railroads, large industrial units, the U.S. army, and other agencies of government.

Let's consider the management career of one remarkable figure in our industrial history, Henry Ford. The story of his life illustrates the growing maturity of management practices and the specific actions of one man, and their consequences, both positive and negative.

Ford's lifetime (1863–1947) witnessed the growth of industry in the United States from its childhood to maturity. As a young man, Ford watched the growth of huge corporations like that of Andrew Carnegie in steel and John D. Rockefeller in oil, as well as the overall development of the U.S. economy. During Ford's youth on a farm near Dearborn, Michigan he became a chronic tinkerer with machinery and showed an enduring curiosity about all things mechanical. In his teens he left the farm to explore the industrial world of Detroit.

By the early 1890s he was experimenting with a "horseless carriage" and produced an operational model in 1896. His was by no means the first, since a number of others had been previously produced by Europeans and Americans alike, but his model was the lightest in weight. People who have studied Ford's career speculate that he was already thinking of a vehicle that could be priced within the means of the average consumer. By 1903 Ford managed to acquire funds sufficient to form the Ford Motor Company.

It is difficult to fully appreciate the technical difficulties and economic challenges that Ford faced in his new automobile venture. At the time, he was only one among literally hundreds of others who were trying to make a go of it in the auto business. At first the autos Ford produced were indistinguishable from those of many other manufacturers, yet within six years his firm was among the industry leaders.

How did this come about? The initial ingredient appears to have been the topnotch group of engineers, production, and financial specialists that Ford brought into his firm. Although he customarily made all final decisions, he drew freely on the talents of his staff and encouraged maximum involvement in the functions of the enterprise. It became apparent to Ford and his associates that their *goal* of producing an auto for a mass market at a modest price required heavy investment in production technology, tooling, and related capital. And this investment would have to be made *before* it was known if the product might strike the public fancy. Ford decided to take the financial plunge. The eventual result was a car and concept incorporating the best design technology and methods of the day including the moving assembly line. Virtually all of the design features of the car were standardized. With respect to precision, synchronization, and the degree of labor specialization, Ford's automobile far surpassed other applications of **mass-production** assembly that then existed.

The famous Ford Model T was introduced in 1909. When its production was finally halted in 1927, more than 15 million had been built. Its success had several explanations; the most basic was probably that the American public had developed a real craving and need for automobiles as both population and markets expanded. Ford appealed to these desires by making the Model T very durable, easy to operate, and economical to buy and maintain. It was a formula that worked superbly for many years. By the early 1920s Ford had captured 60 percent of U.S. motor vehicle output. His policy of *lowering* the *selling* price of the Model T each time production efficiencies were achieved was certainly another key factor in his reaching such a commanding position in the industry.

Advertisement pointing out the virtues of the Ford Model T.

Ford was also outstanding in other respects. He gave the country a new concept of the industrial worker, namely, that the worker was also a *consumer* and should be paid the highest possible wages. Ford was substantially ahead of his time when he introduced the $5 a day pay level for eight hours work, at a time when the standard work day was ten hours or more and the daily pay only a few dollars.

Managerial careers are not always success stories in every respect, and Ford's history illustrates this point, too. Ford failed to recognize that his single minded commitment to one idea—the mass-produced, cheap, *unchanging* Model T—would in the longer run be his downfall. Some skeptics point out that production economies and the reduction of selling price also carried a hidden cost to consumers, namely, little or no choice in car features and options. This situation was certainly a far cry from the wide variety of models and options available to purchasers today. By the early 1920s, the American consumer had become more affluent and was more willing to pay a higher price for a better automobile. Ford remained unresponsive to change until he lost his lead to General Motors, which had been masterfully reorganized by Alfred P. Sloan, Jr. Ford brought out the Model A in 1929, but it was too late. The Model A surged in sales for a few months, but then dropped back, permanently, behind General Motors. Of course, the general economic depression, which had already begun to settle in, definitely affected this outcome. However, Ford's loss in product and market momentum to General Motors was an undeniable fact.

Aside from his refusal to acknowledge that the concepts behind the Model T were no longer valid, Ford contributed to his problems by attempting to run a "one man show" almost to the day of his death. In the early days of the Ford organization, when the number of people involved was relatively small and the company situation rather simple, it was practical and effective for one man to make all the important decisions. But by the time Ford Motor had become a massive enterprise, it was entirely unrealistic and downright harmful. One by one Ford's key subordinates became disgruntled and departed for more congenial employers. Control over the ailing Ford Motor Company eventually passed to his grandson Henry Ford II a few years before Ford's death in 1947.

What in summary may be said about Henry Ford? First, he was largely self-taught, which was by no means unique in his day, with respect to his engineering and financial skills, as well as to the management pattern he adopted within his firm. Next, he made a career commitment at an early age. He knew what he wanted to do and possessed the intelligence, boldness, and tenacity to take the actions that led to his spectacular rise. By using highly qualified engineers and specialists and employing the mass production technology to build efficient, low-cost automobiles, he was able to dominate the automobile industry for almost 20 years. He also established more reasonable work hours and compensation for his workers. Later, however, it became evident that Ford lacked other qualities critical to long-term success in management: a willingness to develop the skills of those about him, to share responsibility, and to question the current soundness of past practices, as well as the flexibility to change or move in different directions as circumstances shifted.

Recent Management Developments

Management Science

Management science, which developed mainly out of the military experiences of World War II, combines systematic approaches and quantitative methods to improve organization and system performance and to produce better economic decisions. It uses mathematics, statistics, models, and computers to define, analyze, and solve problems.

Management science has been used in a wide range of situations, in companies and industries, and in tackling all kinds of problems. A few examples of the types of problems handled by management science follow.

1. Determining the most economical combination of ingredients, given an economic objective and various material and resource costs.
2. Reducing the distance traveled by sales people, given what is to be accomplished, the effectiveness of the sales people, and the costs of their time and transportation.
3. Determining how many people to hire, given turnover and retirement rates and customary promotion paths.
4. Establishing industrial research designs to analyze quality problems.

All of these examples represent ways in which management science can improve managerial planning, analysis, problem solving, and decision making.

Management science has a number of career-related implications; an obvious application is for people who are management scientists and who work with managers. Most management scientists have at least a bachelor's degree from a four-year college, and many often have a master's degree or even a Ph.D. Programs that prepare one for management science concentrate on mathematics, statistics, and systems and computer usage. However, there are related fields in which management techniques are used but that do not require such intensive preparation. One such field is **production or operations management,** which has been a growing area for jobs. This field uses

Keeping the manager's "tool-bag" up-to-date is a life-long process.

management science techniques in dealing with inventory, scheduling, and planning problems. Operations management can be found in use in production plants, warehouses, distribution and transportation facilities, and even in banks, airlines, and other service industries. All of these application areas require people who know some of the basics of management science, yet even the nontechnical manager needs to have a basic understanding of the potential applications of management science.

Situational Analysis–Contingency Approaches

Modern approaches to management such as those in operations represent an important direction for managerial thinking and analysis, since they recognize that managers must deal with widely varying situations. **Situational analysis** and other **contingency approaches** acknowledge that many models, techniques, and theories have emerged, but that not all of these are equally suited for particular situations.

These situation-oriented approaches require that managers have a broad base of knowledge. Managers must be equipped with a variety of techniques, theories, and available assumptions, and they must know the uses, advantages, and limitations of each. This equipment makes up the managerial "tool bag," that managers must use in dealing with particular problems and situations. It takes broad knowledge and a wide range of experience to understand what combination of "managerial tools" to utilize in a particular circumstance. In order to know what tools to use the manager must first be able to carefully define the situation. He or she has to identify the individual needs involved and to analyze other situational factors that come into play. Once the situation has been clearly defined, the manager can explore possible solutions to the problem. Situational analysis and other contingency approaches enable the manager to examine a particular situation to discover which combination of management techniques, theories, and assumptions to test out in attempting to solve a problem.

FORMALIZING MANAGEMENT ANALYSES AND APPROACHES

Management Thinking

The predecessors of the current field of management thought include such a significant set of contributions that it is essential to cover them briefly here. The history of management "thinking" differs from general social or political history in that it concerns the action guidelines, rules of thumb, unique insights, and decision-making patterns that certain practicing managers employed or were encouraged to employ, by management analysts.

The intellectual history of modern management is quite short compared to social and political histories. Management books or related documents that are still significant today date back only to the early 1900s. However it must be acknowledged that in Europe, particularly England, some general descriptions go back to the late 1200s! Moreover, it was not until the late 1800's that formal courses in management were added to the curricula of a few colleges. Then almost 40 more years went by before college-level programs in management became widely available. In the sections that follow four types of management thought or "schools" are discussed as necessary background for and inputs to modern management developments. The four schools are: (1) **scientific management,** (2) **human relations,** (3) **administrative management,** and (4) **bureaucracy.** The first two schools use a grass-roots approach, and the others use a top-down approach.

Two Grass-Roots Approaches

Scientific Management   The type of management thought represented by *scientific management* was the brainchild of Frederick W. Taylor (born in Germantown, Pennsylvania in 1856). A gifted student, Taylor earned a mechanical engineering degree through self-study, went to work in a steel mill, and rose to the position of chief engineer at the age of 28. A few years later, he became general manager of a group of paper mills. Then, at the age of 37, he set himself up as a consulting engineer in New York City. He was also a very successful inventor of cutting tools, milling machines, and hydraulic equipment.

Rather early in his management career Taylor became convinced that two major problems plagued American industry: (1) inefficiency of the great majority of managers at all levels and (2) "systematic soldiering," that is, holding back on work effort of the average employee. Taylor embarked on what might be termed a self-styled crusade to eliminate both problems, and scientific management was born.

Frederick Taylor
(1856–1915)

The essence of Taylor's approach was the creation of a highly efficient work environment in which the roles of manager and worker and the content of each job were to be completely clarified. Each job or task cluster was rigorously analyzed in order to redesign it into its most efficient form, an approach that is typically called **job analysis** today. The persistent question was: What is the best way for the *worker* to perform this job? Also there was the equally important question: How can one plan for, organize, and supervise work activities to achieve high-level performance? Taylor was committed to the idea that management can become a true science, based on clearly defined laws, rules, and principles that are applicable to *all* forms of work activity. In actual practice, Taylor concentrated on common types of manual labor, but he also dealt with supervision, plant organization, planning, scheduling, employee training, and incentive compensation.

Taylor advocated the following steps in the implementation of his approach. First, management must see to it that each basic job is studied in sufficient detail that the *best way* to perform each job is identified. Next comes the *scientific selection* and systematic training of workers in the best way to do the job. Taylor helped to develop certain employee selection tests, for example, one that measured the perceptual skills of quality control inspectors. Once good "fits" had been accomplished between worker and job, scientific management required the establishment of performance standards for each job, that is, a specific level of work output that man and machine should be capable of performing without undue fatigue and under safe operating conditions. Taylor was often openly critical of managers who ignored what constituted a "fair day's work" in their companies. Finally, employees must be paid on the basis of incentive wages: that is, a basic payment for the accomplishment of a standard, but extra compensation for various levels of output beyond the standard (basic payment), up to 60 percent in some cases. The incentive wage played a very special part in this picture. It provided a financial reward beyond what most workers were earning, and it promised something that management valued, increased output and efficiency. Worker–management cooperation was the key.

Taylor's ideas were remarkable for their understanding of industrial engineering science. They included the detailed study and design of work, personnel practices highly unusual in his day, a theory of motivation based on a belief that workers will strive to improve output if offered incentives to do so, and an elaboration of the role of management in making all parts of this system function together. Managers were urged to exert themselves in the continual expansion of job studies, the planning of work schedules, the assigning and reassessing of employees depending on shifts in work loads, the performance of cost analyses, and the keeping of work records.

What have we learned from Taylor's experiences? It is difficult to summarize a career that touched so many lives and whose effects are still so evident today. Scientific management brought a new appreciation of the central importance of well-designed systems of work as a common link between the employee and the employer. The realization of efficient performance requires that the needs of both parties be satisfied in a cooperative environment. For this reason, engineering the work system for good results had to be matched by engineering the management system in an appropriate fashion. For its day, scientific management represented a high point in the application of management analyses and practices. Many of them are used today in factories, offices, hospitals, supermarkets, and fast-food businesses such as McDonald's. Not surprisingly, some of Taylor's ideas are inappropriate today, since social circumstances have changed. For example, there may well be several best ways to perform many jobs, and although money is still very significant as a satisfier of individual needs, it is by no means the only thing that employees expect to get out of their work today.

As a final note, Peter Drucker (1977), a major figure in management practice, sums up Taylor's lasting contribution by saying, "Taylor was the first man in history who did not take work for granted but looked at it and studied it. His approach to work, and his logic of efficiency, is still the basic foundation" for work design and improvement.

Human Relations   The second grass-roots approach to understanding work, workers, and the dynamics of behavior in organizations is most often called the *human relations movement*. The human relations movement grew out of the most significant and pioneering research study of employee job behavior conducted in the United States. The research site was the Hawthorne Works of the Western Electric Company in Chicago, Illinois.

Western Electric is the manufacturing and supply arm of Bell Telephone Systems, and Hawthorne Works is one of a number of production facilities that make up Western Electric. The research that is briefly described here (and discussed in detail in Chapter 10) included the puzzling results obtained by several Western Electric engineers in analyses they made in 1925 and 1926. The engineers were testing the effects of varying intensities of illumination on employee productivity in the hope of supporting scientific management principles. The puzzle was that with a number of different light settings, bright or dim, productivity frequently improved when the lighting was changed. The plant researchers finally concluded that the workers were responding the way they thought the researchers wanted them to respond, namely, by improving their output whatever the illumination level.

It further occurred to the research team that if a small group of employees was assigned to a physically isolated test room and was observed over a long period of time, the psychological factor that had thrown the illumination study into confusion would disappear. At this point, in 1927, the Hawthorne research group sparked the interest of several faculty members at Harvard University, who began giving advice and taking an active part in future studies. The best known of the Harvard people were Elton Mayo and Fritz Roethlisberger.

As the research team improved working conditions, and with the active cooperation of the women in the group, production in general went steadily up. Then when the original working conditions were reinstated, production *still went up!* There were also numerous other experiments conducted over a number of years.

The major conclusions drawn by the researchers from these Hawthorne studies suggested strongly that production was affected not only by a worker's ability or the working conditions (lighting, pay, etc.) but also by the work group itself and various social and psychological rewards.

It should be stressed that these conclusions were drafted about 40 years ago. They should not be regarded as the "last word" on all the topics covered. Still, there is much of enduring value that can be traced to the Hawthorne research. Applications of the Hawthorne conclusions will come up elsewhere in this book, especially in Chapter 10.

Career Value   Of what use to people in industry is an understanding of the two grass-roots approaches just presented, that of scientific management and of human relations? Do they contribute to improving a work situation in which we are currently involved? The answer is "yes," if, like Frederick Taylor, we don't take the job for granted but assume that it can be improved and regard it as an object for our creativity.

Scientific management, as developed by Frederick Taylor, centers on the systematic analysis and understanding of individual jobs. A person who is familiar with the various methods for job analysis is better able to determine, in advance, what types of skills, attitudes, and abilities a particular job requires and how to best use one's own talents in a work context. In addition, the individual is now better equipped to restructure his or her given job to create maximal job efficiency and satisfaction.

The career values stemming from human relations center on the importance of informal, social behavior among members of a work group and the social learning new members need to accomplish. This learning involves matters such as behavioral norms, namely, what is "in" and what is "out" with respect to interpersonal dealings, to pace and amount of work, to relations with the supervisor, and to other related matters. Human relations is also helpful to understand the effects of management-initiated changes on employee attitudes and behavior, enabling the individual to understand change within a larger context and to gauge his or her reaction according to this widened perspective.

Two Top-Down Approaches

Administrative Management and Henri Fayol In this section and the next we examine a point of view that both contrasts with and complements the views of scientific management and human relations. Instead of concentrating upon the grass-roots analysis, that is, employee behavior and organizations from the bottom up, the approach here and in the following section is *top down*, and centers on the concerns, duties, and responsibilities of the head of an organization.

This top-down viewpoint is important in the general study of management for completing the background sketch of where it has been and where it is today. Yet there is a second important reason for considering top-level administration; this level is involved in actions and decisions that affect all of us as members of an organization, be it a school, government agency, or business organization. Simply put, powerful and influential forces exist within organizations beyond any one individual's work sphere that can reinforce, cancel out, or otherwise affect how we respond to work. Thus the managerial perspective requires both the administrative top-down and the job-level grass-roots approach to achieve a balanced understanding.

Henri Fayol (1949) is generally credited today with the formulation of the body of thought usually called **administrative management.** He is also among the first to have developed a rational approach to the design and operation of an enterprise.

Fayol was born in France (in 1841) and graduated as a mining engineer at the age of 19. He went immediately to work for a large French mining and metallurgical firm, and within six years had become manager of a group of mines. Six years later, when he was only 31, Fayol was appointed general manager of the organization. He would ultimately become the managing director, a position usually referred to as chairman of the board in the United States, and he remained in that position until his retirement in 1918.

As we would say today, Fayol was a "man of many bags." He was a prominent mining engineer, who did research and published important findings. He was a management innovator, credited with putting organization structures on paper by drafting organization charts and with developing *written* descriptions of job contents and employee requirements. He had a genius for leadership and late in life became a successful author and the recipient of both scholarly and government awards. He was also a pioneer of the view that management can and should be formally taught, a rather radical idea when he first expressed it in 1907.

Fayol's formulation of administrative management is notable for its emphasis on the proper use of management authority and the *universality* of the *functions* of managers, especially planning, organizing, and controlling; the formulation of action guidelines for managers; and the design of organizational structures.

Fayol placed heavy stress upon the *setting* of *organizational objectives*. He said that managers cannot make the best decision among alternatives unless objectives are clear. Once they are clarified, plans can be drawn for their accomplishment. He defined *planning* as determining, in advance of taking any action, what factors will be required to reach the objectives and what the relationships among them should be, which he termed *organizing*. Once an organized set of activities has been set in motion, Fayol urged managers to establish *controls*—for example, records, inspections, and surveillance by supervisors—so that work activities go forward in conformity with plans.

Fayol is best known for formulation of action guidelines for use by practicing managers, many of which are still used today. He labeled these action guides, "principles" and believed that managers who correctly applied them would likely be successful. These principles are discussed in detail in the following chapter.

Thus in a good organization, overall objectives must be clearly established first. Then and only then can these objectives be passed down from the top to establish plans at lower levels in the organization. In this way even the lowest-level supervisor will have an understanding of organizational objectives and how his or her own tasks are related to the fulfillment of these goals.

Bureaucracy   At the time that Henri Fayol was distilling his experience as a manager and putting it into writing, a scholar of enormous talent and scope was independently pursuing certain intellectual challenges complementary to those of Fayol. This scholar, Max Weber, was born in Germany in 1864 and was educated at the universities of Heidelberg and Berlin. Unlike Frederick Taylor and Fayol, Weber had very little experience working in organizations as a manager. His forte was scholarly research and teaching. Although Weber traveled rather widely during his lifetime, his research into organizations appears heavily focused on those of his native Germany, most particularly German governmental and military organizations.

Of the wide range of intellectual contributions Weber made to economics, political science, the sociology of religion, and the sociology of law, our central interest is his contributions to the analysis of organization structures, functions, and staffing—**bureaucracy** and *bureaucrats*, in today's common parlance. Weber's research in organizations led him to formulate the *bureaucratic model,* a term that at that time suggested an idealized model of how organizations should be organized and operated. Basic characteristics of this "ideal" organization included specialization of function, a hierarchy of authority, a system of rules and regulations, good work attitudes on the part of employees, and the treatment of employees in an "even-handed," but impersonal, way. Weber considered *rationality* to be the most important feature of a bureaucracy. It was the governing principle for organizational design and employee treatment. A rationally governed organization, he thought, had the potential for greatest efficiency.

Career Value   In what ways are the top-down views just presented relevant to career planning and enhanced career progress? Fayol's belief that management can be taught and learned is clearly still of value. His position strongly counters that argument that "leaders are born, not made." Furthermore, administrative management provides a general understanding of how people who design organizations think, what they do, and what action guidelines they can apply. We gain an appreciation of the types of issues and decisions that face our superiors and thus can see their actions in perspective, including their relationship to us.

Weber's mode of thought is valuable since it recommends that career-minded members of organizations ask questions such as: Why is this activity of the organization here? What does it do that is necessary? Why is this policy or work rule in effect? Why are things done this way? In studying the bureaucratic model in more detail in the next chapter, we see better how we fit into the organizational structure, how the decisions of others affect us, and why certain decisions are made.

Learning about bureaucracy also shows us that there is nothing intrinsically negative about it. However, since so many people have had bad experiences being part of or dealing with bureaucracies, we should be forewarned about what can go wrong in coping with any large organization; the individual may feel virtually helpless and alienated, for example.

We should start to visualize the management of needed activities within an organization to better cope with the human dimension and to reduce the sense of impersonality.

CONTEMPORARY MANAGEMENT ISSUES AND PROBLEMS

Management on the Current Scene

Virtually all of the major management concepts, ideas, and guidelines that we have just reviewed in relation to management thinking are still important to managers today. The continued significance of scientific management has already been mentioned, particularly its present applications in various work-study and engineering fields including the design of work systems. Fayol's principles, although they hardly provide today's managers with serviceable guidelines for a great many occasions, are nonetheless still respected. Max Weber's assertion that "the development of the bureaucratic organization is the most crucial phenomenon of the modern Western state" now has vastly expanded significance in that this organizational model characterizes the government and corporate structures of every major world power. His observation is also evidenced in many other components of every developed economy. The lessons growing out of the Hawthorne research, although they often need to be modified to be applied in particular situations, nonetheless have given the "human factor" and work group a central and permanent place in modern managerial practices.

Today's managers could never survive if they simply tried to make do with past events and developments. They face demands, issues, and challenges that are simply at a far higher level of complexity than ever before.

The Organization's External Environment

Some of the most important demands on modern managers arise in the environments *outside* their organizations. These demands influence what managers do *inside* their organizations. For example, this is true with respect to:

- The implementation of *equal employment opportunity,* as required by law.
- Increased competition due to deregulation, technological innovations, or changes in international trade.
- Coping with legal restraints regarding pollution of the physical environment (water, air, soil, noise, etc.).
- Consumer protection demands on the part of organized groups representing a range of consumer interests such as product safety, truth in advertising, and fair pricing.

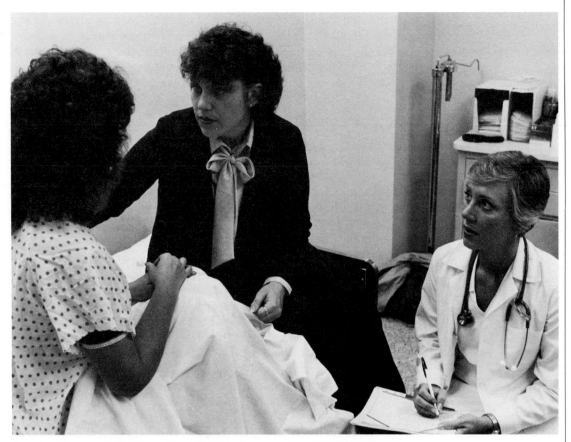

An inventory control clerk from Xerox Corporation organizes the office and serves as a part-time counselor for Rape Victim's Advocates for six months as part of the company's social responsibility commitment.

- The "Washington Watch," that is, pressures to keep on the lookout for new legal requirements coming out of the capitol.
- The conduct of business in a host of foreign countries and the complex demands growing out of government attitudes toward "outsiders," finance and taxing policies, type of business activities permitted, and many similarly complicated matters.

A somewhat new theme runs through nearly all these current concerns—the **social responsibility** of management. This theme arises from the pressures being placed on the managers of U.S. organizations, and to some extent, managers in other countries, to be less self-seeking and less committed to purely organizational objectives. Instead, they should develop a social conscience and put the organization's talent and some of its money to use in such projects as pollution control, the improvement of neighborhood facilities and the quality of education, training programs for the culturally disadvantaged, and the development of minority-operated enterprises, to name a few. Responsible company actions and good community relations can make good business (economic) sense.

Developments within the Organization

Other significant developments calling for effective managerial responses stem largely from sources *internal* to organizations. Sheer growth in organizational *size* in itself is a serious management challenge. Let us take a look at Holiday Inns, Inc., as an example.

Since the opening of the first Holiday Inn hotel at Memphis, Tennessee in 1952, the number of hotels bearing this name has grown to over 1750 in 58 countries throughout the world. How does management keep track of the hundreds of separate operations spread all over the world? One way is by entering into franchise agreements with individuals or groups who then build and operate one or more Holiday Inns more or less independently. By "more or less" we mean that each franchise holder is expected to operate each inn using a manual of standards developed by Holiday Inn headquarters. This manual is intended to help achieve a similarity of conduct at all inns and to maintain a consistent quality of service among Holiday Inn employees. Quality standards are monitored through regular, unannounced on-site inspections of more than 1000 items from linen quality to front desk hospitality.

Another method that the Holiday Inn headquarters management uses to facilitate service, leadership, and control is a communications network that has been described "as second only to that of the U.S. Department of Defense." Important information is readily communicated and operations of an inn can be improved through the use of the Operations Management System that helps control inventories and product quality. Good communications also means careful training of people; Holiday Inn's own training center plus on-site training at inns help to assure uniformity of services provided.

Let us look at W. R. Grace & Company as another example. Here size is even more significant than in the case of Holiday Inns, and there is the added factor of great *complexity*.

W. R. Grace is a *conglomerate* organization. It is not simply involved in one type of business or even in a few types. It is involved in many kinds of businesses. Further, the various kinds of businesses bear little or no relation to one another, with respect to the products or services they provide. All this adds up to a very high degree of organizational complexity and presents management with a host of challenges.

During the 33 years in which J. Peter Grace, Jr. has been the

Typical front desk hospitality at a Holiday Inn hotel.

chief executive of the company, the organization has been completely transformed. Every business unit that was part of W. R. Grace in 1945 has been closed or sold. Gone are the sugar plantations in Peru and textile mills in Bolivia and Chile. Gone also is the Grace Line, once a leading fleet of luxury ocean liners and Grace's most public symbol. Since 1945, W. R. Grace has purchased about 130 businesses and sold about 60. The buying and selling reflects the continual search by top management for the most effective and profitable "mix" of businesses, a search for which there is no standard operating procedure.

W. R. Grace's complex makeup can be best understood by regarding it as consisting of five major *groups* of businesses. These groups are listed below, along with an illustration or two of each:

- Agricultural chemicals (e.g., fertilizers).
- Specialty chemicals (e.g., sealing compounds).
- Natural resources (oil and natural gas wells, coal mines).

- Restaurants and stores (restaurant chains such as El Torito–La Fiesta, Pix of America shoe stores, Herman's World of Sporting Goods).
- Other consumer products (e.g., auto parts manufacturers).

It is natural to ask at this point: Why would W. R. Grace's top management deliberately create such a large, complex, and potentially unmanageable enterprise? Business diversity and size appear to have been the goals of management, in the belief that increases in size and business derived profitability go together if the right combination of businesses can be achieved. Management also appears to believe that with size comes another sought for goal, corporate security; that is, size (and diversity) reduces economic vulnerability, particularly if the organization has not "put all its eggs in one basket." To put the matter positively, the presence of W. R. Grace in various businesses with different levels and patterns of competition and risk helps to reduce its overall economic vulnerability.

A related question is: How does W. R. Grace top management keep on top of this diverse organization? A complete answer would require a great deal of research, so for present purposes we simply note the major roles played by:

- Energetic, forceful, and seasoned top leadership, including the appointment of a senior executive to manage each of the five major groups of businesses that comprise the overall organization.
- A sophisticated communications and information-processing system, which makes possible a constant flow of needed management information to company headquarters in New York City, as well as between separate units of the organization.

Other Challenges Facing Today's Managers

The examples of Holiday Inns, Inc., and of W. R. Grace & Company have illustrated the interplay between management actions and the economic goals of the firm, where large size and complexity pose specific management challenges. Major as these challenges are to Holiday Inn, to W. R. Grace, and to thousands of other similar organizations, there are still other management challenges that should be part of this discussion.

Changing employee expectations with respect to *fair and equitable treatment* is one challenge that takes many specific forms. One change is that many employees want a greater sense of participation in organizational decisions, especially those affecting their careers or opportunities. Also, many employees believe they should be paid for certain activities that in the past were done with no expectation of additional pay—for instance, training a new employee or filling in for a supervisor who is on vacation. Another change is that of government employees who want, or have acquired, the right to unionize and to strike, if they regard this as necessary. There are also major changes affecting hours, working conditions, shared work, permanent part-time employment, and so forth. Management must learn to cope with all of these elements of change.

Of equal importance in the work scene is the *changing character of managers*. At one time, the management field was regarded as a man's world and a "white" man's world at that, at least in the United States. Women, Blacks, and Latins are now becoming managers. The incorporation of women and racial minorities into management is a major and radical change. It is ongoing and likely to continue for many years to come. In 1980, women comprised some 50 percent of the overall work force. Ten years earlier, this figure was only about 40 percent. This change is truly dramatic and suggestive of changes taking place in the United States, Canada, England, and many other countries.

The **quality of life** theme is another development of managerial interest. It has been imported into the workplace, where it has become the theme, quality of *working* life. This theme reflects changing employee expectations regarding the quality of physical conditions of work, but even more to the point is the growth of elevated expectations about the nature of work itself. More and more employees expect their work to be worthwhile and interesting and to challenge their abilities. The growing push to redesign work in these directions stems, in part, from the changing composition of the work force and the decline of the work ethic in the United States. The fastest growing segment of the U.S. work force in the past decade has been *professional and technical* worker, although this segment is still a minority of the overall work force. Typically, professional and technical employees are well educated and view themselves as "underemployed," that is, as having their skills wasted if the work they perform does not call for the full exercise of their capabilities. Expectations like these are infectious; they can easily spread throughout employee ranks in an organization and severely strain management's problem-solving abilities.

Finally, attention needs to be paid to the complex challenge posed by ever-growing *foreign competition,* particularly in product markets. Certain industries, such as shoes and other apparel, automobiles, electronics (radios, televisions, calculators, etc.), and steel, have been particularly hard hit by imports from many parts of the world. Managements in these and other industries are hard pressed to discover and implement strategies to improve products and productivity and thus meet competition. In a number of cases, the chosen strategy has been to open subsidiaries in countries with low labor costs (such as Taiwan) and then to export the finished product such as

Evidence of increased foreign competition at the New York Automobile Show.

television sets to the United States or to other markets. Another strategy is *production sharing*. In this case, the stages of production are handled in different countries. For example, textile yard goods are manufactured in the United States, then shipped to, say, Hong Kong or Singapore for making into various kinds of clothing, and finally returned to the United States. These types of strategies require that U.S. managers learn the intricacies of international trade and of dealing with foreign governments and with workers who come from cultural backgrounds very different from their own.

Management, Where It Is Going

Many uncertainties get in the way of making firm predictions about the future realities of managerial work. Continuing technological change and its unstabilizing effects is one uncertainty. For instance, the fourth generation of computers is already upon us; is the "fifth" very far away? In what way will this change the behavior of managers? Other uncertainties are related to the fact that new organizations are continually being formed at the same time that many existing ones continue to expand, thus "packing" the environment with even more organizations. Interaction rates between organizations increase, stresses traceable to greater business competition build, and frictions between private organization and units of government grow. Still other uncertainties are tied to the question: Is economic inflation now a permanent problem? If it is, managers in all sorts of organizations must learn different long-term strategies than otherwise would be the case.

But not everything is uncertain. It appears likely that management will continue to become "professionalized," to develop a larger and more consistent body of knowledge and related skills. This strongly implies the increasing future necessity for *formal education in management* in order to qualify for consideration as a manager. In the light of continuing change, it is likely that future managers will need to develop their capabilities and sensitivities to *managing change itself.* A later chapter is devoted to this subject.

The behavioral sciences and the management sciences appear to represent the twin domains of the successful manager. The manager must be able to combine the knowledge and handling of people with a thorough understanding of his organizational function and of the business itself.

Career Implications: Leo Bertucci and Foreman Memorial Hospital

Multiple implications for choosing a career in management and attempting to be successful in that choice are apparent throughout this chapter. We wish to illustrate some of the implications by tracking important stages of an individual career as it took shape in the health care field.

Foreman Memorial Hospital is a general community hospital located in a medium-sized city on the West Coast. It has 310 beds and offers typical health-care services: medical–surgical, maternity, pediatric, intensive and intermediate care, laboratory services, and out-patient clinics. Overall, Foreman Memorial has established a reputation for high-quality patient care and its nursing, medical technician, and radiography training programs are well regarded.

Leo Bertucci joined the hospital organization nine years ago, shortly after having acquired a bachelor's degree in management at the local branch of the state university. Andy Fromholtz, the Personnel Director who hired him, was dubious at first, since Bertucci was light on practical and related experience, having worked only at a series of odd jobs during summers and on weekends while attending school. But Bertucci's good academic record, the fact that he had been active in student organizations, plus his enthusiasm won Fromholtz over. Fromholtz was also impressed with the pertinent questions Bertucci asked during the job interview, indicating that he had done his homework.

Over a period of time Bertucci's performance validated Fromholtz's judgment. Leo took a fresh, inquisitive look at the whole process of recruiting, screening, and selecting job applicants, and he suggested several changes in procedures that proved to have merit. For example, he revised the application form in a way that more quickly identified qualified applicants. After 15 months at Foreman, Bertucci was reassigned to wage and salary administration and became supervisor of this section a year later, when the incumbent supervisor took a job elsewhere. Bertucci found this position far more technical than his former one, since he had to learn quickly as much as he could about the hospital's organizational structure and method of classifying personnel for wage purposes (personnel classification system). He also had to learn about the hospital's management philosophy, practices regarding wage and salary levels (compared to local labor markets), and a number of related matters before he could be effective in his new role. He felt it was also essential that he be seen as competent by the two clerks he now supervised.

As time went on both Bertucci's situation and that of the hospital continued to change. Foreman's top administration entered into a merger agreement with a nearby nursing home and added new treatment centers for alcohol and drug abuse. These changes expanded and complicated the hospital's organizational structure and led to the recruiting of new kinds of employees, which pleased some people but definitely displeased others. Some members of Bertucci's informal "coffee klatch," which met in the cafeteria each morning before work, felt Foreman's administration was "empire-building" and making changes that threatened employee job security. Bertucci personally concluded that these changes would be of long-term career value to him, since they would generate more work for the Personnel Department. This was indeed the case. As the department grew, Bertucci told Andy Fromholtz of his interest in taking over responsibility for employee training and supervisory development, activities that in the past had been handled in an unsystematic way. In his new position, Bertucci had the opportunity to handpick three assistants, which brought his employment interviewing skills back into play. He also now had the opportunity to circulate throughout the hospital and interact with a number of department heads and supervisors in the planning of training activities. These experiences, while often very interesting, were often equally frustrating. Some department heads came across as "little bureaucrats," married to their rule books and unresponsive to the benefits Bertucci argued would follow from the sponsorship of training programs. After asking himself what action guides might help him, Bertucci decided to demonstrate the success of training at one or two places in the hospital. He hoped word would get around and change the attitudes of the doubters. In the months that followed, Bertucci found this strategy was only partially effective and he gained a valuable object lesson.

About the middle of his eighth year at Foreman Memorial, Bertucci had worked in or supervised all the functions of the Personnel Department. At that point, his department boss was promoted to assistant hospital administrator and recommended that Bertucci succeed him. After being interviewed by top administration, Bertucci was named the new head of Personnel, a department now comprising 14 people. By this time in his career, Bertucci had developed his own management point of view, and he recommended the department's name be changed to Employee Relations and that his title become Manager of Employee Relations. When asked why, Bertucci replied that employees today, particularly young employees, are more sensitive to fair and equitable *individual* treatment through open relations with management. They don't care to be all lumped together as "Personnel." Leo Bertucci won his point.

After eight years of dealing with grass-roots issues, Bertucci had reached a top level in the organization, where he could put into practice his own ideas and use perspectives gained from many years of experience. He was now in a position to establish hospital objectives dealing with employee relations. He would need to utilize his conceptual abilities to a much greater extent than previously to ensure that the objectives of his department helped to fulfill organizational objectives.

SUMMARY

Managers are responsible for monitoring the many changes occurring inside and outside an organization. Through the four basic skills of conceptualization, analysis, organization, and execution, they are able to ensure the effective operation and continued success of an organization. Looking back on history, we find numerous examples of good leaders like Thomas Jefferson whose intelligence, vision, and determination enabled them to become good managers. We have seen that the field of management can be examined from a grass-roots approach or a top-down approach, depending on whether we want to focus on the individual, job, and work elements of an organization, or whether we are concerned with the big picture of management functions, namely, the establishment of goals, purposes, and strategies of the enterprise and the organization design required for effective implementation. Taylor's scientific management and the human relations movement at Hawthorne Works are excellent examples of grass-roots approaches. Fayol's administrative management and Weber's bureaucracy exemplify the top-down approach. Modern managers must learn to combine both the grass-roots and top-down approaches to deal effectively with current management problems. The problems faced by managers today are compounded by the rapid changes and increased complexity and uncertainty within the world community. Managers must deal with worker concerns such as fair and equal treatment and quality of work life, as well as production efficiency and profitability. Management science, situational analysis, and other modern contingency approaches attempt to deal with some of these problems in a systematic way, using computers, models, and statistics.

A knowledge of management theory and practice will not only enable us to become better managers within an organizational setting, but it will also give us some insights and ideas on how to manage our personal lives, including establishing our own career goals and plans. We hope that this book will be beneficial to you in a very practical and personal sense and will help you to deal effectively with the problems and situations you encounter daily.

Questions for Study and Discussion

1. Why does every organization need managers?
2. Describe the grass-roots and top-down approaches to management and give two examples of each.
3. How long is the history of management scholarship?
4. Are successful leaders necessarily managers?
5. In what way did Thomas Jefferson demonstrate managerial qualities?
6. What strengths did Henry Ford demonstrate as a manager? What weaknesses?
7. What have been the central contributions of scientific management?
8. What is distinctive about the human relations research results at Hawthorne Works?
9. What contribution did Fayol's administrative management make to management thought?
10. To what central feature did Weber attribute the bureaucratic organization's potential for greatest efficiency?
11. What special characteristics does the conglomerate organization have?
12. Name several contemporary changes in employee attitudes and expectations, and discuss one that you especially notice among your peers.

13. Discuss the Leo Bertucci case with respect to the skills needed at different levels in the management hierarchy shown in Exhibit 1-2.

CASE: FRANK SWIFT AND DIAMOND FOODS

Background

Frank Swift started thinking about the alternatives of college and work before he even completed high school. Frank was not especially interested in much additional schooling but had heard much about the importance of a college education for getting a job. He certainly heard plenty of that around the house from his parents—only his mother had attended college for a year before going to work. His father had been an electrician for most of his working life. He went into an apprenticeship program right after high school and continued on in electrical work; for the most part he earned a good living.

Frank made a career decision upon graduating from high school that seemed to satisfy several different personal needs simultaneously. He decided he would go into a community college program that would require only two years for completion and he would start working part-time to get some experience and earn some money. When Frank was enrolled in one of the city community colleges, he started looking for a job—and had what he felt to be really good luck! He was accepted into the Diamond Foods *student intern* program. Diamond Foods was a large regional supermarket chain with almost 100 stores in five states. Its student intern program had the dual purpose of providing needed experience and money for the student, while giving both store *and* student a chance to consider permanent employment possibilities.

Frank was assigned to the retail stores at first, and got much practical experience. He really liked working in the stores, since he had a variety of jobs and met people with whom he enjoyed working. When Frank received his certificate of arts degree, he had already received a new assignment to Diamond Foods' administrative and warehousing center. The management was very pleased with Frank's work and offered him the opportunity to join the company's *store management training program*. Frank was very pleased with the job offer, and he was especially happy for the chance to join the management training program, since it had a good reputation and seemed to offer a sure step to meaningful work, while paying a good salary. He accepted.

Frank Swift, Night Manager

Frank was assigned to several different stores and locations during his first two years of employment to build his familiarity and confidence in dealing with a variety of situations, customers, managerial problems, and sales–traffic problems. Before taking over his "own store," Frank received an assignment as Night Manager at a Diamond Foods store located in a changing neighborhood of a large city.

The organization of the store (see Exhibit 1-3) was much like that of other Diamond Foods units. The Night Manager was "second in command" and assumed responsibility for the evening store hours and closing at midnight. The supervisors working in the evening had areas of responsibility similar to those on "days," except there was no meat preparation, and extra people ("inventory & supplies") were assigned to help restock shelves and supplies for the opening of the store in the morning.

Realistically, the job of the Night Manager was more difficult in some ways than that of the Store Manager during the day. Less help was available if things went wrong, there was nobody around to check requisitions or records, employees were harder to retain, and many of the customers were different than those who usually shopped during the day.

Diamond Foods, because it had been in business for many years, had developed a rather complete set of work rules and procedures for store operations. Also, it had a large number of policies in areas such as customer relations, stocking, advertising, theft, returns, displaying, pricing, sources of supply, and store appearance. Corre-

Exhibit 1-3 Typical Diamond Foods Store Organization

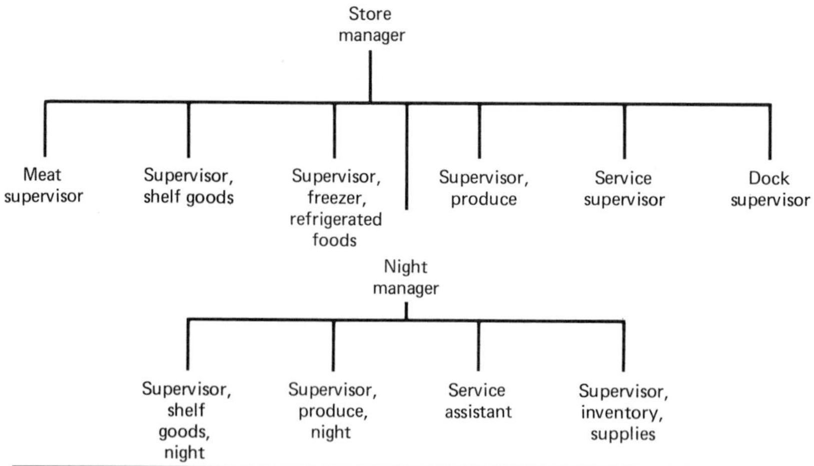

spondingly, it had a large number of personnel rules covering such things as working hours, employee behavior and dress, making out of reports, and reporting on how time is spent. All employees were expected to punch in and out on the time clock whenever they finished an assignment or were reassigned to a new responsibility. To further improve employee performance, standard operating and work procedures were used. As of several years ago, all important store jobs had been studied and a group of standardized job descriptions and specifications developed. These documents provided a detailed description of employee work responsibilities and many details of how various activities were to be carried out.

A Particularly Difficult Problem

When Frank was first assigned to the store, he was told that the store had some serious employee problems. Shortly after starting work there, the Manager confirmed the difficulties and further described an especially troublesome area: "Frank, one thing you'll have to really watch for is to make sure your crews put in a full evening's work. One group that will give you a hard time is the 'shelf goods' crew. First, I think their Supervisor, Tom, is weak and really doesn't push them. Second, we've had a lot of turnover in the group—of the four evening crew members (aside from Supervisor), only one has been there more than six months. I admit their work is tough, moving all those cartons and goods around, but they're getting paid for their work."

The Shelf Goods Crew

Tony was the most senior member of the shelf goods group and more or less took it on himself to make minor assignments to the other three. He had worked in the store about a year and was 28 years old. Jim, Arturo, and Peter were other members of the evening shelf goods crew. Jim and Peter were working full-time evenings to put themselves through school. Arturo was 35, a bachelor who lived by himself—he found little in common with the others and generally left right after work. Tony and Peter had struck up a friendship and on several occasions got together for a drink after work.

After Frank Swift had been in the store about a month, he started to turn more of his thinking and attention to trying to improve evening operations. In particular he wanted to work more closely with the shelf goods crew. One evening after store closing, the evening Shelf Goods Supervisor stopped by and remarked, "It looks like we're going to have some more turnover; I hear Arturo is looking around for another job."

Questions

1. From an overall managerial perspective, what is the nature of the authority structure, policies, and regulations used to achieve store performance?

2. From a grass-roots perspective, what are some of the factors that might affect how workers and crews respond to employment at the store?

3. How would you assess climate of the store from managerial viewpoint?

4. How would you diagnose the evening shelf goods crew problem? Be sure to name and state your assumptions and the management approaches described in this chapter that are used as the basis for your response.

5. From the standpoint of management training, how would you evaluate the
   a. Diamond Foods student intern program?
   b. store management training program?

6. What appear to be some of the critical managerial abilities of a
   a. Store Manager?
   b. Night Manager?

References

Boone, Louis E., and James C. Johnson, "Profiles of the 801 Men and 1 Woman at the Top," *Business Horizons* **23** (February 1980): 47–52.

Drucker, Peter, *Management: Tasks, Responsibilities, Practices.* New York: Harper & Row (1974).

———, *An Introductory View of Management.* New York: Harper & Row (1977).

Fayol, Henri, *General and Industrial Management.* Translated by Constance Storrs. London: Sir Isaac Pitman and Sons (1949).

Fry, Louis W., "The Maligned F. W. Taylor: A Reply to His Many Critics," *Academy of Management Review* **1** (July 1976): 124–129.

George, Claude S., Jr., *The History of Management Thought,* 2d ed. Englewood Cliffs, N.J.: Prentice-Hall (1972).

Koontz, Harold, "The Management Theory Jungle Revisited," *Academy of Management Review* **5**(2) (April 1980): 175–187.

Luthans, Fred, and Todd I. Stewart, "A General Contingency Theory of Management," *Academy of Management Review* **2** (April 1977): 181–195.

Rae, John (Ed.), *Henry Ford.* Englewood Cliffs, N.J.: Prentice-Hall (1969).

Robbins, Stephen, "Reconciling Management Theory with Management Practice," *Business Horizons* **20** (February 1977): 38–47.

Roethlisberger, Fritz, and William Dickson, *Management and the Worker.* Cambridge, Mass.: Harvard University Press (1939).

Ross, Joel, and Robert Murdick, "What Are the Principles of 'Principles of Management'?" *Academy of Management Review* **2** (January 1977): 143–146.

Smith, H. R., and Archie B. Carroll, "Is There Anything 'New' in Management? A 'Rip Van Winkle' Perspective," *Academy of Management Review* **3** (July 1978): 670–674.

Taylor, Frederick, *Scientific Management*. New York: Harper & Row (1947).

Weber, Max, "Bureaucracy." Translated by H. H. Gerth and C. Wright Mills (Eds.) From Max Weber, *Essays in Sociology*, Chapter 8. New York: Oxford University Press (1946).

Wren, Daniel, *The Evolution of Management Thought*, 2d ed. New York: John Wiley (1979).

CHAPTER 2

THE FORMAL ORGANIZATION STRUCTURE

KEY
QUESTIONS
ADDRESSED
IN CHAPTER

1. Why is the formal organization structure classified as part of the top-down approach?

2. What are some basic principles and features of formal organizations?

3. What are some of the benefits and drawbacks of specialization and division of labor?

4. What are some ways in which organizations departmentalize, and why have they been developed?

5. What are some newer approaches to organization design?

6. How do technology and environmental conditions affect structure?

7. How can you use your knowledge of organization structure to aid your career?

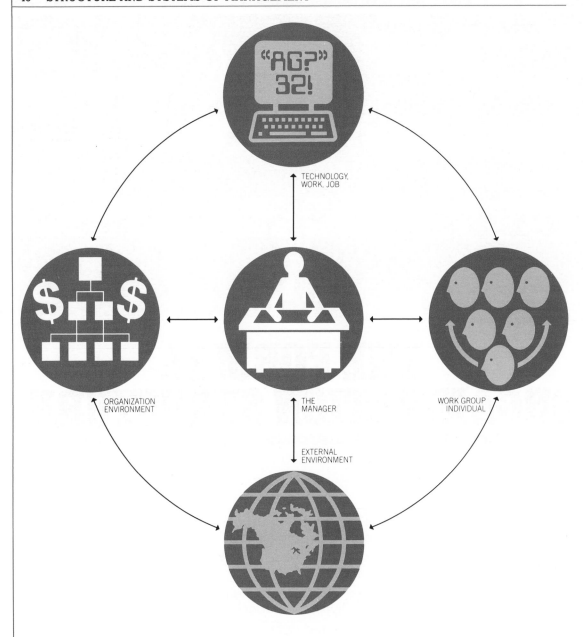

TECHNOLOGY,
WORK, JOB

ORGANIZATION
ENVIRONMENT

THE
MANAGER

WORK GROUP
INDIVIDUAL

EXTERNAL
ENVIRONMENT

The Manager's Work–Life Spaces

When all else fails, read the rules.

THE CHAPTER IN BRIEF

In this chapter we examine the organizational structure that is often the result of deliberate design or strategy, namely, the formal structure. The formal structure of an organization consists of the rules, functions, responsibilities, and relationships that provide the framework for carrying out organizational activities aimed at meeting the needs and goals of the organization.

This is the top-down approach that was discussed in Chapter 1. Most managers, especially those at lower levels, have little if any control over this aspect of the organizing function. In other words, the features presented here really serve as additional constraints, much as external environmental constraints do, to limit the "potential" actions of the manager. For this reason we have placed the features of the formal structure that relate to top-down approaches here and address "bottoms-up" approaches to organizing in later chapters. For example, in Chapter 6 we discuss how managers can establish orderly and efficient uses for all resources within the constraints of the formal structure. In Chapter 10, such elements as interpersonal relations, small group behavior, informal leadership, and "grapevining," which make up the informal structure of the organization are discussed. The student should be aware that this approach represents a significant change from traditional treatments of the organizing function.

What Is Formal Structure?

Regardless of the size of an organization, some formal structure is indispensable. For economic organizations, structure not only facilitates the delivery of goods and services but also ensures continuity and readiness to meet future requirements. Structure must incorporate, either through the designation of individual jobs or units or the assignments of responsibilities, functions that plan, organize, direct, control, administer, coordinate, and acquire. It must also encompass activities that permit the flow of production, processing, marketing, distribution, and finance.

There are those who cringe when they hear the word *structure,* as if it were an evil in itself. Structure as such is neutral. It is a means of achieving the goals established by the organization. How managers and policy makers use structure determines its degree of usefulness. Structure can be used to stifle creativity and self-expression, or it can be used as a framework for guiding and directing action into productive and beneficial channels.

BACKGROUND

Two individuals are particularly noted for their contribution to the study of the formal organization structure. They are Max Weber, who developed the ideal organzational model—termed bureaucracy, and Henri Fayol, who established 14 principles of organizing, which largely still hold true today. Both of these top-down contributions to the study of structure are worthy of detailed discussions here.

Weber's Bureaucratic Model

Max Weber (1864–1920)

Max Weber's *bureaucratic model* is an example, par excellence, of formal organization structure. As we discussed in Chapter 1, Weber envisioned a highly rational and formal organization governed by rules, regulations, and procedures that clearly allocated work responsibilities and procedures and ensured maximal efficiency. Weber's bureaucracy featured a hierarchical authority structure, and members were treated equally and impersonally. Two important features of Weber's ideal organization were specialization and division of labor. We shall return to these issues shortly, in our discussion of *key features of formal structure*.

It is important to understand the purpose that Weber's bureaucratic model served in the period in which he lived. In the late 1800s the German civil service was beleaguered by gross inefficiency. Many civil servants had not been appointed on the basis of their qualifications but, rather, on the basis of their family ties. If one had a relative in the civil service, one stood a good chance of getting a job.

It was Weber's intention to rectify this chaotic, ineffective system, by restructuring the civil service according to rational, orderly principles. His bureaucracy succeeded in eliminating many of the biases and inefficiencies that plagued the German civil service.

Weber's bureaucratic model, in its more elaborate form, is best approached by first presenting those features that Weber attributed to the *organization*, and then those features that he attributed to the *officials* and *employees* working in them. The *organizational features* Weber felt to be most significant were:

1. The activities required by the objectives of the organization are assigned to organization members as official duties. These assignments are made to avoid overlap of responsibilities, and all critical ones are accounted for. Clear-cut **division of work** requires the employment of specialized experts in each position.

2. Positions should fall in a *hierarchy,* with each lower-level position under the control and surveillance of a higher one. The **authority,** the right to direct others, belonging to each position should be limited to what is needed to carry out its duties. Higher officials cannot delegate away their responsibility for the actions of their subordinates; that is, although authority can be passed down to subordinates, the superior official is still *responsible* for how subordinates make use of their authority. (This subject is treated in more detail in Chapter 6.)

3. The organization's work is governed by a comprehensive set of rules and regulations—what is frequently called today *standard operating procedures*. These rules and regulations specify the responsibilities of each member of the organization and the relationships among the members, in a way similar to Fayol's job descriptions.

4. The ideal official in a bureaucracy conducts assigned duties in a "spirit of **impersonality**," that is, without personal preferences or biases. Weber saw such conduct as essential for both the efficient and impartial workings of the organization. Since his time, however, this impersonality has been widely criticized and resented, for example, by citizens dealing with government agencies and by employees dealing with department heads. Impersonality has usually been interpreted as indifference and callousness on the part of "bureaucrats."

From a purely technical point of view, Weber felt that the net result of the workings and interaction among the organizational features just presented would enable bureaucratic organizations to perform with the highest degree of efficiency—higher than any other organizational form. But to further understand how he stood on the matter, it is necessary to describe some *special features* relating to officials and other members of organizations:

1. Employment in a bureaucracy should be based upon technical qualifications, that is, special expertise.
2. People should be protected from arbitrary dismissal, as is true today, for example, of employees in the federal civil service.
3. Job advancement should be on the basis of merit, seniority, or both, and members of the organization should be expected to remain for a lifelong career.
4. The members of the bureaucracy should join the organization of their own free will, should be given written contracts, and should regard their work as a full-time occupation.

Bureaucracy in Perspective

What Weber has actually done in the above is to present what is currently called a **functional analysis** of bureaucracy. This analysis dissects the structure of an organization, identifies its elements, and shows how each element is needed for the whole to survive through time and to operate effectively. Weber realized that things can go wrong in bureaucratic organizations, but he did little to elaborate on this perception. He also stressed that law must prevail in a society before bureaucratic organizations stand any chance of operating successfully. This observation can be appreciated by asking: Why would members of an organization obey those in authority, follow the rules and regulations, and conduct themselves impersonally on the basis of *what* they knew rather than *who* they knew, if being "law-abiding" were not a well-established custom?

Weber felt that *predictability* of action and behavior was a central feature of bureaucracies. The quality contrasted sharply, for example, with the whims and surprises often characterizing the actions of feudal lords at the time. In an organization that operates under written rules and regulations and in a spirit of impersonality, decision making is predictable, Weber's reasoning went. Students of modern organization are likely to criticize most severely this notion of predictability, in the light of the uncertainty of economic and competitive factors in the environment. The presence of widely different human needs and situations requires that these be approached with imagination and variety. Weber further stressed the *staying power* of the bureaucratic form, that is, its capacity to continue beyond the life spans of the many generations of people who work in it.

Weber's ideal organizational model had two major shortcomings. The first was that it failed to take into account the human element. The highly impersonal and formalistic bureaucracy often left workers with a sense of alienation and dissatisfaction. Everything was conducted "by the book." "Equal" and "impersonal" did not always mean "fair," because the bureaucratic model discounted differences in individual needs and the existence of unique circumstances. Sometimes fair treatment would have required "bending" the rules because of differences in personality, temperament, talent, and experience; or a sudden event like an accident or illness might have created a situation in which treating the individual fairly might not have meant treating him or her equally or impersonally. A second shortcoming of Weber's bureaucracy was its ineffectiveness in handling change and uncertainty. The relative inflexibility of the rules and regulations made them poorly equipped to meet the changing and often unpredictable demands of the future.

The fact that the bureaucratic model was not able to accommodate the human element and future demands and uncertainties does not imply that formal structure is doomed to alienate workers or crumble in the face of change. Modern structural approaches have attempted to build flexibility and contingencies into formal structures, enabling them to meet these demands.

It should be pointed out here that the intended purpose of structure may be different from the actual result. Most designers or organizations intend the structure to facilitate both institutional and social processes. Various economic measures such as profit and productivity and human performance measures such as job satisfaction, can be used to determine to what degree the formal structure is an aid in the achievement of organizational goals.

Fayol's Principles of Administrative Management

Noting that **principles of management** are flexible, not absolute, and must be useful in a changing environment, Henri Fayol listed 14 principles based on his experiences (Fayol, 1949). They are summarized in Exhibit 2-1 and discussed in greater detail in later sections.

Some Observations

Our attention to Fayol's *principles* indicates the continuing widespread use of these terms and the continuing relevance of some of his principles. However, we need to know which ideas or portions of his work remain useful, or what the conditions are under which they still apply. A partial answer is provided here. More of an answer is presented in subsequent sections that describe the core of modern management approaches.

Fayol's 14 principles on organizing are similar to those of Weber.

Government Simplification Department

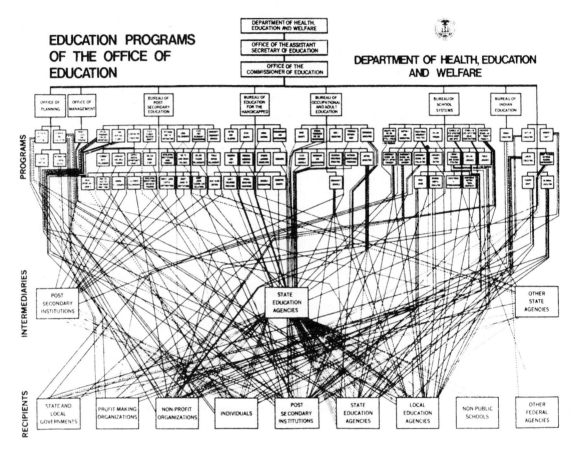

Figure 2-1 Government simplification department. (*Source: Wall Street Journal,* January 25, 1977. Reprinted with permission of the publisher, Dow-Jones & Company, Inc.)

They point out the need to arrange organizational resources, including people, into a structural hierarchy that is more or less permanent. Although both approaches are fairly mechanistic, they established a foundation for organizing that is still appropriate. Thus contemporary thought on organizational design has built on the concepts of Fayol and Weber and integrated findings from the behavioral sciences.

Changes in the social and economic context of work have led to much more **complex** and **uncertain** conditions today. For example,

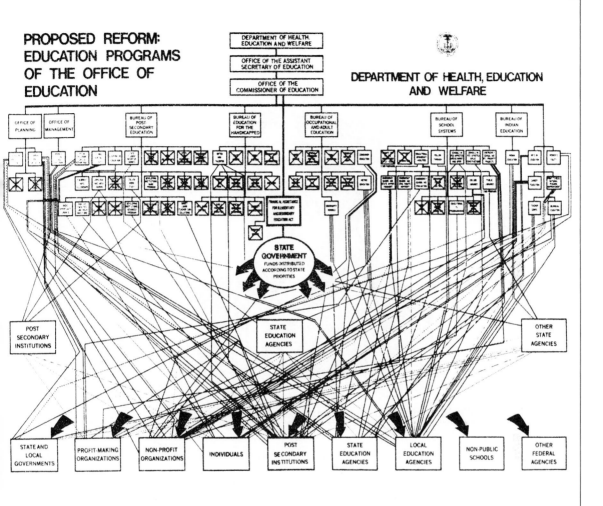

**PROPOSED REFORM:
EDUCATION PROGRAMS
OF THE OFFICE OF
EDUCATION**

complexity has grown as a result of the extension of business competition, laws affecting the operation of private enterprises, and the advancement of technology used in information processing and production of goods and services. Uncertainty has grown because of the increased vulnerability of individuals, organizations, and governments to multiple sources of change. We might infer from Fayol's principles that they should apply quite generally and with little or no variation. But wide ranges of complexity and uncertainty are very much a part of the management scene today, and play an integral role in our personal lives as well. Modern management is concerned with handling complexity and uncertainty and with dealing with the numerous situations where principles of management simply do not apply. What are some key features that should be considered by managers when designing the formal structure?

Henri Fayol (1841–1925)

Exhibit 2-1 Fayol's 14 Principles of Administrative Management

1. *Division of work*

   Fayol argued that every employee's abilities, confidence, and accuracy improves as he or she becomes highly skilled or specialized in a particular activity. More work is accomplished with less effort. However, Fayol recognized that this principle has its limits, in that work can be so minutely subdivided as to be totally boring.

2. *Authority and responsibility*

   Fayol felt that authority has two components: (1) *official* or formal authority, that is, the permission an organization gives a manager to issue orders and instructions, make decisions, and the like; and (2) *personal* or informal authority, which is made up of factors distinctive to the individual, such as intelligence, past experiences, and the ability to lead. Importantly, authority and responsibility should be coequal; that is, no manager should be held responsible for achieving certain objectives unless he has been granted sufficient authority to secure the resources required to meet the objectives.

3. *Unity of command*

   This principle is most easily understood as "one employee, one boss." Fayol was forceful in saying that no employee should be caught in a crossfire of orders from multiple supervisors. When this principle is violated, authority becomes confused, employee resentment builds, and stability is threatened.

Exhibit 2-1, continued

4. *Unity of direction*

This principle is connected to Fayol's stress upon planning. At no time should a unit of organization be operating on the basis of more than one overall plan, and no more than one manager should be in charge of its execution.

5. *Subordination of individual interests to the general interest*

When individual employees, be they managers or otherwise, are not effectively led, "every man for himself" tends to predominate. Thus Fayol urged managers to set good examples in pursuing the overall aims of the organization, and to do a good job in communicating work requirements to each employee.

6. *Centralization*

In Fayol's day, as well as in our own, this principle refers to the degree of concentration of authority and decision making power—the point "where the buck stops." Just where this point is located varies among organizations. Fayol advised managers to proceed in an experimental frame of mind and determine, over time, the degree of centralization best suited to their particular organizations.

7. *Scalar chain*

This principle should be visualized as the formal structure of the organization, the so-called *reporting relationships*. When charted in full, what can be seen is a "chain" that identifies the formal authority linkages and the entire network of superior–subordinate relationships in the organization. Some typical charts are illustrated in Exhibit 2-2. Fayol stressed the advantages of formal organization charts, both from the standpoint of clarity of relationships and of uncovering excessively long authority chains and muddled communication channels. However, the real organizational structure is the total pattern of human relationships that exist.

8. *Order*

By this principle Fayol meant that management is responsible for neat and orderly physical conditions of work, efficient use of physical space and equipment, and related matters. Even more important, management is responsible for deciding how many job classifications are needed in the organization, how many people should be hired for each, and what the employees will be expected to do. He advised the drafting of job descriptions so that the "fit" between people's abilities and job requirements could be improved.

9. *Discipline*

Fayol declared that discipline requires good superiors at all levels and viewed it as respect for agreements that are directed at achieving obedience, application, energy, and the outward marks of respect.

10. *Remuneration*

Methods of payment should be fair and afford the maximum possible satisfaction to employees and employer.

11. *Equity*

Loyalty and devotion should be obtained from employees by a combination of justice and kindliness on the part of managers in their dealings with subordinates.

Exhibit 2-1, continued

12. *Stability of tenure*

Excessive turnover is the result of bad management practices and should be eliminated since the hidden costs of turnover can be severe.

13. *Initiative*

Initiative is the thinking out and execution of a plan and one of the "keenest satisfactions for an intelligent man to experience." Fayol exhorts managers to "sacrifice personal vanity" and allow subordinates to exercise it through delegation.

14. *Espirit de corps*

Fayol emphasizes the need for teamwork and the importance of communication in obtaining it.

Structure and the Life-Space Model

Structure is a central feature of the *organizational life space*. The degree of specialization and amount of **decentralization** define the constraints within which a manager can operate. For example, a manager in a decentralized organization is likely to have more discretion in dealing with problems than his or her counterpart in a highly **centralized** structure. The added responsibility usually given to managers in decentralized organizations also enables them to use their abilities and to develop their skills more rapidly.

We have mentioned the need for organizational structures to adapt to changes in the environment. Too often structural arrangements that were suitable in meeting organizational (and individual) needs under a certain set of circumstances remain in place too long. The Ford Motor Company in the 1920s and A&P Food Stores in the postwar years are prime examples of organizations that once dominated their industries but failed to make structural modifications to deal more effectively with changes in the environment. Changing environmental conditions affect organizational objectives and suggest a need for structural arrangements to be altered or at least to allow for greater flexibility in meeting new demands placed on organizations from external sources.

Comments such as "We've always done it this way" are indicative of the inflexible attitude held by some managers. An over-reliance on rules, policies, and work arrangements are negative effects of structure; yet some order is needed so that everyone doesn't simply "do his own thing." What is called for is structural arrangements that allow for both individual growth and organizational goals to be achieved.

Organizational structure can affect individuals' attitudes and feelings about themselves, their work, their supervisors, or fellow employees. Highly structured organizations may stifle creativity and initiative, while specialization may restrict a worker or manager to

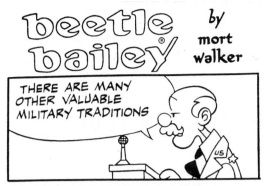

beetle bailey by mort walker

THERE ARE MANY OTHER VALUABLE MILITARY TRADITIONS

A SOLDIER MUST OBEY HIS OFFICERS NO MATTER WHAT. OBEY FIRST, ASK QUESTIONS LATER, IF YOU MUST.

I'M SORRY, SIR. BUT I DISAGREE WITH YOUR LAST STATEMENT

HEH! HEH! QUITE ALL RIGHT. I LIKE YOUR SPIRIT, YOUNG MAN

OUR COUNTRY WAS BUILT ON DISSENT. SPEAKING OUT IS THE ONLY WAY DEMOCRACY WORKS

IN THAT CASE, THERE WERE A **LOT** OF DUMB THINGS IN YOUR SPEECH

WELL, UH...

ALL THAT BULL ABOUT MILITARY TRADITION --- WHO NEEDS IT?!

AND THAT CHAIN-OF-COMMAND STUFF...WHAT A BOTTLENECK

MORT WALKER

5-29

HEY! WHAT ABOUT MY RIGHT TO DISSENT?!

THIS IS **MY** WAY OF DISSENTING

narrowly defined duties so that his or her full range of talents is not used. To avoid these possibilities, organizations have begun to modify traditional structural relationships. These approaches will be discussed in a later section of this chapter.

KEY FEATURES OF THE FORMAL STRUCTURE

Division of Labor

We often associate the concept of **division of labor** with Frederick W. Taylor, founder of scientific management. Taylor demonstrated that the execution of a task could often be facilitated if it was subdivided into individual elements or subtasks. Each of these subtasks could be performed with greater efficiency when handled individually. The division of labor enables the laborer to focus his or her energies and skills on one element of the work task. The relative simplicity of the individual work or job element means that it can be performed more quickly and with less chance of error. The automotive assembly line as developed by Henry Ford, is an excellent example of the efficiency that is accomplished by subdividing the task of assembling an automobile.

Division of labor does have its drawbacks. Many tasks are made so simple that they often become routine, tedious, and boring. Many assembly-line workers complain that their work is very unsatisfying because of its repetitiveness and lack of challenge. If human resource needs are to be taken seriously, these will have to be increasingly considered along with economic criteria. A number of studies are currently underway to establish or design work systems that meet both economic needs *and* behavioral requirements (see the discussion on quality of work life).

Specialization

A feature of formal structure related to division of labor is **specialization.** Aristotle, one of the greatest minds that ever lived, was among the first to systematically present the benefits of specialization. He demonstrated that it was extremely difficult for an individual or even a family to master all the tasks necessary for providing the necessities of life, like food, clothing, and shelter. The idea of a man being a "jack of all trades" was very romantic, but highly impractical. Society could only sustain itself through the development of specialization. Each person gained expertise in a particular vocation and traded his or her goods or services to others. Specialization permitted the individual to concentrate his or her energies on developing particular skills, abilities, and knowledge, the fruits of which could be shared with others. Specialization thus permitted progress through the channeling of productive energies. Interestingly, although Aristotle was a strong supporter of specialization, he was a jack of all trades himself. He mastered such diverse disciplines as physics, poetry, philosophy, mathematics, and ethics.

Specialization, too, has its drawbacks. Sometimes an area becomes so specialized that an individual spends most of his time trying to master it to the exclusion of gaining a more general understanding of other areas. Many specialists become isolated and cut off from other developments in related fields because they are caught up in mastering or progressing in their particular subfield. They may even fail to develop necessary communication links with others and thus may not benefit from discoveries or advances in related fields. Specialization increases the need for coordination and communication between functions and for the establishment of common purposes and a general framework for providing broader scope and direction in organizational activities.

In the modern era, specialization has usually involved the application of systematic bodies of knowledge for studying and improving work performance. Specialists, for example, work in engineering, product development, and statistical quality control. An internist is considered a specialist in the medical profession. The words *specialization* or *specialist* are, of course, only relative terms. A biologist is a specialized scientist, a microbiologist is a specialized biologist, and so on.

In modern organizations, specialization often comes to mean the gathering together of people educated and trained in particular areas who demonstrate competency or expertise. *Professionals,* for instance, are usually considered specialists. Usually a person enters an organization because of a particular expertise or special skill, but as the person moves up a career ladder he or she is expected to develop more general managerial skills. (Recall our discussion of different skills at various levels in the hierarchy in Chapter 1.)

Specialization contributes to the widespread belief in the *Peter principle*, which states that individuals rise to their levels of incompetency. Many specialists are not properly trained to handle generalized managerial tasks, yet they often are selected for these positions on the basis of their performance in their specialties. They may have been great "doers," but they are now failures at getting other people to do things. Simply put, the best worker does not always make the best supervisor. We need only look at professional sports for an example. Most good managers or coaches have had rather ordinary playing careers, and very few "stars" have ever risen to become successful managers.

Departmentalization

Organizations are made up of a wide variety of tasks and duties that must be performed if organizational goals are to be achieved. The method of grouping these jobs together is called **departmentalization.** Organizational units and task assignments can be structured in a number of ways. We deal only with the more common groupings here.

By Function or Process

Production, marketing, finance, and engineering are all examples of structural division by **function** (see Exhibit 2-2, no. 1 for an example). Function pertains to the type of work or activity being performed. These divisions are rather simple and straightforward and

Exhibit 2-2 Illustrations of the Formal Authority Structure of Organizations

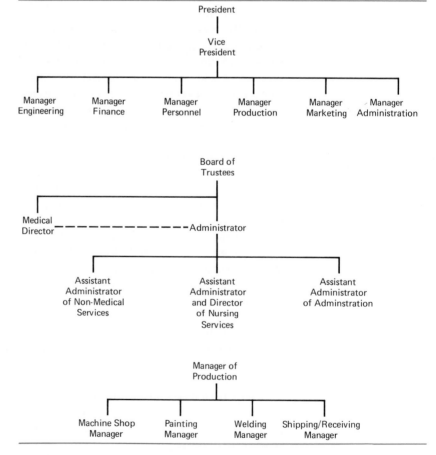

Exhibit 2-2, continued

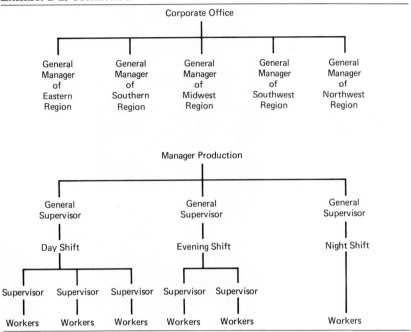

are particularly useful in smaller organizations. However, functional divisions can be unwieldy in large or decentralized organizations where close coordination and a faster response to local situations may be required.

The functional pattern of organization is widely used at higher authority levels within enterprises. When used at lower levels, some authors use the term **process** instead of function. For example, within the functional department, "production," work may be further subdivided on the basis of the process, or type of work, performed (see Exhibit 2-2, no. 2). Organizational components at this level may include machining, painting, welding, and shipping and receiving.

Functional arrangements permit the specialization and development of skills by professionals and other specialists that, in turn, can lead to efficiency and well-defined career ladders. However, the functional pattern may promote a narrow viewpoint. Many functional managers look at a problem with regard to the effect on their own specialty rather than the effect on the company as a whole. This problem is discussed more extensively in Chapter 6.

By Product

Some organizations are structured by product. For example, at IBM there is a Computer Systems Group and an Office Equipment Group.

Which way do you go?
Functional departments
in a university.

Each division handles a different product or service line. General Motors has a Chevrolet division, a Buick division, a Pontiac division, a Cadillac division, an Oldsmobile division, and a truck division. Unlike functional organizations, product organizations allow managers to gain experience in various functional specialties. In this way some of the disadvantages of specialization can be avoided. For example, the general manager of a product department is responsible for dealing with problems in such functional areas as sales, production, research and development, and engineering. His or her career path is likely to have included jobs in some or all of these departments.

In organizations structured by product, however, it is difficult for a person to move from one product division to another, especially if the product lines are significantly different. For example, General Electric has both a Consumer Products Division and a Power System Division. Transfers *within* these divisions are much easier than are transfers *between* divisions, because of the differences in product lines that may require different knowledge of products and technology. There is evidence, however, that organizations are beginning to realize that the *universality of management skills* can allow for more transferability than previously thought. As this view is shared by more companies, career paths can be broadened.

By Geographic Location

Many sales organizations and insurance companies are structured primarily by geographic location. This regional (southern, western, midwestern, etc.) basis enables the companies to cater to the specialized needs or legal requirements of a particular region of the country or world. For example, agricultural needs of the Midwest differ from those of the South, so that a farm equipment company may have a different division for each region, specializing in the types of farming equipment needed there. Regional home offices of an insurance company would be headed by a general manager who directs the overall operation, including the selling and servicing of insurance, in his or her territory (see Exhibit 2-2, no. 3). The underwriting staff in the region has the freedom to secure new business within the standards set by the corporate office.

The geographic structure has advantages in common with those of the product arrangement. Managers can gain broader experience on the regional level. Financial control is also facilitated, since budgets can be prepared for each geographic (or product) area to determine its contribution to corporate profits.

By Type of Client or Customer

Occasionally the type of client or customer using an organization's product or service varies greatly. In these situations it makes sense to structure the company to meet these special needs. For example, publishing houses have separate sales forces within the same geographic area selling the same books but to different clients such as postsecondary schools and bookstore chains. Similarly, the same product may be sold to both an industrial market (factories and offices) and a consumer market (retail stores) in the same geographical area, but by separate sales forces who require different skills and training to meet the special needs of these two markets.

By Time or Shift

Organizations that require around-the-clock operations present unique organizing situations. Highly capitalized industries such as those for steel, automobiles, and oil, as well as service areas such as health care, are examples of organizations requiring shift work. In education there are day and evening divisions in many colleges and universities. Exhibit 2-2, no. 4 shows an example of a production organization in which the number and type of staff available for each time period vary. Usually evening and night shift managers (and sometimes workers) are given broader areas of responsibilities, since there are fewer staff specialists on hand to solve problems that arise.

Span of Control

The **span of control** (sometimes called the *span of management*) refers to the number of individuals reporting directly to a manager. The more individuals a manager supervises, the greater his or her span of control. Conversely, the fewer individuals a manager supervises, the smaller his or her span of control.

The central idea behind the span of control concept is the determination of how many individuals a manager can *effectively* supervise. If managers supervise too few individuals, they may be wasting part of their productive capabilities. They may also cause frustrations for their subordinates by supervising too closely. On the other hand, if managers supervise too many individuals, they may be overextending themselves and may become frustrated. In addition, their subordinates are likely to receive too little guidance or control. Once they

Manager briefs his building maintenance crew.

Exhibit 2-3 Wide and Narrow Spans of Control

a. *Wide span of control—flat structure*

b. *Narrow span of control—tall structure*

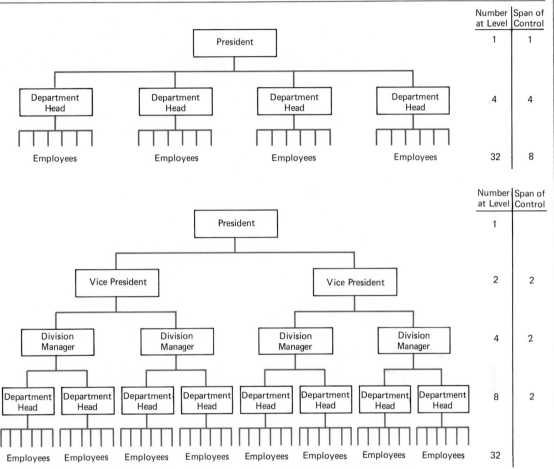

are assigned a number of individuals to supervise, however, managers do have control over how to delegate responsibility. This "art" of delegation is discussed in Chapter 6, which deals with bottoms-up approaches to organizing.

A definite relationship exists between the span of control and the height of an organization chart. If the spans of control are *narrow,* the resulting structure will be *tall.* If they are *wide,* the structure will be *flat.* Exhibit 2-3 illustrates this effect. In Chapter 6, we discuss the factors that affect a manager's span of control and problems associated with wide or narrow spans.

Centralization–Decentralization

The terms *centralization* and *decentralization* can refer to the geographic *or* authority structure of an organization. Geographically speaking, the degree to which an organization is (de)centralized depends on the extent to which its physical plants are dispersed. A highly decentralized company like Coca Cola Bottling Company has production plants located in many parts of the world. The Kitchens of Sara Lee, on the other hand, was geographically centralized when they had only one production facility. *Centralization* and *decentralization* are only relative terms.

Centralized authority means that major decisions and responsibilities are made by upper management. Middle managers have routine responsibilities and do not actively partake in the decision-making process of the organization. Centralized (authority) organizations often have narrow spans of control so that upper management's influence on control can be extended. Decentralized organizations (in terms of responsibility) have wider spans of control and middle managers are given considerable responsibilities.

Decentralized (or divisionalized) organizations delegate operating authority and responsibility to division or department heads. Decentralization is usually accomplished along product (service) or geographic lines with the corporation or headquarters unit remaining responsible for general policy, capital allocation, coordination, and overall strategies. For accounting purposes, each division or department is a "profit center" so that managerial performance can be more easily evaluated.

Sears, Roebuck and Company is an example of a decentralized organization. Major operating responsibilities are in the hands of area and store managers. Each store becomes a profit center, and middle managers are encouraged to develop self-reliance and "run their own show." Decentralization at Sears promotes managerial development and allows store managers to respond quickly when faced with changing market conditions and strong competition (Khandwalla, 1973).

A&P, on the other hand, is an example of a highly centralized organization. Despite its financial strength and size, A&P saw its market share erode because of changing market conditions and severe competition from more decentralized companies such as Safeway and Jewel, whose store managers had major responsibility for store operations. A&P store managers often could not even control the items and prices in their stores, for these were determined by corporate-level decisions in New York. Although purchasing economies resulted, many inappropriate items were stocked in individual stores, and the store managers had little authority to improve the situation.

Increased decentralization or divisionalization in large organizations, however, may have its negative results. The size and complexity of large organizations have often forced them increasingly to centralize key operations (or functions) to improve the communication of information, the interchange of managerial manpower to compensate for manpower shortages, and the consolidation of company-wide hiring requirements and development programs. The greater the *common dependence* of financial, operational, and other functions on common tasks, activities, or markets, the greater the need for coordination and centralization of decision making in the areas affected. The less the dependency of one function on another, the greater the opportunity for decentralization of management responsibility and differentiation of activity.

GREAT PERSON PROFILE

Alfred Pritchard Sloan (1875–1966)

Born and raised in New Haven, Connecticut, Sloan graduated as an engineer from M.I.T. in 1895. He later attended Princeton and Duke universities, acquiring a solid academic base for his management career. Hired as a manager for Hyatt Roller Bearing Company, he quickly advanced to president of the company. After the company was acquired by General Motors, he worked under William Durant, but he disagreed with Durant's centralized authority and intuitive decision-making procedures.

In 1920, Sloan wrote a 28-page memo outlining how he thought GM's management should be restructured, with the centralized power structure replaced by a structure that delegated authority and decision-making power within a *divisionalized* organizational structure. He was about to resign from General Motors over the issue when Durant was forced out by shareholders in 1921, and Sloan was offered the job as president. He quickly accepted and so successfully restructured GM in the 1920s that Ford's previous dominance over the auto industry was overthrown. Sloan *decentralized* much decision making to the divisions, yet maintained a central staff to

monitor their performance and coordinate their operations to avoid duplication of effort. He became chairman of the board in 1937, a post he held until 1956, when he turned his organizational talent to the presidency of the A. P. Sloan Foundation for science as well as other philanthropic interests.

Sloan was the first of a new breed of managers in the United States. His organizational principles and methods have been successfully applied by many major corporations.

Structure and Your Career

You can use your knowledge of structure to improve your understanding of your current organization or the organizations you are now exploring for career purposes. An understanding of structure should help you to determine practical ways of progressing within your organization.

Your knowledge of organizational structure will help you to create career opportunities and **mobility.** Movement (mobility) within an organization is possible in many directions. The traditional **career ladder** involves vertical movement within a particular organization unit, as in the case of the sales trainee who eventually progresses to sales manager. However, many organizations today offer alternative career paths and career ladders. Horizontal, vertical, and diagonal movement is possible if, for example, the sales trainee is able to eventually cross over into the production department and move up the ranks into production management.

If you are presently working in an organization you should look into the career opportunities available to you. A job is more than *just a job*. It is part of an organizational structure, and thus is linked to many other jobs. Frequently there are good opportunities for job mobility within an organization. If you are not presently working for an organization, you might ask organization recruiters and interviewers about the type of career ladders available or how people generally progress within their organizations. For example, Atlantic Richfield Company (Arco) presents recruits with charts that show the type of inter- and intradepartmental movements available for each company position. Research has shown that the more realistic your expectations about a job, the more satisfied you are likely to be with it. One way of having more realistic expectations about a job is to understand how it fits into the organizational structure. This understanding helps you to realize why certain rules and regulations are necessary and what purpose they serve. You will be able to see your job responsibilities within a larger organizational perspective and so may more strongly identify with the organization and its goals. You thus will have a better sense of the extent to which your career plans can be fulfilled within a particular organization.

RECENT STRUCTURAL APPROACHES

In the past two decades, a number of new approaches to organizational structure have been developed to deal with more complex organizational environments. These flexible structural arrangements are project management, matrix structure, and colleague management.

Project Management and the Use of Task Forces

Project management is necessary when special tasks must be done that cannot be easily handled by routine organizational procedures and traditional formal structures. A *temporary* group, or **task force,** is formed combining and integrating members from various functional departments or units with whatever equipment or procedures are required to achieve task goals. Group members return to their respective departments and positions at the completion of the project or of their particular phase of the project. The unique aspect of project organization is that it cuts across traditional departmental lines, and thus combines horizontal, vertical, and diagonal communications.

A project group emerges in response to a need for (1) considerable planning and (2) coordination or research to deal with a specific and complex task(s) that usually must be completed in a specific period of time. The planning of newer generation computers, construction projects, and new products are examples of project situations that, to be successful, must combine diverse social and technical skills and various resources in flexible and creative ways.

Project managers play a unique role. They assume responsibility for successful project completion in connection with specialists who typically have no direct or formal authority relationship with them or with each other. As such they require general management skills related to planning (or seeing the big picture), coordinating, communication, and motivation. For example, a given project may have engineers, architects, estimators, systems people, and a cost accountant. These people represent a number of different functional departments and specialties and may have had little interaction with organization members outside their individual departments.

In effect, the project group superimposes another work and communications structure on top of the existing formal relationships. The project manager evaluates individual performance on the task, while the individual's formal supervisor continues to assess other personal performance or activity aspects and assumes responsibility for preparation of an overall evaluation of the person. This type of dual-authority situation calls for increased cooperation and communication to reduce the opportunities for conflict of authority between the project manager, the individual, and the individual's formal supervisor. Formal authority within a project team is largely on a colleague basis; that is, it relies on persuasion and a demonstration of expertise. The nature of authority is dealt with in detail in Chapter 6.

The project team must contain the necessary range of social and technical abilities to complete the project successfully. Frequently,

Successful project teams use the expertise from different specialties.

not all members will be needed at the same time; they will phase in at appropriate stages or as needed. Team size could range from as small as 3 to as large as 40 (or more).

An extension of project management is the **venture structure.** This structure has evolved largely to foster innovation and creativity within organizations. Many existing departments or divisions become concerned over time with maintaining the status quo regarding existing products. In fact, the reward system may reinforce this behavior. Under these circumstances new products often do not obtain a fair share of resources needed for growth within these units.

By establishing a separate new venture unit within existing departments or divisions and supplying the necessary resources, sufficient autonomy can be established to improve the chances of a new product's success. Also, with more control over resources needed by the new venture, the manager can be held more accountable for overall product performance. Once established the product usually becomes part of the parent department or division.

Matrix Structure

In some industries project organization is needed regularly. When project teams become a permanent feature of the organization we say that the organization has a **matrix structure** (see Exhibit 2-4). Industries that deal with complex situations requiring the integration of diverse areas of knowledge, like the architectural, space, and weapons industries, often have a matrix structure. For example, a large architectural firm may take on several long-term projects that may take years to complete. Groups consisting of engineers, architects, designers, computer analysts, accountants, and others work together as teams during the design and completion of the projects. The problems of conflict of authority and need for coordination encountered in project management are magnified in a matrix organiza-

Exhibit 2-4 The Matrix Structure

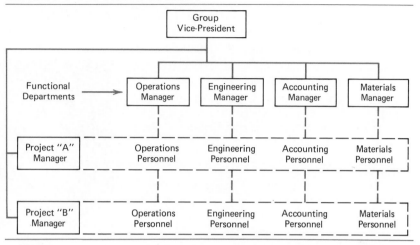

tion. This is because of the number of project or team efforts going on at the same time. Project members may begin to lose contact with their formal supervisors since they are involved in projects that take them away from their departments for long periods of time (sometimes years). Strong lines of communication have to be developed between project members, their project managers, and their formal supervisors. Project management and participation within a matrix organization call for training in techniques of communication and interaction that go far beyond the normal requirements of traditional structures.

Colleague Management and Office of the President

Colleague management is a highly participative management style that is often practiced among a group of individuals considered to be peers. It is based on business and organization skills, experience, education, or the potential contribution to organization welfare.

The **office of the president** was established as part of the colleague management approach. The *office* may consist of a number of people who share the responsibilities of the office and reach consensus on important issues. The concept of office of the president has been most often used when shared responsibility is required to deal with complex problems or situations. Such organizations as General Electric and General Motors now have offices of the president.

The benefits of the structure include the dividing up or sharing of responsibilities along functional lines and the feeling of teamwork this can foster. It does, however, require greater attention to the development of interpersonal relationships and communication skills within the "office."

There are also drawbacks. Individuals at this level often have

GREAT PERSON PROFILE

Stephen Davison Bechtel, Sr. (1900–   )

Stephen Bechtel was the son of a Kansas farmer who had founded Bechtel, a small specialty construction company. He grew up with his brothers in construction camps, but by 1933, when his father died and Stephen took over, Bechtel Corporation had grown to become one of the eight companies building the Hoover Dam.

Owing to the growth in size and the increased complexity of projects, Bechtel saw the need to increase the efficiency of the company by becoming the general contractor for entire projects, including engineering and procurement. This required introducing a new concept in organization, similar to the matrix structure.

The task of reorganization was considerable and required new skills related to project management for it became necessary to coordinate the varied resources of many subcontractors. Top management and professional staffs were selected and trained to carry out these new tasks. It proved to be a wise move—Bechtel Corporation was involved early in work for the Atomic Energy Commission and is a leader in this field today, having built 45 percent of the nuclear power plants in the country. Stephen Bechtel retired from his job as president in 1960, but remained a senior director. At 81, he was still actively pursuing new ideas and innovative organizational approaches. This pioneering organizational effort helped to build one of the largest private businesses in the United States, a multibillion dollar business with more than 100,000 employees.

strong personalities. This can lead to infighting, internal power struggles, and a greater emphasis on politicking as individuals seek to become *the* president. Whether this is more prevalent than in "normal" structures is dependent on the atmosphere or climate that has been developed and rewarded in the organization concerning cooperation versus competition.

OTHER ASPECTS OF STRUCTURE

The Dynamics of Structure

Structures are dynamic, they evolve over time. They are changed in form and character in response to changing needs and demands from the environment as well as from organization leadership. A number of different circumstances and factors shape structure; these include organizational size and complexity, managerial capability, philosophical and environmental considerations, and functional work activities.

Let us examine the shaping effects of a few of these factors. We begin with organization size and complexity. Research has shown that as organizations grow in size and complexity the proportion of professional groups, representing the pool of technical expertise, grows more rapidly than do managerial positions. Increased size brings about new work roles and new needs for coordinating more diverse processes and activities. The professional staff becomes increasingly involved with general direction, control, and coordination of work to provide senior management with a firmer hand on the larger, more complex organization. The use of these professional groups provides an effective alternative to a continued growth in the number of managers and/or the proportionate growth of the managerial structure.

Environmental considerations include such things as population changes and competitive pressures. Also, innovation sets in motion new needs, pressures, and opportunities for the firm. The executive's "reading" of these trends and developments may lead to new goals for the enterprise, which in turn lead to managerial strategies for reaching these goals. These strategies can create internal strains or demands on existing organization structures that set into motion necessary structural adjustments to avoid ineffective organization.

Uncertainty is both a characteristic of the organization's external environment and a feature of the work task. **Environmental uncertainty** refers to the relative instability of the forces surrounding an organization. Greater uncertainty means that events become more difficult to predict. Under such conditions as intense competition and rising inflation, organizations are often forced to develop *flexible* and *contingent* approaches. Sometimes uncertainty can be met head-on with the development of new structures. For example, a manufacturing firm faced with greater uncertainty because of technological innovations may decide to create a department for technology research.

Task uncertainty has to do with the difficulty and variability of the work performed. High task uncertainty may force the exercise of individual judgment or discretion (as opposed to predetermined rules) and decentralizes decision making in the organization. Supervisory decision making is reduced, and nonsupervisory, or colleague, decision making is increased.

Interdependence deals with the extent to which organizational units depend on each other for performance resulting from the interchange of units of work, materials, or information. Interdependence, which is often a result of **automation,** requires a more complex communication network and greater coordinating demands. **Departmentalization** (or divisionalization) by product or location frequently has low levels of interdependence between units, but often has dependent activities *within* units requiring coordination.

Where there are interrelationships between structural elements within an organization, a cohesive network must be designed that guides and channels individual work processes. The *complementary* nature of some organizational structures often permits the substitution of one structural element for another. For example, the use of certain types of regulations and procedures may reduce the need for supervision, since these regulations and procedures (may) provide the type of direction and guidance that a supervisor would exercise if present. Removing the pressure of supervision, in some circumstances, could have the potential for creating increased self-direction.

Technological changes also affect the character and structure of organizational relationships. New technology requires a competent technical support group with well-rounded skills, a comprehensive system of work procedures and controls, and a broadly focused staff to develop new products and product lines. Continuing changes in technology lead to internal reorganization of operations. In manufacturing, highly mechanized production technologies may discourage decentralization of authority to plant managers in favor of higher authority levels and various staff support units at the corporate level. Centralized authority is more suited to overall planning or the engineering of complex systems. In some corporations, authority has remained decentralized to encourage leadership growth and individual development, even though economic benefits seem to be linked with centralization. This is an example of longer run considerations and human resource needs taking precedence over purely economic needs.

Advances in computer technology have resulted in the upgrading of information and production processes. Computers are used to develop more effective means of monitoring and controlling work operations and processes of many different types. Their ability to process and transmit information has provided new options with regard to decision making, planning, coordination, and control. When computers are provided at the field office or plant level, their ability to support administrative control and coordinate activities permits the (re)establishment of management autonomy and increased decentralization. Sometimes, however, the uncontrolled use of computers across organization units makes it necessary to recentralize and consolidate these activities.

Changing technology dramatically affects jobs and people. Certain jobs that were previously performed by people are now performed by machines. Other jobs have been modified, and often technology has

Personnel employees being trained to enter payroll data into a computerized payroll system.

created new jobs, as in word processing units in offices. People's abilities and skills will have to be channeled in ways to both blend and cope with the advancement of technology. The operation, maintenance, and development of new operations and control systems will require sophisticated training and technical skill development—more "specialists" will be needed. Sometimes teams of specialists will be required to perform a complex task. On the other hand, certain operations will be made so simple and routine as to require only minimal skill development.

Structure and Power

Structure sets out formal paths of communication and types of working relationships. It creates formal authority—the right to direct others—but does formal authority create real power? Certainly, in some organizations, the level of formal authority at least loosely corresponds to level of power or influence. One's influence on organizational decision making and operations increases as one rises in the organizational hierarchy. People on the same authority level have comparable levels of *organizational power*. However, in some organizations, positions that have the same level of formal authority differ in their level of real power. For example, within a particular organization the vice-president for finance traditionally might wield more power and influence on organizational operations than the vice-president of marketing, even though they are both vice-presidents.

An individual's influence within the organization is affected by personal knowledge and informal channels of communication and relationships. Sometimes an employee who is known to be particularly knowledgeable or innovative will be encouraged to provide inputs into organizational matters beyond what the formal position would suggest. At times, an individual may be highly competent in his or her particular unit, but may not have the broad base of knowledge and skills necessary to have a major impact on areas outside the unit. People frequently will resist changes in structure because they perceive these as changes in power relationships.

Application Example—Motorola

Motorola, Inc., has long been known as a leader in the high technology fields of communications and consumer electronics. Its pioneering work in car radios had spawned the successful development of sound systems and televisions for the consumer market. These products had even given the company its name, a blend of "motor" and "Victrola."

During the 1970s, however, legislation and competitive forces made it increasingly more difficult for Motorola to improve performance in some long established product areas. Cost containment efforts, including the assembly of product components overseas, were attempted. These efforts, however, could not keep its Quasar television subsidiary from continuing to lose money. In 1974 the subsidiary was sold. The decision recognized that competitive and technological forces required Motorola to focus its leadership in high technology areas in new directions.

Strategic plans developed in the mid-1970s determined that Motorola should take advantage of its leadership in high technology fields. It needed a third business area to go with its strong semiconductor and communications operations and to replace its original consumer electronics business, which had become too mature. This third area, the Information Systems Group, emerged with the acquisitions of Codex Corporation in 1977 and Four-Phase Systems, Inc., in 1982 that raised Motorola's sales to $3.3 billion. The resulting technology triad of semiconductors, communications, and computers gave Motorola the basic building blocks it needed to compete in the fast-growing market for distributed data processing, office automation, and the coming era of remote briefcase-to-computer communications.

These strategic moves have resulted in a quickening of the management restructuring that goes back to the 1950s when Motorola, under Paul E. Galvin, began the decentralization process by forming three distinct business sectors (semiconductors, communications and consumer electronics). At the same time Paul Galvin began to transfer some of the power and decision making to his son, Robert W. Galvin, who is now the chief executive officer of Motorola.

It took until the 1970s, however, to put in place the necessary control systems to allow division managers their autonomy while ensuring the necessary feedback for control purposes. These controls include programs such as corporate fixed asset reviews, capital approval cycles, and tool management programs. Most important are five-year and one-year plans with monthly operating reports that allow the corporate office to evaluate a division's actual performance against its plan.

There has been a conscious effort to reduce the locus of managerial responsibility within the structure. It was hoped that decentralization would support growth opportunities without requiring additional layers of management to be put in place. To further aid in this effort, Motorola has installed a formalized system for human resource management and has restructured its management so that all major business sectors and groups are managed by a two-person "office of" arrangement.

Motorola is also looking at diversification outside its three primary business sectors. Recently, a separate New Enterprises sector reporting directly to Chairman Galvin was formed to ensure that the necessary attention is given to this effort. This New Enterprises sector appears to be the testing ground for new applications of technology that often cross organizational divisions. The use of task forces that possess expertise from various functional and product units link traditionally separate organizational activities. If successful, these pilot operations may some day develop into another business sector.

Whether competition and unforeseen environmental forces will allow Motorola to achieve its sales goal of $15 billion by the early 1990s, of course, cannot be predicted. What is important, however, is that planned changes in structure to decentralization and formalized control systems have been put in place. These structural modifications support Motorola's strategy and allow it the flexibility to deal with the rapidly changing and unpredictable environmental forces certain to be encountered in its high technology areas.

SUMMARY

Thus far we have spoken about the top-down and grass-roots approaches to management. Max Weber's bureaucratic model and Henri Fayol's administrative management are representative of the first approach. Frederick Taylor's scientific management and the human relations movement at Hawthorne Works are examples of the grass-roots approach. This chapter considered the formal *structure* as a *top-down* approach that defines the constraints within which the manager operates. Both Weber and Fayol focused on developing a hierarchy of authority relationships, the underlying connections and lines of communications between jobs, and the rules and regulations for efficient organizational operations. In essence, they created the formal structure, or framework, for the organization. Structural features—such as the degree of specialization, degree of (de)centralization, the manner in which people are grouped together (departmentalization), and the manager's span of control—all act to define a manager's role within the organization.

The formal structure is affected by many factors. Technological change, increased size and complexity of the operation, environmental uncertainty, and changing organizational goals are just a few. Therefore, they should be dynamic and allowed to evolve over time to fit changing circumstances.

Newer approaches to organization have been developed to allow for greater flexibility in dealing with changing environmental conditions. These include the project management, matrix structure, and office of the president.

Decisions affecting organizational structure involve values and goals for both the organization and its individual members. Although conflicts may occur, they should not be irreconcilable. In fact, the appropriate structure is one that achieves (1) organizational purpose, (2) individual self-development and growth, and (3) social satisfaction.

Questions for Study and Discussion

1. What is formal structure? How does it differ from informal structure?
2. What are some of the benefits and drawbacks of division of labor?
3. What are some of the benefits and drawbacks of specialization?
4. In what ways can organization units and task assignments be structured?
5. Compare centralized and decentralized authority.
6. What are some circumstances and factors that shape structure?
7. In what ways are uncertainty and independence considered overall structural features?
8. How can structure reduce the need for supervision?
9. How can you use your knowledge of organization structure to further your career?
10. What are some ways in which technological advances affect structure?
11. What are some of the factors that lead to the emergence of project organization?

12. Name some of the problems that project and matrix organization face.

13. How is formal authority related to power?

CASE: TONI'S DRUGS

"Toni's Drugs" was a long-time dream of Toni Hopkins, who had worked in the prescription department of a large national drug chain. Toni liked her work, and she liked meeting people. But most of all she wanted to get into her own business. To open the door in the morning and know that this was hers was a long-standing ambition and dream. Toni budgeted her expenses carefully and finally put together enough money to go into business. She found an ideal location in a shopping center containing several high traffic stores. When she wanted to get a loan to cover some of her working capital needs, however, several of the banks were reluctant to lend her the money—something about "women" in their own businesses and their not being committed. Fortunately, Toni found a bank that had confidence in her and in her project, and she got the needed capital. From the first, Toni's Drugs was a success. She put in several specialty lines. Novelties and an exceptional department for "women only"—cosmetics and the like. (See Exhibit 2-5 for a typical store layout.) She had a good feeling for hiring and training people and quickly built their loyalty and respect. When the store located beside her lost its lease, she expanded into this area, and sales continued to grow rapidly. Three years later she added still another store when somebody else went out of business.

At that point, Toni's Drugs offered prescriptions, standard drug items, small novelty items, a "women only" unit, watches, radios, and cameras, plus a photo service. When the city's liquor ordinances were changed, she acquired a license and relocated things so as to stock low-alcoholic-content beverages (beer, wine, etc.). The same year that Toni Hopkins secured a lease on the additional store, she spotted another location that looked ideal for a "Toni Store." Interestingly, at this point several banks offered Toni loans at very competitive rates, and she was able to work out a good, low-interest arrangement. The new store was as large as the three stores "put together" at the original location. In the years that followed, Toni's Drugs No. 2 proved to be quite successful, and other stores were added. All told, Toni's had grown to a relatively successful five-store chain with locations throughout the city (see Exhibit 2-6). Although the chain was relatively successful, it was not without its managerial problems.

Exhibit 2-5 Layout of a Typical Toni's Drugs Store

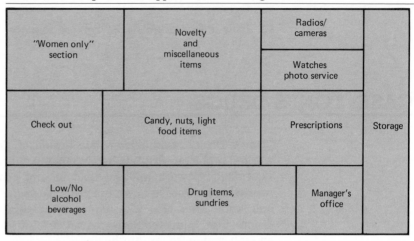

Staffing for Typical Store (Two Shifts)[a]

Manager	1
Assistant manager	1
Check-out	4
Sales people	14
Druggist	1 (days only)
Stock clerks	3

[a]Includes full-time and part-time.

Exhibit 2-6 Organization Chart, Toni's Drugs Chain

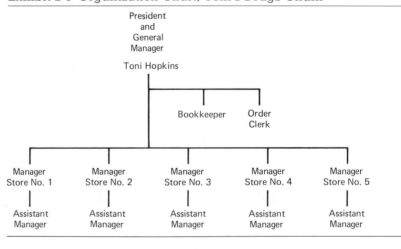

Toni had been in business for quite a number of years, but she was not as young and energetic as when she started her business. Having to move around constantly between her stores and the fact that they were open 12 to 16 hours a day, seven days a week, proved to be a very heavy schedule. Toni decided to talk to Helen France, a long-time friend and also successful business person. They met for lunch.

Toni: Helen, how do I get on top of it?

Helen: What do you mean, Toni?

Toni: I'm talking about this business of mine. It's making money, but the business isn't as profitable as it used to be.

Helen: Do you mean you're actually making less money with five than with four or even three stores?

Toni: Oh, no. . . . It's just that the profit per store isn't as great. I set up a manager for each store, and we even have an assistant manager who takes over each store in the evening or on weekends. But I keep moving around between the stores, and all I get is problems. I've set things up so that I make a complete round of visits between the stores every two to three days. At the store, I spend time with the manager . . . check sales, work out order plans on all the big ticket items, and . . .

Helen: Toni—I can't believe it! You mean that you do all of these things? No wonder you're beat! What are your managers for??

Questions

What type of organization structure has developed at Toni's? Describe its chief features.

Is it a formal or informal structure?

How are responsibilities distributed—to Toni? to Store Managers? to Assistant Store Managers?

What has been the basis for specialization? What has been the basis for the division of labor? Is this a centralized or decentralized organization? Why?

Comment on Toni's basis for structuring the organization as it has grown. Will her mode of growth and structuring be satisfactory for the future? Why?

What should Toni do *now* regarding the structuring of her organization? Name your assumptions.

If Toni's grows to say 8 or even 10 stores in the city, how should she then structure it? Name your assumptions.

If you were employed at Toni's, what do you think you'd have to do to move into a managerial position?

What would be your prospects for future growth and advancement in this organization? What would be your prospects for moving into a managerial position?

References

Barnard, Chester, *The Functions of an Executive*. Cambridge, Mass.: Harvard University Press (1938).

Bird, Mary, "Organizing in a Changing Environment," *Magazine of Bank Administration* **57**(4) (April 1981): 20–27.

Bobbitt, H. Randolph, Jr., and Jeffrey D. Ford, "Decision-Maker Choice as a Determinant of Organization Structure," *Academy of Management Review* **5** (January 1980): 13–23.

Carlisle, Howard M., "A Contingency Approach to Decentralization," *S.A.M. Advanced Management Journal* **39** (July 1974): 9–81.

Davis, Louis E., "Evolving Alternative Organization Designs: Their Socio-technical Bases," *Human Relations* **30** (March 1977): 261–273.

Davis, Stanley M., and Paul R. Lawrence, *Matrix*. Reading, Mass.: Addison-Wesley Publishing Co (1977).

Drucker, Peter F., "New Templates for Today's Organizations," *Harvard Business Review* **52** (January-February 1974): 45–53.

Dugger, William, "Corporate Bureaucracy: The Incidence of the Bureaucratic Process," *Journal of Economic Issues* **14**(2) (June 1980): 399–409.

Duncan, Robert, "What is the Right Organization Structure? Decision Tree Analysis Provides the Answer," *Organizational Dynamics* **7** (Winter 1979): 59–80.

Fram, Eugene, "Changing Expectations for Third Sector Executives," *Human Resource Management* **19**(3) (Fall 1980): 8–15.

Greiner, Larry, and Virginia Schein, "The Paradox of Managing a Project-Oriented Matrix: Establishing Coherence within Chaos," *Sloan Management Review* **22**(2) (Winter 1981): 17–22.

Hutchinson, John, "Evolving Organizational Forms," *Columbia Journal of World Business* **11** (Summer 1976): 48–58.

Ivancevich, John M., and James H. Donnelly, Jr., "Relation of Organizational Structure to Job Satisfaction, Anxiety-Stress, and Performance," *Administrative Science Quarterly* **20** (June 1975): 272–280.

Jackson, John H., and Cyril P. Morgan, *Organization Theory: A Macro Perspective for Management*. Englewood Cliffs, N.J.: Prentice-Hall (1978).

Kerzner, Harold, and Paul Serpentine, "Designing Project Control Forms," *Journal of Systems Management* **31**(3) (March 1981): 27–33.

Kolodny, Harvey F., "Evolution to a Matrix Organization," *Academy of Management Review* **4** (October 1979): 543–553.

Lawrence, Paul R., Harvey F. Kolodny, and Stanley M. Davis, "The Human Side of the Matrix," *Organizational Dynamics* **6** (Summer 1977): 43–61.

Mackenzie, Kenneth D., *Organizational Structures*. Arlington Heights, Ill.: AHM Publishing Corp. (1978).

Mann, John, "The Training of Project Managers," *Industrial and Commercial Training (U.K.)* **13**(3) (March 1981): 101–103.

Miles, Raymond E., Charles C. Snow, Alan D. Meyer, and Henry J. Coleman,

Jr., "Organizational Strategy, Structure, and Process," *Academy of Management Review* **3** (July 1978): 546–562.

Perrow, Charles, "The Bureaucratic Paradox: The Efficient Organization Centralizes in Order to Decentralize," *Organizational Dynamics* **5** (Spring 1977): 3–14.

Rehder, Robert, "What American and Japanese Managers Are Learning From Each Other," *Business Horizons* **24**(2) (March-April 1981): 63–70.

Sayles, Leonard R., "Matrix Management: The Structure with a Future," *Organizational Dynamics* **5** (Autumn 1976): 2–17.

Simon, Herbert A., *Administrative Behavior,* 3d ed. New York: The Free Press (1976).

Wilson, Scott, "Productivity Means Delegating Responsibility to Avoid 'I Told You So' at Project End," *Computerworld* **15**(13) (March 30 1981): 14–15.

CHAPTER 3

A SYSTEMATIC APPROACH TO MANAGEMENT

KEY
QUESTIONS
ADDRESSED
IN CHAPTER

1. How can the organization be compared to a system?
2. What is the relationship of the personnel aspects to the technical features of work systems?
3. How does uncertainty affect systems management?
4. What are some of the common situations faced by managers using systems management approaches?
5. What is the systems approach to management?

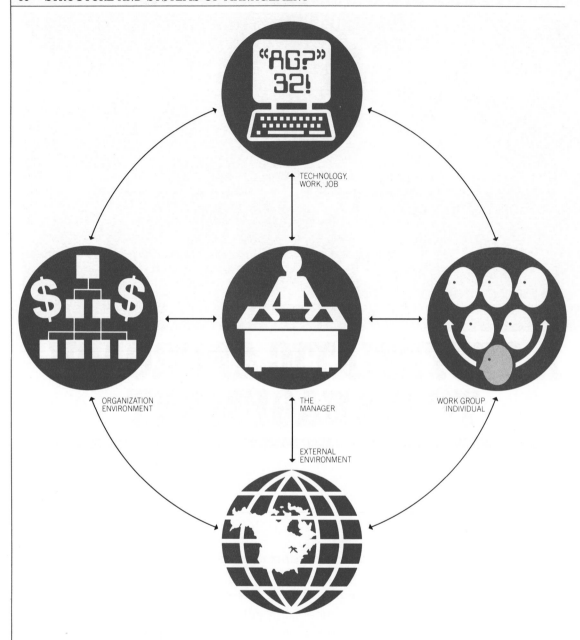

The manager's work–life spaces

*At some point in the **life cycle** of virtually every system, its ability to succeed in spite of itself runs out.*

THE CHAPTER IN BRIEF

In the context of systems theory, the organization can be thought of as one element that acts interdependently with a number of other elements, and can be described as a flow of inputs and outputs. External, or environmental elements are a part of these relationships. They include competitors, suppliers, the community, customers, creditors, and government (local, state, and federal) agencies. Simply, the organization takes its inputs as resources from a larger system—the environment—processes these inputs, and returns them to the environment in a changed form (see Exhibit 3-1).

For example, in an automobile manufacturing firm the inputs are raw materials—glass, steel, and rubber—purchased from other large firms. The engineering and production departments transform these into the end product—cars. Transformation of inputs into outputs is characteristic of all types of systems. Whether one considers hospitals, colleges, and other service organizations, it is clear that something is still being transformed.

At the same time, the enterprise can be viewed as an **open system** because it is an interdependent unit that is greatly affected by the forces and factors in the external environment. The open-system concept is a fundamental idea in systems theory. Prior to systems theory it was conventional to consider factories and other organizations as self-contained entities whose boundaries were neatly proscribed by their property lines. After the introduction of systems theory concepts, one was likely to acknowledge that even the most simple organization is not self-contained but relies upon and is affected by many others beyond the property lines.

Exhibit 3-1 The Organization as a System

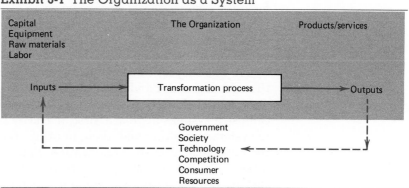

GREAT PERSON PROFILE

Theodore N. Vail (1845–1920)

Theodore N. Vail joined the then-troubled Bell Telephone Company in 1878, after having worked in the railroad industry and the U.S. Postal Service.

His goal-oriented planning and foresightedness envisioned the telephone service as an *open system*. With the rapid advances being made in technology at the time, Vail felt that the public would be better served by one large organization rather than many small companies in direct competition with each other. Yet he was also aware of the public's distrust of monopolies.

His *systematic approach* in the development of the Bell Telephone Company took into account that its survival relied upon the ability to integrate the interests of the company with those of society. Vail had an uncanny ability to anticipate future demands, and he saw that the company's goals should place customer service ahead of profit maximization. From this overall systems view came the ideas of a strong orientation to meeting customer needs for quality service, the establishment of a strong financial base that relied on many small investors in its stock, a strong emphasis on technological research, and even contro-versial initiatives to strengthen public regulation of the company.

The attempts to consolidate these varied interests gave birth to many distinctive policies that served to integrate the different parts of the company. They helped form the basis of the system we know today as A.T.&T.

To be successful an organization needs to be dynamic (adaptive), for static systems rarely survive when all else is changing. Organizations need to change their goals and objectives, their products, their personnel, their markets, suppliers, and locations, when forces in the environment dictate it.

In this chapter we view the organization as a system. We discuss the inherent social and technical aspects of this system and the environmental changes that affect it. We also examine how managers can use a systems approach, first, to clarify trends and relationships in systemic thinking and, then, to utilize these thoughts to improve the management of the organization. Finally, we explain how these ideas are related to managerial growth and the skill building necessary for dealing with a variety of organizational situations.

BACKGROUND

Systems Are People—Too!

In discussing the structural aspects of the organizational system, it should be kept in mind that the system is composed of people and is therefore highly dependent on their individual performance and effective cooperative working relationships. A poorly designed system can reduce its members' growth, development, and sense of competence and accomplishment. The needs of the individual member and the organizational goals can at times present conflicts. A systems approach can reduce both present or potential conflicts by forging a network of linkages that permit the communication of information and facilitate work flow. The organization can help develop conditions that allow the people who make up the organization better to achieve their own goals while also furthering the goals of the organization. In this way the performance of the members of the organization is more directly compatible with the organizational system and structure. In most organizations, individuals form themselves into subsystems, or groups. Groups have their own structure, goals, and leaders. Any large organization has a great number of groups or subsystems. They arise because of the *social needs* of individuals, friendships, physical proximity, or similar interests. Informal groups are formed out of these social needs; they are discussed in detail in Chapter 10.

Environmental Changes Affecting the System

The organization is highly vulnerable to forces and factors in the external environment. In recent years changes and trends in government, society, and cultures have had increasing impacts on organizational systems. These changes usually filter through and affect all levels of the organization and each of its members. One example of this is the increasingly complex pattern of legislation affecting freedom of decision making; reporting of information; constraints on managerial action, hiring, and recruitment policies; and the structure of the organization as a whole. Many organizational activities and social responsibilities that at one time were voluntary are now mandated by the law.

As government and legal regulation increases, its effect on the organization is often one of restricting the role of the manager. Much more attention must be given to such matters as hiring and promotion practices, employee safety, product evaluation, and developing and reporting new types of information. Adaptation to legal regulation and control has become an integral part of the manager's job.

National and international developments have also had a significant effect on organizations. Inflation, high interest rates, the oil crisis, and high unemployment are all examples of external factors influencing the organization. Although some of these changes may seem far removed from the everyday business process, systems thinking necessitates that these changes be viewed also in the narrower scope of their effects on the lives, decisions, and behavior of the individuals comprising the organization. For example, concern about inflation is likely to be translated into higher wage demands among employees. High unemployment may bring about increased concern about job security. In this sense, then, seemingly uncontrollable political or economic forces can be brought into a perspective that is much narrower and in which the issues are more clearly defined.

Consumerism has also created external pressures on the organization. The increasing diversity of consumer decisions, the complexity and technology of consumer products, and the high costs of product liability insurance have all contributed to a changed consumer–seller relationship. Consumers expect increased responsibility and service from the organization, causing changes in operations, management, and almost every phase of the organizational system. A systems view considers not only the people comprising the organization but extends the consideration to include the entire scope of individuals participating within *and* interfacing with the organization.

Increased government regulation has also given employees

Pressman reads the last edition of the Philadelphia Bulletin.

greater protection concerning work-related activity in areas found objectionable, hazardous, or illegal. For example, Occupational Safety and Health Act (OSHA) violations can be reported by employees directly to OSHA officials. Equal Employment Opportunity (EEO) violations can be handled in a like manner. The increased autonomy and power of the worker changes the nature of the employer–employee "contract" and in many cases may even reduce the need for unionization. Equalizing power levels and increasing the possibility of repercussions from hasty managerial decision making expands the need for systems thinking. It becomes increasingly important to view any change as one that will affect many parts of the organization eventually and to consider how these changes relate to external forces. This forces the organization and its managers to look at decisions from the viewpoint of the people it will affect. The cost of neglecting the systems approach can become very high indeed in the light of possible government actions, class action suits which are increasingly being filed by female workers and minorities, and the increasing desire for unionization by formerly nonunionized working groups such as engineers.

A final external effect to be considered is that of rapidly advancing technological change with which the organization is confronted. Its effects, though originally external, may diffuse through many areas of the organization, affecting managers and workers alike.

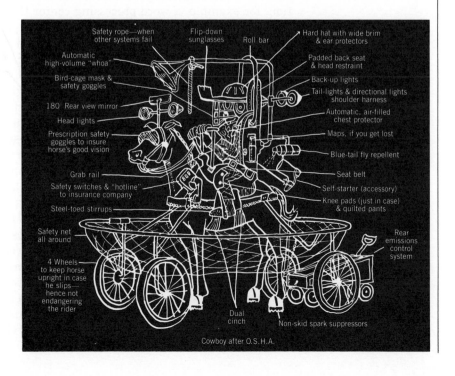

Cowboy after O.S.H.A.

Computerization and computerized information systems are common forms of change that bring with them the need for increased training and personnel requirements. Additionally, the forces that resist change and innovation must be dealt with in order to help assure organizational continuity and renewal of its human and technical resources.

Sociotechnical Systems

Organizational systems are often thought of as **sociotechnical systems**. This concept arises from the consideration that a work system requires both a technical organization, composed of methods or equipment and processes, and a social organization that includes those who carry out organization tasks. The usual definition of technology as "industrial arts" or "industrial science" is overly restrictive. Over time, technology has functioned as a major factor in societal improvements and gains in performance and output and the concept is equally applicable to service and production units. It embodies the total of work procedures, knowledge, machines, tools, and experience for bringing about societal improvements. **Technology,** for our purpose, is defined as the human employment of an aid, physical or intellectual, in generating structures, products, or services that can increase man's productivity through better understanding of, adaptation to, and control of his environment.

The technological system can place constraints on social interaction, for example, a word processing center that confines workers to their stations. Since people are an integral part of these systems, various social and psychological aspects need to be considered. For example, people may be fearful of new technologies because they have unknown elements. People question their ability to learn new things. Studies indicate that certain technological changes affect the (re)organization of jobs, performance, productivity, and work relationships. Employee fears may thus have a sound foundation.

The concept of performance as a joint result of technology and people holds true regardless of how the system is designed. This relationship can be found in hospitals and government as well as in the traditional business setting. Because of the relationship between the technological and social systems, human behavior factors cannot be ignored. Behavioral analyses of organizations include a close look at supervisory attitudes and leadership qualities, worker characteristics, and the informal groups that influence worker behavior. These factors also influence productivity, motivation, and job satisfaction. Top-down attempts by top management to control these factors and to discover the right combination of technologies and social relationships must often deal with reshaping organizational objectives in order to produce the desired levels of productivity and psychological satisfaction. At the same time, grass-roots or bottoms-up approaches at lower levels of management are concerned with implementing new(er) or modified technologies and gaining acceptance of them while maintaining good morale among the work force. This often requires that a manager possess good interpersonal skills.

Certain factors affect the degree of compatibility of the elements within a sociotechnical system. These factors are the technology itself, the expertise of supervision in dealing with human problems, and the ability of workers to cooperate and work together. Work technology can be viewed as a **man–machine system** in which workers have a significant (though different) influence on the quality and quantity of output as compared to traditional work systems. Many highly advanced systems have failed to achieve their potential because of people being unable or unwilling to cope with the technology. Technological change also creates the need for different worker skills, .and more rapid changes place more strain on present skills. Also, as the technology becomes more automated, mental, rather than physical, skills are emphasized.

Supervision can influence the sociotechnical system performance through supervisory direction and leadership skills. The more highly skilled supervisor is able to improve human relations and communications, and develop the best qualities of subordinates. Since structural considerations, such as scope of responsibility and division of labor, may influence the supervisor's ability to utilize these skills, units that are small or decentralized in terms of responsibility are often thought to be more receptive to supervisory influence.

Informal groups influence the system to the extent that they often determine standards of output for the group. Informal groups are groups that exist primarily to satisfy the social needs and requirements of people. Certain rules, or patterns, are established by the informal group that affect work as well as non-work-related behavior. These groups often determine work pace, which procedures or rules to obey or ignore, which supervisors deserve more respect, and many other significant work-related behaviors (the details of which are discussed in Chapter 10). Groups can be a strong influence on the acceptance or rejection of work methods and new techniques. Thus, experienced supervisors and managers attempt to effectively utilize group behavior in encouraging the acceptance of technological change.

Several important elements constitute the relationships found in the sociotechnical complex, including the following (see Exhibit 3-2).

1. Formal work roles, including workers, supervisors, managers, and technical (staff) support groups.
2. Formal prescribed relationships (discussed in Chapter 2).

Exhibit 3-2 Relationships in Sociotechnical Systems

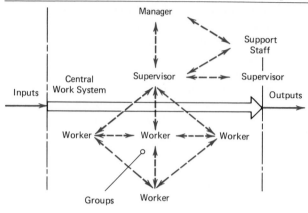

External system	Technological:	specific to job, job relations—confers authority status.
	Formal:	organization requirements to maintain affiliation.
Internal system	Informal:	voluntary interaction.

^aConcepts clarified in R. Dubin, *The World of Work,* revised edition (Englewood Cliffs, N.J.: Prentice-Hall, 1974).

3. The links between communication and the work system that provide the basis for the conduct of both formal and informal relationships and functions. These communication links are crucial in determining the effectiveness of the system.

4. The range of behaviors within work systems, from the purely "technical" to the "social."

The work-related activity of the worker is constrained by the technology, supervisory directives, and organizational controls (see Exhibit 3-2). The performance of the individual is also affected by motivational processes that reflect his or her perception of the environment, personal needs, and colleagues. The worker, manager, or professional staff exhibits a variety of behavioral patterns, including those that pertain specifically to the job or that typically are prescribed by rules and regulations. The combination of these behavioral patterns constitutes an **external system,** within which are other patterns, designated the **internal system.** When reliance on formal authority and structural relationships does not "get the job done," an informal (internal) system will usually spring up to fill this vacuum. With two systems "operating" side by side, confusion and delay can result. Rather than attempting to stifle the informal system and its leader, a good manager should realize that the existence of the informal or social system is (also) a distinct need and, therefore, modification of the formal (or external) system may be indicated. (A more detailed discussion on leadership will be found in Chapter 9.)

Relevance of Systems to the Individual

As individuals, our careers take us into complex systems within all types of organizations. The challenge to personal development and career growth becomes one of understanding the role we play in these systems, what our role ought to be, and the forces that affect us. As a supervisor or manager, we not only define and recognize change but also react to it. We must define and clarify not only how we do things but also how we react to situations. These considerations become extremely important, since the improvement of managerial skills depends on the flexibility and understanding one shows by adaptation to many different kinds of systems. Since the systems approaches involve the external organization environment and various internal events at every level of the organization, it touches and affects (you) the manager, throughout the organization. No matter what level you may be at, sooner or later changes in the system will affect you—your strategy for dealing with this change must be developed. In the following section we discuss ways in which the systems approach can be more clearly defined in order to apply it to your individual managerial needs.

The Manager's Life Space and the Systems Approach

The material in this chapter emphasizes the impact that the organization's external-environment life space has on the manager. Forces in the external environment are outside the control of the manager and most organizations. Of particular importance are the advancements in technology that have raised critical issues concerning managerial obsolescence within many companies. It is a fact that the technical knowledge and information you are now learning in school will become outdated quickly as changes in legislation, societal values, and new discoveries occur. This does not mean that what you are learning is unimportant. Rather, it means that learning is a lifelong "adventure" that is a requirement for managers and others to improve their knowledge and skills.

Technological changes have resulted in some work systems that are highly structured, with many routine and highly specialized jobs. Often work activities become much more complex. Specialization tends to restrict worker (and manager) mobility and presents to the manager additional problems in job assignments. These same changes require a greater degree of coordination among more specialized jobs. The need to coordinate widely different activities becomes a

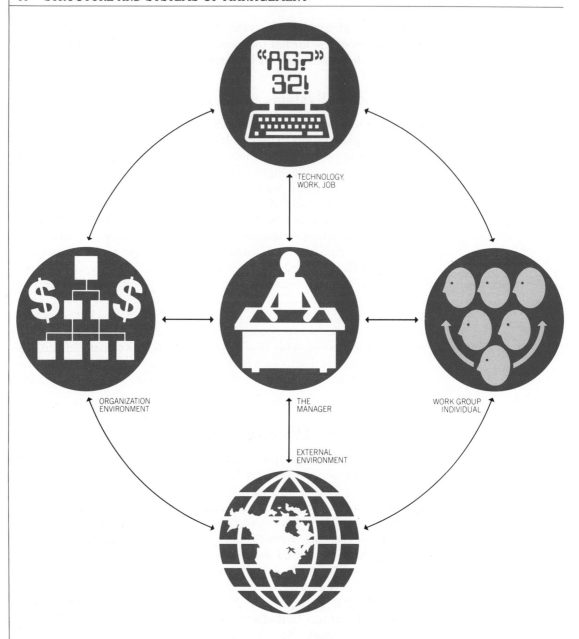

The manager's work–life spaces

central part of many supervisors' responsibilities, as they find themselves dealing with other supervisors and technical support specialists to a greater extent so that the overall operation will continue to run smoothly.

Take the example of a customer complaining about slow service in the supermarket. The store manager may have a number of ways to solve the problem. Some of these include:

1. Identify the peak periods, and schedule additional checkers.
2. Redefine job descriptions to have other store personnel (such as stockers) help out in peak periods.
3. Invest in computerized registers to speed checkouts.
4. Add an express line for those customers with few items.

Which solution prevails is dependent on a variety of factors. Yet the manager can likely implement solutions Nos. 2 and 4 quite quickly while solution No. 1 may require some additional data-gathering time. Solution No. 3 may be a long-term solution, but it is likely to require corporate approval and more detailed financial justification. All solutions, however, will affect the worker and work-group relationship with the manager. They are also likely to result in changed organizational relationships and may require the workers to adapt to new work processes.

Much change is required of a manager as one progresses up the hierarchy. Managers are faced with the challenge of broadening their

Computerized registers in supermarkets speed check-outs while making more information available to managers.

perspective that requires an understanding of the big picture and good planning and conceptual skills. Yet his or her performance at lower levels is likely to be judged by his or her knowledge in a highly specialized area and his or her ability to carry out directives in detail.

NEWER DEVELOPMENTS AND APPROACHES

Properties of the System

Systems have properties that determine the responsiveness or unresponsiveness of an organization. These properties, or features, also affect the organization's ability to monitor change and to respond rapidly to that change. The variation in response time can be attributed to several factors. Some of these factors are barriers in the form of people, technology, personal habit, or in a tendency toward the old way of doing things. Once workers are entrenched in a comfortable, habitual way of doing things they often resist changes. A procedural or technical change represents a stressful situation in which the worker is forced to accept new jobs, learn new procedures, and abandon the old (and nonstressful) routine he or she has become used to. This fear and resistance to change is one basic barrier. "Technology" barriers can be caused by the inability of an organization to respond to change as a result of size, financial situation, or legal or personal constraints. A manager's attention must then be directed toward many aspects of the situation, including the ways in which others will view these changes and attempt to block them. The manager's challenge is to be able to identify key factors and set priorities.

Barriers to change also may occur through constricted information flows to managers. If the organization is not tuned in to the advances and changes in knowledge and new technologies, its response to these changes could be significantly slower than industry leaders in innovation. **Programmed responses** for "routine" situations that involve predetermined handling of given situations in an organization can also reduce abilities to respond owing to inflexibility. When managers are directed to respond in predetermined ways to certain situations, their ability, and therefore that of the company, cannot help but be affected. The organizational capability for handling the situations that arise should also be considered. If an organization does not have the supervisory personnel capable of making effective *non*programmed decisions, or workers who are adaptable, or an organizational structure that is flexible, an organization's change-readiness may be adversely affected.

Uncertainty

A major challenge of systems management is that of dealing with **uncertainty.** The key to understanding this force is that each element of a system contributes different degrees of variability or unexpected behavior on performance of the system. Some of these elements are more easily understood than others and are therefore more controllable or more easily dealt with than others. For example, technological elements such as machinery failure or computer downtime are more easily understood and handled than may be the psychological forces operating behind absentee problems, worker dissatisfaction, or supervisory problems.

Even though some internal matters may be very difficult to deal with, they are generally easier to handle than external problems. Examples of external factors that are not easily controlled are the social, economic, and political changes that occur in the system's larger environment and that were detailed previously. Good systems management requires the ability to analyze organizational activities and adapt to these environmental uncertainties. Adaptations such as new organizational functions or products or expansion of services may be internal ways of dealing with external uncertainties.

These considerations give us a firm basis for understanding the factors contributing to uncertainty. In addition to the uncontrollable external factors already discussed, information and individual judgments of uncertainty also play a significant role. The amount and quality of information the organization is able to collect and process from both internal and external sources will help determine its ability to cope with uncertainty. The more aware and knowledgeable the organization is of possible changes and alternatives, the more prepared and adaptable it will be. This information will be of little value, however, unless it is timely enough to be utilized before changes occur and complete enough to ensure the correct response to impending change.

Individual judgment is also a factor contributing to uncertainty, because just as every individual is unique, so is his or her judgment and response to situations of uncertainty. Each individual has a different risk-taking outlook. The reasoning judgment and action of a high risk taker would certainly differ from that of a low risk taker in the face of an uncertain situation. An individual's personality would, in fact, change his or her reaction to uncertainty. Levels of aggressiveness, competitiveness, optimism, and self-confidence are just a few of the personality traits that contribute to how an individual responds to uncertainty.

The concept of uncertainty is not, however, as totally uncontrollable as it may seem. There are measures that may be taken to deal with system uncertainty. These measures include better training in the analysis of and adaptation to change and uncertainty. Also, increased information processing and analysis is also an important tool in coping with systems uncertainty. It is greatly facilitated by the increasing use of computerized management information systems. These systems are becoming more effective in accumulating and disbursing the type and amount of information that is most relevant and useful to the unique needs of the manager. This "tailored" information tends to be much more general in scope than that provided for lower-level personnel, yielding the type of information that is most useful in facilitating systems thinking. It gives an overall view of the internal as well as the external system and provides the manager with as much knowledge as is possible with which to make a judgment in the light of system uncertainty.

An effective **management information system** (MIS) allows the manager to monitor more closely the vital factors affecting his or her organization. These critical factors might include information on the structure of his or her particular industry, environmental factors, industry position, and competitive strategy. By reviewing just the critical factors, the manager is saved from trying to dig through mounds of time-consuming information that is useless for his needs.

By keeping a finger on the pulse of the organization, the manager is better equipped to establish appropriate performance standards. He or she will have a working knowledge of where the organization stands when events are occurring, and the current level of performance. This overall knowledge gives the manager a better grasp on needed approaches in **contingency planning,** that is, fall-back ac-

Will you fit comfortably into the manager's desk of the future?

tivities to use in case "such and such" develops. This is a very important ability to develop because of the presence of change and uncertainty.

Nature of Work and Managerial Skills

Managerial growth is dependent on acquiring skills that are useful in dealing with a variety of organizational situations and that build on the systems notions and approaches that have been discussed throughout this chapter.

Technological change has an impact on the supervisor's directive functions, control activities, and both the technical and nontechnical aspects of his or her administrative responsibilities (see Table 3-1). Table 3-1 illustrates one type of change. However, these changes are not uniform in the sense of requiring more or less directive effort. For example, as the table suggests, increased dependence upon machines on the part of workers might require more supervisory direction because of the absence of appropriate worker skills. From the broader point of view of organizational systems, planning may assume additional importance, impersonal controls may increase, and technical staff support groups may become more important.

As jobs become more interrelated with increased technology, the need for improved coordination among managers becomes apparent. Coordination requires that supervisors and managers interact with a wide variety of staff specialists and other line managers. This demands on the part of the manager both increased knowledge and understanding of the new technology and its system effects and the ability to communicate effectively with subordinates and others. It

Table 3-1 A Common Effect of Technological Change on Workers, Supervisors, and the Work System

Workers	Supervisors	System
Job knowledge (down)	Need for knowledge (up)	Impersonal controls (up)
Routinization (up)	Directives to workers (up)	Use of technical specialists (up)
Subdivided tasks (up)	Machine responsibility (up)	Broader planning for production and quality (up)
Mobility (down)	Maintenance of flow (up)	Authority levels (up)
Work pace control (down)	Short-run planning (up)	First-line supervisory span of control (up)
Dependency on machines (up)	Work with colleagues (up)	
Craft lore (down)	Work with technical specialists (up)	
	Responsibility to develop (down); to carry out (up)	
	Service workers needed (up)	

Source: Elmer H. Burack, *Organization Analysis: Theory and Applications.* Hinsdale, Ill.: The Dryden Press (1975).

also suggests that managers need to develop a more systematic approach to problem solving.

The Systems Approach to Management

A practical systems approach can be viewed as a series of steps each of which calls for thorough analysis before the next is taken. The four steps are as follows.

1. Establish the main parties or factors in a situation. Does the change or problem affect only you, an entire group, a department, or the whole organization?
2. Clarify the relationships. Are those affected supervisors, managers, workers, or combinations of groups?
3. Identify the forces at work. Are these forces internal or external to the organization? Will it be a one-time problem or one that must be dealt with on a recurring basis, requiring the development of specific approaches to deal with a chronic problem? Define the problem as you see it.
4. Establish actions or goals. Strategies must be determined. Long- and short-range problems must be dealt with in different time frames. Priorities for action must be determined.

Each step is part of systemic thinking in managerial problem analysis. It is crucial to be sensitive to the interrelationships that are involved in the definition and resolution of organization change or problems. Exhibit 3-3 illustrates this systemic approach.

Applying the Systems Model: An Example

All too often, the types of models for "systems analysis" illustrated in Exhibit 3-3 seem to be far from real problems. Thus, the purpose of this section is to illustrate how this model can be applied to a specific company's situation.

Frank Marteri was the general supervisor of a steel processing unit. He was concerned because it was becoming more and more difficult to encourage people from the bargaining unit (union) to try out for supervision. In discussions that Frank had with the men they often mentioned job security (risk in leaving the union) and pay (supervisors made little more than experienced workers) as reasons for not taking on a supervisor's job. Although many of these objections were real ones, he started to suspect that there might be a deeper problem. Growing competition in the steel industry had forced the company to modernize many of its processing units. In Frank's unit, new lines, instruments, controls, and procedures had been in-

Exhibit 3-3 A Systems-Oriented, Problem-Solving Model

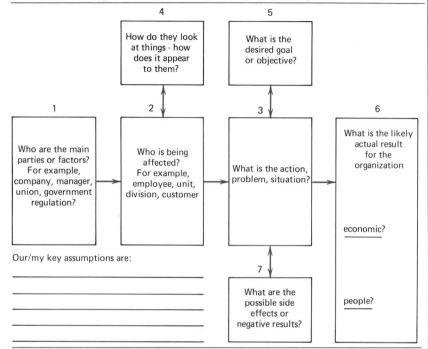

Source: Based on Elmer H. Burack, "Personnel Problem Solving Approach," in *Cases in Personnel Management.* St. Paul: West Publishing Co. (1978).

stalled. He started to suspect that the members of his unit were fearful regarding their ability to deal with the new technology and what it all meant in their personal lives.

The use of Exhibit 3-3 in Frank Marteri's situation could be aproached from several different viewpoints—all using systems thinking but each emphasizing a different aspect of the situation. For example, Frank might have tried first to analyze things as they were likely to be after the change and how they might have affected his crew. This approach, in turn, could have led to several forms of solution approaches. For purposes of illustration, what follows (in Exhibit 3-4) is a systems approach to problem analysis for Frank's situation—to crystallize key issues within a complex sociotechnical activity.

Simulation: A Quantitative Technique of Systems Management

Often, management is faced with a decision that is much more complex than that faced by Frank Marteri. When this occurs, simulation is often the method of analysis chosen. **Simulation** basically means

Exhibit 3-4 Frank's Initial Problem-Solving Approach

1. *Who or What Are the Main Parties or Factors?*
   Competitive events
   Technological improvements
2. *Who Is Affected?*
   Bargaining unit people
   Current supervisors
   Maintenance people
   Technologists
   Frank himself
   . . .
   Plant planners
3. *What Is the Problem?*
   (a) Massive internal changes affecting machines, procedures, and the character of the work environment
   (b) Greater uncertainty as to impacts and meaning for the individual
4. *How Is the Problem Seen by Parties Affected?*
   Threatening
   Many unknowns
   Move away from past habits
5. *Desired Goals?*
   Improve economic performance
   Retain competitive edge
6. *Results (Possible)?*
   Economic: High operating costs
   Potential for turnover
   Damage to equipment
   People: Low morale
   Loss of confidence
   Afraid of supervisor
7. *Side Effects?*
   Make union more militant
   Block progression of people from "ranks"

the representation of a real-world situation. In business situations, it usually refers to the use of a computer to perform experiments on a model of the real-world relationships. Such experiments may be done before the system is in operation as an aid in its design, or to evaluate the system's response to changes once it is in operation.

Simulation models are found in all functional areas of business. In marketing, they are used to investigate the effectiveness of proposed sales promotions. Accountants use simulation in forecasting

GREAT PERSON PROFILE

John Henry Patterson (1844–1922)

John Henry Patterson was born on a farm near Dayton, Ohio. After attending Dartmouth College, he took a job as a canal toll collector. Since the job was too boring and undemanding for Patterson, he left to become a supervisor for a coal company. In those days companies had no orderly means of accounting for cash sales. After Patterson analyzed the problem, he ordered two cash registers—a technological innovation that was designed both to prevent theft by clerks and to bring more order into business transactions.

He quickly foresaw the future for cash registers, and with $6,500 he acquired control of the business. Having little knowledge of selling or manufacturing, he capitalized on the experience of his best sales agent to develop a systematic sales·approach using an organized set of sales procedures.

When $50,000 worth of defective products were returned from Britain, Patterson became aware of the need for better quality control and improved working conditions. He moved his desk to the factory floor and improved working conditions as well as pay to increase

morale and the quality of work performed. He emphasized a systematic approach to all problems and demonstrated the worth of *systematic analysis* in business. His National Cash Register Company brought cash registers to the most distant corners of the world and thereby helped introduce more orderly and honest business methods to organizations.

the future financial condition of the firm. Inventory control managers simulate the cost-effectiveness of various inventory control policies. Simulation is particularly appropriate to situations where the size or complexity (or both aspects) of the problem makes the use of mathematical or statistical techniques either too difficult or impossible.

In addition, simulation is useful in training managers and workers in how the real system operates, in demonstrating the effects of changes in a system, and in developing new theories concerning organizational relationships. A list of the areas in which simulation methods are currently used is given in Exhibit 3-5.

Simulation has been especially useful in solving problems dealing with physical facilities and their capacities. For example, in the steel industry entire plant operations have been simulated to determine how various alternative production methods could reduce the effect of bottlenecks.

Exhibit 3-5 Application of Simulation Methods

Air traffic control queuing
Aircraft maintenance scheduling
Airport design
Ambulance location and
   dispatching
Assembly line scheduling
Bank teller scheduling
Bus (city) scheduling
Circuit design
Clerical processing system design
Communication system design
   Computer time sharing
   Telephone traffic routing
   Message system
   Mobile communications
Computer memory-fabrication
   test-facility design
Consumer behavior prediction
   Brand selection
   Promotion decisions
   Advertising allocation
   Court system resource allocation
Distribution system design
   Warehouse location
   Mail (post office)
   Soft drink bottling
   Bank courier
   Intrahospital material flow
Enterprise models
   Steel production
   Hospital
   Shipping line
   Railroad operations
   School district
Equipment scheduling
   Aircraft
Facility layout
   Pharmaceutical center
Financial forecasting
   Insurance
   Schools
   Computer leasing
Grain terminal operation
Harbor design
Industry models
   Textiles
   Petroleum (financial aspects)

Information system design
Insurance manpower hiring
   decisions
Intergroup communication
   (sociological studies)
Inventory reorder rule design
   Aerospace
   Manufacturing
   Military logistics
   Hospitals
Job shop scheduling
   Aircraft parts
   Metals forming
   Work-in-process control
   Shipyard
Library operations design
Maintenance scheduling
   Airlines
   Glass furnaces
   Steel furnaces
   Computer field service
National human resource
   adjustment system
Natural resource (mine) scheduling
   Iron ore
   Strip mining
Numerically controlled production
   facility design
Parking facility design
Personnel scheduling
   Inspection department
Petrochemical process design
   Solvent recovery
Police response system design
Political voting prediction
Rail freight car dispatching
Railroad traffic scheduling
Spacecraft trips
Steel mill scheduling
Taxi dispatching
Traffic light timing
Truck dispatching and loading
University financial and
   operational forecasting
Urban traffic system design
Water resources development

Source: Based on James R. Emshoff and Roger L. Sisson, *Design and Use of Computer Simulation Models.* New York: Macmillan Co. (1972), p. 264.

In general, simulation allows the manager to evaluate system performance before an action is taken. With the aid of a computer, the manager could know the answer to the question, "If maintenance expenses are increased by various percentages (say 10, 20 or 30 percent), what will happen to our operating cost per unit?"

Inventory decision rules also are commonly tested on computers. The manager specifies such things as the quantity to be ordered and the frequency of orders, and the computer generates the total cost for some time period, say, five years. Then the manager specifies different quantities and frequencies until, after the series of simulation runs, the best policy is selected. Similarly, dozens of related questions could also be answered.

The trial-and-error approach of simulation models is also useful in the development of future managers. There are several computerized business games available on a commercial basis that provide managers an opportunity to test their decision-making skills against other players in a competitive environment. Decisions regarding price, marketing policy, capital, and product improvements all affect a hypothetical firm's financial statements. The simulated outcome gives managers feedback concerning the type of decisions that are likely to work in the real world.

Laboratory or experimental exercises are another management development approach that simulates reality. These are best suited to illustrating specific points and can frequently be conducted in as little time as one hour. For example, leaders in competing groups may be given different sets of instructions as to how they are to go about accomplishing the same task. These instructions can reflect the various styles of leadership, and participants may be shown the impact of leadership styles on group performance. A creative trainer can develop or revise laboratory situations to illustrate most of the major management concepts.

An even simpler simulation format involves the use of 'in-basket' exercises. These present the trainee with some samples of letters, memos, telegrams, and other communication devices that require judgment as to appropriate action. Within a given time limit, the participant must deal with a variety of situations. After the participant has dealt with each communique, the exercise is reviewed by the trainer or the class to see if each individual has properly allocated his time, recognized all of the dimensions in a particular situation, and reached the "best" decision. In-baskets are an interesting training technique because the participants are involved in problems that are realistic to them. These exercises are relatively easy to construct and can reflect the problems that a group is experiencing. They provide a good test of a manager's organizing and problem-solving skills. With continued advancements in computers and mathematical modeling we are likely to see additional uses of simulation models for training and development purposes as well as problem solving.

Systems and Your Career

The early emphasis of systems thinkers and analysts was on various types of business, technical, war-related, or strategic national problems. Only in recent years has the attention of behavioral scientists turned toward the use of systems approaches in helping people to improve their chances to realize career possibilities and potential through systems thinking. The keys to using these approaches are the very same points mentioned above but applied instead to events, activities, personal skills, aptitudes, and interests that shape career opportunities. In short, career opportunities don't just happen—opportunities are *made* to an important extent by the guided thinking and direction we generate for ourselves.

Responsibilities, skills, and educational needs for each are affected by change but *not* uniformly. For example, if technological changes are introduced that shift the bases of work processes from mechanical to electronic systems, process support groups (e.g., maintenance, planning, quality control, and scheduling) will be forced to master a significantly different industrial art. Linear programming models, sophisticated continuous-quality monitoring equipment, job–shop scheduling models, and simulation are among the newer tools used by such supervisory–support groups.

Finally, technological changes of the type described affect the general administrative groups. Increased work interdependencies require the revision of procedures to provide the basis for coodination of work-related units. The personnel function is now confronted with a new set of human resource needs and skill requirements that accompany technological changes in system operation.

Exhibit 3-6, which shows the need for skills in relation to the state of the technology, suggests that the required job skills vary widely in low-level (unit or small batch) work systems, ranging from purely physical exertion—as a laborer in a road gang (manual skill)—to such occupations as tool-room polisher, which demands a low level of physical labor but a high level of craft art. If change takes place so that intermediate states of technology are reached (as in mass production, automotive assembly, or appliance lines), the range of worker aptitudes required by the system narrows: skill requirements decrease for people who formerly used craft arts but increase for the manual work groups. This phenomenon has caused a great deal of confusion in reporting changes in the level of skill required by changes in production technology, and the confusion is due to differing bases for comparison. For automated systems, some uncertainty exists as to the levels of skill required. In this situation the confusion results from the fact that the definition of "skill" for automated systems varies greatly, but often represents a shift from physical to mental skills (Burack, 1975).

Exhibit 3-6 Variations in Skill Requirements According to Level of Technology

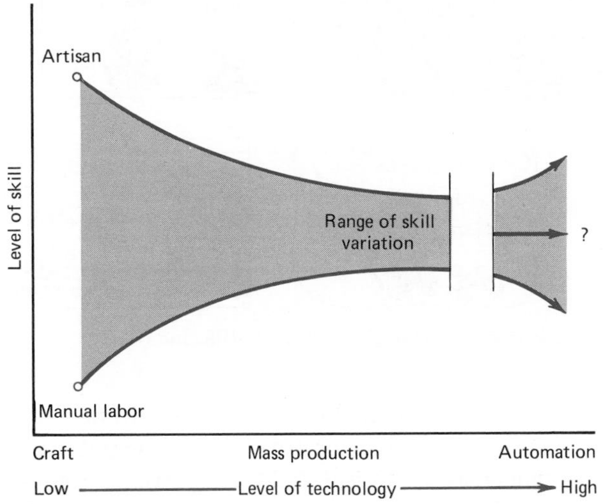

Source: Elmer H. Burack, *Organization Analysis: Theory and Applications.* Hinsdale, Ill.: The Dryden Press (1975), p. 115.

The needed modification of worker skill requirements reflects the interaction of worker features and job requirements. Worker features are based on education, experience, and personal traits; on job duties, decision making, and influence on productivity; and on seniority, location, and work conditions. When these features or attributes of the worker and job requirements are considered together, different levels of mechanization and automation seem to involve conflicting skill trends. For example, when machine operators are replaced by automated machines, equipment adjustment is more complex and requires a wider range of technical knowledge and competence. This situation may even require new job functions, such as an "electronic maintenance person." However, there may be a reduced need for traditional, craft-oriented skills of operators who now are "merely" required to monitor or oversee the automated equipment. *Fewer operators* are required while *more* (and different types of) *maintenance* and other *support people* are needed. Occasionally, even engineering graduates may be hired as line or maintenance supervisors to deal with new technical demands related to equipment operation and the costs of breakdown.

Technological changes seem to involve two different types of *skill*. In one, skill is interpreted in terms of the traditional motor skills, such as strength, dexterity and coordination. These are associated with older production-oriented systems, including both craft and mass production operations. As newer, more advanced systems ap-

We're being replaced by automation. (Copyright © 1976 by NEA, Inc.)

pear, skill has had to be redefined. In newer automated technologies, worker and superior are often spread out over wider production areas; concentrated in isolated work stations; removed from direct interpersonal contact in the work process; and engaged in more monitoring positions. The emphasis thus shifts to "mental skills," which demand such abilities as prompt, accurate response; problem-solving ability;

Worker operating computer controlled turret lathe.

and mental dexterity. In short, the shift in emphasis is from physical to mental skills and a greater emphasis on systems thinking.

From a career viewpoint, systems thinking involves a greater personal sensitivity to the relationships between one's skills, interests, and job needs and educational choices. An individual needs to think through the actions that will better the match between these factors, as well as occurrences likely to prevent a "successful marriage." Consider a person who is supposed to graduate next year. She, say, has had a part-time job with a national concern that has an office in Denver, and she happens to like skiing. Without systems thinking and in a reactive approach she might say, "I'll wait till I graduate then I'll talk to them about transferring me to the Denver plant. I'm too busy to worry about it now." On the other hand, a more planned approach capitalizing on systems thinking would start to consider the following interrelated activities that just might greatly increase chances for the transfer:

1. What's the job situation in Denver? What types of skills do they need, and what kind are they likely to need next year? What departments, units, and managers are involved, and how can I establish a communications link with them?

2. Are there outside events or developments coming up that may affect the company's plant there? What if they were planning to close the plant as an economy move or because of energy costs?

3. Are there courses that I can take in my last year at school to help me better qualify for jobs that may be available out there? Are there personal qualities or skills I need to develop to increase my chances for locating there?

4. What's my fall-back job or position in case nothing will be available in Denver or I can't locate permanently with them?

5. In general, what kind of information do I have to develop to better understand my possibilities and reduce uncertainties?

SUMMARY

Clearly, systems thinking has come a long way from its early emphasis on more traditional types of organizational problems. In recent times, these approaches have helped managers improve their performance by alerting them to new areas or sources of change, to how events combine in dynamic relationships, and increasing their sensitivity to the manner of how these diffuse in the organization. Systems thinking also means understanding the "properties" of the sociotechnical system, how these are affected by the events of the external environment, and how information and other approaches can improve personal performance.

Trends and change in the external environment affect organizations and often create uncertainty among its members. Whether managers are aware of these changes is partly a function of its management information system and monitoring devices. Whether a system is prepared to change is often related to the fears and insecurity of its members. This, in turn, can be related to the degree to which the system has supported people in the past. These are issues to be discussed in later chapters.

However, just as important to the individual are the substantial benefits of systems thinking for one's own career. Recognizing how forces or events shape one's career possibilities and the interdependencies of these with one's skills, contents, and goals promises more rewarding careers for those who conscientiously use the tools that are presented in this and the following chapters.

Questions for Study and Discussion

1. In brief, what is the systems view of organizations?
2. What are some environmental changes that are currently affecting organizations?
3. What are the beneficial outcomes of a system?
4. What is meant by a sociotechnical system?
5. What are the properties of a system?
6. Name some key steps of a managerial growth strategy. How can these be applied to work systems concepts.
7. Use Exhibit 3-3 to analyze the following situation:

   Maryann Falk was recently promoted to the position of Director of Training for the First National Bank of Glen Forks. One of the bank's biggest problems is turnover among the cashiers serving the personal savings department. The work tends to be boring, and many former employees, when interviewed upon leaving, complained that they felt like a number. Maryann feels that an employee program of recognition, solution, and chances for better bank jobs will help the situation greatly.

   a. Account for the current situations in terms of how management has approached its employees in the past, the goals, functions and problems.
   b. Interpret Maryann's planned program, the goals and possible results she anticipates.

   For both (a) and (b) name your key assumptions.

8. What is meant by simulation? Give some examples.
9. Differentiate between motor and mental skills.

CASE: MARY MURPHY—COORDINATOR

Mary Murphy finished high school when she was 17 years old, but instead of going to college like many of her friends, she decided to work "for awhile." "Classes, papers, experiments, projects. . . . It all seemed so unrelated to the real world," said Mary, "I needed some thinking time to sort things out for myself."

Fortunately, Mary had taken some typing and "commercial" classes at school so that she was able to get a job shortly after graduation. She was hired as a clerk-typist at Clark–Thompson, Inc. (C–T), a public relations and advertising firm. C–T performed a variety of advertising and public relations activities including the preparation of ads for newspapers; development of designs and art work for posters and outdoor advertising; design and writing of short paperback books on leisure-time subjects; and even assistance to some clients such as hospitals and schools in fund raising.

Mary really loved the people at C–T: "They're so alive and creative and just terriffic people!" Mary didn't like her own work that much, but every day she was learning so much that she set aside thoughts regarding her own job—at least for awhile.

When Mary had been at C–T for about six months, she sat down with her supervisor for the "new employee–six months' performance review." Her supervisor, Kathy Stevens, indicated that her work had been really good and that she seemed to have potential for more demanding work. Opportunities were there, but certain qualifications were, too. "We have jobs around here that open up regularly, some pretty good ones. The trouble is that we do much specialized work at C–T, we meet clients, and that usually means at least some college, on-the-job training, and sometimes special training in art, graphics, design, or writing."

It was at that point that Mary decided to take some classes at one of the state universities located just outside of the city where she lived. With the agreement of the people at C–T, Mary was allowed to work a 25-hour-per-week schedule that permitted her to take a full load at school, attending afternoon and evening sessions. She found that she enjoyed college much more than she had thought she would since it seemed more related to matters at C–T. About a year later, a job opening was posted for the Leisure Time Books department. The job, described as a Coordinator–Expeditor, seemed attractive to Mary. She applied for it and was transferred to the department.

The job consisted of working with C–T writers and designers to ensure that writing and art were completed on time. Her work also involved some work with clients for whom the books were being printed. Mary found this work interesting but demanding: "There are a lot of things to keep organized, people to keep happy, and schedules to meet. On top of all this, I've got my schooling. It's surely a full week for me."

After Mary had been in her new job for about nine months, her supervisor was promoted to another unit, and Mary was asked if she would like to apply for the supervisory position. Although it meant a full work week and having to go to school part-time, she felt it well worthwhile and told them she would try it out.

As the Supervisor of Coordination and Planning, Leisure Time Books, Mary did many of the same types of things she did previously but now worked with more department heads and, of course, had overall responsibility for the projects flowing through her department. The department itself was a small one in terms of the number of people assigned to it—there was just Mary, a coordinator, and a clerk-typist. However, the work was extremely important, since on-time completion at budgeted costs was mostly in her hands.

When she was a coordinator, Mary ran into various problems and situations that she felt could be improved or even avoided. As supervisor, she had the opportunity to introduce some procedural changes in order to improve the work of planning and coordinating. One area that was a constant problem concerned the timing and coordination of the activities of the writers and artists (see Exhibit 3-7).

Exhibit 3-7 Typical Work Flow: Leisure Time Books Department

1. C–T sales representative   ← Planning and coordinating unit
   "sells" project to client.   ✓ responsibilities
2. Budget worked out
   with accounting.
   3. Job released to   ← (Mary Murphy, Supervisor)
   book editor.   ✓ responsibilities
      4. Editor outlines project,   ↓   ↓
      assigns writer, and artist/designer.
         5. Rough draft and sketches completed.
            6. Corrections, test ad out.
               7. Get bids for printing.
                  8. Release printing.
                     9. Receiving of proofs.
                        10. Proofread—OK for production.
                           11. Deliver finished books.

Mary was thinking to herself. "These people never seemed to be able to get their work done on time." Another concern of Mary was the fact that too many books seemed to be over budget or were delivered late to their customers.

In order to correct some of these problems, Mary decided to try out, as an "experiment," a modified procedure on several books that were to be processed. In order to gain some "extra" time, she decided to release the first stage of the project to the printer before final revisions.

One technique that Mary wanted to try out in order to create "extra" time was to overlap some of the editorial and printer's time. She had noticed that on many book projects, only minor corrections were done after the second revision. "Why not send the material to the printer at this point (by making a copy) so that they could get started and possibly save two to four weeks of time?" If only clean manuscripts were sent to the printer, "the costs of added change would be minimized and they would be weeks ahead of the schedule or there would be time to charge against delays incurred elsewhere."

Mary tried out her approach on four different projects. On two of the books, considerable and costly changes resulted when in one case the customer requested a major change in format; in the other case, the editor had "second" thoughts regarding the manuscript and asked for (additional) changes. In the other two books, the modified approach resulted in a savings of about two weeks on one and better than three weeks on the other book.

When Mary finished her analysis of results, she remarked to a friend; "I think it was a good idea, but everything we gained on two of the books was canceled by our added costs on the others. I guess I've got more to learn about how this business operates."

Questions

1. Describe some general ways in which the various businesses of C–T displayed system features, especially interrelatedness.

2. Mary's remarks regarding problems in Leisure Time Books dealt with costs and time delays. From a systems viewpoint, what might have accounted for these?

3. Mary's experiment on reducing time delays and potentially excess costs had mixed results. Comment on this from a systems viewpoint. State your assumptions.

References

Boem, George A. W., "Shaping Decisions with Systems Analysis," *Harvard Business Review* **54** (September-October 1976): 91–99.

Bowers, David G., and Gregory J. Spencer, "Structure and Process in a Social Systems Framework," *Organization and Administrative Sciences* **8** (Spring 1977): 13–21.

Burack, Elmer, *Organization Analysis: Theory and Applications.* Hinsdale, Ill.: The Dryden Press (1975).

Couch, Peter, "Learning to be a Middle Manager," *Business Horizons* **22** (February 1979): 33–41.

Davis, Louis, "Optimizing Organization-Plant Design: A Complementary Structure for Technical and Social Systems," *Organizational Dynamics* **7**(2) (Autumn 1979): 2–15.

Diebold, John, "IRM: New Directions in Management," *Infosystems* **26**(10) (October 1979): 41–42.

Edstrom, Anders, "User Influence and the Success of MIS Projects: A Contingency Approach," *Human Relations,* **30** (July 1977): 589–607.

Ein-Dor, Philip, and Eli Seger, "Information-System Responsibility," *MSU Business Topics.* **25** (Autumn 1977): 33–40.

Ferreira, Joseph, and James Collins, "The Changing Role of the MIS Executive," *Datamation* **25**(13) (November 25, 1979): 26–32.

Katz, Daniel and Robert L. Kahn, *The Social Psychology of Organizations.* 2d ed. New York: John Wiley (1978).

Kelly, John, "A Reappraisal of Sociotechnical Systems Theory, *Human Relations* **31**(12) (December 1978): 1069–1099.

Longenecker, Justin, "Systems: Semantics and Significance," *Advanced Management Journal* **35** (April 1970): 63–67.

Moore, Jack, "A Computer Modeling Approach to Manufacturing and Distribution Strategy," *Interfaces* **10**(4) (August 1980): 16–21.

Shapira, Zur, and Roger L. M. Dunbar, "Testing Mintzberg's Managerial Roles Classification Using an In-Basket Simulation," *Journal of Applied Psychology* **65** (February 1980): 87–95.

Vardi, Yoav and Tove Hammer, "Intraorganizational Mobility and Career Perceptions Among Rank and File Employees in Difficult Technologies," *Academy of Management Journal* **20**(4) (December 1977): 622–634.

Von Bertalanffy, Ludwig, "The History and Status of General Systems Theory," *Academy of Management Journal* **15** (December 1972): 407–426.

Zentner, Rene, "2001: Can Management Science Keep Up?" *Interfaces* **11**(1) (February 1981): 56–58.

PART TWO

FUNCTIONAL ASPECTS OF MANAGEMENT

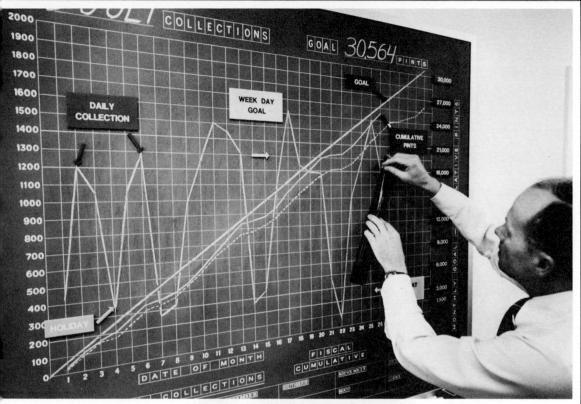

CHAPTER 4

PLANNING

KEY QUESTIONS ADDRESSED IN CHAPTER	
	1. What is planning?
	2. Why is planning important?
	3. What steps are involved in the planning process?
	4. How does planning differ at various levels in the hierarchy?
	5. How does planning affect you? What useful ideas can you derive for your own career-planning purposes?

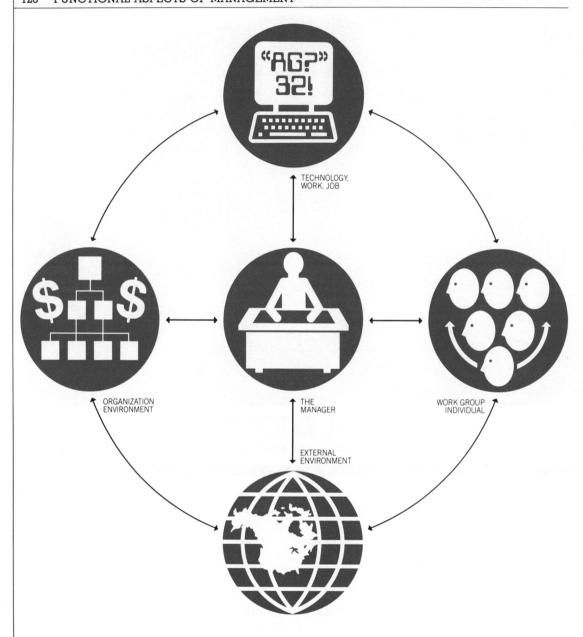

The manager's work–life spaces

Don't proceed with vast projects based upon half-vast plans.

THE CHAPTER IN BRIEF

Planning is an activity that is as useful in our daily lives as it is essential to organizations. With the possible exception of Alice in her own little "Wonderland," we all plan, some in greater detail than others. Whether you are going on a vacation, to work, or to school, or contemplating a change in an organization, planning is a basic process by which you determine how best to meet your objectives.

To draw out these points regarding planning more sharply, our personal choices often come down to being either **proactive** or **reactive.** Do we attempt to take advantage of the range of possibilities that the future may hold, and anticipate needs (proactive) or are we content to bounce along and deal with whatever arises on an hourly, daily, or weekly basis (reactive)? In a situation where little or no knowledge is available regarding the future for ourselves or the organizations where we may now be employed, the reactive approach is probably as good as any: "Why waste time planning when what we choose to do or decide on might just as well be resolved by the flip of a coin?" In simpler days this approach to life (and *non*planning) was permissible, and perhaps even desirable. Today, however, many compelling reasons exist for planning. In essence, the need for planning is the central theme of this chapter.

In this chapter we begin by relating *why* planning is so important both to organizations and individuals. It is no accident that most management textbooks place a discussion on planning at or near the beginning, because it forms the foundation for other functional activities such as organizing, leading, or controlling.

Next we clarify the specific steps in a planning approach and discuss several forecasting approaches used in planning. The effect of environmental change and various organizational factors on planning is also described. It is also important to distinguish between planning approaches at different authority levels in an organization.

(Copyright © 1977 United Feature Syndicate, Inc.)

Clarification of such planning terms as goals, purpose, mission, objectives, strategy, tactics, rule, policy, procedure, and budgets is made—especially as they relate to general management functions and approaches.

Planning and the Life-Space Concept

If performed properly, planning helps to establish a basis for coordinating the various life spaces with which the manager must deal. Organizations facing unstable or changing environments require more flexible planning processes than do institutions in more stable environments. If organizations are highly centralized, a significant degree of planning may be limited primarily to only a few managers or staff at the very top levels, or the type of planning carried out at different levels will vary greatly.

The results of planning can improve the allocation of resources within the organization and serve to better utilize people's skills and abilities. Planning can also provide a basis for defining relationships between individual workers, groups, and the work system itself. In addition, the process of planning improves communication within the organization as managers and staff interact with one another. Planning helps to make change manageable and do away with "potential" conflicts by establishing priorities. Yet the nature of planning that does occur will likely be greatly affected by the climate that exists within the organization. Autocratic managers are likely to be less willing than their more participative colleagues to share planning responsibilities with their subordinates.

BACKGROUND

The Planning Process: What Is It?

Planning is the predetermined course of action that an organization or individual follows to accomplish a specific set of objectives which have been established.

This definition of planning suggests several things. First, the process is essentially *future-oriented,* since we must examine and forecast the environment within which the organization will be operating. Second, there is usually a sequence of steps associated with the planning process that includes "setting goals" and "developing alternatives."

Planning thus can be a highly systematic arrangement in which, knowing where the organization is *now,* one analyzes *where* the organization is going and *how* it's going to get there. Let's consider one typical model for the planning process (the necessary steps of which

Exhibit 4-1 A General Model for Planning

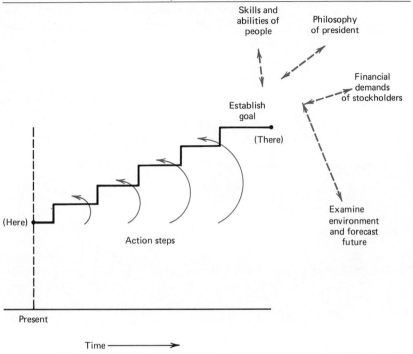

are explained in the next section). It starts with the establishment of long-range objectives (item 1 in Exhibit 4-1). This is the most difficult part of the planned, or proactive, approach. The difficulty arises partially from the fact that, since good understanding is needed of future developments, an accurate (to the degree possible) forecast of the future is needed (item 2a in Exhibit 4-1). Forecasters talk about a "workable level" of accuracy, realizing the uncertain nature of various, future events.

Simultaneous with this activity is the need to "inventory" the skills and abilities of people in the firm (Exhibit 4-1, 2b) as well as the philosophy and personal interests of the president (Exhibit 4-1, 2c) and the financial requirements of the stockholders (Exhibit 4-1, 2d). Although the president and other officials who are involved in the planning process should represent the needs of the stockholders (or of the public in an institutional setting), conflicts can occur. In fact, conflict between the personal needs and abilities of participants in the planning process and organizational objectives is a reality of life (this is dealt with in later chapters). This information gathering and examination (2a through 2d) introduces constraints that often result in a modification of the planner's objectives.

A third part of the process is the development of action programs

Board members establishing long-range goals.

(item 3) or steps. In an organization, a hierarchy of plans is developed to fulfill company objectives.

Steps in the Planning Process: How to Plan?

Although plans can take on many forms, the process of planning usually follows similar steps, even though organizations may have different purposes, goals, or missions. For example, the Environmental Protection Agency's goal to "clean up the air we breathe and the water we drink" may cause conflict with corporate goals of making a profit. Common models for planning often follow the process as described by George A. Steiner (1982) or Peter Lorange (1980).

Step 1. Set Goals

Whether for an individual or an organization, setting goals is the most critical step in the entire planning process. Thus it is crucial that the organization spend sufficient time and effort analyzing where it is now, especially in terms of its strengths and weaknesses. This self-examination becomes especially important in a highly competitive environment. In such a case the organization most suited for the particular goal will likely be most successful.

Organizations can select many goals, but the type of goal selected is likely to depend on such factors as the basic purpose of the organization, the values held by its managers, and its underlying strengths and weaknesses. One organization chose the following goals in order of priority.

1. Provide a fair return on investment to stockholders.
2. Maintain a good share of the market.
3. Develop good managers for executive positions.
4. Be a good corporate citizen.
5. Provide safe working conditions.
6. Manufacture goods efficiently.
7. Maintain and improve employee satisfaction.

Notice that this organization's **mission** could not possibly be described adequately by any single goal or even small number of them. Also, the goals conflict with each other at times. For example, "being a good corporate citizen" and "providing safe working conditions" may not allow them to "manufacture goods efficiently."

Step 2. Analyze the Environment

The environment presents both opportunities and threats to organizations and individuals alike. Whatever goals have been selected at step one, they will in some way be affected by factors outside of an organization's or individual's control. For example, it might be unrealistic for a baby food manufacturer, like Gerber's, to expand aggressively if the forecast is for far fewer babies to be born over the next ten years. Similarly, it may be just as risky for you to prepare for a career in primary education in light of the current surplus of teachers and trends in population. On the other hand, if you pick a location or school system wisely, employment opportunities may be good, since "surpluses" don't occur uniformly. Each situation must be treated individually!

Step 3. Establish Measurable Objectives

Regardless of the goal selected, it will be more effectively carried out if it is spelled out in terms as specific and measurable as possible. For specific objectives make it easier for managers to understand what it takes to achieve them and also to know when these have been accomplished. They also serve as better motivators because managers can tell whether they are succeeding or failing when goals are measurable.

For example, the organization above that had set a general goal of "being a good corporate citizen" further refined it by establishing

GREAT PERSON PROFILE

David Sarnoff (1891–1971)

Born in Russia, David Sarnoff grew up in poverty among thousands of other Jewish immigrants on New York's lower East Side. Self-taught in telegraphy as a teenager, Sarnoff began his career as a radio operator for the Marconi Wireless Telegraph Company. His big break came on April 15, 1912. Sarnoff was the telegraph operator who picked up the SOS from the Titanic and alerted the world to the disaster by staying at his key for 72 hours. The incident stimulated interest in radio communication in general and Sarnoff in particular. He soon became Marconi's commercial manager and in 1916 wrote a memo about his *plan* to put a radio in every household.

After Radio Corporation of America (RCA) bought Marconi, Sarnoff became general manager. In 1922 he convinced RCA to mass-produce "radio music boxes." In the wake of its success, Sarnoff formed the National Broadcasting Company (NBC) to produce programs for radio.

As early as 1923 he turned his attention toward developing television. In later years, he gambled $130 million on a color TV system that initially lost out to CBS. Sarnoff was not to be defeated, however, and three years later, after much research, RCA developed a compatible color TV system that won the approval of the Federal Trade Commission (FTC).

With his commanding personality and his vision of the future, Sarnoff anticipated *environmental trends*, developed plans to meet future needs, and worked hard to implement them. In the process he helped to build RCA, one of the leaders in the communication field.

specific objectives of "reducing air pollution by 15 percent" and "contributing $50,000 to local community groups over the next two years."

Step 4. Develop Subunit Plans

Once specific objectives have been established, lower-level managers must then decide how their own units can best meet them. This is necessary because only in the smallest organizations will top management be able to produce detailed plans for all units. Besides, involvement in the planning process by managers should also result in their increased commitment to goal achievement.

In developing their own plans, lower-level managers repeat steps 1 through 3 for their own subunits. They too set unit goals, assess their units' strengths and weaknesses, and analyze how the environ-

Exhibit 4-2 Means–End Staircase

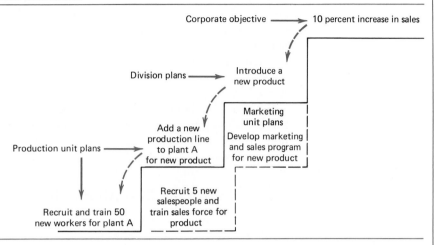

ment may affect them. In this way they develop concrete measurable objectives for their particular unit. **Management by Objectives (MBO)** programs that follow these steps will be discussed in a following section.

Thus, the measurable corporate objective of a 10 percent increase in sales over last year can serve as the basis for a divisional plan to introduce a new product. In turn, the divisional plan then serves as the basis for lower-level, more detailed plans within the division's research and development, work units, and marketing department. The entire process is illustrated in the **means–end staircase** in Exhibit 4-2.

It gets its name from the fact that each stair serves both as the means to achieve the next higher stair and as the end or goal for the stair immediately below it. Just as you must climb stairs to reach the top, managers realized the need to meet lower-level targets if overall objectives are to be met. During the planning cycle, planners proceed from the goal or targeted objective to general plans to detailed plans. When plans are actually launched, plant activities and marketing programs help meet division objectives that in turn help reach corporate goals.

Step 5. Compare Lower-Level Plans with Overall Objectives for Possible Revision

Once lower-level plans are developed they should be communicated up the organizational hierarchy for review, revision, and approval. These plans should be examined to determine how close they come to meeting higher-level divisional and corporate objectives. For example, when all divisional units are reviewed together, it may be decided that the division needs to do more than merely introduce a new product in order to realize the overall corporate goal of a 10 percent increase in sales.

Any gap that potentially exists between the overall corporate objective and those of its units will likely require changes in the plan. A variety of possible alternatives is likely to be forthcoming from managers at various levels to help achieve its long-range goals. For the example given, these may include a speeded-up introduction of new products, increased sales promotion on existing products, hiring more salespersons, or developing new customers.

Step 6. Select the Best Alternative

Although managers may develop a number of alternatives that would fulfill the corporate objective, it is crucial that the best alternative(s) be chosen in light of available information and within cost constraints. Some alternatives may not be feasible except under extreme conditions. For example, one company was prepared to bring out a new product line if "forced" to do so by competition—the alternative was unattractive because it required a major capital expenditure. For division A, it might need to hire additional research talent before it could realistically expect to introduce a new product. It might be better, therefore, to emphasize existing products in the short run for the required sales increase. The alternative finally selected then becomes part of the revised overall (**strategic**) plan of the organization. By strategic is meant the kind of planning needed to carry out particular corporate goals or objectives.

Step 7. Implement the Plan

Once the final (revised) strategic plan has been formulated, its broad objectives must be translated into detailed day-to-day tactics. Here lower-level managers would be involved in the formulation of the appropriate programs and budgets for their units. For example, the planned new product introduction would likely require the following: the Personnel department would need to develop a recruiting program that would satisfy the personnel requirements of the production, marketing, and research departments. Marketing would have to develop a program for preliminary market testing of the product. Production would need to develop preliminary cost estimates and be more actively involved with R&D as the new product reached the final stage of development. In this way the strategic plan is translated into a series of closely integrated plans by appropriate subunits of the organization.

Brand managers and marketing specialist discussing advertising copy (tactical planning).

Step 8. Measure and Control the Plan's Progress

As a plan is being implemented its progress must be monitored to ensure that nothing has occurred to cause the plan to go "off course." Performance standards are needed to measure a plan's progress. Then, if the actual progress in not according to plan, corrective action can be taken quickly. This step is part of the control process and will be taken up in detail in a following chapter. For example, when introducing a new product in division A, the following specific objectives could be established as indicators of the plan's progress:

- Complete product prototype by March 1.
- Install production line by May 1.
- Recruit and train production workers by June 1.
- Complete market test of product by September 1.
- Train salesforce in new product applications by September 1.

We have described an orderly stepwise planning process to make it easier to understand. In practice, however, most individuals and organizations are engaged in a number of planning steps simultaneously.

Why Plan?

Success usually cannot be guaranteed, yet many studies do indicate that planners tend to outperform nonplanners. One such study by Stanley Thume and Robert House (1970) matched 18 sets of firms by size, industry, and other characteristics. Such industries as drugs, petroleum, food, steel, and chemicals were included. In each pair of companies, one firm had begun planning at a particular point, while the other continued to do no active planning. After seven years the results showed that the companies that initiated planning outperformed both their own past performance and the performance of the nonplanning companies on such measures of success as return on investment.

A recent study (1981) by the Bank of America, and documented many times by the Small Business Administration (U.S. Department of Commerce), found, "A predominant cause of failure among small businesses is a lack of planning. Well-laid plans allow a business to take advantage of opportunities and to cope with setbacks by anticipating them."

Planning also allows managers to deal more effectively with change. Our world is rapidly changing, and planning can help us cope with the "shock" of an uncertain future in many areas. For example,

> **technology**—in a few short years watch manufacturers saw their entire industry changed due to competition from electronic companies that developed digital watches. The merging of these quite different technologies drastically altered the mode of business operations and marketing programs of watch companies.
>
> **society**—attitudes can change quickly as witnessed by the reaction to the accident at the Three Mile Island nuclear generating plant in 1979. The threatened explosion of a nuclear reactor led to an emotional reaction throughout the United States. Its effects (i.e. the response of people and the legislative machinery) were felt for months, even years later by the whole utility industry and the companies that build nuclear power plants. Companies whose products are greatly affected by fashion and fads must be especially aware of changing attitudes. Trends in fashion toward physical exercise helped to launch booms in tennis, racquetball and jogging. Smaller or delayed families have affected nearly all organizations in some way. The unavailability of gasoline in 1973 directly affected consumer demand for small cars in a matter of months and the price of gasoline has changed many people's attitudes about big cars.

We all need direction in our lives. Lacking goals we are like a ship without a rudder—buffeted about in whichever direction the wind blows. Having goals gives meaning to our life and work. The planning process requires that managers define organizational objectives so that employees may be able to relate the importance of their particular tasks to organizational or unit objectives. If employees are involved in this process, they can more effectively connect what they are doing (the means) to the organizational objectives (the ends). Through employee participation, a greater commitment to organizational objectives often results, along with improved performance and increased personal satisfaction.

Planning serves as the basis for all other management functions. As such it is absolutely necessary to manage the organizational resources effectively. How can employee performance be evaluated without standards or targets? How can people be directed if they don't know where they are headed? How can people and resources be organized without a knowledge of what is to be accomplished? The quick response is that these accomplishments may be possible but only with great difficulty and sometimes are even incapable of accomplishment.

Finally, planning helps the manager feel in control of things. It reduces uncertainty and can build self-confidence. Nonplanners often blame the things that are happening to them on so much bad luck. Those who look ahead and attempt to foresee change, on the other hand, are more prepared to act correctly. By being ready to take advantage of these opportunities planners are often viewed as "lucky" by the nonplanners. Nonplanners are like the student who takes courses out of sequence and wonders why they are always running into scheduling conflicts.

Obstacles to Planning: Why People Don't Plan?

"Tomorrow's another day" is an apt description of most people's attitude toward planning. Despite its importance, many managers and people in general are reluctant to plan. This occurs for a number of reasons.

- Planning competes with many other activities for our time—and there are only so many hours in the day available.
- We like to perform activities that give immediate feedback. Since planning deals with future events, the rewards of good planning are likely not to be seen for some time.
- Planning is hard work. It requires much thought and careful analysis.
- Finally, planning establishes objectives that can be used to measure results. Many people are reluctant to be evaluated.

Management by Objectives: A Technique for Planning

Management by Objectives (MBO) has attracted many proponents since it was first introduced in 1954 by Peter Drucker, based on ideas expressed by Alfred Sloan and others in the 1920s. Peter Drucker describes MBO as follows.

> . . . the objectives of the district manager's job should be defined by the contribution he and his district sales force have to make to the sales department, the objectives of the project engineer's job by the contribution he, his engineers and draftsmen make to the engineering department. . . .
>
> This requires each manager to develop and set the objectives of his unit himself. Higher management must of course, reserve the power to

approve or disapprove these objectives. But their development is part of a manager's responsibility; indeed it is his first responsibility. . . . (Drucker, 1954)

Since this early work by Drucker, many management authors have written about MBO: George Odiorne (1965) is the most well-known. In general, they describe three guidelines for MBO:

1. Superior and subordinate meet and discuss objectives for the subordinate that are in line with overall organizational objectives.
2. The development of objectives is a joint project of the superior and subordinate, but subordinate should initiate objectives.
3. Later the superior and subordinate meet again to evaluate the subordinate's performance in terms of the objectives. This *feedback* ensures that subordinates know where they stand with regard to their contribution to the organizational unit.

Proponents of MBO claim the following advantages.

- Improves individual and organizational performance.
- Increases employee commitment and job performance.
- Clarifies what is expected of the employee.
- Improves communication between superior and subordinate.
- Eliminates vague performance appraisals.
- Provides the data to reward employee "objectively."

Of course, not everyone agrees with these claims. Several studies have indicated that MBO may not work wonders. These problems include *lack of top management support*. Without proper follow-up and support throughout the year, the program is not likely to be integrated adequately with the reward system. Also, there often is a problem of *poorly defined objectives*. The objectives must be easily measurable to be most effective. They must also be important to the meeting of organizational objectives.

Another problem encountered in MBO is *overreliance on quantifiable objectives*. Many important objectives cannot easily be measured. These are often downgraded in many MBO programs.

Insincere commitment by superiors is another situation encountered. Many managers "play" at allowing their subordinates to participate in the objective setting process. At the joint meeting the superior merely tells the subordinate "what is expected of them." Of course, this defeats the whole purpose of MBO. Finally, too often there is an *overemphasis on paperwork*. Many organizations design sophisticated procedures and forms to provide evidence that MBO is being used. This merely increases the time needed to operate MBO, which is usually resisted by both managers and employees.

In general, studies show that MBO must be implemented thoughtfully or it will not work. This requires an active participation and involvement on the part of top management, the people being coordinated, and the inclusion of the program into the organization's reward system. Successful MBO programs require constant, almost daily, effort if they are to be accepted and useful in gaining important organizational objectives.

Planning at Different Levels in the Organizations: Strategic Versus Tactical Planning

All levels of management are involved in planning. A first-line supervisor may need to schedule the department's activity for the following day or week. The office manager may need to develop the department's budget for the coming year. The marketing vice-president may need to identify the organization's product needs and sales estimates for the next five years. Although all of these are planning activities, there time horizons are certainly different. The first activity is more concerned with short-range, **tactical** types of plans (usually less than one year), whereas the last activity is more involved with long-range, **strategic** planning (usually more than two years).

Managers at higher levels in the organization generally spend more time planning than do lower-level managers. In addition, because lower levels tend to derive their plans from the plans of higher levels, these higher-level plans must be established before lower-level plans are developed. In other words, the higher one is in the organization, the farther into the future one must plan. This relationship is shown in Exhibit 4-3. Thus, the president may spend the majority of his planning activities establishing broad (long-term) company objectives to be met over 5, 10, or 20 years. The first-level supervisor, on the other hand, is much more concerned with meeting (short-range) daily and weekly targets. In some complex or fast-paced industries, tactical planning may be on an hourly or daily basis.

Strategic, or higher-level plans, focus on the opportunities available for the organization to fulfill its mission in the most *effective* way by determining *what to do* and *providing* the necessary resources. Tactical, or lower-level plans, focus on the most *efficient* means of fulfilling strategies by *utilizing* resources in the least costly way.

Planning properly at all levels is important; since strategic planning precedes all others, however, it is more crucial to the organization than tactical planning. In the words of Peter Drucker (1977):

> Whether he works in a business or in a hospital, in a government agency or in a labor union, in a university or in the Army, the executive is, first of all, expected to get the right things done.

GREAT PERSON PROFILE

Robert E. Wood (1879–1969)

During his 26 years as president of Sears, Roebuck and Company, Robert E. Wood showed that one key to success in business is *strategic planning*. Wood transformed Sears from a mail-order operation into a successful retail chain of more than 700 stores.

Wood's emphasis on strategy stemmed from his military background and his interest in statistics. In the early 1900s he used census studies to forecast that the population was shifting into the metropolitan areas. To take advantage of this trend and the increased number of automobiles in use, Wood established neighborhood stores throughout the metropolitan areas. His stores became an instant success.

Wood also recognized the need for his stores to be serviced by dependable suppliers with goods that were of consistent quality. He convinced potential suppliers to locate their factories close to Sears stores. Recognizing that withdrawal of their support could lead to financial difficulties, he then entered into arrangements with them that were mutually

beneficial. Thus, Sears was freed from dependence on one major supplier.

Wood's career is an illustration of the importance of planning and the formation of strategies that anticipated future developments. The manager must be able to correctly interpret and respond to trends in the business environment.

Without setting the right objectives and devising the right strategies, organizations will not succeed. They may do things right (**efficiency**), but they will not be doing the right things (**effectiveness**).

Developments at Texas Instruments suggest some of the critical relations between organizational objectives and planning at lower levels in the organization. Also, a direct connection is indicated between change and other external environmental events that affect organizational policies and strategies. Of interest in this section are the following.

1. How is planning related to the goals of an organization?

2. How does an organization effectively plan its future staffing in the midst of uncertainty and rapid change?

Scenario: Texas Instruments (TI)

Texans tend to think big. That's just what chairman Mark Shepard and President J. Fred Bucy of Texas Instruments have done. In 1976, TI re-

Exhibit 4-3 Types of Plans at Various Levels in the Organization

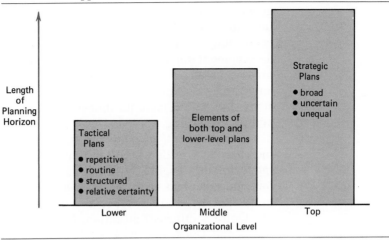

ported profits of $97.4 million on sales of $1.7 billion (Forbes, 1977). Although both were records, the figures were only one half of the 10-year goals that were set in 1966.

Undaunted, TI's bosses promptly proceeded to set a $10 billion sales goal for 1989, all to be achieved from internal growth.

In an industry faced by rapid technological change, strong Japanese challenges, and domestic competitors, TI became a major leader in producing chips for electronic circuitry. These miniature circuits brought TI into more and more product areas that, a few short years ago, seemed to be unconnected in both a marketing and production sense. For example, its digital watch, priced at $19.95 in 1977, was the functional twin of the $100 watch sold by TI a year earlier. In addition, future advances were planned for such diverse areas as auto components and home computer centers.

This rapid change placed severe pressure on both organization and manpower planners to ensure that structural relationships as well as needed people skills would be able to meet the needs that an uncertain tomorrow might bring.

TI is one of the largest nonunion employers in the United States, and its success has been attributed largely to its ability "to keep its people adaptive, intense, and driving."

Notes on Planning and Texas Instruments

The situation at Texas Instruments illustrates several specific points regarding planning. First, in the organizational hierarchy of planning, general business planning serves as the basic input to the functional planning cycle. This means that financial, operational, sales, and human resource plans emerge from the overall business plans. But each, in turn, influences the thrust and feasibility of the overall plan. Thus, when TI set a $10 billion sales goal for 1989 to be generated from internal growth, plans had to be initiated almost immediately that would eventually meet the massive personnel needs suggested by such a projection. The combination of internal development and external recruiting would have to meet such diverse product areas as auto components and home computer centers. The long-range accomplishment (1989) called for shorter-range action steps that would have an immediate impact on personnel planning and programming.

The problems associated with trying to achieve a sixfold sales increase ($1.7 billion to $10 billion) in 12 years amid rapidly changing technology boggle the mind. To accomplish the goal entirely from internal resources required that large-scale planning and follow-up in all functional areas, especially in personnel, were necessary.

Quite a different situation, for example, faced American Telephone and Telegraph (ATT) in its people planning. Improvements in technology had resulted in electronic switching systems replacing the mechanical crossbar systems. The result was declining personnel needs in many areas at a time when the company was attempting to meet Affirmative Action targets for race, sex, and age. Technological improvements displaced people and thus complicated human-resource planning that also had to take into account mobility of people, seniority, transferability of skills, and early retirement.

Planning the Future and Uncertainty: How Far into the Future Should You Plan?

Since planning involves forecasting future conditions, the greater the time span between a prediction and the actual event, the more likely it is that the prediction will be wrong. However, the key point is often not the absolute correctness of the decision, rather that planning provides a focus for organization activities and a base point against which to compare progress and refocus programs as needed.

Uncertainty in the future is often the key to determining the length of the planning period (horizon)—as well as the detail of the plan. Exhibit 4-4 summarizes some factors that affect uncertainty.

As the future becomes less certain, planning horizons are shortened. For example, at one time, when environmental conditions were quite stable, especially in the political and economic areas, utilities planned far into the future, 20- and 30-year projections being quite common. In the middle 1960s, however, a rapidly changing regulatory and economic climate resulted in the need for drastic forecast changes concerning the future. Environmental concerns (pollution) of the public in the 1970s further affected the accuracy of 20- to 30-year projections so that most utilities today feel that information from long-range forecasts must be treated in quite a different way. Therefore,

Exhibit 4-4 Uncertainty and the Length of the Planning Period

Creating Uncertainty— Shortening the Feasible Planning Period	*Promoting Stability— Permitting the Consideration of Longer Planning Periods*
Relatively small organization size	Large organization size, commanding competitive position
Many new competitors, ease of entry into industry	Evolutionary rather than rapid change in the economic, social, political or technological situation
Rapid changes in the social climate, technology, or economic situation	Stable demand patterns
Unstable demand patterns	Good management information system
New legislation that may affect organizations—equal employment, regulation	Understanding of underlying structural forces in environment
Poor management methods reflecting training, available information, analytical tools, internal organization, and so on	Predictable, stable technology
	Good training
	Thoughtful use of analytical tools

Source: Based on Elmer H. Burack and Nicholas J. Mathys, *Human Resource Planning: A Pragmatic Approach to Manpower Planning and Development.* Lake Forest, Ill.: Brace-Park Press (1980), Chapter 5. Reprinted with permission of the publisher.

many have dramatically shortened their tactical planning horizons and developed less detailed or alternate plans in strategic planning.

The actual time horizon for planning in organizations also depends on the particular resources or activities being considered. Exhibit 4-5 shows some representative times for various planning areas within an organization. Of course, these lead times vary from organization to organization or by industry. A good example of this variation is in the lead times for new medical facilities. The figure shown in the exhibit is 4 years. Yet the lead time for a specialized care unit with its equipment, building and public review of plans could easily require 5 or 6 years. Conversely, an expansion of a general care hospital unit might be accomplished in a two- to three-year period.

When operating in an uncertain future, firms need to maintain flexibility by developing **contingency plans.** By contingency plans is meant alternative plans or programs that can be implemented if the original plan becomes unworkable. Managers must constantly monitor the environment to determine whether organizational objectives and the programs required to achieve them should be changed. For example, many plans and commitments made in the early 1970s when energy was "cheap" had to be drastically altered or scrapped altogether as energy became more expensive. Planning involves a continuous process of updating and examination of the "hidden" assumptions under which the original plans were made. Contingency

Exhibit 4-5 Planning Horizons within an Organization

Resource Areas	Lead Time (years)
Planning for materials procurement	½
Planning for operating expenses (budget)	1
Planning for capital expenditures (budget)	1½
Planning for recruiting engineers	2
Planning for major financial needs	2
Planning for new product development	3
Planning for new medical facilities	4

Source: Taken from Koontz, Harold, and Cyril O'Donnell, *Principles of Management.* New York: McGraw-Hill (1980).

thinking has become so much a part of planning that some large companies have set up departments to identify or forecast *possible* future conditions and to trace out the effects of these possibilities on the firm's operations. The Delphi technique described in the following section has proven to be quite useful in contingency planning.

Nonmathematical Forecasting Approaches

The Delphi Method: An Intuitive Forecasting Approach

Reliance on mathematical forecasting techniques to project likely future occurrences often is inappropriate when organizations are engaged in long-range planning over a time horizon of five or more years because much change can occur to reduce the techniques' degree of accuracy. Here, a judgmental technique such as the **Delphi** method is usually more valuable. This technique involves a group of experts who are queried by a coordinator regarding their expectations of certain future situations occurring. The most prominent feature of this method is the lack of direct interaction among the panel itself; that is, interaction occurs only through the group coordinator by the use of written communications. This anonymity reduces the pressure to conform to group opinion and avoids dominance of group opinion by a single member.

Developed by Rand Corporation in the early 1960s, in its most common form the Delphi method consists of several rounds of a series of questionnaires distributed separately to a panel of experts by a coordinator. The responses to the first round of questions are then compiled and fed back to the original panelists, who are asked to submit revised answers together with reasons for agreeing or disagreeing with the initial consensus. Questions for succeeding rounds are determined from previous responses. The ultimate outcome desired is for a consensus of expert opinion regarding the likelihood of future occurrences of concern to the organization (Delbecq et al., 1975).

The following example illustrates a typical application of the Delphi method. The expected rate of inflation over the next five years is considered by a large bank to be a major variant in their five-year plan. Inflation affects their cost of services, supplies, wages, pension, liability, and many other budget items. The causes and effects of inflation need to be identified. A panel of experts from widely diverse backgrounds was chosen by company planners, which included economists, corporate board members, a consumer advocate, business leaders, an expert on city government, a demographer (for population trends), and several government agency staff members.

A typical first-round question was: What are the factors that may contribute most to inflation over the next five years? The respondents answered by listing such items as the increased price of oil, government spending on defense programs, city taxes, and food shortages.

On the second round the experts provide additional information in response to the first-round answers. The idea here is to identify the importance of each answer and to reach a consensus as to the cause and rate of inflation that might be expected. A typical response follows:

Item	Importance (1 = Most Important)	Comments
Increase price of oil	2	If new sources of oil are found, price increases will be less.
Government defense spending	1	Increased foreign pressure on countries supplying our strategic resources is likely.
Food shortages	4	Worldwide demand for our food because of weather problems and war will continue.
City taxes	3	Growing deficit of city services, transportation system, and educational units.

Once this round is analyzed the comments are summarized and results are aggregated. On round three, reactions to the aggregated results are obtained. One respondent's reaction to the item "government defense spending" may be "unrest in southern Africa is likely to accelerate owing to recent guerrilla activity." Finally, once all reactions are circulated, a final round of comments and estimates occurs to obtain some consensus.

What does this application tell us as managers? A projection of sales based mainly on what has occurred in the past often ignores changes that are starting or likely to occur that would impact on the situation of concern to us. This is especially true when such projections are over long time frames. A panel of experts is likely to be aware of contrary trends, especially in one's area of expertise. The result is a "balanced" forecast of sales in which the best information available has been used in a way that no simple model or mathematical extrapolation could hope to duplicate.

In addition to its use as a forecasting device, the Delphi method has been used by organizations to:

1. Establish goals and priorities.
2. Identify the dimensions and attributes of a problem.
3. Clarify positions and delineate differences between group members.
4. Gather information from a group whose members do not meet face-to-face (either by choice or practicality) and who wish to retain their anonymity.

An Illustration of an Extrapolation Forecasting Approach

Many forecasting techniques rely on sophisticated mathematical or statistical models that can be quite complicated. Yet there are graphical approaches available that are gaining wide usage because of their simplicity for picturing complex relationships or providing a basis for planning (Burack and Mathys, 1980).

The following graphical approach and solution illustrate how a forecast of future sales or service levels can be converted to determine the requirements for a particular personnel category. This forecasting technique uses **extrapolation** or projection of past results. Unfortunately, the technique is often misused because the assumptions of "general conditions remaining pretty much the same over the planning period" do not always hold true. This example is a simplification of a much more complex situation found in a dealer service organization for major home appliances.

The company needed to determine the number of customer service personnel to be trained to support their rapidly expanding sales of appliances. In Exhibit 4-6a the company's sales in hundreds of thousands of units are shown (exact numbers modified to avoid disclosure) over time along with the number of customer service personnel required to support various sales levels. Next their sales were extrapolated for a three-year period to judge the approximate scope of their future training program. They carefully examined the business, economic, and internal factors affecting their sales and decided that extrapolation would provide a good initial estimate. Note that the three-year extrapolation suggests a further sales gain in units of some 300,000 or a total sales of about 1,050,000 units (Exhibit 4-6b). It was agreed that future figures could be off by as much as 10 percent and that these should be incorporated in the sales projections and demands for service personnel. This is illustrated by the use of the upper and lower limits in Exhibit 4-6b.

The next step was to examine their experience in growth of the dealer service group. It appeared that a relationship existed between

Exhibit 4-6a Manpower Planning Analysis of Appliance Sales Service Personnel Initial Sales–Manpower Relationships

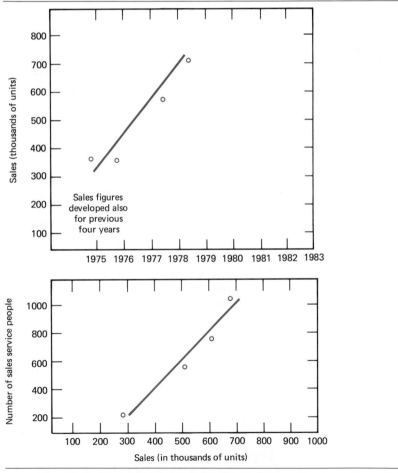

Source: Elmer H. Burack and Nicholas J. Mathys, *Human Resource Planning: A Pragmatic Approach to Manpower Planning and Development.* Lake Forest, Ill.: Brace-Park Press (1980), p. 141. Reprinted with permission of the publisher.

Exhibit 4-6b Dealing with Uncertainty in Sales Extrapolation

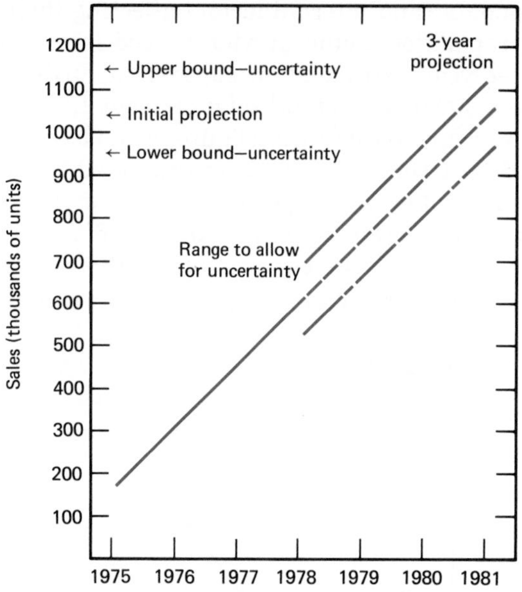

Source: Elmer H. Burack and Nicholas J. Mathys, *Human Resource Planning: A Pragmatic Approach to Manpower Planning and Development.* Lake Forest, Ill.: Brace-Park Press (1980), p. 142. Reprinted with permission of the publisher.

overall unit sales and the size of the service group (see Exhibit 4-6*a*). Although product improvements had taken place that might have lessened manpower needs, they were counterbalanced by added demand for customer service. The net effect was that one canceled out the other. It was expected that these two effects would continue in the future and, thus, that the relationship between sales and dealer organization would likely hold.

Based on the three-year projection, the customer service group could grow to as many as 1700 people (the middle line in Exhibit 4-6*c*) or possibly even 10 percent higher (to 1870 people). With this relationship in mind, the company embarked on an extensive training program since *at least* 700 additional customer service people (1700 less 1000 currently) would be needed. By putting in place this program, the company has been able to achieve planned sales targets and had good reports from the field regarding the level of customer service.

Types of Plans

The hierarchy of plans in an organization can be divided into three broad groups: goals, standing plans, and single-use plans. The rela-

Exhibit 4-6c Dealing with Uncertainty in Staffing Extrapolation

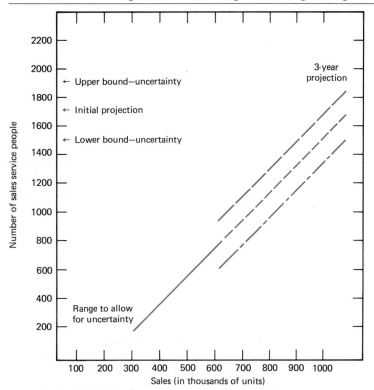

Source: Elmer H. Burack and Nicholas J. Mathys, *Human Resource Planning: A Pragmatic Approach to Manpower Planning and Development.* Lake Forest, Ill.: Brace-Park Press (1980), p. 141. Reprinted with permission of the publisher.

tionships are shown in Exhibit 4-7, and the terms are defined in Table 4-1.

Goals are the broad ends of the organization toward which more detailed plans are directed. **Standing plans** are devised to handle recurring or routine situations that require a consistent and standardized approach. A routine for reporting fires, a merchandise return policy in a store, and admission procedures in a hospital are all examples of standing plans. **Single-use plans,** on the other hand, are developed to meet a unique, one-of-a-kind situation, such as introduction of a new product.

Goals

Goals provide an organization or an individual with a sense of direction, or guide, for its actions. Although many authors use the terms *goals* and *objectives* interchangeably, we view *goals* as the broader

Exhibit 4-7 The Hierarchy of Organizational Plans

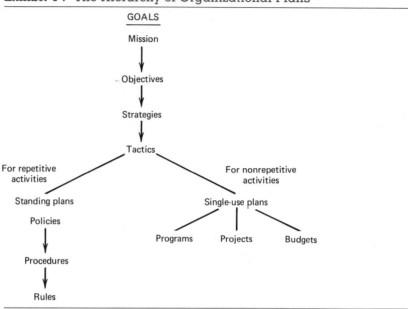

term. We have avoided making this distinction previously, but it is now appropriate in the context of a more specific discussion of types of plans. Starting out with the basic mission of an organization, objectives are developed that attempt to define the mission in more measurable terms. Also, objectives tend to be closer (in time). These objectives then become the basis for strategies or carefully worked out programs that, in turn, are carried out by more detailed tactical plans.

The **mission** of an organization is what uniquely sets it apart from others in its industry. Thus, the Mayo Clinic has a mission uniquely different from that of Cook County Hospital in Chicago. Mayo specializes in highly involved and often complex medical diagnosis and treatment; Cook County Hospital is a general hospital that includes a large public welfare service load. General Motors (full car–truck line) differs from American Motors (jeeps and small cars), as does McDonald's (hamburgers) from Arby's (roast beef). But even these differences are weakening due to competition—McDonald's now features breakfasts and Arby's has numerous food items besides roast beef.

The way in which organizations define their mission is often crucial to their growth or very survival. For example, at the turn of the century many buggy manufacturers saw their mission as "making quality buggies." Others saw it as "providing transportation." Most of the former went the way of the horse and buggy, while some

Table 4-1 Definitions of Terms Used in Planning

Goals	Broad and basic end accomplishment of the organization
Mission	General purpose that organization attempts to achieve
Objective	Specific, measurable end that must be achieved to fulfill organizational mission
Strategy	Broad action oriented programs designed to meet organizational objectives
Tactics	Specific, detailed action steps that implement strategies
Strategic planning	Broad planning designed to meet specific organization goals or objectives
Tactical planning	Detailed planning of the specific steps needed to achieve broader goals, objectives, plans, or strategies
Policy	General guideline to action
Procedure	More specific guide to action than policy; usually spells out sequence of steps to be taken
Rule	Statements that define a specific action to be taken in a given situation over an extended time period
Program	Statements that define a group of activities or projects to achieve specific objectives at a given time
Projects	Plan with a time dimension and focus on a specific end accomplishment—usually part of a program
Budget	Plan with a financial dimension and for a specific time interval

of the latter successfully built automobiles when "the automobile's time came."

If the goal of a hospital, for example, is "to give quality health care to the surrounding community," then objectives must be developed to more concretely define that statement in measurable terms. Some specific objectives might include "conducting at least one off-site preventive health workshop at local civic and educational organizations" and "attracting quality professionals by offering above-average salaries."

Finally, strategies give a unified direction to the organization so that resources can be allocated in a manner that will meet its many objectives. Tactics, on the other hand, are specific, detailed action steps that carry out strategies. Both are described in Exhibit 4-3.

Standing Plans

Whenever an organizational activity occurs repeatedly, standing plans are useful to serve as guides for the repeated actions. They also ensure that tasks are carried out with more consistency while freeing the manager's time to handle less routine occurrences.

The major types of standing plans are policies, procedures, and rules. All establish boundaries so that actions will be consistent with organizational objectives. Policies are usually established formally by top managers to (1) emphasize basic beliefs or areas of committment, (2) resolve conflicts at a lower level, or (3) reflect their own personal values (i.e., dress codes). Procedures, on the other hand, provide a detailed set of instructions for performing a sequence of actions that occur repetitively. The routing slip in an office ensures that sales orders will reach particular units or people for action. The procedure followed by the McDonald's clerk that starts with "Can I help anyone?" also ensures consistent treatment aimed at achieving the organizational objective of "quick and friendly service to customers."

Like procedures, **rules** are statements that require that a specific action must be taken in a given situation. The development and communication of rules provide ways of informing organizational members exactly what the boundaries of acceptable behavior are. A major problem with enforcing rules in practice is for managers to do so in a fair and consistent manner. Exhibit 4-8 illustrates a set of rules for teachers, in use a little over 100 years ago.

Single-Use Plans

Organizations must often deal with special situations or are often engaged in activities that are somewhat unique. Standing plans usually don't cover these circumstances. Additionally, special situations or those somewhat unique because of time frame or focus, require details or analyses tailored to the circumstances. The major types of single-use plans are programs, projects, and budgets.

A **program** covers a relatively large number of activities. The program should include (1) the major steps needed to reach an objective, (2) the individual or unit responsible for each step, and (3) the sequence and deadline for the completion of each step. Programs are usually accompanied by budgets. Programs can be quite large and costly—like the U.S. space program to put a man on the moon before 1970. Other examples include equipment replacement programs, training programs, and expansion programs.

A **project** is similar in nature to a program but usually does not cover as many activities. Building a new plant and marketing a new product are examples of two projects that may be part of a larger expansion program.

A **budget** is a statement of an organization's plan in financial terms, and covering a specified time interval. As such, budgets are also primary devices used to control all kinds of organizational activities. In fact, the budget process is often the key planning process in

Exhibit 4-8 Rules for Teachers (1872)

1. Teachers each day will fill lamps, clean chimneys.
2. Each teacher will bring a bucket of water and a scuttle of coal for the day's session.
3. Make your pens carefully. You may whittle nibs to the individual taste of the pupils.
4. Men teachers may take one evening each week for courting purposes, or two evenings a week if they go to church regularly.
5. After ten hours in school, the teachers may spend the remaining time reading the Bible or other good books.
6. Women teachers who marry or engage in unseemly conduct will be dismissed.
7. Every teacher should lay aside from each pay a goodly sum of his earnings for his benefit during his declining years so that he will not become a burden to society.
8. Any teacher who smokes, uses liquor in any form, frequents pool or public halls, or gets shaved in a barber shop will give good reason to suspect his worth, intention, integrity and honesty.
9. The teacher who performs his labor faithfully and without fault for five years will be given an increase of twenty-five cents per week in his pay, providing the Board of Education approves.

most organizations because managers control dollar expenditures that are considered the life blood of the enterprise, and also use this process to make critical resource allocations. If these allocations do not take strategic objectives into account, organizational effectiveness will almost certainly suffer.

Organizations develop budgets for all major uses of funds. These normally include the following.

- Sales budget.
- Advertising budget.
- Computer budget.
- Production budget.
- Raw materials budget.
- Personnel budget.
- Equipment purchasing budget.
- Cash-flow budget.
- Cost budget.
- Profit budget.

All these budgets must be coordinated if the total organizational effort is to be a united one. Once again objectives play a unifying role, for each budget should be related to organizational objectives.

Behavioral Considerations in Planning

Plans affect people; therefore, their reactions should be considered throughout the planning process. In fact, for successful implementation to occur the commitment of people in the organization to the plan is essential. Studies show that participation is linked closely to gaining commitment. Do you feel more committed to activities you have had a voice in planning?

The determination of how much and what kind of participation employees have in the planning process will likely affect the quality of plans developed. Employees can add much information and "realism" that is not otherwise available. In fact, many organizations have discovered that one of the benefits of their management by objectives programs is the inclusion of more people in the planning effort.

The question of who participates in planning must also be determined. A number of organizations have established special units devoted especially to planning. These planning staffs can save much time and effort and avoid needless duplication by having a central place to gather and analyze information. Both planners and operating managers can then concentrate on the tasks to which they may be best suited.

Planning groups, however, cannot do all the planning. Too often they are isolated from the firing line. Sometimes what they come up with appears to line managers, who may have been excluded from the process, as being totally unworkable. To offset this problem, some organizations rotate operating managers into planning assignments. This can add more reality to planning processes and usefully develop the planning abilities of those managers selected.

Broad participation in planning can bring unexpected results. People bring their own knowledge, values, needs, and even prejudices to the planning activity. This often results in better plans if the staffing of these groups is thought out carefully and the procedures are worked out in detail. If participation is used, managers must be willing to listen and respond to the suggestions and ideas given. Otherwise, employees will feel manipulated and will likely withdraw from future participation and commitment.

To be effective, plans must be realistic. They should reflect goals that are attainable yet challenging. Realistic plans will encourage commitment when they meet, as much as possible, both individual and organizational needs. Nevertheless, some plans that satisfy the needs of a particular group may have to be discarded because they do not mesh well with overall organizational objectives. Explanations should be given in these instances. Connecting the chosen plans to the organizational reward system will help to ensure successful implementation.

Planning and You: Personal and Career Planning Applications

If you are like most people you have probably been asked many times, "What do you want to be?" or "What do you want out of life?" These questions posed by parents, school counselors, friends, or spouses bring out the need for planning in our daily lives. Personal career planning also relies heavily on establishing and implementing career and life objectives. The following situation is quite typical of many.

Betty Baily had always wanted to be a teacher as far back as she could remember. She had majored in social science at Oakland Teachers College and taught social studies in the Taft Junior High for four years before leaving to raise a family in 1969. While her children were young she remained active in various social and charitable organizations, but now she desires to "renew her career."

Because of declining enrollments, teaching opportunities were quite limited. Besides, Betty felt that she wanted some work that "would allow her to help other people while at the same time making good money and providing the opportunity for a life-long career." Betty had always been able to get along well with people and had received satisfaction from helping others.

Betty's husband suggested the possibility of working in Personnel since this was a growing field in many organizations. She also remembered reading an article recently about the opportunities available in Personnel for women, and she wondered just what qualifications were needed. She decided to talk to a counselor at Thorndale Community College to find out what opportunities were available and what qualifications were required in the field. During the discussion she discovered that her courses in psychology were pluses but that she could use more background in the business area. The counselor also suggested that she talk to someone who works in Personnel to obtain more specific information.

After doing so she decided to enroll in several business courses at night while actively seeking employment in the Personnel field.

How has Betty approached planning her career?

How has Betty dealt with uncertainty?

Betty's situation highlights the fact that the planning process is often filled with indecision and uncertainty. Betty had no concrete idea of what her career goal should be. All she knew was that she "liked to help people." In fact, initially most of the planning effort was invested in gathering information that would reduce the uncertainty of making an initial choice and allow her to make a better one.

She established an immediate target of investigating an occupation such as Personnel that might also fulfill her need to help people. Taking the business courses would serve as a "necessary step" by giving her a better understanding of how organizations work. In dealing with uncertainty involved with future events, she began to plot a specific course of action while remaining flexible enough to change direction as new information was obtained. Her situation pointedly brings out that the planning process requires that "one step at a time be taken" to fulfill one's longer-range goal(s).

Individual Planning and the Life-Space Concept

Another way to look at Betty's planning needs is to consider them from the standpoint of the life-space model. Betty's life space is influenced by the spaces of groups to which she belongs, her work, the organization, and the external environment. They all affect the type of planning Betty does and even how useful their contributions will be in thinking through her career possibilities. For example, her relationships with her family, her fellow workers, and major developments on the national scene affect her selection of goals and priorities. Needless to say, energy shortages would likely affect even how she plans her vacations, employment, or work activities.

Some typical questions that affect individual career planning include the following:

What are advancement opportunities like in my organization?

How do their policies affect my career?

Is my work enjoyable?

Do I like the people I work with?

Do I want to spend more time with my family?

Will inflation reduce my standard of living?

A Note on Personal Career Planning

As with business planning, career plans should also be flexible because one never knows exactly what the future holds. As Betty considers new information, whether through courses taken, actual work experience, or changes in her family circumstances, her plans are likely to be revised.

Despite the increased emphasis on career planning in schools, a majority of students still change major fields of study during their college years. Although some may suggest that this action results from indecision on the part of the student, we view it as a natural part of maturing and necessary to the planning process in the sense of adapting to changes in one's thinking as new information is obtained. Efforts *should* be redirected toward a new goal once information is obtained that suggests that the old goal is no longer desirable or achievable. To do otherwise in fact would be "acting indecisively." Thus, earlier thinking, planning and (possible) personal change require a careful integration of the factors indicated here. Taking too much time to change is as serious as being overly reactive. Good balance is required.

It is most important to search out information (using one's own Delphi panel) in areas having the greatest impact on one's career plans. After all, professional baseball teams send out advance scouts to discover what pitchers are giving opposing players the most trouble and what players "have the hot bat." This information is then used to plan the proper game strategy when playing that team. In a career sense it pays to obtain information on the company you are thinking of joining or the job you are thinking of accepting. It has been our experience that many students who begin a course of study in engineering, accounting, or most other fields have little idea of what engineers or accountants actually do, how they spend their work day, or what skills or abilities they require. Many companies, in cooperation with educational institutions, have established career days, cooperative education programs, internships, and other programs that provide this career-related information so that dissatisfaction and "lost time" can be avoided by both employee and company.

SUMMARY

In this chapter we discussed why planning is important for both individuals and organizations. We also looked at how planning varied among managers at different levels in the organization. The effect of time and other organizational and environmental factors was also described, especially in relation to the accuracy of forecasts. Two nonmathematical forecasting approaches were presented to give the reader an idea of techniques used in planning.

Various types of plans were defined, and the steps in the planning process were explained in detail, that is, how to plan. Finally, behavioral considerations in planning were discussed.

Planning takes time and effort; therefore, it is best to do it in a place and manner that is free of distractions. Too often managers find it difficult to do this, yet they must if they are to be successful. For an organization to survive and grow, it too must establish a commitment to planning by pursuing realistic objectives.

For individuals planning is also essential. It is ironic (and somewhat sad) that some individuals spend days, even weeks, deciding what car to buy or what dress to wear while not "investing" as little as one hour in planning their careers and life.

Questions for Study and Discussion

1. What is planning? What steps does it include?
2. Why is planning important for individuals? for organizations?
3. How are planning, decision making, and control related?
4. How does planning differ at various levels in the hierarchy?
5. How would planning be different for larger organizations versus smaller ones? Stable organizations versus ones faced with much uncertainty?
6. How would the time horizon for planning differ for a petroleum company? A hospital? A fast-food restaurant?
7. What are the advantages and disadvantages of MBO?
8. What is the difference between effectiveness and efficiency?
9. Why is it important to set measurable objectives?
10. How would you reply to a manager who said, "I never have time to plan. I have trouble enough just surviving the daily crisis around here"?
11. How would you measure whether a firm was achieving its mission to "be a good corporate citizen"?
12. Three major areas of goal setting for most firms are sales, production, and quality. What are some of the potential conflicts among these areas?
13. What is the Delphi method of forecasting? When should it be used?

CASE: VALUE SUPERMARKETS

Value Supermarkets is a chain of 30 successful supermarkets in medium-sized cities in the Southeast. It has always been the company's policy to have one leading store in each of a number of cities of approximately 50,000 to 100,000 population. In each city large, attractive stores were developed that provided complete product lines of food and related products sold at competitive prices. Although the company had to close a few poorly located stores over the years, it relied for store locations almost entirely on the instincts of its president and founder, George Knudsen. The company's record of profits indicated that his judgment had generally been correct during the company's 25-year history.

George's son, Kevin, had recently graduated from a university with a degree in business administration and joined the company as assistant to the president. His major responsibility involved developing a "system for planning."

Kevin's management courses had often stressed the importance of planning. His summers spent working at various company stores reinforced his thought that there was a need for a more formalized planning effort since not a day seemed to go by without some "fire having to be put out." The more he thought about it the more he felt that management by objectives was a technique that could be useful not only in determining new store locations, but also in planning day-to-day store operations.

He discussed his ideas with his father, who responded, "Management by objectives is nothing new here. We have always had important company objectives toward which everyone strives. As you know, I expect $15,000,000 in sales, a profit on sales before taxes of 2 percent, a return on investment of 15 percent, employee turnover to be stabilized at 8 percent, an on-going training program to be in effect by June 30, and two new stores to be built by the end of the year."

"But I am more interested in how these goals have been developed and who was involved in their determination," replied Kevin.

"Well, they were primarily my thoughts after discussing the situation with the controller and the vice-president of store operations, Wayne Harding."

In later discussions with both the store operations vice-president and the controller, Keven discovered that they felt little direct involvement in planning except for compiling financial information that they were asked to give George. Wayne felt that a more formal planning process that involved the store managers was needed but also realized that the latter's time commitments were already very burdensome.

Kevin was somewhat confused as to the direction to take in planning.

Questions

1. How would you characterize the planning that is taking place at Value Supermarkets?
2. Is management by objectives being used at Value?
3. Would you implement a management by objectives program at Value? If so, how?
4. What should Kevin recommend in regard to planning?

Experiential Exercise

Divide into groups of four or five. Each group is to devise a plan to collect and sell used books on a campus and through a student organization. The project's objectives should be determined. Appropriate standing and single-use plans should be developed and implemented. Include sales projections and an analysis of environmental problems in each group's presentation to the class.

References

Abouzeid, Kamal M., and Charles N. Weaver, "Social Responsibility in the Corporate Goal Hierarchy," *Business Horizons* **21** (June 1978): 29–35.

Aplin, John C., Jr., and Peter P. Schoderbeck, "MBO: Requisites for Success in the Public Sector," *Human Resource Management* **15**(2) (Summer 1976): 30–36.

Bhatty, Egbert F., "Corporate Planning in Medium-Sized Companies in the U.K.," *Long Range Planning (UK)* **14**(1) (February 1981): 60–72.

Blankenship, J. E., II, "Goal Setting in the Diversified Company," *Managerial Planning* **26** (November-December 1977): 8–14.

Blanning, Robert, "How Managers Decide to Use Planning Models," *Long Range Planning* **13**(2) (April 1980): 32–35.

Bourgeois, L. J., III, "Strategy and Environment: A Conceptual Integration," *Academy of Management Review* **5** (January 1980): 25–39.

Drucker, Peter, *The Practice of Management.* New York: Harper & Row (1954).

Drucker, Peter, *Management: Tasks, Responsibilities and Practices.* New York: Harper & Row (1974).

Edmonds, Charles P., III, and John H. Hand, "What are the Real Long-Run Objectives of Business?" *Business Horizons* **21** (October 1978): 49–60.

Emshoff, James R., and Ian I. Mitroff, "Improving the Effects of Corporate Planning," *Business Horizons* **21** (October 1978): 49–60.

Hollmann, Robert W., and David A. Tansik, "A Life Cycle Approach to Management by Objectives," *Academy of Management Review* **2** (October 1977): 678–683.

Hopkins, David, "Improving MBO Through Synergistics," *Public Personnel Management* **8**(3) (May-June 1979): 163–169.

Koontz, Harold, "Making Strategic Planning Work," *Business Horizons* **19** (April 1976): 37–47.

Lorange, Peter, *Corporate Planning: An Executive Viewpoint.* Englewood Cliffs, N.J.: Prentice-Hall (1980).

Lorange, Peter, and Richard F. Vancil, "How to Design a Strategic Planning System," *Harvard Business Review* **54** (September-October 1976): 75–81.

Miller, Danny, and Peter H. Friesen, "Strategy-Making in Context: Ten Empirical Archetypes," *Journal of Management Studies* **14** (October 1977): 253–280.

Mintzberg, Henry, "Patterns in Strategy Formation," *Management Science* **24** (May 1978): 934–938.

Morasky, Robert L., "Defining goals—A Systems Approach," *Long Range Planning* **10** (April 1977): 85–89.

Moskow, Michael, *Strategic Planning in Business and Government.* New York: The Committee for Economic Development (1978).

Odiorne, George S., *Management by Objectives*. Belmont, Cal.: Pitman Publishing (1965).

Paine, Frank T., and William Naumes, *Strategy and Policy Formulation: An Integrative Approach*. Philadelphia: W. B. Saunders (1974).

Palesy, Steven R., "Motivating Line Management Using the Planning Process," *Planning Review* **8**(2) March (1980): 3–8+.

Paul, Ronald N., Neil B. Donavan, and James W. Taylor, "The Reality Gap in Strategic Planning," *Harvard Business Review* **56** (May-June 1978): 124–130.

Steiner, George, *Management Policy and Strategy*. New York: Macmillan (1982).

Thume, Stanley, and Robert House, "Where Long-Range Planning Pays Off," *Business Horizons* **13**(4) (August 1970): 81–87.

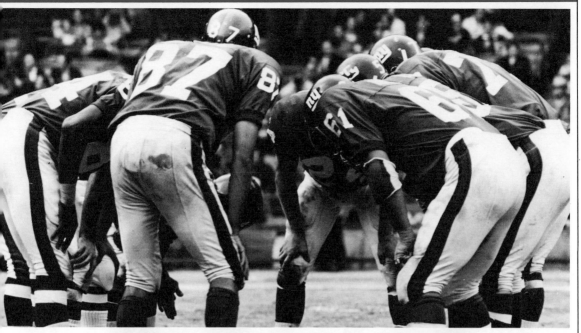

CHAPTER 5

DECISION MAKING

KEY
QUESTIONS
ADDRESSED
IN CHAPTER

1. What is decision making?
2. What factors affect decision making?
3. How do you make decisions?
4. When should group decision making be used?
5. How can decisions in organizations be improved?
6. What techniques are available to make decisions under various conditions of certainty?

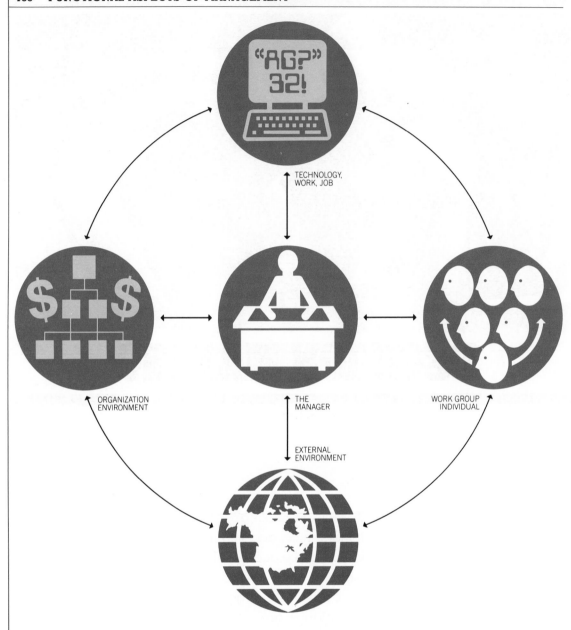

TECHNOLOGY,
WORK, JOB

ORGANIZATION
ENVIRONMENT

THE
MANAGER

WORK GROUP
INDIVIDUAL

EXTERNAL
ENVIRONMENT

The manager's work–life spaces

*When you're up to your neck in alligators, it's difficult to recall
that your original objective was to drain the swamp.*

THE CHAPTER IN BRIEF

Every day each of us is faced with many decisions. Some are rather
routine:

- What clothes should I wear today?
- What should I eat today?
- How should I get to school or work?

Some are more complex:

- What part-time job should I get?
- Should I sign up for public speaking or take racquetball?
- Should I buy a house or rent?

During the workday managers are also faced with many **decisions**—
choices to be made among alternatives. For example,

> Should Tom or Dick be hired? What about Jane?
>
> Should product A or product B be introduced into the product
> line?
>
> Should more heating oil or gasoline be refined from crude oil?
>
> Should John or Mary be assigned the Jones' account?

Decision making is an important part of a manager's activities. It
plays a particularly key role, however, when managers are engaged
in planning. It is for this reason that decision making follows the
chapter on planning. When planning, managers decide what goals
and opportunities their organization should pursue, what resources
will be used, and who should perform the tasks necessary to achieve
planned objectives. If plans go awry, they must also decide what new
actions to take. The quality of their decisions, in fact, will largely
determine how effective their plans will be.

Although decision making is an integral part of all managers'
responsibilities, it is particularly important that top managers make
good decisions. A wrong decision at this level is likely to be very
costly and, on occasion, can result in the organization going out of
business. Major decisions at this level are often more complex and
require judgment that only comes with experience. Lower-level managers, on the other hand, face just as many decisions (maybe more),
but their mistakes are usually less costly to the organization. However, the direct cost of a mistake is only part of the issue because

"I'm going back to plain white shirts! I can't make co-ordinate decisions this early in the morning!"

(From *The Wall Street Journal*; permission—Cartoon Features Syndicate.)

businesses can be damaged in many different ways. Good decisions are needed at all organization levels.

So much of a manager's time is spent making decisions that some management authors view managers primarily as decision makers. These same authors view other managerial activities—such as directing, communicating, controlling, and motivating—of lesser importance. Although this view may overstate the importance of decision making in the management process, whether we like it or not managers are usually evaluated and rewarded on the basis of the number, importance, and quality of their decisions.

Making sound decisions is difficult enough, but further compounding the problem are the many outside forces affecting any given situation that may be beyond our control. Often decisions that seemed "right" at the time they were made may turn out "wrong" later. And sometimes "wrong" decisions, through luck, turn out to be "right" later. It is no wonder that to be a good decision maker it sometimes appears that one must be an accurate economic forecaster, expert psychologist, knowledgeable mathematician, and just plain lucky, all at the same time.

Decision Making and the Life-Space Model

Individual decisions are affected in many ways by the groups to which we belong, the organizations for which we work, and the environment in which we live.

Groups often exert pressures to conform that result in many people "following the leader." Everyone, at one time or another, has conformed to group pressure by agreeing to a decision that, if left alone, he or she would not have made.

Organizations also affect the manner in which decisions are made. Autocratic managers are unwilling to share decisions with others, whereas participative managers are likely to consult their subordinates before making decisions. The size and the complexity of the organization also affect decision making. Large, international conglomerates may have sophisticated, formalized management information systems, that attempt to replace "intuitive" decisions by a "rational" process. On the other hand, smaller organizations or ones in such rapidly changing industries as fashions and toys often must rely on "the feel of the market" rather than "the numbers."

Generally, managers find the external forces in the environment outside their control, whereas organizational resources are more controllable. Therefore, when they face environments that are quite turbulent and subject to rapid change, they must be more alert and remain flexible to respond to the sudden changes that occur. Isn't that why rubber rafts used to shoot rapids are flexible while ocean-going vessels are sturdy but rather inflexible?

People in jobs little affected by change can usually draw on organization history or experience for decision making. Here decisions are usually quite routine and automatic. People in jobs that are at the threshold of change, however, face much uncertainty when making decisions because there is no history to rely on. They are spading new ground and thus face much uncertainty.

Decision Making and You

Although the process of decision making is fairly straightforward, many decisions are not as simple as they appear. Consider the example of Robert Morse.

Robert Morse, a second-year student at Trenton Community College, is trying to decide his course schedule for the following semester, which will be his last. He works part-time as a sales clerk in a local clothing store because he needs the money for his school expenses, and the hours usually fit in nicely with his class schedule. Being captain of the school tennis team, he cannot take afternoon classes four days a week.

Bob has been thinking of what he would like to do after he finishes college and has talked with his counselor at Trenton and also one at the local university. He is still undecided, however, except that he is leaning toward "something in management."

Next semester, he must take three required courses but has to choose two electives. He wonders what two electives would be best, considering his time constraints and interests. His management instructor, Chuck Balskus, has suggested that he take a business report-writing course for one of his electives because written communication skills will be important in almost any field he chooses as a career. On the other hand, many of his friends are going to take a history course because the instructor is known to be quite lenient. Both courses are offered at the same time, and he must register on Thursday—two days from now.

What should Robert decide?

How should he approach this decision?

What does this scenario tell us about decision making?

One factor affecting the decision-making process is the amount of time a person has to make a decision. Time pressures are significant because they affect the amount of information that can be gathered before deciding and, in turn, the quality of the decision itself. In Robert's case the time pressure may preclude him from getting additional advice from others that might, in fact, increase the number of alternatives under consideration (i.e., other elective courses could also be appropriate). As in this instance, decision makers must often comply with deadlines that are set by others. For example:

- You may have to decide between a job at company A or company B, but company A wants your decision before you know if company B will make you an offer, much less whether it's a good one.

- Company C offers your company an order that is only marginally profitable. If accepted, you will have no additional capacity to accept more profitable orders that are possible. However, C must know whether you will accept the order *now*.

The importance of a decision also affects how a decision might be made. **Programmed** or routine decisions such as what to have for dinner can be dealt with quickly although in some households this may be a "big deal." Organizations usually develop rules, policies, and procedures to handle situations that occur repeatedly (see our discussion of standing plans in Chapter 4). Policies, such as "all employees receive two weeks of vacation after one year of service," allow managers to free their time for other decisions that are more unique, more complex, or more important. Without such a policy, deciding how to handle each individual employee's vacation request would be both time consuming and costly.

Nonprogrammed nonroutine decisions, such as what should be done to improve community relations, who should be assigned a specific task, or how to handle a chronically late employee, take up much of a manager's time. In fact, the success in making these kinds of decisions will often distinguish effective managers from ineffective ones. Managers rely heavily on their creativity, judgment, and problem-solving ability in handling nonroutine situations. Established procedures are likely to be of little use. For this reason, many management development programs attempt to improve a manager's decision-making ability by teaching them to make decisions in a logical manner.

GREAT PERSON PROFILE

Joyce Colon

Joyce Colon grew up on her family's peanut farm in Virginia, where she was exposed early to managerial tasks. At eleven, her father put her in charge of the hired workers. This sparked an interest in business and management that led her to major in business administration at Virginia State University. Her first employer was Equitable Life, and after two years as the only black woman among 30 management trainees she became a junior analyst. Within two more years she was a project manager responsible for four other analysts. Feeling the need for more varied managerial experience, she took an Equitable-sponsored leave on an executive loan program, training disadvantaged youths for corporate jobs.

When Colon's husband got a directorship at Virginia State, she did what most women have done in the past; she resigned her job and took an administrative job with the university at half her previous pay. After two years, she was contacted by Equitable and offered a position as executive assistant to their Senior Vice-President of Human Resources. After going through a conscious *decision-making* process regarding her own career, she accepted the offer and became assistant Vice-President after only three years.

In 1980 she was contacted regarding a post as executive assistant to an Executive Vice-President at Westinghouse. Again she studied the situation carefully, evaluating her future career potential with each employer, and chose to accept the job with Westinghouse, viewing it as a springboard. In less than two years, she became Strategic Planning Manager for one of the Westinghouse businesses. Thanks to careful evaluation, foresight in career planning, and *applying* the *decision-making process* to her career, Joyce Colon is one of the highest ranking black females in U.S. corporations.

BACKGROUND

The Decision-Making Process

Managers make decisions in a variety of ways. Some rely on tradition with the hope that "what worked in the past will work again." Others may appeal to a higher authority by relying on expert advice or allowing their boss to decide. Still others may rely on their intuition or simply flip a coin. Although all of these have been used in the past, most decision makers use a more rational approach to decision making that is likely to result in better decisions.

There are generally thought to be five stages to this process of thought and deliberation that we call **decision making.** Although it is normally presented as a sequential process, the stages need not be rigidly applied. Their value lies in aiding the decision maker to structure the problem in a meaningful way and to deal with it systematically.

Stage 1. Problem Identification and Definition

Many decision-making situations are the result of incomplete plans, lack of attention to converting plans into activities, or unanticipated developments. Identifying and defining the problem—the reason for not meeting one's objectives—is not easy. We often "feel" something is wrong before we really know that a problem exists. The more information one has concerning both the external realities and the internal forces at work in a situation the easier it will be to define a problem. For example, someone who knows little about the operation of an automobile is unlikely to make meaningful observations about what might be wrong with his or her car. An auto mechanic, however, because of his experience and knowledge, is able to observe, locate, and define the problem with much more reliability. The relationship between planning and decision making can be observed at this stage. The severity of a problem for an organization is measured by the difference (or gap) between the planned level of performance expected and the levels of performance attained. For example, assume an automotive manufacturer has established a realistic market objective of a 20 percent market share within five years. If market share at the end of the period were only 15 percent, this would be a serious fall-down in terms of planned market share—unless good reasons for this result had been established sufficiently far in advance.

Many people try to define problems before sufficient information has been gathered. If a car does not start or a person has a fever, these are indications or symptoms that a problem exists. But these symptoms are not problems themselves. To cure the fever, a doctor must search for various symptoms that will identify the cause of the fever.

It is important to distinguish symptoms from problems, for too often symptoms are treated while problems remain unsolved. See if you can distinguish between the problem and the symptoms in each of the following situations.*

1. (a) Radiator smoking.
   (b) Broken radiator hose.
2. (a) House lights won't go on.
   (b) Fuse burned out.
3. (a) Employee morale is low.
   (b) Absenteeism is high.
   (c) Boring jobs.
4. (a) High number of mistakes on orders.
   (b) Lack of training program.
   (c) Payment on basis of time only.

Stage 2. Search for Information and Identify Alternatives

Once the problem has been defined, decision makers must decide what they are going to do about it. In other words, what are the best means or alternatives to solve it? In order to identify possible solutions it is necessary to search for as much information as possible, that is relevant and within time limits.

But how long should one continue to search out information? Search is costly in terms of time, effort, and money. The amount of search is therefore usually dependent on the importance of the problem and whether it is a new one or a recurrence of an old one.

For old problems, managers are likely to try programs (as solutions) that have successfully worked in the past. Here care is needed in applying programs when the problem does not exactly fit the program. Since conditions and people both change, a program that worked with a work group some years ago is not likely to work today.

For new problems, managers spend much time searching for information that will help define issues and generate alternatives. Past experience, organizational policies, resource limitations such as money, availability of people and equipment, and personal desires are some of the factors that influence what a decision maker will include on a list of feasible alternatives. But, even under the best of conditions, *all* feasible alternatives cannot be developed because of human or situational limitations. Herbert Simon (1961) has called this process that limits the list of desirable alternatives **bounded rationality** (Taylor, 1970). Since these factors vary among individ-

*Answers: Problems are 1.(b), 2.(b), 3.(c), 4.(b).

GREAT PERSON PROFILE

George Stevens Moore (1905–   )

George Stevens Moore was born and raised in Missouri, which provided him with a heritage to which he accredits his pragmatism, an important ingredient in *decision making*. While studying at Yale, he edited the student newspaper and developed a lifelong habit of getting the facts. His quick, alert mind processed the facts as he collected them, and he developed a reputation for having "the fastest financial mind in existence." This was instrumental in developing his successful decision-making patterns.

During a bank investigation in 1933 he was exposed to bank practices that resulted in near disastrous results. This experience further reinforced the need for fact finding and caution in making decisions.

Through Moore's aggressiveness, Citibank, one of the major financial units in the United States, became a forerunner in two major developments in U.S. banking. These developments were broadening the range of banking services and overseas expansion. These ideas were controversial when they were first introduced, but the energetic and bold Moore convinced his superiors of their

worth with detailed facts. Under Moore's guidance Citibank entered real estate and factoring and opened numerous foreign branches. The latter part of Moore's career centered around restaffing departments and identifying new executive talent. He realized that fresh ideas are necessary to maintain the vitality of an organization. He brought to Citibank a new momentum of which his decision-making patterns were an important part.

uals and organizations, it is likely that one person would rule out certain alternatives that another, either in the same or a different organization, would consider. In our example, Robert Morse has eliminated all but two alternatives, the business writing and history courses, because they "fit" his long-term career interest, personal interest, and/or time constraints better than others. It is likely, too, that if his friends were not "thinking of taking" the history course, neither would he.

Stage 3. Evaluate Alternatives

Actually, as alternatives are being searched out or uncovered, analysis of one's ability to solve the problem is likely to take place simultaneously. A conscious effort is needed therefore to allow sufficient time for thoughtful analysis. But whether the alternatives are analyzed quickly by the decision maker alone or analyzed rigorously by a team of experts, the value of the alternatives will have (at least) two criteria: how realistic or probable is each alternative in terms of the goals and resources of the organization (or an individual), and how well will each solve the problem.

The probability that an *alternative* is likely to solve the problem is often quite *subjective* (or judgmental), especially when past information is not available or the problem is new. Under these circumstances assistance by others, who are "experts," can often improve the accuracy of this **subjective probability** (estimate) or at least make it more "logical." Haven't we all, at one time or another, sought advice or counsel of close friends or others in whom we had confidence when making important decisions in areas that we lacked experience? Robert Morse did this when he sought help from several counselors concerning the courses that would be best suited for his career choice.

Alternatives are also evaluated in terms of how well they will solve the problem or meet the objective. Since most decision situations have multiple objectives, a ranking of the importance of these objectives is desirable. Some objectives are more important than others, and the decision maker may analyze them differently. For example, a college graduate seeking a job may analyze job offers as to how well they meet his or her objectives related to salary, degree of responsibility, advancement opportunities, security, amount of travel involved, and others. How the graduate ranks these objectives will determine largely what job is chosen. If the graduate requires at least a $18,000 annual salary to be satisfied with pay and all job offers *satisfy* this criterion, then other needs become more important in choosing the job. Similarly, Robert Morse's choice of an elective will be dependent on the importance he attaches to his long-term career interest, his social need of being with his friends, and the time constraints posed by his part-time job and participation in sports (tennis).

Let us use a simple weighting scheme to help the college graduate in the above example more objectively evaluate job offers from two companies, A and B.

In Table 5-1 are listed the factors that the graduate considers important in a job. These are his or her job objectives. Alongside these factors are the degree of importance or weight attached to each factor—on a scale of 1 to 10 with 10 being most important.

During the evaluation process the graduate rates each company's offer against the factors that are important to him or her, based upon the information he or she has gathered. For example, the pay and the work being "to my liking" are most important and thus are each weighted 10. Since the actual pay offer of company B was 90 percent

Table 5-1 Factors Considered in Choosing a Job

Job Factors	Weight (Degree of Importance)		Company A	Company B
Pay and fringe benefits	10		10	9
Work to my liking	10		7	10
Advancement opportunity	8		4	8
Boss who will teach	6		4	6
Amount of travel	4		4	2
Hours of work	3		2	2
Job security	3		3	2
Reputation of company	3		1	3
Total possible points	47	Score	35	42

that of company A, it was given 9 out of 10 possible points as a score. On the other hand, the job offered by company B involved work that was more to the graduate's liking and, therefore, received a score of 10 (out of 10 possible). The job offered by company A involved work that was rated a 7 (out of 10 possible). Other factors are similarly rated.

As is seen in the table, out of 47 possible points company B's job offer received 42 points, while company A's job offer received only 35 points despite its offering the higher salary. Based on this evaluation the college graduate should seriously consider company B because such factors as advancement opportunity, work to my liking, boss who will teach, and reputation of company together outweigh the lower pay offered.

Although this method may help to evaluate more objectively alternatives, what is also important here is the reliability of the information used. The college graduate in the example must take sufficient time to gather information that is reliable enough to use in making the decision.

Stage 4. Choose the Best Alternatives

Once the criteria for choosing an alternative have been determined the selection itself appears to be rather routine. The best alternative, however, is limited by information that is available at the time of the decision analyses. Often this is not sufficient to meet long-run requirements. This further emphasizes the need to remain open-minded and allow for sufficient discussion of the issues especially when the decision is "breaking new ground" or will have considerable impact on the organization or group. Eventually, however, a decision has to be made, and more likely than not it will represent a compromise between all factors that have been considered. For example, the problem may involve substandard productivity in the machine shop.

There is evidence that the department supervisor is the cause. Our search also determines that he is quite popular with the employees, and if he were demoted or dismissed, low morale would likely result. Our "best" alternative might then be a developmental program aimed at retraining the supervisor that also supports our commitment to people. This may be a longer-term, more expensive alternative for the organization, but it might be the "best" one when all relevant factors are considered.

Stage 5. Implement the Decision

Many good decisions fail because little has been done to "prepare" people or units. The decision must be communicated properly, support for it must be organized, and the necessary resources must be assigned to implement it. Managers often unrealistically assume that once they have made a decision, their role is over, for action on it will automatically follow.

Proper implementation of a decision involves much the same steps as implementation for plans. Individuals or groups whose support will be needed to implement the decision effectively should be considered from the very beginning of the decision-making process. Often their support can be obtained by allowing them to contribute in some way to the decision. Finally, feedback systems should be installed that serve as "early warning" signals or controls by providing progress information. If implementation is not proceeding according to plan, then a new decision or redirection may be warranted.

DECISION MODELS

The environment within which the decision maker operates also affects the decision-making process. Conditions in the environment change, and prediction of the future is difficult (as already noted in the planning discussions). Yet managers must make decisions based on the information that they have available. For example, Robert Morse may indeed decide to sign up for the history course anticipating an easy A. However, instructors may be changed or the course could be canceled. These future facts, if known when the decision was made, would likely alter the decision reached. Likewise, a person may be hired based on his or her past experience and references. But a manager cannot be confident about how well the employee will perform in the organization until some time passes.

All of this illustrates that managers make decisions under various degrees of certainty (see Exhibit 5-1). These conditions tend to

Exhibit 5-1 Decision-Making Situations Reflecting Understanding and Time Horizons

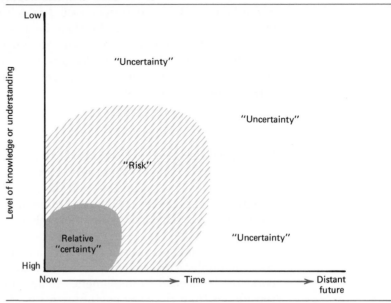

vary with the time frame that encompasses the decision. That is, the longer the future time period involved in the decision, the less certain we are concerning what environmental conditions will occur. Of course, some organizations can predict with much certainty what their future environment may be like over the next two years, if it is quite stable; whereas others, operating in a more dynamic environment, may feel uncertain what the next two *months* will bring. This, in turn, affects the way in which we approach decisions and, indeed, the techniques that are used when evaluating alternatives.

Decision Theory: A Management Science Tool

As suggested earlier, managers are faced with three kinds of decision situations (see Exhibit 5-1): (1) certainty, (2) risk, and (3) uncertainty. The following discussion of decision theory attempts to explain how the kind of decision situation or degree of certainty faced by the decision maker can affect the type of decision that is made. In the Appendix of this chapter we provide a specific problem to illustrate how decision theory can be used in a real-life situation under the three conditions of certainty.

Decision theory may be defined as a set of general concepts and techniques that can assist a decision maker in choosing among alternatives in a given decision situation. Decision-theory problems are commonly cast in a standard framework, termed a **payoff** (profit) or decision table. (See Table 5-3 in the Appendix at the end of this chapter.)

Conditions of Certainty

Under conditions of **certainty** a decision maker has enough information to know what the results of the decision will be. For example, if you must leave the house during a rainstorm, it is likely that you will take an umbrella or other appropriate raingear to avoid being drenched. The environment—rain—is known, and the outcomes of the possible alternatives are also known. A decision under conditions of certainty consists simply of choosing the alternative that will maximize (staying relatively dry, for example) whatever objective is desired by the decision maker. Under conditions of certainty, management science techniques such as linear programming, breakeven analysis, capital investment models, and inventory control models have been used effectively. These techniques are discussed in a later chapter.

Conditions of Risk

Since conditions of certainty are becoming less common in today's complex and rapidly changing environment, it is often only possible to estimate the likelihood or probability of various events occurring in the future. This condition is called **risk.**

Let us use the weather again as an example. You must leave the house now and will be outside for most of the day. Although it is not raining now, the weather forecast is for a 60 percent chance of showers. Do you take an umbrella or other raingear? The event that is presently occurring—no rain—is known with certainty, but since your decision includes a time frame within which another event—rain—is possible, your decision becomes more complex. Under risk conditions various statistical (or probability) techniques are helpful in making decisions. In the insurance industry, actuaries develop risk strategies by analyzing the claims experience of various individuals (that make up a group), and under many different conditions.

In decision making under conditions of risk, managers are faced with the possibility of the occurrence of several **states of nature.** The probability that a given state of nature will occur is known and is based on the manager's research, experience, and other information.

Conditions of Uncertainty

When we are *not* able to estimate the probabilities of various future events occurring, a condition of **uncertainty** exists. Many changes or unknown facts can occur when decision time frames are long, for example, in a decision to build a new refinery. To predict what is likely to occur with any degree of certainty therefore is quite difficult. In such situations, managers frequently apply their past experience, judgment, and intuition to the events so that the range of choices can be narrowed. Also, input from others may help reduce some of the uncertainty and improve reliability. Under these circumstances the inclusion of additional, knowledgeable people in the decision-making process *may* be beneficial. We discuss this in detail in another section.

Nevertheless, under conditions of uncertainty many decision makers will delay decisions until the environment stabilizes or take a path of least risk (many managers tend to be **"risk avoiders"**). For example, oil companies were reluctant to commit large sums for expansion of facilities in the mid- to late-1970s. The uncertainty of pending government legislation and the long time needed to bring new facilities "on stream" resulted in cautious behavior because billions of dollars were at stake. An already tight supply situation was aggravated while companies waited for "signs from Washington" in the form of a national energy policy that would clear up the uncertainty.

> *Parkinson's 5th Law*
> If there is a way to delay a decision, the good bureaucracy will find it.

Several decision-making approaches under uncertainty are presented in the Appendix at the end of this chapter. Each approach suggests a somewhat different personal philosophy of the decision maker.

Implications for Your Career

Many of the career-related decisions that you are presently making are being made under conditions of risk or uncertainty. Like those of Robert Morse, your career goals may be "something in management." Yet, despite the fact that much information is not easily available, decisions must be made *today* that are likely to affect you for many years. For instance, some job related questions are:

- Will there be a demand for my skills when I graduate?
- What are certain jobs really like? Will I enjoy the work?
- How does company XYZ treat its people?
- How do I advance from job A to job B?

Changes will occur in the future that will affect the decision you make today. In some occupations, like education, advancement opportunities are poor, *as of a particular time,* and salary increases are below average. This has forced many to seek new opportunities to maintain their families' standards of living. Questions suggesting other changes are:

- How are technology and economic conditions likely to affect your career choice?
- What will be the demand for X occupation in Y years?

Your personal situation and interests are also likely to change over time. For example, a sales position that offers much travel may seem quite attractive now for a single person, but will it continue to be true if you decide to marry or raise a family? If not, will a sales manager's position that reduces travel demands likely be available?

As suggested by the above discussion, decision making concerning careers is full of unknowns. To improve the handling of this type of situation, one must search out relevant information. One helpful approach is to obtain advice and counsel from other people who "have been through it" or who are more expert in a particular area.

Maintaining flexibility is also important. One of the benefits of general study requirements in the early years of college education is the possibility for young people to discover a major field of interest. At the same time, students must start "getting their act together" by thoughtfully exploring their own career and life goals so that career decisions can be made more soundly. We all know individuals who have taken many courses that, in looking back, were of little or no use in preparing for their chosen career. The time and effort that was lost may have been saved if effective career planning had begun. Conversely, the courses may also have been a useful exposure of things that the individual did *not* want to do. This is a topic for a special chapter at the end of this book.

ADDITIONAL DECISION SITUATIONS

Individual versus Group Decisions: When Is Each Appropriate?

When should a decision be made by a group rather than an individual? This issue is greatly debated. Traditionally in the United States, most decisions have been made by individuals, whereas the Japanese are noted for their adherence to group decisions. Whether decisions should be made by an individual or group is largely dependent on factors such as the complexity and importance of the problem, the time available, the degree of acceptance required, the amount of information needed to make a decision, and the accepted manner in which decisions are made within the organization (see Exhibit 5-2). There are several possibilities for managerial decision making.

Exhibit 5-2 Some Conditions for Individual versus Group Decisions

Factor	(1) Individual	(2) Compromise (Some Amount of Participation)	(3) Group
1. Complexity and importance of problem	Simple, straightforward	⟷	Very complex
2. Degree of acceptance required for success	Little or none	⟷	Crucial to success
3. Time constraint	Extreme time pressure	⟷	Sufficient time to obtain needed information
4. Amount of information required	Little information is required for effective decision	⟷	Much information is needed from a variety of sources for proper interpretation
5. Accessibility of information	Decision maker has all information necessary	⟷	Information needed for decision is held by people other than decision maker
6. Organizational climate	Autocratic, centralized structure	⟷	Participative, decentralized structure

1. **Individual Decision.** Managers can make decisions themselves using the information that is available to them.
2. **Combination Decision.** Managers can make the decision after consulting with others (these may include subordinates or members of various groups affected by the decision).
3. **Group Decision.** Managers can allow the decision to be made by the group (with the manager usually being one of the group).

Group decisions are often more appropriate and more accurate than those of individuals when conditons are changing rapidly (there is much uncertainty) or when the problem is complex. These circumstances usually require skills and experiences that one person is unlikely to possess. The NASA Survival Test exercise at the end of this chapter is a good demonstration of these points.

For successful implementation, many decisions require acceptance by those affected. Decisions made by a group, or where the group participated in some way in the decision, will likely be accepted by its members and will be implemented more readily. Many a "good" decision has been sabotaged by people who felt they were denied a role in the decision-making process.

When the decision requires much information and the information is housed in many places within the organization, group participation is again called for to ensure that all available information is analyzed and to help in its interpretation. Some decisions, like moving a plant or opening a branch office, affect widely different areas in the organization. Bringing together the people who will be affected by the decision will improve the coordination that will be required during its implementation.

Finally, most organizations have established leadership styles that are closely connected to patterns of decision making. Whatever the pattern, whether group- or individual-oriented, expectations are built up and, in turn, subtle pressure is exerted to continue that style.

There are a number of questions that managers can ask themselves to determine which of the three decision-making styles may be more appropriate (refer to the three types previously described).

Marketing specialists working on the development of a new product.

- Do we have sufficient information and knowledge to solve the problem ourselves? If yes, then style 1 (where the individual makes the decision) would be more appropriate. Otherwise, style 2 or 3 would be better.
- Is acceptance by the group crucial for successful implementation? If yes, then style 2 or 3 is more appropriate.
- Is time a major factor? If yes, style 1 may be our best choice when the problem is relatively straightforward. Otherwise, style 2 would likely achieve a sufficiently good decision in view of the time pressure.
- Is our decision likely to be different from the group consensus? If yes, style 3 would be inappropriate. Giving up our authority to make the final decision would not have the objective quality that is necessary. Style 2 would be more appropriate.

These questions suggest that managers have much flexibility in choosing a decision style for a given situation. In the end, regardless of the style chosen for a particular decision, the final responsibility does rest with the individual manager. Nevertheless, both the increased complexity of problems faced by many managers and the increased expectations of individuals to share in the decisions that affect them suggest broader participation in the decision-making process.

Decision Making and Level in the Hierarchy

From a structural standpoint committees are organized at all organization levels. Key decision making, however, is confined typically to top management levels where problems involve more important and complex issues than at lower levels. In addition, lower-level managers generally have policies and procedures to guide them in making decisions, and thus committee activities here serve as advisory to higher levels or for purposes of communications or coordination.

Top-management decisions also take in a much longer time frame than do those of managers at lower levels. For example, the top managers may be considering strategies such as developing a new product line. The time frames of top management decision making often involve extended time periods into the future (e.g., two, three, or even five years), thus much uncertainty is involved in them (see Exhibit 5-1). On the other hand, first level managers are more often concerned with short-term tactical decisions including what workers to assign to certain tasks or schedule on certain shifts. These latter decisions are much more routine (certain), and there are likely to be procedures in place to serve as guides. If there are employee unions present, supervisory decisions may be further restricted to relatively routine matters.

The Japanese and Decision Making

The success that many Japanese organizations have enjoyed of late has focused worldwide attention on their managerial practices. Many researchers and American managers who have had the opportunity to observe Japanese management in action feel that their decision-making activities are quite different from our approach (Noda, 1980).

Peter Drucker (1974), for example, highlights the fact that in America we focus on getting the *answer,* whereas in Japan the emphasis is on the *question* and its implications.

The Japanese tend to be quite deliberate in the initial stages of information gathering, and benefiting from the Japanese business managers' opinions of group members or others may consult with people throughout the company and over a longer period of time to gain a true consensus about what to do. Although American decision makers may attempt contacts with the rank and file, there are usually token communications; many Japanese make decisions on the basis of majority opinion. Some American managers might be horrified at such a loss of control, but the success of the Japanese approach cannot be denied. For once the decision is made, there is

Japanese Plant Manager listening to an inspector's suggestion at a Tokyo assembly plant.

almost no need to imitate clever programs to "sell" the decision to the troops.

Drucker also praises the Japanese idea about which decisions need to be made at the top and their sense of what aspects of the decision process to emphasize in study or analysis. He recalls experiences in which Americans wanted to establish cooperative business relations with a Japanese company. While the Americans waited impatiently to discuss licenses and other critical particulars, the Japanese continued to discuss basic ideas at length. Once the basic decisions were made, the Japanese were able to polish off the details in record time. Certainly, the Japanese approach cannot be transferred intact to the United States because of the cultural differences. Even so, American decision makers could benefit from more emphasis placed on participative decision making.

How Organizational Structure Affects Decisions

Decisions link yesterday, today, and tomorrow and bring life to an organization by instituting actions toward specific goals. Better decisions will result in the organization more effectively accomplishing its goals. Organizational structure can play a large role in this regard.

In organizations, important responsibilities typically rest with line management, but many line managers do not have the appropriate authority to make necessary decisions. Instead, specialists in staff positions or in (subordinate) nonmanagerial roles find themselves making critical or more decisions because of their specialized knowledge. This situation often creates conflict and friction between line managers and staff specialists (this is discussed in the next chapter). To reduce this conflict and improve decision making some organizations have restructured the organization around groups that have sufficient expertise within them to make effective decisions in a particular field. The project or matrix form of organization discussed in Chapter 2 is an example of this trend.

Computerized management information systems (MIS) have given top management new options as to what level decisions should be made. One result has been that unique nonprogrammable decisions have been given to upper levels in the organization while programmable decisions have been relegated to lower levels. But the fact that computers can make information more available to all levels in the hierarchy has made this aspect of designing decision systems a most important one. Recent studies indicate that the decentralization of decisions is more effective for those organizations faced with rapidly changing, more turbulent environments. Since the environments surrounding many organizations seem to be changing rapidly, it is possible that greater flexibility in decision systems and placing decisions at lower levels in the organization may improve their effectiveness.

The flow of information (quantity, type, and direction) in the organization also greatly affects who is likely to make decisions. The manager who has access to the best information or who gets it first is often in the best decision-making position. Such *information-sensitive* positions in organizations hold much power and are likely to increase one's career mobility. Thus, it is well to recognize that by setting up an organizational structure to channel the flow of information, the organizations' decision makers are also being created.

SUMMARY

Managing is often a process of decision making. As such, the development of this skill is extremely important for career advancement. Since "practice makes perfect," it is never too early to start making decisions. Indeed, many graduates choose their first job on the basis of the amount of decision-making authority they will be given. Organizations that are considered developers of managers such as IBM, Proctor and Gamble, Xerox, to name a few, have well-developed information systems that allow managers the ability to make relevant decisions at an early point in their career.

In this chapter we have looked carefully at the five-stage systematic process of decision making and have discussed how the actual approach to decision making may vary based upon the degree of certainty faced by the decision maker. Also presented were the circumstances under which group, rather than individual, decisions may be more appropriately used. Finally, differences between the Japanese and American approaches to decision making were noted.

Although there is a science to decision making, much of it is still an art that takes careful nurturing and much practice. The types of decisions managers make and the conditions under which they make them will change. Therefore, managers must tailor their decision-making style to their particular problems and circumstances. In the end the quality of their decisions will mean the success or failure of the organization.

Questions for Study and Discussion

1. What is the relationship between planning and decision making?
2. What is the difference between programmed and nonprogrammed decisions?
3. Give examples of programmed and nonprogrammed decisions that you make in your everyday life.

4. How is decision making under conditions of certainty different from decision making under risk? From decision making under uncertainty?

5. Describe the steps involved in the decision-making process.

6. Under what circumstances would group decision-making likely be effective?

7. Why is it that many authors argue that decision making is the most important managerial function?

8. Consider an important decision that you have made recently. Describe how the five steps discussed in this chapter could have helped you in making the decision. In doing so, identify what step, if any, was most crucial.

9. How can creativity be of use in the decision-making process?

10. Can there ever be too many or too few alternatives to consider before making a decision?

11. Why is it important to accurately define the problem or issues when making a decision?

12. How does the Japanese approach to decision making differ from the American approach?

13. Describe the four selection criteria that could be used when making decisions under conditions of uncertainty (see Appendix).

Experiential Exercises

1. Complete the NASA Moon Survival Test. Rank-order the items in terms of their importance for survival as indicated. After you have done this individually, take the test again using a group of at least four people. The group must reach a consensus on the ranking of each item. Allow 15 minutes for group discussion. Now compare the group error score (column 5) with each individual's error score (column 3) once the correct answers are given. Was individual or group decision making more accurate? Why?

NASA Moon Survival Test*

Your spaceship has just crash-landed on the moon. You were scheduled to rendezvous with a mother ship 200 miles away on the lighted surface of the moon, but the rough landing has ruined your ship and destroyed all the equipment on board, except for the 15 items listed below.

Your crew's survival depends on reaching the mother ship, so you must choose the most critical items available for the 200-mile trip. Your task is to rank the 15 items in terms of their importance for survival. Place number 1 by the most important item, number 2 by the second most important, and so on through number 15, the least important.

Item	(1) Your Ranking 1 to 15	(2) = (3) − (1) Your Error Score	(3) NASA's Rankings 1 to 15	(4) Team Rankings 1 to 15	(5) = (4) − (3) Team Error Score
Box of matches	――	――	――	――	――
Food concentrate	――	――	――	――	――
Fifty feet of nylon rope	――	――	――	――	――
Parachute silk	――	――	――	――	――
Solar-powered portable heating unit	――	――	――	――	――
Two .45-caliber pistols	――	――	――	――	――
One case of dehydrated milk	――	――	――	――	――
Two 100-pound tanks of oxygen	――	――	――	――	――
Stellar map (of the moon's constellation)	――	――	――	――	――
Self-inflating life raft	――	――	――	――	――
Magnetic compass	――	――	――	――	――
Five gallons of water	――	――	――	――	――
Signal flares	――	――	――	――	――
First-aid kit containing injection needles	――	――	――	――	――
Solar-powered FM receiver–transmitter	――	――	――	――	――

Your total error score ☐   Team's total error score ☐

*Reprinted from *Psychology Today* Magazine, November 1971, Copyright © 1971, Ziff Davis Publishing Company.

CASE: RELIABLE INSURANCE COMPANY

The Reliable Insurance Company is a medium-sized regional insurance company located in the Northeast that specializes in automobile and homeowners' coverage. Recently the company has been experimenting with a four-day work week at a number of their regional offices.

Regional offices presently work a 40-hour week, and the bulletin sent from the home office has suggested that four 10-hour days be scheduled for each employee. The schedule that has proved most effective is 7:00 A.M. to 6:00 P.M. with a half-hour for lunch and two 15-minute coffee breaks.

Joyce Duncan has been a manager for the Rochester, New York office for six months. Previously she had been an assistant manager for a larger branch office for three years. She originally started with Reliable eight years ago as a claims adjuster after graduating from college with a degree in business. Joyce is 29, single, and looking forward to a career with Reliable.

Each regional office must be open five days a week, and it is the manager's responsibility to schedule his or her employees. Joyce has eight employees who are described in Table 5-2.

Joyce is trying to decide whether to experiment with the four-day work week and is discussing the matter with her assistant manager, Dick Munter.

"I think I should let the group decide whether they want to work the four-day week. After all, they have to live with it. They may as well decide on the hours and schedule too. What do you think?" asked Joyce.

Dick replied, "Are you crazy? You won't be able to get this group to agree on anything. They're too different. Besides, you're being paid to make the decisions."

Table 5-2 Employees of Rochester Regional Office

Employee Name and Title	Age	Sex	Marital Status	Number of Dependents	Time with Company	Education
Dick Munter Assistant Manager	34	M	Married	Wife	4 years	3 years college
Harry Johnson Claims Adjuster	23	M	Single	None	1 year	1 year college
Alice Pela Clerk-Typist	38	F	Married	Invalid mother, 2 children	5 years	High school
Sandy Wheeler Claims Processor	35	F	Widowed mother	2 children	6 years	High school
Ann Hunter Clerk-Typist	18	F	Single	None	6 months	High school
Sam Darnell Claims Adjuster	36	M	Married	Wife, 1 child	5 years	2 years college
Roberta Young File Clerk and Typist	19	F	Single	None	9 months	High school
Lynda Merrill File Clerk and Typist	20	F	Married	Husband	1 year	High school

Questions

1. Do you think that this situation calls for a group decision?
2. What other information would you like if you were Joyce?
3. What should Joyce do?

APPENDIX

The following illustrative example presents a *payoff (profit) or decision* table (Table 5-3) for a *chain of retail stores*. This table includes the payoffs to be expected if certain alternatives (or strategies) are implemented within a given economic climate (state of nature) and with the **probabilities** that the states of nature will occur.

The following terms are important in understanding the model.

1. **Alternatives or Strategies (A).** Alternatives are under the control of the decision maker and are designated by the symbol A. For example, "make" and "buy" would be two alternatives in a make-or-buy decision problem.

2. **States of Nature (N).** These are characteristic of the environment and are beyond the control of the decision maker. States of nature can be weather conditions or, in business decisions, various levels of demand for a product, governmental actions, or the like. They are represented by the symbol N.

3. **Payoffs or Outcomes (O).** These are the values associated with each combination of alternative and state of nature. The values are for a specified period of time. For example, the payoff when A_1 (open five stores) is chosen and N_1 (inflation) occurs is $50,000.

4. **Probability (P).** This is the likelihood of a state of nature actually occurring. If a particular state of nature is sure to occur (p =

Table 5-3 Payoff Table (Payoff in Thousands of Dollars)

| | States of Nature (N) | | |
| | N_1, Inflation | N_2, Recession | N_3, Stagflation |
Alternatives	P_1	P_2	P_3
A_1—Open five stores	50[a]	−15	3
A_2—Improve existing stores	25	4	6
A_3—Expand downtown store	10	6	5

KEY: A = alternatives
   N = states of nature
   P = probability
[a] Payoffs in thousands of dollars.

nature, with no one state given a value of 1, the decision situation is *risk*. Finally, if the decision maker has no idea of the probabilities of occurrence of any state of nature the decision situation is *uncertainty*.

Decision Making Under Conditions of Certainty

Under conditions of certainty only one state of nature exists. Referring to Table 5-3, if it were certain that inflation (state of nature, N_1) existed, then the decision or payoff table would be

Alternatives	N_1, Inflation
A_1, open 5 stores	50,000 ($50,000)
A_2, improve existing stores	25,000 ($25,000)
A_3, expand downtown store	10,000 ($10,000)

With only one state of nature possible and an objective of obtaining the maximum profit, the manager would select alternative A_1, the one with the highest payoff of $50,000. Likewise, if a recession (N_2) were certain, the best payoff we could expect would be $6000 by choosing alternative A_3 (A_1 = loss of $15,000, A_2 = $4000), expansion of the downtown store only. Obviously the existence of a single state of nature simplifies decision making, but certainty in our daily lives does not often occur. Rapid change in a complex society seldom permits a problem situation to be stated with complete assurance. If certainty be assumed it would likely be for a brief time horizon. More realistically, managers deal with probabilistic (likely) occurrences of various states of nature.

Conditions of Risk

Using payoff Table 5-3 and assigning probabilities to each state of nature (meaning, the chance that the state of nature will occur), the decision maker can determine the expected value (EV) for each alternative. The expected value of an alternative is the summation of the probabilities of the various states of nature multiplied by the particular payoffs* (see Table 5-4 and sample calculation). It is basically a *weighted-average* approach.

---

*For any alternative j the expected value is

$$EV_j = \sum_{i=1}^{n} O_i \times P_i(N_i)$$

where O_i is the conditional value of each outcome, $P(N_i)$ is the probability associated with a given state of nature, and $P_i + P_2 + \cdots + P_n = 1.0$.

As we "look back" on results, it can be seen in Table 5-4 that the opening of five stores, A_1, produces the best payoffs when inflation occurs. Likewise, A_2 is best when stagflation occurs, and A_3 is best when a recession occurs. In the expected value approach, the decision-maker, being unable to identify with certainty a particular state of nature in advance, may opt for a balanced (average) approach. The explanation underlying this approach follows.

We are no longer certain which state of nature will exist, but we do know (from experience and research) the probabilities of occurrence of each state of nature. The choice of any alternative incurs risks. For example, if A_1 is chosen, there is a 50 percent chance of losing \$15,000 and a 25 percent chance of making \$50,000. Our task is to determine which alternative seems superior under these conditions.

Using the expected-value approach as a selection criteria, the expected value for opening five stores, A_1, is

$$EV(A_1) = (50) \times (.25) + (-15) \times (.50) + 3 \times (.25)$$
$$= 5.75 \text{ thousand dollars, or } \$5750$$

Likewise, the expected value for improving existing stores, A_2, is

$$EV(A_2) = (25) \times (.25) + (4) \times (.50) + (6) \times (.25)$$
$$= 9.75 \text{ thousand dollars, or } \$9750$$

and the expected value for expanding downtown store, A_3, is

$$EV(A_3) = (10) \times (.25) + (6) \times (.50) + (5) \times (.25)$$
$$= 6.75 \text{ thousand dollars, or } \$6750$$

Table 5-4 Payoff Table (Payoff in Thousands of Dollars)

Alternatives	States of Nature (N)			Expected Value, EV
	N_1, Inflation ($P_1 = .25$)	N_2, Recession ($P_2 = .50$)	N_3, Stagflation ($P_3 = .25$)	
A_1—Open five stores	50[a]	−15	3	\$5750
A_2—Improve existing stores	25	4	6	\$9750 (best)
A_3—Expand downtown store	10	6	5	\$6750

Sample calculation (e.g., A_1, open five stores):
$EV = \$50,000 \times 0.25 + (-\$15,000 \times 0.50 + \$3,000 \times 0.25)$
  $= \$12,500 - \$7,500 + \$750$
  $= \$5,750$
KEY: A = alternative
  N = state of nature
  P = probability
  EV = expected value
[a] Payoffs in thousands of dollars.

By deciding on A_2, it should be understood that the EV of $9750 is not an assured profit. At any point in time only one state of nature can occur. As little as $4000 or as much as $25000 can be obtained. The *EV* means that on the average and for many similar decision situations, A_2 would produce a profit of $9750.

The decision maker is still playing the percentages, and thus this criterion is best used when the decision is a repetitive one. For if the probabilities are reasonably accurate, the expected values should be realized over time.

Conditions of Uncertainty

When we are *not* able to estimate the probabilities of various future events occurring, there are several decision-making approaches or criteria that can be used. Four are presented below.

The Maximax Criterion. If a decision maker is completely *optimistic* concerning the outcome of certain events, it would be natural to select the strategy providing the maximum payoff. For example, using payoff Table 5-3 we see that the maximum payoff for each alternative is 50, 25, and 10 for A_1, A_2, and A_3, respectively. With an optimistic attitude, the decision maker would choose A_1 to *maxi*mize the *max*imum payoff. This approach is referred to as the **maximax criterion.**

The Maximin Criterion. A decision maker, on the other hand, may be very *pessimistic* or cautious. In order to be as rational as possible with this attitude, the decision maker would attempt to *maxi*mize the *min*imum payoffs (the **maximin criterion**) for each alternative and would then choose the maximum one (best of the worst). Referring to Table 5-3, the minimum payoffs for each alternative are as follows:

Alternatives	Minimum Payoff	
A_1	-15	
A_2	4	
A_3	5	Maximum

This criterion is a conservative approach and is favored by many decision makers. Note that by choosing A_3 (the maximum of the minimum payoffs), we expect "at least" a $5000 profit, whereas with other alternatives there are possibilities of making less than $5000. In fact, if "luck shines on us," we can make either $6000 or $10000.

The Regret (Minimax) Criterion. Often decision makers feel *regret* when decisions in retrospect do not achieve their expected results owing to uncontrollable environmental conditions (states of nature). The regret criterion is an approach that attempts to minimize the regret or remorse one might feel relative to a decision that was made.

Referring to Table 5-3, if the decision maker chose A_3 and inflation (N_1) occurred, there would be no regret since other alternatives could not have produced a higher payoff under the conditions. But if the decision maker had chosen A_1 and a recession (N_2) occurred there would be $21,000 regret [$6000 − (−$15,000) = $21,000] because A_3 could have been chosen and have provided $21,000 more profit. Likewise, if stagflation (N_3) occurred there would be $3000 ($6000 − $3000 = $3000) regret because A_2 could have been chosen and have provided $3000 more profit. Regret, therefore, is similar to the lost opportunity of obtaining more profit. Table 5-5 shows the completed regret table.

In figuring the regret table for each state of nature, a zero value is assigned to the alternative that has the largest payoff in the payoff table. The regret values of the other alternatives for each state of nature are determined by subtracting their payoffs from the largest payoff. These differences (opportunity losses) give the amount of regret in the regret table.

Once the regret table is obtained, the next step is to select the largest (maximum) regret for each alternative. These are shown in Table 5-5. Logically the decision maker would choose the alternative that would *mini*mize the *max*imum amount of regret possible. In the example A_1 would be chosen, and the decision maker would be guaranteed not to have regret more than $21,000, regardless of which state of nature occurred.

The Equiprobable (or Ignorance) Criterion.   Even though decision making under uncertainty implies that managers do not have enough experience or knowledge to determine probabilities of occurrence, they sometimes take the position that one state of nature is just as likely to occur as another. Thus, equal probabilities are as-

Table 5-5 Regret Table (Regret in Thousands of Dollars)

| Alternatives | States of Nature | | | Maximum Regret |
	N_1	N_2	N_3	
A_1	0	21	3	21 Minimax
A_2	25[a]	2	0	25
A_3	40	0	1	40

KEY: A = alternatives
    N = states of nature
[a]Values in thousands of dollars.

signed to each state of nature and the expected value criteria used. In our example the calculations are:

$$EV(A_1) = \tfrac{1}{3}[50 + (-15) + 3] = 12.7 \ (\$12,700)$$
$$EV(A_2) = \tfrac{1}{3}(25 + 4 + 6) \quad = 11.7 \ (\$11,700)$$
$$EV(A_3) = \tfrac{1}{3}(10 + 6 + 5) \quad = 7.0 \ (\$7,000)$$

In this instance, A_1 would be chosen since it has the highest expected value.

Using the four approaches to decision making under uncertainty, alternative A_1 was chosen by optimism (maximax), regret (minimax), and the equiprobable criteria, while A_3 was chosen by the pessimism (maximin) criterion. Determining an alternative under conditions of uncertainty can be very dependent on the personal philosophies of decision makers. In reality there is no "one best" criterion. Rather the choice of criteria is dependent on (1) the specific situation facing the decision maker, (2) personal attitudes of optimism or pessimism, and (3) the financial conditions of the organization.

References

Argyris, Chris, "Single-Loop and Double-Loop Models in Research on Decision Making," *Administrative Science Quarterly* **21** (September 1976): 363–375.

Beach, Lee Roy and Terence R. Mitchell, "A Contingency Model for the Selection of Decision Strategies," *Academy of Management Review* **3** (July 1978): 439–449.

Brightman, Harvey J., "Differences in Ill-Structured Problem Solving Along the Organizational Hierarchy," *Decision-Sciences* **9** (January 1978): 1–18.

———, "Constraints to Effective Problem Solving," *Business* **15**(2) (March-April 1981): 28–44.

Ebert, Ronald J., and Terence R. Mitchell, *Organizational Decision Processes: Concepts and Analysis*. New York: Crane, Russak, and Co (1975).

Higgins, James M., "Strategic Decision Making," *Managerial Planning* **26** (March-April 1978): 9–13.

Howard, Ronald A., "An Assessment of Decision Analysis," *Operations Research* **28** (January-February 1980): 4–27.

Humphreys, Luther Wade, and William A. Shrode, "Decision-Making Profiles of Female and Male Managers," *MSU Business Topics* **26** (Autumn 1978): 45–51.

Janis, Irving L., and Leon Mann, *Decision Making: A Psychological Analysis of Conflict, Choice and Commitment*. New York: The Free Press (1977).

Lang, James R., John E. Dittrich, and Sam E. White, "Managerial Problem Solving Models: A Review and a Proposal," *Academy of Management Review* **3** (October 1978): 854–866.

Mintzberg, Henry, Duru Raisinghani, and Andre Theoret, "The Structure of

'Unstructured' Decision Processes," *Administrative Science Quarterly* **21** (June 1976): 246–275.

Radford, K. J., *Information Systems for Strategic Decisions*. Reston, Va., Reston Publishing Co (1978).

Rockart, John F., "Chief Executives Define Their Own Data Needs," *Harvard Business Review* **57** (March-April 1979): 81–93.

Schwenk, Charles and Richard Cosier, "Effects of the Expert, Devil's Advocate and Dialectical Inquiry Methods on Prediction Performance," *Organizational Behavior and Human Performance* **26**(3) (December 1980): 409–424.

Shrieves, Ronald, "Uncertainty, The Theory of Production, and Optical Operating Leverage," *Southern Economic Journal* **47**(3) (January 1981): 690–702.

Turecamo, Dorrine, "Making Decisions in Three Dimensions," *Supervision* **42**(7) (July 1980): 5–7.

CHAPTER 6

ORGANIZING RESOURCES

KEY
QUESTIONS
ADDRESSED
IN CHAPTER

1. Why is organizing important?
2. What factors affect the manager's options when organizing resources—given the constraints of formal structure?
3. What are some factors that affect the number of people one can supervise effectively?
4. How does the delegation process work?
5. How can you improve the use of your time?
6. How can a mathematical technique such as linear programming be applied to help managers organize and allocate scarce resources?

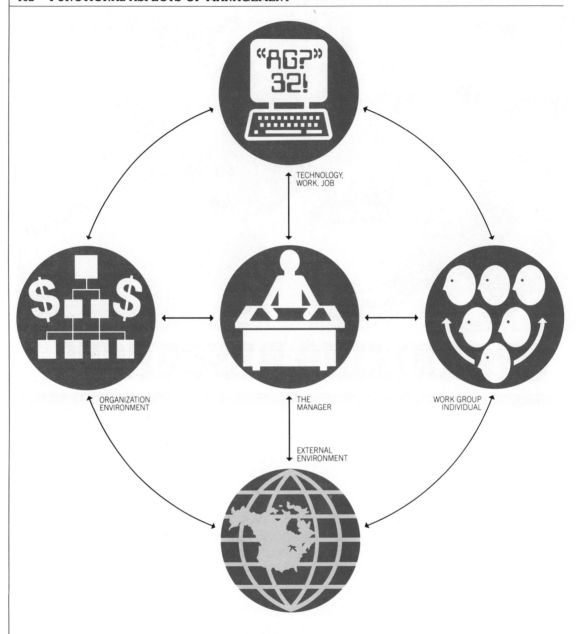

TECHNOLOGY,
WORK, JOB

ORGANIZATION
ENVIRONMENT

THE
MANAGER

WORK GROUP
INDIVIDUAL

EXTERNAL
ENVIRONMENT

The manager's work–life spaces

Work expands so as to fill the time available for its completion.

C. Parkinson

THE CHAPTER IN BRIEF

The word **"organization"** has two distinct meanings: one refers to an organization as an *entity* in itself, whereas the other refers to organization as a *process*. All kinds of institutions and business units can be thought of as entities—schools, business firms, government agencies, and social institutions. Each has a degree of formality in its *structure* that results in limiting the behavior of its members. The elements of this structure, such as division of labor, specialization, departmentation, span of control, and centralization, are the subject of Chapter 2. Thus in this chapter, the emphasis is on organization as a process of establishing orderly and efficient uses for all resources within the constraints of the formal structure. Good organization supports the attainment of organizational objectives. It helps managers use the product of other activities, such as planning and decision making, to efficiently use those resources chosen to fulfill organizational objectives.

We have often heard the phrase, "what this place needs is more organization." But the question arises—what is being organized? Is it work?, people?, the system? And how much *discretion* does the manager have to organize critical resources within the limitations of the formal structure and system?

This chapter begins with a discussion of the critical design elements of an organization from the view of the manager—a "bottoms-up," or micro, approach. This view of organization considers the discretion available to managers when organizing critical resources within structural constraints. Current studies of the manager's organizing activity emphasize the importance of understanding various environmental, technical, and behavioral factors *before* deciding how an organization should be designed. These are the next series of discussions. Finally, a discussion of organizational aids, such as time management and quantitative techniques, is presented.

(Copyright © 1966 United Feature Syndicate, Inc.)

Organization and the Manager's Life Space

This section explains some of the mechanics of the life-space model and how various sectors are referenced depending on the specifics of a situation.

In work situations, the manager's *primary responsibilities* may be any one or a combination of the life-space sectors. For example:

1. **In the External Environment Sector.**   Advertising managers, sales, and marketing people deal regularly with outside clients and customers. Other managers also do a good job of "managing" the external environment. Purchasing agents deal with suppliers. Engineers work with outside consulting engineers, customers, or suppliers. These are just some examples of managers deeply involved with this sector of the manager's life space.

2. **In the Organization-Environment Sector and the "Work-Group–Individual" Sector.**   A manager may have responsibility for internal accounting within the organization. This manager would work with many different departments comprising the enterprise. A manager primarily responsible for wage payment or compensation would be responsible for designing or improving compensation systems that are part of the "organization-environment" sector. To the extent that a compensation manager would also have to work extensively with many different departments, the heads of the work-group individual sector of the manager's life space would be involved. If a compensation question arose regarding individual employees, the compensation manager would need to work with individual organization members and department heads, both of whom are part of the work-group– individual sector.

Thus, from an organizational viewpoint, the assignment of responsibilities to a particular managerial position defines the life-space sectors that make up his or her major area of concerns. Although more than one may be involved simultaneously, the management of each life-space sector often involves substantially different activities, skills, approaches, and even styles on the manager's part. In managing the external environment sector, the ability to work well with people and influence them (as in a sales capacity) is important, often critical, for success. Work in the "technology–work-job" sector often demands technical abilities and insights regarding problems that are technical in nature, and this requires technical abilities and systematic approaches. Thus, understanding one's work–life space area of activities and what it implies in the way of needed skills and work patterns represents a practical use of the model.

Another way of viewing the life-space model as it relates to organizational matters is the managerial impact of responsibilities that involve primarily single versus multiple sectors. The manager who must be able to work regularly within different sectors must be able to display a breadth of skills and the adaptability to meet widely different conditions and demands. If a manager is formally assigned the responsibility to work with several sectors, one of his or her main areas of work would be coordinating the personnel and the duties that are a part of their job.

Another feature of the life-space model from an organizational standpoint is the communication needed to discharge the manager's responsibility effectively. Although more of these considerations are brought out in the chapter on communication, there are some important ideas that need to be developed here.

There is also a need to identify the personnel and units with whom the manager must communicate. If these units involve other managers or different departments, which can often happen, communications become more complex. It becomes important to understand the practical politics of getting things done without stepping on toes. The politics of the situation means knowing who has the influence and being able to communicate effectively with them.

Implications for Your Career

One way of thinking about the organizing process is to reflect on your own work experience. Work brings one in contact with other people. Someone in that organization at some time had to specify what each person, including you, should do and how he or she should do it. Early on your boss likely told you what your job would involve—what equipment you would use, and what and how many you would produce or service. For example, if you were employed as a clerk in a retail store, you may have been trained and directed to take inventory, stock shelves, service customers, and transact sales.

You were probably taught, or you quickly learned from experience, which other people in the organization you had to work with to complete your job satisfactorily. For example, you may have been required to get the approval of another person before you could refund a customer's purchase. In this situation you were acting on directives or orders that defined the limits of your authority.

You likely remembered the name of your boss before anything else, for he or she was the individual who supervised your work and ensured that you stayed within the bounds of your authority. More importantly, your boss had authority over you. He or she had the right to tell you what work to do, to assign your various tasks, and to evaluate your performance.

The names of other people in your department unit or group were also important. Some of your co-workers may have had more tasks than others and also more authority to do those tasks. When you

GREAT PERSON PROFILE

J. P. Morgan (1837–1913)

John Pierpont Morgan was born in Hartford, Connecticut in 1837. After attending the University of Göttingen in Germany, he returned to the United States in 1857, where he applied his analytical mind to mathematics and finance with the bank of Duncan, Sherman & Co. In 1860, he became agent and attorney for George Peabody & Co., Bankers of London, in which his father, the leading U.S. banker in London, was a partner. In 1871 he helped form the investment security firm of Drexel, Morgan & Co., known today as J. P. Morgan & Co.

Morgan played a dominant role in the major *reorganization* of both the Pennsylvania and New York Central Railroads, persuading them to stop wasting money, resources, and time by building competing, parallel tracks. Morgan placed $62 million worth of U.S. Bonds during the Cleveland administration, and in 1901 his firm supported the reorganization of U.S. Steel Corporation.

J. P. Morgan had a way of supporting his client's "visions" through sound financial analysis. He commanded enormous power and earned the trust and confidence of his political and business peers through his ability to organize financial resources while maintaining high moral standards. He was a significant contributor to the development of business in the industrialization of the United States.

discovered these differences, you probably discovered that they had more experience or possessed greater skills than other co-workers.

Your work experiences should suggest that your employer had devised a system of jobs, departments, and authority that enabled the work to get done apart from the particular people who were employed at a given time. The following sections of this chapter present the concepts of organizing.

BACKGROUND

Early Work of Organization Theorists

Early classical theorists, such as Frederick Taylor, set forth basic guidelines for the design and maintenance of large organizations while realizing that good organization is only an aid to the efficient achievement of organizational objectives. The reader may wish to review the discussion of Taylor's ideas in Chapter 1 as well as the works of Max Weber and Henri Fayol, two macroorganization theorists, which are discussed in detail in Chapter 2.

Frederick Taylor believed that the critical elements in the management process revolved around relationships between manager and worker which, in turn, were influenced greatly by work design and structural arrangements (Taylor, 1947) (see Exhibit 6-1).

He saw the test of a good manager as the degree to which the satisfaction of *both* organizational and employee objectives could be achieved. He indicated that satisfaction depends on an organizational arrangement that allowed for functional specialization and effective coordination.

Taylor noted that many supervisors had abilities and skills that were not used to their fullest. His solution to this waste of supervisory talent was to employ the supervisor as overseer of those who were working in his area of expertise as well as overseer of those who fell within the administrative scope of his department. Thus, under this **functional specialization** the supervisor would have dual responsibilities: functional responsibility for certain specialized activity of workers in his and another department, and general administrative responsibility for all the workers in his or her own department, regardless of the specialized jobs they performed. This arrangement was not accepted by industry in the form Taylor recommended, but was the beginning of the concept of functional authority (Taylor, 1911). This concept is developed later in the chapter.

As Peter Drucker notes, "Taylor was the first man in history who did not take work for granted but looked at it and studied it."

Exhibit 6-1 Role of the Manager in the Organizing Process

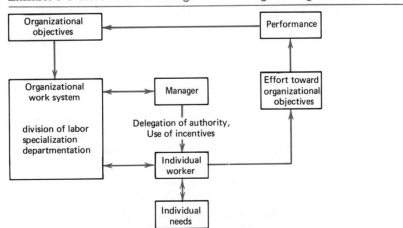

Through detailed analysis of the activities to be accomplished by a worker his aim was to *make the work role more predictable* so that both managerial and worker efficiency could be improved. For Taylor and others felt, as many still do today, that workers were producing significantly less than they could (which he termed "soldiering"). Improved productivity could be realized if the roles of manager and worker and the content of jobs could be clarified. Taylor saw managers as having a largely untapped role in the organization. He urged managers to go beyond direct supervision. Exercising managerial discretion included activities such as reassigning employees as work loads varied, performing cost analyses, planning work activities, and even performing studies that investigated how jobs could be redesigned. The emphasis was always on cooperation between management and worker.

Taylor believed that once performance work standards were developed for various jobs, then incentives could be offered to workers to increase their effort toward greater performances in achieving organizational objectives. His emphasis was largely on monetary rewards as a motivating device. We will take a closer look at other motivation factors in Chapter 8.

Organizational Design and Managerial Discretion

Classical organization theory was built largely on structural elements such as specialization and departmentalization. These were already discussed in Chapter 2. The remainder of this section deals with such additional and important design features as the span of control, the unity of command principle, and the twin concepts of authority and responsibility and their effect on managerial discretion.

Span of Control

Most managers agree that there are limits to the **span of control** or the number of persons one can effectively manage. What factors determine this limit then? There are many, but the major factors are the people involved, the jobs involved, and the situation.

Personal Factors. Two personal factors could influence the span of control. The first is abilities or competence. A more competent supervisor may be able to supervise a larger group, thus his or her span of control may be larger. Similarly more capable subordinates may also result in less direct supervision and wider spans of control.

The second personal factor is managerial preference. Managers, having a high need for power, may prefer a wide span of control. Likewise, managers, having strong social needs, may also prefer to interact with more subordinates, again resulting in wider spans of control.

Job Factors.   The first of these factors is the similarity of functions or degree of specialization. When activities performed by subordinates are similar, wide spans of control are possible. Managers of specialists usually can supervise more individuals than their own bosses, whose expertise must span many specialty areas.

A second job factor is the level of the position in the hierarchy. Despite the fact that individuals at higher levels in the organization are considered more expert in some matters than those at lower levels, spans of control tend to decrease (become narrower) because tasks become more important and complex. Also, a much greater degree of coordination tends to be required as managers must deal with many functional specialties.

Situational Factors.   Technology also influences the span of control. In general, more sophisticated technology requires more specialists and a need for greater control. This typically results in narrower spans of control than at lower levels of technology.

The degree of physical or geographic dispersion is another factor. The closer subordinates are physically, the wider the span of control that is possible.

Unity of Command

Another basic concept in organizing is the vertical relationship referred to as the **unity of command.** This principle is based on the idea that a subordinate should have only one boss. This one-person–one-boss guideline has held up rather well over the years as a fundamental premise upon which organizations should be structured. The underlying reason behind this idea is the belief, which has all too often been supported by experience, that an individual cannot entirely serve two masters. The conflict, tension, and frustration that occurs when several bosses are giving orders to one person usually results in ineffectiveness, low job satisfaction, and breakdowns in communication.

In Chapter 2 some organizational forms were presented, such as the matrix structure, that have successfully overcome some of the problems in "violating" the unity of command principle. These newer forms allow greater discretion to the manager in the choice of subordinates for various work functions. They also require greater cooperation among managers when "lending" or "giving up" important group members to other groups. Additionally, when subordinates serve "more than one master," questions also arise concerning how the subordinate's performance will be appraised by the managers involved, since the managers may view the individual under different circumstances.

Authority and Responsibility

An effective organizing effort would be incomplete if it did not specifically channel the activities of organization members to achieve high performance levels. The organizing concepts that assist in accomplishing this are authority, responsibility, and delegation.

Authority.   This is the right of a manager to direct others and take actions because of the position one holds in the organization. The granting of such rights flows from the top of the organization down. Thus the right of a manager to take action is delegated down the hierarchy in those areas so designated by upper management. A sound organizing effort, therefore, includes specific job activities for each position in the organization. This is accomplished through the use of **job descriptions**—a listing of specific activities and responsibilities that must be performed by anyone holding the position.

Responsibility.   This is the obligation to perform an assigned activity. If a person accepts a job, they agree to carry out the duties or activities or to see that someone else carries them out. Since responsibility is an obligation that a person accepts, there is no way it can be delegated or passed to a subordinate. That is, the obligation still remains with the person who accepted the job.

It has been argued frequently that authority and responsibility should be equal. This means that individuals should be given sufficient authority to be able to carry out their responsibilities or obligations.

The following example illustrates this relationship between authority and responsibility. Two tasks for which a maintenance department manager is responsible are planning the department's operational budget for next year and repairing equipment. The manager has complete authority to perform either task. If the manager chooses, however, he or she can delegate the activity of repairing equipment to the assistant manager. Along with this activity of repairing, the assistant should also be delegated the authority to order parts, to direct certain workers to help when necessary, and to do other things necessary to carry out the obligation of repairing equipment. Without the proper authority the assistant manager may find it impossible to complete the delegated job activities.

Delegation

Delegation.   This is the process of assigning job activities to specific individuals within the organization. It is through this process that authority and responsibility for performance are transferred to lower-level personnel in an organization. In a sense, delegation is the essence of management, since only by getting work done through others can managers justify their existence.

Many managers do not delegate as much as they should because in the short run it often takes additional time and effort (1) to clearly communicate to others what they want done, and (2) to check to ensure that the task is proceeding well. When certain jobs have tight time schedules or crisis situations are involved, they feel that it is often "easier to do it yourself."

Offsetting these short-term disadvantages are the longer-term advantages of delegation. Effective delegation is probably the most important means managers have of developing their subordinates and allowing them to reach their potential. As subordinates are able to take on additional tasks, managers also are freed to do more planning and other important activities. Through careful delegation, then, the effective use of people is assured.

For effective delegation to occur, three vital elements must be present.

1. **Specific Tasks Must Be Assigned.** Clear communication is vital so that the subordinate has a clear understanding of the specific duties to be performed. Whenever possible, activities should be stated in operational terms so that the subordinate knows exactly what action must be taken to perform the assigned duties. How specific the communication is will depend on such factors as the importance of the task to be accomplished, the time available, the abilities of the people involved, and the manager's previous experience.

2. **Sufficient Authority Should Be Granted.** The subordinate must be given the right and power within the organization to accomplish the duties assigned. This transference should be clearly communicated by the manager to others whose cooperation is required by the subordinate to complete the task.

3. **Responsibility Is Created.** A sense of accountability must be conveyed to the subordinate to complete successfully the duties assigned.

Types of Authority

Three main types of authority exist within most organizations: (1) line authority, (2) staff authority, and (3) functional authority. Each type exists so that individuals can carry out different types of responsibilities.

Line Authority. Line authority reflects superior–subordinate relationships and, as stated earlier, is the right to direct others because of one's position in the hierarchy. The vertical connecting lines that are depicted in the organization chart in Exhibit 6-2 illustrate this relationship.

Staff Authority.   Staff authority is simply the right to advise or assist others. It exists in most organizations as their growth requires that more expertise be present in a variety of specialized areas.

Functional Authority.   Functional authority is the right to give orders involving particular work activities and responsibilities both within and outside of one's organizational unit. It is typically possessed by individuals, most often in staff positions, who must exercise some control over organization members in other areas in order to meet their responsibilities.

The Vice-President of Personnel can be used for illustration purposes. Among his or her basic responsibilities is the obligation to develop programs and systems for the use of human resources within the organization. To accomplish this task he or she must be delegated the functional authority over other departments in many matters related to personnel (see dotted lines in Exhibit 6-2). Thus in carrying out the responsibilities of the office, a Vice-President of Personnel is likely to determine such matters as the range of pay for *all* organizational positions, the type of performance evaluation system used by *all* departments, and, in some cases, whether a person can be hired or selected by another department because of "affirmative action" guidelines. Similarly, other positions, usually in staff areas, would also possess functional authority to meet their obligations.

More Recent Work of Organization Theorists

Recent managerial studies indicate the importance of understanding various environmental, technical, and behavioral factors before adhering to any arbitrary (organization) rules. Consideration needs

Exhibit 6-2 Functional Authority

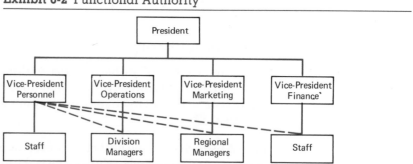

to be given to the technical makeups of jobs, how people are assigned to them, and the need to cope with environmental change. The 1960s saw a number of new(er) concepts of organizational design proposed in these areas. Prominent among them are the works of Burns and Stalker (1961), Lawrence and Lorsch (1967), and Woodward (1965).

Managers face quite different organizational settings, in part because of such factors as the stability of the environment, technology, work demands, and the personal characteristics of organizational members. Yet there are many similarities in organizations that allow us to classify organizations in ways that increase our understanding of organizational processes.

Mechanistic and Organic Organizations

One useful classification was developed by Burns and Stalker (1961). They researched a number of plants in Great Britain to examine the relationships between organizational processes and systems and their external environments. Specifically, they conducted field research in a rayon factory, a large engineering concern, and a number of firms in the emerging electronics field. The rayon manufacturer was the company that operated in the most stable, or most predictable, environment. The engineering company operated in a rapidly changing commercial environment, and the electronics firm operated in the most turbulent, or least stable, environment.

Identifiable patterns of organization tended to depend on the predictability or certainty of the organizations' environments. In the more certain, or stable, environments, the organizational design that seemed most prevalent was termed "mechanistic." In the more dynamic or turbulent environments, the organizational design that seemed most prevalent was termed "organic." From this the researchers concluded that organizations' styles or structures were dependent upon the certainty of the environment in which the organization operated.

Mechanistic organizations, which seemed to fare best in stable environments, had characteristics similar to those of the classical form of organization described in Chapter 2. Positions in the mechanistic structure tended to be highly specialized and defined. Authority was concentrated at the top of the structure and in the hands of a few. Communications and interactions seemed to be unidirectional— downward only. In general, mechanistic systems seemed to be closed, rigid systems.

There is little managerial discretion in mechanistic organizations. Middle- and low-level managers are likely to emphasize technically improving the means of achieving organizational objectives, sometimes losing sight of the objectives themselves. For example, service managers may become so committed to using the rule book

Parade at U.S. Naval Academy.

that they lose sight of the fact that competitive changes require a different approach to servicing accounts. Decision making is often highly centralized, with middle- and low-level managers expected to carry out decisions rather than make them; a highly directive or authoritarian management style is the rule. Finally, specialized knowledge and skills are valued more than broad-based experience.

Organic organizations, as described by Burns and Stalker, possessed characteristics more conducive to conditions of environmentally induced change. Authority was more decentralized and more closely located to where competence resided. Positions in the structure tended to be less specialized. Jobs were not as closely defined and distinguished from one another. Communications and interactions were more *multi*directional; lateral, consultative communications tended to predominate over vertical commands. In general, organic systems seemed to be more open, and flexible—a necessity when dealing with uncertainty.

There is room for much managerial discretion in organic organizations. The emphasis on cooperative problem solving encourages the delegation of tasks and duties to those individuals in the work group whose abilities and knowledge enhance the achievement of group goals. However, it is important to recognize that some managers may not possess these needed qualities.

Other researchers since Burns and Stalker have also investigated the various characteristics of organizations that fit the

Researchers working on optical fibers for possible undersea application.

mechanistic and organic models, but the message that comes through almost consistently is that basic organizational design and structure are related to, and dependent upon, the nature of the organization's environment. The most important characteristics of these organizations are summarized in Exhibit 6-3.

Differentiation and Integration

The work of two other researchers on the subject of organization and environment also deserves attention. Lawrence and Lorsch (1970) concluded that because the environments that organizations face are different—varying in certainty–uncertainty and in diversity–homogeneity—organizational structures need to be altered to accommodate these differences. The concepts that describe such management efforts at accommodation are differentiation and integration.

Differentiation is the process of dividing the organization into subsystems so that each subsystem can better adapt to the requirements of its part of the total external environment. This process of developing subunits in the organization is similar to the notions of specialization and departmentation discussed in Chapter 2. The differentiation concept, however, goes one step further and specifies the dimensions along which these subunits will vary, once differentiated. Examples of these are (1) the unit's or department's structure, (2) the members' time orientation (such as immediate problems versus long-

Exhibit 6-3 Characteristics of Mechanistic and Organic Organizations

Mechanistic	Organic
Closed system	Open system
Stable environment	Turbulent environment
Certainty, homogeneity	Uncertainty, heterogeneity
Centralized	Decentralized
Many hierarchial levels	Few hierarchical levels
Precisely defined jobs	Broadly defined jobs
High position-based authority	High knowledge-based authority
Low differentiation	High differentiation
Little discretion available to managers	Much discretion available to managers
Appropriate for medium levels of technology	Appropriate for low or high levels of technology

term research), and (3) the orientation of the unit's members toward task or interpersonal relationships.

Lawrence and Lorsch assert that, depending upon the environment the organization faces, it will differentiate itself to deal with that environment. The end result, for example, is a highly differentiated organizational structure in the face of a turbulent or dynamic environment. Conversely, a less-differentiated organization will function more effectively in a stable or placid environment.

The companion concept to differentiation is **integration.** An organization may differentiate itself to more effectively deal with the environment, but integration must also be achieved. **Integration,** or coordination, is defined as the "process of achieving unity of effort among the various subsystems in the accomplishment of the organization's task" (Lawrence and Lorsch, 1970). Integration, then, refers to achieving coordination among the differentiated units of the organization.

Differentiation and integration might appear to be basically contrary forces operating on organizational design, but the work of Lawrence and Lorsch shows that both high-differentiated firms and low-differentiated firms were able to achieve a high level of integration. The difference between the two seems to lie with the *type of integrating tools* used in the respective organizations. Organizations that are more highly differentiated tend to require more sophisticated integrating tools.

The integration tools available to managers to ensure coordination between organizational units range a great deal in complexity.

One of the most straightforward integrative tools used is the *management hierarchy* itself. As the organization structure is built by grouping activities into logical units, the management hierarchy of the organization can be designed so that coordination is built in. For example, if it is decided in an organization that sales units need to be differentiated according to territory or region, these units can then be coordinated with a superior to whom both units report. Similarly, if the marketing unit needs to understand what is being done in the research and development department in a high-technology electronics firm, then a common superior, such as a vice-president, may have reporting responsibility for these two units. Thus, integration is designed into the structure by considering at the outset what functions must especially be integrated.

Once units have been grouped and the hierarchy has been established, other integrating tools may also be necessary. These other integrating tools can range from prescriptive rules, operating regulations, and plans for organizations that are basically "mechanistic" (Hellriegel and Slocum, 1973) to the use of liaison individuals, integrating departments, or cross-functional teams for more complex organizations. The former are structural arrangements that allow little room for maneuvering on the part of the manager, whereas the latter do allow managers some discretion in assigning or delegating those individuals or teams to perform coordinating or integrating functions.

Liaison individuals, sometimes referred to as coordinators, are individuals who, although they may officially reside in a given functional department of the organization, have the responsibility for coordinating the activities of two or more departments. An example of this role is the design engineer who may officially be a part of the engineering department but who works in a special office out in the plant to ensure close coordination between design and manufacturing. The use of *coordinating departments* and *cross-functional teams* are also effective integrating tools.

A number of authors have argued for a **contingency approach** to organizational design. They feel that the differentiation of an organization is a function of the organization's environment among other things. Likewise, the integration tools needed will vary depending upon the kind and degree of differentiation. Exhibit 6-4 is a simple grid that shows the basic combinations of differentiation and integration needed by organizations in response to environmental uncertainty or turbulence. It also illustrates the different types of integration or coordination tools that can be employed under each set of circumstances. A brief explanation follows.

Cell 1 (High Differentiation–Low Integration).   An example is the corporate level at General Motors (GM). Since GM is differ-

Exhibit 6-4 Companies and Integrating Tools for Differentiation–Integration Grid

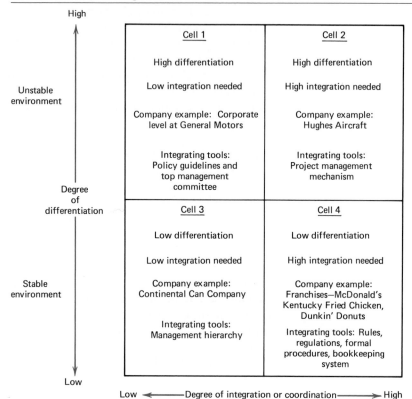

Source: Adapted and summarized from Hellriegel and Slocum, "Organizational Design: A Contingency Approach." *Business Horizons* (April 1973), pp. 60–68.

entiated along product lines that are profit centers—Chevrolet Division, Pontiac Division, Buick Division, and so on—there is little need for integration. This can be achieved by top-management committees that provide policy guidelines for the semiautonomous units.

Cell 2 (High Differentiation–High Integration). An example is Hughes Aircraft Company, which is organized into seven product lines. The company works on the basis of awarded contracts that call for many people in various divisions to work closely together. The shifting of highly trained personnel between projects and the constant technological change that characterizes the firm's industries (such as electronics, space, and research) demand special integrative devices such as matrix management or a project management structure. These were discussed in Chapter 2.

Cell 3 (Low Differentiation–Low Integration). Illustrated by Continental Can Company. The environment and technology are stable in this firm's industry and thus there is a low need for differentiation and integration. High-performing firms in the container industry are able to successfully achieve integration by employing the management hierarchy.

Cell 4 (Low Differentiation–High Integration). Franchises such as McDonald's, Kentucky Fried Chicken, and Dunkin' Donuts are examples. Individual units of these organizations require low differentiation but high integration. Homogeneity and integration of the units are achieved by rules, regulations, formal procedures, and bookkeeping systems to which all units are expected to adhere.

Thus different companies, facing different combinations of differentiation and integration needs, employ varying kinds of tools to achieve coordination. The environments of these organizations assume a prominent role in influencing their organizational design and thus the amount of discretion available to managers within them.

Technology and Organization

The research of Joan Woodward (1965) and her colleagues into the relationship between technology and organizational design has also stimulated considerable thought regarding the design of organization. Woodward investigated the organizational structure of 100 manufacturing firms located in the south of England. Having found no relationship between organizational characteristics and size of firm or business efficiency, the researchers looked at the relationship between organization and technology. The firms studied were classified according to *simple technology features* into three major subgroups.

1. Unit or small-batch technology.
2. Large-batch and mass-production technology.
3. Continuous-process technology.

This classification scheme provided a rather crude scale of technology, but it enabled the researchers to examine organizational characteristics that varied with technology. Wide differences were found on such measures as number of levels of management authority, span of control, and ratio of managers and supervisors to other personnel.

As a result of examining the organizations that fell into the various technology classifications and the success (profit) indicators of these firms, Woodward observed that organizations deviating from the general pattern within a classification were often least effective.

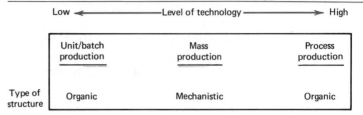

Exhibit 6-5 Woodward's View of Technology and Structure

Organizations that were most effective in the unit or small-batch and process-production categories tended to be more flexible. Organizations that were most effective in the large-batch or mass-production technology were those that were more hierarchically organized, specialized, and with clearer chains of command and tighter controls.

These observations led Woodward (1965) to conclude that:

> Successful firms inside the large-batch production range tended to have mechanistic management systems. On the other hand, successful firms outside this range tended to have organic systems. [See Exhibit 6-5.]

In any organization one must coordinate the work of individual members into a unified whole. As individuals and organizational units carry out increasingly specialized activities, the overall goals of the organization may become secondary, or conflicts among organizational members can develop. For example, production managers in a manufacturing company may desire lengthy production runs to hold down costs. However, the interests of the company may be better served by shorter runs that allow salespeople to meet customer requests for fast delivery. Coordinating mechanisms enable organization members to focus on organizational goals, reduce inefficiency, and avoid harmful conflicts.

Thus far we have examined the classical concepts of organizing, organizational relationships, and processes. In the following section we take a close look at some "organizational" techniques that are useful in efficiently using scarce resources like time.

ORGANIZING TECHNIQUES

Organizing and You: The Management of Time

Do you find that you are always behind schedule? That you have not accomplished the things you really wanted to? Are worried about what you have to do? At work do you find yourself constantly interrupted by phone calls, visitors, or meetings?

Do you find yourself complaining about being overworked, or not having enough time to explain things to others?

Do you have enough time for your family or your hobbies?

If the answers to any or all of these questions is yes, then you need to use your time more efficiently.

Time is one of your most important resources, but it has some unique characteristics that pose problems for its use. It is a fixed resource; everyone has the same total amount of time. Time is completely perishable, it cannot be stored. It is also inelastic—the supply of time does not increase even when demand for more time increases dramatically. Once time is used, or is wasted, it is gone forever. Because time is a fixed quantity, your only recourse is to use—invest—it wisely and effectively, to get as much out of your time as possible.

Not using time efficiently leads to constant worry. You cannot even enjoy yourself during evenings, weekends, or vacations, because you have unfulfilled responsibilities "hanging over your head." You may even find yourself waking up in the middle of the night worrying about a task that you have not completed. Thus your inefficiency leads to worry, which leads to periodic sleeplessness, which leads to further inefficiency . . . carried to an extreme this pattern produces great amounts of stress that can lead to other physical and psychological problems.

To make sure that you fulfill your responsibilities in a timely manner, leave time for your family or those whose company you value, and provide time for career and personal development. It is imperative that you make good use of your time. Remember, it is not *how much* you (attempt to) do that matters, but *what* gets done.

Analyzing Your Use of Time

Before you can begin to make improvements in managing your time, it is necessary for you to discover how you presently utilize your time. There are a number of techniques that can be used, ranging from compiling a detailed log of virtually all of your activities on a minute-to-minute basis, to a random sampling of your activities, to the generation of a list of your activities. The important point to remember in conducting such an analysis is that you do not rely on your memory, because you will quickly learn that you will list what you *think* you do rather than what you *actually* do.

Once you have completed what you do with your time, you can then begin to analyze each activity. You will be able to quickly identify habitual patterns, for example, using meetings for purposes other than the reason for which the meeting was called, inviting interruptions from co-workers or subordinates, discussing non-business-related issues during phone conversations. All of these are time wasters. You will also have the basic information needed to determine which activities are most important or which activities you have the most significant impact upon. Using this information you can now prioritize your activities and begin to delegate important ones to others. The analysis of your daily activities will probably illustrate that many of the activities you routinely perform make very little contribution to performance results. These activities can be delegated or dispensed with, thereby freeing more time for the more important facets of your job.

There is a frequently cited phenomenon that aptly relates to your efforts. The rule of thumb states that 20 percent of your time is spent on activities that produce 80 percent of the results. Conversely, 80 percent of your time is spent on activities that produce 20 percent of the results (see Exhibit 6-6).

Basically, the analysis of how you spend your time will enable you to identify those activities that are *time wasters*.

Time Wasters

Exhibit 6-7 lists 15 leading time wasters identified by a leading authority on time management (Mackenzie, 1973). Comparing these time wasters with the list of activities you have generated can help identify time wasters that plague you. One technique that you may find useful is to identify which of the activities lie within your control and which are not within your control. One author categorized activi-

Exhibit 6-6 The Time Trap

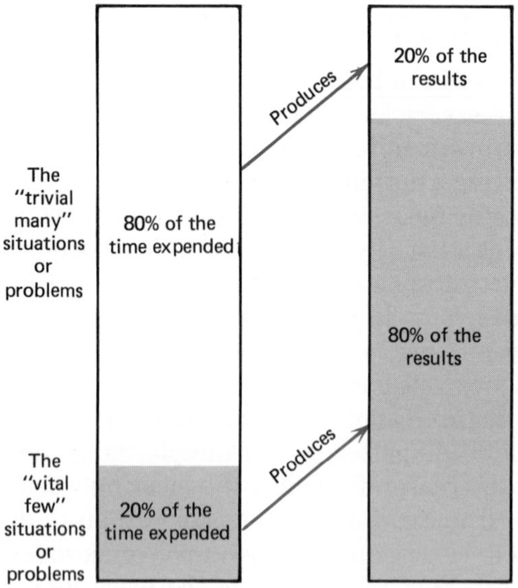

Exhibit 6-7 The 15 Leading Time Wasters

Based on experience of managers in 15 countries, Mr. Mackenzie ranks time wasters as follows:

1. Telephone interruptions
2. Visitors dropping in without appointments
3. Meetings, both scheduled and unscheduled
4. Crisis situations for which no plans were possible
5. Lack of objectives, priorities, and deadlines
6. Cluttered desk and personal disorganization
7. Involvement in routine and detail that should be delegated to others
8. Attempting too much at once and underestimating the time it takes to do it
9. Failure to set up clear lines of responsibility and authority
10. Inadequate, inaccurate, or delayed information from others
11. Indecision and procrastination
12. Lack of clear communication and instruction
13. Inability to say "no"
14. Lack of standards and progress reports that enable a company manager to keep track of developments
15. Fatigue

Source: Interview with R. Alec Mackenzie, "How to Make the Most of Your Time," *U.S. News & World Report* (December 3, 1973), pp. 44–48, 53–54.

ties as those that are boss-imposed, system-imposed, and self-imposed (Oncken and Wass, 1974).

This categorization will further assist you in analyzing and prioritizing your activities. To illustrate its use let us look in on a typical morning of a social worker who is working for an organization called Big Brothers–Big Sisters, which attempts to develop ties between "problem" children and specific individual volunteers who would act as Big Brothers or Big Sisters to these children (See Exhibit 6-8).

In analyzing this scenario, you can readily see that there are several activities that Frank performed that easily could have been delegated. These are looking up a phone number, calling the printer, picking up the materials from the printer, and getting a cup of coffee. Further, it may be possible to delegate certain facets of the special event, and Frank may have been able to delay meeting with the director to provide "input" to help solve the problem that has arisen.

Frank certainly has been a victim of time wasters and is in need of a program to more effectively and efficiently use his time. The

Telephone interruptions are the leading time waster for managers.

Exhibit 6-8 Scenario

Last night, just before leaving the office, Frank Nelson was asked by the director to schedule a special event for unmatched Little Brothers for this weekend. As Frank begins to make the arrangements this morning, the phone rings, and an unhappy mother tells him that her son is threatening to leave home because his Big Brother failed to show up yesterday, the second time in a row this has happened. As Frank is looking for the Big Brother's phone number his eye happens to fall on a "reminder note" on his desk. The note informs him that he has a luncheon meeting with a potential money donor. He decides to call the printer to see if the brochures are ready. The aroma of freshly brewed coffee reaches Frank's desk and he decides that a cup of coffee would really hit the spot about now. While getting his coffee, the Director asks, "Frank, do you have a few minutes? I ran into a problem and I'd like your input."

After leaving the Director's office Frank looks at his watch—11:30. What has Frank accomplished?

Boss-Imposed

System-Imposed

Self-Imposed

System-Imposed

Self-Imposed

Boss-Imposed

following section provides a list of guidelines for improving the management of time.

Time-Management Guidelines

The management of time can be viewed from the perspective of each of the functions that a manager performs. The guidelines of time management listed below refer to the planning function.

Planning

1. Determine objectives and goals that you want to accomplish. Focus on *results* to be achieved rather than activities to be performed.
2. Prioritize your objectives and goals, establishing realistic time tables for completion.
3. Develop a "to-do" list to achieve your prioritized objectives and goals.
4. Establish procedures for getting the job done—particularly when you will not be available to answer questions or provide direction.
5. Set aside a time to plan. This can either be before a day begins or before you leave at the end of a day. It is important to always plan at this time to develop the proper habit of planning.
6. Use a calendar to ensure planning over a longer period of time. Do not rely on your memory.

Organizing

1. Learn what to do yourself, what to do first, and what not to do at all.
2. If you have a secretary, work with him/her to
   a. Screen, and even answer incoming mail, phone calls and visitors. All of these can lead to interruptions.
   b. Learn to dictate letters.
3. Handle paperwork only once. Write answers on original, have copy made for file, and have original returned to sender.
4. Work on one or at most two projects at one time.
5. Keep your desk top uncluttered, using desk drawers or a file cabinet for "tickler" files.
6. Be punctual and expect punctuality from others.
7. Identify your most productive time, and establish an uninterrupted block of time to begin your "to-do" list.
8. Accumulate small tasks to be handled in "free" time or waiting time.

Controlling

1. Take periodic samples of your workday to ensure that time wasters do not creep back into your activities.
2. Review "tickler" file to ensure that assignments are proceeding according to schedule.
3. Review procedures and systems to ensure that they are as efficient as possible. Also review to ensure that procedures are still necessary.
4. Learning from your mistakes will enable you to become better in the future.

Directing

1. Give clear, simple, and specific instructions to others.
2. Use others effectively by delegating activities that are within their abilities to perform.

GREAT PERSON PROFILE

Henry John Kaiser (1882–1967)

Henry John Kaiser was born to German immigrant parents in Sprout Brook, New York. He eventually dropped out of high school and took a *payless* job with a photo supply company in Lake Placid on the condition that, if he doubled business within a year, he would become a partner. By the age of 23, he owned it! From then on, his administrative talent and organizational ability resulted in a multitude of ventures, mostly involved with construction projects.

For example, his company was one of six involved with a contract that completed the Hoover Dam two years ahead of schedule. Kaiser's companies were a major factor in U.S. wartime naval production—the famous Liberty ships. A steel mill, an aluminum company, a bad "miss" in the auto industry (remember the Kaiser-Fraser), and vacation resorts, as well as a health plan serving three million people are parts of the diversified group of more than 100 companies founded by Kaiser, many which bear his name.

He had great respect for *time* as a cost

factor, which made him attempt always to minimize the use of this "commodity" in his construction projects. Kaiser truly felt that "time is money" and treated it as an important organizational resource. This, combined with his administrative abilities, contributed greatly to his success in business.

3. Do not overmanage. Let subordinates have as much freedom as possible to get the job done. Remember to focus on results, not efforts.

A manager's job is to "get things done through others." In order to ensure that objectives are achieved, it is imperative that the manager effectively utilize both his time and that of his subordinates. Remember that it is results that count, not the efforts expanded.

Allocation Techniques: Quantitative Organizing Tools

As an aid in the organizing process, the manager has available to him or her a number of quantitative techniques that, through the aid of a computer, can save much time and effort when attempting to allocate resources to meet organizational objectives. However, a quantitative model, like **linear programming,** does not just mysteriously appear for managers and others to use. Rather, it is the end product of a substantial organizational commitment to deal with important problems that are sufficiently complex that human logic would be unworkable.

Most organizations (and people) are faced with a variety of situations in which scarce resources, including capital, labor, and equipment time, need to be organized in a way that will achieve predetermined objectives. In these situations, a manager wishes to find the best or optimum way, from a mathematical and economic standpoint, to allocate the scarce resources, given objectives and operating within certain constraints or limitations. For example, major refineries must decide daily how to refine crude oil, which has varying characteristics, into products that will give them the greatest return or profit. There are literally hundreds, even thousands, of different product possibilities, and each of their prices in the marketplace may have changed since the last decision was made. For a manager to attempt to deal with such a complex situation would go beyond the ability of human logic. For even if one were able to keep track of many interrelationships, the calculations would take so long without the aid of a computer that the market conditions (and hence the problem) would likely have changed.

Linear programming models are among the most widely used allocation models. As the name implies, linear programming is concerned primarily with those situations that can be expressed in terms of linear or directly proportional relationships. The objective to be achieved is expressed in the form of a mathematical function to be maximized (for example, profits) or minimized (for example, costs). The constraints serve to limit the number of possible alternative solutions.

The use of linear programming is not really new. Since World

War II, linear programming models have been used increasingly to solve a wide variety of allocation problems. With the growth of the management science school and the advances made in computers, more complex linear programming models are now being used on a wide scale.

A complete discussion of the mathematics involved in linear programming is beyond the purposes of this text. Rather, emphasis is placed on the specific applications in which the technique has found widespread use.

Application of Linear Programming to Problems Faced by Managers

In a typical application of linear programming the manager must interpret output generated by staff specialists in order to decide the production levels for a given time period. For example, take the situation of the ABC Manufacturing Company shown in Exhibits 6-9 and 6-10. This firm manufactures two products, A and B. Each of these products uses up available capacity (or production time) of three production processes (resources) differently. It takes 20 hours to fabricate, 12 hours to paint, and 16 hours to assemble one unit of product A. It takes 12 hours to fabricate and 24 hours to assemble one unit of product B, which requires no painting.

Exhibit 6-9 Summary of Capacity and Performance Features

Production Centers (Resources)	Product A (Hours Used per Unit)	Product B (Hours Used per Unit)	Capacity Available (Hours)
Fabrication	20	12	300
Painting	12	0	144
Assembly	16	24	456
Contribution per unit	$10 per unit	$5 per unit	

Total Contributions for Various Product Mixes

Point	Units of A	×	Contribution ($)	+	Units of B	×	Contribution ($)	=	Total Contribution ($)
A	0		10		0		5		0
B	12		10		0		5		120
C	12		10		5		5		145
D	6		10		15		5		135
E	0		10		19		5		95

Exhibit 6-10 Linear-Programming Graphical Method

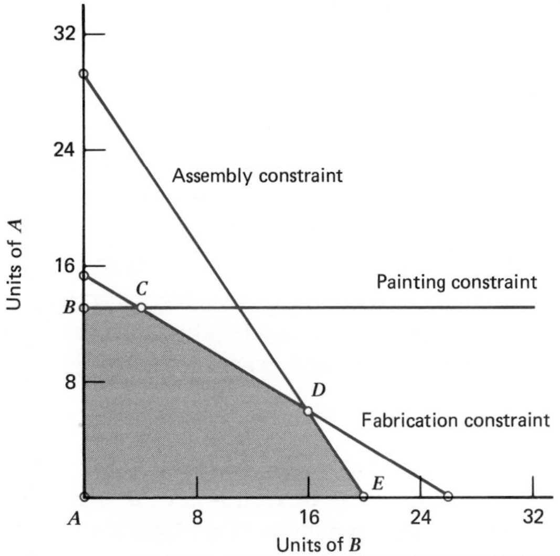

The limited capacities available for each of the production centers limit our ability to produce each product and therefore the amount of profit we can make. Furthermore, the products vary in profitability. Product A contributes twice as much as product B ($10 versus $5 for each unit sold).

Given these facts and an objective to make as much profit as possible, common sense tells us that the manager should produce as much of product A as possible, since it is twice as profitable as product B. However, product A also uses up more time of the scarcest resources (painting and fabrication) than product B in its production. The manager faces a dilemma—does product A contribute sufficiently more to profit than product B to offset the additional use of resource time, and therefore cost, in its production? The mathematics of linear programming provides the answer.

Limitations in production capacity define the amount of either product A or product B that can be produced (the shaded portion in Exhibit 6-10). Points B, C, D, and E use up all of one or more resources needed to produce products A and B. Exhibit 6-9 shows that the best profit in this situation is obtained by producing 12 units of A and 5 units of B (point C in Exhibit 6-10). Limited painting capacity keeps us from producing more than 12 units of A (144 hours are available, and it takes 12 hours to paint one unit), while limited fabrication capacity keeps the production of B from increasing beyond 25 units (300 hours divided by 12).

What does this example tell us as managers? First, internally, products use up varying amounts of scarce resources, some of which are more scarce than others. Second, owing to external market conditions, products contribute differently to our profit picture. The relationships that exist both internally and externally, therefore, affect production-level decisions that must be made. Yet, other less tangible factors that we have thus far ignored may further complicate this situation. For example, if producing only product A is the most profitable thing to do (which it is not), would we, in fact, consider it? How would our product B customers react? Would it be looked on favorably by government? These are just two of many questions that would have to be addressed and that could be included in a more complex version of the linear programming model presented here.

Linear programming has been applied successfully to solve problems in many different areas. Here are just some of the typical applications.

- **In Advertising.**   The technique is used to determine how budgeted funds for advertising can be allocated over various media to maximize the exposure of a client's product or service message.
- **In Sales.**   The technique is used to route salespeople in a way that will reduce travel costs and improve their time utilization.
- **In Distribution.**   A special application of linear programming is called the *transportation method.* This technique is used to evaluate the cost advantages of shipping from various locations to various destinations. If a company has only one facility it has little choice but to ship to all outlets from that facility. However, a company with many facilities that can ship to many distribution centers must evaluate the cost of shipping from any of the facilities to any of the distribution centers.
- **In Institutional Settings.**   Many large institutions such as hospitals and prisons can meet their residents' nutritional requirements at minimum cost using linear programming.
- **In Farming.**   Cooperatives often purchase and mix together several types of grains. Each grain contains different amounts of various nutritional requirements that will enable them to bring an animal to market at the lowest cost possible.
- **In Banking, Retailing, and Service Settings.**   Linear programming can be used in scheduling of jobs to particular machines or departments and the assignment of various tasks.

Through the use of linear programming improved resource allocation can occur. A word of caution is in order, however. Before the model is ready to be solved and after it has been solved, human judgment and ingenuity are important. For only a manager can decide which objective should be attempted or interpret various constraints on resources. The technique, through the use of a computer, merely manipulates and computes the conditions presented by you.

SUMMARY

Organizing makes it possible for the organization to achieve its goals. It lets organizational members know what their responsibilities are so that they can carry them out. It frees managers and subordinates to concentrate on other tasks. It coordinates organizational activities so that there is no wasteful duplication of effort. The organizing process reduces the chance that confusion will develop so that the organization can move rapidly and efficiently toward its goals.

In this chapter we have considered a variety of organizational design features that allow managers discretion in their dealings with others in the organization. These features include span of control, unity of command, delegation, and various types of authority. We have also compared the more recent work of organization theorists, which shows the dependence of organizational design features on factors such as environmental change and level of technology. Finally, we discussed organizing techniques, for instance, time management and linear programming, that are useful tools for the manager to better allocate resources within the organization.

Organizing resources is a crucial responsibility of management, and managing time, probably the most important individual resource, is equally important for individuals. The organizing process is of vital importance to the management system because it is the basic mechanism with which managers activate plans. Organizing creates and maintains relationships between all organizational resources by indicating which resources are to be used for specific activities and when or where or how such resources are to be used.

Questions for Study and Discussion

1. Keep a detailed log during the next week (including the weekend).
   a. Using Exhibit 6-7 as a guide, identify how many time wasters interrupted your typical day.
   b. Plan for the next week to reduce the two most common time wasters. What would you do?
2. What is the difference between functional and scalar processes?
3. What is meant by the span of control? What factors determine how wide or narrow the span of control will be?

4. Distinguish between authority and responsibility. How is each related to delegation?

5. What are the three essential features of delegation? What would happen if one feature was not considered?

6. Your boss comes to you and says, "Get started on this right away, and let me know next week how you're doing." Is this effective delegation? Discuss.

7. Distinguish between line, staff, and functional authority, and give examples of each.

8. Distinguish between organic and mechanistic organizations. Under what conditions would each be more appropriate?

9. How do the terms *differentiation* and *integration* apply to organizational design?

10. How did Woodward's research suggest that technology influences organizational design?

CASE: A MATTER OF DEBATE, ORGANIZATIONALLY SPEAKING

Mr. Frank Elwood, president of Elwood Electronics Company was explaining his firm's organization.

"I founded this firm in 1965, when I was a professor of electrical engineering at State University," he said. "By 1970, I was doing over $20 million in business, mainly with the federal government for advanced process control devices. It's still our major customer, although now our control systems are used by many major firms. Our gross sales are now over $85 million per year.

"I realize that our organization [see Figure 6-1] may seem somewhat disorganized to an outsider," Mr. Elwood goes on, "but it works for us. I read where spans of control of key executives shouldn't be more than five or six. But my key men are highly specialized, and they know what they're doing. Most are personal friends of mine. Why we've worked together for years, and I rarely have to tell them what to do. We don't seem to have any coordination problems and, generally speaking, we do all right."

The president of Ajax Electronics, Inc., Mr. Morse, had a different view of his organizational problem.

"We compete with Elwood Electronics, and feel that they have some real organizational problems. We're about the same size, and sell competing equipment. But we believe that it is critical to have only a few people report to the president. Our business is complex, and that means there'll be frequent consultations among key people. I

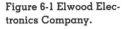

Figure 6-1 Elwood Electronics Company.

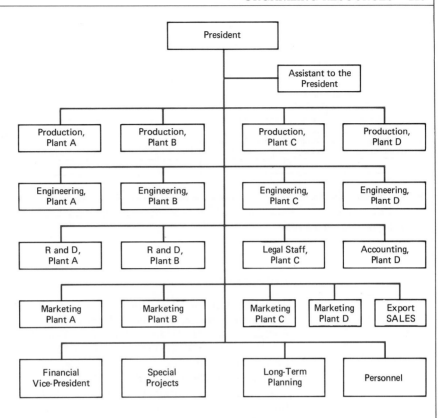

can't expect to have 15 or 20 people report to me. Our organization is quite narrow [see Figure 6-2]—only five people report to me. This way we can easily work out any complex problems. It's impossible to have a broad span of control at the top in a high-technology, complex industry like ours. I respect Frank Elwood, but he's all wet on this point."

In 1979, Elwood Electronics grossed $85 million and netted $5.8 million. Ajax Electronics, Inc. grossed $95 million and netted $2.4 million. The former has consistently shown better profits and growth than Ajax while competing closely for over a decade.

Questions

1. Which structure do you prefer? Why?

2. How could the organization of each firm be improved?

3. Is the organization potentially responsible for the different growth and profit results of each firm? If so, in what way? If not, what might account for the different results?

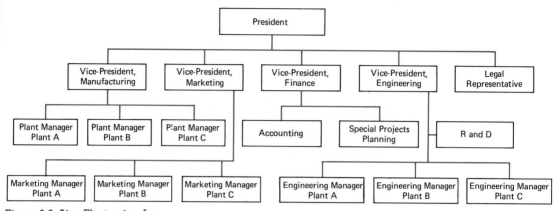

Figure 6-2 Ajax Electronics, Inc.

References

Alper, S. William, "The Dilemma of Lower Level Management: Freedom Versus Control," *Personnel Journal* **53** (November 1974): 804–808.

Bistline, Susan M., "How to Survive on Your Way to the Top," *Association Management* **33**(2) (February 1981): 116–121.

Browne, Philip J., and Robert T. Golembiewski, "The Line-Staff Concept Revisited: An Empirical Study of Organizational Images," *Academy of Management Journal* **17** (September 1974): 406–417.

Burr, Jonathan, W., "The Planning of Time," *Managers Magazine* **55**(11) (November 1980): 28–31.

Ford, Jeffrey D., and John W. Slocum, Jr., "Size, Technology, Environment and the Structure of Organizations," *Academy of Management Review* **2** (October 1977): 561–575.

Gabarro, John J., and John P. Kotter, "Managing Your Boss," *Harvard Business Review* **58** (January-February 1980): 92–100.

Hellriegel, Don, and John W. Slocum, Jr., "Organizational Design: Contingency Approach," *Business Horizons* **16** (April 1973): 59–68.

Hodghinson, Douglas, "If I Only Had Time," *Canadian Manager (Canada)* **5**(4) (August-September-October 1980): 14–15.

Hrebiniak, Lawrence G., "Job Technology, Supervision, and Work-Group Structure," *Administrative Science Quarterly* **19** (September 1974): 395–410.

Keren, Michael, and David Levhari, "The Optimum Span of Control in a Pine Hierarchy," *Management Science* **25**(11) (November 1979): 1162–1172.

Limerick, David C., "Authority Relations in Different Organizational Systems," *Academy of Management Review* **1** (October 1976): 56–68.

Lorsch, Jay W, "Organization Design: A Situational Perspective," *Organizational Dynamics* **6** (Autumn 1977): 2–14.

Lorsch, Jay, and John J. Morse, *Organizations and Their Members: A Contingency Approach*. New York: Harper & Row, Publishers (1974).

McConkey, Dale D., *No-Nonsense Delegation*. New York: American Management Association (1974).

Oncken, William, Jr., and Donald L. Wass, "Management Time: Who's Got the Monkey?" *Harvard Business Review* **52** (November-December 1974): 75–80.

Porter, Lyman W., and Edward E. Lawler, "The Effects of 'Tall' Versus 'Flat' Organization Structures on Managerial Job Satisfaction," *Personnel Psychology* **17** (Summer 1964): 135–148.

Shetty, Y. K., "Managerial Power and Organizational Effectiveness: A Contingency Analysis," *Journal of Management Studies* **15** (May 1978): 176–186.

Udell, Jon G., "An Empirical Test of Hypotheses Relating to Span of Control," *Administrative Science Quarterly* **12** (December 1967): 420–439.

Urwick, L. F., "V. A. Graicunas and the Span of Control," *Academy of Management Journal* **17** (June 1974): 349–354.

Van Fleet, David D., and Arthur G. Bedeian, "A History of the Span of Management," *Academy of Management Review* **2** (July 1977): 356–372.

Woodward, Joan, *Industrial Organization: Theory and Practice*. London: Oxford University Press (1965).

CONTROL

KEY
QUESTIONS
ADDRESSED
IN CHAPTER

1. Why is control important?
2. How does the control process work?
3. What are the important features and elements of a control system?
4. How is the "right" amount of control determined in a particular situation?
5. How does control affect the behavior of individuals?
6. What are some useful quantitative or analytical approaches that can be used by managers in achieving control?

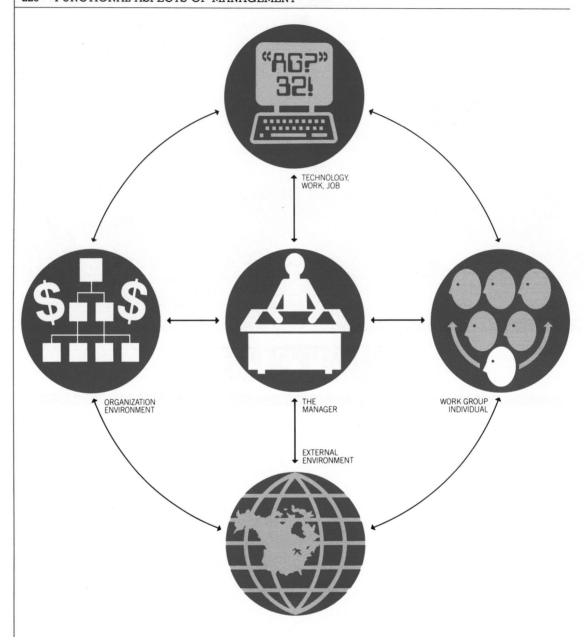

The manager's work–life spaces

Worker: *You can't measure the effects of what I do.*

Boss: *Why not?*

Worker: *They're intangible.*

Boss: *Oh? Why should I pay you for intangible results?*

Worker: *Because I've been trained and educated to do them.*

Boss: *Hmm . . . alright. Here's your money.*

Worker: *Where? I don't see any.*

Boss: *It's intangible!*

THE CHAPTER IN BRIEF

For any organization to accomplish its goals, the efforts of the individuals and systems comprising it must be coordinated. That process that helps to achieve coordination is termed **control.** Stated simply, **control** is assuring that actual performance conforms to planned results. Planning and control, as implied in this definition, are closely interrelated.

Planned and actual results very often are not the same. Plans are based upon imperfect information and upon estimates about the future. Management may be faced with changes in the environment or other circumstances that were not indicated when plans were first made. In these cases it may be more desirable to modify the original plan than to continue using it. Once activity begins to take place and plans are implemented, however, adequate controls should be in place to measure actual performance, such as unit sales, number of units produced or costs per unit, against the standard or planned figure. Some level of managerial control is required in all organizational processes. What varies are the amount and type of control. In effect, costs and benefits need to be jointly considered.

Murphy's Law

Captain Ed Murphy, a development engineer from Wright Field Aircraft Laboratory and the namesake of Murphy's law (Bloch, 1977), explained why control is so important when he said:

> If anything can go wrong, it will.

Other corollaries of Murphy's law include:

1. Nothing is as easy as it looks.
2. Everything takes longer than you think.
3. If there is a possibility of several things going wrong, the one that will cause the most damage will be the one to go wrong.

4. Left to themselves, things tend to go from bad to worse.

5. Whenever you set out to do something, something else must be done first.

6. It is impossible to make anything foolproof because fools are so ingenious.

7. Under the most rigorously controlled conditions of temperature, pressure, volume, and other variables, the organism will do as it damn well pleases.

Murphy's general philosophy could be summed up by the following:

Smile . . . tomorrow will be worse.

If you are like us, no doubt you have experienced many occasions when it seemed that Murphy was an optimist. Yet, Murphy in a lighthearted way was making the serious point that managers need to regularly control or check to make sure that organizational activities are proceeding as planned. To do this one must first understand why control is necessary, how the control process works, what its essential elements are, and what types of control approaches are available to the manager.

Control and the Manager's Life Space

That control systems are needed in organizations cannot be debated. The nature of the control system, however, can greatly affect the relationships between organizational members, including the manager and his or her subordinates. Some organizations may have rigid policies and procedures that are to be adhered to without exception. Other organizations may allow for greater flexibility among individuals' behavior so long as organizational objectives are being met.

Technological advancements in the workplace have also significantly affected a manager's control over the work process. Automatic or continuous-control systems in the factory and on-line computer systems in the office are just two examples of the more timely information possessed by managers. When present, more rapid and less drastic corrective actions are likely to result.

A later section of this chapter discusses the behavioral implications of the discretionary control that can be exercised by a manager. Although essentially a quite positive element in the managerial process, control can have dysfunctional behavioral effects that should be guarded against to ensure that organizational and unit objectives are being met.

BACKGROUND

The Need for Control

If plans were never in need of revision and were executed flawlessly, there would be no need for control. However, "even the best laid plans of mice and men often go astray." Unplanned events or environmental factors often prevent actual performance from meeting expected results in spite of how well plans were originally developed. Consequently, managers need to give close attention to the control function to adjust it to changing needs and to guard against undesirable surprises. Some areas for which control is commonly needed are:

1. **Cost (Financial) Control.** Ensuring that budgets are met.
2. **Quantity Control.** Standardizing performance to improve efficiency.
3. **Quality Control.** Monitoring quality to meet customer and technical specifications.
4. **Performance Evaluation.** Evaluating on-the-job performance of organizational members.

In each of these areas, managers have a key role to play. This chapter will discuss managerial control activities that are useful in achieving or strengthening control in a variety of organizational situations.

The Control Process

Exhibit 7-1 illustrates the three main elements of the control process: establishing standards (no. 1), comparing actual performance to the standard (no. 2), and taking corrective action as necessary (no. 3). If actual performance meets standards, no action is needed. If actual performance does not meet standards, however, corrective action occurs. This action may be directed to improve operating performance or to change the standards or goals that have been established.

Establishing Standards

Before standards can be established, current organizational performance must be capable of being measured. Some unit of measure must be established that gauges the performance.

For example, if a sales manager wanted to measure the performance of five salespeople, the manager would first have to establish units of measure that represented sales performance. Such units of measure could be the number of sales made, the number of new accounts opened, or the dollar value of sales. Once those measures of sales performance had been determined, the sales manager would

Exhibit 7-1. The Control Process

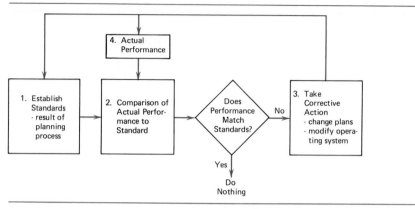

then have a basis to determine the number of these units that should be associated with a particular salesperson's efforts—a standard of performance.

A **standard of performance** is the level of activity that serves as a model for evaluating individual or organizational effort. In essence, standards are "benchmarks" that determine the adequacy of organizational performances. Companies set performance standards for themselves in a number of different areas.

1. **Profitability.**   In general, these standards indicate how much money a company would like to make as profit over a given time period, that is, return on its investment.

2. **Market Position.**   These standards indicate the share (or percentage) of total sales of a particular market that a company would like to have relative to its competitors.

3. **Production.**   How much various segments of the organization should produce relative to costs or effort is the focus of these standards. The same also applies to individual performance.

4. **Product Leadership.**   Companies often desire to assume one of the lead positions in product innovation in the field. Product leadership standards indicate what must be done to attain such a position.

5. **Employee Attitude.**   These standards indicate the types of attitudes or the level of some behavioral variable (e.g., job satisfaction) that management should strive to develop in its employees.

6. **Personnel Development.**   Standards in this area indicate the type of training programs to which company personnel should be exposed to develop appropriately.

7. **Public Responsibility.**   Standards in this area outline the level and types of contributions that a company will make to society.

One must also keep in mind that a wide range of organizational activities can be measured as part of the control process. However, the degree of difficulty or reliability of established standards is largely determined by the type of activity being measured and can vary greatly. For example, it is likely to be more difficult to measure performance regarding employee attitudes and the contributions that a company is making to society than a company's profit or productivity. Both can be done, but the latter's activity is more concrete.

A more specific example of standards established to help judge performance is the case of ABC Airlines. This company set the following standards for performance at their airport ticket offices: (1) at least 95 percent of the flight arrival times posted should be posted accurately within 15 minutes of the arrival of "equipment" at the airport; and (2) at least 90 percent of the customers coming to the airport ticket counter should not wait more than 5 minutes to be serviced. Many other standards, in addition to these two, could be set. In general, organizations try to pinpoint all important areas of organizational performance and establish corresponding standards in each area.

Comparing Actual Performance to the Standard

Once standards have been established the control system should have the capability to **monitor** actual performance to determine whether it is within the desired range of performance. The frequency of monitoring is dependent on factors such as:

1. The reliability of the process.
2. The cost of monitoring.
3. The cost of the system being out of control.

Managers are often tempted to measure performance at some convenient time, rather than at times that are potentially critical. For example, they may wish to check costs of returned merchandise at the end of each month. Because of advances in computerized information systems, however, it may be possible to quickly and inexpensively monitor costs on a daily basis. This could greatly reduce the cost of the system being out of control and allow for less drastic adjustments to be made if they are needed.

Taking Corrective Action

Corrective action is that activity aimed at bringing organizational performance to the level of performance standards. In other words, corrective action focuses on correcting the mistakes in the organization that have hindered organizational performance. Before taking

Manager discusses control reports with a group of circuit board assemblers.

any corrective action, however, one should make sure that the standards being used were properly established and that measurements of organizational performance are valid and reliable.

People make mistakes—this is the nature of things. Realizing this, managers can encourage and clearly acknowledge suggestions made to correct mistakes rather than viewing such suggestions as "rocking the boat."

Although it is easy to state that corrective action should be taken to eliminate a problem, in practice it is often extremely difficult to pinpoint the problem(s) causing some undesirable organizational effect(s). The difficulty in analysis is caused by the numerous and simultaneous events that create a complex organizational environment. For example, observation may indicate that a worker is not cooperating with fellow workers. But what accounts for the lack of cooperation? Is the individual not cooperating because he or she does not want to? Or does the job itself make cooperation difficult? Another possible explanation is that the individual does not have the training needed to enable him or her to cooperate in an appropriate manner. The manager must determine whether the lack of cooperation on the part of the individual is a problem or merely a symptom of such possible problems as poor job design, clumsy organizational structure, or improper training. From a control viewpoint, the initial and essential task is that something must "signal" an activity or event that is off-standard.

Types of Control

There are three types of control: (1) preventative, or precontrol; (2) concurrent control; and (3) feedback control. Each type is determined primarily by the time period in which the control is emphasized in relation to the work being performed.

Preventative, or Precontrol

Control that occurs *before* work is performed is called **precontrol.** Precontrol eliminates significant deviations in desired work results before they occur through good system design. Thus, management creates policies, procedures, and rules aimed at eliminating (in advance) a behavior that may cause future undesirable work results. Other examples of precontrol include the safety goggles hanging near a machine's on-off switch, the one-way supermarket turnstile, and the inspection of incoming raw materials.

A considerable amount of thought may go into the design of control systems to make them as foolproof as possible and to minimize (direct) supervision. For example, the scoop at McDonald's is designed to hold just enough french fries to fill a bag. However, if the counter person consistently overfills or underfills the scoop, the management or the customer can be expected to object. Managerial control is required, even in this "foolproof" system.

Quantitative precontrol techniques include quality control models, inventory control models, and the financial methods of payback, rate of return on investment, and cash-flow statements.

Precontrol systems are rarely sufficient, however. They must usually be supplemented by concurrent and feedback control systems to handle exceptional circumstances.

Concurrent Control

Control that takes place *as* work is being performed is called **concurrent control.** Concurrent control relates to human performance as well as areas such as equipment and administrative procedures. Charts that help keep track of daily production or sales are examples of concurrent control. Another example is the strict rule at McDonald's regarding the length of time food should be "stockpiled." The manager and register people meet this time requirement by monitoring the traffic flow and stating the number of hamburgers "being taken from stock." The stock, in turn, is replenished by the cooks. Ideally, each hamburger would be made "fresh" when ordered, but as a practical matter the ideal is not possible at a busy lunchtime.

Managers can exert much influence in these types of situations. What does a manager emphasize? Equally as important, what does a manager deemphasize or ignore? What is rewarded or punished? What is watched closely or indifferently? Often, managers are not aware of the cues they themselves give to employees regarding what work is worth doing and what is not. In a later section we look more closely at the manager's role in the control process.

Some control situations have grown too complex or are too fast moving for the manager to attempt to affect directly. Various computer based or quantitative models have been devised to handle these situations. Several examples of quantitative models are presented later in this chapter.

Feedback Control or Postcontrol

Control that concentrates on improving future performance based on past activity is **feedback control.** Here managers actually are attempting to take corrective *future* action by looking at *historical* information. This information is "historical" in the sense that it comes from events that have already occurred—even if only a few moments in the past. The period of time between the sequence of action, feedback, and correction can be as short as a few seconds or hours, days, or even longer. Thus the term "historical information" must be interpreted in terms of situational needs. For example, if a profitable order is in danger of being lost, prompt action through feedback may mean minutes or an hour or two—but no longer.

Feedback control systems are diverse and include: employee performance evaluations, exam grades, time clocks, sales receipts, Gallup polls, applause, and even roving managers. Common to all of these feedback control systems is the providing of information in an appropriate form and in a timely way so that corrective action can take place. Budgets are also control mechanisms and are typically used in both a preventative and feedback context. We discuss this valuable managerial planning and control tool in a following section.

As might be expected the majority of feedback systems involve human intervention, usually in the adjusting activity. As a result they are typically much more expensive than precontrol systems. This gives meaning to the saying, "an ounce of prevention is worth a pound of cure."

How Much Control Is Desirable?

As with any organizational undertaking, control activities should be pursued only if the expected benefits are greater than the costs of

GREAT PERSON PROFILE

George Washington (1732–1799)

So much has been written about George Washington's political and military success that his talents as a business manager have been virtually ignored. Early in life, Washington began buying and selling land. At his death his estate, including Mount Vernon, totaled some 64,000 profitable acres.

Washington achieved success as a farmer by keeping accurate records concerning all his financial dealings and crop yields for *control* purposes. Like most Virginians, Washington grew tobacco; through analysis of his records, however, he recognized early that the crop was depleting the soil. Thus, he switched to the cultivation of grains and grasses, including wheat, and subsequently organized an elaborate system for the division of labor during a wheat harvest. His system of controls also alerted him to the fact that mules were more efficient than horses for farm work.

Washington's penchant for record keeping and his analytical mind also carried over into his military and political careers. He demanded strict discipline from his troops yet was able to command their respect and kept his underpaid and ill-fed troops together.

As a politician he realized that trade between the coastal cities and "western" outposts in the Appalachians would help to develop a stronger national government. His

attempt to develop water routes to the interior created awareness among the states of their common dependencies. This led to the Constitutional Convention of 1778, where Washington helped to develop our Constitution with its system of checks and balances.

George Washington's experiences point out the importance of the use of information as a *feedback* and *control* device. Based on accurate records, managers are able to plan more effectively and make more rational decisions.

control. Exhibit 7-2 shows the relationship between the degree of control exercised and the value of the control activity. According to this figure, control costs increase steadily as more control is exercised. Since certain start-up costs usually are incurred in control systems, for example, training, the costs of controls exceed benefits until the initial costs have been recouped. Point No. 1 in Exhibit 7-2 indicates where costs just balance benefits.

As more control is added beyond point 1, the benefits from increased control exceed the added costs of this control. However, a second point (No. 2) is reached where, because of the rather rapid growth of the costs of control, the added benefits of more control are

Exhibit 7-2 Value of Additional Control

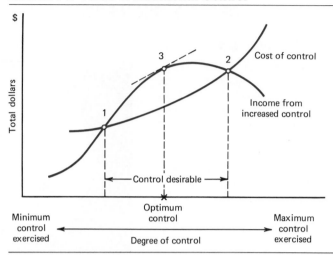

once more canceled by the costs. Put another way, as managers or organizational systems atempt to bring about more and more controls, there are **diminishing returns** so that one receives relatively less benefits for the costs of control incurred.

Points 1 and 2 thus define the limits within which control is profitable, while point 3 shows the optimum, or most desirable, degree of control. In many situations, organizations cannot precisely measure the actual returns obtained by increasing control activities; therefore, points of control such as 1, 2 and 3 can only be approximated. Nevertheless, the basic concepts remain valid and provide guides to managerial action.

The cost of control is largely centered in the financial and accounting departments, for it is they who provide many of the necessary reports for line management. To keep this cost as low as possible, therefore, it is important for all parties to communicate effectively with one another for coordination purposes. Then line departments, such as sales and operations, will receive more meaningful (control) reports rather than being "overburdened with too much paperwork," as is the complaint of many line managers.

Managers often think that if a little control is good, more is better. We have already seen that diminishing returns can negate this assumption. There are additional considerations too. Over-reliance on the use of rewards or punishments as a control device can have adverse effects. Some employees who receive excessive praise or very large salary increases grow uneasy as a result of receiving "more than they deserve." Often they are not sure that they can live up to the high standards expected of them. Similarly, excessive punishment is deeply resented and may produce an opposite effect from the one intended, that is, a determination to get back at those responsible.

The "right" amount of control has many behavioral aspects and to some extent depends on the employee's expectations. Too little control can result in excessive errors and increased anxiety in employees who actually require more direction. Too much control, on the other hand, can result in a system that stifles individual development and creativity. In a later section we examine the behavioral implications of the amount of control exerted.

ISSUES AND ASPECTS OF CONTROL

Control and Information Systems

For control systems to be effective they must deal with information in an effective manner. The study of how systems maintain a state of equilibrium in the midst of environmental influences by processing and interpreting information effectively is called **cybernetics.** Examples of cybernetic systems are all around us: the thermostat that maintains temperature at a predetermined level, the photoelectric cell that turns lights on and off or opens and closes doors automatically, and the speed (cruise) control on a car. All of these systems are designed to process information efficiently and thus meet particular sets of performance standards.

Characteristics of information systems that are particularly relevant for control purposes include:

1. Timeliness of information.
2. Reliability of information.
3. Validity of information.
4. Channeling information to proper organization members.

Chapter 11 on communication also discusses information systems, however, there the behavioral aspects of information are stressed.

Timeliness of Information

To be useful, information must reach the manager in time for him or her to take corrective action. Often managers rely too much on accounting information and fail to develop other sources that can be useful for control purposes. Accounting statements are usually prepared at the end of a given time period. Even with efficient procedures, one or two weeks may be required to prepare statements of the preceding month's operation in many organizations. For some control purposes such as long-term trends in the use of certain materials or labor, this accounting information may be acceptable. However, many control applications require good information much more quickly. This is the key; control information must be designed for the needs of the system.

Ideally, managers of each operating unit should have information so that he or she can take (immediate) corrective action if necessary. Advances in computers have resulted in a closer approximation to this ideal. For example, on-line computerized cash registers allow retail store managers to know the up-to-date status of inventory of goods and the immediate effectiveness of sales.

Although establishing formal reporting systems for control purposes is important, *informal* control mechanisms can be more efficient. Timely control information can be obtained through telephone calls, daily reports, or personal observation without having to wait for information to be prepared and distributed by formal reporting systems.

Importance of Information Lag.   An important aspect of the feedback process previously discussed is the information lag relative to the time when the event occurred. If the feedback of information is delayed, decisions can be made to take corrective action that is no longer warranted by the changed conditions.

Reliability versus Accuracy of Information

When working with data, the manager must consider two quite different terms that describe its characteristics, namely, *reliability* and *validity*.

Reliability relates to data or results that can be reproduced, given the same (initial) work conditions, machine function, or situation. For example, if we were gathering data on how much it costs to produce a radio, several observations and checks could have been made at various times. The reliability question here is "If we (again) check the same type of production for processing cost, will the results be similar?" In short, can we come up with similar or identical results under the same conditions as existed when the estimates were first made?

Validity has to do with the manager's ability to generalize possibilities based on the initial results. For example, in the above situation, could we now say that radios in general take $X to produce? Could we infer that, based on the indicated results, *similar* types of radios would also cost X dollars? These are validity questions.

The manager is constantly faced with the challenge of the *validity* of his or her understandings based on observations or experiences that in reality are simply *samples* of a complex sequence of events. Another example may sharpen the differences in these two concepts.

If a secretary processes 20 bills per hour today, the following questions could be raised.

> Will the secretary be able to handle 20 units per hour tomorrow under the same office conditions?

This question has to do with *reliability*.

> Could the manager infer that the secretary *normally* processes 20 bills per hour, or even more?

> Could the manager infer that the secretary is a poor worker because he or she only processes 20 bills per hour?

These questions have to do with *validity*.

In case there is any question as to the correct inference on the part of the reader, we suggest that the manager would be on very shaky ground to make the types of indicated generalizations, based solely on the data provided!

Validity versus Accuracy: Some Additional Thoughts

It is possible for information to be quite reliable, yet not valid. This relates to choosing an *appropriate* basis for measurement. For example, a paper company used the total number of pounds shipped daily as a measure of its productivity. This measure was inappropriate and lacked validity for several reasons. First, the total number of pounds shipped bore no *consistent relationship* to the dollar volume of sales, profitability, or worker-hours required for production because paper items were packaged in many different ways. Second, the pounds shipped were only indirectly related to daily production since up to 40 percent of the orders shipped daily were drawn from stock in the warehouse.

Managerial decisions usually require a compromise be made between reliability, validity, and timeliness. Many managerial interpretations of situations, and the subsequent corrective actions that are taken, are based on incomplete information. For example, a market research manager must decide whether to recommend a major sales program based on a *relatively small number* of results from a test marketing. Even this partial (sampling) information, if derived in a representative way, can be analyzed and related to an entire activity and provide a relatively accurate basis for corrective action.

A note of caution should be mentioned regarding the reliability of information when data are taken from only part of a cycle or at the start of a new program. Quality, quantity of performance, or worker skills are usually at their lowest point in this phase of the activity.

provement of worker abilities over time, are often represented graphically and are called **learning curves.** These curves have been used extensively in situations where complex operations or products result in long learning periods for workers, sales people, or specialists of various kinds to become proficient at a particular task. The concept of the learning curve applies to many different start-up situations including a manager being transferred to a new job assignment.

Only when (accurate) information is channeled on time and in adequate quantity to the individual who has the authority to take the appropriate action has the final link been made in an effective control system. The right information must be provided at the right time and at the right place. What constitutes the best or the proper channel of information varies with each organization, the information to be interpreted, and the corrective action required to meet expected standards.

Computerized information systems are becoming more commonplace in organizations. Some researchers argue that these systems will encourage centralization of controls. On the other hand, others point out that the speed and variety of information made possible by computers make it possible for first-line supervision and middle-level managers to be supplied with (more) significant control information. Although there is a trend toward centralized control, the trend is not necessarily a function of computerized information systems. Rather, it may be an expression of a desire to place control information in the hands of those possessing the authority to take corrective action.

Behavioral Implications of Control

People are an essential part of the control process because many control systems help to evaluate individual performance. Individuals often feel threatened when corrective actions do not automatically occur or where some corrections take place that they do not understand. Properly designed control systems should, and do, reinforce positive behavior on the part of employees. Controls help to "tell people where they stand" and thereby often reduce their anxiety. Good performance against standards should be praised and rewarded by supervisors. Control systems should help monitor work activity so that sufficient time for corrective action is provided. This should result in less costly and less drastic actions being taken, to say nothing of the peace of mind that managers may possess knowing that such systems are in place. However, control procedures that are insensitive to human behavior may result in people adapting behavior patterns, leading to poor personnel actions or performance. The remainder of this section deals with this situation.

Consider the many possible choices that a claims adjuster in an insurance company faces in the daily performance of his or her job.

> Management has told us we should handle 20 claims a day. One way I can reach this total is to avoid the really tough cases and pass them up to my supervisor.

> My fellow employees often urge me to do less than 20 claims to prove to management we are overworked.

> Sometimes when I hurry, I approve or disapprove claims that I would settle differently if I had more time; I am not sure whether this makes much difference or not.

> I am often asked by the accounting department and our customer relations department to answer inquiries, and I question how much time and energy I should devote to these outside requests.

> If you want to do a really thorough job on some cases, it means a dozen phone calls, lots of checking in files, and even consulting with the more experienced adjusters. How thorough should I be?

> I often am asked by those less experienced than I to help them.

> I ought to spend some time reading some of the old files and policy statements here in the office to improve my ability to do this job. Also, I ought to be studying up on other subjects to qualify for a promotion.

> I've been asked if I wanted to take over temporarily a claims review job—while the woman who handles the job has her baby. It's hard work and very demanding, and I don't know whether it's worth it for a couple of months.

> The company wants you to keep your desk neat at all times and to have everything put away in files. If I do this, I work slower because it means constant filing.

> You're only supposed to have one customer record out of Central Filing at a time. If I take several, I can work on another while I am waiting for some information on the first.

> I have a typist working for me, and I can let him fill in some of the more routine things, or I can meticulously spell out every detail.

> I've got some ideas on how this job could be improved, and I wonder whether it's worth trying to get the company to listen.

This list could easily have been made longer, but it shows that an employee's use of his or her day is not entirely dictated by a specific job assignment or set of controls. What you emphasize or deemphasize, what you do quickly or indifferently or what rules or norms you follow or ignore are all choices that can be made. Other options include: whether you are responsive to the requests of others or ignore them, or whether you concentrate on present problems or future events. Their choices are not (entirely) *pre*determined by the organization or through the definition of job responsibilities. Even on relatively programmed jobs, there is likely to be a good deal of discretion.

Conditions that organizational members are likely to see as threatening and that can result in dysfunctional consequences include (McGregor, 1967):

1. Direct hierarchical pressure to reduce costs and increase productivity.
2. Employee anxieties due to negative feedback on performance.
3. A decline in trust and confidence in management.
4. An overreliance on quantitative measures of performance.

Hierarchical Pressure

Constant management pressure to increase output may simply cause employees to disregard performance ratings and resign themselves to lower production levels. Management may even believe that the lowered production stems from poor supervision or, more likely, from the caliber of the worker. Although any of these assumptions can be true, the problem may be centered in the design and administration of the control system.

When imposed standards are considered to be unrealistic, employees can be quite creative in getting around them. In fact, there are numerous documented examples, going back to the Western Electric studies referred to in Chapter 1, of work groups that have deliberately restricted or adversely affected performance.

For example, in one company:

> Certain employees were encouraged to produce as many units as possible by being told that their production was the primary measure of their effectiveness and by being offered extra pay for what they produced above a given standard. Gradually management discovered that the employees were becoming very careless about how much material they used and about keeping their equipment well maintained and their work areas cleaned. Quality was a continuing problem because, in rushing the job, employees produced a great deal of marginal work.
>
> Other organizational problems emerged. When management changed the material from which the parts were produced, the workers wanted the standard lowered (to enable them to get to bonus earnings more quickly), claiming that the new material was harder to handle and slowed down the machines. Also, when management attached new feed-

ing devices to the machines (to lessen employee effort and make high production easier), the workers fought against management's raising the standard. When management argued that it was not fair to pay workers for the additional production that would be possible because of the new feeders (which were quite expensive), the employees charged that this was just a trick to lower their bonus.

Managerial actions on behalf of control are also a major determinant of individual behavior. What is emphasized or not, rewarded or punished, watched closely or indifferently—all give cues to employees concerning how to behave on the job. Consider these examples.

A bank teller learns that, while his boss talks a lot about being pleasant to customers, the one thing that really makes him fuss is inaccuracy. The teller is therefore brusque at the window but spends a great deal of time counting his cash.

There is no workbreak scheduled during the day, but employees walk over to the cafeteria every day—and nobody says anything.

An engineer devoted a great many hours to preparing a special report and came up with some very startling conclusions that would save the company money. He even worked on it at home on his own time, concentrating harder than he ever had before. The report was two days late, and he was sharply criticized. A few months before, he had done a routine job on another assignment but turned in the report two days early. He was told he had done fine work on the first report.

A programmer notices that the people who get promotions appear to have several things in common: they do not wear "mod" clothes, they have reasonably short hair, and they use standard English. Their work in many cases is less good than that of others who are not promoted.

A manager who is being pressured by his own boss is likely, in turn, to threaten subordinates if appropriate behavior is not forthcoming. Such threats when communicated down through the hierarchy often result in *behavior that is opposite or quite different to the one desired*. This is called **dysfunction**.

Employee Anxiety Due to Negative Feedback

People tend to be defensive about their behavior even though criticism may be offered in a constructive manner. If feedback adversely affects an individual's employment status or career plans, much anxiety is likely to occur. Therefore, feedback should be directed toward performance matters and not people as such. The focus should be on isolating differences between (actual) performance, work standards,

Feedback should be presented in a positive manner.

objectives, and positive approaches to improvement rather than aimed at the individual. Support should also be offered so that the individual can make the corrective actions required to meet the established standards.

Particularly when the threat of punishment is great, the employee can become extremely tense and be unable to accomplish much of anything. Effects of excessive threats of punishment can be seen when employees "change" data to avoid admitting problems or otherwise find ways to dodge the main issues.

For example, a department head had been relaxed about production quality in the die-casting group because it had not varied over several months. He learned later that the supervisor had neglected to note the change in the type of work being performed. The men were now producing very simple parts where the rejection rate should have been much less than the 5 percent rate that had been acceptable when they were working on highly complex and intricate parts. He also learned that the same supervisor was hiding rejected parts in scrap barrels. This behavior followed an announcement by middle management that any increased scrap would have serious consequences for the jobs of the supervisors involved.

Decline in Trust and Confidence in Management

Individuals also feel insecure when conditions occur that bring into question management's ability to establish workable control systems. Factors that contribute to a decline of confidence or trust include: (1) unrealistic or poorly defined performance standards, (2) lack of clearly defined work procedures, and (3) lack of authority of the manager to make necessary decisions based on "signals" from the control system.

Restoring employee trust takes much effort and time—it is easily lost and difficult to restore. A central role of managers is to support employee performance. In fulfilling this role, managers need to reach agreement with their subordinates on what and how objectives are to be accomplished and how results will be measured.

Some managers believe that individuals work harder if they are kept guessing as to how they are being evaluated. Thus they keep changing their standards in the hope of keeping "everyone on their toes." In the process, employee confidence in the manager is destroyed. The result is characterized by the following example.

> Karl plays his cards close to his chest as to what he is looking for in these reports we are preparing. So every week we all get together and compare what he has said to each of us about our reports. We purposefully introduce a lot of stuff we don't think is useful to see how closely he reads them and what he'll "bite on." The reports take a lot more time this way—much of it wasted—but, believe me, we're going to figure this guy out once and for all.

Overreliance on Quantitative Measures

Managers often place too much emphasis on control techniques that use numbers almost exclusively to judge performance—and in the process ignore the impact of controls on people. Budgets, quality standards, and financial ratios are all important parts of control mechanisms but must be flexible and used in a common sense way to meet new needs that may arise.

Time or performance standards that allow little room for variation ignore the fact that situations vary and that most people work within a *range of performances*. It should be unnecessary for management to search out causes for every variation. Thus, a salesperson in a given territory may report customer calls in successive weeks of 15, 12, 10, 16, and 11. Even though the targeted figure may be 13 weekly calls, variations in the accounts (e.g., type of customer, extent of possibilities) *plus* some variations in the work pattern of the salesperson, may easily account for these differences in weekly figures.

CONTROL TECHNIQUES

Budgets: A Financial Planning and Control Technique

Many different types of **budgets** are used in organizations. Typically they cover a one-year period. One basic type brings together *estimated cost expenditures* in key personnel or activity categories. If the budget is accepted by management, it may then become the basis for *authorized* cost expenditures.

The budget described here serves as a financial plan, outlining how funds are to be used in a given time period. In addition to being a financial plan, however, budgets are control tools. As information is gathered on actual receipts and expenditures within an operating period, significant deviation from budgeted amounts may be indicated. In such a case, managers need to institute control measures aimed at bringing actual performance (and their costs) in line with planned performance.

Like other types of control, budgets can have both functional and dysfunctional effects on an organization. It is desirable to be aware of their potential benefits as well as to avoid the common pitfalls usually encountered with them. Examples of budgets can be found in Chapter 4.

Positive Aspects of Budgets

One author has described a number of potentially positive aspects of budgeting (Irvine, 1970).

1. Budgets can have a positive impact on motivation and morale by creating the feeling that everyone is working toward a common goal.
2. Budgets make it possible to coordinate units of the entire organization by tying together activities of every unit.
3. Budgets can signal the need for corrective action by alerting members when actual expenses exceed the budget.
4. Budgets improve resource allocation by forcing managers to defend their plans logically in quantifiable terms.
5. Budgets improve communication by requiring managers to communicate their plans as part of the budgeting process.
6. Budgets serve as a means of evaluation because performance can more easily be measured against specific and approved benchmarks.

GREAT PERSON PROFILE

Andrew Carnegie (1835–1919)

Born in Scotland, Andrew Carnegie came from a family of "rebels" who disliked privilege and had a tradition of political activism. At the age of 12, he and his family emigrated to the United States, bringing with them a belief in the "improvement of mankind." His first job in a cotton mill in Pittsburgh paid $1.20 a week, and in various jobs that followed he learned to master various machine operations, to fire furnaces, and to do double-entry bookkeeping. He also became an expert clerk for the Pennsylvania Railroad, for whom he worked for 12 years. In later years he developed an interest in the stock market and a growing interest in the steel business.

In his stock purchases, he used strict *cost accounting principles*, and also saw to it that they were applied in the companies in which he invested. He learned about steelmaking during a trip to Britain and returned to Pittsburgh to set up Carnegie Steel. *Applying cost controls* to each phase of the process, he was able to cut costs and produce more profitably than his competitors. This enabled him to expand faster. He also evaluated his employees carefully and surrounded himself with top-rate managers. In his later years, he was eager to pursue his philanthropic interests; he sold out

to J. P. Morgan for $250 million. Carnegie received payment in U.S. Steel Bonds—Carnegie Steel became the base subsequently for the United States Steel Corporation.

Andrew Carnegie spent his remaining years finding fulfillment in giving his fortune away for various purposes, among them the financing of 2800 public libraries and several educational foundations. His faith in the improvement of mankind never ceased, and his own rise from the bottom to the top of the social order had proved it possible.

Potential Pitfalls of Budgets

When budgets are instituted, unintended and unanticipated responses often result. These dysfunctional aspects of budgets often interfere with the attainment of an organization's goals. These possible pitfalls include:

1. Placing too much emphasis on relatively minor expense items. Although budgets force managers to plan, too much time can be spent on insignificant expenses.

2. Increasing budgeted expenses without adequate information or justification. Perhaps the most well-known method developed to overcome this response is **zero-based budgeting.** This technique requires managers to *justify their entire budget request* annually in detail rather than simply refer to budgeted items of previous years. In other words, the "zero based" approach does not permit additions or subtractions from the budgeted figures for the previous period. Each budgeting cycle requires a complete review of each item.

3. Ignoring changes in the external environment or company circumstances that require budgets to be changed. New laws that are enacted, a worsening economy, or the development of a new technology all signal the fact that a budget, or the bases on which it is developed, may be in need of modification.

4. Emphasizing short-term performance at the expense of long-term performance. When managers are having difficulty meeting their budgets, they will often reduce research and development or maintenance expenses because the effects in these areas usually do not surface for some time. Thus managers may "appear" to be performing adequately while below the surface the seeds for long-term problems are being sown.

Because of these significant "pitfalls," corporate control systems have to have the capability to review regularly the relevance of the assumptions and bases for drawing up the detailed budgets used by organizational units.

People Considerations and Budgeting

Although budgets are useful for both planning and control purposes, they can result in major people problems in an organization. Budgets can build pressures that unite organization members *against* management; this negative result may come from a sense of unfairness or a situation people cannot deal with or control.

The resentment that budget pressures generate can often be reduced when managers and subordinates meet together to develop and agree on various budget items. Establishing targets that are difficult yet attainable will help to motivate individuals to achieve them, especially if they have participated in the budget development process. If individuals consider budgeted items as unattainable, they lose confidence in management. What is worse, they may seek means of covering up activities that would signal "off-budget" performance. The managerial challenge is clear: to create an environment of openness so that realistic targets are mutually agreed upon. The role of the manager then becomes one of ensuring their successful achievement, frequently by providing support or ensuring needed services.

"Management has asked us all to tighten our belts a bit."

(Drawing by Booth; copyright © 1971 The New Yorker Magazine, Inc.)

Quantitative Control Techniques

Managers need a variety of control techniques to meet valued objectives, but their time is limited so that approaches must be selected carefully. For example, take the job of general manager of a small company. It may be likened to a three-ringed circus. Daily demands and decisions are called for in production activities, selling, personnel issues, and financial management. There is little time and information available for in-depth analysis. One must have some basic priorities or strategy clearly in mind to be able to handle the constant flow of interruptions and decisions, or, very simply, the total operation can go rapidly out of control. A number of quantitative and analytical techniques have been developed to handle more routine control decisions so that the manager's time can be freed for more significant matters.

Some of the more important control techniques include (1) charting techniques that ensure "quality" levels are maintained within predetermined limits, (2) inventory models that help to control the quantity of materials kept, and (3) network analysis techniques that aid in meeting scheduling or time commitments.

Charts for Controlling Quality and Other Dimensions

A complete discussion of **statistical sampling** is beyond the scope of this text, but the techniques date back to the 1920s and address such concerns as sample size, random sampling procedures, and the establishment of standards and control limits (Shewhart, 1931). These methods of *quality control* allow organizations to inspect samples rather than the entire lot of work. Thus, less inspection time, and therefore cost, is incurred but at the expense of some risk of accepting an excessive quantity of defective items.

To facilitate the quality-control process, **control charts** are normally used. For example, Exhibit 7-3 shows the upper and lower control limits for the filling of 50-pound sacks of potatoes. *Control limits* are established through statistical techniques. The discussion of these techniques is beyond the scope of this book. Acceptable measures fall between the upper and lower control limits that have been established. When samples are taken periodically, the average measurement of the individual items in the sample is plotted on the chart for the specific time period. By observing successive measurements, an overall trend is indicated. These methods are widely applicable to many non-work situations.

In Exhibit 7-3, one observation is below the lower control limit. This suggests that the process or machine filling the sacks is out of

Exhibit 7-3 Standard Control Chart

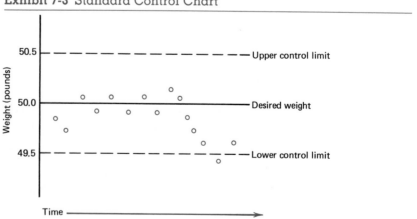

control. An investigation should take place to find and correct the cause of the problem. It is also important to note that the measures declined steadily immediately preceding the out-of-control observation. This pattern should have been questioned because it is highly unlikely that such measurements were due to random behavior.

Of what other use can these charts be to managers? As in the above example, managers can use these charts to tell when any predetermined objective that was decided upon during the planning process is not being met. Work and sales activity levels such as the number of patients per day in a hospital, the amount of deposits per day in a bank, the sales calls made per week by a salesperson, and the number of automobiles manufactured per shift are all dimensions that can be monitored through the use of these charts. This technique emphasizes *control by exception* and recognizes that many deviations or movements of the variable being measured, are normal.

Inventory Control

Operations managers are constantly involved with ensuring that an adequate inventory of materials and supplies is on hand for efficient production. For some companies the amount of money tied up in inventories can surpass their investment in plant and equipment.

There are two key inventory questions: (1) How *many* items should be ordered at one time? and (2) How *often* should an order be placed in relation to existing inventory levels?

A major objective of **inventory control** is to minimize inventory costs. To make these inventory decisions, therefore, the manager must understand and be able to identify the two main cost factors—carrying costs and order costs—that will affect the choices being considered.

Carrying costs are those direct costs of keeping inventory on hand. They include the interest foregone on money tiedup in inventory rather than financially invested, and the cost of storage space, inventory taxes, insurance, spoilage, theft, obsolescence, and handling. The carrying cost figure is usually expressed as an annual percentage; average figures in the past were between 15 and 25 percent but are much higher in times of high interest rates.

Order costs are those clerical and administrative costs necessary to place an order. They include purchasing agents' time, typists' time, mailing or telephone costs, paperwork involved in getting the order placed, and computer time.

To minimize inventory costs, a balance must be found between these two costs. As the size of each order increases, the cost of carrying this larger amount also increases. On the other hand, since fewer orders need to be placed to meet demand, total order costs decrease.

The **Economic Order Quantity** (EOQ) represents the size of order that minimizes total annual ordering costs and inventory carrying costs:

$$\text{EOQ} = \sqrt{\frac{2DO}{C}}$$

where D is the annual demand or items needed per year, O is the cost per order, and C is the inventory carrying cost per unit per year.

EOQ computations are not always as simple as they may appear. For them to be reliable, several conditions must exist. First, the rate of demand should be known and be constant for this particular model, which is not the case in most business situations. Thus, reliable forecasts from the planning function are of great importance here. Second, cost per order (O) and carrying costs (C) must be computed with a workable degree of accuracy. Third, the time between placing an order and receiving the goods must be constant, which is rarely the case in a world of strikes and transportation breakdowns. Last, the cost of materials and inventory must be constant and predictable which it seldom is in inflationary times.

If these conditions can be pinned down or, at least, anticipated by the manager, the EOQ model will still enable the manager to know when and how much to order. The factors mentioned above merely represent added uncertainties with which managers must deal when controlling inventory costs.

Network Analysis Models: Aids to Scheduling Resources

Nothing is ever built on schedule or within budget.

Most of us have followed schedules to meet deadlines. The schedules that are developed in organizations today have been aided greatly by **network analysis techniques,** such as PERT (Program Evaluation and Review Technique), CPM (Critical Path Method), and Gantt charts. In general, network techniques relate planned work activities to time requirements; they are excellent planning *and* control tools. In the latter function they are concerned primarily with concurrent control.

Gantt Charts.   In the early 1900s Henry Gantt developed a number of different types of charts that were the forerunner of network analysis techniques. These charts related types of activities to the amount of time required for their completion by showing work planned and work completed in relationship to time (Clark, 1922).

Exhibit 7-4 shows a Gantt chart for the preparation of a research paper. The Gantt chart shows the sequence in which activities need to occur and the time each task is expected to take. Once the plan is on

Exhibit 7-4 Gantt Chart for the Preparation of a Research Paper

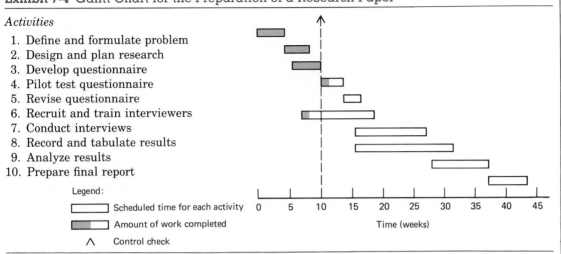

Activities

1. Define and formulate problem
2. Design and plan research
3. Develop questionnaire
4. Pilot test questionnaire
5. Revise questionnaire
6. Recruit and train interviewers
7. Conduct interviews
8. Record and tabulate results
9. Analyze results
10. Prepare final report

Legend:

☐ Scheduled time for each activity

▨ Amount of work completed

∧ Control check

Time (weeks)
0   5   10   15   20   25   30   35   40   45

paper, follow-up and control are made easier because activity deadlines that are not being met or activities that are not meeting the plan, are identified.

Several types of information are shown on the same chart. The scheduled time for each activity is represented by a "trough." As work on an activity is completed the trough is filled (colored) in. Thus at any point in time the progress of the project can be easily monitored to determine where any problems may arise. For example, for the research project shown in Exhibit 7-4 at day 10, activities 1, 2, and 3 are on schedule, while activity 4 is ahead of schedule and activity 6 is behind schedule.

Critical Path Methods.   In project planning the Gantt chart emphasizes the importance of a systematic arrangement of work to be performed. However, this (vertical) arrangement of activities gives no indication of the tasks that must be completed before others can begin, that is, the interrelationships between activities. This shortcoming is overcome in network analysis techniques, such as PERT and CPM, that are often called **critical path methods.**

Both techniques are procedural methods that are typically used for large-scale, complex, one-time types of projects that require the project manager to plan, schedule, and control a great number of interrelated activities. Characteristic of most large-scale projects is the fact that many of their activities are inter-dependent and must occur in sequence. For example, in a building project, the architectural design would occur before construction could begin. It would also be necessary for the foundation to be laid before floors and walls could be built.

PERT was initially developed by the United States Navy in the late 1950s to plan, schedule, and control the Polaris missile submarine construction project. It involved the sequencing of activities and the estimating of three possible times of completion for each activity (optimistic, pessimistic, and most likely time). **CPM,** on the other hand, was developed by The DuPont Co. at about the same time as a tool to reduce the amount of downtime for equipment maintenance projects. Since activity time estimates tend to be more reliable for these latter types of projects, one time estimate is used in CPM. In contrast, PERT models usually use several time and probability estimates. PERT is appropriate for one-of-a-kind projects with which there has been little historical experience, for example, in research and development. CPM, on the other hand, is most appropriate for projects that have been done before so that data are available on time and cost estimates, for example, construction projects.

An example of a network diagram is shown in Exhibit 7-5. The lines in the network represent the work activity required to reach a particular event. Events merely signal the completion of work leading to them and are represented by circles or nodes, while activities, which take time, are represented by arrows. No event can be reached until all work (activities) leading to it has been accomplished. Thus activities CE and BE (and the activities preceding them) must be completed before event E is reached and activity EF can begin. On the other hand, activities AB, AC, and AD will all be carried out simultaneously.

There are three major paths through the project: (1) the upper path, A–B–E–F–G; (2) the middle path, A–C–E–F–G; and (3) the lower path, A–D–F–G. They are expected to take 11, 13, and 10 days, respectively, to complete. The most **critical** or important **path** to ensure that the project is completed on time is also the path that takes the longest time to complete, path A–C–E–F–G; that is, if it is possible to do the things requiring the most time, on schedule, it should be relatively easier to stay on schedule with the other events.

Delays along the critical path A–C–E–F–G must be avoided in order to complete the project within 13 days. Since activities AB and BE combined take only 5 days while activities AC and CE combined take 7 days, however, the former can be delayed 2 days without affecting project completion. From a control standpoint, then, one does not need to control such activities as much as those activities that are critical. In fact, if there are potential delays anticipated on critical path activities (such as AC or CE), resources often are "borrowed" from other activities (such as AB, BE, AD, or DF) that are not on the critical path if these resources are readily transferable.

Network analysis techniques are very useful both as a planning

Exhibit 7-5 Network Diagram of Activities

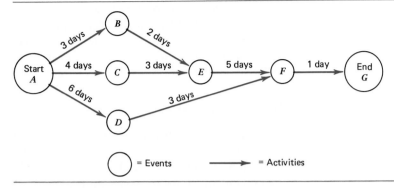

○ = Events   ⟶ = Activities

and a control device. For our purpose we have included it as a control device, emphasizing their use to ensure that schedules are met at the least possible cost by using resources more efficiently. These and other quantitative control techniques allow managers to delegate the actual control activity to others once standards have been developed. This frees their time to handle more important problems of a less routine nature.

CONTROLS BROADLY VIEWED

When one views control broadly—as an effort to channel behavior toward desired ends—the full scope of the concept is achieved. It is important to note that many efforts to channel behavior do not come from management. Gene Dalton suggests that there are at least three major types of control over behavior in organizations, with each having its own standards, monitoring system, and bases for bringing about corrective action. These three types are (1) organization control, (2) social control, and (3) self-control (Dalton, 1971).

Organizational Control

Organizational controls represent those formally designed control efforts originated by management. The general area of application of these controls comes from the objectives and plans of the organization. The standards come from objectives stated in areas such as profit, market share growth, and cost reductions. Monitoring of performance is handled through devices such as budgets and standard cost reports. An MBO interview is a technique for reviewing or monitoring performance. The signal for managerial action is a variance between the planned and the actual result. The reward system of the organization provides one way to correct or reinforce the behavior patterns of individuals. Praise, promotion, and salary increases represent positive rewards, whereas negative sanctions include actions such as a request for an explanation, withholding of praise and rewards, and at the extreme end of the spectrum, dismissal.

Social Control

Although social control does not carry with it formal organizational sanctions, it is often powerful in channeling behavior in directions desired by various informal cliques or social groups. The direction of social control comes from the mutual commitments that members of informal groups have toward one another. The standards here include group norms of behavior that have emerged and crystallized in areas like sharing work or problems, helping each other, levels of work that are acceptable, and dress. Observation and informal communication channels are the monitoring mechanism. When deviations are noted, sanctions will probably result. Negative sanctions may include good-natured kidding, verbal abuse, hostility if a behavior is really disliked, and rejection from the group. Rewards for conformance also exist, and these include membership, approval, and favors.

Self-Control

Whereas social control comes from an external source, *self-control* comes from within. Reliance on this type of control is at the heart of *intrinsic motivation* systems. Self-control comes from individual commitment to personal goals, individuals' sense of goal fulfillment, and their ability to affect the variables related to their goals or commitments. The standards are expectations for accomplishments of established goals. The monitoring system is self-awareness and personal observation, and the signal for corrective action is any indication that goals or personal expectations will not be met. The system for appropriate action includes self-administered sanctions and may range from a mild feeling of disappointment to a deep sense of failure or inadequacy and, perhaps, withholding of a privilege as a form of self-punishment. Positive reinforcers would include feelings of elation, satisfaction, esteem, and self-mastery.

Taken together, the three types of control discussed in this section have the potential to create pressures toward goal accomplishment. The three do not work independently of one another; in fact, they combine to support or negate one another. If one system runs counter to another, optimal control is not likely. If all three operate consistently and in the same direction, the total control achieved can be very great. A general idea exists that "control is usually highest when it is least felt." To the extent this notion is valid, it suggests that control systems be designed that rely more (heavily) on self and social control rather than on organizational controls. In the past, organizational controls received the greatest emphasis; we have now entered an era where greater benefits may be achieved for the organization *and* individual through social and self-control systems.

SUMMARY

The control function is undergoing change but not to the degree of other areas of management. One noteworthy change is the effort to reshape the role people play as *part* of a control system rather than acting solely as the focus of the control effort. These changes are a part of a quality of work life philosophy of management that seeks to harness the creative energies and abilities of people and that emphasizes behavioral guides on social controls and self-control.

In this chapter we began with a discussion of why control is needed and what is involved in the control process. Various types of control were presented including preventative, concurrent, and feedback. Various issues related to control including desirability, timeliness, reliability, and accuracy were then investigated. In addition, both the positive and negative implications of control from a behavioral viewpoint, were discussed, and specific examples were given. A number of control techniques useful to managerial work were presented, including budgets, (quality) control charts, inventory control models, and network analysis models. Finally, the chapter concluded with broad view of control.

The manager depends upon controls to determine when something is going wrong that may require his or her attention. For example, merchandise quality is falling off, absenteeism is climbing among younger workers in the department, or squabbling is increasing among employees over job assignments. Each of these (control) measures requires attention to bring the system back to its normal operation. To do so may require addressing a deep-seated problem. At other times, a simple order needs to be given such as, "Get the machine repaired, and transfer the work to another piece of equipment." The important thing is that action is taken to get the system going.

Questions for Study and Discussion

1. Why is the control function important?
2. What are the three basic steps necessary for control to occur?

3. How are planning and control interrelated?
4. What are the three main types of control? Give examples of each.
5. What are four characteristics of effective control systems? State briefly why each of these characteristics is necessary.
6. Why are budgets useful?
7. What are some dysfunctional effects of budgets?
8. Under what conditions are individuals likely to resist controls?
9. Describe the steps you would take to reduce the usual resistance that develops when controls are installed.
10. Under what conditions would you recommend the use of PERT rather than CPM?

CASE: MALLORY SALES COMPANY

Mary McCarthy was promoted to head up the accounts payable department at Mallory Sales Company. She was formerly a supervisor in accounts receivable and did an excellent job. She got along well with people, learned fast, and was very loyal to the company. Some people were surprised at the promotion, but most realized that Mary was ambitious and knew how to play the "office politics" game.

Some time after Mary had taken over her new job, her manager, John Davis, began receiving complaints from the cost accounting unit about billing errors originating from Mary's unit. John asked Mary to check into the matter and report back to him.

Mary's immediate reaction was that the complaint probably came from Rick Camp, a senior member of the cost accounting unit. He was thought to have been the main contender for the job that Mary received. It was no secret that Rick thought he should have been given the promotion based on his background, training, service to the company, and knowledge of the work.

Mary received the information and discovered that the output of her unit had decreased by about 13 percent during the past month. However, she observed that all of the billing clerks seemed to be busy. She talked to the former head of accounts payable and was told that Janet Johnson, one of the five billing clerks, had done sloppy and inaccurate work when other complaints were received about six months ago. Mary talked individually with each of the billing clerks and asked them to cooperate in eliminating errors in their work. Each one said they would, but the errors continued.

Several days later, Mary decided to have Janet and Diane (another billing clerk) submit their work to her for double checking. After being informed, Diane said, "O.K., if that's what you want." But Janet was taken aback and visibly upset. "You're picking on me!

My work is accurate—I check it carefully! You're just trying to get rid of me so you can get a friend in! All of us have been waiting for you to change things." Mary tried to reassure Janet that what she said was not true, but Janet was not convinced.

The next day, Janet called saying that her car broke down and she would not be able to report for work until noon.

Questions

1. What is the problem in this case?
2. Comment on Mary McCarthy's handling of the billing errors in her unit.
3. What key control considerations does this case bring out?
4. What is your recommendation? Why?

References

Bloch, Arthur, *Murphy's Law*. Los Angeles, Cal.: Price/Stern/Sloan Publishers (1977).

Cameron, Kim, "Measuring Organizational Effectiveness in Institutions of Higher Education," *Administrative Science Quarterly*, **23** (December 1978): 604–632.

Clark, Wallace, *The Gantt Chart*. New York: The Ronald Press (1922).

Conn, Carolyn, "Budgets: Planning and Control Devices," *Managerial Planning*, **29**(4) (January-February 1981): 36–38.

Currier, Benjamin A., Jr., "Management Controls," *Best's Review*, **81**(4) (August, 1980): 100–103.

Dalton, Gene W., *Motivation and Control in Organizations*. Homewood, Ill.: Richard D. Irwin (1971).

Edwards, James, and Roger A. Roemmich, "Scientific Inventory Management," *MSU Business Topics* (Autumn 1975): 41–45.

Flamholtz, Eric, "Organizational Control Systems as a Managerial Tool," *California Management Review* **22**(2) (Winter 1979): 50–59.

Giglioni, Giovanni B., and Arthur G. Bedeian, "A Conspectus of Management Control Theory: 1900–1972," *Academy of Management Journal*, **17** (June 1974): 292–305.

Hitt, Michael A., and R. Dennis Middlemist, "A Methodology to Develop the Criteria and Criteria Weightings for Assessing Subunit Effectiveness in Organizations," *Academy of Management Journal* **22** (June 1979): 356–374.

Hofstede, Geert, "The Poverty of Management Control Philosophy," *Academy of Management Review* **3** (July 1978): 450–461.

Irvine, V. Bruce, "Budgeting: Functional Analysis and Behavioral Implications," *Cost and Management*, **44**(2) (March-April 1970): 6–16.

Lee, Douglas, "Balancing the Budget—Does it Matter?" *Journal of the Institute for Socioeconomic Studies*, **5**(4) (Winter 1980): 25–35.

Machin, John L. J., and Lyn S. Wilson, "Closing the Gap Between Planning and Control," *Long Range Planning*, **12** (April 1979): 16–32.

McGregor, Douglas, *The Professional Manager*. New York: McGraw-Hill (1967).

Nadler, David, Cortlandt Cammann, and Philip Mirvis, "Developing a Feedback System for Work Units: A Field Experiment in Structural Change," *Journal of Applied Behavioral Science*, **16**(1) (January-March 1980): 41–62.

Newman, William H., *Constructive Control: Design and Use of Control Systems*. Englewood Cliffs, N. J.: Prentice-Hall (1975).

Ouchi, William G., "The Relationship Between Organizational Structure and Organizational Control," *Administrative Science Quarterly*, **22** (March 1977): 95–113.

Pekar, Peter Paul, Jr., and Elmer H. Burack, "Management Control of Strategic Plans Through Adaptive Techniques," *Academy of Management Journal*, **19** (March 1976): 79–97.

Rhode, John Grant, and Edward E. Lawler III, *Information and Control in Organizations*. Pacific Palisades, Cal.: Goodyear Publishing Co. (1976).

Ryan, Joseph, "Profitability in the Nonprofit Environment," *Journal of Systems Management*, **31**(8) (August 1980): 6–10.

Schutte, F. Grant, "Budgetary Control Systems for the Eighties," *Journal of General Management*, **5**(3) (Spring 1980): 3–18.

Shewhart, W. A., *Economic Control of Quality on Manufactured Products*. Princeton, N. J.: D. Van Nostrand Company (1931).

"Some Middle Managers Cut Corners to Achieve High Corporate Goals," *Wall Street Journal* (November 8, 1979): 1.

Steinberg, Earle, and Albert Napier, "Optimal Multi-Level Lot Sizing for Requirements Planning Systems," *Management Science*, **26**(12) (December 1980): 1258–1271.

Stumpff, Marlin, "Better Communication Means Better Control," *Magazine of Bank Administration*, **57**(3) (March 1981): 50–52.

Tosi, Henry L., Jr., "The Human Effects of Budgeting Systems on Management," *MSU Business Topics*, **22** (Autumn 1974): 53–63.

Tucker, Jack, "Budgeting and Cost Control: Are You a Businessman or a Riverboat Gambler?" *Public Relations Journal*, **37**(3) (March 1981): 14–17.

PART THREE

BEHAVIORAL ASPECTS OF MANAGEMENT

CHAPTER 8

MOTIVATION

KEY
QUESTIONS
ADDRESSED
IN CHAPTER

1. What do you understand by the term *motivation*? That is, what are its basic components, process, and dynamics?

2. What are the premises, applicability, and shortcomings of the motivation–hygiene theory?

3. Why is Abraham Maslow's "need hierarchy" important? How is it related to Frederick Herzberg's dual-factor approach?

4. What are the expectancy models of motivation—their advantages (contribution) and limitations?

5. Using John Hinrichs's model, how would you describe the entire motivation process?

6. What is meant by the recent "motivation crisis of new lines"? Why are nonfinancial motivating factors becoming increasingly important?

7. How can you apply motivational research findings to your own personal career?

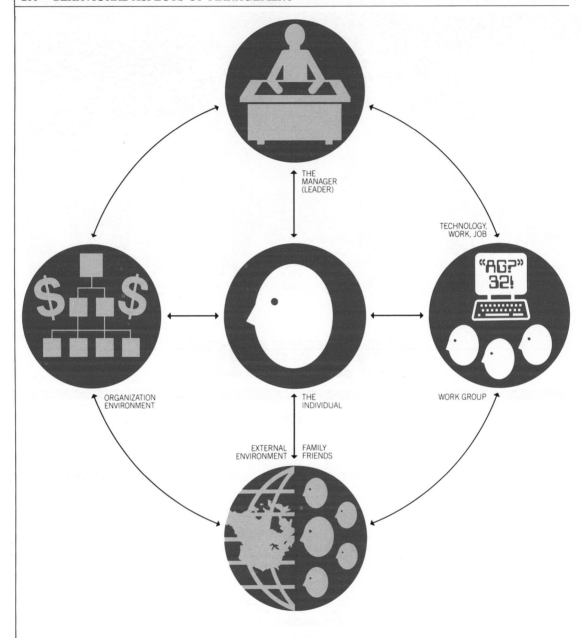

Work–life spaces: the individual viewpoint

When a person says it isn't the money but the principle that counts—it's the money.

THE CHAPTER IN BRIEF

Every manager, whether or not he or she is aware of it, has a philosophy of why people work. This influences not only their own behavior but also that of their employees. Everyone recognizes motivation as the indispensable glue that holds an entire organizational structure and its units together. To be sure, it will remain the critical component of organizational success.

This chapter begins with a general model of the motivation process and discusses some individual needs that are generally thought to be important for motivational purposes. Key theories of motivation are then presented—both content and process related. Finally, the application of motivational theories to work situations is explored, especially as it relates to the role of the manager in motivating employees.

Motivation and the Work–Life-Space Model

The sketch of the work–life-space model heading this chapter differs somewhat from that of previous chapters in order to emphasize for the manager the need to focus motivational strategies on the individual. The sketch shows the individual at the center of the work–life space, and, indeed, this outlook often reflects how each of us sees the world with which we must deal.

From the manager's point of view, it is often helpful to put oneself in the shoes of the employee and attempt to appreciate his or her perceptions of the work–life spaces. Thoughtful managerial strategies for motivation can emerge from this perspective. For example, the individual is affected by his or her view of the manager. How is this relationship perceived—supportive, cordial or open, neutral or indifferent, or distinctly unfriendly?

The individual employee is also affected by other life spaces. The (internal) organizational environment, with its specific rules and regulations, compensation system, opportunities to pursue one's career, and social climate, provides the constraints on the motivating factors that the manager can offer to an individual employee. In addition, aspects of the external environment, including family and friends, also have an impact on individual expectations or demands. For example, increasing inflation can affect income needs and therefore wage or salary demands, increased social awareness concerning sex or race discrimination can result in more assertive behavior related to pay and promotion policies that are perceived to be discriminatory, and new technology that threatens job security can result in renewed interest in unionization.

Research suggests that the work itself may have a major motivational influence on the worker, although the other life spaces should not be discounted. Rather, it would be of distinct value to the reader to begin reflecting on which work–life space is most important or has the most impact in particular circumstances. Also to be considered is how the importance of the various life spaces is likely to change as one's life or career starts to unfold.

BACKGROUND

What Is Motivation?

There are several concepts that are basic to our understanding of human motivation. Before we discuss them, however, it is necessary to agree on some definitions.

Motivation can be best described as "the driving force within an individual that impels him to action." This driving force is produced by a state of tension, which exists as the result of an unfulfilled need. Individuals, whether managers, supervisors, or subordinates, strive both consciously and unconsciously to reduce this tension through behavior that they anticipate will fulfill their needs and thus relieve them from the stress they feel. The specific goals they select and the patterns of action they undertake to achieve their goals are the result of individual thinking and learning.

One model of the motivational process is presented in Exhibit 8-1. It portrays motivation as a state of need-induced tension (2) brought about by individual needs that are not fulfilled (1). This tension "drives" (3) the individual to engage in behavior (4) that is expected to gratify his or her needs (5), thus reducing tension (6). Whether need fulfillment actually occurs, of course, depends on the course of action taken. The specific course of action or behavior undertaken by a manager or employee as well as the specific goal he or she chooses to fulfill are affected by his or her thinking processes (7—called cognition) and previous experiences (8).

Let us now say a few words about needs. Every individual has (motivation related) **needs;** some are innate, others are learned. **Innate needs** are *physiological;* they include the needs for food, water, air, clothing, shelter, and sex. Because all of these factors are needed to sustain life, they have also been called *primary* needs or motives by various psychologists.

Acquired needs, on the other hand, are needs that we learn in response to our culture or environment. They include needs for es-

Exhibit 8-1 A Model of the Motivation Process

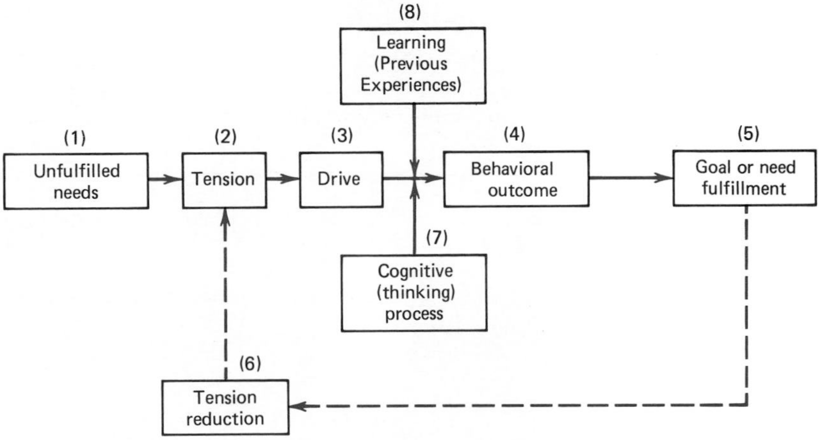

```
                                    (8)
                                 Learning
                                (Previous
                               Experiences)
                                    │
    (1)           (2)          (3)  ▼       (4)              (5)
 ┌──────────┐  ┌─────────┐  ┌───────┐  ┌────────────┐  ┌────────────┐
 │Unfulfilled│→│ Tension │→│ Drive │→ │ Behavioral │→ │Goal or need│
 │  needs    │  │         │  │       │  │  outcome   │  │fulfillment │
 └──────────┘  └─────────┘  └───────┘  └────────────┘  └────────────┘
                   ▲            ▲                              ┊
                   ┊           (7)                             ┊
                   ┊      ┌───────────┐                        ┊
                   ┊      │ Cognitive │                        ┊
                   ┊      │ (thinking)│                        ┊
                   ┊      │  process  │                        ┊
                   ┊      └───────────┘                        ┊
                   ┊          (6)                              ┊
                   ┊     ┌───────────┐                         ┊
                   └┄┄┄┄ │  Tension  │ ◄┄┄┄┄┄┄┄┄┄┄┄┄┄┄┄┄┄┄┄┄┄┄┘
                         │ reduction │
                         └───────────┘
```

teem, prestige, affection, power, and learning. Because acquired needs are generally *psychological* they have been named *secondary* needs or motives. They result from the person's subjective psychological state and from his or her relations with others.

Related to needs are the individual's goals. Goals are the sought-after results of motivated behavior. As Exhibit 8-1 indicates, all behavior is goal-oriented. Finally, rewards are the factors related to motivation greatly affected by the organization.

A distinction also is made between positive and negative motivation. Motivation can be either a driving force *toward* some object or condition (positive motivation) or a driving force *away* from some object or condition (negative motivation). Some psychologists refer to *positive drives as needs* and *negative drives as fears* or aversions. However, though negative and positive motivational forces seem to differ dramatically in terms of physical and sometimes emotional activity, they are basically similar in that they both initiate and sustain human behavior. It is for these reasons that researchers often refer to both kinds of drives or motives as needs.

Goals, too, can be either positive or negative. A "positive goal"— I want to get an A in this course—is one toward which behavior is directed. A "negative goal"—I don't want to flunk this course—is one from which behavior is directed away. Since both goals can be considered objectives of motivated behavior, most researchers refer to both types simply as goals, whether they be individual, as is our concern in this chapter, or organizational, as is discussed in Chapter 4.

To the extent that goals emerge from needs, there are many different and appropriate goals to satisfy these needs. The goal selected depends on the person's subjective experiences, physical capac-

Recognition: an important human need.

ity, prevailing cultural norms and values, and the goal's accessibility in the economic and social environment. Furthermore, the individual manager's or employee's own conception of himself or herself also serves to influence the specific goals he or she selects. Thus, a person who perceives himself as "rough" may choose to adhere to an authoritarian leadership style or smoke a cigar!

Both needs and goals are interdependent. One does not exist without the other. However, many managers and employees are not especially aware of their needs. For example, an employee may not be aware of his or her social needs but may join a union to achieve a specific economic goal—and at the same time be satisfying a social need.

Needs and goals are constantly changing in response to an individual's physical condition, environment, interactions with others, and experiences. As individuals attain their goals, they develop new goals. People continue to strive for existing goals, or they may develop substitutes if they fail to attain particular goals.

Failure to achieve a goal often results in feelings of frustration. The behavior that prevents attainment of a goal may be personal to the individual, or it can be an obstacle in the physical or social environment. Regardless of the cause, individuals react differently to frustrating situations. Some people are adaptive and manage to cope by finding their way around the obstacle or, if that fails, by selecting a substitute goal. Others are less adaptive and may regard their inability to achieve their goals as a personal failure and may experience feelings of anxiety.

Why Is Motivation Important?

Since individuals to a great extent determine an organization's performance, motivating people to acceptable levels of behavior and performance is a must. The study of motivation is also important because it is often difficult to determine *why* employees behave as they do simply by observing the outcomes of their behavior. People's actions cannot always be directly related to their immediate conscious or unconscious thoughts. Futhermore, different individuals may have very different reasons for behaving in exactly the same way. Take, for example, two assembly workers, Ruth and Sam. Both are reluctant to follow a new work procedure but for different reasons. Ruth is fearful that the new procedure will break up her social group, whereas Sam has a fear of failure and is worried about making mistakes. Managers, therefore, need to understand and deal with the underlying motivation behind people's actions so that both individual and organizational performance can be improved.

Diversity and Hierarchy of Needs

For many years, psychologists and others interested in human behavior have attempted to develop exhaustive lists of human needs or motives. Although there is little disagreement about specific "physiological" needs, there is considerable disagreement about specific "psychological" needs (needs that have their origin in the mind).

As far back as 1938, psychologist Henry Murray prepared a detailed list of 28 psychological needs that has served as the basic construct for a number of widely used personality tests [for example, the TAT and EPPS (Murray et al., 1938)]. Murray believed that everyone has the same basic set of needs, but that individuals differ in their priority ranking of these needs. Murray's basic needs include many motives such as achievement, recognition, and dominance or authority, that are assumed to play an important role in motivating employee performance and the general organizational behavior of groups.

The first major proponent of a theory of a universal hierarchy of human needs was Dr. Abraham Maslow (1970), a psychologist who formulated this widely accepted theory of human motivation after some 20 years of clinical practice. Maslow's theory postulates five basic levels of human needs, which rank in order of importance from low-level (physiological) needs to higher-level (psychological) needs. His theory is discussed in the next section of this chapter.

Some Important Needs or Motives

Learned needs have always been considered more important in understanding the dynamics of employee motivation in modern organizations than are the physiological needs that are innate. In fact, certain theorists such as David McClelland have identified various motives that they contend are most relevant in motivating today's employees. These include needs for power, achievement, affiliation, status, and security.

The **power motive** refers to the desire to be in charge, to control and manipulate other individuals. A supervisor is likely to have a greater need for power than a file clerk. The employee who is characterized by a high **achievement motive** takes moderate risks, wants immediate feedback on performance, finds the task intrinsically satisfying, and, in general, is considered to be the *ideal* employee. It

GREAT PERSON PROFILE

William Cooper Procter (1862–1943)

William Cooper Procter was born in Cincinnati, Ohio and was educated at Princeton University before he returned home in 1883 to work for the family partnership of Procter and Gamble, as his father and grandfather had done before him. He started at the bottom and developed sympathy for the worker's sense of economic insecurity and alienation. A growing awareness of problems resulting from unsatisfactory labor relations, such as high turnover and numerous strikes, motivated him to propose ways to improve working conditions, worker morale, and *motivation* and to provide more equitable treatment for the labor force.

As a junior executive in 1885 he persuaded his superiors to establish a reduced (5½-day) work week, followed by the first profit-sharing plan in a U.S. corporation. In 1923 Procter started to guarantee every employee work for 48 weeks per year, a practice literally unheard of till then. He proved that the introduction of these incentives not only motivated the employees, but that their implementation also dramatically reduced turnover and the number of strikes.

William Cooper Procter's accomplishments show that people are an essential part of an organization, and when properly motivated they can have positive effects on the business itself. During his presidency at Procter and Gamble, sales increased from $20 million to more than $200 million.

should also be emphasized that whereas managers and supervisors generally have higher power and achievement needs than employees, the contrary is true with the **affiliation motive.** In other words, employees may be more concerned with being accepted by a group of co-workers than they are about power and achievement. Furthermore, although status and the symbols that go with it (dress, titles, special benefits, etc.) are very important, it seems that managers often fail to assign them the proper importance. Finally, the need for security has been traditionally ranked at or near the top of motives by most workers.

KEY DEVELOPMENTS CONCERNING THEORIES OF MOTIVATION

Content Theories

Maslow's Need Hierarchy Model

As we mentioned earlier in this chapter Abraham Maslow's well-known theory of motivation contends that the basic human needs fall into a hierarchy of importance—the **hierarchy of needs.** The lowest level of *unsatisfied* needs predominates in determining behavior; as the lower-level needs are effectively satisfied, they no longer serve as strong motivators, and higher-level needs move into prominence.

Maslow's theory suggests that the most fundamental needs of people are *physiological*—the needs for food, drink, and the like. When they are unsatisfied, individuals attempt to behave in a way that will satisfy these primary needs. *Safety* needs are the next level in the hierarchy—the need for physical and psychological security. The next level, *belonging,* or social needs, usually does not play a significant role in determining behavior until lower-order needs have been met. Above the belonging needs are *esteem* needs—the need for self-esteem and respect for others. The highest need in the hierarchy is the need for self-actualization, for realizing one's own potential to become everything one is capable of becoming (see Exhibit 8-2).

Maslow's theory contends that all these needs can be satisfied except the highest level, the need for self-actualization. In effect, the theory maintains, that although an individual attains a gratifying goal, his need for self-actualization is not satisfied; rather, new routes are explored. This often results in second, third, and even fourth careers, self-development, world trips, and even older people taking up running and competing in races.

Exhibit 8-2 Maslow's Hierarchy of Needs

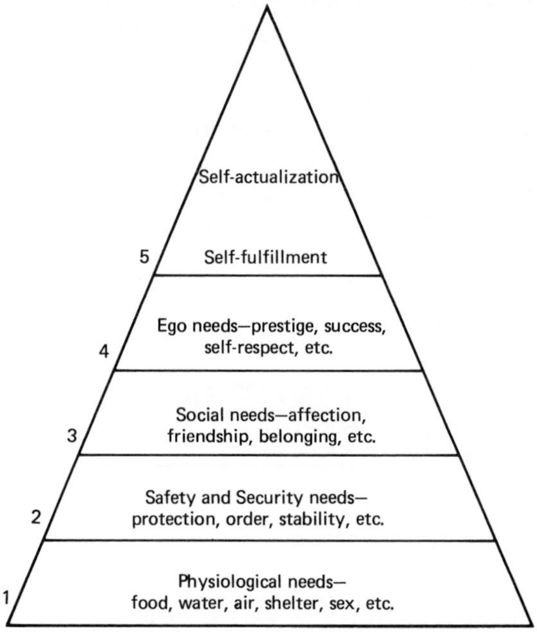

Self-actualization

5 — Self-fulfillment

4 — Ego needs—prestige, success, self-respect, etc.

3 — Social needs—affection, friendship, belonging, etc.

2 — Safety and Security needs— protection, order, stability, etc.

1 — Physiological needs— food, water, air, shelter, sex, etc.

Herzberg's Motivation-Hygiene Model

Frederick Herzberg's concepts of job satisfaction and motivation to work were a post World War II development, originally presented in the book *Motivation to Work* (1959).

In developing his theory, Herzberg was searching for the answers to these three questions.

1. What factors cause job attitudes to change?
2. Are the factors that bring about high job satisfaction different from those that cause dissatisfaction or low job satisfaction?
3. What happens to people on the job as a result of changed job attitudes?

Through research, Herzberg identified 10 major factors that he believed had a significant effect in causing attitudes to change. More recent studies by Herzberg have since expanded the list to 16.

The original 10 factors affecting employees' attitudes were achievement, recognition, work itself, responsibility, advancement, company policy and administration, technical supervision, interpersonal relations and supervision, salary, and working conditions.

In answering the second question Herzberg found that the follow-

Maslow's lower-level needs in action.

ing five factors were mentioned most frequently when men spoke of satisfaction with their work: (1) achievement, (2) recognition, (3) work itself, (4) responsibility, and (5) advancement. He observed that the last three had a longer-lasting effect on attitudes than did the first two. These five factors were rarely mentioned in events that described feelings of job dissatisfaction. Herzberg refers to these factors as **satisfiers;** and they are related to the job content or job task. They strongly correlate with achievement of a task, recognition for this achievement, the nature of the task, responsibility for the task, and professional growth or advancement in task capability. These satisfier factors were (also) named **motivators,** since the 1959 study suggested that they were effective in motivating the individual to superior performance and effort. Two groups of factors, "hygiene" and "motivators" account for the description of this approach as a **two-factor theory.**

The remaining five factors of (6) company policy, (7) technical supervision, (8) salary, (9) interpersonal relations and supervision, and (10) working conditions, were observed to produce negative job attitudes and were rarely involved in events resulting in positive attitudes. These **dissatisfiers** related to the job context or environment. They can prevent job satisfaction but have little effect in creating it. The dissatisfiers can at best lead to job attitude neutrality. Herzberg initially called these factors "maintenance" factors and in his later papers referred to them as **hygiene** factors. Exhibit 8-3 includes all 16 factors affecting job attitudes as reported in 12 investigations conducted by Herzberg.

To answer the third question, Herzberg looked at three general areas of "effect": (1) performance, (2) job turnover, and (3) attitudes toward the company. His findings were:

1. *Favorable attitudes* toward the job had a greater effect on job performance than did unfavorable ones. When performance was analyzed as a result of improved attitudes, productivity was often rated above standard level.

2. Rather large numbers of employees, perhaps 25 percent, showing *low job satisfaction,* withdrew from the job in varying degrees.

3. Of those who felt *high job satisfaction,* one-half said they had a

Exhibit 8-3 A Comparison of Satisfiers and Dissatisfiers

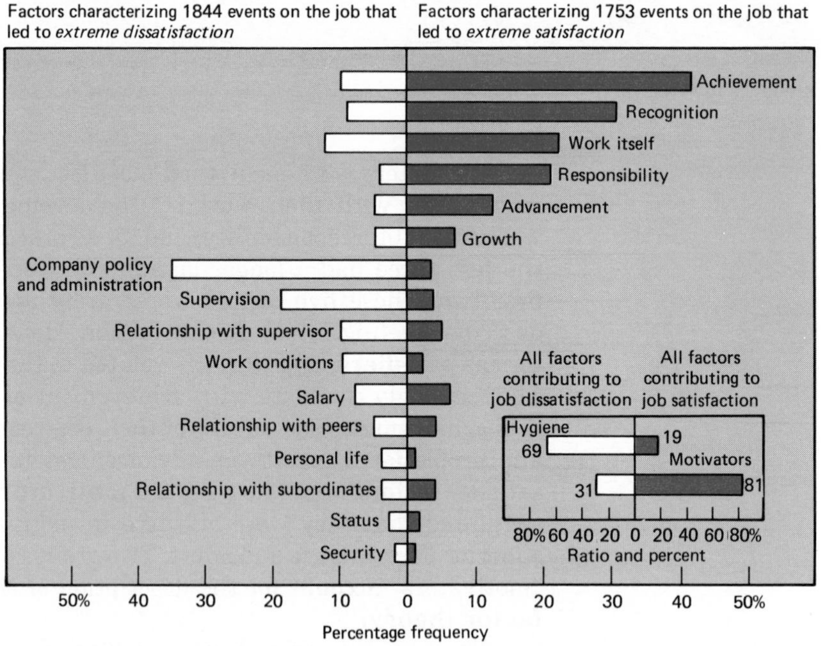

Factors characterizing 1844 events on the job that led to *extreme dissatisfaction*

Factors characterizing 1753 events on the job that led to *extreme satisfaction*

Achievement
Recognition
Work itself
Responsibility
Advancement
Growth
Company policy and administration
Supervision
Relationship with supervisor
Work conditions
Salary
Relationship with peers
Personal life
Relationship with subordinates
Status
Security

All factors contributing to job dissatisfaction
All factors contributing to job satisfaction

Hygiene 69   19 Motivators
31   81
80% 60 40 20 0 20 40 60 80%
Ratio and percent

50% 40 30 20 10 0 10 20 30 40 50%
Percentage frequency

Source: Federick Herzberg. "One More Time; How Do You Motivate Employees?" *Harvard Business Review,* January-February 1968, p. 57. With permission. Copyright © 1967 by the President and Fellows of Harvard College; all rights reserved.

favorable attitude toward the company. It seemed reasonable to conclude that a company may expect the degree of loyalty it gets from its employees to vary with job satisfaction. Positive attitudes seemed to be more potent than negatives ones.

Comparison of the Maslow and Herzberg Models

Although Herzberg used Maslow's framework as a basis for his own theory, he did break with the traditional view of a job satisfaction–dissatisfaction continuum. According to Herzberg the factors leading to job satisfaction are separate and distinct from those that lead to job dissatisfaction. He believed that satisfying Maslow's lower-order needs—physiological, safety, and social—would not lead to job satisfaction because these are now "guaranteed" by society. At best, satisfaction of these needs can lead to job attitude neutrality. Not having them fulfilled, however, would lead to job dissatisfaction. Working from this concept Herzberg formulated his hygiene factors. The motivators emerged from the belief that job satisfaction could only be achieved by satisfying (Maslow's) higher-order needs for self-esteem and self-actualization. A comparison of the two theories is shown in the diagram.

From this comparison chart it becomes evident that managers who try to eliminate factors that create job dissatisfaction can bring about a neutral situation regarding performance, but not necessarily motivation. They will be placating their work force rather than motivating them. When hygiene or maintenance factors are largely fulfilled, people will not be dissatisfied; however, neither will they be

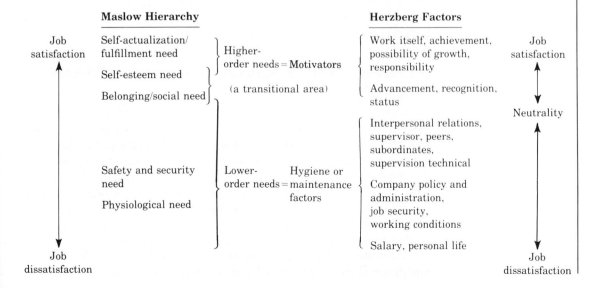

satisfied. To motivate workers requires, according to Herzberg, an emphasis on such factors as recognition, advancement, achievement, and the work itself.

Shortcomings of the Herzberg and Maslow Models

A very common criticism that surrounds Herzberg's model is the research methodology of his two-factor theory. Some researchers suggest that the original 1959 study was seriously biased because it led to a technique of questioning and information gathering that is often viewed as self-confirming: that is, the manner in which questions were asked determined largely the two categories of responses. Furthermore, there is a possibility that factors such as responsibility, achievement, and recognition may be of higher importance with regard to *both* satisfaction and dissatisfaction than factors such as security and work conditions. Finally, it may be that motivators may be no more related to high performance on the job than the hygiene factors, since only satisfaction was explored (Schwab, Devitt, and Cummings, 1971).

Similarly, Maslow's model faces some shortcomings. The major criticism is that this formulation emerged as a purely theoretical statement rather than the outcome of field research. Since people differ greatly in terms of their needs, need schedules, and need preferences, various critics maintain that it is unfair and misleading to group everybody under such a limited Maslowian need range.

Although these criticisms have much merit, the theories are widely known in the work world. The increased popularity since the mid-1960s of work designs that seek to enrich jobs, that allow workers greater responsibility, and other quality-of-work-life issues (which will be discussed in more detail in Chapter 14), are in large part due to Herzberg's findings.

A Process Theory of Motivation: Expectancy Theory

Expectancy theories resulting primarily from the research of Victor Vroom (1964) and others (i.e., Porter and Lawler, 1968), are compatible with need theories. Yet at the same time they are an alternative to the content models of Maslow and Herzberg, which do not explain the complex process of work motivation (Luthans, 1981).

Edward Tolman was one of the first psychologists to take a cognitive, rather than a psychoanalytic or behavioristic approach in analyzing human behavior. In other words, he felt that humans act (largely) of their own free will and are not (or perhaps little) controlled by other forces such as unconscious thought.

According to Tolman, humans behave in a purposeful manner and direct themselves toward a goal or outcome. A baby, for example, quickly learns that saying new words like "ma–ma" gains approval from mother. This personal satisfaction (or goal) derived from gaining a positive response from one's mother will further motivate the child in the future. Learning, according to Tolman, consists of the *expectancy* or likelihood that one's effort will result in a particular outcome.

Expectancy theories state that motivation begins with a desire for something, such as greater status, more autonomy, a sense of achievement, or more recognition. How much an individual desires a particular outcome is dependent on its importance to him or her (termed **valence**). Outcomes are both extrinsic—external rewards such as pay, promotion, or pleasant working conditions—or intrinsic—internal rewards or valued personal goals such as personal growth, increased self-esteem, or fulfillment. Feelings of personal accomplishment (an intrinsic outcome), for example, may be attained in a variety of ways such as good performance on the job, success in off-the-job activities, or even through the accomplishments of others. A simplified illustration of expectancy theory is shown in Exhibit 8-4.

Effort is not the same as performance, as anyone can testify who has worked hard on a task and could not complete it successfully. For performance depends not only on the effort one puts forth but also on one's ability and skills and on channeling one's behavior in the right direction.

Take the case of an employee who desires a greater feeling of accomplishment and believes there are two ways of attaining it: performing well on the job or becoming more involved in community affairs (an off-the-job activity). In each instance the individual will first estimate the likelihood that the effort will lead to the expected performance and hence the desired outcome. Barriers at work such as excessive "red tape," unclear directives, or the inability to obtain needed resources to carry out the task will reduce the chances that one's on-the-job efforts will be rewarded with good performance. Therefore, the employee may become "turned off" regarding work and pursue more likely avenues off the job. The challenge for management, of course, is to recognize the existence of blocks to motivate performance and keep these barriers to a minimum so that expectancies related to on-the-job actions remain high.

Exhibit 8-4 Expectancy Theory

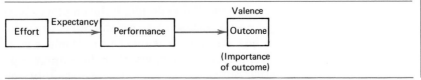

Work is often more than a 9 to 5 job.

The Vroom Model

Two basic assumptions are important to Vroom's expectancy theory: (1) Most individuals act to achieve goals or ends leading to these goals; whether they act or not depends mostly on whether they *believe* their particular action will lead them to the goals they have been seeking. (2) Individuals have the capability to establish preferences among different courses of action and, in fact, they do establish these preferences most of the time, based on the likelihood that the outcomes of these acts will take place (in relation to desired goals).

Vroom believes that an individual's motivation is a function of the *expectancy* that a particular outcome will follow his performance or behavior. For example, if the employee works harder he is likely to get a salary raise. Also considered is the *valence* of the outcome, that is, how strongly he wants this outcome (e.g., the raise). This valence's strength depends on whether the employee prefers a raise more than other outcomes, such as less responsibility or an easier job.

The Porter–Lawler Model

A model similar to that of Vroom's is the Porter–Lawler model (1968). Expectancy-based theories of motivation pay considerable attention to the anticipation of response–outcome connections and rely heavily upon such concepts as value, valence, and perception.

Effort, according to Porter and Lawler, is the amount of energy an employee exerts in a particular job. Effort correlates more with motivation than with performance. However, motivation, satisfaction, and performance are all separate variables that correspond in ways that are different than previously assumed. The gap between motivation and performance is bridged by those abilities and traits associated with the particular individual (Luthans, 1981).

Porter and Lawler's approach to expectancy theory contends that the likelihood of an individual engaging in particular behavior is enhanced to the extent that he or she believes that the behavior will lead to rewards that he or she personally values.

The theorists contend that intrinsic rewards should be excellent motivators for two reasons: (1) higher effort–reward probabilities can be established for them than for extrinsic rewards, and (2) many people place value on rewards of this nature.

It therefore appears from this discussion that job content is a critical determinant of whether employees believe that effective performance leads to feelings of personal growth and self-esteem. Since it influences what rewards are perceived to stem from effective performance, job content can be a powerful motivational force where higher-order needs are concerned. The next task is to determine the characteristics of motivating jobs.

Hackman and Lawler (1971) specified three characteristics that jobs must possess if they are to arouse higher-order needs and create conditions under which people who perform them can receive intrinsic rewards: (1) the job must allow a worker to feel personally responsible for a meaningful portion of the work; (2) the job must provide outcomes that are intrinsically meaningful or otherwise experienced as worthwhile to the individual; and, finally, (3) the job must provide feedback about what is accomplished.

Although both Vroom's and Lawler and Porter's theories have received support from various empirical studies, there are some concerns with regard to expectancy theories that are being addressed in more recent studies. First, more information is needed concerning the factors that influence expectations about both the likelihood that effort will lead to performance and that performance will lead to certain outcomes. Second, an outcome's importance to an individual has been shown to be somewhat unstable (Edwards, 1961); that is, both the relative and absolute intensity of a person's feelings toward a particular outcome tends to change often during his or her life. Third, with respect to managerial effort, there is a need to consider both physical and mental aspects. Many studies thus far have bypassed these considerations and have attempted to explain motivational variations in performance entirely by measuring expectations and the importance of outcomes—these are very crude measures of effort. Nevertheless, both expectancy models provide an excellent basis for further theoretical and empirical development of our understanding of managerial motivation.

The Total Motivational Picture: Hinrichs's Model

John Hinrichs (1974) formulated a comprehensive model of the entire motivational process. This model, shown in Exhibit 8-5, indicates how the various components of the motivation process discussed at the beginning of this chapter interact. We can see that the fundamental links of the model are (a) effort, or energy expended (no. 2); (b) directed effort, or effective performance (no. 4); and (c) satisfaction (no. 6), or job and company commitment. Effort reflects the strength

Exhibit 8-5 Hinrichs's Model of the Motivation Process

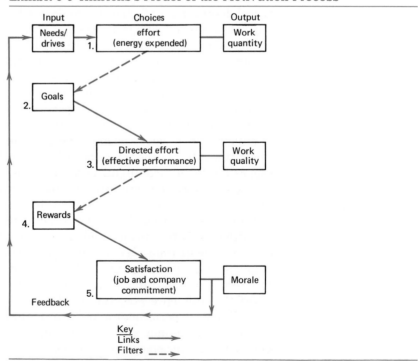

Source: Based on the work of John Hinrichs, "A Replicated Study of Job Satisfaction Dimensions," *Personnel Psychology* 21 (Winter-1968), 479–503 and related works.

of the individual's needs (no. 1) that start the activity in the first place. This effort is goal directed, and it can therefore be thought of as the activity that links needs (no. 1) and goals (no. 3). Also, the model implies that effort will be expended only when the person has reasonable expectations that the goal can be obtained.

We can see here the similarity with Vroom's motivational model. The concept of expectancy implies that blocked goals, whether real or perceived, will lead to frustration and adaptive behavior that will have direct effects on the organization. Finally, the key to work quality is the direction of the expended effort that is determined by the nature of available rewards. Every time effective performance is rewarded and ineffective performance is discouraged, high-quality work is sustained. There are filters in the link between goals and rewards; for example, the employee's ability. These should concern management a great deal because the person has to have the ability to perform his or her job effectively in order for any kind of reward system to succeed. Also, unless the person is confident that his or her performance will lead to rewards that are tied in with his or her personal goals, he or she will not choose to direct his or her efforts toward high-quality performance. Satisfaction, the final link in the system, is the basis of employee morale and derives from the rewards given for effective performance. It was not long ago that satisfaction was seen as an *input* to the motivational system contributing directly to productivity. Research has failed to validate the relationship, however, and it has become clearer that job satisfaction should be viewed as an *outcome* derived from the organizational rewards. For research has shown that, most often, high levels of effective performance are the *cause* of satisfaction, and this in turn may be a very useful strategy for monitoring the motivation system.

Path–Goal and Contingency Models

Many of the newer motivational approaches described in this section have been incorporated in the **path-goal model.** Many elements of this model have already been described in the preceding discussions. Managers like this approach because they find that it is understandable, fits in with their framework of thinking, and squares with past organizational experiences. Also, the same model has been used to help people better understand their own career situations and things they can look at usefully to further their career possibilities. Finally, the model is also one that has gained popularity in the leadership area and thus is described in the next chapter. Clearly, this is a most important way for managers and organizational members to be thinking about their situations.

The path-goal model has six key elements that are diagramed in Exhibit 8-6 and described briefly below.

Exhibit 8-6 The Path–Goal Contingency Model

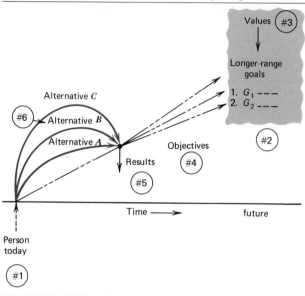

1. **Today.**   The initial orientation of this model starts from the point at which the manager or individual finds himself or herself. The emphasis is clearly on connecting up "today" and future situations. The past is not ignored, because it affects individual objectives (4) and longer-range goals (2). But the emphasis is clearly on where I am going and not where have I been.

2. **Goals.**   Items nos. 1 and 2 represent the extremes in time over which managerial or individual planning takes place. The basic viewpoint is that behavior is goal oriented, but, of course, we must be able to develop goals and know how to accomplish them. Our experience has been that many people do not know how to plan goals and therefore cannot take advantage of this approach. Another feature of the goals is the fact that all of us attempt to satisfy *multiple* goals represented by goal no. 1, goal no. 2, and so on. For example, we may start preparations today to enter a contest (objective no. 4). But even if we win it (no. 6), we may greatly satisfy goal no. 1 (say, the desire to receive recognition or to achieve notable things) but may not touch at all goal no. 4, which is to have a good home life. Another feature of the goals is that these are usually quite general and change slowly over time. In a way, we never fully achieve them, yet they continue to command our interest and attention.

3. **Values.**   Goals are derived from our innermost ideas of the type of person we want to be, a sense of the type of life we want to lead,

and the accomplishments that provide "happiness" or "contentment." These may deal with security, religious belief, peace, and so on.

4. **Near-Term Objectives.** Objectives represent shorter-term (time) means, not longer-term ends (goals). These are the stair steps helping to achieve longer-range goals.

5. **Results.** Somehow we need to be able to evaluate how well we secured our objectives and whether these in fact contribute to reaching goals. At one extreme, the answer may be "no"—they don't help at all. Here, the objective is an end in itself. It may be following some order but with no longer-term values (other than maybe keeping your job?!). At the other end, a particular objective may be of great help and greatly valued in meeting longer range goals.

6. **Alternatives.** It is probably clear that various means may be used to secure objectives and that these are not equally as good. Thus, we have a two-part problem: identifying promising or new alternatives (the creative process, Chapter 13, is extremely helpful here) and determining how to evaluate these alternatives; that is, how long does it take, how much does it cost, what other things are to be accomplished, and so on. For example, to travel from Chicago to Indianapolis can be accomplished in many different ways: walking, bicycling, driving an automobile, riding a train, or flying—to name a few. We can go there directly or by way of other towns or cities, by interstate, or by older highways. How do we decide? Well, in part, the answer is that it depends on what we are attempting to accomplish and the value we place on certain accomplishments, knowing that we may have to pass up other possibilities.

The path–goal model is a vehicle to express motivational ideas. It suggests that individual behaviors are goal oriented and that choices will be made based on the individual's assessments of payoffs for the possible directions or alternatives one pursues. However, individual motivation is likely to shift or to appear somewhat unstable in terms of preferences or evaluations as one becomes more aware of one's goals, gets better information, or has more powerful means to consider alternatives.

EMERGING ISSUES AND APPLICATIONS

The Role of the Manager in Motivating Performance

Having examined some of the more prevalent approaches to motivation we have reached the point where we can ask ourselves the pragmatic questions: How can we improve a manager's motivating behavior? What specific points should be considered in attempting this task?

First, it should be emphasized that morale and motivation are not changed merely by *one* managerial action. But they are changed by numerous actions. Hence, each and every action by a manager counts.

Before a manager can, in fact, motivate others he or she needs to have a clearer understanding of his or her own behavior and how that relates to others. To do this the following points should be examined.

1. Everyone, including managers, should be able to plan a concrete series of attainable steps toward each one of his or her goals.

2. Keeping in mind that physical and mental rest supplies a great deal of the energy behind motivation, we should examine whether our basic plan allows enough time for relaxing and thinking about the future.

3. Everyone has setbacks. The important thing is to learn from our experiences so that they are not repeated.

4. We should be aware of what we do not want—even if we cannot fully describe what we really do want.

5. Our goals should be sufficiently broad to allow for flexibility and high enough to be challenging.

6. There are no two people who are identical, and, as a consequence, general rules for working with individuals do *not* apply to everyone.

7. Acting differently toward employees A and B does not imply that we are "soft-hearted" or "wish-washy" nor does it mean that we agree with A or B.

Nonfinancial Motivating Forces

Motivating forces can be conceived of as a continuous series of concentric environments, with the most powerful factor in the center being the self. This (shown in Exhibit 8-7) implies that the individual, in general, is most motivated by his own personal self-interest, somewhat less by his job, and least by society in general. Few would argue that it takes a highly attractive bundle of fringe benefits and personnel policies to overcome an extremely unattractive job.

Obviously, motivation involves a great deal of communication, which, in turn, has its roots in the personal skills of reading, writing, speaking, and listening. In fact, most managers view listening (communications!) as the personal skill of greatest importance because listening is a key to empathy, and there can be no real motivation without empathy. Finally, the company's image, the employee's su-

Exhibit 8-7 Nonfinancial Motivational Forces

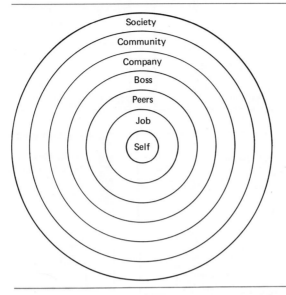

pervisory environment, and his job and group environments all contribute in varying degrees to motivating his performance.

However, the financial motivating force of pay still remains a very unique kind of incentive in that it satisfies both lower- and higher-order needs (Lawler, 1973), contributing directly to lower-level needs and indirectly to higher-order needs by providing status through higher achievement.

Pay tends to decrease in relative importance for those people whose salaries have advanced faster than inflation. For many people, therefore, nonfinancial motives, for instance, psychological and sociological needs, have been substituted in recent years for economic ones.

Young Employees and the Motivation Crisis

Many industrial attitude surveys have consistently noted that newly hired employees are highly motivated (defined as being very satisfied with their job) immediately after they join the organization but that their motivation declines drastically within the first few years (see John Hinrichs, 1974). Exhibit 8-8 indicates this trend. It is appropriate to ask why this decline takes place in such a short period of time. Some studies attribute the fall in job satisfaction of new employees to unrealistically high expectations as they entered the organization. The result is a disillusioned employee who has encountered a quite different organizational reality than he or she expected. In terms of

previous models, reduced expectations and more realistic job objectives may have a positive effect on performance, may lead to more job satisfaction, and also may lessen turnover.

Leadership Strategies for Motivation

Although Herzberg's theory has been criticized for weaknesses in method, his contributions to the concepts of job enrichment are extensive. He has given managers, businessmen, and professionals a way of thinking about motivation that has proved useful in many areas. As illustrated by Exhibit 8-9, the supervisor does have a range of control over (hygiene and motivators) conditions affecting his or her subordinates. The supervisor has the potential to deal with the employee in each of the listed areas in a way that is mutually beneficial (e.g., the supervisor acknowledges worker performance, and the employee receives satisfaction). The supervisor can also adjust or modify conditions of work itself.

The supervisor has the greatest influence on items under his or her immediate control (as shown by the **X**'s in the "high" column Exhibit 8-9). If, for example, an employee does not enjoy working (or is not motivated to work) at a specific work task or piece of machinery, the supervisor has the authority to find someone who is suited to that job. The supervisor may not be able to change a piece of machinery, but he does control "assignment of responsibility," and modifications are possible in methods or procedures. Although his may appear to be a modest approach to job enrichment, it is one that could be employed effectively. As in these two examples it is important to understand that the supervisor plays a role, however modestly, in motivating the work force.

Exhibit 8-8 Satisfaction with Job and Tenure

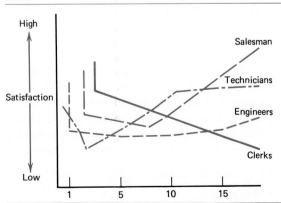

Exhibit 8-9 Influence of Supervision on Work and Job-Related Factors

Work Dimension or Factor	Degree of Supervisory Influence		
	Little/none	Some	High
Worker skill preparation			X
Pay, salary	X ----------------------X		
Social relationship		X	
Sense of closure, achievement	X ----------------------X		
Feedback			X
Task variety	X ----------------------X		
Task significance	X ----------------------X		
Recognition		X ------------X	
Work conditions	X ----------------------X		
Company policy	X		
Advancement opportunity	X		
Responsible assignments	X--X		
Technology	X		
Work procedures	X ----------------------X		

An Alternative Approach to Motivation

Arthur Miller and his associates have been working on a motivational approach called the system for identifying motivated skills (SIMS) since 1958. This system uses a questionnaire-type apparatus to gain information that they feel can prove highly effective to motivating individual performance. In approaches such as those of Miller, carefully designed questionnaires are used in a systematic way to learn features of work and individual interests and abilities that are crucial to gaining motivated job performance. The basic objective of these types of job-worker analyses is to more carefully match the individual and the job. From the worker's viewpoint, they possess knowledge, skills, and abilities. They also exhibit work styles that reflect types of work that are clearly preferred to alternate job assignments or occupations. Of additional interest is the recognition that a current work assignment may fall short of meeting individual capabilities or preferences. Even if a current work assignment is viewed as "satisfactory" by the person, there still may be a desire to make a major job shift in the future to better achieve career possibilities and objectives. These analyses thus provide a rather comprehensive picture of the worker in terms of the following:

- Current knowledge, skills and abilities.
- Work style.

- Degree to which personal needs are met by the current job assignment.
- Career direction and focus for the future.
- Future preferences as to the use of knowledge, skills and abilities.

These alternate approaches to achieving motivated work performance then try to more effectively match what has been learned about the worker and the current work assignment and future possibilities. As already indicated, some degrees of freedom may be possible (now) to the improved use of "motivated skills" of the worker. Additionally, more thought is given to future job assignments and attempts to better approximate individual needs and desires with requirements of the organization. To further gain commitment and harness individual energies to rewarding purposes for himself or herself and the organization, some companies will seek to establish "negotiated" goals with the person. Thus, if the organization agrees to particular assignments, job (re)designs or the like, the worker in turn "agrees" (commits) to a given line of personal actions. This creative approach to identifying the "motivated skills" of workers *and* their greater use by the organization can prove to be very useful for all concerned.

CAREER IMPLICATIONS AND SUMMARY

The so-called individual development phase of any motivation program usually aims to provide both managers and employees with a work environment that is conducive to personal advancement in their careers and personal growth. Every person in an individual development program should be concerned with what constitutes *successful* managerial or employee performance and behavior. "How will I be evaluated about my performance, and how are the criteria related to my success in the future?"

There are a number of techniques, tools, and data inputs that can be built into any self-improvement program. There can be paper and pencil tests, interviews, training programs, performance evaluations, and peer evaluations (Burack and Mathys, 1980).

Motivation considerations discussed in this chapter have a major influence on the advancement and growth of our personal careers. The specific career and personal goals we choose and the particular course of action undertaken by us as managers or employees, are selected on the basis of our thoughts reflecting needs, values, and goal-seeking processes. To the extent that we better understand motivational research, we can make a more conscious effort to alter our thinking or cognitive processes and to adapt to a particular organizational environment or situation.

Also, bearing in mind that needs and goals are *interdependent*, it is important to become as much aware of our needs as we are of our own personal goals. Recognizing the growing emphasis in our culture regarding social and higher-order needs, it is prudent to pay particular attention to them as they impact on both our organizational and personal lives. These higher-level needs may hold the key to success in our work lives.

We also know that needs are never completely satisfied, and we should therefore expect to strive to attain and maintain fulfillment of needs previously experienced. In terms of the theory set out by Maslow, as needs become satisfied, new, higher-order needs emerge that we as managers or employees will have to more consciously identify, explore, and consider in terms of fulfillment. Caution is urged in not setting goals that are too high, because this may lead to frustration and discouragement. Challenge is important in goal attainment, but the goals should be accomplishable. In summary, the hierarchy of needs model indicates that high-order needs become the driving force behind human behavior as lower-level needs are satisfied. We should thus understand that once needs are (largely) satisfied they no longer are a major factor in motivating (current) behavior.

From the viewpoint of career advancement, we should also consider needs for power, affiliation, and achievement. For example, it has been found that individuals with high achievement motivation tend to be more self-confident, enjoy taking calculated risks, and are interested in feedback. Rewards or profits can also serve as feedback by indicating how well a person is doing. High achievers also tend to like situations in which they can take personal responsibility for finding problem solutions (McClelland, 1962). We should understand that the power and achievement motives of managers are often higher than those of rank-and-file employees and that work in the training field indicates that important aspects of achievement motivation can be learned.

Based on ideas incorporated in Herzberg's dual-factor theory, we could identify for ourselves the specific factors of our job that are motivators and those that comprise the hygiene factors. Are the motivators less well defined than the maintenance factors? What effect can this have in our present careers? To what extent can we negotiate with our supervisor a more rewarding or satisfying job which can benefit both the organization and ourselves? In other words, if we work to more consciously think about and pursue our personal careers, we should look for those events on the job that appear to increase or decrease satisfaction as well as those that appear to cause much personal unhappiness with job circumstances. Thus, we can better understand the reasons behind our motivation or *de*-motivation.

In general, our own motivation to work can be strengthened by better understanding the job structure, supervision, and our company's goals and how we can influence these variables.

Bearing in mind Vroom's hypothesis, we should realize that our own motivation is a function of the expectancy that a specified outcome will follow our behavior, and the importance of the outcomes to us. In other words, if we work harder we shall increase the probability of our receiving a raise; but this, in turn, depends on *how strongly* we want this raise! If we value an outcome other than the salary raise more importantly, we may work harder to achieve it.

Another question that we could ask ourselves in an attempt to understand our career is whether the *intrinsic* rewards inherent in our job are sufficient enough to motivate us (as contrasted to *extrinsic* rewards). We discussed earlier Porter and Lawler's finding that intrinsic rewards are excellent motivators because of the high positive value that we tend to place on these rewards as well as the higher effort–reward probabilities that can be established for these rewards. Also, *job content* can serve as a motivational force, and should therefore be constantly reexamined, since it seems to be the initial determinant of whether we believe that effective performance will lead to our personal growth, self-esteem, and fulfillment.

Finally, the results of Vroom's and Deci's study (1971) should warn new employees not to become disillusioned with the company they select. New employees should avoid building unrealistically high expectations when they enter an organization, because they will be subject to severe disappointments and thus, likely to become *de*-motivated and less productive.

Questions for Study and Discussion

1. What is motivation?
2. How does Murray's list of needs differ from those of Maslow?
3. What is the relation of Maslow to Herzberg regarding needs?
4. What are the shortcomings of Herzberg's work?
5. What is meant by achievement theories? Expectancy theories?
6. What factors would you include in a comprehensive motivational model?
7. For your career thinking, how does a knowledge of motivation enter into new(er) areas for job exploration?
8. What options can a supervisor exercise regarding the Maslow–Herzberg-type needs?
9. What is the approach taken by Arthur Miller ("motivated skills")

and other "alternative" approaches (as opposed to leadership) for improving motivation to work and perform?

10. How can Miller's motivational theory be applied by managers?

CASE: MOTIVATION

Frank's Deli was located in the shopping district of a larger suburban town. Frank's was established many years ago by Frank Larsen. He spent much time in making sure that his food and service was tops. No wonder, then, that it turned out to be a highly successful business. As Frank moved on in years, he decided to sell the business because none of his own children were interested in coming into the business. A number of people responded to his "business opportunity" ad. He reached an agreement with Mary and Jim Parsons. Mary and Jim had both had restaurant experience in the past, had retired, and now wanted to become active again. They were both in their early fifties. Mary and Jim talked about the name of the restaurant and decided to retain the old name (Frank's Deli) because it was so well known around town.

For its size, Frank's was a very busy place. The restaurant employed 17 people including *countermen* (3), table help (3), the kitchen crew (3), and the waitresses (8), and was open six days a week from 7 A.M. to 7 P.M. Jim took care of the cash register, supervising the countermen, and ordering supplies; Mary supervised the waitresses and the kitchen.

The countermen in Frank's were highly experienced and had worked counters for many years. Each had his own work position and work at the counter. Since Jim had very little to do by way of supervision, he spent most of his time at the register and placing or picking up orders. Jim felt that he had a pretty good counter crew. The only real trouble occurred when the counter was busy and people were calling in trying to place take-out orders or Jim had to deal with customer complaints regarding quality or quantity.

Mary's problems were quite different from those of Jim. Mary's crew consisted mostly of temporary help who worked part time after school or in the summer between school terms. Three of her crew, however, were permanent and full time. Table service always presented problems because of the need for rapid turnover of customers (to make tables available), quality complaints, and constant problems with help. As a matter of fact, it was Mary's impression that help problems had gotten worse: employees not showing up or coming in late; poor customer handling; and not moving as fast as they should to keep things "humming." But Mary was experienced with these types of problems and knew how to handle them. She simply tightened things up and supervised the girls (temporaries) and women (full timers) more closely.

When Mary and Jim went on vacation, there was a noticeably different climate around the Deli. The girls and women seemed to be much more relaxed and happier, and one was heard to remark, "Hope Mary takes another two weeks of vacation—this is the first time I've enjoyed working since I've been here." The salaries of the countermen and kitchen help were about average for this type of work. The hourly rate of the waitresses was low, and they depended on customer tips to make a "decent" salary.

Questions

1. Do you think the workers at Frank's Deli were "motivated" in terms of job related satisfaction and performance? Be sure to name your assumptions.

2. Compare and contrast the motivational needs of the various employee groups at Frank's, and connect these to their career situations.

3. What advice would you give to Mary and Jim regarding the motivation of their employees to ensure good performance (i.e., customer service, avoidance of waste, efficient customer handling, etc.)? How could Mary and Jim further the career needs of (some of) their people?

References

Burack, Elmer H., *Organizational Analysis: Theory and Applications.* New York: Holt, Rinehart (1975).

Cherrington, David, "The Values of Younger Workers," *Business Horizons,* **20** (December 1977): 5–13.

Deci, Edward, "The Hidden Costs of Rewards," *Organizational Dynamics,* **4** (Winter 1976): 61–72.

Giles, William F., "Volunteering for Job Enrichment: A Test of Expectancy Theory Predictions," *Personnel Psychology,* **30** (Autumn 1977): 427–435.

Grigaliunas, Benedict S., and Frederick Herzberg, "Relevancy in the Test of Motivation–Hygiene Theory," *Journal of Applied Psychology* (February 1971): 73–79.

Hackman, J. R., and E. E. Lawler III, "Employee Reactions to Job Characteristics," *Journal of Applied Psychology Monographs,* **55** (1971): 259–286.

Hall, Douglas T., and Khalil E. Nougaim, "An Examination of Maslow's Need Hierarchy in an Organizational Setting," *Organizational Behavior and Human Performance* (February 1968): 12–35.

Hanson, Marlys, *American Society for Training and Development.* Special Report of the Career Planning Task Force, edited by Tom Gutteridge (1981).

Herzberg, Frederick, Bernard Hansner, and Barbara Snyderman, *The Motivation to Work*. New York: John Wiley (1959).

Hinrichs, John R. *The Motivation Crisis*. New York: AMACOM (1974).

Holpp, Lawrence, "Enhancing Skills Acquisition Through Achievement Motivation," *Training*, **17**(6) (June 1980): 60–63.

Ivancevich, J. M., "Different Goal Setting Treatments and Their Effects on Performance and Job Satisfaction," *Academy of Management Journal*, **20** (1977): 406–419.

Jago, A. G., and V. H. Vroom, "Predicting Leader Behavior From a Measure of Behavioral Intent," *Proceedings, American Institute for Decision Sciences*, **9** (1977): 503–505.

Lawler, Edward E. III. *Motivation in Work Organization*. Belmont, California: Wadsworth (1973).

Levinson, Harry, "What Killed Bob Lyons?" *Harvard Business Review*, **59**(2) (March/April 1981): 144–162.

Lopes, L. L., "Individual Strategies and Goal Setting," *Organizational Behavior and Human Performance*, **15** (1976): 268–277.

Luthans, Fred, *Organizational Behavior*. New York: McGraw-Hill (1981).

Maslow, Abraham, *Motivation and Personality*. 2nd ed. New York: Harper & Row (1970).

Matsui, Tamao, et al., "Expectancy Theory Prediction of the Goal Theory Postulate 'The Harder the Goals, the Higher the Performance,' " *Journal of Applied Psychology*, **66**(1) (February 1981): 54–58.

Mento, Anthony, et al., "Maryland vs. Michigan vs. Minnesota: Another Look at the Relationship of Expectancy and Goal Difficulty to Task Performance," *Organizational Behavior and Human Performance*, **25**(3) (June 1980): 419–440.

Miller, Arthur, *American Society for Training and Development*. Special Report of the Career Planning Task Force, edited by Tom Gutteridge (1981).

Murray, H. A., *Explorations in Personality*. New York: Oxford University Press (1938).

Porter, Lyman, Edward E. Lawler III, and J. Richard Hackman, *Behavior in Organizations*. New York: McGraw-Hill (1975).

Schwab, Donald P., and Lee D. Dyer, "The Motivational Impact of a Compensation System on Employee Performance," *Organizational Behavior and Human Performance* (April 1973): 215–225.

Steers, Richard M., and Lyman W. Porter, Eds., *Motivation and Work Behavior*. 2nd ed. New York: McGraw-Hill (1979).

Tupstra, David, "Theories of Motivation—Borrowing the Best," *Personnel Journal*, **58**(6) (June 1979): 376–379.

Vroom, Victor H., *Work and Motivation*. New York: John Wiley (1964).

CHAPTER 9

LEADERSHIP

KEY
QUESTIONS
ADDRESSED
IN CHAPTER

1. Is a manager a leader?
2. How do personal and situational factors and considerations enter into management development?
3. What are contingency approaches? What is their role in leadership analysis?
4. Is there such a thing as "leadership style"? If so, how does it relate to leader effectiveness?
5. What strategies appear to be useful in developing leaders?
6. How do developments in leadership research affect your career thinking and personal planning?

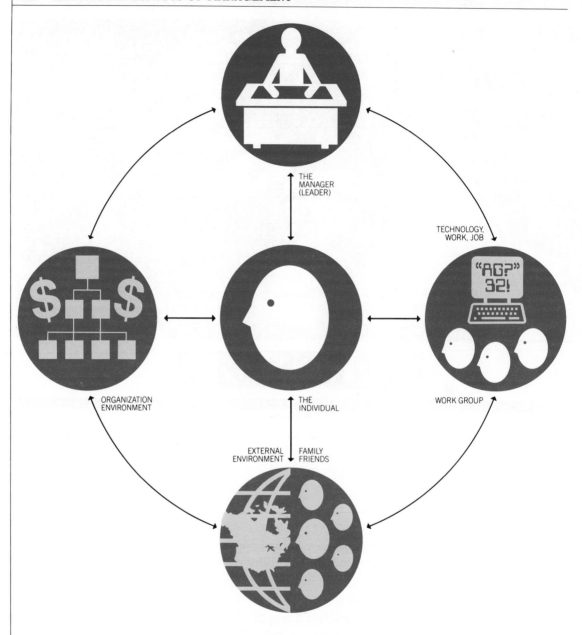

Work–life spaces: the individual viewpoint

When in charge, ponder. When in trouble, delegate. When in doubt, mumble.

James H. Boren

THE CHAPTER IN BRIEF

The early attempts to define the elements of leadership and leadership behavior were basically dependent on the "traits" that leaders were thought to possess. Researchers often conveniently formulated his or her own definitions based on a preferred set of specific traits. Few, if any, universal characteristics were identified as a consequence, since the characteristics depended heavily on the situation or individual involved. The oldest theory of leadership, the "great men" idea, is still prevalent today. When one explains events by referring to the unique qualities of prominent people, he or she uses this approach. The implication is that great leaders are born to be great. But, as we shall see, they are actually developed. They reflect the diversity and uniqueness of the situational factors in a myriad of ways.

What Is Leadership?

Leadership is more than innate traits that certain individuals possess. As the life-space model describes in detail later, it is a rather complex and intricate process involving many personal and situational factors. These factors include:

1. The leader's (personal) characteristics.
2. The organizational characteristics, for example, its purpose, policies, functions, and structure.
3. The followers' attitudes, needs, and other traits.
4. The social, technical, economic and political environment that surrounds individual, group, and organizational activities.

   Leadership is the process of influencing the behavior of an individual or group toward the achievement of some goal. Not all leaders are managers, nor are all managers leaders. Not all leadership behavior aims at the accomplishment of organizational goals and objectives. For example, the vice-president of a large company may be a successful leader and successfully accomplish his or her personal goal of becoming president. But this does not automatically imply that he is an effective manager. The vice-president's efforts to achieve this personal goal may even have a detrimental effect on the functioning of the entire organization! Thus, we should understand the intricate and subtle differences between organizational and individual goals, and between leadership and management, if we are to use the term *effectiveness* appropriately.

Does Being a Manager Make You a Good Leader?

Let us now look at the functions of a manager and the role of leadership. Management functions include organizing, directing, and coordinating organization efforts. To the extent that managers work with people, there are many opportunities to engage in behaviors that facilitate group processes, that help individuals achieve organizational and their own performance goals, and that actively encourage participation in selected management procedures. As a practical matter, these people-related activities involve influence primarily from the formal position the manager holds in the organization. Leadership has its informal dimensions as well, however, to the extent that work-group members can also exert leadership. That is, they can influence others including the formal leader to carry out their decisions.

Traditional assumptions regarding organizations suggest that every employee recognizes that the boss or manager is the source of leadership. Employees in this system are expected to "follow orders," since all authority flows from the top down. Yet being a leader today depends on the *acceptance* of that leadership by those led—the employees or subordinates. This contention that the right to lead actually flows from the bottom up was first developed by Chester Barnard

"And just how long have people accused you of being a 'take charge' type?"

(From *The Wall Street Journal*; Permission Cartoon Features Syndicate.)

(1938). It is called the **acceptance theory** of leadership (*authority*). In other words, leadership is determined by whether or not individuals will follow leaders. For example, cases of insubordination and failure to follow orders during the United States involvement in Vietnam support this observation. Soldiers in the field were simply not willing to accept the traditional concept that rank and the formal designation of authority automatically indicate an ability to lead. Managers are increasingly finding that their subordinates are less willing to follow them without question. Leadership, much like respect, is earned by performance and by the reaction of those led.

Leadership and Power

Leaders do possess **power,** and this power can take various forms. There are five basic dimensions of power, which can be described as follows (see Exhibit 9-1).

1. **Legitimate Power.** This power comes from the *formal* position held by an individual and is usually called *authority*. A vice-president thus has more legitimate power than a supervisor.

2. **Reward Power.** This power comes from a leader's ability to reward others if they follow him or her. Examples of formal rewards are increases in pay or promotions that managers can offer. Informal rewards are also possible, such as the trading of favors that is commonly done among individuals in different departments or units.

Exhibit 9-1 The Dimensions of Leadership and Power

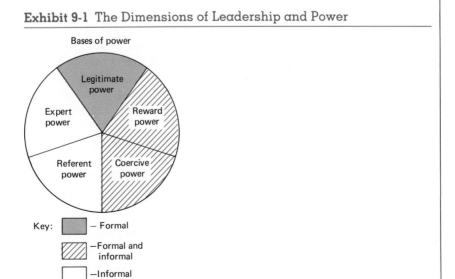

3. **Coercive Power.**   This power is the opposite of reward power. It is the ability of a leader to *punish* individuals who do not comply. In terms of formal authority, managers can fire, demote, or otherwise threaten individuals under them. Informally, many individuals can create difficulties for others by "following procedures to the letter" or otherwise slowing things down if their wishes are not followed.

4. **Referent Power.**   Often called *charisma,* this power is based on individuals identifying with a leader. If followers believe their leader is interested in their welfare or has a pleasant personality then referent power is likely to be high.

5. **Expert Power.**   This power is held by those individuals who are viewed as being *competent* in their job. Knowledge gained through education or experience and a demonstration by the leader of the ability to analyze, implement, evaluate, and successfully carry out tasks results in the acquisition of expert power.

Although all five dimensions of power are important to leaders, expert power has been found to be more strongly related to satisfaction and performance than legitimate power. Coercive power tends to be the least effective means of gaining compliance. Nevertheless, depending on the situation, any one of the five dimensions can be of value to the leader.

Theory X and Theory Y

Up to now we have been talking about the leader and not the circumstances or environment in which managers find themselves. Why are some managers more autocratic than others? Do they tend to follow this style over another? We will investigate these questions in more detail later in this chapter. In describing these styles it is helpful to consider the **Theory X** and **Theory Y** model proposed by Douglas MacGregor (1960).

These two distinct views of human nature, one basically negative—labeled Theory *X,* and the other basically positive—labeled Theory *Y,* relate to basic philosophies or assumptions that managers have regarding the way employees view work and how they can be motivated.

Under Theory *X,* managers assume that:

1. People inherently dislike work. They will avoid it as much as possible.

2. Since people dislike work, they must be coerced or threatened to achieve desired goals.

3. People do not like responsibility. They want to be directed or led.

4. Most people have little ambition. They are greatly concerned about security.

On the other hand, there are Theory Y managers who believe that:

1. People do not inherently dislike work. Work can be as natural and enjoyable as play.
2. Under the right circumstances people will be committed to achieving organizational goals.
3. People will exercise self-direction and self-control and seek responsibility.
4. Creativity and ingenuity are widely dispersed among individuals. They are not the sole province of managers.

These contrasting sets of assumptions lead to different leadership styles among managers and behaviors among employees. Theory X managers tend to be autocratic, whereas Theory Y managers are more participative. Although Theory Y seems logical to most students of management, in practice many managers are Theory X types. They tend to control subordinates closely, not giving them much free rein. In some cases, such as lower-level jobs in organizations, Theory X may be an accurate description. It does not hold in all situations, however, and in more professional occupations the Theory Y description is more accurate. Correspondingly, current research suggests that many workers carry out the role that they believe represents the manager's view—a Theory X worker!

Leadership and the Life-Space Model

In general, the organizational environment of the leader is composed of major components in the life-space model: the leader or manager, the subordinate and other group members, and the work environment. Each of these factors seems to have two critical dimensions— expectations and style. Consequently, all parties involved, both the leader and those led, have expectations regarding style that have an impact on leadership behavior and decision making.

The leader should be competent. That is, the leader should know what he or she is supposed to be doing. The leader must be able to reward followers. He or she should have influence with higher levels of management and should be able to support and represent the subordinates to his or her boss. In determining whether or not the work-group members will accept a leader, their perceptions of the leader as well as their own values and goals are important. What do they want? What do they consider important? What "turns them on"? *Group Cohesiveness* (discussed in Chapter 10) allows the leader to attain organizational goals easily through manipulation, rather than spending time trying to settle disputes or act as a mediator.

Finally, there is the work environment, which includes the conditions under which the leader and the subordinates come together, the nature of the work, and the organizational climate. Are the jobs routine and well structured? Do they require the leader to be frequently available for assistance? Given the type of work, what style of leadership is likely to be effective? If upper management requires many rules and procedures to be followed, then an autocratic style may be necessary. If decentralization is encouraged, however, a participative or democratic style is likely to be best.

The important thing to remember is that many factors affect a leader's style and effectiveness. As we shall see, this requires an individual to be a **contingency-oriented** person. For a good leader should, if possible, be able to adjust his or her personal style to meet the needs of subordinates and the situation. Initial leadership studies that identify traits that distinguish effective leaders and explain leadership in terms of behavior, as well as more recent studies given to situational and contingency approaches, are presented in this chapter.

We also examine certain leadership notions such as leadership styles and sources of power. Thus, our discussion continues with our integrated application of leadership research findings to the individual's career development and enhancement. In particular, we attempt to answer the question: how should the individual leader (manager) employ some of the leadership ideas and findings in his or her own career to increase his or her personal satisfaction and effectiveness, group effectiveness and, ultimately, the major goals of the organization? Finally, we investigate the possibility of developing leaders by discussing various leadership-development strategies.

There are more elements involved with being a good leader than can be pinpointed or charted. Some individuals are **informal leaders** who gain respect and leadership through family, friends, and interpersonal relationships—although it is not formally designated. The individual possesses leadership qualities. Understanding is the payoff. So is being a good listener. A leader/manager must listen in on a four-way band consisting of (1) the organization, (2) the work group, (3) his or her boss, and (4) the external environment (that is, family and friends) and respond simultaneously to all of them. He must mediate among the four—between people and processes. His success is determined by how finely tuned to these factors he becomes. His caring and interaction help to refine his qualities to lead. Leadership within the organization consists of helping the work group to understand where the "boss" is coming from and vice versa. Not all may be leaders, but through appreciating the elements that leaders must possess, a better relation with managers and officials in the organization will be gained. Workers, as do all people, have different needs, learning styles, and life styles. They have different path–goals. The leader can facilitate career plans and act as a sounding board, reality check, or mentor.

BACKGROUND

Leadership Trait Studies

Systematic study of leadership began by concentrating on determining exactly what characteristics or traits make a good leader. The earliest was the ancient Greek philosophers. Their "great man" theory held that a leader is born possessing those desirable traits that cause men to follow, as opposed to having to undergo a process of development. In the early 1900s, attention turned to the search for universal traits possessed by leaders and the fact that traits could be acquired through learning and experience. This school of thought gained popularity until the mid-1900s.

Early **trait studies** focused on physical traits such as size and personal appearance. Even today some managers believe that it is possible to relate physical characteristics to success as a leader. Many military groups used height as a major criterion in choosing leaders. Otherwise intelligent corporate managers occasionally discuss how they still select candidates based on certain physical characteristics. These unproven assumptions, which have been used historically to exclude women and minorities from leadership positions, are today illegal. History reveals that prominent leaders appear in all shapes, sizes, sexes, colors, and ages, with all kinds of physical attributes and handicaps.

There are some personality traits, however, that do appear to have some relevance to leadership success. Nonetheless, a summary of studies in this area showed inconclusive results (Gibb, 1969). The best that can be said is that intelligence, self-confidence, empathy, emotional stability, motivational drive, and the ability to solve problems tend to be associated with effective leaders more often than with those led.

Trait studies had inherent limitations. They ignored the needs of followers and the situational factors. More important, the specific traits identified for successful leaders are also widely found among nonleaders. It is too much to ask that similar physical and personality traits would apply to effective leaders whether they be in charge of the Israeli Army, the Red Cross, the Space Shuttle, the local school board, or the local street gang.

Leadership Behavior Theories

Trait theories are concerned with what people *are*. If they were valid then leaders would be born: you either have it or you don't. Organizations merely have to *select* those with the "right" traits.

Leadership *behavior* theory, on the other hand, is concerned with what people *do* or how they behave. If there are critical behavioral determinants of leadership, then leadership can be taught. Organizations could then design programs to *train* individuals to become effective leaders. This approach offered an exciting route for researchers because it meant that the supply of leaders could be expanded. Although there are a number of studies that looked at leadership behavior, the work done by the Ohio State and Michigan groups will be specifically noted here.

The Ohio State Studies

The leadership studies initiated by the Bureau of Business Research at **Ohio State** University in the mid-1940s investigated certain dimensions of leadership behavior. **Leadership behavior** was defined in terms of two dimensions: **initiating structure** and **consideration.** The first refers to the leader's behavior in organizing work to fulfill organizational goals. The leader who has high initiating structure is greatly concerned with completing tasks. He or she emphasizes maintaining performance standards and meeting established deadlines. The second dimension, consideration, refers to behavior indicative of friendship, mutual trust, and concern for subordinates' ideas and feelings.

Extensive research based on these definitions found that leaders high in initiating structure (or task orientation) and consideration for people tended to achieve high subordinate performance and satisfaction more frequently than did others (Kerr et al., 1974). However, this style did have some negative consequences. For example, leader behavior greatly concerned with task performance led to more grievances, absenteeism, and less job satisfaction for workers doing routine tasks. Also, some studies showed that high consideration was negatively related to the performance rating that the leader received from his or her superior.

The Michigan Studies

In the 1950s investigators from the Survey Research Center at the **University of Michigan** were also examining clusters of traits that characterized leadership behavior and that had a tendency to relate positively or negatively to certain indicators of leadership effectiveness. These studies isolated two major concepts of leadership:

Construction supervisor giving directions to a worker on a construction site. Such situations often require a task orientation.

employee orientation and *production orientation* (Kahn and Katz, 1960). These two ideas seem to run parallel with the authoritarian and democratic ideas concerning leader behavior. Employee-centered leaders were identified by their special emphasis on the human-relations part of their jobs, whereas production-oriented leaders emphasized performance and the more technical characteristics of each job. So, although individuality and personal need satisfaction are the main ingredients of the employee-centered concept, the employees are viewed as "tools to accomplish organizational goals" to the production-centered leader.

The conclusions of the Michigan studies strongly favored the employee-centered leader because they were believed to be associated with both higher group performance and higher job satisfaction among members.

The Managerial Grid

The two-dimensional view of leadership behavior suggested by the Ohio State studies has been portrayed by Blake and Mouton (1978) as the **Managerial Grid.** Following their own research, they proposed a grid based on leadership behavior styles of "concern for people" and "concern for production." These styles basically represent the Ohio

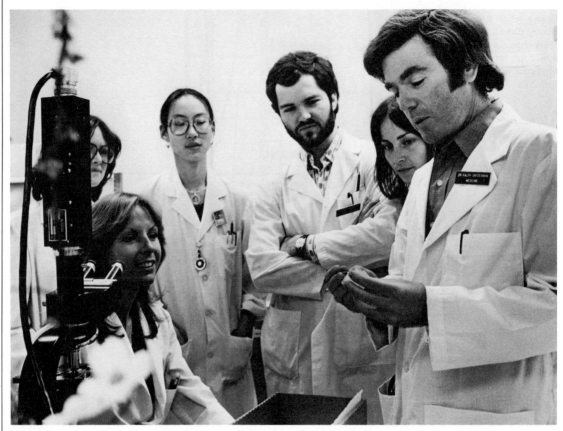

The Director of Cancer Research discusses a problem with his team. Such research situations often require a concern for people.

State dimensions of consideration and initiating structure and approximate the Michigan dimensions of employee-centered and production-centered, respectively.

The grid, shown in Exhibit 9-2, has 9 possible positions along each axis for a total of 81 (9 × 9) possible leadership styles—although only 5 basic styles have been documented widely. The grid has become so popular among some managers that they refer to the styles by number. For example, a 9,9 manager refers to a leader who has a high concern for both people and work. This style is called "team management." A 9,1 (task-oriented) manager has a high concern for work and a low concern for people needs. A 1,9 "country club manager" is just the reverse—having a low concern for work and a high concern for people.

Using the Managerial Grid as a basis for *training,* Blake and Mouton have developed a six-phase program to train leaders to become more effective. Thus their grid not only describes typical leader-

Exhibit 9-2 The Managerial Grid

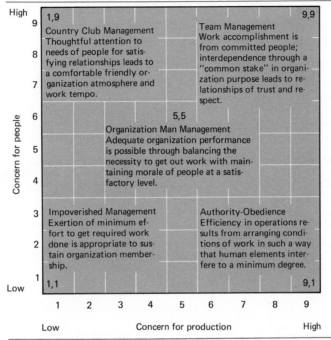

Source: The Managerial Grid figure from *The New Managerial Grid,* by Robert R. Blake and Jane Srygley Mouton. Houston: Gulf Publishing Company, Copyright © 1978, page 11. Reproduced by permission.

ship patterns of behavior but also attempts to apply theory to practice. The grid serves as a basis for leaders to examine their own style, identify the most effective style, and then develop a strategy for implementing it.

Hundreds of researchers have repeated and modified some of the original theories of the Ohio State and Michigan work (Kerr et al., 1973). However, many of the studies focusing on leader behavior seem to lack a basic theoretical background. In addition, the importance of situational factors has been greatly underemphasized. Factors such as the followers' expectations of leader behavior and the influence of the leader in the organization have been paid little attention in this mass of research. In a subsequent section we shall see that Fred Fiedler attempted to fill in the gaps by developing a comprehensive contingency model of leadership effectiveness.

Situational or Contingency Approaches to Leadership

Situational or **contingency approaches** emphasize leadership skills, behavior, and roles that are thought to be dependent on the

CONTRASTING LEADERSHIP STYLES

Henry Ford (1863–1947)
Alfred P. Sloan (1875–1966)

Managerial leadership can assume different styles to achieve goals successfully in dissimilar situations. To illustrate this, let us briefly discuss the respective styles of Henry Ford and Alfred P. Sloan. Henry Ford built a major auto manufacturing corporation while employing a management style characterized by many as autocratic, stubborn, and even willful. It may have been adequate for the time and the situation, if one is to judge by the results. Within a short time he brought automobile prices low enough to create a mass market and make cars household items in the United States. Simultaneously, he raised the workers' wages substantially, creating a historic $5 per day wage. He symbolizes the ability of industrial capitalism to lift workers and consumers to higher levels of prosperity. However, Ford's concentrated decision-making power also carried with it an increased risk of less objective decisions. This ultimately provided the climate for the organization's difficulties, to the benefit of General Motors.

At the other end of the spectrum from the centralized autocracy of Ford, Alfred P. Sloan developed a leadership style that dealt effectively with the problem of making individualistic and independent men cooperate within an orderly framework of policy making. Sloan's managerial career started with the Hyatt Roller Bearing Company. He remained there after its acquisition by William Durant to become part of General Motors. Sloan disagreed, however, with Durant's intuitive decision making. He prepared a report on how management ought to be restructured. He recognized that in such a large organization a high degree of operating authority must be left to the divisions. After Durant's departure from management in 1921, Sloan's ideas were implemented. He built a strong central staff to monitor divisional performance against standards established by a system of forecasts and delegated substantial authority. His effective restructuring of management and his unique ability to marshal facts around the points of a decision took Sloan to the very top of General Motors. His principles are still in use today by many large corporations.

particular situation. This research can be best described as an "insight," rather than a typical "approach" to leadership, because it is based on the hypothesis that behavior of effective leaders in one setting may be substantially different from that in another.

In a review of the research literature, Filley and House (1976) isolated the following situational factors that were thought to have some impact on leader effectiveness.

1. The previous history of the organization, the age of the leader, and his or her previous experience.
2. The particular work requirements of the group.
3. The community in which the organization operates.
4. The kind of job the leader holds.
5. The psychological climate of the group being led.
6. The size of the group.
7. The personalities of group members.
8. The expectations of subordinates.
9. The time required for decision making.
10. The degree to which group cooperation is required.

Most of these situational factors have not been tested by existing research, and there is no existing theory that integrates them into a meaningful pattern. Fred Fiedler's research in this area is an exception, since it attempts to combine and relate the trait, behavior, and situational approaches. Robert House's path–goal theory also integrates the expectancy model of motivation (discussed in Chapter 8) with the Ohio State leadership studies. Finally, Victor Vroom and Philip Yetton relate leader behavior to decision making. Each of these contingency models is discussed here.

The *Situational Leadership Model* (SLM), both prescriptive and diagnostic, was designed to help managers understand differences in interpersonal style. The model and program provide a framework for focusing on specific behavioral components that make up leadership events. The SLM suggests that there is no one "best" way to go about influencing people. Which style to use depends on the maturity level of those to be influenced. Communication skills, including effective listening for information, evaluation, and understanding, and the prevention and minimizing of misunderstandings in one-to-one communication are taught. Research indicates that empathy and acceptance are two ingredients necessary in any relationship that fosters growth and mental health in another. The process of feedback is also important. This can work destructively as well as positively. Feedback provides learning opportunities by using the reactions of others as a mirror for observing our own behavior. Its negative aspects could come from the focus on behavior rather than on the individual. Feedback is most effective when the purpose is a sharing of ideas, rather than the giving of advice, or the exploration of alternatives, rather than the giving of answers or solutions. Leadership style is determined by constant awareness of both the situation and the people and the ability to adapt style to purpose. With increased attention being paid to career programs within the organization today, the role of the manager in providing insightful leadership becomes an important matter for further study.

Fiedler's Contingency Model

Following years of empirical research, Fred **Fiedler** developed the **contingency model** of leadership effectiveness (1967). His model suggests that effective group performance depends on matching the leader's style of interaction with subordinates to the nature of the situation. The three situational factors that Fiedler considers are leader–member relations, task structure, and position power. They are defined as follows.

1. **Leader–member relations.** How well liked, respected, and trusted the leader is.
2. **Task Structure.** The character of work activity and degree to which job assignments are spelled out in procedures, policies, and the like.
3. **Position Power.** The degree of influence a leader has over factors such as hiring, firing, promotion, discipline, and pay increases.

To determine what kind of style leaders use Fiedler developed an instrument that he called the *least preferred co-worker (LPC) scale*. This scale measures whether a person is task or people oriented. To get the leaders' LPC scores, they are asked to think of all the co-workers they have ever had. They then rate the individual with whom they were *least* able to work. Fiedler assumed that if a person described the least preferred co-worker in a relatively favorable way (that is, gave them a high LPC score), then the person or leader was generally relaxed, permissive, considerate, and *people oriented*. On the other hand, if a leader described the co-worker in an unfavorable manner (that is, gave them a low LPC score), then the leader was task oriented.

After studying numerous groups, Fiedler and his associates constructed a contingency theory of leadership. Exhibit 9-3 draws together the three main situational factors and the leader's style (as reflected by the LPC score). Basically, Fiedler implies that task-oriented leaders are more effective in situations that are either very

Exhibit 9-3 Findings from the Fiedler Model

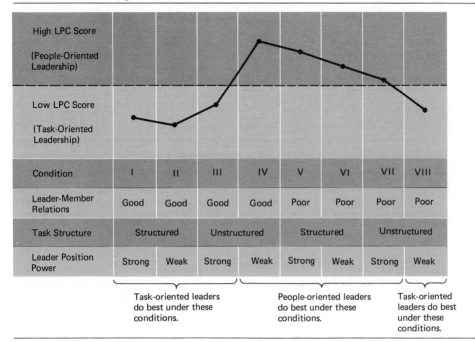

High LPC Score (People-Oriented Leadership)								
Low LPC Score (Task-Oriented Leadership)								
Condition	I	II	III	IV	V	VI	VII	VIII
Leader-Member Relations	Good	Good	Good	Good	Poor	Poor	Poor	Poor
Task Structure	Structured		Unstructured		Structured		Unstructured	
Leader Position Power	Strong	Weak	Strong	Weak	Strong	Weak	Strong	Weak

Task-oriented leaders do best under these conditions.

People-oriented leaders do best under these conditions.

Task-oriented leaders do best under these conditions.

Source: Adapted from Fred Fiedler, "The Effects of Leadership Training and Experience: A Contingency Model Interpretation," *Administrative Science Quarterly* (December 1972): 455.

good or very bad (the right and left sides of the graph). These extremes are characterized by the leader having either a great deal of influence and power or hardly any influence and power over group members. People-oriented leaders, on the other hand, tend to be more effective in mixed situations where they have only moderate influence over the group.

How can these findings improve leadership effectiveness? The answer is found not so much in changing the leader's personality or training him or her to act in a different way but, rather, in *matching,* as Fiedler suggests, *the leader and the situation.* If the situation is very good or very bad, use a task-oriented leader. If the situation is mixed, use a people-oriented leader.

Fiedler's model has been questioned on empirical, methodological, and theoretical grounds (Grane et al., 1972; Korman, 1973). In spite of these criticisms, however, the Fiedler model continues as an important one in the development of the contingency approach to leadership effectiveness. Its greatest value is its attempt to deal simultaneously with (complex) situational factors and leadership style. This work helped to focus leadership research in a new direction.

Path–Goal Theory of Leadership

Other recent approaches to leadership are based on the path–goal theory and emphasize the expectancy model of motivation (House, 1971; House and Dessler, 1974). This theory integrates some of the earlier Ohio State studies using the dimensions of "consideration" and "initiating structure."

The path–goal theory holds that a leader's function is to define a path and clear any roadblocks so that subordinates can achieve their (group) goals. In other words, subordinates should be guided to do things that will increase their opportunity to obtain personal satisfaction. Thus, the best style is a function of both the subordinate and the task.

The path–goal receives its name from the fact that it is described in terms of path clarification, need satisfaction, and goal attainment. Initiating structure acts to "clarify the path," and consideration makes the path "easier to travel."

House's work has helped to explain some of the apparent contradictions of the Ohio State studies. The Ohio State group suggested that effective leaders would score high on both initiating structure (task orientation) and consideration (people orientation); yet there were exceptions. When do these exceptions occur? Based on his research, House concluded that task-oriented leaders are more effective when subordinates are working on loosely defined tasks. When tasks are routine or highly structured, however, people-oriented leaders tend to do better. In this situation explaining tasks in detail would be seen by employees as redundant and even insulting.

The path–goal theory proposes a correct way to lead lower-level subordinates. It is a relatively recent addition to leadership literature, and attempts to validate it have been generally positive. The theory helps to integrate the expectancy model of motivation with contingency leadership style. It encourages the leader to analyze the situation before determining the right amount of concern for tasks or people that will be required. Generally, the theory places a major emphasis on subordinate satisfaction and leader acceptance.

Leader-Participation Model

Victor Vroom and Philip Yetton (1973) proposed a more modern contingency model of leadership that centers around basic styles in the decision-making process. Their approach emphasizes leadership training. Since tasks have varying degrees of routine and nonroutine activities, they suggested that leadership behavior should reflect task structure. Researchers isolated eight situation factors, including the relative importance of the decision and the extent to which information is available to both the leader and his or her subordinates.

The model assumes that any one of five leadership styles may be chosen in an attempt to solve group problems. They include:

1. **Autocratic.**   You make the decision yourself using the information available.

2. The subordinates provide you with information, and then you make the decision.

3. **Consultative.**   You make the decision after consulting with your subordinates individually.

4. You make the decision after consulting with your subordinates collectively.

5. **Group.**   You share the decision with the group and obtain a consensus.

GREAT PERSON PROFILE

Thomas J. Watson, Jr. (1914-)

The electronic computer has revolutionized the American business scene. Today the name IBM is synonymous with the development of the computer. It was largely through the efforts of Thomas J. Watson, Jr., that IBM became the leader in the computer industry.

Before Watson assumed the presidency in 1952, IBM's sales were mostly in the area of tabulating machines. Watson realized that IBM was lagging behind in the computer industry. Therefore, he expanded the research and development departments to meet this need. He refused to depend on just one research team for innovations, but encouraged them to compete.

His first significant step as president was to replace his father's rather autocratic leadership style with a more *participative style*. This style provided the stimulating atmosphere within which ideas flourished. Employees were given greater responsibility and were recognized and rewarded for their achievements.

Watson is also proud of IBM's accomplishments in the area of employee relations. His concern for people resulted in IBM's long-standing no-layoff policy, as well as the fact

that IBM was among the first American companies to establish a weekly wage plan for blue-collar workers.

Perhaps Watson's most awesome accomplishment is the fact that IBM's stock value increased by billions of dollars during his tenure as president. Through reorganization, concern for people, and emphasis on innovation, Watson was able to push IBM to the forefront of a fast-growing industry.

These represent different degrees of participatory styles.

The model is *normative:* it provides a sequential set of rules that should be followed in determining the form and amount of participation in decision making under various situations.

Based on standards related to the quality of the decision, the time needed to arrive at a decision, and the acceptance of the decision by subordinates, the styles chosen by a leader will differ. Participative styles are used more when the quality of the decision is important, the acceptance of the subordinates is required, and time is not a constraint. Generally the Vroom and Yetton model emphasizes the need for increased participation of subordinates but suggests that it makes more sense to talk about autocratic and participative *situations* rather than *leaders*. This is an important difference from the Fiedler model, which emphasizes changing the situation to *match* the innate characteristics of the leader. The leader's style in Fiedler's model is assumed to be rather inflexible. Vroom and Yetton disagree; they assert that leaders (can and do) adjust their style to different situations. Who is right is a matter for more investigation.

Transactional Approach

A typical feature of leadership activities is that of a continuous **transactional process;** there is a dynamic relationship between the subordinates and the leader. An exchange relationship and subordinates *perceiving* and *evaluating* the leader in the context of situational demands are key features of the transactional model of leadership.

This leadership approach is a dynamic one in that it is very much concerned with change. Also, it provides the bases for dealing to a greater depth with some of the actualities of daily life, such as:

1. Leaders gain authority from those for whom they work.
2. Subordinates "consent" to engage in the process.
3. Leadership consists of a variety of tasks that require role differentiation.
4. Subordinates informally evaluate the leader.

The subordinates' perceptions of the leader's actions are central in the transactional approach. Subordinates have expectations about leaders and their contributions, and the work group operates as an interdependent system with inputs from members to produce desired outputs. Also, according to the theoretical framework, leadership is a mutual activity in which the leader is able to be influenced by followers as well as influencing them. This is usually left out by the traditional approaches to leadership.

Consequently, the term *transaction* indicates an active role by followers in an exchange relationship with the leader, including mutual influence. Ideally, this process helps to use human talents and physical resources for effective group functioning.

In a very simple transactional view, the leader directs communications to followers, to which they may react in various ways. The leader attempts to take account of the attitudes and motives of followers. They, in turn, evaluate the leaders with particular regard to responsiveness to their needs. Very important are the followers' perceptions of the leader's effectiveness and how they perceive and evaluate the leader's actions and intentions (Johns, 1978; Greene, 1979).

ADDITIONAL LEADERSHIP ISSUES

The Power of Leaders

Explicit in the formulation of Fred Fiedler is the idea that leaders have the "right" and presumably the ability to exercise power. The sociologist Etzioni has defined power as the ability of the leader to influence the subordinates' behavior. Based on this definition, Etzioni distinguishes between "position" and "personal" power. **Position power** is exerted by individuals who influence the behavior of other members simply because they occupy a certain position in the organization. On the other hand, those people who depend on their followers as a source of power are said to possess **personal power** (Etzioni, 1961).

Contrary to Etzioni's belief that position power is acquired by managers from the organizational office, some recent theorists believe that position power is a matter of the extent to which the manager wishes to delegate responsibility or authority to those individuals lower in the organizational hierarchy.

On the other hand, sources of personal power often come from lower organizational levels, since it represents the extent to which the subordinates are willing to follow their leaders. Hersey and Blanchard (1977) wrote, "Personal power . . . can be earned and it can be taken away." However, personal power does not necessarily reside *within* the leaders *per se* as charismatic power. Yet, it should be noted that most managers are able to control their amount of personal power in one way or another by treating their people appropriately.

Etzioni postulated that the most desirable situation for leaders is the possession of both position and personal power. Since this is a rather idealistic expectation, however, we should ask ourselves whether personal power is more important than position power, or vice versa. Although most of us would wish to conclude that personal power is at the heart of leadership effectiveness, we saw that Fiedler's contingency model and the other approaches that we discussed so far do not seem to confirm this layman's view of power. In other words, the desirability of position or personal power seems to reside in the specifics or "favorability" of the given situation.

Leadership Styles and Leadership Effectiveness

The behavior of leaders has been described traditionally by various leadership styles that they employ. These styles tend to capture the entire range of leader behavior, and, as a consequence, much leadership research has resulted in dozens of leadership style classifications. Tannenbaum and Schmidt (1973) classified the major leadership styles into two general categories. The first category contains those styles that aim at the satisfaction of *task-oriented* activities of which tight controls and close supervision are the fundamental ingredients. On the other hand, the second general category includes styles that are more *person oriented*. That is, the satisfaction of individual needs is of paramount importance in achieving organizational objectives. Limited direction and supervision, as well as a democratic climate, characterize the styles that fall in this general class.

The results of the studies conducted to determine whether task-oriented styles are more or less important than employee-oriented ones with regard to leadership effectiveness are inconclusive. The Michigan studies favored employee-centered approaches. Both general styles are important, however, and no one style is the panacea for every situation or problem. Tannenbaum and Schmidt make the implicit assumption that an effective leadership style tends to maximize the leader's contribution to group effectiveness by his using wisely all the available power sources of leaders. At present, we do not know exactly what leadership style is appropriate for each and every situation. Contingency research, however, has provided us with some useful insights (see our previous discussion of Fiedler and other contingency analysts).

How can leaders choose an effective leadership style? The first critical task of the leader is to uncover the major factors that underlie the specific situation. Second, leaders should be flexible with regard to their leadership style, and they should not be "trapped" by their past styles when overwhelmed by the novelty of a new situation. Leadership styles that are effective in one situation may be obsolete or even result in adverse effects in another. Furthermore, leaders should attempt to carefully identify *where* their power comes from as well as the specific areas where they can best utilize their skills and abilities so that they contribute to their group's effectiveness. Finally, rapid sociocultural changes require leaders to study their jobs carefully and to be very skeptical when they employ or experiment with a particular leadership style.

Studies made some years ago dispel the idea of a single best leadership style. After reviewing more than 25 relevant studies that investigated the relationship between task and relationship dimensions and various measures of effectiveness, Korman (1966) concluded that:

> Despite the fact that "consideration" and "initiating structure" have become almost bywords in American industrial psychology, it seems apparent that very little is now known as to how these variables may predict work group performance and the conditions which affect such predictions. At the current time, we cannot even say whether they have any predictive significance at all.

Various other researchers have also shown that different situations require different leadership styles. We should therefore conclude that there is no single, general leadership style that is effective in each and every possible situation.

Leadership Research and Individual Career Development

Obviously, the different leadership ideas and findings, however inconclusive, have a number of practical implications for the leader–manager who wishes to better his leadership style and effectiveness and his group's satisfaction and potentially their productivity as well. How can the manager apply these notions to his or her personal career effectively?

In terms of one's own career planning, the emphasis on understanding others' views is paramount in realizing there exists a two-way street between the workers and the leader–manager in which the concerns of one directly affect the other. By understanding the makeup of leadership, one can better appreciate the demands of a leader in any context, no matter what one's position in the organization. Whether it be at home or at work or with friends, there exists a leadership situation. An empathetic nature, nurtured with a compassionate concern for the ideals and feelings of others, will yield a better grasp of one's own situation.

Knowledge of the concepts of leadership enables an individual to better self-assess needs and specifics and makes it easier to determine possible areas for strengthening. Strengthening skills and understandings of leadership can help improve social relationships as well as one's relationships and opportunities in a more formal work context.

Leadership thinking is situationally oriented. Knowledge and the understanding of oneself facilitate the understanding and knowledge of others. A leader must tune in to the fact that people learn in so many different ways and at such different speeds. The approach to any given situation must include the need to know how one learns so that the leader can pick and choose those elements of learning style that best suit the makeup of the individual or the person with whom he or she is working.

Leadership thinking helps one to apply and appreciate the fact that a leader can be a career facilitator in the advancement of others. He or she can act as a catalyst in the course of counseling or serve in an important role of sounding board or mentor. With an understanding and empathetic approach, a leader can advance his or her own career as well as the careers and aspirations of others.

Leadership in Perspective

It has been clear throughout our discussion that there is no single dimension to the study of leadership. All leaders should therefore attempt to understand the totality of leadership components such as their personal characteristics, organizational characteristics, the attitudes and needs of their followers, and the sociopolitical context in which both their group and their company operate. He or she needs to bear in mind that his or her group's output is *not* entirely a function of his or her own skills and abilities; leaders may have responsibility for activities over which they may have little control or influence.

With regard to the personal traits of leaders we saw that emotional stability, broadness of interests and activities, high achievement, motivational drive, and an empathetic understanding of the needs and worth of each and every employee may be greatly related to the leader's effectiveness and success. Furthermore, certain situational variables such as previous experience with the job, the kind of job (assigned responsibilities) the leader has, the psychological climate (satisfactions or frustrations), group or individual expectations and the size of the group, the degree to which group–member cooperation is needed, the expectations of the leader's "boss," and the community in which the organization operates often affect the leader's success. Thus the leader's subordinates, boss, and job/work, all form a first level of influencing factors. Organizational climate forms a second layer, and aspects of the external environment establish an additional set of factors potentially influencing the leadership expertise "dictated" by the situation (see Exhibit 9-4).

Fiedler's findings can also provide leaders with some useful guidelines. Leaders should be highly directive and relatively impersonal where situational conditions make it either very easy or very difficult for them to manage the group. However, the leader should be much more permissive and considerate where conditions are only *moderately* favorable for him. Three major factors describe the

Exhibit 9-4 Situational Factors in Leadership Approaches

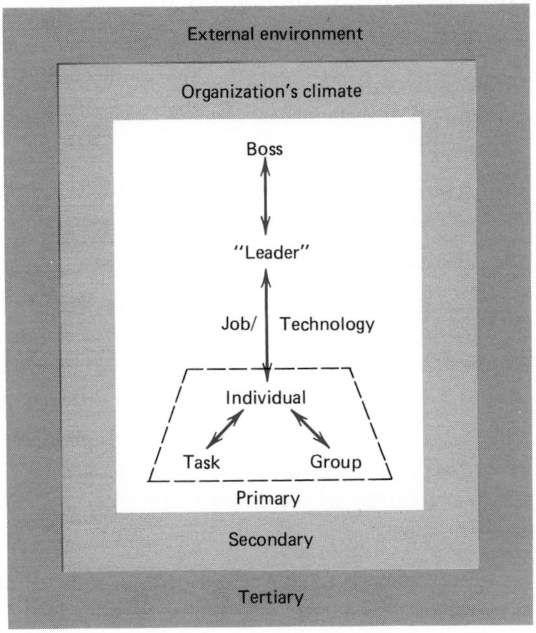

favorability of the situation. These were found to be leader–member relations (the more favorable they are, the more the leader is respected by the group), task structure (the more clearly defined the original task is, the better off the leader), and, finally, position power.

Vroom and Yetton's model emphasized placing greater reliance on subordinate participation and thus somewhat less dependence on the leader being so versatile. However, the leader needs to have confidence in his personal judgment, the model postulates, with regard to the requirement of the specific situation.

The path–goal hypothesis states that the leader should be primarily concerned about defining a path along which the followers achieve both the organization's and the group's goals. The leader needs to increase the number and kinds of personal payoffs for group members in order to motivate his or her subordinates and achieve their work goals. At the same time, he or she must make the paths that lead to these payoffs very clear to their subordinates. Added to these responsibilities, the leader also attempts to keep in mind the external pressures imposed upon the group members.

Finally, the transactional model warns leaders that they should constantly be aware of their subordinates' perceptions of them, since subordinates have certain expectations about leaders and their contributions to the task group. The leader influences his or her followers. They, in turn, influence him or her. In general, in an attempt to advance his or her career and increase satisfaction and group effectiveness each leader should try to:

1. Uncover the factors that underlie the specific situation.
2. Delineate and understand his or her personal skills, abilities, and needs. The latter directly affect the satisfactions derived from one "playing" the leadership role.
3. Identify his or her sources of power and the specific areas where he or she can best utilize his or her skills and abilities.
4. Be flexible with regard to leadership style considering the multiplicity of the existing situations and the rapid sociocultural changes taking place.
5. Understand the consequences of future work changes on situational needs and the opportunities for career fulfillment through his or her work.
6. Regularly review his or her job and be very skeptical (but sincere and spontaneous) when experimenting with or employing a leadership style.

To achieve some of these requirements, leaders would be helped by various self-assessment instruments. Hersey and Blanchard, for example, developed the *Leader Effectiveness and Adaptability Description* (LEAD), which was specifically prepared to deal with three aspects of leader behavior: style, style range, and style adaptability.

LEAD measures the leader's self-perception of how one views oneself as a leader. Therefore, *if* the individual's self-perceptions match the others' perceptions of himself or herself, LEAD may prove to be valuable in establishing a "baseline" against which the individual can start making adjustments to situational needs.

It has been found that managers at different levels of the organizational hierarchy have different LEAD profiles. This implies that if leaders know the specific style *required* by each stage in the organizational structure they may more effectively engage in it and develop it. It has been found that many *effective top managers* tend to engage in more "participating" and "delegating" behavior rather than "telling" and "selling," possibly because as such managers go upward in the hierarchy, the subordinates reporting to them have acquired a higher level of task-relevant maturity.

Training and Development of Lenders

Hersey and Blanchard (1977) have explained that it is difficult to expect quick changes in leadership style because individual change depends on getting feedback from previous experiences (see Exhibit 9-5).

Exhibit 9-5 Feedback Model for Changing Leader Style

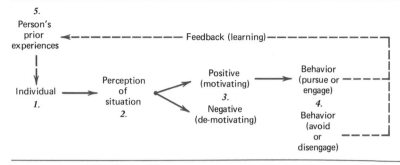

As the feedback loop indicates, when a person perceives a situation (item No. 2, Exhibit 9-5) to be motivating (item No. 3) and behaves (item No. 4) accordingly, that specific behavioral pattern becomes a new input to that individual's previous experiences (item No. 5). Most psychologists would agree that the earlier in life this "motivating" behavioral input takes place, the greater its impact will be on future behavior. Furthermore, the more often this behavior is reinforced (for example, by rewards), the more difficult it is to change it. The implication is that it takes much longer to change people's behavior when it is entrenched in routine ways of doing things. The ability to change behavior patterns may frequently become a matter of the amount of resources an organization can afford and is willing to commit to leadership development.

It has also been observed by behavioral researchers that changing knowledge and skills is much easier than changing deeply seated beliefs or behavioral patterns. To the extent that expectations are built on knowledge and skills, behavioral changes involving these factors are brought about more quickly than where attitudes and beliefs are involved. Also, once the *subordinates understand* the leader's style for the particular situation, they can then adjust their expectations to this style more easily. The emphasis is that adjustments can take place in various aspects of the situation and thereby decrease the sole dependency on flexibility of the leader's style.

Leadership-Situational Alternatives

Fiedler has suggested that instead of concentrating on changing various leadership styles, we could teach the person to understand the situational variables in the presence of which he can perform best and to modify the situation somewhat to adapt to his personal leadership style. This is the philosophy of "organizational" engineering. Organizational engineering is based on the assumption that changing one's personality is a much more tedious task than changing the work environment. A better strategy would be to *combine both* changes in leadership styles with changes in the leader's situational variables rather than to rely on one or the other tactic.

Rensis Likert observed that what a manager expects of his or her subordinates and the particular way in which they are treated determines to a great extent their career progress, aspiration, and subsequent performance. Other researchers have found that superior managers are characterized by their ability to create expectations of higher performance that, in turn, the subordinates fulfill. The implication is that subordinates learn what they are expected to do from their supervisors. A leadership style may thus develop in which high expectations may result in high performance, which further strengthens these high expectations and leads to even higher productivity.

Research tends to support the contention that the criteria for the performance of a person or group should be mutually discussed and decided with the leader. For example, when managers and employees discuss thoroughly various technological changes that are expected, productivity may increase substantially with a corresponding decrease in resistance to change.

SUMMARY

Leadership can be defined as the ability to exert influence on individuals or groups in order to achieve specified organizational goals and objectives. The various functions of a manager include organizing, directing, and coordinating efforts. Leadership may be a critical aspect of managerial activity and involves defining the situation, setting goals, and maintaining the group. Leadership is not a specific individual property but rather a complex relationship among variables. These include the leader's characteristics, the organizational features, the followers' attitudes and needs, and the social, political, and economic environment.

Approaches like the Leader Effectiveness and Adaptability Description (LEAD) instrument exist that permit self-assessment of aspects of one's leadership style. Thus, leaders and managers can further develop their personal leadership skills and abilities.

Researchers have asked: what traits make a leader effective and enable him to get his group to perform well? A leader's effectiveness can be evaluated on the type of personal relationship between the leader and other group members, and the extent to which the leader is businesslike and task oriented. Fiedler found that to be effective the official leader uses approaches appropriate to the favorableness of the situation. For example, the leader's style is highly directive and relatively impersonal when conditions are such that it is either very easy or very difficult for him or her to manage the group.

In general, combining the more traditional approaches with situational variables seems to bring about a more realistic basis for leadership. Furthermore, the character of the work, the followers' needs and limitations, and the specific situation must all be considered in adapting a leadership style. Viewing leadership as a strategy rather than as a specific kind of behavior implies that leaders can be better trained to improve their technical and people-related skills.

Questions for Study and Discussion

1. What is meant by the terms "leader" and "leadership"?
2. On the basis of the various leadership approaches discussed, how do people become leaders?
3. What are the implications of leadership research findings for managers?
4. Compare and contrast the major findings of the Michigan and Ohio State leadership studies.
5. Discuss the limitations of the trait approach to leadership. Compare it to the situational theory of leadership.
6. Compare and contrast the various Contingency Models to Leadership Effectiveness.
7. How do leaders acquire their power?
8. In what ways are various leadership styles related to leadership effectiveness?
9. It has been said that training and developing leaders is a challenging and difficult task. Comment on this.
10. What are the personal career consequences of various leadership notions?

CASE: THE BRIGHT IDEA

It's us or them! You know I've always leveled with you. As your boss, I've always taken care of you. Remember when you didn't listen to me and messed up the Atlanta job? I covered for you, didn't I? I want this operation to be a family. Now, on your idea about changes in the record-keeping procedures, let's not make any waves. If changes are needed, my bosses will tell me, and then I'll assign you to the job. Anyway, I never told you to do that work. What *haven't* you been working on while you have been studying this?

Dana White was stunned. She had come to Fred Singer with the best idea she had ever developed. It would revolutionize the record keeping in the office and would save money, too. Dana liked Fred, and Fred had always looked after Dana as he did the rest of the staff. But Dana figured recommending this new procedure was her best chance of being recognized by top management. She could not understand why Fred would stand in her way.

Questions

1. What leadership style is being displayed by Fred Singer?
2. Which leadership theory best explains this particular situation? Why?
3. If you were Dana, what would you do next?
4. If you choose to go over Fred's head with your idea, what would you expect Fred's reaction to be?

CASE: ALBERTO MARTINEZ

Alberto Martinez, the new supervisor of the Records and Collections Department, had just spoken with Jack Halley, the division superintendent of Alberto's area. As a new supervisor, Alberto was getting acquainted with his own department's and with the division's operation. Since he would begin his supervisory duties the following Monday, Alberto was particularly concerned that the department's former supervisor, Harry Lanson, resigned the position in apparent frustration. Supposedly, he was unable to get along with Grace Arnold, a senior employee in the department. Lanson claimed that Grace had "turned the other employees against me." Since Arnold was the most senior employee in the division and possessed the greatest knowledge of the department's work, it was known that most of the other employees in the department looked to her for guidance. When asked about the impact of Arnold on the department, Jack Halley had assured Alberto that he had "full authority to get the job done." But as Alberto left Halley's office, he wondered if that were really the case.

Questions

1. Analyze the type of power that Grace Arnold apparently has.
2. As Alberto takes on the job of supervisor, what is his source of power?

3. How might Alberto enlarge his power sources? Could Grace be involved? Explain.

References

Abdel, Halim Ahmed, "Personality and Task Moderators of Subordinate Responses to Perceived Leader Behavior, *Human Relations,* **34**(1) (January 1981): 73–88.

Barnard, Chester I., *The Function of the Executive.* Cambridge, Mass.: The Harvard University Press (1938).

Bass, B. M., D. L. Farrow, E. R. Valenzi, and R. J. Solomon, "Management Styles Associated with Organizational, Task, Personal and Interpersonal Contingencies," *Journal of Applied Psychology,* **60** (1975): 720–729.

Blake, Robert, and Jane Mouton, "What's New with the Grid?" *Training and Development Journal,* **32**(5) (May 1978): 3–8.

Etzioni, Amitai, *A Comparative Analysis of Complex Organizations.* New York: Free Press (1961).

Evans, M. C., "Extensions of a Path–Goal Theory of Motivation," *Journal of Applied Psychology,* **59** (1974): 172–178.

Fiedler, Fred E., *A Theory of Leadership Effectiveness.* New York: McGraw-Hill (1967).

Fiedler, Fred E., "Engineer the Job to Fit the Man," *Harvard Business Review,* **43**(5) (September/October 1965): 115–122.

Gibb, Cecil, "Leadership" in *Handbook of Social Psychology.* Gardner Lindzey and Elliot Aronson (ed.). Reading, Mass.: Addison-Wesley (1969).

Greene, C. N., "Questions of Causation in the Path–Goal Theory of Leadership," *Academy of Management Journal,* **22**(2) (March 1979): 22–41.

Griffin, Ricky W., "Relationships Among Individual, Task Design, Leader Behavior Variables," *Academy of Management Journal,* **23**(4) (December 1980): 665–683.

Hersey, Paul, and Ken Blanchard, *Management of Organizational Behavior: Utilizing Human Resources.* 1st ed. Newark, New Jersey: Prentice-Hall (1977).

House, Robert J., "A Path–Goal Theory of Leader Effectiveness," *Administrative Science Quarterly,* **16** (1971): 321–338.

House, Robert J., and Gary Dessler, "The Path–Goal Theory of Leadership: Some Post-Hoc and A Priori Tests," in *Contingency Approaches to Leadership.* James G. Hunt and Lars Larson (ed.). Carbondale, Ill.: Southern Illinois University Press (1974): 29–55.

Johns, G., "Task Moderators of the Relationships Between Leadership Style and Subordinate Responses," *Academy of Management Journal,* **21** (1978): 319–325.

Kahn, Robert, and Daniel Katz, "Leadership Practices in Relation to Productivity and Morale," in *Group Dynamics: Research and Theory.* D. Cartwright and A. Zander (ed.). Elmsford, New York: Row Peterson (1960).

Kerr, Chester A. et al., "Toward a Contingency Theory of Leadership Based

Upon the Consideration and Initiating Structure Literature," *Organizational Behavior and Human Performance,* (August 1974): 62–82.

Korman, Abraham K., "Consideration, Initiating Structure and Organizational Criteria: A Review," *Personnel Psychology,* **19**(4) (Winter 1966): 349–361.

Latona, Joseph, "Leadership and Managerial Effectiveness: An Exercise in Self-Analysis," *Supervisory Management,* **23**(12) (December 1978): 18–24.

Miner, Frederick C., Jr., "A Comparative Analysis of Three Diverse Group Decision Making Approaches," *Academy of Management Journal,* **22**(2) (March 1979): 81–93.

Mintzberg, Henry, "The Manager's Job: Folklore and Fact," *Harvard Business Review,* **53**(4) (July/August 1975): 49–61.

Noda, Mitz, "The Japanese Way," *Executive,* **6**(3) (Summer 1980): 22–25.

Schriesheim, Chester et al., "Leadership Theory: Some Implications for Managers," *MSU Business Topics,* **26** (Summer 1978): 38–44.

Stogdill, Ralph, *Handbook of Leadership.* New York: The Free Press (1974).

Tannenbaum, R., and W. H. Schmidt, "How to Choose a Leadership Pattern," *Harvard Business Review* (May-June 1973): 162–180.

Teas, Kenneth, and James Horrell, "Salespeople Satisfaction and Performance Feedback," *Industrial Marketing Management,* **10**(1) (February 1981): 49–57.

Vroom, Victor H., "Decision-Making and the Leadership Process," *Journal of Contemporary Business,* **3**(4) (1974): 47–64.

Vroom, Victor H., and P. W. Yetton, *Leadership and Decision-Making.* Pittsburgh: University of Pittsburgh Press (1973).

Zaleznik, Abraham, "Managers and Leaders: Are They Different?" *Harvard Business Review* (May-June 1977): 67–78.

CHAPTER 10

INFORMAL GROUPS

KEY
QUESTIONS
ADDRESSED
IN CHAPTER

1. What role does the informal group play in individual job satisfaction and organizational performance?
2. In what way do the structure and processes of the informal group parallel those of the formal organization?
3. In what way do an individual's career thinking and sense of success reflect interactions within the informal group?
4. How do groups emerge?
5. Why do individuals join groups?
6. What practical strategies should a supervisor or manager consider in fostering and dealing with the informal organization?

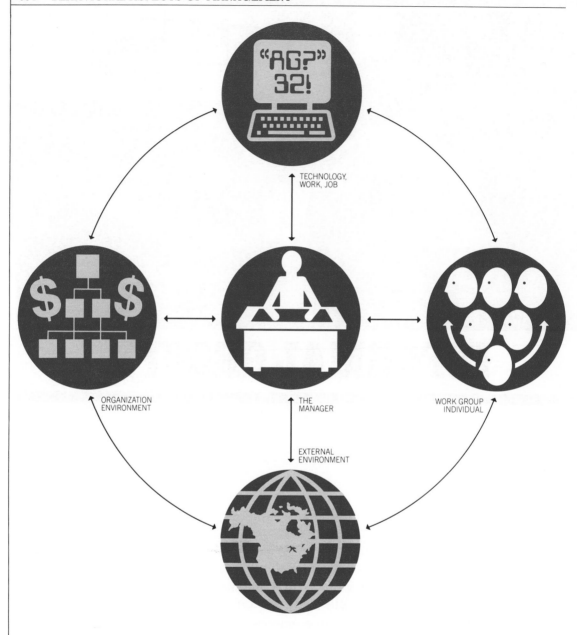

The manager's work–life spaces

We work as a team. I hand him the clubs, and he makes the shots.

Caddy for Arnold Palmer,
commenting on his four Masters victories

THE CHAPTER IN BRIEF

Groups exist at all levels within organizations. Many of these groups are formally designated by organizations, for example, departments, committees, and task forces. These formally designated groups are discussed in Chapter 2. Other groups evolve naturally, or informally, largely in response to the social or work-related needs of people in the work environment. The existence of these informal groups can have a positive, neutral, or, to the chagrin of many managers, negative impact on organizational performance.

By **informal group** we refer to collections of two or more people who band together on the basis of common interests, concerns, or even problems. Friendships or simply cordial relationships may result from this gathering together of individuals for mutual self-interest and support. Although these informal group relationships fall outside those that are formally prescribed by work or organizational responsibilities, there are similarities with the formal structure. They have their own goals and their own leaders, as well as an authority hierarchy and information system. In addition, groups develop their own norms of behavior and well-defined roles that serve as guides to a member's behavior so that group goals are achieved. These goals may or may not be similar to those of the organization.

Although similarities exist between informal and formal groups, it is clear that major differences also exist. Informal groups exist to satisfy the behavioral and work needs of their members, whereas the formal groups exist to satisfy the needs of stockholders and customers by achieving organizational objectives. This difference in focus between formal and informal groups is sketched in Exhibit 10-1. Informal groups are also the basis for much organizational change, for an enterprise *is* people. What it accomplishes and how well it accomplishes its goals are affected importantly by how it is perceived by its members. Organization success depends on the successful integration of informal *and* formal groups and activities. This integration rests largely on the manager, who must work with the informal group and its leader to try to influence them in the direction of organizational goals.

That groups can strongly influence the behavior and, thus, the performance of their members is quite clear. Alcoholics Anonymous is perhaps the most successful example of how group support has helped change the lives of countless individuals. In fact, its success

Exhibit 10-1 Differences between Formal and Informal Groups in Focus

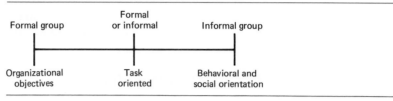

has led to numerous spin-offs that have largely copied its format in helping other members of society deal with problems like drugs, child abuse, and overeating. In fact, managers may have much to learn from what has been discovered by informal groups about the internal organization of task groups, allocation of work, methods, and so on.

Much modern study in management has turned toward the redesign of the job ("job enrichment") as an important source of individual satisfaction and thereby improved performance for the organization. (This is discussed in Chapter 8.) But what has often been forgotten is the fact that certain *pre*conditions must be met if job enrichment, or for that matter supervisory leadership approaches and even organizational rewards, is to be successful! One of the central preconditions is that of the individual's acceptance by and cordial involvement with other organization members. "No man is an island unto himself." He or she needs encouragement, "positive strokes," recognition, and periodic interaction with associates to reap the potential benefits of various motivational or work-related strategies. This is an extremely strong statement. But it is probably realistic in its recognition of the potency of informal groups and the central role they play in the human experience and bottom-line performance. For organization members (and the reader!) involvement with informal groups and acceptance by their members help to fulfill their social needs and may constitute a major reason for remaining in an organization and the main source of satisfaction derived by the individual. Therefore, knowledge of how and why informal groups form is important for anyone interested in understanding the management process and means of better relating to one's work associates. These insights can be used in a positive way by the manager to encourage informal group formation or to assist in the maintenance of various group processes.

These brief notes sound the themes of this chapter, the purpose is to explore the role, activities, and relationships of informal groups to the individual member and to performance. Initially, however, we discuss the general background of research into groups, beginning with the now famous Hawthorne studies of the 1920s. We then introduce the student to group terminology. The role that groups play in bringing about organizational change and various organizational development (OD) techniques is then explored. Finally, the implications that groups have for your career are developed.

Life Spaces and the Informal Group

To this point we have discussed briefly how the existence of informal groups can affect individual behavior and, in turn, the performance of the formal work group to which the individual belongs.

The "organizational space" described in Chapters 2 and 6 contains the factors making up the rewards, procedures, activities, and formal structure of the organization. Even the most casual observer would admit that many different friendships exist in the organization. Yet it is not so obvious how the coffee group, the "brown-bag" group, or the "electronic chess" group forms. It is largely the formal structure relationships that form the initial basis upon which informal groups develop.

By virtue of his or her position in the formal organization, the manager is in the center of things. He or she is the formally designated leader and consequently directs, coordinates, and controls the work group. Communication flows largely from the manager and usually concerns technological or work-related information.

The technology or work space is also relevant because the performance and servicing of the work system depend on the contribution of workers in their work-assigned roles. But, of course, many of these same workers are also members of the coffee or brown bag group. Thus, people play dual roles that, on the one hand, are dictated by work necessities, and, on the other, are dictated by informal processes. If these roles are conflicting, they can add to the stress felt by worker and manager alike.

Managers, therefore, should be aware of the needs and norms of behavior of existing informal groups and should take these into account when carrying out their duties. This suggests that the manager play the role of a facilitator so that group and individual needs are met as well as organizational performance objectives.

BACKGROUND

Key Developments of Informal Group Research
Historical Roots: The Hawthorne Study

Small-group research received its impetus from the pioneering work done at the **Hawthorne Works** of the **Western Electric Company** by Elton Mayo and Fritz Roethlisberger (discussed in Chapter 1). A small isolated work group of six women "volunteered" to assemble relays for telephone equipment in a room called the Relay Assembly Test Room. Working conditions and tasks were identical to those for workers in the main department (Roethlisberger and Dickson, 1939).

The women did not have a supervisor in the usual sense, but merely a "test room observer." Besides keeping piece parts moving into the room and finished relays out, the observer simply kept records on items such as product quality, room temperatures, and humidity, as well as a work log. These records eventually provided some of the most significant information of the entire study regarding the behavior of the women and their gradual growth into a coheseive group.

The experimental concept behind a test room of this sort was to make a series of changes in the conditions faced by the test group and then observe the effects on work behavior and attitudes. Many changes were made during the five-year period; in each case, however, the women were consulted in advance, and their suggestions were asked for. In summary, these changes were as follows. The six women became their own group for purposes of compensation; that is, a group piecework basis was used instead of the group's work being lumped in with the large, main assembly department. Twice-a-day rest pauses of 5 minutes each were (first) introduced and were then later extended to two daily pauses of 10 minutes each. Rests were next increased to six 5-minute pauses per day, then back to two pauses per day, then to two pauses accompanied by light snacks. The *workday* was shortened by $\frac{1}{2}$ hour and later by a full hour. Finally, the *workweek* was reduced from $5\frac{1}{2}$ days to 5.

During this lengthy period, *production in general went steadily up*. Then, with the consent of the women, conditions in force at the beginning were reinstated, that is, no rest pauses or snacks and a return to full workdays and weeks. *Output still went up*. In fact, it continued to rise until it reached a plateau (and apparently the physical limits of the women), which was maintained until the test was ended early in 1933.

The work log kept of test room activities revealed important influences on the behavior of the women. They liked to work in the test room. It was described as "fun" compared to their previous work experiences. They appreciated not being supervised, and could converse freely, something that was discouraged in the regular department. The test room was frequented by company "big shots," thus the women felt they were part of something important.

The women developed close friendship ties that carried over to off-the-job situations. On the job, when one woman was having a "down day" her co-workers would "carry" her. Altogether, results from the Relay Assembly Test Room dramatized the effects of social relations within a work group on the attitudes and productivity of that group. However, the several special aspects of the test room situation need to be kept in mind when attempting to draw conclusions from the research results.

Large-Scale Employer Interviewing. The next phase of employee research initiated at Hawthorne Works was a very ambitious program of employee interviewing. Overall, this program included some 21,000 interviews of employees over a $2\frac{1}{2}$-year period and reached some very important conclusions, which were considered novel in the 1930s.

- Morale improves when employees are allowed to "blow off steam."
- Employee complaints are frequently not objective statements of fact but, rather, symptoms of other problems.
- Job satisfaction is influenced by how an employee evaluates his social status relative to his co-workers and others.
- On-the-job behavior is influenced by happenings off the job.

Study of Male Work Group: The Bank Wiring Experiment. Another phase of research at Hawthorne was a $6\frac{1}{2}$-month-long study of a 14-man work group and their supervisor. This study was decided upon after analyses of the interviews revealed how often employees remarked about the strong influence exerted by on-the-job social groups. A setting was created in which the group members to be observed were isolated from their regular department. Researchers would thus be able to observe the growth of social ties among the workers.

The 14 volunteers were selected from a large department where mechanical switches were wired into banks for use in telephone equipment. They were assigned to a special research room called the Bank Wiring Observation Room, in which care was taken to duplicate the large department in all respects. The group was supervised by a "group chief," the lowest level of supervisor in terms of formal authority, and the members were compensated in a group piece-rate system.

Two members of the research team became part of the Bank Wiring Room. One was an observer, who was to keep records both of work performance and of employee behavior, and the other was an interviewer. As in the Relay Assembly Test Room, the observer's log book came to provide the most important information. It documented how the men followed uniform behavioral patterns that deviated from those set by the organization and how the men formed social ties on the job. They actually formed into two subgroups, or "cliques." There was documentation also of group "codes," or norms, including such items as the informal setting of output levels. That is, the group defined such things as how much output is "enough," how much is "too much," who is alright to trade jobs with, who is expected to help a fellow worker out and why, how the group protects its own by not "squealing" to the supervisor, and other behaviors indicative of intrawork-group social controls. From this standpoint, what was learned from the Bank Wiring Observation Room still has general applicability to what goes on in a wide variety of work groups in all sorts of organizations.

Overall Results.   Major conclusions from the various phases of the research work at Western Electric's Hawthorne plant included the following.

1. The level of production is established largely on the basis of social norms, not by the physical capacities of workers or physical conditions (setting aside technological considerations).
2. Social and psychological rewards, rather than money, can significantly affect the behavior of employees and put limitations on the motivating effects of incentive wage plans.
3. Frequently, employees do not act as individuals but as members of groups.
4. A primary reason for group formation was to resist changes introduced by management.
5. Leadership, both formal, as appointed by management, and informal, as arrived at by consensus among co-workers, plays roles in the setting of social norms and in their enforcement.
6. Building high morale results from open, systematic communication between levels of an organization that involves employees in decisions. This is especially the case in decisions that directly affect them and management practices that take a "democratic" approach to the work force. People feel better when they are given a chance to discuss a problem, even when the trouble is not corrected.

Criticisms of the Hawthorne Research.   In spite of their impact on management thought, the Hawthorne studies have been subjected to various criticisms (Landsberger, 1958; Carey, 1967; Shephard, 1971), largely regarding the research design. Temporary favorable results may occur when special attention of experimenters is given to workers with regard to their sentiments and motives. The biasing of results by the observers' personal involvement in the experiment is referred to as the **"Hawthorne effect."**

The method of research and the small sample upon which major conclusions were based were not statistically appropriate. Much of the research employed relatively unsophisticated design concepts by today's standards and related to only a small part of organizational life.

The premises on which the research was conducted were unrealistic. For example, one assumption was that organizational members exist in such a state of confusion that they revert to the group for solidarity.

Although the Hawthorne studies have some limitations and may be bounded by overzealous humanitarian values, they have had an enduring impact on management thought. At the time of the experiments, more than 40 years ago, a new direction to management was undertaken. Referred to as the "human relations movement," this movement stimulated research into the behavioral sciences that has provided new insights into human behavior.

Management Implications. In general, these findings indicate that modern business organizations should be viewed as both social and economic institutions. They point out that through informal groups individuals can often increase their authority and autonomy over the work situation while reducing their dependence upon the formal organizational structure. In addition, informal groups can often increase the solidarity of employees (this is called **cohesiveness**) and restrict competition between individuals that could work against the goals of the organization. Through a better understanding of the informal status hierarchy and social relationships of these groups, possible reactions to changes in working conditions, wages, job requirements, and hours of work can be predicted by management with greater accuracy.

Implications for Your Career

The following situation involving Hank Webster is typical of the effects that informal groups can have on individuals. At school in shop classes Hank was a whiz with a lathe—fast and accurate. But on the job it's a different story. He is still accurate, but he works at about half the pace he can consistently attain in his home workshop. Why is this so?

After his first few days on the job, a couple of workers took him aside and "wised him up." "There's no sense in killing yourself, kid. A fair day's work around here, for your job, is 40 to 45 pieces an hour. If you keep producing 100 pieces, the supervisor's going to expect that from us. They may even raise the standard on us, and you know what that means! We won't have a chance to make any incentive pay; we'll just be working harder to make the same money. And next thing you know they'll be laying someone off because they don't need so many of us. That someone could be you."

That was the essence of their message. And because Hank was eager to be accepted by his co-workers, he not only got the message—he took it very much to heart. Over the past two years, Hank's production has deviated very little in either direction from the norm set by the informal group.

Several things may strike you about this true-to-life situation. First, in conforming to the standards of the informal organization, Hank is in conflict with his own value system. Second, his behavior also conflicts with the norms of the formal organization—obviously, management wants higher production. Evidently, the informal group can set up norms that motivate employees, on occasion, to behave in ways that contradict both their own value systems and the company goals. The reasons that informal groups are formed by employees are varied and powerful.

When you are recruited by an organization, there is really little opportunity to know or understand the nature of informal group structure. Unless you had a friend there previously, you probably will not know anyone in the organization. However, after employment, your initial work assignment sets in motion a chain of events that are likely to affect greatly your sense of job-related satisfaction, notion of career progress, ability to resolve conflicts, level of performance, and even whether you want to stay a member of the organization!

Unfortunately, job assignments reflect very little by way of social or group concerns—the main emphasis is usually work responsibility and performance. But the ability of the individual to find a satisfying social experience within group processes affects their performance in

(Copyright © 1976 by NEA, Inc.)

ways already suggested. Consequently, whether you "hit it off" with the people you contact in your work experience is important. In most situations people uncover common areas of interest. Mutual dependencies exist because of work, and acquaintanceships or even friendships grow. Yet it is important to realize that if it is hard for you to develop such relationships—after a reasonable length of time—another department member or even the supervisor can be a facilitator in this process.

From a career viewpoint it is important to realize what is happening to you or perhaps what ought to be happening as you get to know others. Over time, there is a strengthening of individual (informal) ties, and cohesion grows. If the group is a good one, you gain a sense of relaxation or belonging due to your acceptance by others besides your supervisor.

As you move into the activities and influence of the group, your sense of accomplishment will be more frequently responsive to the cues of your group. What is good professional progress? What is a good promotion? What skills should you be acquiring? All of these questions and many more come to be affected increasingly by what other group members view as good or bad, desirable or undesirable.

Group members also represent an important source of information regarding career opportunities elsewhere. They are thereby able to extend an individual's knowledge of events or opportunities relevant to his or her career. Also, group members can serve as a sounding board for your career ideas—as they get to know you—and present other sides of you with which you are unfamiliar but that may prove quite useful to you.

An Example

Carlos and Henry work together in the field office of an insurance agency. Although both have their own territories, they meet at sales meetings, occasionally at the office, and at the quarterly regional meetings. After meeting casually for about six months, Henry asks Carlos if he would like to drive together to the upcoming regional meeting. Carlos is happy to have someone to talk to. In subsequent months, they have some occasional meetings together for coffee, and, a little later, the families of both join them for dinner out to get further acquainted. Thus, over a rather extended time period, a relationship emerges beyond simply work concerns.

But this relationship goes beyond only social purposes. For example, Carlos hears that the company is going to revise its incentive system and advises Henry to get his policies processed as quickly as possible. In turn, Carlos has been trying to "sell" a large account but has not been able to write the policy. He does not want to discuss the problem with the field supervisor, because it may make him look bad.

So he goes to Henry, they talk about the situation, and Carlos gets several ideas on how to approach the account. As they become successful, other salesmen may also desire to become part of the group.

Informal Group Terminology and Features

Over the years researchers of informal groups have developed a basic language to describe the formation and activities that greatly facilitates understanding and communication of meaningful ideas. A summary list of these terms are presented in Exhibit 10-2 and are briefly described in this section.

Structure refers to the network or system of relationships and the pecking order that grows and then solidifies group membership. Thus, structure expresses memberships and hierarchy. It may also imply the "responsibilities" or activities "assigned" to each member

Exhibit 10-2 Group Features and Terms: Summary

Terms	Work Concept
Structure	The number and characteristics of the members of the group
Cohesion	The strength with which individual members are attracted to establish or maintain membership
Sentiments	The feeling, sense of comradeship or likings of one member for another
Status	The relative level of individual prestige within the group based on expertise, power, and the like or some combination of these
Leadership	The willingness of group members to accept the influence, advice, or direction of another (the leader—one who guides, inspires, or motivates group members)
Exchange (intragroup)	The reciprocal relations among group members so that each has the sense of some type of balance between the "gives" and "takes"
Norms of behavior	Informal guides or rules that affect conduct; developments viewed as valued ones; by "acceptable" and "unacceptable" actions of group members
Roles	The sum total of expected behaviors that make up each of the parts played by a group member, for example, work role, friendship role, role in the group

in order to stay a member and "perform" in an acceptable way. Carlos and Henry in the above example have similar responsibilities of sharing work-related information. Terms and concepts have been used here that are similar to those used in the chapter on structure because there is much similarity between these notions.

Cohesion refers to the strength of the bonds that exist between group members. In other words, how strong are the forces or considerations that keep Carlos and Henry interacting for mutual benefit? The stronger the bonds are, the higher is the value of group membership, the greater are the costs of losing membership, and the greater is the influence of group members on each other.

A manager should try to strengthen these bonds to the extent that they would support work flow or help various members work out problems or situations that are best not confronted alone. For example, members can be especially supportive to each other in getting through difficult situations like company layoffs or work system changes, or even difficult economic or personal circumstances (inflation, illness).

Sentiments reflect the feelings that each member expresses to the others in terms of liking, respect, cordiality, or whatever. Although groups may be quite cohesive, this may occur for reasons other than the fact that they like each other. It could reflect "association by necessity" or common problems such as layoffs or Carlos and Henry's need to exchange useful work-related information.

Sentiments are also expressed in the "strokes" one gives or receives. Positive strokes can provide good feelings for the receiver and build a good relationship between the individuals involved.

Status reflects the hierarchy or pecking order that exists within a group among members and also refers to the relationships between groups. From the viewpoint of the individual, status is gained on the basis of *valued* accomplishments, abilities, or potential possessed by a member. Individual status may be based on the type of car driven or home owned, experience, level or amount of education, political pull, age, beauty or personal mannerisms, and the ability to solve problems. The important point is that within any particular group the status factor has to be seen as a valued one.

Status also applies to relationships between groups so that there are implied pecking orders here too. One group may have greater prestige relative to others and as seen by others in terms of what it accomplishes for its members, for example. The status among groups is often not clear-cut but can be identified by individuals seeking to join certain groups over others.

Leadership in the informal group builds on the power, merits, or abilities of an individual. The informal leader is able to secure valued services for the individual members or simply may provide recognition that is valued. The informal leader is also able to guide or influence the activities of individual group members along particular lines. But in all instances, the designation *leader* is "voted" by group members, and thereby advice or guidance is accepted by group members. The title of leader in an informal group may reflect past accomplishments of the person, current performance, or the possibilities that he or she holds for group members in the future. It is likely that either Carlos or Henry will soon emerge as the acknowledged leader by the others based on these notions.

Exchange suggests that a trade-off of information, ideas, advice, and work assistance takes place among group members. In addition, there is the idea that some balance must be seen as existing between those who exchange. An exchange can be seen as "balanced" where, for example, advice given provides a good feeling for the giver and utility for the receiver as in the case of Carlos and Henry. This notion also gives the supervisor or manager something tangible to observe among group members and in his or her relationships with group members. "Is he or she a taker but never a giver?" is an important type of question to keep out in front. Reciprocity as part of an exchange may also represent acknowledgement by the receiver that the giver of information has more knowledge and hence more status. This can be a reward in its own right.

Norms of behavior are codes of conduct that develop within groups. These provide the "do's" and "don't's," and serve as guides to individual actions in the future. These "norms" may be dress, personal habits, punctuality, helpfulness, and the like. They are part of the unwritten but indispensable climate of group life that makes it valued but disciplined for its members.

Roles are the activities and behaviors that an individual is expected to follow as part of the group. Members of groups become a part of many areas of life that, in turn, establish a pattern of activities within this area of life space. Individuals have work roles, and these prescribe formal patterns of work relationships, locations, skills, and the like. Within the informal group, individuals also have roles or parts to play. A basic one is simply being a member of the group, which automatically implies certain patterns of behavior. Second, because of special work or social abilities, the individual's role may take on new dimensions of helping, social conduct, and know-how.

The Role of Leaders in Informal Groups: A Special Case

As individual members begin to fill the various group roles and perform various functions, a leader tends to emerge and be accepted by group members. Becoming a group leader depends heavily on such characteristics as aggressiveness, confidence, a desire for recognition, and good verbal communication skills. In the end, though, the ability to get along with other group members and the ability to accomplish group goals are likely to be crucial determinants of group leaders.

Since informal leadership depends upon the needs of the moment, an appropriate leader in one situation may not necessarily be qualified to lead in another situation. Consequently, several group members may be required to fulfill various leadership functions. For example, the union representative who must deal with management may play a leadership role quite different from that of the informal group leader who provides technical assistance and expertise.

Basically, we see the acceptance theory of authority (Barnard, 1938) operating in the selection of informal group leaders. Based on this theory, informal authority depends on the willingness of the group to accept and follow another group member. In gaining acceptance, the goals of a sensitive leader are usually related closely to group goals. Thus, informal leaders are perceived by the group as possessing the best means of achieving group goals.

Informal Communication: The Grapevine

Operating alongside the formal communication flow in an organization is an informal communication flow commonly called the *grapevine*. The informal groups have a great impact on the grapevine, a fact of organization life that is one reason that some managers attempt to break up groups (Kippen, 1974). Often group networks can spread information far faster than formal channels, and this may be necessary if the formal system will not do the trick or is too slow. Of course, there is a danger here because the grapevine may greatly distort what is happening or is supposed to happen and thus cause much needless trouble or delays.

Unfortunately, the grapevine has come to be associated with negative things, but there is also a strong positive aspect. Grapevines can be used in constructive ways: they represent a vehicle to get word to levels in the organization that might not be touched adequately even by good communications systems. Since many grapevines parallel informal group structures, and there are connections between groups due to overlapping "memberships," this system can be exercised to explain things through informal group leaders and to a level not possible with newsletters or releases. Chapter 11 deals with this topic in more detail.

These properties and characteristics of informal groups provide a valued dimension of organizational life for their members and help us better understand how informal groups operate. If used properly by managers, informal groups can further the needs of their members and still achieve organizational purposes.

Much information is informally exchanged during coffee breaks.

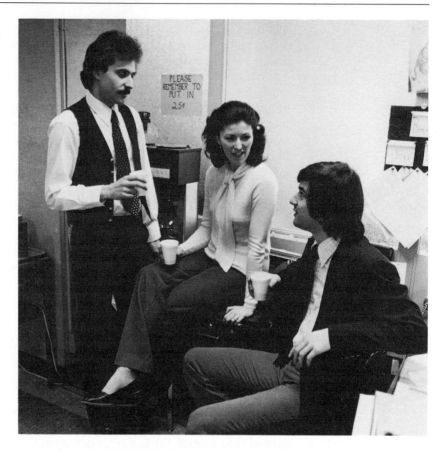

The Formal System and Emergence of Informal Groups: How Groups Form

Work procedures and responsibilities establish an initial basis for work-related activities or interactions. Although such procedures channel individual activity, the extent to which work assignments *restrict* movement depends on the type of work involved. For example, skilled workers in a tool and die shop have assigned benches or work spaces but tend to move about. Workers assigned to a station on an assembly line are almost completely restricted to specific work-station areas. Clerks, secretaries, and other office workers may be assigned to a certain office or desk by a manager but usually can move around more freely than blue-collar workers. However, the office manager may wish to see such "absences" confined to "necessary" trips for personal reasons or to designated break times. Outdoor salespeople or executives have considerably more freedom of movement than the above workers. But even in these cases, the very na-

Work stations can severely restrict movement and the formation of informal
groups.

ture of their assignments dictates geographic areas of travel or types
of people visited. Naturally, the choice of whom to visit first and
sometimes the specific area of selling may be left in the hands of the
individual. These observations point out that one's work establishes
the general boundaries of the number, type, and location of people
contacted, although the restraints vary greatly depending on the
specific job involved. Thus, the way in which work is organized owing
to formally structured relationships forms the basis for personal relationships that often result in the emergence of informal groups (see
Exhibit 10-3).

Whether the latter emerge depends on various personal considerations such as common interest, likes or dislikes, and mutual respect. Yet a new basis of relationships starts to emerge that moves
beyond formal work requirements (see stage I in Exhibit 10-3). An
individual's work responsibilities and assignments (2) as determined
by the organization mission (1) put them in contact with other individuals for work-related purposes (3). The nature of the work system
also either restricts or favors freedom of movement that allows interaction to occur. These formal responsibilities, therefore, establish

Exhibit 10-3 Work and the Emergence of Informal Groups

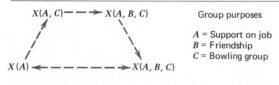

Group purposes

A = Support on job
B = Friendship
C = Bowling group

Stage II. Emergence of informal groups

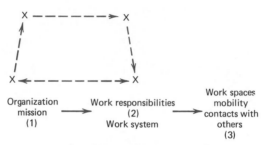

Organization mission (1) → Work responsibilities (2) Work system → Work spaces mobility contacts with others (3)

Stage I. Establishment of work-related activities

the basis for the emergence of the system of informal groups (stage II).

Stage II in Exhibit 10-3 shows some of the possible types of informal groups that can emerge from the formal work relationships of four people. Notice that some members (designated by X) are members of more than one informal group for different purposes (designated by letters A, B, C). Of course, these need not be confined to people who have work relationships, but work does establish an initial point of departure for interactions and possible friendships.

Parkinson's 4th Law

The number of people in any working group tends to increase regardless of how much work needs to be done.

How Informal Groups Evolve

Muzafer Sherif (1969) has identified four evolutionary steps through which informal groups pass. First, there must be a motivational base that causes repeated interactions among group members. Normally, the dominant motivation is the need to perform certain formal organizational tasks.

Second, the group evolves a structure of roles and status relationships as discussed earlier. All groups develop a set of role expectations for their members, and managers would benefit from knowing which roles their subordinates play in the group. In addition, groups evolve a pecking order among their members that becomes quite defined in certain groups.

A third essential in the evolution of groups is the establishment of norms that govern the behavior of group members in matters of importance to the group.

The final ingredient in the evolutionary process is the exercise of group control over its members. Specifying the rules of conduct is not sufficient to influence group members' behavior. Rather, the group must have rewards and sanctions available for use to ensure that members conform to its norms. For example, Sandra is friendly with several of her co-workers in the billing department where she is employed. The group eats lunch together daily, and the members stop work 10 minutes before their designated lunch period in order to get ready to go out to eat. For the last two days Sandra has not stopped work early because of a particularly heavy work load and has not caught up with her friends at the local diner where they normally eat. When Sandra shows up "late" for lunch for the third day in a row, her friends act coolly toward her and make sarcastic remarks about her "showing them up." In this way the group is sanctioning her for violating the group norm of stopping work 10 minutes prior to the company's official lunch period.

Framework for Describing Group Behavior

Complex interrelationships can often occur between group members. This requires the development of a systematic framework for analyzing and describing such behavior that is both practical and workable. George Homans (1950), a small-group theorist, has developed such a model. Homans's model identifies three elements common to all groups:

1. **Activity.**   What members of a group do.
2. **Interaction.**   Relations between and among the group members.
3. **Sentiments.**   The feelings that a member has in relation to other group members (see Exhibit 10-4).

The relationships among these elements can be seen in a situation where the actions of some group members go against the established group norms (sentiments). When this occurs, interaction is likely to be increased as the group attempts to bring the behavior of the deviant members back in line with group sentiments. If the interaction fails, the group is likely to take more drastic action, namely, ostracizing the deviant members or ceasing interaction by giving them the silent treatment.

Homans also distinguishes between internal and external systems. The **external system** includes contact points between the

Exhibit 10-4 Homans's Model: A Way of Viewing Small Groups

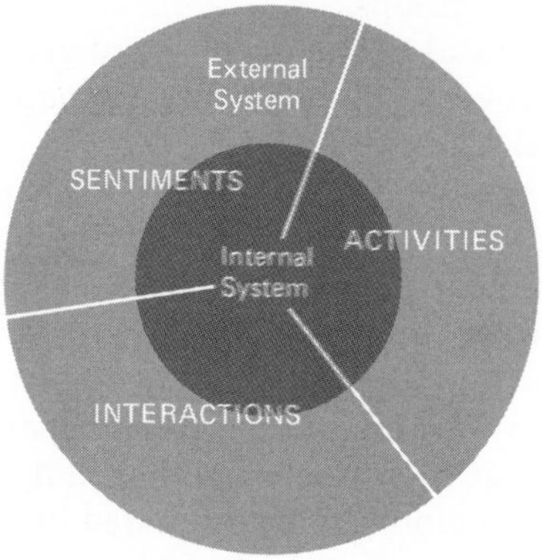

External System—Required behavior in terms of job specifications, work methods, prescribed layouts, and selection of personnel represents the external system.

Internal System—Emergent behavior that results from friendships and cliques, socialization, and helping one another with their work, and so on, refers to the internal systems.

Activities—The things people do, the acts they perform are referred to as activities.

Interactions—When two people come together so that one party has an effect upon the other interaction occurs. Interaction is differentiated in three ways: duration, frequency, and direction.

Sentiments—The internal states of a human (sentiments) include a person's emotions or feelings, beliefs, objectives, frames of reference, and needs.

Source: Data for diagram from George C. Homans, *The Human Group.* New York: Harcourt Brace Jovanovich (1950), p. 82. By permission of the publisher.

group and its environment, such as managers, other groups, governmental regulations, technology, and the work system. In short, the external environment affects required group behavior. The **internal system** is concerned with the sentiments of group members toward each other. It is here that we can witness emergent behavior as the needs of the group and therefore its members change owing to external influences.

The Homans model also provides a systematic view of group behavior. It shows that each element within a system affects others (a concept developed in Chapter 3). By viewing the entire system in relation to the environment, managers should be able to identify more possibilities for a given behavior. Their ultimate solutions, therefore, should result in less spur-of-the-moment decisions. By recognizing those elements that are common to human groups, managers can better understand the general nature of informal group behavior as well as their interrelationship with other organizational entities.

Why Individuals Join Informal Groups

The propensity of individuals to become members of an informal group seems surprising when you consider that they are already members of a formal organization with a specified role and specific duties, explicit channels of communication, and a definite line of command. What more could they need?

It seems they need a good deal more, for employees develop informal groups to meet needs that are left unsatisfied by the formal organization. To what needs are we referring?

Friendship, or Sociability

The simplest need and the one that comes most readily to mind is friendship, or sociability. Man is a social being who spends about half his waking hours at work. He or she needs and enjoys the social contacts with his fellow workers—joking, sharing experiences, expressing his or her opinions, and obtaining a sympathetic hearing to his or her troubles when necessary.

For example, the supervisor of a typing pool learned the importance of sociability the hard way. The supervisor felt that the women in the pool did entirely too much talking, but they ignored her warnings. Finally, she decided on a drastic step and, with the office manager's permission, had plywood partitions installed between the workplaces over one weekend. By Monday noon all work had ceased, and a delegation of the women informed the supervisor that they would not return to work unless the partitions were removed. She had little choice but to yield to the ultimatum. Yes, sociability does count.

Identification, or Need to Belong

Somewhat similar to friendship as a motive for joining an informal group is what is called *identification*, or a sense of belonging (Maslow's social need). We all need to belong, to associate with others in purposes and goals that may encompass and also transcend our individual self-interest. Of course, the formal organization also has its goals and purposes. The problem is that in an organization of any size, these organizational purposes appear abstract, remote, and meaningless to the average employee. What rank-and-file worker can identify with a chairman of the board and his or her purposes?

However, they can and do identify with their immediate work group, which is one of the reasons they join it in the first place. Let us take an example from the military to illustrate this point. Studies

Conformity among workers—dress and gestures often signal acceptance by the group.

conducted during World War II showed that bravery and the willingness to make sacrifices had little to do with a commitment to "honor, duty, country." Rather, they had almost everything to do with the individual soldier's loyalty to his immediate group—his desire not to let his buddies down.

Thus, one reason that Hank Webster in the earlier example, went along with the production quota laid down by the informal organization was that, as an employee, he had subordinated his personal goals to those of the group. He had exchanged the satisfactions of independence for those of association, and, he felt better for it.

Protection or Security Need

Webster's going along with the group in setting production quotas suggests another reason that employees form groups: to attain protection for the membership, especially protection from what the members feel are arbitrary actions by management. This is a primary reason that individuals join unions, for in unity there is strength.

Although it is true that employees may occasionally band together to defend themselves from another work group, most of the time the protection the workers seek is from management's demands for additional output, longer work hours, higher quality, restriction of customary privileges, and other changes. Many organizations, for example, introduce changes in work methods at a faster rate than most individual employees can comfortably adjust to. On their own, they can accomplish little. Their only alternatives are to conform or quit. However, when the group as a whole objects and the supervisor faces the prospect of slowdowns, sabotage, or a concerted campaign to put him or her in a bad light with his or her superiors, he or she is likely to do whatever is possible to make the introduction of the work methods compatible with the group's ability and willingness to accept them.

An individual employee, like Hank Webster, may have his or her personal concept of what constitutes a fair day's work. Alone, the employee has to bend or be fired if his or her personal concept is contrary to management's standards. As a member of a group, however, management faces such unpleasant alternatives as fire the whole group or live with its production quotas. Usually as long as group standards permit what management feels is a reasonable output and a reasonable rate of return, and when the group is relatively difficult to replace, most managements elect to put up with its standards. However, if group standards and organizational goals are significantly different, management's response has often been automation.

Assistance in Problem Solving or Need to Achieve

When the employee has a problem, it is natural to ask for help from a member of the group instead of from the boss. The assistance given is usually just as valuable, and the employee has spared himself the embarrassment frequently involved in admitting failure to the supervisor. In the Bank Wiring Room of the Hawthorne study at Western Electric discussed earlier, members of the group frequently helped each other even though the rules forbade it. The fact that helping and being helped made them feel better was the simple but adequate explanation the men gave for why they violated the rule.

Groups also help to facilitate the use of creativity and initiative even when the job requirements are rigid and the jobs themselves are simple and undemanding. This exercise of initiative is sometimes desirable from management's viewpoint. Exchanging jobs in the Bank Wiring Room, for example, even though contrary to the rules, probably made a positive contribution to morale and efficiency. On other occasions, such as when the group decided jointly to beat a complicated incentive formula, it exercised its creativity at management's expense. The key point is that on jobs that provide little intrinsic opportunity for the use of initiative or creativity, employees often manage to exercise both. The individual employee on his own would not risk it, most such expressions being clearly contrary to the rules. With group approval and support, however, the risk is less, and the satisfaction may be greater.

Managerial Recognition of Informal Groups

Within any formal organization informal groups will arise. People bring an organization to life. Their continuous effort to develop and maintain personal relationships and friendships eventually serves as the catalyst to change the formal structural relationships where necessary. As enduring elements of an organization, informal groups can be used by the manager to achieve organizational objectives. But how can you know if an informal group exists?

The following features of groups serve as clues in identifying whether a collection of individuals is, in fact, functioning as a group.

1. The individuals engage in frequent interaction both on and off the job.
2. The individuals share a common set of rules that govern their behavior, at least regarding areas of common interest.
3. The individuals pursue related goals.
4. The individuals tend to act in a similar fashion toward their environment.
5. The individuals perceive that they are members of the same group (Cartwright and Zander, 1968).

Thus, if a manager notices that the same individuals tend to eat lunch together, dress similarly, talk about accomplishing the same kinds of goals, frequently refer to themselves as "we," and react to changes in organizational policies in the same way, then the manager should realize that he or she is dealing with a social unit rather than a collection of autonomous individuals.

Managers can do several things to better understand informal groups. They can listen to group members, observe group behavior, seek to understand why certain behavior occurs, and identify informal leaders. In dealing with the informal group, managers can gain the group's support if they are willing to work through the informal leaders or the group itself. Promoting group participation in decisions and seeking advice from group members are important when attempting to integrate the formal and informal roles toward goal achievement.

Group Consensus: The Japanese Approach to Decision Making

In the 1960s a new term—*organizational development* (OD)—became popular as a way of describing the process of dealing with systemwide changes within organizations. Today, the term is used for a wide variety of change-oriented activities. For some it is just a fancy name for sensitivity training and other leaderless group-consensus methods that gained popularity in the late 1950s.

Consensus is defined as agreement by all parties involved in some group decision or action. It occurs only after deliberation and discussion of the pros and cons of the issues and when all (not a majority) of the members are in agreement. Each member of the group must be satisfied with the ultimate course of action to be taken (Holder, 1972).

Decision making by consensus has been used by the Japanese with much success. In this country companies such as Yellow Freight System Inc. (since the early 1950s) and General Electric have made organizationwide commitments to is use. The process is not a simple one, and much more time is spent in the early stages of decision making. The result, however, is usually a faster and smoother implementation. (See Chapter 5 for a further discussion on group decision making.)

Nevertheless, there are important differences between decision making by individuals and by groups. Groups can offer advantages on certain kinds of problems when favorable conditions exist such as open communication among group membership and the absence of status and hierarchical distinctions. Training, experience, age, and personality also affect group effectiveness, but groups tend to make fewer errors and are willing to take greater risks than individuals (Hampton, Summer, and Webber, 1973).

The Future and the Informal Group

Change and New Roles for the Informal Group?

We possess no special crystal ball, but it is already clear that many work procedures will undergo redesign in the future. Informal *and* formal work/task groups will often be one and the same. Thus, a base will be established to gain the benefits of new work designs and the mutual reinforcement of each. Reports that have come from early work in this field (see the chapter on work design) indicate good performance results and superior possibilities for their human behavior consequences.

Recognizing the influence of group processes in performance has also led to some specific attempts to develop work designs built

Quality Circle in action at a Toyota plant.

around group concepts. New units at Mead Paper, General Foods, various European concerns, and elswhere incorporate new work designs that attempt to break with the tradition of the mass assembly line. Here groups are established so that a more complete part of a total activity can be accomplished and so that the group and its leadership can better influence how and when things happen. In some plants even floor supervision has been eliminated, and the group largely governs its own affairs.

Too often in the past, management and workers have had adversarial relationships, especially when unions were present. This is a major reason that group consensus and other participative approaches, used so successfully by the Japanese, have seldom been applied in the United States. It is hoped that both management and union leaders will realize that cooperation will be mutually beneficial to the achievement of both group and organizational goals. The early reopening of previously bargained agreements by the United Auto Workers and the Teamsters in 1982 are examples that this realization may be close at hand.

Informal Group: Catalyst or Roadblock for Change?

The title for this section announces the range of possibilities for group processes and influence. As new procedures, technologies, people, or activities are introduced into the organization, groups may feel threatened. Their survival may even be at stake if departments are phased out or new ones are created. It is not reasonable to suggest that these situations could be ignored without a response from the group. If it feels threatened, the group may seek to develop delaying tactics and fight the change most of the way. The manager will seek to judge the likely direction of proposed changes, enlist the group's assistance in the change, or maybe even reconsider the change, if possible, if its effects seem so negative.

Informal Groups in Action: Application Example

Tyung Kim graduated from Lakeview Community College when he was 21 years old and joined United Stores on a full-time basis. Tyung had been in United's sales training program since he entered school. He worked 16 hours per week during the school year and full time during the summer. As a result, he had a good chance to get acquainted with their merchandise lines, policies, and general store operations. United had a nationwide chain of large retail department stores in many principal cities in the United States and in Canada. Tyung did all of his "interning" in United's Baltimore store, but when he went on full time he was transferred to their Cleveland store to gain exposure to a different buying group and slightly different lines of merchandise.

Tyung's first assignment in the Cleveland store was as supervisor–trainee in the men's furnishings department. As a trainee he worked beside regular floor employees, but he regularly met with the department head and attended selected staff meetings with several other trainees who had also been assigned to the store. The three other trainees were Rosa, Michelle, and Nick. Although Tyung had been introduced to the other trainees, they had not had much time to talk and rarely saw each other during the day.

One day the store manager called Rosa and asked her to contact the other trainees. She was to set up a short meeting for the purposes of sharing their store experiences, and then they were to develop a report highlighting strong and weak features of the training program

ALTERNATIVE ORGANIZATIONS IN DIFFERENT COUNTRIES BASED UPON INFORMAL GROUPS

Recent efforts to structure organizations more effectively in the United States have turned attention toward alternative organizational structures and managerial practices used in other countries. These alternative organizational forms often reflect basic differences in political or social philosophy and are the result of a significant investment. Yet they are largely based on our knowledge of informal groups and motivation.

Some of the more recently publicized alternative organizational practices originate in Japan and are commonly referred to as "Theory Z." Briefly, these Japanese management practices include the following concepts: (1) Guaranteed lifetime employment is the norm in large corporations. (2) Management by consensus allows for participation among employees. Although the decisions take longer to make, implementation occurs more rapidly with less conflict and resistance by employees. (3) Not to be ignored is the sense of duty and gratitude toward the employer that is deeply rooted in Japanese society. These factors have all contributed to a greater mutual commitment between employer and employee, resulting in high productivity and a sharing of ideas.

Experiments in Scandinavia in companies such as Volvo have led to the formation of work groups that largely decide their own work pace and what tasks they perform. They also participate in decisions that are usually made by managers in the United States. As a result, productivity and employee satisfaction have usually increased.

In West Germany employee representation on the boards of directors of large companies has been the rule for some time. In 1976 this representation was extended to include all organizations employing more than 2000 people.

The kibbutz system in Israel is another example of an alternative work organization. All members of the kibbutz (self-sufficient commune) have direct influence on the design and operation of the collective through weekly general meetings.

Lagging productivity and deteriorating labor relations in the United States have also led management here to search for new solutions to these problems. Many large companies have undertaken systematic programs related to improving the Quality of Work Life (QWL), including satisfying worker demands for greater involvement in decisions concerning their work. This has led to the formation of semiautonomous production teams and the elimination of many middle-level managers and staff people. Often the number of grievances and rate of absenteeism have been significantly reduced as a result of these changes.

For example, General Foods designed a production facility specifically for self-managing teams that assumed responsibility for large segments of the production process. Team tasks were designed to include both physical and mental skills, and the layout was designed to encourage informal gatherings of team members. The results have been encouraging. The work force has a more positive attitude, and the output has been higher than in most other plants in the system.

In summary, the trend appears to be toward a greater degree of employee involvement using group structures as a basic design element. This involvement results in increased commitment and trust between employee and employer, ultimately leading to improved labor relations and increased productivity. It is likely that these organizational innovations will become more widespread in the coming years.

(as they saw it) and recommendations for future trainees. As a result of their work together they decided that it might be nice to meet now and then and trade experiences. Now there were also occasional coffee breaks together—Tyung might see Nick, Michelle, or Rosa, and if it were toward midmorning they would have coffee together.

As they got to know each other there were also other communications and contacts. For example, Michelle was working in sporting goods and ran into a problem—several expensive pieces of sporting equipment were missing. Michelle suspected one of the part-time workers. She did not know whether to go to the department head or try to get some specific evidence or whatever. Michelle arranged to meet with Tyung after work, and they talked about the situation. After Michelle and Tyung had a chance to talk things out, it became clear that it was a rather complex problem and a serious charge to bring against an employee. It also became clear that it was too delicate for Michelle to handle by herself and that she should discuss the situation with her department head, who was charged with responsibility for department merchandise. A short time later the employee was caught trying to pass merchandise along to a "customer" and was dismissed.

Another situation that came up involved Rosa—she had been assigned to the customer service department. A customer had come in with a complaint regarding his treatment by an employee and demanded to see the *manager*—he didn't want to talk to a service representative! When Rosa tried to calm him down he became very angry, and Rosa became terribly upset.

That evening Tyung, Nick, and Rosa had dinner together, and they had a chance to talk about Rosa's customer experience. By this time, Rosa was able to see things in a different light and thanked Nick and Tyung for "lending an ear" long enough for her to unwind.

Gradually over time, Tyung found that he usually took on the task of arranging meetings for "the group," as they started to call themselves. Michelle even remarked, "I'm glad we have somebody like you [Tyung] around or we would never get together."

Some years later Tyung had become manager of one of the smaller stores in the chain. The regional manager asked him to design a new regional training program for young college people based on his own experiences as a trainee and the information he had gained from continuing contacts with Michelle, Nick, and Rosa.

As Tyung reflected on his experiences and those of his friends he thought about how he and the others had met. One thing was certainly clear—his training program would include a conscious arrangement to ensure that trainees got to know each other well enough to benefit from mutual sharing experiences and also had people available to whom they could turn to talk out problems.

SUMMARY

Informal groups represent the network of people and relationships that makes possible the conduct of formal processes and work activities of an organization. Although there are obvious parallels between the formal and informal, each develops its own unique characteristics and has a special role to play.

The informal structure carries out a wide range of functions—the knowledge of which the supervisor or manager will find highly useful both for individual and organizational purposes. Communications, favorable career experiences, good levels of performance, and a sounding board for individual ideas are only a few of the many roles to be served by the informal group and its members.

The more that performance depends directly on individual actions as opposed to technology, the greater is the ability of the group to affect results or outcomes. However, even where advanced technologies are used, as in highly computerized information systems or petroleum refineries, group actions can affect such things as absenteeism, turnover, cooperation, and the generation of helpful, creative ideas. Groups may affect, if only indirectly, the economic or service results of the organization through the creation of norms of performance and the ability of members to level sanctions against one another. This alone requires understanding of their behavior on the part of managers.

Questions for Study and Discussion

1. Describe and interpret the following situation using the terms described in Exhibit 10-2. Name your assumptions.

    Rebecca Miller supervises a sales department. She has come to know many of the employees and their habits quite well. For example, Jim, Bill, and Maria always seem to take their coffee breaks and lunches together. During the course of the day, if either Jim or Maria has a problem, they are as likely to go to Bill as to Rebecca to work it out. It was also Rebecca's impression that occasionally they stopped by the local disco on Friday nights after work.

    Sean, Bill, and Maria are all in their late twenties, unmarried, and with some college background. Bill is to get his B.A. degree shortly in night school. They have all been employed in the firm for several years. Maria was initially employed by another department but shortly thereafter was promoted to Sales.

2. What part does the informal group play in communications and work performance?
3. What are the career aspects of the informal group?
4. Name two people and briefly describe their backgrounds. Name an

organization and also briefly describe it. Now list and briefly describe status factors for each. Justify your descriptions.

5. What were some of the managerial implications of the Hawthorne studies in relation to informal groups?
6. How do informal groups emerge in a work environment?
7. What are the four steps through which informal groups evolve?
8. What are the three elements according to Homans that provide the framework for the study of informal group behavior?
9. Think of one or two informal groups to which you belong and discuss *why* you joined them.

CASE: ADVANCE ELECTRONICS

Advance Electronics is a space-age company that manufactures a line of consumer products built around newer electronic ideas and applications. Their products include garage door openers, smoke alarms, solar heating units, and household computers. These products are produced in three plants located in northern California so that they are proximate to the capabilities represented by the University of California (Berkeley, Los Angeles) and Stanford University. Each of the plants employs some 200 to 400 people. This case concerns the plant located south of San Francisco and, in particular, employees of the technical staff and plant.

Advance Electronics Plant No. 2 employed almost 400 people—about 300 worked in the plant assembling electronic products, and the balance were employed in the office for business and billing purposes or were part of the technical staff. The technical staff was responsible for the design of the light/solar group of products. A summary organization chart is presented in Exhibit 10-5.

Lester Clark was the Senior Production Engineer. His main responsibility was to work with design engineers and detail people regarding the redesign of existing products or the introduction of new ones. He assumed the key responsibility for moving the product from design model to the production unit. He had joined the company at the time the plant was being erected so that he had gotten to know most of the employees from the beginning, including those in the control departments and in production supervision.

With the expansion of the company's solar products, Lester soon became overloaded with projects and decided that he would have to get help quick or run the risk of falling seriously behind. He got the approval to hire a Junior Production Engineer. After a short search, Lester hired Martha Peterson. Martha had a B.A. in science from one of the state colleges and two years of experience working in a re-

Exhibit 10-5 Advance Electronics Plant No. 2

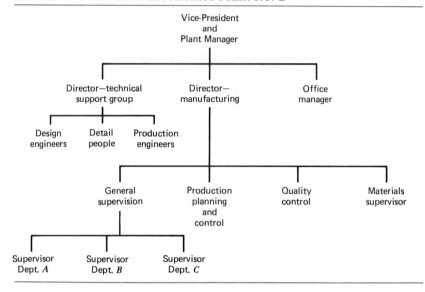

search and development company as a project coordinator. She was 25 years old and recently married.

Martha had a pleasing personality and got to know other members of the technical staff and some of the plant supervisors in the course of following up on projects. Of course, Lester had introduced her around, but he was so overloaded that he was anxious to get back to "his" projects. After a quick tour and round of introductions he remarked to Martha, "You'll get to know the rest when you start to work with them."

Things went well for Martha for several months, and she felt that she was really getting to know the system and how to get things done. Then she ran into a series of problems that made her start to wonder if she had missed something along the line. For example, Martha was supposed to follow up with Sam Davis, Supervisor of Department A, on the installation of new equipment for the production of a new version of an existing product. Sam promised her samples from the new equipment. The time came, passed, and still no samples appeared. Martha checked with Sam almost every day and it was always, "we've got this or that, but we'll have your samples shortly." They were two weeks late on that project.

Another situation concerned her work with some of the assembly line people in Department B. She was working with the Department Supervisor and some of the line people in order to get several different variations of one of the roof-top solar heating units. Martha was carrying the sample when she noticed that it seemed to be missing an "end cap." She brought it over to Jim White, an assembler, and asked to have a cap attached. With a little effort Jim managed to attach a cap. When Lester saw the sample he said, "That's the model I wanted, but that cap doesn't belong on there. Anybody in the plant would know that with that cap attached, the unit will short out!" Martha was really upset over the "wrong cap" incident and was letting her friend Dorothy Kuhn in the design engineering group know about it.

When Martha had finished her story, Dorothy laughed a little and said, "Martha, let me tell you a riddle about people, coffee cups, and getting things done."

Questions

1. What do you think Dorothy meant by her remark to Martha?
2. What differences existed between Lester's situation and his involvement with the informal structure of the plant and those of Martha?
3. List and briefly describe "status" factors related to Lester and Martha. How would these affect their becoming a part of informal groups in the plant? Would certain memberships be more likely than others? If so, why?
4. If you were Lester Clark, how would you have helped Martha better her chances for successful work performance in the organization?
5. From a career viewpoint, what advice would you pass along to Martha?

CASE: THE INFORMAL LEADER APPOINTED SUPERVISOR

Until recently, David Collins was a machine operator in a manufacturing firm. His job was dull and uninspiring, as were most of the jobs in his work crew. In order to relieve the boredom of their jobs, the men would find various ways of amusing themselves. Hardly a day went by without one of them playing a practical joke on someone.

One of the favorite activities of the informal group was to match wits with their supervisor. Although he was fairly well liked by the men, he was a symbol of management and was therefore the "enemy" with whom they had a running "battle." One of their favorite tactics was to play dumb whenever they were assigned a new part to produce or a different machine to work on. They would ask the supervisor many detailed questions about how to produce the new part or how to operate the different machine. If the supervisor became somewhat suspicious of their asking so many questions, they would tell him that they hated to take up so much of his time with their questions but that they were sure he would want them to do the job right and not make any mistakes, since they did not want to run up any extra costs for the company.

Whenever the supervisor was not in the work area, the group would loaf until they saw him returning, at which time the person who first spotted him would signal to the others, and they would all start working hard again. The men also complained about the materials they had to use, the instructions sent down by the industrial engineering department, the quality-control procedures, and many other items.

Collins emerged as the leader of the informal group. This was due partly to his natural leadership ability and partly to his ability to devise new ways of harassing the supervisor. The majority of the men were competent workers and could have produced more if they had desired to do so.

As a result of the poor production record of the group, top management transferred the supervisor to a different department in the plant. An assistant foreman of another department was placed in charge, but after two weeks he asked to be transferred back to his old job. He told the general foreman that someone should be promoted from within the group since he would know the problems of the work crew and would be aware of how the workers were "goofing off." The general foreman thought that was a good idea. He checked with the previous supervisor, who said that David Collins appeared to be the best possibility, since he seemed to be the informal leader and was a skilled worker.

The general foreman talked with Collins about becoming foreman, allowing him several days to consider the offer. Collins accepted the job of foreman and is now faced with some new experiences. He is now part of management—the "enemy" on whom he had previously played tricks. Instead of congratulating him on his promotion, his former fellow workers seemed displeased and have acted somewhat coolly toward him. Collins believes that he can "shape up" the department since he knows all the men's old tricks. Also, the men are capable of good work, if they can be motivated to work for the company instead of against it. He had been supervisor only one week when he caught his men trying to play one of their old tricks on him.

Questions

1. How can Collins persuade the men to work for the company instead of against it?

2. What are the advantages and disadvantages of promoting an informal leader to the position of supervisor over his group?

3. Suppose a new informal leader emerges and attempts to maintain the old activities of the group. What should Collins do?

4. Would it help if the jobs could be redesigned to be more challenging?

References

Baker, Kent, "Tapping into the Power of Informal Groups," *Supervisory Management*, **26**(2) (February 1981): 18–25.

Barnard, Chester. *Organization and Management*. Cambridge: Harvard University Press (1948).

Burton, Gene E., and Dov S. Pathak, "Social Character and Group Decision Making," *S.A.M. Advanced Management Journal*, **43** (Summer 1978): 12–20.

Carey, Alex, "The Hawthorne Studies: A Radical Criticism," *American Sociological Review*, **32**(3) (June 1967).

Cartwright, Dorwin, and Alvin Zander, Eds. *Group Dynamics: Research and Theory*. 3rd ed. New York: Harper & Row (1968).

Cummings, L. L., George P. Huber, and Eugene Arendt, "Effects of Size and Spatial Arrangements on Group Decision Making," *Academy of Management Journal*, **17** (September 1974): 460–475.

Hampton, David R., Charles E. Summer, and Ross A. Webber, *Organizational Behavior and the Practice of Management*. Glenview, Ill.: Scott, Foresman (1973).

Heinen, J. Stephen, and Eugene Jacobson, "A Model of Task Group Development in Complex Organizations and a Strategy of Implementation," *Academy of Management Review*, **1** (October 1976): 98–111.

Holder, Jack J. Jr., "Decision Making by Consensus," *Business Horizons*, (April 1972): 47–54.

Homans, George C., *The Human Group*. New York: Harcourt, Brace Jovanovich (1950).

Isenberg, Daniel, "Some Effects of Time-Pressure on Vertical Structure and Decision-Making Accuracy in Small Groups," *Organizational Behavior and Human Performance*, **27**(1) (February 1981): 119–134.

Ivancevich, John M., and Timothy McMahon, Jr., "Group Development, Trainer Style and Carry-over Job Satisfaction and Performance," *Academy of Management Journal*, **19** (September 1976): 395–412.

Landsberger, H. A., *Hawthorne Revisited*. Ithaca, N. Y.: Cornell University Press (1958).

Noda, Mitz, "The Japanese Way," *Executive*, **6**(3) (Summer 1980): 22–25.

Parker, L. D., "Evaluating Group Decision-Making in the Corporate Environment," *Management Decision (UK)*, **18**(1) (1980): 35–44.

Roethlisberger, Fritz J., and William J. Dickson, *Management and the Worker*. Cambridge, Mass.: Harvard University Press (1939).

Sanders, Bruce, "Avoiding the Groupthink Zoo," *Supervision*, **42**(12) (December 1980): 10–13.

Schriesheim, Janet, "The Social Context of Leader–Subordinate Relations: An Investigation of the Effects of Group Cohesiveness," *Journal of Applied Psychology*, **65**(2) (April 1980): 183–194.

Scott, Sid, "The Design Group in Action," *Training and Development Journal*, **35**(4) (April 1981): 70–72.

Shepard, J. M., "On Casey's Radical Criticism of the Hawthorne Studies," *Academy of Management Journal*, **14**(1) (March 1971): 23–32.

Sherif, Muzafer, and Carolyn Sherif, *Social Psychology*. New York: Harper & Row (1969).

Singleton, Royce, Jr., "Another Look at the Conformity Explanation of Group-Induced Shifts in Choice," *Human Relations*, **32** (January 1979): 37–56.

Smith, Peter, "Working and Learning in Groups," *Industrial and Commercial Training (UK)*, **10**(8) (August 1978): 322–329.

Tasklanganos, Angelos A., "The Committee in Business: Asset or Liability?" *Personnel Journal*, **54** (February 1975): 90–93.

Zander, Alvin, "The Psychology of Removing Group Members and Recruiting New Ones," *Human Relations*, **29** (October 1976): 969–987.

CHAPTER 11

COMMUNICATION

KEY
QUESTIONS
ADDRESSED
IN CHAPTER

1. How does the communication process work?
2. What are the characteristics of good communication?
3. How can barriers to good communication be overcome?
4. Why is the role of listening important in communication?
5. How is communication related to other management functions?
6. Why are written and oral communication skills important for career advancement?
7. When should formal and informal communication be used?

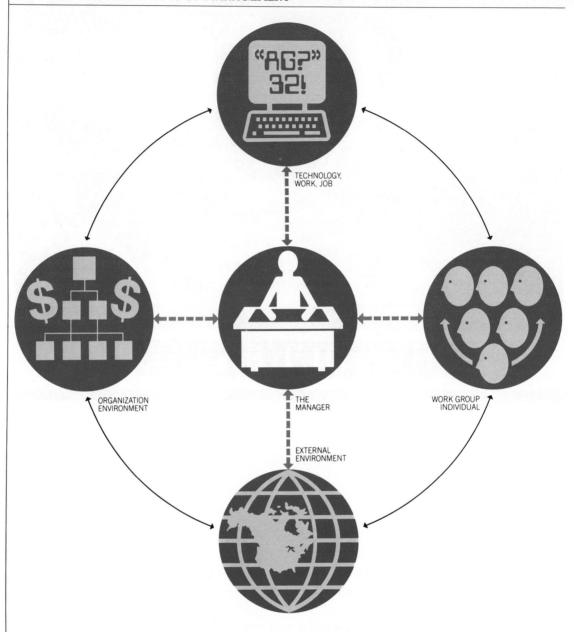

TECHNOLOGY,
WORK, JOB

ORGANIZATION
ENVIRONMENT

THE
MANAGER

EXTERNAL
ENVIRONMENT

WORK GROUP
INDIVIDUAL

The manager's work–life spaces

Organizations require both a chain of command and a chain of understanding.

THE CHAPTER IN BRIEF

We all spend much of our time each day communicating with others at work, at home, or at play. The best idea, plan, or decision is of little use if it is not effectively communicated to others.

Although studies show that managers rely mostly on oral communication, written communication must also be mastered, since the written word is relied on to transmit complex ideas and to establish records. Oral communication is timely and current; it enables managers to be informed about immediate problems or opportunities. Written communication, on the other hand, may have distinct limitations in terms of rapid response.

Communication is the cornerstone of other management activities. It is only through communication that managers can carry out their responsibilities. Information must be transmitted as a basis for planning; plans must be communicated in order to be carried out. Organizing and directing require that tasks be assigned and people be motivated toward group and organizational objectives. Communication of verbal and written information is also essential to the control activity. In short, without interacting and communicating with others, managers could not function effectively.

This chapter describes the nature of the interpersonal communication process, including the important role that feedback plays. An understanding of the communication process serves as a basis for explaining how to overcome communication barriers, which are all too common in most organizations. Distinctions are made between formal and informal communication and when each should be used. Suggestions for improving organizational communication are presented with an emphasis on how to make the grapevine work. Finally, we present an overview of different communication networks or channels in organizations, showing how they affect variables such as group performance, leader emergence, and member satisfaction.

Communication and the Life-Space Model

The manager's world is a world of words. Most of his or her time is spent communicating with others. For this reason verbal skill is often the *most critical managerial skill* needed for managerial success and career advancement.

As shown in the life-space model, the manager is both a translator and a facilitator of information. The manager makes important choices concerning the type of communication media to use. The

COMMUNICATIONS BREAKDOWN

As marketing requested it.

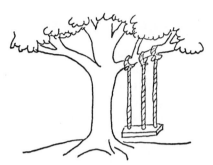

As sales ordered it.

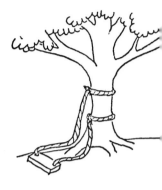

As engineering designed it.

As supplier delivered it.

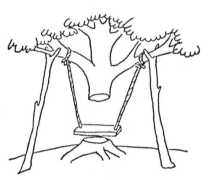

As plant installed it.

What the customer wanted.

choice of media usually depends on the problem or situation faced. Most managers prefer informal, face-to-face communication and work best when dealing with people on a one-to-one basis (Mintzberg, 1973). Other managers are more formal, relying more on written forms such as memos. Still others work best with groups.

The communication process also affects the work/technology space. Examining for clarity, written documents such as procedures, job descriptions, and policies helps to improve job performance. The presence of computerized information systems can change the nature and timeliness of information used by managers, especially for decision-making purposes.

Activity related to organizational life spaces, in fact, demands communication, whether it be downward (as in giving directions), upward (as in reporting results), or horizontal (as in coordinating work of two different departments). Establishing clear communication channels in the formal structure can ensure that things run more smoothly. Clearly defined responsibilities leave less doubt as to job tasks and duties and should reduce the possibility of conflict.

Communication patterns can also greatly affect the relationship between a manager and his or her subordinates. If open communication networks or patterns are allowed, greater two-way communication is likely to occur. This communication can help motivate individuals and improve group morale, but it may also result in more time spent in meetings while "hashing things out."

Finally, a manager is affected greatly by his or her past experiences in the environment; these affect the perception of reality. Past experiences can cause an individual to have preconceived ideas about what others are trying to say. Individuals often infer that something is being communicated when it is not. For example, if a manager believes that work must be painful to be productive, then laughter may mean that employees are wasting time and, perhaps, that their assignments are too easy. On the other hand, if a manager believes contented employees work harder, then the laughter of employees means that he or she is succeeding as a manager.

Communication and You

Everyone has experienced at some time a failure to communicate an idea effectively. This could have occurred when speaking or writing, when interacting with friends, business associates, parents, spouses, or children.

Let us take the example of Mary Smith, a recent college graduate who was hired as an assistant office manager for a medium-size law firm. She is talking with her boss, Sue Thompson.

"Mary, I'm quite pleased with how you've been running the office the past three months. You seem to have corrected the tardiness problem of two of the legal assistants—something your predecessor wasn't able to do. Even the reports are on time!"

"Thanks, Ms. Thompson, I appreciate your compliments."

"There is one other thing I'd like to mention, Mary. I noticed that the office-supplies bill is $250 over budget. Also, I see that you want to fire Tom Witherspoon, one of our most promising law clerks. Did you know that he's been studying for the bar exam and also happens to be the nephew of Joe Taylor, a partner?"

"Tom Witherspoon is studying for the bar? So that's why he's been late so often. No one told me about that! And the $250 over budget is because I ordered the 1200 pens that you requested."

"Oh, my gosh, Mary. I said 12 dozen pens, not 1200!"

It is likely that we have all experienced a situation similar to Mary's. What went wrong here?

First of all, a discussion that began with praise for a job well-done ended up with criticism, which will be remembered long after the praise has been forgotten. But of equal importance is what was uncovered during the discussion about previous communication that was apparently ineffective. There is evidence that Mary failed to understand the personal needs and goals of one of her subordinates, Tom. Also, the failure of communication between Mary and her boss over the exact number of pens to order suggests the need for written communication, so that records can be kept. On the other hand, the communication between Mary and the two legal assistants seems to have positively affected their behavior.

BACKGROUND

The Communication Process: What Is It? How Does It Work?

Communication is the process of exchanging information and transmitting meaning between people.

Since **communication** is such an integral part of all managerial activity, an understanding of how the **process** works is a necessary first step toward improving both interpersonal and organizational communication.

A communication model is shown in Exhibit 11-1. The communication process begins with the sender, who has an idea and purpose for sending a message. Then he or she encodes or transforms the idea into message form: words, body movements such as gestures or facial expressions, or symbols such as pictures, diagrams, or writing. The message is then transmitted through one of various channels, for example, in person, by telephone, or in writing. Alternatively, the

Exhibit 11-1 The Communication Process

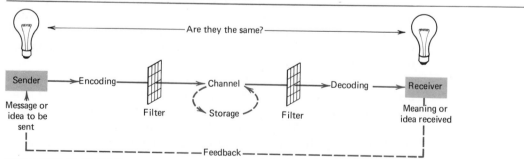

information may be stored for future use, as in the case of reports or analyses. This possibility completes the sender's initial involvement in the communication process.

From the receiver's viewpoint, the message is then decoded into terms that have meaning for him or her. Completing the process, and essential to it, is the feedback from the sender. Whether direct or indirect, feedback indicates whether or not the message was accurately received.

What Makes Communication Effective?

In the final analysis, from the sender's point of view communication is effective if it brings about the intended action or response from the receiver. To achieve this desired outcome, an initial requirement is to send clear messages—ones that can be understood by the receiver. This is easier said than done, however, for talking down to an individual, underestimating his or her ability to understand, can convey an attitude of superiority or make the receiver feel that the speaker does not understand the situation fully. On the other hand, overestimating an individual's ability to understand, talking over his head, can result in feelings of inferiority or the sense that the boss is "trying to impress me," which often leads to tuning out the message.

Empathy, the ability to see the world through the eyes of others, helps us send clear messages because we understand others more clearly.

Managers can communicate better by creating an environment in which employees feel at ease because they feel that their needs are understood. It is no easy task to create such an environment. The entire context in which the message is being transmitted must be considered. For instance, is the timing of sending the message right? Is the physical setting appropriate—that is, is there enough privacy? Is the message compatible with the organizational climate, social customs, or past practices within the company?

The behavior of the sender can also have an impact on whether or not the communication is effective. If the message is verbal, the tone of voice, facial expressions, and apparent receptiveness of the sender are all important cues that the receiver closely "tunes in on." The sender's actions should also be consistent with the message being conveyed, for, in truth, actions do speak louder than words. Take, for example, the department head who continually arrives late for work, yet disciplines subordinates who inadvertently come in late once. Or take the nursing supervisor who wants subordinates "to level with me," but then holds grudges against those nurses who may have been somewhat critical of her or the hospital's practices.

Conciseness, another characteristic of effective communication, is achieved by using as few words as possible to convey an idea completely. Perceptual filters protect us from being inundated with information that is not relevant to us and that we cannot use. Research studies indicate that most people listen with only 25 percent capacity. Attention spans are quite short, especially when messages appear to be redundant.

The following comments illustrate complaints often heard when communication systems are ineffective.

- I receive too much information; it's just not relevant [*lack of clarity and conciseness*].
- I always seem to receive the information two days after I needed it [*lack of timeliness*].
- We receive a great deal of information but often can't tell who sent it [*lack of clarity*].
- The information I get is just not specific enough for my purposes. [*lack of clarity*].

Barriers to Communication

To make communication more effective, managers must become more aware of the barriers to communication that exist within their organizations. By recognizing these barriers, they should then be more prepared to overcome their adverse effects. Barriers can occur at various stages in the communication process and may be classified as semantic, personal, or organizational.

Semantic Barriers

Words often mean different things to different people (**semantic barriers**). As a result misinterpretation may occur (see Exhibit 11-2). It is not only that a given word may have several dictionary meanings but that meanings may vary according to the way they are used in a sentence and the setting in which they are used. In addition, either the sender or the receiver may attach different meanings to words because of the individual's past experiences, backgrounds, attitudes, biases, or perceptions. For example, women are likely to interpret the phrase "women's lib" quite differently from men. For communication to be effective, the area of understanding (or overlap between what is meant and what is perceived) should be large.

Marshall McLuhan, a well-known expert in communication, observed, "Each of us goes through life with our own set of goggles" (McLuhan, 1964). We view the world from our own viewpoint or frame of reference. What our goggles tell us about a situation is not necessarily what someone else will understand about the same situation (see Exhibit 11-2). A group of people on a street engaged in heated conversation could simply be discussing something. However,

Exhibit 11-2 Problems with Perception

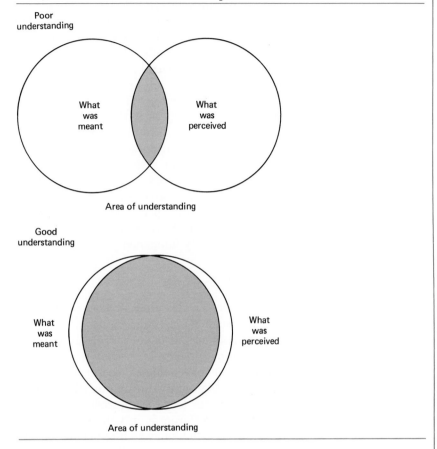

Poor
understanding

What
was
meant

What
was
perceived

Area of understanding

Good
understanding

What
was
meant

What
was
perceived

Area of understanding

passersby, through their goggles, may interpret the scene as a confrontation, a fight, or even a racial incident.

Our goggles come from our experiences. No two people, not even identical twins, have done the same things and been to the same places. Each of us is unique—an individual, one of a kind. Our goggles don't tell us who is right but that viewpoints and perceptions are likely to be different.

As time passes, the meanings of words and other symbols change. New slang words appear, and others fall into disuse. People who were "neat," "cool," or "with it" now "have their act together." One of the most common communication barriers encountered by a new member of a group or organization, in fact, is the use of slang or "shop talk." The unique language of various professions can often be a problem. Nurses give "IVs," computer operators work with "CRTs," and soldiers learn about "KP."

We have all witnessed situations in which the misinterpretation of the importance of symbols has resulted in conflict. For example, a manager may regard the coffee break as a fringe benefit and luxury that does little to help achieve company goals. Employees, on the other hand, may consider it a vital and basic part of their jobs, one that helps fulfill physical and social needs. Status symbols, too, have long played a major role in work (and leisure time). The key to the executive washroom may signal that "one has arrived," as can other symbols such as offices with windows, large desks, carpeting, and selection to a special group or seminar.

Individuals often perceive the same situation differently. Lawyers use this fact in attempting to discredit witnesses or to raise doubts in jurors' minds. The classical Japanese film *Roshoman* depicts the story of a rape as seen through the eyes of three different people: the woman raped, her husband, and the rapist. Think about an event that you have witnessed in which there was much debate about what really happened.

Personal Barriers

Personal factors also create barriers to communication. Despite the fact that much of our time is spent communicating, many individuals are poor listeners. It is not merely a matter of having poor attention spans, although sometimes that is part of the difficulty. Of deeper concern is the psychological distance that people feel between them, which results in one "tuning out" the other. There are a number of possible causes: lack of interest in the topic, differences in personalities, or differences in values.

There is a tendency to like people with whom we agree and dislike people with whom we disagree. If we disagree with someone on one subject, we may quickly tune them out when they are discussing an entirely different matter because we anticipate disagreement when, in fact, it may not occur. Thus we put people and things into neat little categories, like black and white. For example, politicians are labeled liberal or conservative when, in truth, many are somewhere in between, depending on the issue.

Trust between people is essential to effective communication. In fact, if there is distrust, communication may be nonexistent or, at best, greatly distorted. For example, if subordinates have not been allowed to participate in decisions that affect them or are lied to regarding circumstances surrounding the situation, their commitment will likely be reduced. Future attempts at communication may be tuned out or viewed with skepticism.

Communication is also influenced by personalities and physical appearance. Whether an individual is dynamic or introverted, empathetic, or disagreeable does matter. Even though dress codes are

Listening is an important component of communication.

out of favor today, we all become aware of the appropriate attire for different occasions. We would not think of going to a job interview in blue jeans. Likewise, the rock group Chicago would be out of place in three-piece, pin-striped suits.

Our values and beliefs also play a large part in communication. Since values are the result of many years of nurturing, they are difficult to change. In fact, we tend to develop a filtering mechanism that screens out or modifies information that may be contrary to our set of values. Prejudice is an extreme example of communication distortion. Although prejudice is normally associated with feelings about race and sex, one can also be biased against unions, business, or just about anything.

Perhaps the most important personal barrier to effective communication is poor listening on the part of the receiver. Studies show that we forget roughly one half to two thirds of what is said within an eight-hour period.

There are a number of factors that prevent individuals from being more effective listeners. First and foremost is the inability to concentrate. Often our minds wander because the average individual speaks at a much slower rate than we are able to comprehend. We may concentrate or focus on certain emotion-laden words and then subconsciously tune out other statements that may disagree with our values.

To become effective listeners, we need to keep our emotions in check, especially when dealing with emotion-laden topics. It is also important to listen to the full message. Instead of listening many of us spend entirely too much time talking or thinking about how we should phrase our response. Note taking is quite helpful here, especially for accurate recall purposes. For example, studies of students show a high correlation between note taking and good exam grades. Finally, when part of a message is unclear, feedback in the form of a question should be directed to the speaker.

We communicate in other ways besides words, as indicated by the recent emphasis placed on body language as a means of more effectively interpreting communication. The way in which one walks or nods one's head communicates different things. In our personal lives, an affectionate hug, kiss, or even look can be more meaningful than saying, "I love you." In organizations, too, it is not only *what* is said but *how* it is said that gives importance and meaning to the message. Managers tend to pick up on nonverbal cues sent from their bosses much more so than ones sent from their subordinates. Why? It is more important for individuals in subordinate positions to hear their bosses' message (both verbal and nonverbal) accurately than it is for them to hear the messages of others (namely, their own subordinates). Improving our knowledge of body language should also make us more effective listeners.

Organizational Barriers

All organizations establish hierarchies through which most formal communications flow. Differences in status and power help form invisible barriers that are difficult to break down. A company executive may espouse an "open door policy," but most subordinates will probably be reluctant to take advantage of it. In fact, many subordinates will often "bend the truth" to their advantage when communicating information upward through the hierarchy. The effect of **organizational distance** on the content and accuracy of communication is largely due to differences in authority among individuals. Managers should consider this effect when interpreting communications from lower levels in the organization.

The increased complexity and size of many far-flung organizations also pose physical barriers to communication. Despite breakthroughs in technology that may speed communication from one place to another almost instantaneously, effective communication is more difficult to achieve in a financial organization with widely dispersed offices than in a hospital, for example.

Finally, formal channels of communication often follow the organization's chain of command. Information is communicated from division manager to manager to supervisor to sales person, and it is hoped, back up. The free flow of communication between levels is often inhibited. Of course, this has the advantage of keeping higher-level managers from getting "bogged down in detail." Yet it also can keep them from getting the right information quickly. For example, a worker will almost always communicate problems to his supervisor rather than, say, the department head or general manager. This is fine as long as the problem is not urgent or can be solved by the supervisor. However, a number of organizations have gone to *free* forms of communication, which allow individuals to communicate with anyone in the organization who may be of help in solving the problem. In addition, large companies may even have a communication specialist, who will help "poor" communicators (like the one in the cartoon) improve their messages.

A related structural barrier to communication involves the manner in which work groups or departments are organized. Although the specialization of tasks may facilitate information exchange within each group, communication between highly differentiated groups or departments is likely to be inhibited. Differences in group goals, tasks, and jargon largely account for this difficulty and may be especially troublesome in communication between line and staff units.

Individuals in any organization, whether they be line or staff, worker or manager, possess unique information and knowledge about their jobs. For example, a supervisor may have a particularly effective way of handling conflicts among subordinates, or a product planning specialist may have an extremely good "feel for the market."

Proper speech habits are an important managerial skill. (Copyright © 1975 by **NEA,** Inc.)

Many individuals are reluctant to share this kind of information with others. To overcome this reluctance, some organizations require a manager to have identified a replacement before he or she can be promoted. Also, because of the positions they hold, individuals possess much valuable information that gives them power over others who need that information. As a result, completely open communication within organizations is quite rare.

Organizational noise, like static on a radio, can often create distortions in information. Overcrowded work areas, too many individuals competing for the attention of a manager, or even the improper choice of a communication channel (say, a typed letter instead of face-to-face communication to handle a "touchy" matter), are all examples of organizational situations that can cause messages to be misinterpreted as a result of "garbled transmission."

Finally, time pressures or deadlines imposed by the organization can also result in the sending of incomplete or inaccurate communications, as the memo from James Roland to Jim Snow illustrates.

MEMO

DATE: August 15
  TO: Jim Snow, Advertising Manager
FROM: James Roland, Controller

According to the instructions of Wayne Knowland, Division Manager, the printouts you received recently concerning the proposed annual budget should be returned with corrections and comments. Each manager should check that the printout data correspond with previously published budget data.

JAR:cc

P.S. THE DEADLINE FOR THESE PRINTOUTS FOR RETURN TO US IS AUGUST 16.

The memo may be all too typical. In this instance, the short deadline came at a time when Jim Snow was in the middle of a major advertising campaign that had to be completed by August 17. If both deadlines were adhered to, it is likely that one or both of the tasks would suffer.

Organizational Communication: Formal versus Informal

Communication is essentially an interpersonal activity; that is, it takes place between people. However, the form and structure of communication change according to the setting in which it occurs. For example, the type of communication that occurs at a party is quite different from that which occurs at a business meeting, because organizations impose certain formalities on the communication process. Without this formality, chaos can result. Some people may not know what is going on, while others are bombarded with too much information. Thus, *formal* communication channels systematically transmit amounts of information to members of the organization corresponding to the positions they hold. This helps to ensure that members of the organization receive (and send) information that is pertinent to their work responsibilities.

Occasionally, formal communication channels impose such constraints on information that real barriers to communication can develop (as discussed in the previous section). When role and status relationships are strictly defined, supervisors may feel that they will lose status if they "associate" with their subordinates. Employees, too, may be intimidated by differences in status, and they may not communicate effectively with their managers. Thus, communication between organizational levels can be discouraged. On the other hand, if organizational relationships are too loosely defined, assignments may be vague or responsibilities may overlap. As a result, employees may compete for positions of power within the group by withholding needed information or by assuming inappropriate leadership roles.

There are three general types of formal communication in organizations based on the direction of information flow: downward, upward, and horizontal (or lateral). Exhibit 11-3 illustrates each of these, and the following sections discuss the purposes served by each.

Downward Communication

Downward communication provides directions and instructions for individuals to ensure that organizational objectives are met. Written policies and procedures are a primary device by which individuals determine how to carry out organizational objectives. Additionally, supervisors issue orders verbally and assign tasks to their subordinates as a routine part of their workday.

Exhibit 11-3 Types of Communication Flow

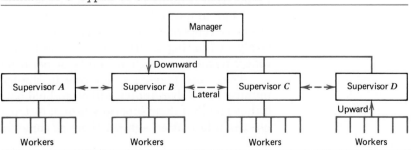

The major function of the formal downward flow of communication in an organization is to ensure that each level has the opportunity to add its knowledge to the overall body of information. Messages that start out as general strategy become specific procedures to be implemented as they move through successive levels of management. Usually this system works well, but certain problems tend to be built in to vertical communication channels. For instance, there is little direct communication between top and bottom levels. If the directives issued by top management bypass immediate supervisors, they may not be taken seriously by lower-level employees. On the other hand, going through all the levels in the hierarchy takes time and can easily result in misinterpretation, as the message is filtered by individual perceptions and needs. To avoid such misinterpretation, some top executives deal directly with the person involved in executing a task. This course, although often required for effective communication, may lead to the erosion of the supervisor's authority. Therefore, it should be used sparingly, with the affected supervisors being kept informed of the directives that are given to their subordinates.

Upward Communication

Upward communication is used primarily to feed back information on the condition of various parts of the organization to upper levels of management. An auditor's report specifying problems uncovered in an audit is a prime example of upward communication being used as part of an organization's control system.

Besides its use in the control process, upward communication is the mechanism that allows employees to have a voice in the operations of the organization. Listening and responding to employee suggestions can foster effective two-way communication and, in turn, improve employee morale.

Since in upward communication lower-status people communicate with higher-status people, distortion and inaccuracy often result. Most employees will tend to transmit only information that is favorable to themselves—telling only what the boss *wants* to hear, not what he or she *should* hear. Studies have shown that upward communication is likely to be less open and accurate when subordinates have a great desire for upward mobility. Often ambitious individuals are more concerned with protecting their self-image than with objectively evaluating a situation, especially if such an evaluation will reflect negatively on their ability or performance.

Trust also plays a major role in the openness of upward communication. Subordinates will often hold back or distort information if they feel that their superiors cannot be trusted to react fairly or will use the information against them at some future time.

The main purpose of *horizontal communication* is to coordinate the work activities in an organization. Lateral communication usually follows the pattern of work flow and occurs often between members of different work units. For example, a systems analyst sends a memo to the product manager, specifying the deadline and the procedures to be followed for a computer analysis that was requested by the product manager. In this way, matters can be handled at the same level in the organization, thereby speeding up action while also relieving supervisors of unnecessary problems.

An added benefit of horizontal communication is the formation of relationships among peers in different departments. These informal communication networks can serve to increase employee satisfaction and also be an important source of information about position openings and needed skills and abilities for lateral transfers.

Informal Networks: The Grapevine

Informal communication networks appear primarily because an organization's formal communication channels do not adequately fulfill all of the information needs of its members. The **grapevine,** as the informal channels are frequently called, can be an effective and necessary supplement to the formal communication system, while also serving the social needs of individuals in the organization.

Some managers refuse to acknowledge the existence of a grapevine for fear that it might be viewed as an indictment of the failure of an organization's formal communication system. It is natural for people often to seek information through informal channels when the formal channels are blocked or inefficient. Although the grapevine may filter or distort messages and occasionally may transmit rumors, gossip, and other negative feelings, its accuracy is probably as good as the formal communication system and its speed has astounded many a manager. The continuing existence of the grapevine in organizations proves its utility.

Rather than spending much time and effort in trying to eliminate the grapevine, some organizations have taken steps to ensure its continued existence as a complement to the formal system. Such steps have included increasing the number and effectiveness of liaison individuals such as counselors and "ombudsmen." Both groups of individuals tell others what they want or need to know and can "cut through the red tape" of many bureaucracies. Informal information that helps to identify career paths and to describe what certain jobs are really like can be helpful, especially when it is not available through formal channels.

Demands for information that arise during the normal flow of work are often inhibited by the reliance of the formal communication system on the organization's chain of command. For this reason, informal communication systems can help to speed the work-related flow of information by making use of the natural interaction of some staff positions across departmental units. Through the improved selectivity of informal communications, information can be transmitted in a more timely fashion than through formal channels.

Any time more than two people come together to work or play, there is a possibility of a grapevine forming. Basically there are two strategies open to the manager: ignore the grapevine, or make it work for you.

Ignoring the grapevine and rumors is a dangerous alternative. A rumor usually has some element of truth in it, and all rumors are symptoms of larger problems. When rumors are rampant or focus on a particular activity, the manager would be wise to look for the cause of the dissatisfaction and take steps to correct it.

GREAT PERSON PROFILE

William Blackie (1907–   )

Caterpillar Tractor Company of Peoria, Illinois has been called one of America's best led, most innovative companies. Much of its success can be attributed to William Blackie, who started with the company as a Comptroller in 1939 and retired from the position of Chief Executive Officer (CEO) in 1972.

Finding itself with thousands of abandoned Caterpillar machines in foreign countries at the end of World War II, the company decided to engage in manufacturing abroad in order to protect its export markets. It was no easy task for Blackie to convince his peers of the necessity for this move. He made himself accessible to people at all levels who were in need of an explanation. In public speeches Blackie showed that every foreign market where Caterpillar was engaged in manufacturing became a better market for the company's exports from the United States. William Blackie was highly effective at communicating what his company was doing and describing the context of world trade in which it operated, observing the rights of labor and the public to question and understand Caterpillar's operations. As with many CEOs today, he felt it was his responsibility to ensure open communication and information flow between management and labor, government, and the general public. This policy helped William Blackie build Caterpillar into one of the world's successful multinational corporations.

The grapevine can and should work for the manager. Whenever possible the manager should present facts as they are known at that time. When people are honestly involved in the information flow of an organization, the desire and opportunity for rumors to develop and grow are drastically reduced. It may sound trite, but honesty is the best policy. It is the most effective weapon against rumor. Managing the grapevine means being open to the information communicated informally, even though it may not be totally correct.

OTHER ASPECTS AND ISSUES OF COMMUNICATION

Communication Networks

Every group is affected by the **communication network** through which its functions are performed. This network may be the result of the formal organizational structure or arise because of the unique behavior of group members. Exhibit 11-4 shows four common networks that have been tested by researchers.

The *circle network* and *all-channel networks* are more decentralized than others, since all members have access to an equal number of people. For example, in the all-channel network, any individual can interact with everyone else; whereas in the circle form, each individual can interact with only his or her immediate neighbors. Conversely, the other networks, the *wheel* and *chain*, are more centralized because communication is forced through a central channel with the result that some members have access to more information than others.

A substantial amount of research has been conducted on which network is the best. The criteria used to make this determination has included the efficiency with which the given problem was solved or the task carried out and the satisfaction experienced by the individuals who participated in the group.

Research indicates that no one type of network is best, in fact. Rather, each network has certain good and bad points. Centralized

Exhibit 11-4 Four Types of Communication Network

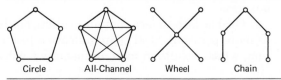

Circle   All-Channel   Wheel   Chain

networks like the wheel and chain are more efficient for solving simple problems; they are more accurate and require less time to produce a solution. Decentralized networks like the circle and the all-channel are able to handle complex and unstructured problems that require much creativity and discussion and where time is not critical. Member satisfaction tends to be greatest in these networks because more individuals have a sense of much participation.

Based on such findings, it appears that the appropriate network for an organization or group depends largely on the nature of the tasks to be accomplished and the extent to which employees are concerned about satisfaction and productivity. If satisfaction is desired, a circular or all-channel network would be appropriate. For simple, routine tasks, the wheel or chain works well. For difficult tasks that require flexibility or creativity, the circle or all-channel network is most useful.

These studies also show that individuals who hold certain positions that may be "information sensitive" can be more influential than their titles suggest. For example, staff positions such as assistant may have little formal authority, yet they may command great influence because of their control over information needed by decision makers.

Written versus Oral Communication: When to Use Each

Although it is not easy to determine when written or oral communication should be used, each has certain characteristics that affect its usefulness.

Written communications in general give the appearance of being more formal and authoritative than oral communications. Written communications tend to be interpreted more accurately, since they can be communicated in the same words to all who receive them. They tend to be used when consistent action is required, for instance, in stating organizational policies and procedures, and where a (written) record is necessary.

A common problem with written forms of communication, especially reports, however, is the proliferation of reports that are of questionable importance. This "paperwork burden" can dull the impact of the really useful reports or other written communications. Effective report writing is increasingly important, and many universities are now requiring a specific course in writing for students majoring in business.

Oral or face-to-face communication, on the other hand, is viewed as more personal. Oral communication fosters two-way communication, which results in more immediate feedback.

Paperwork—A necessary evil?

The major problem with oral communication, however, is that distortion can occur during the transmitting process. Distortion occurs most often when the information requires evaluation or interpretation. When factual information or expected messages are being transmitted, the distortion tends to be minimal.

In a 1972 study of the attitudes of supervisors, Dale Level compared the effectiveness of oral and written communication. The study found that oral communication was more effective in disciplinary situations or in settling a dispute among employees concerning a work-related problem. In both of these situations, evaluative judgments are involved.

Written communication was more effective for communicating factual information required for decision-making purposes or to carry out tasks. Oral communication was least effective for these purposes, the study concluded.

The Importance of Effective Communication to Other Management Activities

Communication is the way people express their feelings or obtain needed information to carry out assigned tasks. Good communication skills play a vital role in the successful performance of a manager's job. It is not just because it takes up a large part of the workday; rather, communication is essential when we want to motivate others or when we ourselves need assistance.

Clearly written policies and procedures will help ensure that organizational members understand not only what goals are important but also how to achieve them. Whether plans are being formulated to introduce a new product, improve an existing service, or establish a new department, clearly communicating these goals to the people involved will improve the likelihood of success.

When organizing work groups and determining structural relationships, their impact on the effectiveness of communication should also be considered. If the emphasis is on communication "following the chain of command," then the lateral communication necessary for coordination purposes will likely be inhibited and, in turn, cause unnecessary delays. Unnecessary delays also occur when there is an overemphasis, as in many bureaucracies, on "putting everything in writing," rather than using oral communication where appropriate.

The use of oral communication is probably greatest when managers are directing or seeking to motivate their subordinates. Crucial information and instructions must be given clearly and accurately. Ideas and emotions become translated into personal expectations concerning qualities such as honesty, loyalty, and trust and organizational requirements concerning abilities and performance.

Finally, the control process relies heavily on feedback. The providing of feedback should have been made during planning to determine how well organizational goals are being achieved. Control reports should be clear, and managers need to understand their interpretation.

Improving Communication

Effective communication is essential to all aspects of managerial work. In fact, without good communication techniques and information systems most organizations could not exist. So far in this chapter we have explored the communication process, its importance in carrying out management functions, and the barriers to communication that exist in organizations. Overcoming these barriers requires certain guidelines for improving communication. Some of these guidelines include:

- The credibility and reputation of the sender greatly determine the degree to which the listener "hears" and filters communication. By their past actions people and organizations show how fair, open, and trustworthy they are. Fairness, openness, and "telling it like it is" will reduce distortion.

- Messages that reinforce the receiver's attitudes will be better received. Receivers also tend to interpret messages in line with their attitudes. The communication of information that is not in line with receivers' attitudes therefore needs to be composed carefully and reinforced more often.

- Mass communication is seldom a successful channel of communication for bringing about change. Rather, more personal kinds of communication, such as meetings, should be used to determine how people feel and to allay their fears.

- The purpose of a message should be clearly defined by the sender. Determining why the message is being sent, who is to receive it, when it should be sent, and the exact relationship between the sender and receiver will largely determine the form that the message will take and what channel to use.

- Messages should be tailored to the specific receiver, so that he or she can respond in the desired manner. It is important that information is relevant, accurate, and clear to minimize misunderstanding.

- Feedback should be encouraged to verify that the intended message was received accurately.

- Effective listening is equally as important as effective sending. Effectiveness in listening can be tested by having receivers repeat messages when they are received and by encouraging senders to read messages before they are transmitted.

- Words should be selected carefully to avoid emotionally loaded terms that may cause the receiver to misinterpret the message.

- Written communication should be used whenever practical. Policies, rules, procedures, and instructions have a much better chance of being understood when they are in writing. Written messages tend to be clearer and are on record for future reference.

- Finally, improving communication takes time and effort. Written communication skills can be improved by a variety of writing courses. Oral communication skills can be improved by public speaking courses. These skills are basic to all career choices and are nurtured and improved through practice. We urge the student to take advantage of electives to improve his or her ability to communicate.

The preceding guides emphasize the importance of being sensitive to others. In fact, increased sensitivity and awareness of others will largely reduce the interpersonal barriers to communication.

Effective Listening: A Key Ingredient to Improving Communication

Listening is a skill that is often taken for granted. We assume that just because we can hear we are listening when something is said. Yet, our confusion is responsible for many unfortunate failures of communication. **Hearing** is a physical process that goes on inside one's head. It is the conversion of vibrations into electrical signals which, in turn, form messages in the brain. *Listening* is an active process, which involves understanding, evaluating, and making a part of one's consciousness the thoughts and expressions of others.

Many of us develop bad listening habits. We assume that we can guess what an employee is going to say; therefore, there is no need to listen carefully. We adopt a "listening posture," sitting or standing upright, eyes open, appearing to concentrate on the speaker. Having done this, we often "turn off our mind" and assume that any failure to communicate is the fault of the speaker. This assumption allows the listener to absolve himself or herself from blame. Ralph Nichols, an expert on listening, identified what he called the 10 bad habits of listening. The best way to overcome these problems is to develop what are called effective listening habits. Often referred to as the "10 commandments" of good listening, the following are excellent guidelines for becoming an effective listener (Nichols, 1959).

1. Stop talking. As long as you are talking, there is no chance for you to listen.

2. Put the speaker at ease. Let the other person know that he or she is free to talk.

3. Show the speaker that you are interested in what is being said. Do not read your mail or talk on the phone while listening. Look and act interested. Also, listen for the purpose of understanding, rather than for a way to find things wrong with what is being said.

4. Remove distractions. Close the door or screen out noise. Tell the secretary to hold all calls. This creates the right environment for listening.

5. Empathize with the speaker. Put yourself in this person's shoes and try to see things from his or her point of view.

6. Be patient. Allow the individual plenty of time to develop what he or she is saying. Do not interrupt the person or start walking

away from the conversation. This will simply turn the person off and diminish the chances you have to understand.

7. Hold your temper. An angry person often takes the wrong meaning from what is being said. Remain calm.

8. Go easy on criticism and argument, as these things put people on edge and make them defensive. If they have a problem with which they relate and then find themselves getting yelled at, it is unlikely that they will come by to discuss such matters in the future. They will bottle it all up inside themselves and let it affect their work. Remember also: if you quarrel and win, you still lose.

9. Ask questions. This encourages the speaker to develop his or her ideas and shows that you are interested in what is being said. It encourages the person to go on with the conversation.

10. Stop talking. This is not only the first rule of effective listening, it is the last. All other commandments of effective listening depend on it.

Good listening is an active process, one that requires concentration, conscious effort, and an open mind. Often employees are reluctant to express their true feelings to their manager. Then the job of the manager is to discover what his or her employees are really thinking. To do this, ask open-ended questions such as: what do you think about this project? A question like this will signal to the employee that more explanation of his or her earlier statements would be useful. As long as there is dialogue going on, the manager stands a better chance of getting to the bottom of the problem.

The Use of Management Information Systems

Within an organizational setting, managers cannot take for granted that the right information will be available at the right time. They must plan ahead to ensure its availability. A Management Information System (MIS) is designed to fulfill management's need for information by identifying *what* information is required *by whom* and at *what time* within the organization. MIS refers to the techniques that are used to select, store, process, and retrieve information that is required by management for decision making and control.

As organizations become larger and more complex, communication networks must be modified to provide the needed information in an efficient and timely manner. The communication needs of a small organization are clearly different from those of a highly decentralized, diversified, and geographically spread-out organization. Where goals are relatively simple and facilities are nearby, traditional information processing is usually sufficient. Advances in computer technology have enabled managers in more complex organizations to obtain the information they require. Proper MIS helps ensure that these needs are met without inundating the manager with useless or inappropriate information.

The management information system in the Chevrolet Division of General Motors illustrates the importance of a well-designed system. During the late 1960s, increased production of various Chevrolet models resulted in inadequate information regarding parts inventories. This incomplete data in turn caused material shortages on assembly lines; parts had to be flown in at great cost using chartered aircraft. The subsequent development of a more timely MIS reduced the response time in placing orders for parts, assigning orders to assembly plants, and therefore delivering cars to customers.

Management needs to be informed of the degree to which various departments are meeting their goals, especially their budgets. Since financial reports are at the heart of most MIS systems, managers at all levels require a basic understanding of financial statements.

Communications technology is perhaps the most rapidly changing area today. Telecommunications and word processing capabilities have significantly changed how communication takes place in an organization. For example, Continental Bank in Chicago has placed video computer terminals in the offices of many of their managers. These managers can now "write" memos directly to other managers. The messages are sent instantly without the need of a secretary. Much paperwork and time are saved in the process.

As communications technology continues to advance, one wonders whether the complexity of the systems will reduce their usefulness. This question is largely one of man–machine interfacing (discussed in Chapter 3).

Questions have also been raised about the protection of privacy when masses of information are kept on people by both government agencies and private organizations. Who can access this information and for what purposes are considerations that certainly need to be thought through carefully, or communications technology will overwhelm us.

SUMMARY

Communication skills are among the most important that individuals can acquire for all sorts of careers. In a survey of college graduates of the past five years, most stated that the single most important skill they require in their careers is the ability to communicate. They further stressed that more course work related to written and oral communication skills would have been beneficial to them. This response was especially striking since it came from college graduates in a wide range of careers. Besides an understanding of the process of communication, practice in the art of communication is also required.

In this chapter we have stressed that communication is at the heart of all management activities. The communication process was described, and common barriers to communication were discussed. The difference between formal and informal communication was then developed, as well as guidelines to make communication more effective.

Although the emphasis in this chapter has been on the interpersonal aspect of communication, the technical, or systems, aspect of communication is certainly also important (this is discussed in Chapter 3).

Questions for Study and Discussion

1. Describe the components of the communication process.
2. What are the characteristics of good communication?
3. What are some examples of personal barriers to effective communication?
4. Why is communication important?
5. How is communication related to the management functions of planning and control?
6. What are the purposes of downward, lateral, and upward communication?
7. What are some examples of formal (written) and oral communications?
8. How can informal communication networks be used by management?
9. How can written communications be improved?
10. What are the advantages of oral communication?
11. What are the distinctions between the different communication networks?

Experiential Exercise 1

This exercise illustrates the relative effectiveness of two-way communication (where there is feedback) compared to one-way communication (where no feedback is allowed).

Choose two individuals who will serve as the senders to the rest of the class. Each sender should make a *distinct* figure composed of a combination of seven geometric shapes, including triangles, squares, and rectangles. Each of the seven shapes (except those at each end)

Exhibit 11-5

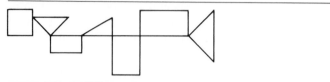

should touch two other components. A possible figure is shown in Exhibit 11-5.

To illustrate one-way communication, the sender should sit or stand with his or her back to the class. He or she should then verbally describe the figure, taking as much time as necessary but *without* using any gestures or facial expressions. Group members should attempt to reproduce the figure, again *without* asking questions. No feedback is allowed!

To illustrate two-way communications, the second sender should face the class and verbally describe the figure he or she has constructed. The second sender may use gestures and may answer the group's questions.

After each sender has completed his or her communication and each figure is drawn, information on the following criteria should be discussed with the class.

1. The similarity between the figures drawn by the group and the one held by the sender.
2. The amount of time required to complete the communication process in each situation.
3. The different feelings experienced by each sender and the class (the receivers) during two-way and one-way communication.

The following questions should also be discussed.

1. What are the trade-offs between accuracy and speed in one-way communication?
2. What is the effect on behavior of one-way communication?
3. Under what conditions would one-way communication be appropriate?

Experiential Exercise 2

The second exercise illustrates the relative ineffectiveness of oral communication for recalling facts. Select two volunteers from the class and have one leave the room. Read the following story to the first volunteer in front of the class, while the second volunteer waits outside the room. The second volunteer should then be called into the room and told the story by the first volunteer. The second volunteer should then tell the story to the class (or to a third volunteer).

The class should be given tally sheets listing the 20 facts in the original story to use as a checkoff when the story is retold. Discussion should revolve around how many facts were "forgotten" from one telling to another.

The Story

A farmer who lived in western Kansas was presented with a very peculiar problem. The tin roof on his barn was torn off by a small tornado. The twisted and mangled metal was found two communities away from his home. A friend and lawyer advised him to sell the scrap metal to the Ford Motor Company. The lawyer was sure that he could get a good price for it; so the farmer decided to ship the metal to the company to see how much he could get for it. He put it in a very big wooden box and sent it to Dearborn, Michigan. He left a return address and told the company to send the check to him. Twelve weeks passed without his hearing a word. He was on the verge of writing, when finally he received an envelope from the company. A message inside asked, "What hit your car?" The letter also informed the farmer that the company would have his car fixed by the 15th of the next month.

	20 Key Facts		
Original Story	**Version 1**	**Version 2**	**Version 3**
1. Farmer			
2. Western Kansas			
3. Tin roof			
4. A small tornado			
5. Two communities away			
6. Twisted and mangled			
7. A friend and lawyer			
8. Ford Motor Company			
9. A good price			
10. Ship the roof			
11. How much he could get for it			
12. Very big wooden box			
13. Dearborn, Michigan			
14. Return address			
15. Send the check			
16. 12 weeks passed			
17. Verge of writing			
18. Received an envelope			
19. What hit your car			
20. 15th of the next month			

Any new items?
In which version?
List:

CASE: DUNCAN MANUFACTURING COMPANY

Duncan Manufacturing Company is a medium-size supplier of automobile parts. Its parts are sold (1) directly to the major automobile manufacturers for use as original equipment and parts supplies and (2) through jobbers to a number of automotive supply houses that specialize in selling replacement parts, both on a wholesale and retail basis. Sales to the replacement market have increased steadily over the years and now account for 65 percent of all sales and 75 percent of profits. Duncan's organization chart is shown in Figure 11-1.

After a recent meeting, Juan Ramirez, a supervisor, returned to his office quite angry. "The boss had done it again!" he thought. Juan had just been advised of pending changes affecting his department that everyone else at the meeting seemed to have been aware of except him. The changes included the addition of a third shift, as well as the installation of some labor-saving equipment.

Juan's boss, Steve Hanson, was quite enthusiastic when he announced the changes to those assembled. The group included Joe Peters, the personnel manager; Ann Davis, the purchasing agent; and three supervisors from other departments that also reported to Steve. The other supervisors seemed to have expected both the announcement and the other information related to the pending changes that was presented by Joe Peters and Ann Davis.

Juan had reservations about the company's ability to staff a third shift with the kinds of skilled workers that would be required to maintain quality standards. He also had some concern about the

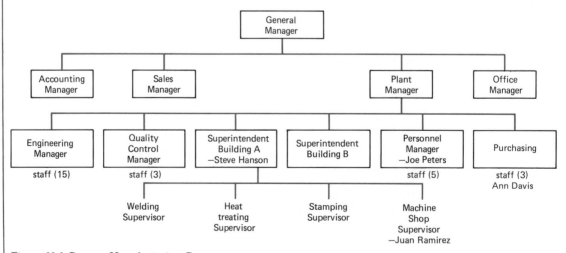

Figure 11-1 Duncan Manufacturing Company

company's ability to deliver the machinery on schedule. Juan had not expressed these concerns in the meeting, since he had no opportunity to discuss them beforehand. Therefore, he decided to say nothing, since the decisions had already been made.

Upon Juan's return to the department, Mike Demming, one of his subordinates and a union steward, asked Juan, "What do you think about the addition of the third shift?"

Questions

1. Why did Steve Hanson not discuss the proposed changes with Juan Ramirez prior to the meeting?
2. What might be the consequences of this failure to communicate?
3. Why do you suppose that Ann Davis, purchasing agent, and Joe Peters, Personnel Manager, knew about the changes?
4. Suggest two reasons that Mike Demming, the union steward, knew about the change before Juan Ramirez.
5. Comment on the barriers to communication that seem to exist in this situation.

References

Allen, Richard K., *Organizational Management Through Communications.* New York: Harper & Row (1977).

Anderson, Mel, "Communication Barriers and How to Scale Them," *Supervision,* **41**(3) (March 1979): 14–16.

Bacharach, Samuel B., and Michael Aiken, "Communication in Administrative Bureaucracies," *Academy of Management Journal,* **20** (September 1977): 365–377.

Baird, John E., Jr., *The Dynamics of Organizational Communication.* New York: Harper & Row (1977).

Baskin, Otis W., and Craig E. Aronoff, *Interpersonal Communication in Organizations.* Santa Monica, Cal.: Goodyear (1980).

Brown, Alan, and Frank Heller, "Usefulness of Group Feedback Analysis as a Research Method: Its Application to a Questionnaire Study," *Human Relations,* **34**(2) (February 1981): 141–156.

Clutterback, David, "Breaking Through the Cultural Barrier," *International Management,* **35**(12) (December 1980): 41–42.

Cross, Gary P., "How to Overcome Defensive Communications," *Personnel Journal,* **57** (August 1978): 441–443ff.

Denny, William, "Remedies for the Excelsior Syndrome," *Business Horizons,* **23**(5) (October 1980): 37–39.

Huegli, Jon, and Harvey Tschirgi, "An Investigation of Communication Skills Application and Effectiveness at the Entry Job Level," *Journal of Business Communication,* **12**(1) (Fall 1974): 24–29.

Kikoski, John F., "Communication: Understanding It, Improving It," *Personnel Journal,* **59** (February 1980): 126–131.

Level, Dale, Jr., "Communication Effectiveness Method and Situation", *Journal of Business Communication,* 10, (1), (Fall, 1972): 19–25.

"Listening and Responding to Employees' Concerns: An Interview with A. W. Clausen," *Harvard Business Review,* **58** (January-February 1980): 101–114.

McCallister, Linda, "The Interpersonal Side of Internal Communications," *Public Relations Journal,* **37**(2) (February 1981): 20–23.

McLuhan, Marshall, *Understanding Media: The Extensions of Man.* New York: McGraw Hill (1964).

Miller, George, "Management Guidelines: Being a Good Communicator," *Supervisory Management,* **26**(4) (April 1981): 20–26.

Mintzberg, Henry, *The Nature of Managerial Work.* New York: Harper & Row (1973).

Muchinsky, Paul, "Organizational Communication: Relationships to Organizational Climate and Job Satisfaction," *Academy of Management Journal,* **20**(12) (December 1977): 592–607.

Nichols, Ralph, "Listening: What Price Inefficiency?", *Office Executive* (April 1959): 15–22.

Roberts, Karlene H., and Charles A. O'Reilly III, "Some Correlates of Communication Roles in Organizations," *Academy of Management Journal,* **22** (March 1979): 42–57.

Samaras, John, "Two-Way Communication Practices for Managers," *Personnel Journal,* **59**(8) (August 1980): 645–648.

Tortoriello, Thomas R., Stephen J. Blatt, and Sue De Wine, *Communications in the Organization: An Applied Approach.* New York: McGraw-Hill (1978).

Wofford, Jerry C., Edwin A. Gerloff, and Robert C. Cummins, *Organizational Communication: The Keystone to Managerial Effectiveness.* New York: McGraw-Hill (1977).

PART FOUR

NEW MANAGEMENT PERSPECTIVES

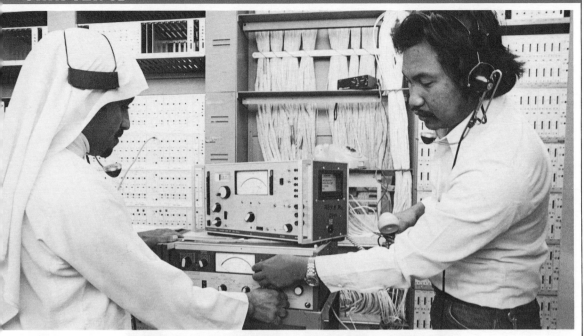

CHAPTER 12

CHANGE AND ITS MANAGEMENT

<table>
<tr><td>KEY
QUESTIONS
ADDRESSED
IN CHAPTER</td><td>
1. To what extent does change surround us in our business and personal lives?

2. What concepts can assist managers in better understanding and interpreting change?

3. What techniques and approaches are available to help people better cope with change?

4. What are the managerial skills and action capabilities crucial for success in initiating and guiding change?
</td></tr>
</table>

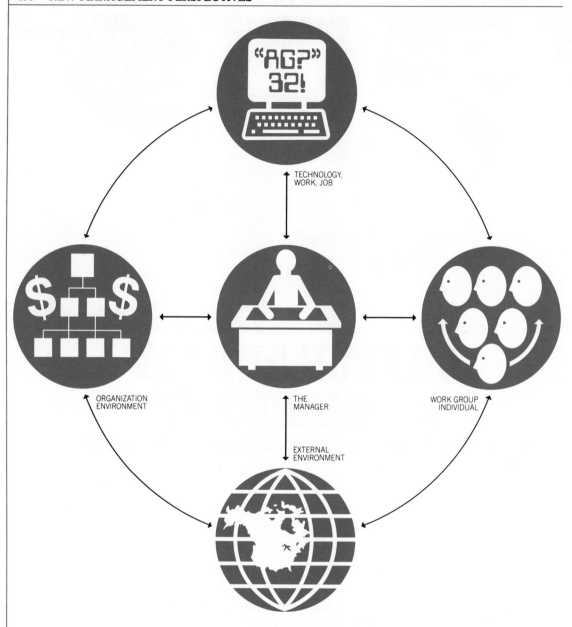

The manager's work–life spaces

All progress is precarious and the solution of one problem brings us face to face with another.

Martin Luther King, Jr.

THE CHAPTER IN BRIEF

Why should a chapter on change and its management be included in this book? Understanding and dealing with change may well appear to be less urgent, for private individuals or managers, than trying to stay on top of ordinary affairs on a day-to-day basis. Simply maintaining the status quo is, after all, a demanding affair.

In truth, few of us are able to maintain the status quo for more than brief periods. Change is the much more usual condition. In its various forms and in many ways, change surrounds us. It can neither be avoided nor ignored. Although in earlier periods of history, change was "a big deal," in the contemporary world it is regarded as "business as usual." But this does not mean that the thoughtful treatment of change is either usual or ordinary—on the contrary. In essence, the theme of this chapter is improving people's ability to understand and deal with change, both as managers and in their personal lives. Change can be either a positive or threatening force in our lives, depending on what we make of it.

The basic rationale for devoting considerable attention to change is that facing up to specific situations in which change is involved is challenging for all of us. This is the case in our individual lives, as well as in our occupational roles, whether we are professional managers or otherwise. None of us need search very long to find instances in which we, or people we know, have met inadequately the challenge of change.

Change can be disruptive, uncomfortable, or worse. For these reasons many of us do not bring out capabilities to bear on it very effectively. We may delay, hoping that the pressures of change will "blow over," or we may pretend that our circumstances require no change. Responses like these suggest that dealing successfully with change may require modes of behavior that go beyond intuition or the use of so-called common sense.

It is important that the capacity to understand and cope with change be seen as a deliberate thought process. One that can enable us to initiate, guide, and control the components of change, so that the end results are at least close to those we desire and value. For managers, the management of change means that they should be aware not only of how change affects them but also of how change should be managed to overcome their subordinates' resistance to change. Managers must employ a unique combination of insights and skills in reaching decisions about change. Just what is involved in the application of these talents and skills will be elaborated at some length in the pages to follow.

Change and the Life-Space Model

There is little value—in fact, there may be potential harm—in dealing with all aspects of change in a similar fashion. Only confusion results from an analysis of change that lumps together very different types of events, treating them as if they fit into the same mold. A better approach is to use the life-space concept. In this approach, events and processes involving change are distinguished from one another by being assigned to different spaces within our total life experience. Exhibit 12-1 provides a guide to the discussions that follow. The diagram, similar in format to those heading up each chapter, structures life experiences into five "spaces" identified as individual, group, work, organization, and environment. Except for individuals who do not work at all, the five spaces fit together in some design or configuration to make up the total round called life.

The *individual–life space* is positioned at the center of Exhibit 12-1. This position indicates that, as individuals, we typically take part in all of the other life spaces. Also, we maintain for ourselves a space that is not overlapped by the concerns and demands of the work group, organization, or environment spaces. One might expect that changes which occur within the individual–life space are entirely self-initiated. Yet the motivation for individual change may be traced to one or more of the other spaces. For example, a decision to join a sports club and "get into shape" may be a self-initiated change; however, at times the pressure of friends or a mate may also be a factor. Similarly, it is likely that volunteering to substitute for one's supervisor while he or she is on vacation stems from group and organization influences.

The individual–life space is a useful starting point to understand how we recognize changes in ourselves and in our particular situations. To some extent we serve as our own reference points. Probably more often, however, we look to people and events around us in drawing conclusions about the type or degree of change. We can take note of shifts in the way we should think and behave, in the way relatives and friends differ from the past, and in the way group or organizational circumstances can present us with potential benefits or dangers. Of course, we do not perceive many of these shifts accurately or with clarity. This often results in individual problems that arise from our failure to act forcefully enough or in the right way.

The *group–life space*, like the individual, has meaning for change both on and off the job. We are all familiar with change as it affects members of our families or of social and community groups. In

Exhibit 12-1 Work–Life Spaces: The Individual Viewpoint

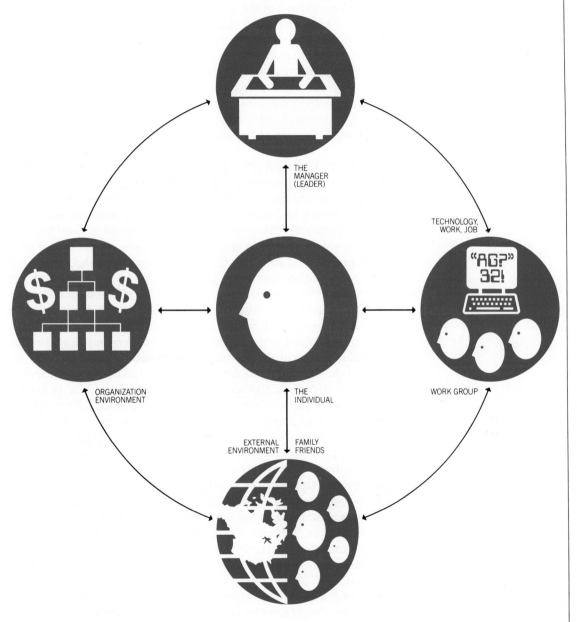

most cases, group memberships are unstable over time, and this characteristic alone causes other changes. Groups take on new leaders, group goals shift, and even the spirit of group participation may assume a different form. In Chapter 10, we considered the role of friendship on the job (recall the Hawthorne experiments) and ways in which the codes of conduct of a group mold individual actions that result in organized group responses to change. There are also the formal staff or support groups with which one must interact to accomplish work or receive assistance. We shall return to the study of groups at work later in this chapter, when we analyze *resistance to change*.

Turning to the *work–life space*, we see that this space concentrates on certain well-known properties of work systems. It is tempting to use the assembly-line model for discussing these systems, since it is so well known and does possess all the basic features necessary for such a discussion. This mode of work exhibits a *flow* from an *upstream* to a *downstream* point. It encompasses the use of required tools, equipment, and supplies. It makes use of work rules and procedures that employees are expected to follow. It is not a complete system in itself but functions as an input to still another system. Illustration of this work–life space can also be accomplished in a nonassembly-line context, which is important because so many people today are involved in nontechnical, or service oriented, activities.

Consider a typical elementary or high school teacher. Such an individual takes groups of students at an early point in their learning development, and over the course of the school year, it is hoped, moves them to a point of more advanced development. This process involves tools, equipment, and supplies appropriate to the schoolroom, shop, or gym. Also, rules and regulations are supposed to be followed by both students and teachers. The end products are inputs or prerequisites to other parts of the system, such as to the next grade level or perhaps to college or a job.

Change, particularly technological change, is a very common feature of work situations. If we consider some examples of new technologies—such as the pocket-size calculator, computer-assisted instruction, and closed-circuit television—the connections between these devices and changes in how "school work" is done are easily appreciated.

The *organization—life space* is also dealt with at considerable length in this chapter. Some individuals are unaware of changes in this life space, because they have had little experience in actual organizations. But even people with little or no work experience can identify some changes that are initiated by organizational sources— for example, changes in key government officials at federal, state, and local levels; the constant increase in the cost of goods and services that can be traced to numerous organizational decisions; the continual change in the content and scheduling of commercial television programming; and the compact appearance of current automobile models, which reflect major design decisions of the major automobile producers.

Experienced employees have little difficulty in noticing some instances of change, such as when their organization offers new or revamped goods or services or adopts new marketing or public relations strategies. Another well-known facet of organizational life is the frequency with which "reorganizations" occur. These changes signal shifts in "who is in charge of what," and the redirection of the activities of some or all parts of the organization. For example, the matrix structure discussed in Chapter 2 has been introduced by many organizations to deal with change. Employees may also detect subtler changes, such as in the quality of organizational climate. In such cases, employees take "readings" of management behavior regarding employee welfare, the openness and credibility of communication to employees, the competence of managerial leadership, and other matters affecting the quality of the work climate.

Last, in this overview of life-space concepts, we come to the external *environmental–life space.* As its name suggests, this space typically refers to those external events over which organizations, let alone individuals, have little influence. For organizations, the external environment consists of other organizations plus economic, legal, technological, political, and social trends (and changes!) that shape its policies, programs, and priorities. In addition, the organization's environment is made up of competitors, suppliers, customers, and government agencies whose actions affect the conduct of business in a multitude of ways. If the business organization operates internationally, the numbers of organizations in the environment increase dramatically.

In recent times, large-scale changes have been taking place in the external environment. All of us are familiar with social changes regarding such matters as careers—multiple careers, dual careers, and new careers for women (re)entering the work force; in vocabulary—what choice of words is acceptable among communicators; and in recreational pursuits—what currently qualifies as pleasurable for different individuals and groups. On a more significant level, the "rights explosion" is an environmental fact of life that is also very much with us.

On a still broader front, the current external environment is notable for its inclusion of international opportunities, issues, and problems on a scale unmatched in the past. If we only point to the energy dependence of the United States upon foreign imports and the weakness of the U.S. dollar relative to several foreign currencies in recent times, the pervasive importance of environmental change is clearly established.

Life Spaces, Managerial Role, and Change

For the manager, change may be initiated in any of the sectors or life spaces with which he or she deals. Also, the manager often initiates change. Therefore, the manager's ability to manage or cope with change is very complex, since the sources of change literally surround him or her. The situation is made even more complex by the fact that the sources of change may be activated either by individuals or by groups and that eventually a change initiated in one sector often affects another. Thus, the life-space model is transformed into a dynamic mass of interacting forces and variables, for which managers must establish priorities: which can they handle given their own abilities, availability of funds and staff, and time constraints?

GREAT PERSON PROFILE

Donald Wills Douglas (1892–   )

Donald Wills Douglas was instantly and permanently converted to a belief in the airplane by watching a demonstration by the Wright Brothers in Ft. Myers, Virginia in 1908. Douglas was educated as an aeronautical engineer at Massachusetts Institute of Technology, and after working several jobs in the field of precommercial aviation, he formed his own business. In 1920 he set about designing and building wooden airplanes for the U.S. Navy at a small workshop in Santa Monica, California. Through steady progress, he made a pioneering industry come of age with the introduction of the DC series in 1932. He combined a sense of purpose with insistence on perfection. As an acquaintance once said of him, "He never built a bad plane."

The aviation industry is characterized by rapid changes and competition, and during a long career, no one introduced more changes than Douglas. The ability to change and to adjust to change is symbolized in Douglas's rise to leadership in commercial aviation. Along with others in the industry, Douglas foresaw the rapid change to jet-powered aircraft after World War II. An inability of Douglas to meet the increased competition led to the rapid decline of his company's leading position in the industry. Failing to regain this position, Douglas was forced to merge with McDonnell in 1966.

Students of management can learn both from Douglas's success and failure: managers must not only be *sensitive* to the changing needs of the marketplace but they must also be able to implement their plans into profitable products or services.

Within the framework of this model, the ability of a manager to **manage change** (change management) can be interpreted as the management of life-space sectors over which he or she has varying degrees of influence or control. For example, in an insurance company, a major change in client coverage needs for risk (external environment) required that a new type of policy be developed (internal environment). However, all policies at the time were handled using standardized computer programs (technology–life space), so that the field salesperson (individual–life space) and the manager had to work out a temporary procedural arrangement. The new procedure required senior management approval (organizational–life space), but it could not at that point be adapted to the computer system. The only feasible approach was a temporary manual procedure that required more work on the part of the field salesperson. Needless to say, the manager was faced with considerable internal administrative problems and a motivation problem, insofar as the salesperson was concerned.

BACKGROUND

Forces Impelling Change

The forces that generate change and the explanations for them are implicit in a number of examples that have already been presented. Yet, this type of discussion often risks leaving these ideas in a somewhat uncertain state. A better procedure is to deal with them specifically, and this is the subject of the following discussion.

Those changes that occur within the individual–life space, although having certain general properties, are not usefully dealt with outside of specific individual situations. Various features of these are treated in the chapters on motivation, leadership, and informal groups.

The changes of most immediate relevance to our understanding are those stemming from *interactions* between the work, organizational, and environmental life spaces. Several major forces for change and the impetus behind them are examined—with no order of importance implied.

Responses to Societal Needs and Trends

Let us first consider a very general example of environmental change, but one ultimately having important managerial implications. In the past, the trend toward suburbanization in the United States led to further development of transportation networks that were needed to meet the needs of a more scattered, traveling public. Service facilities, including drainage systems, streets, and expressways, also had to be greatly expanded. In some areas, the response has meant a larger metropolitan or regional unit of transportation, communications, or government. Now, with the growing complexity and uncertainties of the energy situation, people are moving back into the city. This is causing new pressures to update or renovate many previously neglected urban facilities. Accompanying these population and transportation shifts are managerial questions regarding the source, number, and types of employees for staffing existing units. There will also be growing and serious problems of employee transportation to work, in the light of the high cost of energy and lack of mass-transportation development.

The energy situation (external environment) is influencing still another area; it has started to affect internal organizational priorities. High energy costs are now a major factor to be reckoned with in managerial decisions. The four-day week and whole new sources of supplies and resources are likely results (among others) of rapidly rising costs in this area.

Technological change or scientific innovation and the opportunities and threats embedded in these are another important area of developments. In the electronics industry, for example, innovations in circuitry led to the incorporation of a succession of new concepts and processes into all kinds of electronic and communications devices, excluding radio and television. In a 10-year period, three different generations of circuitry concepts were introduced by manufacturers of these products. Lesser known, but of equal importance, were the numerous changes that the organizations were forced to undertake in manufacturing methods, skill training of personnel, recruitment of engineering help with knowledge of the new concepts, and the redevelopment of marketing strategies.

Organizational Goals as Forces in Change

Although sheer survival is the most basic of all organizational goals, once an organization's existence is no longer actively threatened, it is very likely to attempt to grow and expand. A key explanation of this widespread phenomenon is the *positive value* managers in organizations place upon growth—although we are aware of some glaring exceptions to this development. A growing organization is generally viewed as a successful organization.

This growth further serves as a measure of managerial competence. Managers thus become committed to growth as a goal, and with growth comes change. To the extent that an organization's growth correlates with its success in entering new markets, in

Industrial Robots: Once
an Idea, Now a Reality.

generating increased investment returns, in hiring new employees, or other relevant indicators, success feeds success. Various employee skills, knowledge, and experience that contribute to this success lead to the realization that "we are doing something right." In addition, an organization with a record of success finds it easier to borrow money for further expansion, to attract talented new employees, to interest new customers, and to achieve other objectives that it values.

Involuntary Change

Governmental laws and regulations are currently among the best known sources of involuntary organizational change. Examples are easy to find.

The hiring and promotion practices of most organizations are being forced to adhere to Title VII of the 1964 Civil Rights Act and the 1972 Equal Employment Opportunity Act. The thrust of both acts, as they bear upon employment, is frequently to require the internal restructuring of work forces: the proportion of minority and women employees must approach the proportion found in the organization's particular labor markets. Increasing numbers of minority group members and women in positions and occupations where they were seldom found in the past are generating widespread changes in employee relations, supervisory practices, and the management of human resources.

Equally well known are the changes required of the automobile manufacturers to comply gradually with the federal government's miles per gallon and exhaust emission standards. It has been necessary to design a whole new generation of automobiles. Also, many new employee talents and skills have had to be acquired, and marketing strategies and customer education efforts have had to be revamped. Change in many forms has also radiated to the thousands of supplier organizations that provide the auto makers with component parts and services.

Involuntary response to government-initiated change is now also prominent on the college and university campuses, an environment often regarded by the general public as not part of the "real world" and thus protected and isolated. Not so today. These institutions of higher learning have been the specific target of many regulations. Aside from "equal employment opportunity," Title IX of the Higher

The role of women and minorities in the labor force has been broadened by changes in employment practices.

Education Amendments of 1972 provides for the equal treatment of women students. The Family Education and Privacy Act of 1974 affords students the right of access to their record files. The Student Consumer Education Act of 1976 requires institutions of higher education to publish policies and practices and to be held accountable for them according to "truth" in advertising standards. The many regulations have changed the lives of university administrators in drastic ways. Much time must now be spent responding to regulations. Organizational structures have had to be expanded, and a great deal of money has been spent on compliance measures as well as on expensive legal advice.

Pervasive as government regulations seem to be, they are not the only forces impelling involuntary change. Challenges from competitors may equally effect change. Two examples from contrasting industries are sufficient to make this point.

Commercial airlines in the United States began to be deregulated in the 1970's. The Civil Aeronautics Board (CAB), which has ruled on airline route patterns and pricing practices for many years, was scheduled to go out of existence in 1982. The prospect of operating without CAB restraints led to many changes within the airline industry, as new airlines were formed and existing carriers sought to improve their competitive positions through the addition of new routes, innovations in passenger fares, and related matters. Thus, the top management of the airlines was forced to deal with increasing uncertainty, as the known quantity of regulation gave way to the lesser known one of competition.

On another front, a major department store chain made plans to build hundreds of new stores in the first half of the 1980s. To help raise the required financing, it proposed to offer notes to its customers. The notes would earn interest higher than rates available from banks and savings and loan institutions. To the extent that this innovative financial approach is implemented successfully, competitors of this chain face a new challenge.

Finally, with respect to involuntary sources of change, attention needs to be paid to certain new or strengthened forms of organizations that are making their demands felt. Unions of public employees—policemen, firemen, teachers—and a wide variety of government clerical and service workers have shown much more willingness in recent years to act in ways more traditional for industrial or private-sector unions. As sources for increased funding of governmental units "dry up," these groups have been involved in picketing, withholding services, and in many cases going on strike. Actions such as the Air Traffic Controllers' strike in 1981 forced changes in the policies of government employers and have very likely also changed the general public's image of government employee unions.

The Role of Information in Change

Every situation or event involving change introduced in this chapter could have been examined from the standpoint of the information possessed by the participants. Had this been done, it would have become evident that individuals, groups, and whole organizations were variously well informed, misinformed, or uninformed with respect to the appropriate content of plans, the availability of information sources, and the extent to which one or more decision alternatives might lead to success. Consequently, the projected outcomes of an individual, group, or organization's actions can range from high certainty to high uncertainty.

Clearly, the quality of planned change or the reaction to change that is thrust upon an individual, a group, or an organization varies as widely as the quality of the information inputs. It should be stressed that these inputs are not confined to information flows from the environment, but also include information already possessed by individuals in the form of education, special training, and work experience. Effective Management Information System (MIS), as discussed in Chapter 11, therefore have a crucial role to play in the management of change.

Readiness for Change: A Four-Step Test

The experience of the authors and others with change in many different organizations has been helpful in identifying certain regularities that seem to be present frequently, regardless of the situation. Of course, the importance of this finding for managers or individuals dealing with change is the fact that their own situation can be examined in systematic fashion. The ability to describe change in a systematic way helps us to understand better the problems, issues, or frustrations confronting us now—and to start pointing the way to solutions. The outline for a *change readiness* test is shown in Exhibit 12-2.

The most immediate and basic test for change measures the *awareness* of the fact that change has taken place. People, and the collection of individuals called the organization, often get wrapped up in today's problems and issues. For many, it is business as usual even though major changes are coming, have already taken place, or cumulatively have already had great effects. Thus, people may be only vaguely aware that change has taken place, and they may have mentally perceived it as "nothing special." The energy situation, described previously, is a good example of this. In the mid-1960s, energy experts had already forecast problems of international scope arising from supply, demand, and pricing policies. By 1980, the widespread implications of the situation still had not been recognized by many

Exhibit 12-2 Change Basics[a]

A   Awareness of the fact that change has taken place

I   Impact on individual or organization—that is, "Does change affect me?" "Does change affect us as an organization?"

M   Motivation—"Do I desire to change?" "Are we as an organization willing to change?" "Do we have to change?"

S   Skills—"Do we possess the skills or abilities to change successfully?"

AIMS = Readiness for Change

[a]For more details see Elmer H. Burack and Nicholas J. Mathys, *Human Resource Planning: A Pragmatic Approach to Manpower Planning and Development.* Lake Forest, Ill.: Brace-Park Press (1980), Chapters 1, 2.

Elmer H. Burack and Florence Torda, *A Manager's Guide for Change.* Belmont, Ca.: Lifetime Learning Press/Wadsworth (1979).

individuals and organizations, despite the major dislocations that occurred in the mid-1970s.

The second test for change is establishing that, in fact, it affects (*impacts on*) one's organizational department or oneself. It is true that change may be acknowledged as lurking on the sidelines, but it is clearly an additional step to establish one's involvement with it. Several examples help to illustrate this point. In the 1970s, it was common knowledge that changes in the school-age population were already underway that had major consequences for the number of needed teachers, facilities, and so forth. Yet many young people continued to set their career "sails" on teaching programs, although there were few real job prospects—"I don't have to worry, I'll find a job." In the automotive industry, big cars were still on the drawing board and being produced, despite the dramatic rise in small foreign-car imports and the energy problems. In one consumer products firm, a marketing manager remarked, "I know competition has this new copier coming out, but ours has been around for years, and they aren't about to pick off our customers." (Postscript: the manager's company lost almost one fourth of its market before it brought out a newer version of its own copier.)

The third test for change asks that the *motivation* or desire to undertake change be examined thoroughly and honestly. Change can be threatening—at the very least, it means uncertainty related to new learning and leaving the familiar behind. "Will I succeed?" "Will we be pouring dollars down a bottomless hole?" These are questions not easily dismissed. Thus it is not realistic to think about pressing ahead with change unless people or the organization are, at the very least, willing to go along with change and desirous of active involvement.

The fourth test, measuring the *skill* or ability to undertake change, is a necessary ingredient for successful change. People may need training. Organizations may require new systems, procedures, product lines, technical staff groups, or more resources. Picture a situation we recently encountered in which a small company, experienced in the sale of industrial products, decided to enter the highly competitive consumer products field of plastic housewares. More than two years passed before the company was able to assemble the product design skills needed for regular introduction of new products, and a sales force skilled in selling to customers completely different from those dealt with in the past.

Having the skills or abilities to change also affects an individual's or company's desire to enter into change. The fact that we have the skills or capability for change will often give us encouragement—a sense that we can be successful because we have the necessary skills.

Implications for Your Career

The discussion of change already presented has major implications for individual careers. Let us briefly recount key points already described. First, change is the normal state—we all experience it within our own individual life spaces and through interaction with other life spaces. Change, in its various forms, is seldom a random process. Identifiable forces and understandable reasons usually set change apart from chance. Change can be studied systematically as a four-step process. The management of change requires a unique combination of talents and knowledge, but it is a combination that can be learned. Demonstrating the manner in which this learning can take place on the individual level is the logical next step in our discussion.

Donna Cardelli: A Scenario

Donna's story is actually a composite based on the lives of several young women who have much in common. Donna is now almost 26 years of age. She has her own small apartment, though it is in the same part of the city where she grew up. After finishing high school, Donna attended the local branch of the state university but dropped out after two years. She lost interest in the liberal arts program she was pursuing, since she simply saw no point in it.

Since that time she has held the following unrelated jobs: (1) combination receptionist–telephone-console operator, (2) cashier–attendant at a racquet club, (3) driving instructor, and (4) veterinarian's assistant at an animal hospital (her current job).

During a recent evening visit to her older sister, Donna was brought up short when her sister asked, "What's going on in your head? Have you done any real thinking about where you're going?" Donna replied rather lamely that she did "like animals," had a good boss at the animal hospital, and got along well with her co-workers. As the conversation continued, however, Donna had to admit that the job was a dead end and provided a minimum of benefits and future salary potential. Her sister further pointed out that Donna was doing something very common for a person of her age and experience, namely, thinking only in job-by-job terms with no real objective in mind. Since the two sisters had an excellent relationship, Donna soon felt more comfortable talking about becoming career-minded and about the related concerns of marriage and family. For the time being, her sister advised, Donna should treat these matters separately and first look at the career question.

Donna's next step was to take a mental inventory of her assets. She had completed some college work with a respectable grade-point average. Her job experience had provided her with a few skills, although they fit into no pattern. Still, she was not "typecast," and this might prove an advantage. She also had a real sense of restlessness, hopefully an indication of a willingness to change and a desire to achieve. Then there was her youth; at almost 26 she was still young without being completely "green."

In examining the obstacles to her new interests, Donna wrote out her liabilities and problems. These rather quickly emerged as a series of "I don't knows."

- I don't know what I might be good at, because I've never tried to find a real career.
- I don't know enough about the availability, types, and trends in jobs that might interest me.
- I don't know how this information may affect me.
- I don't know what skills and experience are the best bets for me.
- I don't know what to do first to cope with my liabilities.

Confronted with so many unknowns, Donna felt it was reasonable to ask for help from some reliable sources, her sister and brother-in-law. She made arrangements to see her sister and brother-in-law the next evening. From this three-way discussion came the following inputs to Donna's plan for changing her life.

- Advice from relatives and friends was not enough. Donna should seek out professional counseling. The Psychological Institute at her old university offered an occupational assessment service. She made an appointment for this and applied for help from the college placement office, where she hoped to learn of *current market trends* for recent graduates. As mentioned earlier, societal needs and trends change over time.

- She would begin systematically reading the help-wanted advertisements in local newspapers to develop a "feel" for the pattern of opportunities available and the kind of personal credentials that various employers required. She would also study the jobs and careers section of these papers.

- She would spend time at both the public and the university library concentrating upon: (1) the "how-to-do-it" and "how-to-get-into-it" literature on occupations, and (2) a sampling of industry and trade magazines in search of career information, trends in demand, and case examples of individual successes and problems.

About three months later, Donna was able to sit back, review the highlights of what she had learned, and do additional planning.

Donna's occupational assessment indicated, overall, that she was strong in verbal skills and showed an orientation toward "human services." By contrast, she was relatively weak in quantitative skills and in technical inclinations. The college placement office told her that engineering, computer sciences, and business administration graduates were in strong demand; however, graduates with liberal arts, teaching, social work, and journalism degrees faced much dimmer prospects. Her study of the want ads backed up the placement office's summary of trends.

Through Donna's library reading she learned, among other things, of projections that in the 1980s the U.S. labor force will be 50 percent female, if not higher. But the internal distribution of female employees will change slowly—many women will still hold traditional "women's jobs" (secretarial, clerical, food service, and teaching positions). Also, the percentage of women in professional and managerial positions will grow, but not steeply.

Donna received the strong impression that, unless she resigned herself to rather routine white-collar work, she would have to make a determined effort to break out of her current mold and assume some risks for the sake of productive change. Despite her weakness in quantitative skills, she decided to begin study in two areas that had never tempted her before—computer science and business. She would continue in her job at the animal hospital, enroll in evening courses during the next term, and do her best to see if a new pattern of interests began to emerge.

Her approach would be experimental, open-minded, and outreaching. Hopefully, she would discover new or untapped potentials and, given some time, see where these might lead, if they seemed to promise a more satisfying life style.

Comment on Donna Cardelli

No attempt to bring about a significant change in a person's life goes smoothly—and this was very much the situation with Donna Cardelli. There will always be problems. People who seek advice, professional or otherwise, may be misadvised or simply become confused. They may also reject advice, since it may be uncomfortable. Still, the elements of action sketched using Donna as an example are basically sound and represent a commitment to planned individual change. If we examine Donna Cardelli's experience in terms of the life-space model and the four-step change test, constructive approaches for dealing with change become still clearer.

Individuals are affected by those people or events occupying other life spaces. Donna's outlook on careers and possibilities for herself were shaped by her family, schoolmates, and friends, as well as supervisors in her employer's organizations and various counselors. Note, however, that the period and form of influence differed in time, space, and content. Donna's family affected her outlook in her early growth and had some influence even after she went to school. As possible influences of her career direction, the professional counselors did not enter into the picture until relatively late.

To some extent, Donna was also affected by the organizations she worked in and the type of work she did. Yet the possible benefits to be gained from these were largely lost, since Donna lacked a plan to guide her and the background to distill information from her experiences with organizations. Change in the external environment and newer social trends had affected Donna's social existence except in ways that were a mystery to her—she sensed she should be changing but did not understand how, where, and when.

From the viewpoint of the change test, Donna was only vaguely aware of changes in the external environment and still more uncertain as to how these affected her. There is no point in worrying about an individual's ability or motivation to change when his or her involvement with change itself is not established. But note what happened when, almost by accident, Donna's sister asked her about her career. It is not clear that everything followed from this incident, since Donna was likely stewing about the problem for a long time. But the incident did trigger Donna's questioning. Notice how from that point, clarification of the *awareness* and *impact* of change were answered quite quickly and in a forceful way. Second, building the skills to change by gathering information and through self-study probably helped Donna over the hurdle of wanting to make changes in her life even though they were threatening to her. Her final strategy still had no specific answer attached to it, but it represented a systematic course of inquiry that was likely to turn up workable answers at a later point.

Of importance in Donna's case is the provision for a *rolling* plan, one that is responsive to new developments, much in keeping with the way the planning process is carried out within groups and organizations.

Aspects of Change at the Organizational Level

We are now ready to proceed to an analysis of change in an organizational context, one that will occupy much of the remainder of this chapter. Readers will discover that although organizational change is a more complex, protracted, and demanding affair than individual change, it, too, should deal with questions very similar to those individuals should ask of themselves in their efforts to change.

Key Questions about Change

As already noted, the most basic question is whether the organization is aware of the need to change, or of change that may be already ongoing. Since organizations, as such, have no "awareness," this question points to the necessity of assigning responsibilities for the awareness of change to certain individuals and groups. As with the carrying out of any responsibility, this job may vary widely in quality and completeness. Means of improving this quality will be taken up shortly.

Assuming that imminent change has been detected and the need for it is understood, the next question is how change will affect organizational relationships. Dealing with this question calls into play the skills of systems thinking (developed in Chapter 3). In particular, the skills of perceiving interrelationships among events, of sensing the motivation of participants, and of predicting the possible benefits or problems in the wake of change are required. Clearly, these complex skills lie at the very center of any repertoire for managing change.

Are there sufficient organizational or individual incentives to change? As was evident in the case of Donna Cardelli, incentives are crucial for any break with the status quo. On the organizational level, incentives for change become a complicated matter, in that no one type or magnitude of incentive will appeal to all organizational participants. Thus, as we see in examples to be introduced later, the incentives involved in change require "programming." Management, through a process of delegation to subordinates, needs to establish which combination of economic, psychological, social, and possibly legal incentives appear to be most workable in the situation of change. The chosen combination would then proceed, step by step, with different incentives quite likely offered to different groups affected by the change.

The last key question focuses upon resources; namely, does the organization have the human resources, technology, and financial capacity to cope with the demands of change? Raising this question is obviously much more sensible when change is *anticipated*. The manager needs to know whether these resources are at his or her disposal to meet these demands. In such cases, an audit or inventory approach can be taken to evaluate the adequacy of resources available and, at least, approximate the organization's ability to deal with change successfully established.

Role and Relational Features of Change

The roles that individuals and groups take on with respect to organizational change tend to be specialized because of the largely specialized forms of behavior displayed in organizations overall. Specialization varies with both hierarchical level and role, that is, according to individuals' positions in the organizational structure and what individuals or groups are expected to do.

At the top management level, chief executives and their immediate associates are expected to play the role of *initiators* of change, through the formulation or modification of policies intended in some way to change the behavior of some or all organizational participants. It should be recognized also that in a number of instances top managers decide on change initiatives on the basis of work done, advice given, or recommendations made by people at lower organizational levels. Here, accuracy in communication is very important to ensure that the "right" policies are developed and that these are, in turn, communicated in the right way to those groups and individuals in the organization whose support is essential for success.

All organizations, except for those on a very small scale, employ technical specialists. Large organizations may have many hundreds; medium-sized firms employ similar types, but fewer numbers, of experts. Such people play key roles in the *design* of organizational change. They bring their specialist knowledge to bear on the problems of discerning the need for change, analyzing the alternative responses to change pressures, and mapping out designs to be recommended when confronting problems arising from change or initiating change. This knowledge is relayed to the department manager, who is able to organize and use these resources for effecting change. An example is in order.

The personnel director and the financial services officer of a medium-size hospital in a southeastern city of the United States both came to the conclusion that the demands on their respective departments had become increasingly complex and urgent. At the same time their access to the overall hospital administrator had become more limited. Although technical experts in their own areas, both officers were unable to make a number of important decisions without the administrator's knowledge and approval. They sounded out a few other department heads on an informal basis and discovered that they all shared the same problem. Rather than simply going to the administrator with a broad, general complaint, they resolved to approach her with a *design* for change, which would break the logjam then located in the administrator's office. The design posed a choice between two alternatives: (1) the creation of a new position of associate administrator, who would function as increased access for decision making needed by department managers; (2) the delegation to department managers of greater decision-making power, the specifics of which would be worked out through discussions with the administrator. Both choices aimed to streamline management action.

In this example the department managers each acted as technical experts in different functional areas, and their ideas for change were communicated upward to the hospital administrator. Her agreement was obviously necessary for their ideas to have any meaning.

Another significant role in organizational change is that of **facilitator,** whose key responsibility is the "debugging" of problems and obstacles and creating the acceptance of change in all those affected. Facilitators are in many cases located at the lower level of the management hierarchy or at the grass-roots level of technical or operating employee classifications. Ideally, lower-level managers communicate the need for change to subordinates and are expected to make change "work" in their area. To this end, they frequently enlist the talents of "troubleshooters" or "expeditors," people who have a nuts-and-bolts understanding of change requirements (for instance, quality-control technicians, employment recruiters, cost analysts, and production schedulers), and have ideas on how change may be implemented most smoothly.

A quite different approach to facilitation is brought about through individuals who act in the capacity of a change agent, and whose formal designation is consultant. In large organizations, these change agents are often internal consultants, that is, employees of the corporation who are usually assigned to the headquarters staff. Outside consultants are also used for the same purpose. In either case, the consultants can often bring a degree of objectivity that the line managers or regular staff members find difficult to achieve.

At times, the facilitation of change may even be carried out on a large scale through the attempt to strengthen work teams. This approach is termed Organization Development.

At this point we can look back at the set of roles related to organizational change. Top management initiates change; technical experts design programs for change, including their details; and finally there are facilitator roles played by most managers, who carry out the plans and designs of others and make them work in the organization. Obviously, this is a simplified description. Nothing thus far has been said about the large majority of employees, who, in any organization, determine the success or failure of any attempt at change. In the main, most employees are on the "receiving end" of change; they typically have no responsibility for its initiation. Yet, change would neither begin or become the new mode of behavior without the interrelated actions of initiators, designers, and facilitators.

GREAT PERSON PROFILE

Harry Blair Cunningham (1907–   )

Harry Blair Cunningham started his career as a journalist for the *Harrisburg Patriot* in 1927. However, an executive from S.S. Kresge Co. soon convinced him that his future would be more promising in retailing. Cunningham joined S.S. Kresge in 1928 as a stockboy, and through hard work he advanced to the position of vice-president in 1957. In the next two years, Cunningham traveled extensively, visiting almost all of S.S. Kresge's stores nationwide. He used the opportunity of his travels to analyze the company's position in the industry and its specific needs to survive in the future.

From the information gathered on his travels, Cunningham realized that a change in the company's direction and focus was needed. He felt that, because of demographic changes, Kresge's future was in discount merchandise. Since this concept was a radical departure from the company's traditional line of business, Cunningham decided not to disclose his intentions until he was made president in 1959.

Before a conversion was undertaken, further extensive research was done, all of which confirmed Cunningham's "vision" or plan for the future. The overwhelming evidence, together with Cunningham's communication skills, helped him sell the discounting concept to his directors and shareholders.

In 1962 the first K-Mart store opened, with a philosophy of low prices and high turnover of nationally advertised products. By 1980 there were more than 1500 K-Marts nationwide.

The responsibility for this spectacular success can largely be attributed to Harry Blair Cunningham. He was able to foresee the need for change, plan the change, and sell the idea to other company officials while preserving organizational strengths through the transition. He relied on the expertise of store managers and effectively used the strategic talents of the real estate department in site selections. Remarkable foresight combined with thorough planning and sound execution are key words in the remarkable growth record of K-Mart Corporation.

One of the most intriguing aspects of social and organizational change is the rate at which it proceeds. Many factors affect this pace, not the least of which are the attitudes of those people exposed to change. The extremely slow acceptance in the United States of the goals of the civil rights movement is dramatic evidence of the hostile attitudes widespread among majority members of our society. By contrast, new fashions in clothing, handshakes, and "in" talk occur practically overnight. In these cases, there is little resistance due to attitudes, and change occurs rapidly.

In established organizations, any change process is typically guided by certain features that are characteristic of most organizational structures. One of the most evident features is the network of communication that ties individuals, groups, and the whole organization together. It is across this network that plans for change are formulated and transmitted among initiators, designers, and facilitators of change and later passed on to other organization members.

Since the formal communication network corresponds to the authority hierarchy of an organization, it follows that the formal change process conforms to the working of the hierarchy. Those people with less authority, power, and control over organizational resources must gain approval for effecting changes from those "higher up." Those people with more power, authority, and control can *order* changes, but they usually find such unilateral action inferior to motivating subordinates to accept change. A final point to note here is that change also moves through informal channels, at times reinforcing formal efforts but also at times working against organizational purposes.

Wherever individuals or groups may be located in a hierarchy, the desire to initiate change, guide it, hasten it, or even block it often brings the political realities of the organization into play. Here, organization "politics" should be understood to mean efforts on the part of individuals or groups to gain a "constituency" through providing incentives for conforming behavior. Usually the successful "politician" takes something of value away from the less successful; often this is control over some of the organization's resources. The taking can be skillful and painless, or crude and traumatic. A case in point is relevant here.

Twenty-two years ago, Eric Henson joined the Engine Division of Topco Industries as a mechanical engineer (all names have been changed). At the same time that he began applying his engineering skills, he was acquiring insights helpful to his career progress. From this evolved the following personal strategy. He would do his utmost to merit promotion and to see to it that his accomplishments came to the attention of the "right" people. As he began to rise, first in the engineering hierarchy and later on the general management ladder, he would do his best to handpick the successor for each position he vacated. As the years went by, he successfully "planted his people" step-by-step behind him. When the time came for the division president, Peter Burgos, to fill a senior vice-president position, Eric asked his constituency to boost his cause with Burgos. This executive was impressed with the show of loyalty on Eric's behalf and selected him for the position in the belief that a man with a strong, established "team" could get more done if the need for change came about. Eric's case illustrates one of the many ways in which organizational politics can be played for the benefit of both the individual and the organization.

Major Types of Managerial Responses to Change

Two distinctly different approaches to the realities of change are readily found in the management scene today. Broadly speaking, these may be called *reactive management* and *proactive management*, and each will be dealt with next in some detail. Before proceeding, readers should be warned that few if any managers are *always* reactive or proactive, but we feel that drawing strong contrasts between the two approaches has analytical value.

Reactive Management: Why Does It Happen?

Reactive approaches consist of after-the-fact adjustments to an event or situation that has already taken place. The result is generally "crisis management." Frequent reasons given for reactive adjustment include unanticipated shifts in competitive conditions, government legislation, economic circumstances, and other environmental influences. For example, many energy-importing countries are still independent, reactive positions vis-à-vis the plans and actions of the energy-exporting countries. Similarly, the firing of the air traffic controllers in the United States resulted in long-lasting adjustments by the airline companies in particular and by many other organizations dependent on transportation.

Why do so many managers simply react? Some reasons are simply not known. However, it seems likely that poor execution of their planning responsibilities is very frequently why managers find themselves in a reactive bind. Planning calls for reasoned, deliberate attempts to anticipate or forecast the future, a type of mental activity that many managers find far afield from their normal action or intuition. More often their preference is for "live action," for the "here and now." By contrast, planning is slow paced and low key. In their distaste for it, managers may relish the challenge of "putting out fires" and continue to neglect habits that would improve their future readiness and reduce the number of fires. Too often organizations reinforce such preferences by rewarding fire-fighting activity rather than long-term accomplishments.

Closely allied to the neglect of planning is the leadership style usually referred to as "head-in-the-sand." Rather than choosing an aggressive and forceful reaction to anticipated changes, the manager decides to "wait and see," probably in the hope that the change will disappear or turn out to be insignificant. Considerable risk may very well accompany such a decision. Furthermore, such a choice does nothing to upgrade future decision skills.

Poorly organized or outmoded organizational arrangements are another important explanation for why managers simply react. If the organization does a poor job of providing a monitoring system, some managers will be faced with making crisis adjustments that good information could have prevented. Organizational arrangements may be relatively inflexible and not permit "bending" and coping actions in the face of change. For example, more and more foreign buyers are now attending various trade shows in the United States. Many of these buyers complain that American firms do not give any real authority to their sales representatives at the trade shows. Instead, the firms force representatives to clear sales arrangements for other than trivial amounts with headquarters and in general get in the way of making sales. Such rigidities are enemies of effective anticipation of opportunities and indeed encourage reactive failures.

Underestimation of the human problems involved in change and a concurrent overreliance on the powers of technology work together to produce great amounts of reactive management behavior every year. Managers often make the mistake of believing the performance potential of a new or improved technology will be more or less automatically realized. They overestimate the power of technology to overcome human resistance to change. This often results in techno-

logical change being delayed for some years. For example, when General Motors committed itself to construction of the Vega assembly plant at Lordstown, Ohio, the new technology promised production of 100 cars per hour in the near future. But as a result of gross underestimation of the human problem, production timetables were badly missed and many costly errors were made, causing employee morale to flounder. Managers had to "pick up the pieces" as best they could. Vega is no longer even in production.

An organization that develops a reputation for simply reacting to pressures and developments can readily acquire a "follower" label. Such a label may well become a significant problem in recruiting new employees, particularly for professional and managerial openings. Such employees often shy away from organizations that appear to lag behind their competitors. Thus, over a period of time, the reactive organization may suffer an overall decline in the caliber of its work force, which, in turn, affects its ability to compete.

Proactive Management: Systems Thinking and Change

Proactive management can be thought of as a systems orientation to change and its likely consequences. Proaction places a premium on managers' ability to understand the relationship between elements and forces in the change environment, to anticipate the nature and pace of specific changes, and to initiate such action as appears needed to guide the effects of change in desired directions. (This systems approach to change is developed in Chapter 3.) It should be immediately obvious that successful proaction is difficult and challenging. It is a mode of management seldom, if ever, carried out completely, even to workable levels of need.

A particularly striking and complex example of the need for systems thinking in the application of proactive management can be taken from the changes affecting the huge American Telephone and Telegraph Company (AT&T). As a result of recent court decisions and deregulation efforts, AT&T is experiencing unprecedented competition. Customers of AT&T and its 23 associated telecommunications companies (the Bell System) no longer have to purchase equipment from AT&T but can buy it from a large number of alternative sources and still have access to AT&T lines. Competition is also springing up with respect to long-distance communication service. Anticipating and trying to cope creatively with these newly emerging competitive conditions is now a very high management priority throughout AT&T, and its soon-to-be-divested Bell System. Aggressive marketing strategies are being implemented, in contrast to the old-style thinking of simply taking customer orders. Managers who cannot adapt to the new competitive circumstances will likely be relieved of their responsibilities.

Strategy Development and Implementation

Fundamental to the proactive mode of management, and to the initiation and management of change, is the process of organizational strategy development. A strategy is the long-range commitment of an organization's resources in coordination with plans approved by top management. Of course, "long-range" is a relative term. A contrast can be drawn between a steel producer and a motel operator. The steel maker has to think 10 years ahead about replacing old facilities, raising money for expansion, changing demand patterns for steel, and trends of foreign competition. The motel operator thinks in much more limited time intervals—this year compared with last, getting ready for this summer's travel peak or this month's room remodeling schedule. Of course, there are longer-term travel patterns and changes in energy costs and availability. This they deal with in the initial location analysis and decision. However, for general operations of the motel, planning horizons of 1, 2, or 3 years would be more likely.

The significance of the term "commitment" in change strategies requires special attention. As discussed in Chapter 4, once top management has decided to pursue a certain strategy, it is essential that both a sufficient amount and a correct mixture of resources be committed to the strategy. Otherwise it stands little chance of success. This requires the implementation of controls to ensure that lower-level managers are following sound tactics. Take the case of one company that sells franchises in certain kinds of specialty restaurants. The components of its strategy include increasing its share of the market by gradual expansion from one southeastern state to several neighboring ones, as income from franchise sales and fees makes this possible; concentrating on shopping mall and motel-related locations; and providing management training plus regular management audits for franchise holders. Each element of this strategy is related to the others. Taken together, they indicate the kind of resource commitment and monitoring system that is needed for success.

Management Strategies and Resistance to Change

Strategy formulation must anticipate the sources of *resistance to change* within the organization and develop coping actions that solve difficult resistance problems. Since resistance to change is often centered at lower levels in the organization, strategies for change must be understood and implemented by managers at those levels. Critical to successful strategic choices in such actions are decisions that seek to (1) change people's attitudes and motivation, (2) change the structure of the work situation, or (3) take a combined approach. A decision to change people's attitudes and motivation rests on the assumption that, given the relevant inducements and rewards, people will accept change. This would be the opposite of an aggressive, "take it or leave it" approach. On the other hand, if the decision is to focus upon restructuring the work situation, the underlying assumption management makes is that trying to change attitudes is too unpredictable, costly, and time consuming. Research suggests that changing attitudes is indeed difficult and developing positive motivational approaches takes time. Therefore, management approaches to deal with resistance to change require much understanding of human nature and the possible effects of a given action.

It is not enough for a manager to be aware of changes occurring around him or her. As a facilitator of change, he or she must overcome the resistance to change among subordinates. In a proactive mode, this can be accomplished by (1) avoiding surprises through open communication, (2) explaining the reason for the change thoroughly so that it is understood, (3) establishing a program that shows the benefits of the change to the employees, and (4) generally developing a trusting atmosphere through effective leadership.

Practical Approaches in Dealing with Change

One helpful device in dealing with change is **force field analysis.** During any specific time interval, the attitudes and behavior of members of a work group are the net result of a combination of social and psychological forces to which the group is subject. Some forces encourage change in one direction, while other forces push in different directions. The analyst using this device attempts to make a paper-and-pencil sketch of a particular force field. An illustration is in order.

Force Field Examples. In the recent past a corporation in the industrial chemical field found itself facing a difficult decision concerning the oldest of its 11 plants. Over the years this plant, known in the corporation as South Point, suffered increasingly from inefficient physical design. Further, it seemed clear that the plant manager was a major factor in the unprofitable plant performance. There appeared to be only two choices: phase the plant out or take drastic measures to make it productive. The top management committee assigned to this problem picked the latter choice and began by requesting that the current South Point manager take early retirement. An up-and-coming assistant manager from another unit was appointed plant manager. He was given instructions to conduct a quick, intensive study of plant problems and what was needed to remedy them.

The new manager proceeded to do this with the help of a personnel specialist on loan from corporate headquarters. Together they applied the force-field approach and produced the analysis shown in Exhibit 12-3.

Exhibit 12-3 Plant Problems and Force Field Analysis

Plant Problems

Poorly maintained physical plant	Reputation of being a "loser"	Some "clinkers" in middle and lower management	Rigid union–management relations	A very high seniority work force
↓	↓	↓	↓	↓
↑	↑	↑	↑	↑
Budget approval for a "clean-up, fix-up" campaign	Successful bid to produce a new product	Replace "clinkers" through personnel actions	"Last chance to make it" approach to union officers	"Gains-sharing" plan plus improved early retirement benefits

Strategies to Deal with Plant Problems
(Positive Forces for Change)

As can be appreciated from the force-field sketch, the basic idea is to cause a *thickening* and *lengthening* of the *up* arrows through a combination of the indicated actions. In other words, the new plant manager should increase the impact of the positive forces for change. If the necessary budget is approved to upgrade the plant, then it may compete successfully as the production site for a new product recently formulated by the corporate research laboratory. Candid meetings with union leaders, it is hoped, will convince them that the plant has one last chance to succeed. The chances for improved union cooperation should be increased by transferring certain members of management, an indication that management is willing to clean up its own ranks. Finally, it is hoped that by offering improved retirement benefits some of the "peaked-out" employees will choose to retire and that those who remain (plus some new employees) will respond to a productivity gains-sharing incentive plan. This same type of analysis can be usefully applied to a wide range of change situations.

Strategic Alternatives in Working toward Renewal of Human Resources

There is a continuing need in a great variety of organizations to combat the kind of stagnation brought on by skill, knowledge, or motivational **obsolescence** on the part of some employees. Obsolescence means essentially the growing irrelevance or "lack of fit" between what the individual brings to the work situation and what that situation currently demands. If obsolescence of this sort goes unrecognized or unremedied, the overall achievement level of the organization will decline.

For example, in the 1960s, the U.S. steel industry began to replace open-hearth steel-making technology with the basic oxygen furnace (BOF). The BOF technology makes use of pure oxygen injection to speed the production cycle. Employees caught up in this technological change found the BOF work pace much faster, and the threat of costly errors greatly increased. Actually, the strains in adjusting to the new work circumstances, as often occurs, fell most heavily upon first-line supervisors. Workers with much seniority, who were used to the previous methods, found the new demands threatening. Many requested to be reassigned to nonproduction work, feeling that they could never handle the new requirements. Others chose to retire early. Younger men, some with college degrees in engineering, were in many cases hired and trained to replace the older workers. In this way, needed skills and knowledge for the new technology were put in place.

There are several individualized approaches to the renewal of human resources to avoid or reduce obsolescence. *Coach and understudy* is one such approach. It can be particularly effective when one individual is being developed to succeed another on a planned basis. Recently a senior lending officer in a medium-size bank sensed that his career progress would be blocked if he did not groom a capable replacement. On the basis of performance records and other positive qualities, he singled out a younger man in his department and talked to him about his own ambitions. They developed a mutual plan to achieve both of their ambitions. When the relationship between coach and understudy is an open and trusting one, it is excellent for meeting specific renewal needs.

The *developmental transfer or job rotation* is another individualized method. Although this method has many possible applications, it tends to be restricted to professional and managerial-level employees. It is intended to broaden perspectives of professionals who have spent their entire careers within one part of the organization. By transfer to a different function, for instance, from product engineering to market planning and research, the transferee potentially gains a whole new point of view and set of skills, and the organization gains a "broader" employee.

Problems in Developmental Approaches

Sometimes job rotation or developmental transfers can go wrong. To ensure against the process being a waste of time: (1) the *trainee* needs to be enthusiastic about the opportunity, since he or she will be physically moving around, (2) at each different rotation point, a specific and well-selected person (trainer) needs to be responsible for provid-

Experienced city planner coaching a protege.

ing the conditions under which the trainee's learning may be enhanced, and (3) the trainee should be required to record the new learning in some systematic way and present this accomplishment to the appropriate members of the organization, after completing the series of assignments.

In thinking through the alternative approaches to individual renewal, it must be recognized that the choices are not always positive. The demotion or discharge of an obsolete person is sometimes absolutely necessary. In the case of the industrial chemical plant cited earlier to demonstrate the use of the force-field analysis technique, we found that certain members of management who were slowing down or actively fighting progress were removed. Of course, in preparing for such action the plant manager and his personal adviser had to identify qualified and willing candidates to fill the impending vacancies. Not to be ignored is how this situation came about in the first place. Some of the blame must be placed at the "door" of top management.

Organization Development: A Group Approach to Renewal and Change

Organization development (OD) is the most ambitious of various group-oriented approaches to the renewal of human resources. For our purposes, *development* should be understood as the strengthening of skills or individual motives in a way that supports organizational commitments and contributions. OD attempts to overcome the limitations of typical *management development* programs that take individuals out of their work roles and relations and place them off site in *management seminars* or *institutes*. OD deals with actual work groups, established status relations (for example, superiors and subordinates), and work-related attitudes and motivations as they actually exist. Generally, OD strives to improve the quality of overall group effort among related work groups. Management interest in the potential benefits of OD appears to be increasing, since what it aims for is of such vital organizational importance.

The social values underlying OD are both positive and optimistic. Advocates of the OD approach accept differing views among people, the expression of real feelings among work colleagues, the airing of conflicts, the use of candid and honest communication and the building of trusting relations, and the gaining of commitments from OD participants to improve the workings of the organization. However, these newer values clash with the traditional way things are done by ordinary workers, technicians, and managers. Everyday events usually teach employees that divergent opinions are not welcome, real feelings should be masked, conflicts are simmering below the surface, and open, "tell it like it is" communications simply gets one in trouble. This is what we meant in calling OD ambitious. It confronts strongly entrenched attitudes and behavior, and the prospects for changing them is never known at the beginning.

Example

An example of OD in action may be the best way to make the various components of and steps in the process more concrete. A hospital in a midwestern suburb was undergoing expansion and change. Its work force of about 225 employees was scheduled to gradually increase by 100 workers on completion and staffing of an outpatient clinic and a geriatric wing. The hospital administrator got approval from his Board of Trustees to conduct an employee attitude study, on the grounds that the existing attitudes and work motivation would be a crucial indication of the organization's readiness to grow successfully.

The survey was conducted by an outside consultant, and the results were analyzed and reported back. Although the results suggested some grounds for optimism, there was just as much reason for concern: most employees believed that the hospital's top management was out of touch with "the troops." People's concerns never got a hearing at the top. Communication about future plans was erratic. Secrecy was said to be the order of the day respecting pay policies and promotion opportunities. Finally, the white majority was upset about "favored treatment" of minorities.

The hospital administrator and his subordinates wondered what to do next. The consultant's advice was to engage the services of an organization development specialist and to use the survey data as the starting point for an OD process. In the consultant's opinion, the hospital was ready for a major renewal effort. An OD consultant was identified, and after acquainting himself with the hospital as an organization and with the nature of the survey results, he recommended that the following steps make up the OD effort.

1. The hospital administrator and his top staff should hold several in-depth meetings to ponder the survey results, with the consultant on hand to help guide the interaction and to make sure the participants faced up to the basic issues. That is, under the watchful eye of the consultant "outsider," the hospital's top group was to determine why employees took such an overall dim view of management's behavior. In doing this, it was expected that the managers would discover better ways of working together.

2. Later, each of the administrator's key subordinates should repeat the process within his or her own functional department. At this level, the survey results were to be used in a more specific way, namely, for what they revealed about employee attitudes regarding their department manager and the quality of work relations in the department. Meetings should be held by the department manager with the next lower level of management or supervision, again with the consultant present. Efforts should be made to improve communication on the job, and to face openly current problems and the ways to resolve them.

3. Still later, first-level supervisors should initiate the same type of meetings with people in their immediate work groups. Again using the outcome of the attitude survey as a point of departure, and still drawing upon the help of the consultant, they should move toward fuller identification of their problems and the changes needed to cope with them. At this lowest management level, prior experience is most lacking in holding employee meetings and exchanging frank and open views. Thus, it usually takes a great deal more time for progress to be made. The consultant's role is particularly vulnerable during this phase, in that some supervisors may simply prefer that the consultant take over and run things, a tendency the consultant must guard against. What is needed is to establish relationships between supervisors and workers—a challenge that is the major responsibility of the consultant.

Interpreting OD as a Change Process

Let us examine the prerequisites for change that were represented in this example. First, the hospital administrator was *aware* that changes in the environment were occurring. Faced with expansion of facilities, he wanted to discover the attitude climate in his organization and how this climate related to planned changes. The survey results suggested that change had indeed already *affected* the organization and that individuals at all levels of the organization, including the administrator, seemed to be *motivated* to change organizational relationships. Since the organization did not possess the necessary *skills*, in the person of an OD specialist, to bring about change successfully, such a person was hired on a consulting basis. Once hired, the outside consultant was a regular participant in the meetings and analyses. It should also be noted that the employee-attitude survey was a research step that provided basic information for further steps in the change process.

At any one organizational level and within any one group, the object of the OD interaction was the building of more effective work-team relations. *Team building*, in fact, is the most accurate description for the mode of interaction described. This was to be accomplished, hopefully, by the development of a consensus on the problems to be solved and the formulation of plans to deal with them. In the months ahead, of course, the effectiveness of these actions would have to be monitored and the need to redirect some of them decided on. In these ways, the necessary "cementing" of change behavior into enduring forms would best be accomplished.

SUMMARY

Change affects all of us at different times and in different ways during our lives. Some individuals change within their personal lives while still others are affected by it within the framework of an organization. For our purposes, however, we have mostly been concerned with change and its relationship to the business world.

Because of trends in such major areas as transportation and technology, the organization has had to be keenly aware of external conditions that may very well affect their livelihood. In addition, governmental laws and regulations are a greater cause of organizational change than they ever were in the past. Relatively new legislation in such areas as equal employment also has brought about the need for change.

To deal with change properly, timely and accurate information must be provided. This information not only flows from the environment, but is also often possessed by the personnel of the firm.

Readiness for change is often thought of as a four-step test. The individuals must first be aware that the change has occurred. Second, the business, or individual, must decide if this change will affect it (him or her). Following this step, an organization must ask itself if it desires change and, if so, whether it has the pool of skills demanded by the coming changes.

The roles that individuals take on with respect to organizational change are specific, in keeping with the specialized behavior in the overall organization. Change tends to be implemented by individuals at the top of the business hierarchy, who often gain necessary information through specialists in the field of change.

There are two principal managerial responses to change. In the first, reactive management, the manager simply reacts after the change has already taken place. Failure to anticipate change can lead to great losses. The nature of the loss varies with the nature of the unanticipated change.

Proaction, an alternative form of management, is highly favored over reactive management. Through this method, a situation is analyzed before it is critical, and the chance to deal with it effectively is greatly increased.

One major maneuver in dealing with change is called the force-field approach. Internal problems are analyzed, and qualified individuals (often specialists) are brought in to come up with workable solutions to these problems.

Other strategies are concerned with the renewal of human resources. In some cases, obsolescence is avoided through job shifts within the work force. Another strategy is that of coach and understudy. When an individual rises in an organization, he or she may train a person who will soon fill the vacated position. This strategy prevents individuals from leaving their positions without adequate replacements.

Organization development (OD) is an ambitious approach to human resource renewal. OD works through groups and deals with the attitudes, motivation, and feelings of the workers. Management works with personnel (often through a mediator) to attempt to resolve any conflict and increase potential productivity. Plans are drawn up to open the vital lines of communication that make an organization run smoothly.

Questions for Study and Discussion

1. Identify and explain at least three concepts that are important in understanding the management of organizational change.

2. In what ways may individuals become alerted to the need for change and of ways to adapt to change?

3. Why are organizations the most relevant forms for appreciating the dynamics of change?

4. What two or three managerial skills are particularly challenged in situations of change?

5. In what ways is information a cause of change in society? In organizations?

6. What are the four steps that determine one's readiness for change?

7. Discuss the following: Organizations are essentially at the mercy of forces of change. Their only practical response is to react to change.

8. What is meant by systems thinking with respect to change? Give an example.

9. Identify two ways in which the management of an organization might reduce uncertainty in decision making. Apply one of these to a specific situation.

10. What is the basic meaning of organizational renewal? Does renewal only apply to the human resources of an organization?

11. Contrast the pros and cons of conflict management and organization development as strategies for managing change and achieving organization renewal.

CASE: DMITRI POULOS

Dmitri Poulos was manager of personnel planning for a large diversified corporation, organized on the basis of three main divisions that were operated for the most part independently. Dmitri was hired by the Director of Personnel because the Director believed that the company was about to enter a new and critical phase of its corporate life, in which there would be a dependency on human resources much greater than in previous years.

After Dmitri had been with the company for about two years, he started to work on a human resource planning program designed to strengthen greatly the organization's abilities in handling people. Management was to play a key role in the development of unit plans, based on the knowledge of their people and a sense of future needs.

To start the program, the company President issued a brief order concerning the program and asked for the managers' cooperation with the personnel planning department.

All of the managers complied with the request for information and carried out the procedures without too much difficulty. The following year, when Dmitri again issued the forms for reporting information from the units, a number of the managers asked, "What was going on—we did this last year, wasn't that enough?"

Questions

1. What went wrong in this case?
2. Based on the four-step change model, what did Dmitri miss?
3. How might Dmitri have approached this situation initially?

References

Alpin, John C., and Duane E. Thompson, "Successful Organizational Change," *Business Horizons* (August 1974): 61–66.

Blake, R., J. Mouton, and L. Greiner, "Breakthrough in Organization Development," *Harvard Business Review*, **42** (1964): 133–155.

Edrich, Harold, "Keeping a Weather Eye on the Future," *Planning Review*, **8** (January 1980): 11–14.

English, Jon, and Anthony Marchione, "Nine Steps in Management Development," *Business Horizons*, **20** (June 1977): 88–94.

Giegold, William, and R. J. Craig, "Whatever Happened to O.D.?" *Industrial Management* (January–February 1976): 9–12.

Guest, Robert, Paul Hersey, and Kenneth Blanchard. *Organizational Change Through Effective Leadership*. Englewood Cliffs, N. J.: Prentice-Hall (1977).

Heizer, Jay, "Managing a Changing Workforce—Does Equality Mean Sameness," *Management World*, **9**(6) (June 1980): 21–36.

Hersey, Paul, and Kenneth Blanchard, "The Management of Change," *Training and Development Journal*, **34**(6) (June 1980): 80–98.

House, William C., "Environmental Analysis: Key to More Effective Dynamic Planning," *Managerial Planning*, **25** (January–February 1977): 25–29.

"How Companies Overcome Resistance to Change," *Management Review* (November 1972): 17–25.

Humphries, George E., "Technology Assessment: A New Imperative in Corporate Planning," *Planning Review*, **4** (March 1976): 6–9ff.

Huse, Edgar, *Organizational Development and Change*. St. Paul: West Publishing Co. (1975).

Jacoby, Neil H., "Six Challenges to Business Management," *Business Horizons*, **19** (August 1976): 29–37.

Kleiner, Brian, "A Manager's Guide to Organizational Change," *Personnel*, **56**(2) (March–April 1979): 31–38.

Leifer, Richard, and Andre Delbecq, "Organizational/Environmental Interchange: A Model of Boundary Spanning Activity," *Academy of Management Review*, **3** (January 1978): 40–50.

Nicholas, John, "Evolution Research in Organizational Change Interventions: Consideration and Some Suggestions," *Journal of Applied Behavioral Science*, **15** (First Quarter 1979): 23–40.

Organ, Dennis W., "Linking Pins Between Organizations and Environment," *Business Horizons*, **14** (December 1971): 73–80.

Sheldon, Alan, "Organizational Paradigms: A Theory of Organizational Change," *Organizational Dynamics*, **8** (Winter 1980): 61–80.

Steiner, George A., "New Patterns in Government Regulation of Business," *MSU Business Topics*, **26** (Autumn 1978): 53–61.

Terborg, James, George Howard, and Scott Maxwell, "Evaluating Planned Organizational Change: A Method of Assessing Alpha, Beta and Gamma Change," *Academy of Management Review*, **5** (January 1980): 109–121.

Wilson, Ian H., "Business Management and the Winds of Change," *Journal of Contemporary Business*, **7** (Winter 1978): 45–54.

CHAPTER 13

CREATIVITY

KEY
QUESTIONS
ADDRESSED
IN CHAPTER

1. Why is the study of creativity important to managers?
2. What developments are occurring on a societal and organizational level that affect creativity?
3. How does the creative process work?
4. What are some techniques that organizations and managers use to foster creativity?
5. How does creativity affect basic management activities?

TECHNOLOGY,
WORK, JOB

ORGANIZATION
ENVIRONMENT

THE
MANAGER

WORK GROUP
INDIVIDUAL

EXTERNAL
ENVIRONMENT

The manager's work–life spaces

Discovery consists in seeing what everyone else has seen and thinking what nobody else has thought.

Albert Szent-Gyorgyi

THE CHAPTER IN BRIEF

Our first aim is to establish the overall significance of creative behavior, as seen from management's point of view. This includes both a *micro* perspective, the viewpoint of a single organization, and a *macro* view, the focus of our economy and society as a whole.

We examine the distinctions between creative and conventional thought, as well as the stages apparent in the creative thinking of individuals, paying attention to the many forms that creativity and innovation may take. New products and services are widely recognized by the general public, but innovations in technology, such as construction, transportation, and information processing, have equal significance. We also examine creativity in organizational structure and management policies and practices, as well as in the personal lives of individuals.

Next, we move to discussion of creativity as it relates to the management activities of planning, leadership, decision making, and coping with individual and organizational change. All four of these basic functions of management require creative approaches. Management's responsibility for translating creative ideas into plans for action and then capitalizing on them is necessarily involved here. In one's personal life, innovative or creative thinking and skills can be learned, at least to the extent that they can noticeably improve work performance and activities. Correspondingly, managers can greatly enhance the emergence of creativity by providing the proper support, identifying and encouraging creative talent, building a positive organizational climate, and rewarding creative individuals and groups. We also make a point of examining here the ways in which behavior in organizations can function to hinder or completely stifle creative tendencies.

Organizations also institutionalize creative action by establishing particular groups, departments, or units as temporary or permanent parts of their structure and processes. We discuss here specific successes in the stimulation of creativity and innovation within the context of particular organizations.

Personal and Career Applications

Although our primary interest in creativity concerns its value in job roles and careers, creative behavior has many implications for personal lives as well. One of the most potentially productive and satisfying applications of creative thought is to solve problems. Typical examples include the problems of how to stay within a modest budget, how best to make use of the space and furnishings in our living quarters, how to choose topics for class projects, and how to cope with the demands of a heavy work load *and* school schedule. Each of these problems, and many others like them, affords opportunities for new and creative paths to a solution.

The same is true for the key relationships in which the great majority of us are parties. These include relations with parents, brothers, sisters, other relatives, and good friends, both on and off the job. Creative examination of how these relationships might be made more satisfying can be beneficial in our personal lives. This requires a decision not to take these relationships for granted or as static states but to view them as subject to improvement. The relationship between an employee and his or her supervisor can also be improved through creative effort.

Are there ways in which a person can gain an understanding of his or her creative potential? Although this is a complex question, it appears that different forms of creative thinking are possible, and that these are affected further by one's knowledge or information in related areas. Considerable research and experimentation is going on in the early identification of employees' (or students') creative potential, in finding and testing creative problem-solving techniques, and in the training of creative leadership behavior. Also, methods are in sight that will enable people to assess their own creativity.

Creativity, Innovation, and the Manager's Life-Space Model

Creative thinking is an idea very much associated with the *individual*. Yet research and experience clearly indicate that the *organization* itself and various other people and groups also greatly affect creative thinking and activities. These influences on creative activity are represented in the life-space model. The interpretation of the sketch is as follows: there are five spaces that make up the manager's life-space model. For creative activity, the individual is actively involved (shaded area). At the same time, the individual's work, groups, and organization are also involved (heavily shaded area). This chapter deals not only with the individual's role in this program but also the nature of the interactions and relationships with the group and organization.

In today's environment, creative solutions are being called for to improve productivity within organizations. Toward this end, organizations have tended to emphasize improvements in work technology. In the previous chapter we discussed some of the technological changes affecting organizations. In Chapter 3 we emphasized the need to systematically and creatively connect work and the technology used with the individuals who perform it. In the next chapter we further explore some newer work designs that increase participation among employees and improve the motivational climate within the organization.

A structural approach can also be used to foster flexibility and creativity in dealing with a changing environment. This approach includes instituting better ways to sort the mass of information available to managers for decision-making purposes. Along these same lines, more creative use of people in problem-solving situations is also needed. The latter can be accomplished by rewarding creative thinking, either formally through incentive pay or informally by praise—a pat on the back or improved status.

BACKGROUND

A Macroview of Creativity and Innovation

When viewed from a macro perspective, that is, from the standpoint of a total society, creativity and innovation are seen to be crucial for increasing economic productivity, improving the level of public health, and mounting an attack on social problems, such as unemployment or the quality of educational systems. The role of creativity and innovation in the development of culture and the arts goes without saying. Currently, the people of Japan are widely regarded as an exceptional example in these respects. In spite of the fact that Japan must import virtually all the raw materials it needs for manufacturing, as well as much of its food, it has succeeded in becoming the world's leading exporter. At the same time, Japan is meeting its social needs more effectively than at any time in its history. This success has been largely due to continual innovation in production processes, to new organizational forms, particularly the trading companies, and to unusual degrees of collaboration between the Japanese private and public sectors. Any country's experience might be used to trace the roles played by creativity and innovation in determining that country's overall progress. If one were to catalogue the history of major inventions and the exact times when each made its impact, certain trends would become visible. One is that the rate of economic growth and expansion in any society is closely tied to the creative contributions of its members, as well as to effective application of innovations made elsewhere. In fact, no society merits the description *developed* or *advanced* that does not exhibit a significant history of creative behavior and its implementation.

Another trend that emerges from historical analysis is that the frequency of important innovations has been increasing, and the interval between the "drawing board" and practical application has been decreasing. The combination of these considerations provides substance to the idea that "things are changing fast."

A Microview of Creativity and Innovation

If we turn to a micro point of view, it quickly becomes evident that organizations of all types need creative contributions of many kinds to pursue goals of growth and expansion, or perhaps simply to survive. One of the more obvious illustrations of this point is the major U.S. television networks, which, season after season, change programming and scheduling, revamp formats of shows, and search for the "fresh faces" that each network hopes will enable it to outdistance the audience ratings of its competitors. Well-known organizations such as McDonald's also have a major stake in creative action. With its international system of some 4200 restaurants, McDonald's is known for experimentation in new types of locations, such as in expensive major business centers; in restaurant design and layouts; in menu expansion toward a more "full-service" concept; and even in internal policies, which get the executives into individual restaurants periodically to ensure that they don't "lose touch." Such actions are evidence of creative activity within the organization. The same may be said of the recent appearance of generic, "no-name," lines of products at certain supermarkets. The no-name products afford lower prices and substantial savings to shoppers, while still providing good quality. Of course, if quality were highly variable, the attraction of this approach would be lost. Who makes the creative contributions we have just described? A partial answer lies in observing that one of the major responsibilities of management in any organization is to foster the conditions and to allocate the resources that support and guide creative behavior. The ways in which this is done are detailed in a later section.

What Is Known about Creative Thinking and the Creative Process?

It is best to begin with another question: what do we mean by *creativity?* At a general level, **creativity** is the recognition or discovery of a significant novelty that has a social value or a degree of importance. It should be stressed that unless the "creation" is accepted by at least some segment of society, it is of little value. At the individual level, an answer or approach is creative if it produces a significantly different and more valuable response than might otherwise have been the case. There is a subtle idea behind these definitions of creativity that needs to be noted. In some situations, there is tangible evidence of creative action because we have *improved* something that already *exists*. That is, there are ways to determine if it is an improvement—for instance, more sales. The newer version can then be compared against that which existed previously.

There are, however, many situations in which ideas or approaches are used as part of an initial effort. For example, we may assemble a group of designers, sales representatives, and managers to "brainstorm," to come up with a new sales promotion. Here the creative action is in the organization and conduct of the meeting. There may be no internal benchmarks with which to judge the quality or success of the effort at the time of the meeting. Research reported in the literature indicates the creative potential of **brainstorming.** The final answer, however, will be the bottom-line result when the program is launched. It is characteristic of creative thought that it typically consists in making new associations among existing ideas, concepts, objects, or phenomena. Put somewhat differently, it makes a connection between two things previously regarded as dissimilar. One of the most renowned examples of this is the case of Sir Isaac Newton, who observed an apple falling from a tree and deduced the similarity between the pull of the Earth's gravity on the apple and the attractions between cosmic bodies. He concluded that the force causing the apple to fall was also responsible for holding planets and other bodies in their orbits. The same observations could have been made by many others, but Newton was the one to achieve this classic insight.

Cross-Fertilization

Creative thinking often takes the form of *cross-fertilization* between related fields. One of the most significant examples may be taken from the career of Charles Darwin. Darwin saw a connection between his work in botany and biology, on the one hand, and the work of others in the field of human population trends. Population scholars had reached the conclusion that human populations tend to increase faster than available food supplies, thus causing a struggle for existence. Darwin found a similarity between this conclusion and his many observations of a struggle for survival in the plant and animal world. His insight enabled him to formulate the principle of the "survival of the fittest" and to put thinking about evolution on an entirely new path.

Individual Traits and Characteristics

The points just presented mostly concern the end products of creative thought. We now turn to what is known about the *process* of creativity, as it takes place in the human mind. How can this process be

A brainstorming session
in progress.

described? First, it appears that it is *not* based on some simple, undifferentiated mental capacity, but on a complex set of abilities that are only partially understood. The correlation between creativity and intelligence is one of the difficulties. The consensus is that highly intelligent persons are not necessarily creative, since their intelligence may make them overly self-critical. On the other hand, it is widely agreed that many forms of creativity require *substantial* intelligence, although creative actions can be displayed by many with appropriate training and self-discipline.

Elements of the Creative Process

A clearer picture emerges from the analyses and reports of many individuals who have had creative experiences and who have analyzed and relived the stages they went through. From this has come general agreement that creative thought is a **process** that has a beginning stage, usually called *preparation,* and subsequent stages of *incubation, illumination,* and *verification.* Each will be discussed in turn. The overall process is illustrated in Exhibit 13-1.

Preparation.   *Preparation* means building a knowledge foundation and skill base in a chosen field. Without such an underlying struc-

Exhibit 13-1 The Creative Process

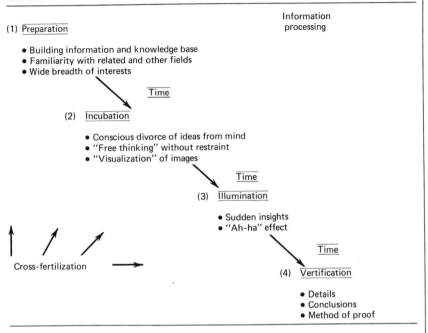

(1) Preparation

- Building information and knowledge base
- Familiarity with related and other fields
- Wide breadth of interests

Information processing

Time

(2) Incubation

- Conscious divorce of ideas from mind
- "Free thinking" without restraint
- "Visualization" of images

Time

(3) Illumination

- Sudden insights
- "Ah-ha" effect

Time

Cross-fertilization

(4) Vertification

- Details
- Conclusions
- Method of proof

ture, an individual would have nothing to draw on for either conventional or creative thought. New ideas and insights do not emerge full bloom from blank minds but rather from ones that have become progressively more immersed in the facts, tools, research results, and so forth that make up a particular line of human endeavor. And, to repeat, a wide breadth of interest and familiarity with aspects of another field will be of more service to the individual than exclusive concentration on a specialty. This is why a broad-based educational curriculum is important.

Incubation. *Incubation,* the second stage, seems to require relaxing, and partially "turning off" the process of conventional thinking. This involves a backing away from normal tendencies to criticize and judge the value of what is taking place in the flow of thought. To the extent that the individual is successful in not immediately censoring the thought flow, deeper mental functions within the mind can be reached. These deeper functions are believed to take two forms, *free thinking* and *visualization.* In free thinking the individual must allow the mind to wander in any direction without restraints or organization, until later when organization is reimposed. Visualization is a mode of thought employing visual images rather than verbal or numerical symbols, a process having a lot in common with the content of dreams. During this phase, the mind seems to scan pictures of possible new relationships, structures, and objects in an effort to solve a problem or satisfy a need. Recent research indicates that dreams can play an important part in creative thinking. It appears that information processing during dreams and meditation is faster or more efficient than when one is awake.

Illumination.   If incubation is successful, there follows the moment of *illumination,* which often is depicted as a light bulb going on. This sudden insight of people is likened to a mystical experience. It should be added that there is no known standard manner for predicting when illumination may occur and whether it will occur at all. Persons having such an experience have reported being engaged in many different kinds of activity, and inactivity, at the moment of insight. We do know that with appropriate training and individual effort, the odds favoring a creative experience can be improved.

Verification.   The final stage of creative thought is *verification.* Here, the mind returns to the pursuit of more conventional patterns and works out the creative solution in detail, polishes it into a more final form, and chooses some test or method of proof so that the idea achieves credibility and acceptance. As we see later, when we discuss creativity and innovation in an organizational context, gaining credibility and acceptance is by no means automatic. Many creators have found themselves up against tough political battles in the process of unveiling their contributions and seeking to have them implemented.

> ### Saying
> Every revolutionary idea—in Science, Politics, Art, or Whatever—goes through three stages of reaction.
>
> 1. It is impossible—don't waste my time.
> 2. It is possible, but it's not worth doing.
> 3. I said it was a good idea all along.

Pioneers in Creativity Technique

Perhaps the best-known pioneering work in the field of creativity and innovation is that of Alex F. Osborn. In exploring ways to improve "how to think," Osborn hit on the brainstorming technique: to illustrate, imagine a group of a dozen or so people having some common interest or relationship (for example, students, fellow workers, friends). As they sit around a table, they consider the question: To what other uses might an ordinary garden hose be put? Under the "rules" of brainstorming, people call out their ideas as quickly as the ideas come to mind. No one is to criticize any idea expressed, and a large *quantity* of ideas is sought. Only after the idea flow has stopped

is judgment about the quality of ideas invoked. Also, during this phase ideas are improved by combination, substitution, modification, and other changes.

Since Osborn's early work other *idea stimulation techniques* have been formulated and are currently being applied. These include the checklist technique, forced relationships, attribute listing, and the morphological approach. Let us illustrate the use of these four techniques as they might be applied to the question: how can we go about giving a really unusual and enjoyable party?

Checklist Techniques

The *checklist technique* tells us to think of a series of action verbs that could apply to a party situation, such as magnify, minimize, rear-

---

GREAT PERSON PROFILE

Thomas Edison (1847–1931)

Students of management can look toward Thomas Edison as a prime example of the creative spirit. The volume of his work—1,093 patents in 20 different areas—is staggering. Among his many inventions were the incandescent light bulb, the phonograph, the alkaline storage battery, and the motion picture.

Even though the principles of electricity on which his work rested had been previously set forth, Edison found ways to use this knowledge in a practical way. His inventions were things that people could *use*. Edison once said, "An inventor is essentially practical." He felt that theories were essentially meaningless without application in the real world. In the business world, he was a realist; he would not market a product without a firm belief that people would buy it because it was useful.

Edison displayed a high degree of curiosity and determination. He immersed himself totally in the problem at hand, often working as many hours as necessary to find the solution. When asked, "What is genius?," he replied, "99 percent perspiration and 1 percent inspiration."

On the other hand, some of Edison's ideas came about quite by accident while he was

involved in other projects. Here the inspiration comes into play. Sometimes ideas come to us in a flash when our conscious minds are involved in other activities.

Although we cannot perhaps involve ourselves as totally in the creative process as Edison did, we can look at his life as an example of what can be accomplished when we develop creative thinking skills.

range, combine, substitute, adapt, invert, refocus, and so on. We might think of *combining* a special date (the birthday of our favorite poet, athlete, or politician), a special dish (soft-shell crabs, steamed sweet corn), and a special costume (funny hats). In the process of using the checklist technique, critical judgment is to be temporarily suspended, as in brainstorming.

Forced Relationships

Forced relationships is another creativity technique. It involves taking anything in your own or a group's awareness and attempting to relate it to the problem or question at hand. The objective is to force a mental connection between sense impressions and the problem, thus stimulating ideas. Suppose while trying to plan our party, we glance out the window and see a squirrel. We know squirrels hoard food in advance of winter. Aha, we will "squirrel away" some prizes for guests to hunt at our party.

Attribute Listing

In *attribute listing,* we take specific aspects of a situation and then focus separately on each aspect. The checklist or forced relationship techniques can be applied to the aspect being focused on. Say we choose that aspect of a party known as "breaking the ice." We might decide to try to force relationships between strangers by having them trade funny hats or by playing brief roles from cue cards that they are asked to select.

Morphological Approach

The most ambitious technique, the *morphological approach* is the study of patterns. It uses a combination of attribute listing and forced relationships to fill the cells of a matrix (see Exhibit 13-2). Imagine a grouping of squares, as in a checkerboard, with the heading *attributes of a party* across the top and a vertical heading along the right or left border reading, *possible forced relationships.* Each vertical row of squares would have a specific attribute label—*people to invite, date and time, place, food, special effects,* and the like. The objective is then to create relationships of a novel sort among the attributes.

Process Education

To date, the above techniques and a number of others have been applied to numerous industrial, organizational, and school situations. For example, during the 1960s, with the aid of both government and private grants, a number of exemplary programs of *process education*

Exhibit 13-2 Application of the Morphological Matrix in the Creativity Process

Possible forced relationships	People to invite	Special effects	Food	Etc.
Prizes for best, worst guess who?	Neighbors	Costumes	Cake and candy	
Only "cool" things and people	Friends	"Dry ice"	Cold cuts	
Have people bring wierd soundmakers and have others guess	People one works with	Wierd sounds	Apples for dunking	
	Etc.	Etc.	Etc.	

were developed in the United States. In these programs the stress was upon *how* to think, not *what* to think. The role of the teacher changed from one of imparting facts to students to one of teaching them problem-solving methods, the use of instructional technology, and ways to access effectively learning resources, such as periodicals, reference works, and data bases. Other novel elements now in use at some schools are team teaching, with more than one teacher in any one course or program, and project-based learning, in which the focus is not on topics or subjects but on integrating knowledge from several fields into a larger whole. Of course, the teachers currently involved in process-education programs had to receive the training necessary to be successful. Each year a number of training institutes throughout the country offer courses, sponsored by such organizations as the Creative Education Foundation and the National Institute of Education. It should be noted, however, that process education applications had highly mixed results. It is likely that too little attention was given to student capabilities and limitations for this style of individual learning.

The creative approaches to thinking and education just presented represent novel "invasions" of schools and school systems, many of which were well known for inflexibility and resistance to change. It is not surprising that much resistance has been met in attempting to redevelop educational approaches.

Improving one's powers of observation in identifying significant differences promotes creative behavior because being able to detect differences and noting the out-of-the-ordinary among ideas, objects, or human behavior is an important aspect of creative behavior. Creative responses sometimes can be elicited by asking a person to examine an ordinary object, like an orange, and to describe as many attributes of the object as he or she can discern. Examples are the texture of the orange peel, variances in color and shape, "veins" in the orange segments, and so forth.

It is also generally agreed that the wider an individual's breadth of interests, the more likely it is that the person will produce creative accomplishments. The advice is clear—diversify your interests and branch out into new areas of study and skill building. This can be accomplished by getting involved in a variety of activities, diversifying your reading habits, meeting different types of people, and working on developing a well-balanced set of skills. From this wider base, cross-fertilization of ideas is more likely to occur.

Creativity also requires motivation. An impelling need to solve a problem or to discover a novel combination of ideas seems to be required to spur on individuals to creative attempts. Studying the problem or situation, while delaying a response until you have literally "slept on it," Can improve the quality of the idea or solution. Our level of enthusiasm about a particular field of study or line of work furnishes an important clue as to whether we are likely to make creative contributions in that area. The moral would seem to be: exert yourself; creative opportunities will not come looking for a creator.

Creativity also involves risk taking—the willingness to take chances on the unknown rather than being secure and content with the known. The previous chapter showed the need for creative solutions. For the career-minded student, some industries like steel and auto currently present particular challenges for creative approaches to production and marketing efforts. Indeed, the challenges may be great in these industries, while resistance to new ideas is likely to be entrenched. All things considered, there may be a greater opportunity to use one's creative talents in newly emerging companies in growth industries.

CREATIVITY AND MANAGEMENT

The Varying Forms Creativity and Innovation May Take

Creative and innovative contributions are by no means limited to new products or services, although these are probably the best

GREAT PERSON PROFILE

Cyrus Hall McCormick (1809–1884)

Cyrus Hall McCormick was born and raised on a farm in the Shenandoah Valley, where he and his father experimented with farm machinery to improve the farmer's job of reaping wheat during a short harvesting period. The first successful machine built by McCormick was patented in 1831. His background as a farmer, combined with his innate mechanical skills, resulted in a unique *creativity*.

Although he is widely known for his invention of the reaper, McCormick also developed *innovative business practices*. In 1855, he provided the first written guarantee for his products. Realizing that farmers were often hard pressed for cash, McCormick also introduced installment selling, with generous credit terms that included time extensions without interest during periods of bad harvests. These practices swept the industry and are now deeply embedded in all facets of American business.

After Cyrus McCormick's death, the McCormick Company and four other manufacturers were merged to form International Harvester.

known. Supermarkets, shopping malls, discount stores, selling on installment credit, condominiums, and discotheques were all creations at one time or another. The same may be said of such new developments as *flexible work hours,* which permit some individualizing of the workweek, and *job enrichment,* which calls for redesign of job content with the objective of making work more interesting and challenging.

Institutionalizing Creativity

There are equally good examples of innovations that are intrinsic to organizations or to the functions of management. Market research was "invented" to provide managers with a systematic method of investigating new market opportunities, testing consumer responses, and the like. The result of this research often leads to new services or products or revisions of existing ones. Technological forecasting came into being in response to managers' needs to anticipate the nature and speed of adoption of future technologies, such as solid-state circuitry in electronics, and laser-beam technology. Another rather recent innovation is establishing units for the purposes of human resource planning and programming. This activity involves inventorying the organization's current work force, estimating future needs in terms of numbers, knowledge, education, skills, and experience, and then drafting plans to achieve future requirements. Yet another, and extremely important, innovation was the engineering of computer-based management information systems. Systems departments had to exercise much imagination and ability in these applications. The ability of computer systems to process huge volumes of data at incredible speeds made it possible for even managers of very large and complex organizations to be constantly informed in ways never before feasible. Newer forms of creative action have involved new and novel uses of computer-derived information.

The *departmentalizing* of creativity and innovation must itself be regarded as creative. That is, management in many organizations has decided to make creativity and innovation the special assignments of employees in departments with names such as Research and Development, Advanced Systems, Engineering Design, and Advertising Research, to mention a few. In all such cases, there is a common thread: to hire people who possess the credentials that may enable them to be creative, and then place them with others similarly prepared, in the hope that a good deal of mutual creative stimulation will take place.

The level or intensity of creative action needed by an organization is affected by the nature of the organization, its competition, the pace of change, and related considerations. Institutions vary widely in terms of their needs for innovative actions. For example, for years the design department of the Oldsmobile Division of General Motors assumed leadership for "the corporation" in introducing new and creative designs for exterior appearance, transmissions, and motors. A company that was licensed to use or produce the "hydramatic" transmission, originally designed by Oldsmobile, required little creativity in design, but possibly a great deal in recognizing that the licensing could be arranged with a *competitor!* Another instance of the need for creativity is found in the architectural field. A firm specializing in the redevelopment of older areas of major cities requires a high level of creative action. In this same field, the Skidmore, Owens, and Merrill firm that designed well-known skyscrapers in Chicago and New York pioneered a new and highly creative concept for constructing a tall building on a relatively small base. It accomplished this feat by using bundles of steel tubes anchored firmly below ground and extending to the top of the building (as in the Sears Tower in Chicago).

Training People for Creative Thinking and Problem Approaches

The advances in work on creative thinking and problem solving have reached a point where managerial training in this subject matter has been undertaken. Representative of these efforts are the programs conducted by M. D. Edwards (1975). Edwards has developed a five-step approach to *creative problem solving,* quite similar to the steps in the creative process described previously. These steps are:

1. **Fact Finding.** Often it helps to ask oneself the questions: *Who* started the activity? *When* must initial information be provided? or *What* kinds of activities stimulate me?

2. **Problem Finding.** Here the challenge is to "see" the problem or issue from several different view points, since these almost always bring out new points or ideas. It frequently helps to ask others to state their ideas of "how things look" or what they think to be the key problem.

3. **Idea Finding.** Brainstorming techniques, talking to others, and looking at reference sources are some ways that people start to develop potentially useful ideas and approaches to their situations. Making notes to oneself is also a common and useful technique. In all cases, "mulling things over" is important so that things start coming together—and one should not disregard one's own viewpoint; it is always important.

4. **Solution Finding.** Ideas have to be evaluated. Consequently, criteria should be developed that will be used to reach a solution or make a decision. Then, each of the ideas or approaches can be evaluated against this set of criteria, realizing the limitations of resources.

5. **Acceptance Finding.** Creative ideas or approaches must be implemented, and here one leaves the area of largely mental or intellectual processes. The challenge is to anticipate problems or select out those approaches that give one's creative solution the best chances for success.

When Edwards conducts various training seminars and workshops, he provides a number of suggestions to help managers or other participants strengthen these creative approaches (see Exhibit 13-3).

Individual and Organizational Aspects of Creativity

Before proceeding further, it will prove helpful if some of the themes surrounding creative action are brought together. Creativity has been discussed at several different levels.

Creativity being taught to executives.

1. **Individual.** Personal qualities influence creative actions and learning in terms of individualized methods and processing of information. Also to be considered is creative action that enhances one's personal experience, as compared to creative action that can contribute directly to performance in an organization as part of one's responsibilities.

2. **Managerial.** Managers can catalyze creative actions through their relations with members of their group and the quality of their leadership.

3. **Organizational.** Organizations require different levels of creative action, depending on their mission, competition, and numerous other factors. Creativity is institutionalized within groups, departments, or units set up expressly for these purposes.

4. **Environmental.** Invention and change are characteristic of advanced societies. Creative actions by individuals or organizations are multiplied many times over throughout society. In the United States, Canada, England, France, and other countries, innovation and creative action have expanded to create a realistic sense of increasing change.

These points are summarized in Exhibit 13-4. One could rightfully conclude that creativity does not take place as an isolated action. Rather, creativity is connected to all types of events in our personal lives. In an institutional framework, creative actions reflect the interconnections between individual, manager, organization, and environment.

Exhibit 13-3 Hints on Creative Thinking

Personal Habits

Start questioning the "why" of things.

Try to develop habit of free association. Be able to "disconnect" and move between ideas and approaches.

Challenge common assumptions if doubts exist.

Identify the best time of your day and the appropriate time to spend.

Find ways to change your habits or viewpoint.

Outlook

Assume: there's always a better way.

You can be a thinker as well as an action person.

Avoid attachment to an idea at too early a point.

Don't disregard the unfamiliar.

Look to your past successes and build confidence in "can do."

Be persistent. Don't be easily discouraged.

Techniques

Track previous actions and learn from past experiences.

Keep a file on ideas or "different" approaches.

Use multiple criteria to judge "goodness" of an idea.

Devise alternate ways to state your problem or situation.

Source: Based on the work of M. D. Edwards, "How to Make Training Decisions—Creativity," *Training HRD* (July 1978): 21–23.

Creativity, Innovation, and the Basic Functions of Management

There is a creative dimension to the fundamental responsibilities managers shoulder. If we examine the nature of planning, for instance, it is easy to appreciate that planning is "a time for ideas," a future-oriented activity. During planning, a search is most needed for new ways to anticipate problems and challenges, prior to any commitment to a specific line of action. The generation of creative ideas can be aided by certain forms of interaction. For example, one or more specialists may be asked to make presentations at a management meeting, with the intent that the presentations will include recommendations for solving some significant problem or for taking a specific future course of action. Discussing and arguing over such recommendations may well lead to creative inputs to future plans. On occasion, brainstorming may also be productive.

Exhibit 13-4 Creative Action

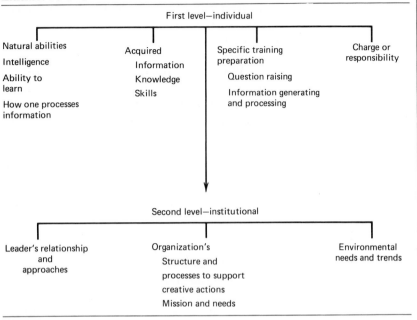

First level—individual

| Natural abilities | Acquired | Specific training preparation | Charge or responsibility |

Natural abilities
Intelligence
Ability to learn
How one processes information

Acquired
Information
Knowledge
Skills

Specific training preparation
Question raising
Information generating and processing

Charge or responsibility

Second level—institutional

Leader's relationship and approaches

Organization's
Structure and processes to support creative actions
Mission and needs

Environmental needs and trends

Leadership Quality

Leadership, too, may involve creative activity. What is significant here is that leaders who make use of widely different "styles" can be equally creative, depending upon the "goodness of fit" between leadership style and the makeup of the situation. We illustrate this point by referring to an account taken from David M. Ogilvy's *Confessions of an Advertising Man*. Ogilvy related that early in his working life, before he turned to the advertising business, he was one of 37 chefs employed in a large and famous Parisian restaurant. It was here that he came under the domination of M. Pitard, the head chef.

Pitard is described as "ruling with a rod of iron" and keeping the entire staff terrified of him. He kept people under ferocious pressure, especially the "section specialists" for such items as poultry, salads, sauces, crepes, and pastry. He seldom praised any of his subordinates, but when he did, he gave all the credit to them and thereby gained the complete loyalty of the person praised. Pitard also had a sense of timing. One evening he took Ogilvy to where he could observe the President of France eating with delight a soufflé Ogilvy had prepared.

Pitard would not tolerate incompetency. He knew how demoralizing it is for professionals to work alongside bungling amateurs. He was on the constant lookout for evidence of poor performance, personally inspecting everything that left the kitchen before it was served to his customers. Finally, Ogilvy recounts, Pitard made no effort to conceal that he had become a wealthy man because of his long, successful career. Rather, he flaunted his possessions, "thus stimulating the ambitions of all of us to follow in his footsteps," Ogilvy writes.

What is notable in this account is that a very "heavy," taskmaster style of leadership fits this situation perfectly. The assistant chefs all knew that the past and current reputation of the restaurant had been achieved by the determined, driving, no-nonsense leadership of the head chef. They also knew that Pitard was more skilled in every phase of cooking than any of them. That is, he was an outstanding role model. Finally, they realized that for all his blustering and pressure tactics he was showing them how to succeed in their chosen profession.

Innovative behavior also enters into managers' roles as decision makers. The various forms this behavior can take are well illustrated by certain events that transpired at a new automobile engine plant of the Saab-Scandia Corporation, near Stockholm, Sweden. In the late 1960s, at the time when the new engine plant was being planned, Saab management was plagued by problems of high employee turnover, high rates of absenteeism, and difficulties in recruiting new workers at one of its truck manufacturing plants. A key decision was made to create a new mode of interaction between management and the work force by developing a network of *idea and consultation groups,* made up of supervisors, engineers, and rank-and-file production workers. The concept was to enlist the best thinking of these groups in an attack on the plant's current problems, as well as to seek their advice about the design and operation of the planned engine plant. Although wholesale changes were not feasible in the existing truck plant, nonetheless various innovations recommended by the network of groups were implemented and were successful in drastically reducing turnover and absenteeism, while improving product quality.

Based on this experience, Saab management decided to create a project development group consisting of three workers, one supervisor, one assembly instructor, and the plant physician. This group was directed to evaluate the ideas initiated by the idea and consultation groups, as well as to generate new ones and to bring all the ideas to bear on the design of the new engine plant. After considering various alternatives, including conventional assembly-line technology, the group finally recommended the adoption of a system under which parallel groups of 10 workers each would be responsible for the production of complete engines from engine block and piece parts. Under this system, the allocation of tasks would be decided on by the group, as would be the pace of work. Engine production has been functioning in this fashion since late 1972. In terms of the conventional criteria of management, it has been an overall success. The new method is no longer considered an experiment, and neither workers nor management appears to entertain any notion of returning to former methods.

In the above example, Saab management's creative decision to present company problems to the work force included a real element of *risk,* since there was no adequate precedent for this action. By opening up new lines of communication with employees, there was the chance that management might hear some things it would prefer not to know. And, as another facet of risk, by asking employees for solutions to problems, management was making an implicit commitment to accept at least a significant number of these ideas. If it did not accept at least a significant number of the employees' recommendations, its credibility would be badly damaged.

Being Creative in Managing Change

The management of change is still another managerial responsibility that calls for creative contributions, on both the individual and organizational level. One contemporary problem of individual change is that of *obsolescence,* a process in which the skills, knowledge, and motivation that a person brings to the job are no longer consistent with the demands of that job. In such a case, the manager is faced with a creative challenge: what to "do about" the employee who no longer meets job requirements. Simply discharging the individual may not be possible, perhaps because of a union contract or civil service protection. Also, it may not be humane, in the light of many years of previously productive service. Ways to deal with obsolescence include personal counseling, discussion of possible job reassignment on a transfer basis, and exploration of the appropriateness of "retreading" through additional training and education.

Creative coping with change on an organizational level may be illustrated by the case of the agricultural and technical college whose top administration, with the agreement of the faculty, decided to upgrade its academic program. The college president and the vice-president for academic affairs addressed themselves to the question: what will the proposed change do to the college as a social organization? It was plain, they reasoned, that upgrading academic demands would require more and different kinds of work from students. If students were to make the transition successfully, they would require new forms of support. First, open forums were held with leaders and officers of student organizations with college "top management" and several faculty members. At these meetings, the rationale for upgrading standards was communicated, questions were answered, and criticisms were gathered. Next, the same process was expanded to large open meetings of the student body as a whole. Through the give and take of this process, it became evident that other, concurrent changes would be necessary: strengthening the faculty–student advising system, expanding the staff and capabilities of the Dean of Students office, adding to library holdings and study facilities, building communication links with high school student counselors, and providing an appeal process for use by students in academic difficulty. The point of this story is that prior to implementing change, the college administration did its best to anticipate the unwanted consequences of the change. It guarded against this by involving the students in how the changes were to be carried out.

Requirements for the Management of Creativity

Since the creative process is not likely to be understood by intuition, and since creativity is of such importance to organizational functioning, it is important for managers to make the understanding of how creativity works a matter of formal learning. Deliberate examination of their own experiences, as these relate to creative events and creative people, can be very useful.

Identification

Identifying people with creative abilities is another type of skill that is of increasing value. This is not a problem *if* a person within the manager's group already has a "track record" of creative accomplishment. But managers rarely have the good fortune to recruit individuals with established reputations. More often, managers are involved in the process of screening and selecting from a group of fresh, young aspirants or working with assigned management trainees.

Let us assume that a manager is the head of the Department of Economics and Planning in a bank. The fresh, young aspirants with whom he is dealing are recent graduates of Ph.D. programs in economics. What is needed by the bank is a person who, aside from possessing the usual economist's tools, can develop "creative interpretations of many complex governmental actions and environmental developments." What problems does the department head face in selecting the person most likely to become a creative performer? First, the candidates have very little, if any, work history. Next, the hiring interview is not a situation that facilitates behavior suggesting creative potential. Let us assume, for example, that a candidate exhibits behavior often thought to suggest creativity, such as display of "free spirit" nonconformity. But there is no sure way to distinguish this behavior from simple conceit. Is close study of the candidate's resumé, a summary of his or her work and educational experience, the way out? Of course, what is learned from resumés is helpful, but only up to a point. For instance, let us suppose that the resumé conveys the impression that the candidate has great persistence, which is often thought to be another clue to the creative individual. Persistence can also characterize the plodding "workaholic." It is likely that the department head, and other managers facing similar problems in hiring, would do better by arming themselves with recommendations provided by former teachers, peers, and superiors who know the various candidates in some depth. These ratings are additionally valuable if they can be acquired from individuals who themselves have already demonstrated creative capabilities. Still, there is always the difficulty of getting an open, objective recommendation.

Climate

Managing creativity also requires active management involvement in the creation and maintenance of a supportive organization **climate.** In the present context, climate should be understood as the quality of an organization's *internal* environment, *as experienced by insiders.* The following adjectives, and their opposites, are suggestive of the qualities people discern in judging what type of climate they work in: friendly, accepting, helpful, productive, cooperative, supportive, responsive, and dependable. If most people in the organization perceive these *positive qualities,* rather than their opposites, then management has done a very creditable job in bringing about circumstances productive of high morale and creative contributions.

It is also essential that top management show support for creativity through the reward system and by reducing resistance to change among employees.

Size.   Characteristics of the organization must also be factored into managerial interpretations and efforts to develop creativity. Sheer organizational size is one such feature. In a small organization, it is possible for members of top management to be on a first-name basis with most employees, thus making it much easier for warm, friendly, mutually trusting relations and a positive climate to emerge. This becomes more difficult for the large organization with many layers of hierarchy and great social distances between the worlds of management and of other employees. Some large organizations attempt to deal with this difficulty by a policy of decentralization. That is, they grant managers of the organization's various units substantial autonomy in the day-to-day operation of these units, including the freedom to build a climate according to their interpretation of the needs of their situation. The potential variability in climate among organizational units can be a serious problem warranting the attention of officials and policy makers.

Leadership Styles.   Leadership styles clearly play a critical role in the quality of climate. Consider the contrast between the style employed by the head chef, M. Pitard, and that of top management of Saab-Scandia's engine plant. Pitard was a heavy-handed autocrat; Saab management, in this instance, chose a participation–consultation style. Both styles were successful, in that each fit the particular set of circumstances. Because of the differing sets of circumstances, the two styles produced contrasting climates.

Communications.   The communications network in an organization is another basic factor that influences the quality of climate. Consider the likely result if, in a particular organization, communications behavior is very formal, for example, a heavy flow of memos or the building of voluminous files. Alternative communications channels are few, so that communication "jams" are frequent, the content of communication is heavily loaded with controls (budgets, work rules and regulations, personnel policy constraints). Top management takes the attitude: "What employees don't know won't hurt them." This kind of climate is almost certain to be perceived by people as heavy and punitive.

Goals.   Goals represent "what the organization was created to pursue," and they serve several functions. First, they exert directional pressures on the behavior of participants in an organization. That is, each person's contribution is expected to be in a direction that serves the organization's goals. Second, goals function as measurements of success, and the members of an organization may well assign different values to goals and their pursuit. These values will color their perception of the organizational climate. Let us suppose that, on the one hand, we are talking about a typical community hospital in which employees are likely to associate positive social values with the goal of providing high-quality patient care. They, therefore, will be inclined to enhance their efforts to accomplish this goal. On the other hand, consider the likely climate where employees are working to produce toy guns intended for the children's market or horror movies intended for general audiences. Certainly, some employees would assign little or negative social value to these goals, and this attitude might adversely affect their performance.

Policymakers and Officials: Climate and Creativity

This textbook on managing and managers has intentionally concentrated on positions and actions besides those of policymaking and strategic actions. These fields are so large and specialized at this point that they cannot be adequately covered in a single volume. But this does not mean that policy actions can be disregarded. The matters of climate and creativity are good examples of this. Climate is "constructed" through specific pronouncements and consistent actions over an extended time period. The failure of officials to recognize the potentially wide range of variability in climates among units can seriously impede efforts to build the *creative organization*. Second, officials as well as those assuming managerial responsibilities must be able to visualize the connections between organizational purposes or goals and the part played by creative activity: what is the type and scope of creative actions, and who is to carry these out? These are all questions that will have to be answered. Officials and policymakers will have to deal directly, and on a continuing basis, with climate and its determination by managerial actions, if creativity is to achieve success as an institutional strategy.

How Organizations Often Hinder the Creative Process

Although management's job includes the responsibility to foster creative work, in many cases individual managers exhibit anxiety over the impact of creative ideas upon the status quo. Creativity, in its essence, often means change. Change may be unwelcome to managers as well as to rank-and-file employees, for a variety of reasons.

Fear of becoming obsolete as a result of change has been an obvious problem for some managers. For example, 10 to 15 years ago managers were hearing dire predictions about how high-powered computer installations would absorb the work of many managers, particularly at middle-management levels. The fact that these fears have proved largely unwarranted has not reduced the tendency for many managers to be wary of proposed changes. Since managers are often in a position to veto changes, they may, for personal reasons, be doing a disservice to their organization.

Also, some managers appear fearful of creative people or are, at least, made uncomfortable by them. This seems especially likely if a manager is faced with requests, perhaps even demands, for additional support (money, equipment, people) from a subordinate with a record for creative performance. The manager's response may well be to apply tight rules regarding the use of more resources and to supervise the subordinate's progress in a way that supresses creativity. Close supervision of employees performing potentially creative assignments virtually guarantees failure.

Problems of Specialization and Creative Action

Specialization

Departments "specializing" in creativity have been instituted in some organizations to expand or coordinate creative efforts, but they may also have some dysfunctional results. When people are set off from one another by departmental boundaries, they develop a tendency to regard their activities in a very possessive way and to resist any effort by "outsiders" to intrude on their "turf." When this occurs, it is also very likely that specific departments will develop *inward* orientations regarding their own goals, with the accompanying risk that the overall goals of the organization will fade from attention. Thus, it may turn out that creative work at the departmental level will not advance the large organizational purpose.

Another well-known kind of functional specialization in organizations is that of *line* and *staff* units. In this context, line functions are those functions needed to provide the services or products of the organization's basic purpose. For example, in a health care setting, the line functions and people provide direct patient care and medical activities. Staff employees provide important support, service, and advisory functions, such as the maintenance of patients' medical records, financial and accounting services, and custodial care. The problem that may arise to plague creativity stems from tendencies for staff units to enlarge the scope of their activities and to attempt to get their creative ideas accepted by managers of line functions. An adversary relationship counterproductive to creative accomplishments may result.

Political Realities

The typical workings of organizational hierarchies, including the requirement that all or most actions taken at lower levels be checked in advance by a higher level, confront creative individuals with the problem of getting a hearing at some appropriate but higher point in the organization. Such people often learn that they require a well-placed *sponsor*. This need to "play politics" to gain acceptance of new ideas may be distasteful to creative people—but is often a part of organization life.

Location of Groups

Still another damper on creativity is the tendency demonstrated by many organizations to locate groups presumed to be creative, in remote or relatively inaccessible places. They proceed on the theory that isolation will promote "thinking" by lessening distractions. Many research and development groups find themselves in such a situation, and they experience a real loss in productive interaction with the rest of the organization, which retards their efforts. Furthermore, unless R&D and similar groups are made up of people with many different backgrounds and types of training, cross-fertilization of ideas will suffer.

Top Management

Finally, as noted under the preceding topic, upper management may reduce the chances for creative accomplishment by not setting out and communicating sufficiently clear goals and expectations about the roles creative individuals and groups are to play. Sometimes this situation occurs when top management has itself paid insufficient attention to the long-range goals of the organization, and to the specific areas in which creative ideas or solutions to problems will most likely be needed. It is plain that companies must narrow the ways in which creative groups devote their talents so as to have reasonable assurance of furthering company goals.

Structural and Behavioral Approaches Used to Facilitate Creative Activity

A basic challenge to managers is to build creative motivation into all the regular day-to-day work processes of the organization, instead of limiting creative behavior to designated, special groups. This process means taking a responsibility or work assignment formerly limited to a few employees and making it "everybody's business." However, the difficulties involved in doing this must be faced. Earlier we described how setting up boundaries between departments encourages "turf mentalities" and the like. Such attitudes must be responded to with official actions. A significant degree of change is required if creativity and innovation are to be elicited from employees at every level and within each function, rather than confined to specialized groups.

Upper management must function as positive role models for lower-level managers and supervisors, or desired changes will not "take." Upper management must support and respond to subordinates' ideas and suggestions and reward subordinates for doing a good job. In this context, *reward* includes a variety of possibilities, including recognition, individual sense of contribution, as well as some obvious economic incentives. Even if support is widespread, much time and management patience will pass before notable achievements are likely to occur.

A number of approaches that exist for the achievement of creative results have been implemented by various organizations.

Think Tanks

Various companies and some governmental agencies have introduced the concept of **think tanks** to expand creative outcomes of their units. In this approach, a think tank represents a structure and a process to improve creativity. Consider as an example the approach taken by a large "fast food" organization. The rapid growth and economic success of the organization was due to a notable series of innovations in services and products. These, in turn, were attributed to the formation of a think tank, supported by the president. It was recognized that the success of the food outlets would depend on the introduction of noticeably different products and services, consistent in quality and superior to many competitive products. Accomplishing this objective meant that highly creative, but practical, approaches would be needed. Strong competition further reinforced the need for creative, but practical, approaches. The answer was a think tank consisting of key officers, managers, and, at various times, suppliers, customers, and employees. The group recognized that competition was extremely tough and that ideas must be drawn together from many different sources—and carefully screened and integrated.

The think tank met regularly for the specific purpose of innovating new products and service approaches. The agenda would consist of a problem or suggestion. Combinations of brainstorming techniques and individualized approaches were used *after* the product or service had been carefully researched for available information.

Extensive and carefully prepared records of background research and group discussions ensured continuity between sessions and the ability to build upon previous accomplishments. Also, appropriate time was allowed between discussions for the incubation of ideas.

In sum, the think tank represented the infusion of the creative process into an active and on-going organizational activity that brought superior results.

Task Forces and Venture Teams

Task forces and *venture teams* are well-known special-purpose groups with well-established potential for creative ideas and problem solving. An illustration of the use of each should make this clear.

A major corporation in the food industry decided to evaluate the economic logic of producing one of its major product lines at four widely scattered locations around the United States, instead of consolidating all production at only one location. Top management decided to assign this problem to a task force composed of one person from each of the following functions: production, engineering design, accounting and finance, transportation and distribution services, information systems, and personnel. The specific people were chosen on the basis of recommendations of their immediate managers. They were relatively young and were well motivated to take on this assignment. The task force was authorized to visit each production site, conduct interviews, review all facilities, examine records, explore a number of possible new sites, talk with people in local governments as required, and do anything else they deemed necessary. Although choosing a group leader was not necessary, they decided that the man with experience in production management should be in nominal charge.

The task force ultimately produced a report summarizing its various investigations and recommendations. The key decision was to consolidate all production of this particular product line at one site, a site different from any of the existing four. Top management was very impressed with the thoroughness and overall quality of the group's work, including the suggestion that a consulting firm be hired to conduct a labor market study.

Although this whole process was not nearly as simple as this account suggests, you can see the major elements of the task force and its creative accomplishments.

Venture teams have a good deal in common with task forces. They are usually formed to explore the feasibility and advisability of engaging in some form of business opportunity, while recognizing the accompanying risks. For example, two companies in the wood products industry were, at one point, conducting negotiations about joining forces in order to bid on a large tract of forest land that was being sold by a third company. To expedite the process of deciding how best to combine their efforts, top management officials of both companies agreed to form a venture team. They would assign the team the responsibility of working out all the necessary details and making a recommendation on the nature and amount of the bid. In this case, the team was composed of representatives of both bidding companies. They possessed various skills and experience that straddled forestry and forest land management, wood pulping, transportation and materials management, cost accounting, and finance.

As was true in the example of the task force, the particular specialists were appointed at the recommendation of their managers. Unlike the task force, however, the venture team had to work against a tight deadline, since there was always the possibility that competitors would also enter bids for the same property.

Pilot Plants

Pilot plants in many instances are the best devices to test the potential value of creative ideas. Usually, the test is of a piece of equipment, an equipment complex, or a production process. More often than not the pilot plant is a miniature, scale model. If the pilot test proves successful, a full-scale version will then be built. The act of building and operating a pilot plant often causes the people involved to discover ideas better than the ones with which they began.

Employee Forum

Another manner in which some organizations attempt to generate creative inputs is through use of *employee forums*. Forums may take a variety of shapes, but the following example contains the more common features.

A company in the automobile parts manufacturing industry decided to implement the forum concept by asking employees in each of the plant's departments to elect a person to represent their department in meetings to be held with members of top management. The rationale given to employees was that management wanted to create a new means for two-way communication with the work force. This communication channel would be used for contributing ideas and suggestions for new products or product modifications, for changes in personnel policies, for changes in the plant safety program, and anything else that might make for a stronger organization and higher morale. Meetings between management and forum "delegates" took place twice a month. Minutes were kept and were later published and distributed to all employees. A record was also kept of the accomplishments. This system was instituted 15 years ago. The company's top management is planning to continue it indefinitely, on the basis of its many valuable contributions to both morale and profitability.

Less ambitious and less personal forms of communication with creative ends are illustrated by the *suggestion system*, with its well-known forms for submitting ideas and suggestions for changes through interoffice mail directly from the initiating employee to a designated office. Also used are several variations of the *speak up* system, an auxiliary communication medium between employees at large and a specific delivery point within the organization. By "speaking up," any employee can contribute a useful idea or pose questions indicative of problems that may need to be solved. Here, too, pre-printed forms are provided for use by employees at a number of locations in the organization.

Two related approaches having the same objective, that of "recharging the batteries" of individuals or groups expected to play creative roles, are the *retreat* and the *sabbatical*. The retreat usually involves assembling a group of employees having professional or managerial assignments at some secluded location. By having "freewheeling" discussions in an environment relatively free of distractions, but providing adequate comforts, it is hoped that innovative thinking will be stimulated. The same general hope is held out for the sabbatical, which calls for release of one or a few individuals at one time from their normal duties to take a sharp break from the usual round of activities. This might be accomplished by the individual entering a university program of studies or research, or by becoming a staff member for six months or a year at a technical institute, industry association headquarters, or government agency. In some cases, spending the sabbatical in another country may strengthen the individual's knowledge base, motivation, and creative potential, all of which can be effectively utilized upon return to the home organization. Unfortunately, the negative attitudes and actions of certain employees cannot always be changed. Such individuals can easily "infect" and "poison" the work climate for their fellow workers. Consequently, there are times when remedial measures may be painful, such as forced resignation, early retirement, or transfer to other jobs.

The various approaches just covered, when taken in combination, offer excellent potential for achieving **"organizational renewal"** on a periodic basis. By "renewal" is meant the recapturing of organizational vitality and the accompanying drive to accomplish organizational goals. Creative people are the particular spark for this process, but all organization members can take part in renewal-oriented activities, and in their benefits.

Creativity and Innovation: The Case of "Hamburger Hamlets"

It should be stressed at the outset that we are dealing here with a "developmental situation," one that has taken substantial form but does not have a discernible end point. The selection of "Hamburger Hamlets" as an illustration of managerial creativity is to dramatize the emergence of a particular success strategy and to suggest the directions it will take in the future.

First, let us present a bit of organizational life history, the reasons for its founding, and the principal persons involved. Marilyn and Harry Lewis met in Los Angeles early in 1950, married, and swiftly discovered they had a strong common interest centering around food. She liked to cook, and he wanted to own his own restaurant. They pooled their meager financial resources, leased a small building, completely remodeled it with their own hands, and opened the first "Hamlet" in October 1950. It had seating for 80 people and a very limited menu. Marilyn and Harry soon settled into a routine of 18-hour days, with Harry acting as the greeter, broiler man, and cashier, and Marilyn handling all the other cooking chores. From the beginning, they attempted to set themselves apart from other places identified with hamburgers by adding blintzes, crepes, and flaming desserts, and by highly personalized service coupled with rock-bottom prices, which are possible when the owners do all the work. This combination of food items rapidly caught on, and the Lewises found themselves confronted with the problems of success: a continually growing and demanding clientele, an increasingly complicated menu, and an exhausting pace of work with little or no time off.

A crucial decision point had been reached. In order to implement several truly innovative design and decor ideas, the Lewises knew they would have to expand to new locations. Expansion required that they hire other people in management roles to whom they would delegate authority, something they had not tried before. This involved the real risk that others would not succeed with the Lewis formula of high-quality food, personalized service, and low prices. Nonetheless, they went forward, designing a management system that included a complex training program for all new employees, a manual of work rules and procedures which gradually became more extensive, and a system of supervision that kept Harry Lewis "in the field" almost continually, visiting each Hamburger Hamlet on a round-robin basis.

By the mid-1970s, 20 Hamlets had been established and more were being planned, moving outward from the California base to Arizona, Illinois, and Washington, D.C. In each new location, the basic design and decor resemblances were maintained: bright red seats, dark paneling, white silk walls, thick red rugs, chandeliers, and quality paintings on the walls. At a number of locations one or more special features were added, such as a greenhouse or patio, a library, or collections of theater programs, art posters, and engravings. Very few if any of these features would ordinarily be associated with a lunch-counter-sounding name like *Hamburger Hamlet*.

Further pressure on management's energy and ingenuity stemmed from growth of the basic Hamlet menu to 106 items. To serve all the items on the menu without pricing itself out of business, management had to recruit, screen, and train excellent cooks who could handle heavy, complicated work loads and would take the initiative to maintain rigid portion controls on customer orders. Another requirement was excellent table service. Here, the Lewises hit on the creative notion of recruiting waitresses from among the wives, sisters, and daughters of retired Pullman coach railroad waiters, who in their heyday were widely reputed for their quality customer service.

As the success of the chain continued and the distance between the various units increased, additional care had to be taken by management not to make casual assumptions about applying past thinking patterns to new situations far removed from familiar territory. Thus, in the case of "checking out" the advisability of adding a new unit in Scottsdale, Arizona, a research team of management trainees interviewed a number of merchants and suppliers in that area. They performed extensive price calculations for locally available ingredients for the Hamlet menu and for others that would need to be shipped in from elsewhere. The team also purchased several meals at restaurants with which they would be competing; "comparison-shopped" their prices, menus, and service quality; and performed estimates of customer volumes for various hours of the day. All of this indicates how far, and relatively fast, the Lewises and their colleagues had come in terms of the quality of their managerial ideas and their implementation.

Career Values Gained from the "Hamburger Hamlet" Example

It is well known that starting a small business can be a very risky proposition if the founders do not have sufficient "working capital," that is, the financial resources needed to begin the business and pay its operating expenses until income from sales builds to a successful volume. The Lewises brought barely sufficient capital to their enterprise to open its doors, but overcame this risk by the special ingredients they brought to the venture: a distinct menu, personal service by the owners, and low prices. Once they had the resources, they began adding all the design, decor, and menu elaboration features described earlier. All this provides an object lesson for others thinking of going into business for themselves.

Another prominent aspect of the Hamberger Hamelt story is the obvious total commitment of time, effort, and talent made by the owners. Opening a business is usually an exhausting affair, at least in the beginning, and requires the complete dedication of those involved.

Other items of career value include the instinct for "market differentiation" displayed by the Lewises—how they managed to set themselves apart from other restaurant chains associated with hamburgers. This is a prime necessity in any highly competitive industry. They also had the creative knack for finding the new in the old, as is evidenced in their hitting on the idea of hiring the relatives of Pullman car waiters to wait on tables, in the belief that providing good service is a tradition in these families.

A final career pointer is the need to anticipate the challenges and problems of growth as the business succeeds. This involves finding ways to apply the success formula that worked well on a modest scale to a much expanded operation. The key to continued success, in this case and many others we could have examined, turned out to be a change in roles for Marilyn and Harry Lewis, from "owners" to "managers." This required very real changes in behavior: delegating authority, building a system of communication, constructing an elaborate manual of policies and procedures, and designing a training program, as well as a number of other novel departures. Thus, growth in a business requires accompanying growth on the part of the individuals who run it and the ability to adapt *new* solutions to *old* problems, which is crucial for managers at all levels.

SUMMARY

Creative thinking and approaches have become part of the necessary preparation for managing. The growing complexity and uncertainty that characterize the work and world of the manager require new ways of thinking about and dealing with the resources within the domain of management. To some extent, it appears that people are born with various talents or abilities permitting creative behavior. Yet, the presence of this potential provides no assurance that it will be used, or that the person understands the methods to tap these. Correspondingly, work in this field suggests that many people can learn elements or procedures of creative thinking, which can improve both their work and personal lives.

Creativity goes beyond individual considerations to those associated with the organization and its approaches to implementing creativity. Creative capabilities are established through departments, divisions, committees, project groups, and workshops. Some of these represent permanent functional arrangements expected to make creative contributions on a continuing basis. Others may be temporary arrangements, as with project groups or workshops. In all cases, creative behavior can be improved through the use of training approaches, whether these be directed at departments or individual organization members.

Questions for Study and Discussion

1. What is creativity at the personal level? On a more general level?
2. Are only artists, musicians, and people in other "arty" occupations truly creative?
3. What is brainstorming? How does it work?
4. Why worry about being creative? How will it help me?
5. Can creativity be learned, or does it simply emerge under the right conditions?
6. In what ways do managers utilize creativity and innovation?
7. What is known about the creative process at the individual level? Describe the four stages of the creative process.
8. What is meant by "organizational climate"? What significance does "climate" have for creativity and innovation?
9. How and why do organizations often hinder the creative process?
10. How may departmentalization interfere with creative accomplishment? How may "line" and "staff" distinctions be troublesome in the same fashion?
11. What is meant by "organization renewal"? How can it be done?

CASE: DOROTHY GOLDEN, MARKET RESEARCHER

Dorothy Golden, Market Research Manager for Modern Care Company, was sitting at her desk one evening wondering, "How in the world am I going to get market research *really* going here? I don't know if Modern Care is doing that much better since they formed this department than without it(!)"

Dorothy had been a marketing major at Britton University, a small, private university located in Georgia. She had a number of job interviews during her last year at school. Because of her good academic performance, outside activities, and self-confidence, she received a number of job offers. She took a position with Modern Care Company (MCC), headquartered in Atlanta, because they were well established, offered training, and had a good-sized sales department.

Company Background

Modern Care Company employed approximately 3000 people at four different locations in the United States. It produced a large line of health products under its own name as well as items for large drug chains and retailers, such as Sears, Inc., that used their own brand. The Sales Department for MCC was a large one with more than 100 people, including field sales people and the office and administrative staff. An organization chart for the sales department is attached (Exhibit 13-5).

The Training Program

Dorothy's training at MCC was aimed at familiarizing her with all phases of their operations. She spent almost a year working in various sales departments including "Field Sales," as well as some time in gaining familiarity with "production" and "purchasing." At the completion of her training, she felt that her time had been well spent, but she was eager for an assignment.

Ralph Churchill, Vice President of Sales, held a "feedback" session with Dorothy at the end of her training period. Churchill told Dorothy of her performance and the uniformly *good ratings* given her by the heads of departments where she had worked. She was very pleased after receiving the information, since she had been extremely tense during her training period, not being sure what the "feedback" would be. Then Churchill went on to talk about her job assignment:

Exhibit 13-5 Sales Department, Modern Care Products

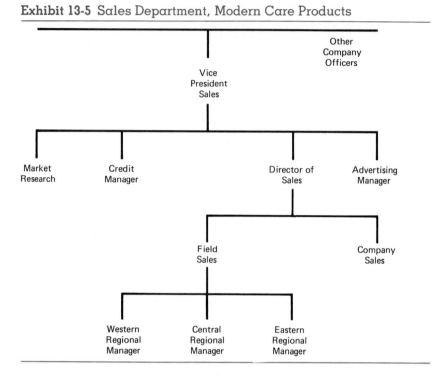

Dorothy, we have been selling health products for almost 20 years, but we still don't know much about our customers and the sales of our products. "We don't know why we are successful!" For a long time, I've discussed with the Executive Committee the need for a market research department—it could benefit everyone and really affect our "bottom line"—point the way to new and better products; show us where we've been falling down on existing products or sales to customers; and why we've been successful with many of our older customers. They've okayed our setting up the department. If you are willing, I'd like you to take the job. I'll assign Jim Weatherall to work with you—he had plenty of selling experience before being assigned here and also wants a change. Okay?

The Market Research Department

Since setting up the department almost three years ago, Dorothy had hired one additional person, an "analyst," Cathy Burns. Cathy compiled and analyzed figures based on the computerized sales reports, special notes and reports from the sales people, and various reports published by government agenices. Jim Weatherall's work came to deal more and more with developing information from customers, working with sales people, and then meeting regularly with Dorothy and Cathy. Dorothy set up a schedule of monthly sales meetings. The second Monday of each month, Cathy and Jim met with Dorothy and spent most of the day analyzing sales figures and marketing information that became the basis for Dorothy's presentation at the monthly Sales Department meeting.

Dorothy's Working Style

When Dorothy majored in marketing at Britton University, the program was developed pretty much along the same lines as other professional management programs: many courses in her major field plus general requirements in economics, management, accounting, and organization behavior. The courses provided a good general background, but never seemed to deal very much with "putting the stuff to work," and not at all with an individual's own way of doing things required by organizations. It was just assumed that students would acquire the practical side as they gained experience with their employers.

Dorothy had little to go on regarding her own work habits other than what she observed as she worked in various departments during her training, or when visiting with customers, field people, and members of other organizations. She had hired Cathy when it became clear to her that there just was too much information and data to be analyzed. She simply did not have the time to do that and carry out her other administrative responsibilities.

Dorothy hit on the idea of having her own monthly meetings as a way to keep track of what was going on, and to help her digest information for the monthly sales meeting and report.

Market Research Meeting Format

The first week of each month Cathy received the computer printout of sales, which she then analyzed for trends, problems, and general performance. Cathy's analysis was recorded on a standardized form, which along with her verbal commentary became the basis for her report at the monthy market research meeting. If she analyzed other figures during the course of the month, they, too, were brought along for discussion at the meeting. Jim worked with various people and organizations during the month, some assigned by Dorothy and others representing routine calls. He usually summarized his individual "field research reports" during the first few days of the month, and then brought these to the market research meeting. Since the format for each meeting was about the same, no agenda was made up. If Dorothy had something special to discuss, she brought it up at the meeting. Otherwise, most of the time was taken up with discussing the reports of Cathy and Jim.

During the month, Dorothy talked to a number of other company managers on various problems or needs they had. Usually she spent one or two days traveling; visiting companies, customers, and government agencies; or talking to companies developing new products. Some of the things that she came across, or ideas that occurred to her, she discussed with Cathy or Jim individually, or sometimes brought them up at the monthly meeting. At times, she discussed ideas with some of the other managers she had gotten to know.

Reflections

"Deep down," Dorothy knew that "market research" was doing some good, because the Vice President, managers, and sales people had a lot more information to go on, and it was better than any they had had previously. Yet, she felt that somehow her department was not really getting to the bottom of some problems. Nor were they really coming up with many new ideas. Somehow, new product ideas and even analyses of sales often seemed to have a familiar ring—not much new was being developed.

Questions

1. What was the mission of the market research department?
2. What are some of the areas where there was a real need for creativity?
3. Were there some important skills that Dorothy was *not* likely to acquire from her schooling or even the Modern Care Company training program? If so, what are these? How might they best be acquired?
4. Develop a preliminary consultant's report for Dorothy. Consider yourself a member of Creative Management Associates, a firm specializing in helping its clients to develop better techniques so as to improve planning, problem analysis, and solutions. It bases its approaches on modern ideas of processes contributing to innovation and creativity. With approval of the Vice President of Sales, Dorothy has asked for assistance from your firm. The report should therefore be addressed to her. Since it is a preliminary report, 400 to 500 words should be enough to communicate to her some of the high points of your thoughts.

References

Arieti, Silvano, *Creativity: The Magic Synthesis*. New York: Basic Books (1976).

Burton, Gene, "Unleashing the Creative Flow Through NGT," *Management World*, **9**(8) (August 1980): 8–10.

Carl, L. M., "Wart-Hog Brainstorming," *Public Relations Quarterly,* **25**(4) (Winter 1980): 14–15.

Crosby, Andrew, *Creativity and Performance in Industrial Organization.* London: Tavistock Publications (1968).

Edwards, M. D., *Doubling Idea Power.* Addison-Wesley (1975).

Engel, H., *Handbook of Creative Learning Exercises.* Houston: Gulf Publishing (1973).

Feldhusen, J. F., D. J. Treffinger, and P. A. Pine, *Teaching Children How to Think.* Technical Report, National Institute of Education (1975).

Howard, Niles, "Business Probes the Creative Spark," *Dunn's Review,* **115**(1) (January 1980): 32–38.

Journal of Creative Behavior, published by the Creative Education Foundation, Buffalo, New York.

Miller, Ben, *Managing Innovation for Growth and Profit.* Homewood, Ill.: Dow Jones-Irwin (1970).

Ogilvy, David M., *Confessions of an Advertising Man.* New York: Atheneum (1963).

Osborne, Alex F., *Your Creative Power.* New York: Charles Scribner's Sons (1948).

Parnes, S. J., *Creative Behavior Guidebook.* New York: Scribner's (1967).

Polon, L., and W. Pollitt, *Creative Teaching Games.* Minneapolis: Denison (1974).

Rothenberg, Albert, and Carl R. Hausman, Eds., *The Creativity Question.* Durham, N.C.: Duke University Press (1976).

Scott, Sid, "The Design Group in Action," *Training and Development Journal,* **35**(4) (April 1981): 70–72.

Seferian, A., and H. P. Cole, *Encounters in Thinking.* Occasional Paper no.6, Buffalo, N.Y.: Creative Education Foundation (1970).

Steiner, Gary A., Ed., *The Creative Organization.* Chicago: University of Chicago Press (1965).

Upton, Albert, and Richard Samson, *Creative Analysis.* New York: E. P. Dutton (1961).

CHAPTER 14

WORK AND WORK DESIGN

KEY
QUESTIONS
ADDRESSED
IN CHAPTER

1. What are the quality of work life issues and arguments?
2. What descriptions of work and workers have been found to be useful in crystallizing behavioral and design issues?
3. What behavioral models, theories and bases for studying work have proven useful in the analysis and redesign of jobs?
4. How can a knowledge of work design notions improve the analysis of your own career possibilities?

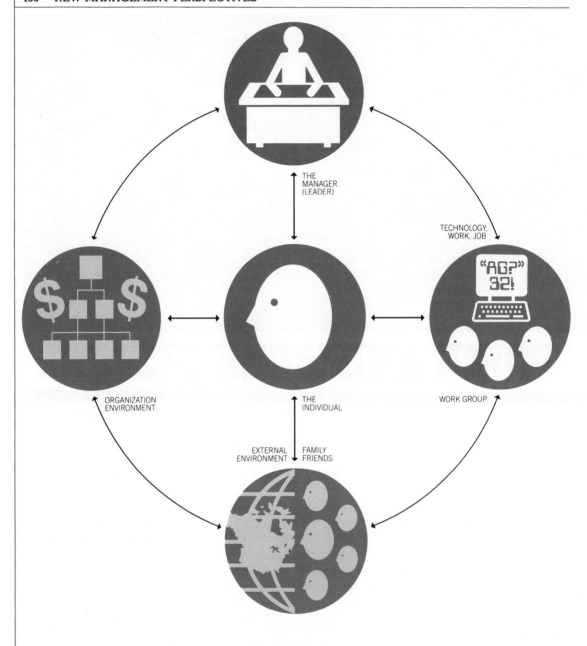

THE
MANAGER
(LEADER)

TECHNOLOGY,
WORK, JOB

ORGANIZATION
ENVIRONMENT

THE
INDIVIDUAL

WORK GROUP

EXTERNAL   FAMILY
ENVIRONMENT   FRIENDS

Work-life spaces: The individual viewpoint

In any organization work seeks the lowest level.

THE CHAPTER IN BRIEF
The Quality of Work Life

Adam and Eve sinned. Their punishment? To be tossed out of the Garden of Eden—Eve was to bear the pains of childbirth and rearing; Adam was to till the ground for food all the days of his life. Adam's curse, in short, was that he would have to work. This "curse of life" view of work was shared by the wealthy of ancient Greece, who preferred to spend their time developing their minds and indulging their senses. This was a time when leisure was seen as a worthy activity. Almost 2000 years later Karl Marx attacked the organizations of his times for alienating the worker from his work. He saw the worker as being powerless in the face of an overwhelming technology and massive organization. A worker, who was isolated from the central goals and outputs of his organization, became estranged from himself because he lacked purpose and identification with his work. Also, Marx felt that this alienation left the worker with a sense of meaninglessness because of excessive specialization and division of labor and separation from responsibility, decision making, and working at worthwhile tasks. William Faulkner, the famous American novelist, once said that the only thing man can do eight hours a day is work, which is why he is so miserable and unhappy. In short, work is a necessary evil—to be participated in but not enjoyed. Perhaps the reader shares some of these views of work and working. But there is another side to this picture.

Possibly contrary to popular belief, work has also been looked upon as quite a positive factor in people's lives. In the formative years of America, many subscribed to the Protestant work ethic. This ethic stated that work is good in itself and that it is through working that a people can better themselves. One of the Biblical writings, the Midrash, also supports this idea that a man who works is blessed. Clearly, much difference exists in these alternate views of work— blessing or curse, burden or challenge, or just what? If work is seen as a means of gaining a sense of self-worth, social acceptance, or personal growth rather than just a means of more productivity and profits, its positive effects can be extensive. In addition, is it not possible that the historical views of work as good or evil may all contain elements of the truth? In a sense, work is what we make it, *and* we can make it much more than it often is! This is one of the themes of this chapter: work, what it is and what it can be.

Many individuals have stood up and challenged traditional organizational authority. They are questioning the use of the *efficiency standard* as the sole determinant of organizational operations and are demanding the right to "job satisfaction." The dominance of the efficiency standard and emphasis on productivity has often created people-related differences in the work setting that workers demand should be rectified. The human needs of employees no longer can be neglected. This challenge to organizational authority is symptomatic of larger societal changes involving the erosion of arbitrary authority in all walks of life. Morals, values, and norms are no longer seen by most people as absolutes. This means that there is no one right ethical or political system to which everyone must conform. In fact, the importance of conformity, which at one time was viewed as a sign of commitment or allegiance, is now looked upon by many people as the surrender of personal independence and insensitivity to individual differences. The absolutist approaches to ethics and politics have gen-

GREAT PERSON PROFILE

Eli Whitney (1765–1825)

Eli Whitney was born in Westboro, Massachusetts. He entered Yale University at the age of 23. He had an inquiring and innovative mind, always searching for better ways to do things. The changes he initiated eventually brought about social as well as political development and helped shape American society as we know it today.

After his graduation from Yale, he visited Georgia and was surprised by the difficulty of removing seeds from cotton on the plantations. Within 10 days he had developed an engine (cotton "gin") that allowed one operator to do what used to be the work of 50. From 1792 to 1800, American cotton production increased from 138,000 to 18 million pounds a year! With the increase in cotton production there followed an expansion of slavery, creating a tension between the North and South that eventually brought about the Civil War. Some years later and on the verge of bankruptcy (he had made little off his invention owing to many patent infringements), Whitney was given a federal contract to manufacture 10,000 muskets. Instead of making them by hand, he employed mass production techniques and introduced the principle of *inter-*

changeable parts. This gave the products exactness and uniformity, while expediting manufacture. Whitney's method brought about major changes in *work design* and *quality of work.* These changes relieved workers of many strenuous tasks by designing tools to fit the job and each particular product. These innovations increased industry's profitability and, with it, the welfare of owners as well as workers. They also influenced the course of American industrial development.

erally given way to more flexible, pragmatic, open-ended systems, based not on conformity to authority, but on *rational thinking* and *empirical study*. These two elements have been borrowed from philosophy and the natural sciences. **Empirical study** involves the systematic examination of phenomena and events. In general, the scientific method has been applied in a large number of sectors of society—to the study of human behavior, to the design of organizations, and even to the understanding of fundamental works such as the Bible.

Young People in the Work Force

Robert Katz and Basil Georgopolous (1976) have identified the emergence of four value patterns that have had a major impact on the way today's youth relate to work and organization. The first idea has to do with the emphasis upon self-determination, self-expression, or "doing one's thing," as in the case of the "hippie" movement of the 1960s. The second value pattern deals with the "sense of need for self-development and making the most of one's own talents and abilities." The third idea refers to the "unleashing of power drives," a concept emphasized by some leftist leaders. The fourth pattern to emerge was "the outcome of the other three—a blanket rejection of established values—a revolutionary attack upon the existing system as exploitive and repressive of the needs of individuals." These four value patterns are reflected in the attitudes of youth toward organizational work life. They are dissatisfied with organizational work life because it has become so fragmented as a result of growing specialization or growing insensitivity to individual needs and possibilities. The emphasis on maximizing output and technological efficiency has furthered the need for increased specialization of knowledge and skill and the continued subdivision of work responsibility. This growing fragmentation of work life is seen by many as producing dull, routine, impersonal work roles incapable of offering broader personal satisfaction in which more of the needs of the whole personality are met. Opportunities for self-expression and self-development are often viewed as minimal in such a work setting or as much below that which is possible.

Another major objection of youth to organizational life according to Katz and Georgopolous "concerns the exploitative character of bureaucratic structures." People with positions in the upper levels of the authority hierarchy are seen by some to receive disproportionately high rewards, of both an extrinsic (in terms of economic returns, for example) and intrinsic (in terms of psychic rewards, for example) nature. Some feel that reward structures in organizations are "distorted toward the immediate interests of the elite and away from desirable social goals of the many."

These points are made rather strongly to emphasize the sense of

"*There are plenty of jobs around. People just
don't want to work.*"

frustration and concern shared by many young people *and* mature
people on the work scene. Issues in this area have now bubbled up to
the surface and raised the consciousness of managers and public
officials for positive approaches to study the nature of work. Many
work improvements have been launched in organizations. Here, work
design plays a key role.

What Is Work Design?

Work design may be defined as the function of specifying the work
activities of an individual or group in an organizational setting. Its
objective is to develop work assignments that meet the requirements
of the organization and of the technology and that satisfy the personal and individual requirements of the job holder. The term *job*, in
the context of nonsupervisory work, and the activities that make it up
are defined below.

1. **Micromotion.**   The smallest work activities, involving elementary movements such as reaching, grasping, positioning, or releasing an object.
2. **Element.**   The combination of two or more micromotions, usually

thought of as a more or less complete entity, such as picking up, transporting, and positioning an item.

3. **Task.**   The combination of two or more elements into a complete activity, such as wiring a circuit board, sweeping a floor, or cutting a tree.

4. **Job.**   The set of all tasks that must be performed by a given worker. A job may consist of several tasks, such as typing, filing, and taking dictation in secretarial work, or it may consist of a single task, such as attaching a wheel to a car as in automobile assembly.

Work design is a complex function because of the variety of factors that determine the ultimate job structure. Decisions must be made as to who is to perform the job, what task is to be performed, and how it is to be performed. As can be seen in Exhibit 14-1, each of these factors may have additional considerations. This chapter focuses on performance measures and the motivational factors related to "who" and "why" (as illustrated in Exhibit 14-1 and discussed in Chapter 8). The other key factors shown in Exhibit 14-1 are largely a consideration of the organizing process (see Chapters 3 and 6).

Work Design and the Life-Space Model

A number of different life spaces can have an impact on the individual and the satisfaction that he or she gets from work. Initially, the organization, through its policies and procedures and the general way that work has been "organized," certainly provides the overall atmosphere or climate within which work is performed. For example, procedures can be detailed or authority can be so centralized as to reduce individual initiative. On the other hand, advancement through the organization can be planned so as to broaden and enrich human experiences while giving people greater responsibility.

The technology of the work place can also affect the nature of work and hence the degree of job-related satisfaction possible. Technology can be a liberating force—freeing workers from drudgery and poor working conditions. However, it often has replaced hard physical labor with dull, monotonous mental activity that destroys the link between the worker and the results of his or her "labor." Thus, monitoring automated equipment and "pushing paper around" become tasks that some workers feel lessen their importance in the overall productive activity of the organization. Additionally, technology can result in highly specialized tasks that pose problems for individual growth and development.

The manager can play a large role in the individual's work–life.

Exhibit 14-1 Factors in Work Design

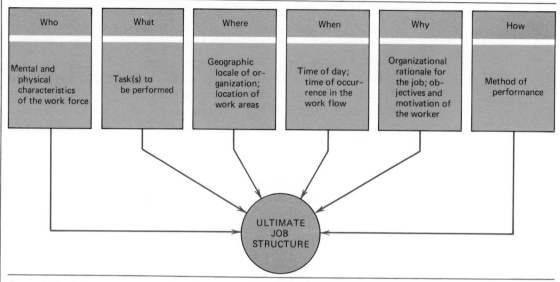

Source: Richard Chase and Nicholas Aquilano, *Production and Operations Management.* 3rd ed. Homewood, Ill.: Richard Irwin (1981), p. 333.

Through work assignments and the judicious delegation of responsibility individuals can be given a real voice, through participation in decision making in matters concerned with their job, and be allowed to develop their talents.

The manager may have little say regarding the nature of work, since that is usually an organizational decision based on economics and technological advancements. However, he or she can play a mediating role between the worker and the job and organization life spaces by giving encouragement and support to workers through timely communication—whether it be a "pat on the back" or crucial feedback of information needed for the job.

We have discussed those factors dealing with individual satisfaction related to work. Of course, equity issues related to pay and security may be equally important to individuals. Whether organizational policies show concern for employee needs in this area quickly becomes apparent.

A sense of inequitable treatment or lack of concern often leads to unionization attempts as employee groups seek protection against what they consider to be an "unfeeling" organization.

BACKGROUND

Key Developments

Scientific Management: A Traditional Approach to Work Design

Frederick Taylor's work in the early 1900s was the first major, systematic attempt at job analysis and design. As noted in Chapter 1, his work formed part of the basic underpinning of modern management thought. He has been called the prophet of **scientific management,** with the stopwatch as his Bible. Taylor got the idea for developing his system of scientific management while watching a Dutchman named Schmidt and his fellow workers shovel pig iron. He noted that Schmidt worked much more efficiently than his co-workers. In fact, it is told that he worked so efficiently that he was able to shovel pig iron 10 hours a day and still have enough energy to run home 5 miles to tend his garden. Taylor thought that if the other workers could be taught to shovel pig iron like Schmidt, then as a group they would be able to work more effectively. As a result, Taylor decided to study Schmidt's work technique. He analyzed every aspect of Schmidt's technique in great detail: the size of the shovel, the bite into the pile, the weight of the scoop, the arc of the swing, and the length of the rest periods that Schmidt took. This method of analysis is now known as **time and motion study.** Schmidt served as the "standard" for efficient pig-iron shoveling, and it was clear that the others could be taught to follow his example. *Scientific management* sought to break a job down into smaller components and to determine the most effective way of combining elements and performing each subtask.

Taylor thought the workers should be matched mentally and physically to the job on which they were to work. Overqualified individuals were to be excluded. Workers were trained to perform their tasks exactly as prescribed, since the best work procedures had been determined by **job analysis.** Taylor's goal was to obtain increased productivity from workers, at less cost to management. This increased productivity and worker efficiency would also have benefits for the worker in the form of higher pay. In effect Taylor made two assumptions about worker satisfaction. First, he assumed that an individual will work with the greatest satisfaction, both for himself and his employer, when he is given a definite task each day to be performed within a given amount of time. This will provide the worker with clear-cut standards (goals) by which to assess his accomplishments and progress. Taylor's second assumption was that the worker's *primary motivation* was for economic gain, and that he would make rational choices that would provide the greatest monetary payoff. These assumptions have guided much organizational practice until the present, although in recent years these assumptions have been vigorously challenged, at least for today's workers.

Taylor's time and motion study technique makes use of the **standard time** concept. The standard time represents the amount of time it takes for the *average worker* to complete a task. The assumption is made that the work is done under **representative work conditions** and at a *normal work pace*. The **average worker** concept takes into account a fair distribution of physical skills, intelligence, motor abilities, and even such qualities as susceptibility to boredom and attention span.

Representative working conditions involves the individual's ability to adjust to such things as periodic delays, absenteeism, shortages, lighting, and temperature. Work events are analyzed and averaged over time to give representative conditions. **Normal work pace** takes into account the average level of energy that can be expended over long periods without undue fatigue. Resting periods are also figured into the normal work pace.

Today, standard times serve as the basis for determining the expected level of work performance, managerial control, and monetary compensation. The concept of standard time is derived from a series of assumptions about technology, working conditions, and the amount of energy needed for the work. Disagreements about the fairness and accuracy of these assumptions create conflict between management and workers (especially union workers).

Hawthorne Works

As discussed in previous chapters and contrary to management's expectations at the Hawthorne Works, group members did *not* try to maximize their wages by working harder. Instead, they established their own production norms and encouraged each other to keep to these production levels. Clearly, this was in opposition to Taylor's motivation assumptions. Supervision, interpersonal relations and communication, group norms and values, participation, and morale were all thought to have an important impact on worker motivation, satisfaction, and productivity based on the findings of the Hawthorne research. The work conditions, performance, and individual morale or satisfaction are some of the main work design considerations in this chapter. Since work plays an important role in people's lives, it is tied in with one's notion of longer-term career progress as well.

Career Implications

The main theme of this chapter is that work can be approached as more than merely a means of providing economic gain, or of paying the weekly bills. From a time perspective alone, working is an integral part of your life. You spend one third of your waking hours on the job. Work can be satisfying and enjoyable, if it is a means of satisfying needs that you value highly—whether this means spending time in good company or in the pursuit of higher-order needs like self-esteem, a sense of accomplishment, personal growth, and independence. You should be aware of your priorities and how different work situations, duties, activities, and supervisory responsibilities help to meet your personal requirements. That knowledge will help you find jobs or select activities to fulfill your needs, or may help you approach your current job in more satisfying ways.

As a worker you need to recognize that there are key elements in any job. For example, does the work involve mainly people or analyzing information? Are you closely supervised or left largely on your own? Do you have to meet tight schedules, work under pressure, or maintain a steady pace? Is the work mental or physical? Is the work challenging or boring? These and many other factors will impact on whether a job will meet your personal work needs.

Many individuals who are reentering the work force, such as homemakers, have found that their technical skills may have become somewhat dated because of changes in the workplace. On the other hand, their non-work-related activities (in PTA groups, social clubs, and the like) have often given them new skills that can help support other careers.

Finally, as managers you need to support and empathize with your subordinates' career concerns. An awareness of their work needs can help you in counseling efforts and in providing useful information.

Contemporary Thinking and Approaches

Job Satisfaction

The concern for the "people" side of work, rather than just the performance or efficiency side, has led researchers to investigate those aspects of working life that bring about job satisfaction. Job analysts have discovered that **job satisfaction** arises from dimensions of the work situation, four or five of which have been identified. The nature of the *work itself*, that is, the job content, is one dimension from which an individual can attain a sense of job satisfaction. Individuals must feel that the work they are performing is intrinsically meaningful (*task significance*) and that they are exercising a variety of skills and abilities that they consider to be worthwhile (*task variety*). If workers feel that their efforts are insignificant or lack real importance, they will work less efficiently and will also be less satisfied. The type of work being performed has its impact on the worker's self-image and self-esteem. Valuable work reflects positively on the worker's sense of self, and insignificant work casts a veil of negativism over his sense of self. In addition, individuals have to be able to identify with the work they are performing and also relate to the overall operation of the organization (*task identification*).

Another dimension that affects the worker's sense of job satisfaction is the *worker's influence or control over his work*. It is essential that workers sense that they are responsible for their work performance, that success of failure depends on their efforts (*autonomy*). Also, only when individuals feel a relationship between their efforts and accomplishments or an *opportunity for upward mobility,* can they gain a sense of self-esteem from the work. A sense of independence and opportunities for growth or decision making and for exerting influence all heighten self-esteem. True, some workers are not interested in these factors. But sufficient numbers are to justify careful study of these approaches.

The supervision received by workers is another dimension in which job satisfaction can be attained. It is important that individuals establish a comfortable and cordial relationship with their supervisors. They need to feel that they are receiving proper guidance and recognition and are being fairly evaluated. Information must be appropriately conveyed to individuals about their work performance and ways in which they can improve (*feedback from task*). The research work at Hawthorne already established that one's co-workers have a major bearing on individual performance and their sense of accomplishment or recognition. Finally, work *compensation* contributes to a sense of job satisfaction. Aside from the obvious monetary satisfactions associated with wages, there are also other elements of compensation that are of major importance. One's level of compensation or economic status is often closely associated with one's social status. The social–economic status of an individual has a major influence on the individual's self-esteem. Increases in compensation are also linked with promotion and an accompanying sense of advancement, which further increase job satisfaction. In short, compensation has potential in two directions, in satisfying economic needs and for what it represents psychologically or sociologically.

Maslow's Need Hierarchy Theory

Abraham Maslow first presented his *need hierarchy theory* in the 1940s. This model, discussed in detail in Chapter 8, suggests that man's basic needs are divided into five classes: (1) *physiological needs* (for example, desire for food or water), (2) *safety needs* (for example, desire for security or avoidance of physical danger), (3) *social needs* (for example, desire for affection or friendship), (4) *esteem needs* (for example, desire for self-respect and a positive self-image), and (5) *self-actualization needs.*

Although Maslow's theory was meant to be a general theory of human nature and development, it has obvious implications for the work world. It suggests that a number of different classes of needs come into play in a work situation and that job analysts and designers need to build into jobs opportunities for satisfying a variety of needs classes. Frederick Taylor postulated that workers will be satisfied if their monetary gains are maximized and if they can make definite task accomplishments on a daily basis. In contrast, Maslow theorized that higher-order needs of workers must also be met so that they can achieve their full potential.

It is thought that many organization members today are motivated largely by higher-order ego and social needs, especially those involving personal gratification, independence, self-expression, power, and self-actualization (Argyris, 1971; Blake and Mouton, 1968; Herzberg and Zautra, 1976; Likert, 1967; Morrow, Bowers, and Seashore, 1967; McGregor, 1960; Schein, 1965; Katz and Georgopolous, 1976, p. 126). Social or psychological incentives, as opposed to economic rewards and incentives, are increasingly being used to improve the compliance and role performance of organizational members and, in general, to improve organizational effectiveness.

The research of Payne (1970) and Schneider and Alexander (1973) has produced evidence, however, that Maslow's classes of basic needs are not separate, distinct entities. Rather, they overlap with multiple needs existing simultaneously.

Herzberg's Motivation–Hygiene Theory

Frederick Herzberg and his *motivation–hygiene theory* is also discussed in detail in Chapter 8. This theory rests on the assumption that two different sets of needs come into play in the work situation: (1) *basic biological needs* and (2) *psychological growth needs*. In the industrial setting, the *job environment* factors "extrinsic" to the job determine the gratification of man's basic biological needs. These factors, which include physical working conditions, pay, supervision, and interpersonal relationships, were termed *hygiene factors* by Herzberg. On the other hand, *job content* factors "intrinsic" to the job influence the degree to which psychological growth needs are met. These factors, which include sense of achievement, independence, responsibility, recognition, growth, and advancement potential, were termed *growth or motivation factors* by Herzberg.

Herzberg's research seemed to indicate that job satisfaction and job dissatisfaction were separate and distinct individual states. The factors that give rise to one were different than those affecting the other. In short, providing for basic biological needs lessened *dis*satisfaction; providing for psychological growth needs directly affected job satisfaction. These findings emphasize the need for job designers to concentrate their energies not only on improvement of the *job environment* but especially on the *redesign of the jobs themselves,* so that the job content will be intrinsically more satisfying.

Although Herzberg's motivation–hygiene model is quite attractive in theory, there are the problems of the validity of the theory let alone assessing the level of job enrichment of a particular work setting. Although this theory has been questioned because of shortcomings in the research methods used, behavioral scientists have found some support for Herzberg's motivational formulation and some of the general concepts. Especially relevant, however, is the emphasis on work and job design that has proven helpful in modern studies of work.

Major efforts have been launched to apply the behavioral models and theories described in this chapter and the one on motivation. Job enrichment efforts based on Herzberg's work have run into difficulty because of theory problems as well as some practical application and measurement problems. An alternative approach to job enrichment is described in a subsequent section. What follows now is a brief description of a concept, "job enlargement," that has historical importance because of its relationsip to job enrichment. Differences between the two have become quite blurred.

Job Enlargement

Specialization leads to the breakdown of work into simple, often routine and tedious, subtasks. In an effort to counteract the low job satisfaction accompanying overspecialization, job designers have begun to enlarge, rather than simplify, some job responsibilities. There are two approaches to **job enlargement:** *horizontal* and *vertical* approaches. Horizontal job enlargement involves adding similar elements to the job without altering the job content. The employee is given more of the same kind of work to do. This tends to reduce routinization and may also increase variety somewhat. In vertical job enlargement, however, the actual job content is altered as new activities are taken on. Employees may be given increased responsibility in the planning, control, or supervision of their own jobs.

An Alternative Approach to Job Enrichment

Research in the area of **job enrichment** has isolated five* factors that help to describe critical work-related factors that are useful in

---

*Although the descriptions that follow are for five factors, recent research indicates that, the "magic number" may be four. Regardless, work–worker dimensions have been identified that are highly useful for work in this area.

establishing the level of job enrichment. These include (1) task independence, (2) task identification, (3) task importance, (4) task variety, and (5) feedback. They are explained in Exhibit 14-2.

Four of these five factors describe a feature of how work appears to the individual—independence, identification, importance, and variety. By the way, there is no reason to assume that all organization members want a full measure of each of these factors. In fact, there is plenty of evidence to indicate that the "right amount" is very much an individual matter. Thus, if profiles were to be drawn for these four factors to illustrate how much each person feels they now have, or want, the profiles or numerical values would differ greatly.

The fifth work dimension, feedback, is important to the individual in order to judge "How am I doing?" "Where are areas in which I might improve?" and so forth. If this information is carefully developed, the manager can help the individual worker exercise self-regulation. For example, Betty Samuels is a supervisor in a large business-center bookstore. Monthly, figures are compiled as to sales in various departments and for titles carried in these departments. Information is also provided on the number of employees in each department and the hours worked. This type of information permits supervisors like Betty to act as managers of "their" units. They have the kind of information needed to make intelligent decisions regarding their people and books based on the "feedback" from their accounting unit.

These five factors represent specific criteria for judging the degree of enrichment of a particular work situation. This is an improvement on the Herzberg model, which failed to present specific criteria that can be applied in a wide array of job situations.

Exhibit 14-2 What to Look for in Job-Enrichment Approaches

1. **Task Independence.** Is the degree of autonomy in a job. Can the person excercise choices and guide his or her own activities?
2. **Task Identification.** Considers the degree to which the individual can associate with the work being performed or product produced. Does his or her activity have recognizable features?
3. **Task Importance.** Is the task seen as significant by others in overall work accomplishment, servicing customers or clients, profitability, and the like?
4. **Task Variety.** Considers the number of different activities or elements that make up a job and therefore the different skills to be applied.
5. **Feedback.** Has to do with information provided for the job holder regarding performance, quality, and timeliness that can become a basis for self-improvement.

Source: Based on the work of Frederick Herzberg et al. *The Motivation to Work.* 2nd ed. New York: John Wiley (1959).

The aim of the job-enrichment approach to job analysis and design is to improve job performance and satisfaction by changing the job content itself, instead of altering extrinsic work conditions. Unfortunately, some jobs are not easily enriched. It is possible to see how the job environment of a production assembly line could be improved (for example, improving physical working conditions, increasing pay, and better supervision). But changing the nature of the work itself often involves major technical problems. Yet even in the face of this difficulty, improvements have been made, for example, in the automatic assembly lines of several European manufacturers and here in the United States as well.

There is another side of job-enrichment approaches that should be discussed. It is the notion that all people *will* experience job satisfaction if their psychological growth needs are met. What if a person does not consider it important to gain a sense of achievement, advancement, or recognition from his or her work? Work is seen by many people in largely economic terms, as a means to satisfy basic necessities. Consequently, it is likely that job-enrichment programs would only be successful for those who desire motivator–growth needs satisfaction.

Job-enrichment programs have encountered a number of obstacles, including the attitude of management and employees toward these programs. Some people have the unrealistic expectation that a job-enrichment program will be a cure-all for organizational problems and are disappointed when this does not materialize. Others who are distrustful of job designers tampering with their jobs may close themselves off from the beneficial effects of enrichment. Additional pitfalls to the successful implementation of job-enrichment programs include failure to educate the affected groups adequately (Rush, 1971), organizational and technological limitations, superficial attempts to change the work itself, and incompatibility of traditional bureaucratic practices with job-enrichment approaches. To avoid these pitfalls, several job-enrichment strategies and procedures have been devised. A more extensive discussion of these approaches is provided in Burack and Smith (1982) and is summarized in Exhibit 14-3. These concepts have the potential to increase an employee's motivation because they satisfy various growth–motivator needs. In other words, Herzberg has proposed some concrete things that managers, job analysts, or others can do to modify work and thereby make it potentially a more satisfying experience. For example, the first "concept" talks about "removing some controls while retaining accountability." Here managers might negotiate with the employees the specific end accomplishments of a task, *when* they are to be completed, and *how* the results are to be measured. The worker may even receive needed information for accountability directly (the fifth con-

Exhibit 14-3 Seven Job Design Concepts in Enrichment Approaches

Concept	Motivators Involved
1. Removing some controls while retaining accountability	1. Responsibility and personal achievement
2. Increasing accountability of individuals for own work	2. Responsibility and recognition
3. Giving a person a complete natural unit of work	3. Responsibility, achievement, and recognition
4. Granting additional authority to an employee in his activity—job freedom	4. Responsibility, achievement, and recognition
5. Mailing periodic reports directly to the person himself rather than to the supervisor	5. Recognition
6. Introducing new and more difficult tasks not previously handled	6. Growth and learning
7. Assigning specific or specialized tasks not previously handled	7. Responsibility, growth, and advancement

cept). But now the worker, rather than the manager, would assume responsibility for accomplishment.

Job Enrichment: A Career Note

The previous section described five different characteristics of organization members at work. Four of the five are highly personal in the sense that they reflect how people feel about their jobs. There is no issue here of right or wrong in an absolute sense but, rather, what is right for you *now*—in your current job or for the job you are considering in the *future*. This distinction gives a valuable basis for helping us to establish future job goals containing features that we desire—and for which we can plan our careers in a more specific way. Since these features of work and workers appear to be important to individual feelings of job-related satisfaction, sense of worth, or even frustration, it is well to think through these features of work for ourselves.

One other point should be mentioned that has to do with change—more precisely, the fact that how we feel about these work characteristics changes over time. Quite naturally, as our life situation changes so do our ideas as to what is important for us. For

Autonomous work groups assembling autos in a SAAB plant (in contrast to assembly line approach shown in opening picture to this chapter).

example, considerations such as *high* independence or variety might be quite unimportant in an initial job (say, at age 20)—we want the experience. At age 28, job "importance" could be a major job consideration. At age 35, "independence" and "identification" might be all important to us.

Path–Goal Expectancy Approach to Work Design

This approach has grown in importance because it builds in much of the current thinking regarding people, goals, orienting activities toward goals, and individual differences. This model also provides a framework of approaches that can incorporate the Maslow and Herzberg work as well. The **expectancy theory approach** to work design assumes that a number of work options are available to every individual and that each individual has the capacity to make a conscious choice among alternatives. Not all alternatives have the same payoff value for the individual. He or she must therefore exercise (good) judgment in choosing the paths whose outcomes will most effectively fulfill his needs and goals. The satisfaction of worker needs and goals can be viewed from two perspectives: (1) the short term and (2) the long term. Short-term satisfaction is concerned with the immediate payoffs of a work situation. Short-term outcomes may satisfy lower-order needs of the individual, like physical and economic security, or higher-order needs like sense of achievement, self-esteem, and growth. Individuals find their jobs satisfying to the extent that these personal needs are met. However, the benefits of working do not only apply to the immediate circumstances surrounding the individual. Work also has long-term consequences for the individual, intrinsically in terms of satisfaction of higher-order personal needs and extrinsically in terms of satisfaction of lower-order needs from such things as general working conditions. Path–goal theory suggests that people make conscious decisions and perform deliberate actions aimed at fulfilling goals in the more distant future. It has been emphasized throughout this book that good career planning calls for examining both the short-term and long-term benefits of a job. There must be a connection between short-term and long-term outcomes if the latter are ever to bring personal satisfaction. Properly oriented, short-term outcomes are the means by which valued long-term outcomes are accomplished. Thus, the whole issue of job satisfaction has to be seen in a broader context in which immediate and long-term satisfactions are taken into consideration. The sociotechnical systems approach is another way to think about how improved work conditions can be accomplished.

Sociotechnical Systems Approach

In the 1950s researchers at the Tavistock Institute of Human Relations in London, England developed a sophisticated systems approach to job analysis and design. This approach, known as the **sociotechnical systems approach,** recognizes that both *social* and *psychological needs* and *technical needs* must be considered in the systematic analysis and design of work performance, work conditions, and organizational output. An organizational environment has to be created that is technically efficient and productive and that leads to job satisfaction for organization members (Davis and Taylor, 1978). The satisfaction of social needs is important for two reasons. First, changes in society have created a new concern for improving the quality of working life. Second, job related satisfaction seems to have its benefits in improved worker cooperation, sense of loyalty, identification with the employers, and decreased turnover and absenteeism. In the past, great consideration was given to improving technical efficiency, and social concerns were almost completely neglected.

The sociotechnical approach views the organization as a system. What is a system? It can be defined as a set of components in active organized interaction that are bounded to form a common whole and have a common purpose. An organization is a system in that it represents a set of people, services, work, or goods-production facilities and procedures that interact in an organized and integrated fashion for the purpose of carrying out the goals of the enterprise.

Organization Subsystems

Katz and Georgopolous (1976) have pointed out that organizational structure is comprised of three *subsystems:* (1) *production or instrumental* subsystem, (2) *maintenance or social* subsystem, and (3) *managerial* subsystem. The production or instrumental subsystem is concerned with the basic work task of converting inputs (material, resources, labor) into products or services. The maintenance or social subsystem involves the ways in which organization members relate to each other and to the operation and aims of the organization. This subsystem serves psychologically and socially to integrate organizational members into the larger system and to bind the organization together. It deals with rewards and sanctions as well as with social values and norms. The managerial subsystem, through the processes of direction, coordination, control, and decision making, integrates the production and maintenance subsystems. Management represents the necessary link that bridges the gap between organization norms, values, roles, and production requirements and worker needs, values, and abilities.

Organization members are "connected" with the organizational system in various psychological and sociological ways. These organizational ties are affected by individual norms, values, and roles. The behavioral norms of an organization will be accepted by its members as legitimate if they are seen as necessary and equitable. Employees will be responsive to formal authority in the organization because ("if") they understand that certain procedures and regulations are required for the smooth operation of the enterprise. Those who come to internalize organizational *values*, namely, those who identify rationally and morally with the goals of the enterprise, will have the strongest sense of organizational commitment. This is in line with McGregor's Theory *Y* approach that is discussed in Chapter 9.

Organizational programs further employee identification with company goals when the goals are also valued by the employees. Thus, organizational *work roles* and informal *group roles* will be interdependent and require cooperative behavior to make these systems work.

The discussions that follow fit into the sociotechnical approach in two ways. First, the worker and work task are described in some detail in an approach that benefits from Taylor's type of scientific management study. Second, work activity is viewed in a broader, systemic context that takes into account behavioral considerations, communications, and the total impact of work itself—the so-called quality of work life.

METHODS OF JOB ANALYSIS AND WORK DESIGN

Traditional Approaches

Prior to the industrial revolution, production workers were craftsmen who had their own, sometimes secret, methods for doing work. However, as products became more complicated, as mechanization of a higher order was introduced, and as output rates increased, the responsibilities for work methods were necessarily transferred to management. It was no longer logical or economically feasible to allow individual workers to produce the same product by different methods. Furthermore, work specialization brought the concept of craftwork to an end as less-skilled workers were employed on the simpler tasks.

Today, the responsibility for developing work methods in large firms is often assigned either to a staff department that is called "methods analysis," or "systems analysis" or to an industrial engineering department. In small firms this activity is often performed by individual specialists who report to the operations or administrative manager.

The principal approach to the study of work methods is the construction of charts (such as operations charts, man–machine charts, activity charts) in conjunction with time study or standard time data. The choice of which charting method to use depends on the focus of the analysis. That is, is the focus on (1) the overall operation, (2) the stationary worker at a fixed work place, (3) a worker "interacting" with equipment, or (4) a worker interacting with other workers (see Exhibit 14-4)?

Process charts are valuable in the study of an overall system. They provide detailed sequences of operations performed, the distances materials are moved, and the times required to perform operations. The focus may be on a product being manufactured, a service being created, or a person performing a sequence of activities. An example of a process chart and flow diagram for a clerical operation and common symbols used is shown in Exhibit 14-5.

The objective in studying the overall work system is to identify delays, transport distance, processes, and processing time requirements in order to simplify the entire operation. Once the process has been charted, the following questions may be asked:

What is the essential task to be done? *Must* "this" particular activity be done?

Where is the task performed? Is it critical that it be done there? Could it be done in combination with some other step in the process?

Exhibit 14-4 Charting Techniques for Various Work Methods

Activity	Objective of Study	Charting Techniques
Overall operation	Eliminate or combine steps, shorten transport distance, identify delays	Flow diagram, process chart
Stationary worker at fixed work place	Simplify method, minimize methods	Operations charts, simo charts; apply principles of motion economy
Worker interacts with equipment	Minimize idle time, find number or combination of machines to balance cost of man and machine idle time	Activity chart, man–machine charts
Worker interacts with other workers	Maximize productivity, minimize interference	Activity charts, gang process charts

Source: Chase and Aquilano (1981), p. 339.

How is the task done? Why is it done this way? Is there another way?

Who does the task? Can someone else do it? Should the worker be of a higher or lower skill level?

These thought-provoking questions usually lead to elimination of much of the unnecessary work, as well as to simplification of remaining work, by combining a number of processing steps and changing the order of performance.

Many work tasks require the work to remain at the same place. When the nature of the work is primarily manual (for example, sorting, inspecting, making entries, or assembly operations), the focus of work design is on simplifying the work method and making the required operator motions as few and as easy as possible—while maintaining or improving performance.

There are two basic ways to determine the best method when studying a single worker who is performing an essentially manual task. The first is to search among the workers and find the one who performs the job best. That person's method is then accepted as the standard, and others who are assigned to that job are trained to perform it in the same way. This was basically Taylor's approach. After determining the best method, he searched for "first-class men,"

Exhibit 14-5 Process Chart for Clerical Operation

A. *Work Flow*

			PROCESS CHART	

Present Method ☒
Proposed Method ☐

SUBJECT CHARTED ___Requisition for small tools___ DATE _____

Chart begins at supervisor's desk and ends at typist's desk in ___ CHART BY J. C. H.

purchasing department ___ CHART NO. R 136

DEPARTMENT ___Research laboratory___ SHEET NO. 1 OF 1

DIST. IN FEET	TIME IN MINS.	CHART SYMBOLS	PROCESS DESCRIPTION
		●⇨□D▽	Requisition written by supervisor (one copy)
		○⇨□D▽	On supervisor's desk (awaiting messenger)
65		○⇨□D▽	By messenger to superintendent's secretary
		○⇨□D▽	On secretary's desk (awaiting typing)
		●⇨□D▽	Requisition typed (original requisition copied)
15		○⇨□D▽	By secretary to superintendent
		○⇨□D▽	On superintendent's desk (awaiting approval)
		○⇨■D▽	Examined and approved by superintendent
		○⇨□D▽	On superintendent's desk (awaiting messenger)
20		○⇨□D▽	To purchasing department
		○⇨□D▽	On purchasing agent's desk (awaiting approval)
		○⇨■D▽	Examined and approved
		○⇨□D▽	On purchasing agent's desk (awaiting messenger)
5		○⇨□D▽	To typist's desk
		○⇨□D▽	On typist's desk (awaiting typing of purchase order)
		●⇨□D▽	Purchase order typed
		○⇨□D▽	On typist's desk (awaiting transfer to main office)
		○⇨□D▽	
		○⇨□D▽	
105		3 4 2 8	Total

B. *Common Notations*

○ **Operation.** Something actually is being done. This may be work on a product, some support activity, or anything that is directly productive in nature.

⇨ **Transportation.** The object of the study (product, service, or person) moves from one location to another.

□ **Inspection.** The object is examined for quality and correctness.

D **Delay.** The object of the study must wait before starting the next step in the process.

▽ **Storage.** The object is stored, such as finished products in inventory or completed papers in a file. Frequently, a distinction is made between temporary storage and permanent storage by inserting a T or a P in the triangle.

Source: Chase and Aquilano (1981), p. 340.

rters
tal em-

such as Schmidt, to perform according to the method. The second way to determine the best method is to observe the performance of a number of workers, analyze in detail each step of their work, and pick out the superior features of each worker's performance. This results in a composite method that combines the best elements of the group studied. This was the procedure used by Frank Gilbreth, the "father of motion study," to determine the "one best way" to perform a work task. However, in fairness to their approach, once the work activity was studied, the final result also reflected the creativity of the analyst. New work implements and redesign of the entire work area were not uncommon results.

Whereas Taylor observed actual performance to find the best method, Frank Gilbreth and his wife Lillian relied on movie film. Through *micromotion analysis*—observation of the filmed work performance frame by frame—the Gilbreths studied work very closely and defined its basic elements, which were termed *therbligs* ("Gilbreth" spelled backward, with the *t* and *h* transposed). Their study led to the rules or principles of motion economy listed in Exhibit 14-6.

Work Measurement: Time Studies

Knowledge of how long it takes to make a product or perform a service is helpful, if not necessary, for such activities as:

- Cost estimating.
- Price quoting.
- Budget determination.
- Performance evaluation.
- Wage incentive and merit payment systems.

Exhibit 14-6 Principles of Motion Economy

Use of the Human Body	Arrangement of the Work Place	Design of Tools and Equipment
1. The two hands should begin as well as complete their motions at the same time.	10. There should be a definite and fixed place for all tools and materials.	18. The hands should be relieved of all work that can be done more advantageously by a jig, a fixture, or a foot-operated device.
2. The two hands should not be idle at the same time except during rest periods.	11. Tools, materials, and controls should be located close to the point of use.	19. Two or more tools should be combined wherever possible.
3. Motions of the arms should be made in opposite and symmetrical directions, and should be made simultaneously.	12. Gravity feed bins and containers should be used to deliver material close to the point of use.	20. Tools and materials should be prepositioned whenever possible.
4. Hand and body motions should be confined to the lowest classification with which it is possible to perform the work satisfactorily.	13. Drop deliveries should be used wherever possible.	21. Where each finger performs some specific movement, such as in typewriting, the load should be distributed in accordance with the inherent capacities of the fingers.
5. Momentum should be employed to assist the worker wherever possible, and it should be reduced to a minimum if it must be overcome by muscular effort.	14. Materials and tools should be located to permit the best sequence of motions.	22. Levers, crossbars, and hand wheels should be located in such positions that the operator can manipulate them with the least change in body position and with the greatest mechanical advantage.
6. Smooth continuous curved motions of the hands are preferable to straight-line motions involving sudden and sharp changes in direction.	15. Provisions should be made for adequate conditions for seeing. Good illumination is the first requirement for satisfactory visual perception.	
7. Ballistic movements are faster, easier, and more accurate than restricted or "controlled" movements.	16. The height of the work place and the chair should preferably be arranged so that alternate sitting and standing at work are easily possible.	
8. Work should be arranged to permit easy and natural rhythm wherever possible.	17. A chair of the type and height to permit good posture should be provided for every worker.	
9. Eye fixations should be as few and as close together as possible.		

Source: Ralph M. Barnes. *Motion and Time Study.* New York: John Wiley (1968), p. 220.

Although there are several accepted ways to derive the time required to perform a task, time study (stopwatch and micromotion analysis) is perhaps the most widely used. Exhibit 14-7 lists some of these methods and the tasks to which they can best be applied. The use of historical records to estimate future performance is generally bad practice. Experience has shown that tasks that are performed without any formal analysis (that is, based on records) range widely in "fairness." Some tasks are very easy—the allowed times are too long, and some are too difficult—inadequate time is allowed. Therefore, good practice requires that tasks be measured formally.

Exhibit 14-7 Types of Work Measurement Applied to Different Tasks

Work Measurement Method	Type of Task Best Applied
Film analysis	Very short interval, highly repetitive
Stopwatch time study	Short interval, repetitive
Elemental time standard data	Task in conjunction with machinery or other fixed-processing-time equipment
Work sampling	Infrequent work or work of a long cycle time

As discussed earlier, time study was formalized by Frederick W. Taylor in 1881. A time study is generally made with a stopwatch, although in some instances film analysis or a timed recording device may be used. Procedurally, the job or task to be studied is separated into measurable parts or elements, and each element is timed individually. After a number of repetitions, the collected times are averaged. To make this operator's time usable for all workers, a measure of speed or "performance rating" must be included to "normalize" the job. The application of a rating factor gives what is called *normal time.* For example, if an operator performs a task in 2 minutes and the time study analyst estimates him or her to be performing about 20 percent faster than normal, the normal time would be computed as

2 minutes + 0.20 × (2 minutes), or 2.4 minutes

In equation form:

Normal time = (Observed performance time per unit)
× (Performance rating).

In the above example, denoting normal by NT, the equation would be:

NT = 2 × (1.2) = 2.4 minutes

When an operator is observed for a period of time, the number of units produced during this time, along with the performance rating, gives the normal time as

$$NT = \frac{\text{Time worked}}{\text{Number of units produced}} \times \text{Performance rating}$$

Standard time is derived by adding allowances to normal time for personal needs (washroom and coffee breaks, and so forth), unavoidable work delays (equipment breakdown, lack of materials, and so forth), and worker fatigue (physical or mental). Thus:

$$\text{Standard time} = \text{Normal time} + (\text{Allowances as a percentage} \times \text{Normal time})$$

To illustrate, suppose that the normal time to perform a task is 1 minute and that allowances for personal needs, delays, and fatigue total 15 percent. Then, using ST for standard time:

$$ST = 1 \text{ minute} + (.15 \times 1 \text{ minute})$$
$$ST = 1 (1 + 0.15)$$
$$ST = 1.15 \text{ minute}$$

Once standard times are determined, a performance standard is available for use in cost estimation, performance evaluation, and merit-pay determination. However, time and motion analysis does not readily account for the behavioral aspects of most jobs. For this reason, other job analysis methods have also been developed.

Additional Methods of Job Analysis and Design

Critical Incidents Approach

The **critical incidents approach** to job analysis focuses on direct, objective indicators of what individuals have to do in order to satisfy job and organizational requirements, rather than on indirect measures like personality assessment tests. Key job elements are described. Important hourly, daily, and weekly activities of the job are identified, compared, classified, and simplified. For example, the head of the women's clothing department in a retail store might be responsible for such financial activities as: "At beginning of each day make sure cash register has $100 in cash." "At end of each day bring all cash register receipts to store auditor." "Sign all sales refunds of more than fifty dollars."

Job Descriptions

Job descriptions serve two very important purposes within an organizational framework. First, they define and describe the nature of the tasks and responsibilities of a particular job. Second, they define the position of the job in the overall organizational structure. Job descriptions are therefore valuable to the organization, its employees, and prospective employees. From the point of view of the organization, a *precise* and *detailed* job description furthers efficient job performance, enhances organizational communications and authority lines, and serves as a basis for recruiting new employees and assessing current employees. Recruiters, knowing the position of the job within the organizational structure and thus aware of possible career ladders, will look for skills and qualifications not only suitable for the entry-level job but also those appropriate for higher-level positions. At the same time recruiters will also have a clear idea of the kinds of duties, responsibility, and activities expected from new employees and will be able to see the career opportunities available to them after entry into the organization. The employees will therefore have a realistic, informed concept of the career ladders available to them.

Finally, job descriptions precisely indicate to current organizational members the types of activities and responsibilities they will be involved in and the standards according to which their job performance will be evaluated. Current organizational members will also be aware of available career ladders. Unfortunately, job descriptions are almost completely useless in many organizations, which makes this section especially appropriate. Failure to keep these up to date or distortion of their content for other purposes (for example, justifying wage differences) has contributed to this sad state of affairs.

Job descriptions usually contain *four* main elements. The first element involves the *organizational (structural) position and descriptors.* This part gives the title of the position and describes where the job fits within the organizational hierarchy—namely, to whom the job holder reports (immediate superior) and whom the job holder directly supervises (immediate subordinates). The second portion of a job description gives the *summary highlights of the job,* that is, the critical achievements required for successful job performance. The third section, called job specification, *details major responsibilities,* often stating organizational requirements in descending order of importance. The fourth section presents *principal working relationships.* Communications and interpersonal relationships are spelled out here, especially with organizational members outside of one's department.

Job descriptions should be flexible and creative, not ironclad. For example, circumstances in the labor market sometimes arise in which there are no applicants who meet all of the requirements of the job description. If a job is to be studied it is important that a job description be reviewed by the appropriate supervisor before it is issued. This ensures that the job description reflects the supervisor's conception of the job responsibilities and activities. It has proved beneficial for both the supervisor and the job holder to discuss the preparation of a job description. There is the opportunity to expose differences in philosophy and arrive at shared purposes. Personnel people should also have the opportunity to review job descriptions, since changes in the structure of a position may bring about the need for wage or salary modifications. An upgraded job will deserve a higher salary, but this upgrading process may create a "domino effect" within the organization in which job changes are desired so that salary increases can be justified or equitable relationships maintained.

Another problem that must be faced when job descriptions are changed is that such changes may alter the wage relationships of positions within the organizational structure. Also, realistic adjustments may have to be made in training and the type of person selected for the job.

It should be pointed out that *job descriptions* are not synonymous with **job specifications.** The latter specify the educational experiences, knowledge, and mental and physical abilities required to carry out the job activities. Job descriptions detail the responsibilities, activities, and relationships that make up the job, as well as how the job fits into the organizational structure. Newer job description approaches increasingly emphasize work-related behaviors or results needed for job success. In turn, job analysis then seeks to identify these critical work activities or "incidents."

Functional Job Study Approach

Service organizations, like banks, insurance companies, and government units, have traditionally relied on people and information to carry out their work activities. In recent years there has been considerable growth within the service industry. As a result, many job analysts and designers have channeled their efforts into this industry. Information systems need to be developed to handle and to coordinate the large number of service workers. The government has improved job-related information systems by developing and refining the **Dictionary of Occupational Titles (DOT),** which classifies more than 20,000 jobs and provides important information about them for employment and statistical purposes.

The DOT job analysis approach classifies job features into three categories: (1) data, (2) people, and (3) things (DPT). Each job is studied in relation to these three categories, and the level of ability, judgment, or complexity required for the job is determined. More difficult jobs are characterized by unstructured situations, poor information available (not available or hard to secure), and a need for exercising judgment. These receive "high" ratings. "Low" ratings are assigned to jobs requiring little experience or formal education, routine procedures, and readily learned approaches.

Another DOT job classification is called the MPSMS—the materials, products, subject matter, or services connected with a particular job. Approximately 600 categories are divided into 55 MPSMS groups (for example, banking, bacteriology). The DOT also classifies jobs according to education, vocational preparation, experience required, and the like. There are, however, other systems that are receiving attention, such as the Position Analysis Questionnaire (PAQ) developed by Dr. Ernest McCormick and his associates at Purdue University. The PAQ contains almost 200 descriptions of jobs and work conditions that have proved highly useful in job–work-design studies.

Other Considerations for Job Analysis and Design

The Function of Education: A Newer Perspective

As Havighurst (1967) has indicated, in the past education served an *opportunity* and a *production function*. In the first case, "opportunity" education served as a means of social mobility.

In terms of its "production function," education supplied the training for technical, industrial, and professional roles. Today, a third function of education has become operative, the *consumption function*. This means that people are viewing education as a process (product or service) to be enjoyed for its own sake and for the purposes of personal growth and satisfaction, rather than as merely a means to greater economic opportunity or production (Havighurst, 1967). Development people who have worked with adult learners believe that there is also another function of education—it is to meet the need of people to stay up to date and avoid obsolescence.

The value of higher education as opportunity and production functions has been brought into question in the last 30 years. The college degree that almost assured a good job and a high socio-economic status before 1950 now seems to have lost much of its power. Since a majority of the population is now attending colleges and universities, some see the college degree as a competitive "necessity" that keeps the person abreast of the mainstream of society—it is no longer a special accomplishment. These are realities that must be considered in the career thinking of individuals.

However, the important news in education is the rapid growth of newer educational modes involving short courses, institutes, seminars, learning centers, and self-paced study. The emphasis of past decades on primary, secondary, and college education is shifting toward life-long learning for the future.

Communications: A Critical Work-Design Factor

At one time communications between people involving work took place only when needed. Supplying information or directions, counseling, or gaining agreement just seemed to happen as a response to the obvious requirements of the situation. However, as pointed out in an earlier chapter, the systematic study of communications has revealed that such factors as timing, content, accuracy, and choice of medium are extremely important to performance and even to the sense of well-being that people feel toward work. These developments have caused communications in organizations to be considered in a much more formal way, especially when it is realized that communications can act either to motivate or integrate organization members or to confuse and alienate them. Communications is a two-way process. Consequently, management has the responsibility of monitoring and being responsive to the work needs of employees and their responses to particular work conditions. For example, it might be that a task group is overburdened with responsibilities. Management in this case has to be responsive to this situation by either reducing those responsibilities, refashioning the group so that it will be able to perform its function, or maybe even introducing new technology into the situation. Thus, the information flowing from workers to management influences the degree, direction, and content of communications flowing from management to workers. This process is known as *feedback*. The information output of management is constantly being adjusted or modified according to worker output and worker responses. From a design viewpoint, it becomes desirable to build in this feedback capability.

The information content that is communicated may be impersonal—such as economic data and company policy, or personal—such as the emotional reactions of employees. Impersonal content usually flows from management to workers and is requisite for organizational activities. The information feedback of employees is frequently of a personal nature. When employees feel that their responses are reaching management and that their feedback is being responded to, they gain a sense of increased participation in the organization and therefore a stronger loyalty to and identification with it. Communications is the cement that binds together people, units, and work activity within the organization. The quality of communication can be ensured through completeness, objectivity, accuracy, and timeliness—and as a conscious strategy in work design.

Quality of Work Life Designs

Restructuring Using "Democratic Principles": Participative Management

Katz and Georgopolous (1976) have examined successful and unsuccessful ways in which democratic principles can be applied to organizational operations. The **representative form of democracy** has been under attack because some feel that it gives too much decision-making power to its representatives. They have abstracted some useful notions from the observation of this political "arena" with organization design implications. Katz and Georgopolous suggested that this difficulty can be reduced if the number of levels of authority within the organizational hierarchy is kept to a minimum. Close proximity between the levels ensures accountability for decision making and responsiveness to the needs of organizational members and customers. Clearly this arrangement would be unworkable in many real-life organizations, but it does crystallize a form of structuring—fewer authority levels—likely to receive more attention in the future.

Implementing the principles of representative democracy (participative management) within an organizational framework could certainly enhance the involvement and commitment of organizational members. There would also be the psychological satisfaction of their having a determining influence on the course of organizational operations and activities.

Even though the **direct form of democracy** (people involved in discussions) has often been shown to be slow moving and ineffective when a large number of people is involved (electorate), it does provide two important functions. First, "direct democracy" serves as a check on policy decisions made by the elected representatives. If, for example, organizational members feel that their leaders have abused their powers in certain policy decisions, the members have the opportunity to veto these policies. (This would certainly stir up some controversy among policy makers.) Second, direct democracy has been shown to be effective within smaller groups. Thus, whereas the overall organization may be structured on the principles of "representative democracy," or professionally managed units, units within the organizations could be structured along the lines of principles of "direct democracy." The relatively greater sense of decision-making power afforded to the individual in the context of a unit run on these principles will act to tie him or her into the larger organizational system where that influence is more indirect (Georgopolous and Katz, 1976). The notion of direct democracy has actually been implemented in the design of task groups at plants here in the United States (for example, Mead and General Foods) and in Japan, where "quality circles" have had great success.

The kibbutzim in Israel provide an interesting example of combining direct and representative democratic principles. Each kibbutz is a collectively governed community, a direct democracy. Most kibbutzim are agricultural communities, but many have factories that manufacture furniture, agricultural equipment, and other products. The kibbutz has community meetings in which all members participate. All major decision-making positions, including farm manager, are chosen by direct election, and these positions are usually rotated among kibbutz members. Each kibbutz belongs to a larger movement

Workers share respon-
sibilities in an Israeli
kibbutz.

of kibbutzim, which may involve between 15 and 50 other communities. Each larger movement has its own religious, political, and
ideological persuasion and is organized on the basis of a representative democracy. Kibbutzim are known throughout Israel for their
exceptionally high agricultural productivity, low crime and delin-
quency rates, and their large contribution to Israel's young leadership. Other forms of collective effort also exist in Israel.

It must be pointed out again that the application of principles of
direct or representative democracy to organizations has its limitations. In a large, complex organization the decision-making powers of
any particular organizational unit may be modest, although it is
possible to involve organizational members in matters more directly
affecting them—for example, training, working relationships, and
the social climate within their unit. Where organizational activities
need to be coordinated on a rigorous timetable, as in production
schedules or new product introductions, overall coordination may be
a necessity and thus restrict the decision-making powers of organizational units. Third, in the case of a public institution, the administration has to function within the laws (of a representative democracy)

already established. However, there may be flexibility in terms of how the legislative guidelines are carried out. It has been suggested that the *whole concept of centralization of authority should be examined and a determination should be made as to the types of control that are really necessary and effective* (Katz and Georgopolous, 1976).

Reduction of Process Specialization

In most large organizations the service personnel are separated physically *and* psychologically from operations personnel. This division of labor is based on what Katz and Georgopolous call *process specialization*. They advocate that this artificial barrier be removed so that service and operations personnel can be in direct personal contact. The result would be a boost in morale for the service personnel, since operations personnel usually enjoy greater recognition and rewards for their work than, say, clerical workers. Also, the integration of these two groups would lead to improved interpersonal relations. Besides being beneficial in its own right, this would have a positive influence on organizational operations. Katz and Georgopolous suggest the creation of groups and teams in which personnel of one division (for example, service) would have primary membership in the one group (service) and secondary membership in the other group (operations). The dual membership would serve to build social bonds within the organization. This has been accomplished in some organizations by assigning related clerical or production workers to liaison or communications tasks.

SUMMARY

Innovation and change are major themes of this chapter on work design. In past years, job improvements or design efforts were confined mostly to improvements in methods. Now the growing emphasis is on performance *and* the human experience. Job–work design now encompasses the job, the work, the organization, *and* the individual. Furthermore, it takes into account the nature of supervision, the demands imposed on workers, and the realistic limitations of individual physical or psychological capabilities. On the other hand, in the past there was a tendency to make assumptions about what people can't do and to discount motivation, "drive," and the will to be successful.

Sociotechnical perspectives and approaches have been applied in a number of real-life settings. The results from these are providing a growing body of information likely to prove of much help in the future.

In a realistic sense, job–work design is a capstone for much of the subject matter described in this book. If we return to the life-space perspective, we see that *all* life spaces are involved in these newer approaches:

Job.   Redesign of methods, arrangements, and responsibility assignments.

Group.   Participation, greater self-direction, improved training, and more group-oriented work activity.

Work–Job.   Redesign for better linking between work-related activities, more group-related arrangements, more responsibility to the group itself as opposed to supervisory direction.

Organization.   Reexamining the assumptions of centralization of direction or power or the need for close supervision, reexamining the place of rules, regulations, and the appropriateness and completeness of job descriptions.

Individual.   Taking account of individual needs, motivation, skill preparation, and even social compatibility with other group members; attempting to create more harmonious relationships using motivational concepts and models.

Questions for Study and Discussion

1. According to Georgopolous and Katz, what are the four value patterns that have emerged among today's youth? What is the overall impact of these value patterns on the work world?
2. Name two assumptions that Frederick Taylor made about worker motivation. Compare these assumptions with Maslow's need-hierarchy theory and with Herzberg's motivation–hygiene theory.
3. Explain Taylor's "standard time" concept.
4. Name the four dimensions of the work situation from which job satisfaction derives.
5. Compare horizontal and vertical job enlargement.
6. What are the implications of Herzberg's motivation–hygiene theory for job designers?
7. What are two limitations of the job-enrichment approach to job analysis and design?
8. What are the basic ideas of the expectancy theory approach to work?
9. Describe the critical incidents approach to job analysis.
10. What purposes do job descriptions serve? What are the primary components of job descriptions?
11. According to Havighurst, how has the function of education evolved?

12. Describe the basis of contingency leadership approaches.
13. Explain how a two-way communications process works in an organizational setting.
14. Name the basic elements of the sociotechnical systems approach.
15. In what ways can an organization be considered a system? An open system?
16. Describe the three organizational subsystems cited by Georgopolous and Katz.
17. How can organizations be restructured using democratic principles?

CASE: ALPHA ELECTRONICS DIVISION, INDUSTRIAL COMPUTER SYSTEMS, INC.

Industrial Computer Systems, Inc. was a product of the space age. Founded in 1950 by physicist and computer expert Barry White, it went through many years of financial losses before industry started to "catch up" in its use of industrial computers. Industrial computers are used to guide and direct all kinds of manufacturing and industrial processes, provide continuous quality and central monitoring, and perform various complex analysis and control functions. In the 1950s, many industries were still employing the technology of the 1940s. But as new oil refineries, steel mills, chemical plants, and manufacturing appeared, the newer computer technologies started to take hold. Suddenly Barry and his company found that they had a "tiger by the tail." They were swamped with installation and design contracts.

Computer Systems, Inc. survived the turn of events and by 1978 had become a $50,000,000 corporation with four major operating divisions. The company used many modern management techniques, including a general corporate employee-attitude survey run every two years. The events in this case concern Alpha Division, a unit of some 300 people charged with manufacturing various components for their industrial computers.

Alpha Electronics Division, Organization and Activities

Industrial computers were always customized to specific application conditions. Yet they used many standard components, housing, instruments, and the like. As a result, much of the production at Alpha was concerned with the routine manufacturing of standard components. The industrial processes involved all kinds of metal forming and stamping machines. Additionally, some units specialized in electronic circuitry, building small subassemblies and painting, inspecting, and testing them. The plant was organized by departments corresponding to each of its major activities. The General Manager, Fred Stein, was responsible for all division operations and reported directly to the President, Barry White (see organization chart in Exhibit 14-8). Alpha Division was the oldest unit in the corporation, since its products were essential for the manufacture and assembly of the industrial computers.

The "People's Age" Catches Up with the Space Age

For many years as Alpha Division expanded, most employees were caught up in the excitement of its products, growth, and the eventual financial successes of the business. However, around 1979, certain problems started to appear that had been minor ones previously or simply nonexistent. For example, turnover started to creep up among younger, skilled plant workers, supervisors, and even some "staff" people. A second disturbing sign of trouble was the figures that Fred Stein had regarding plant performance and delivery schedules. In the last 18 months plant performance measures became quite uneven

Exhibit 14-8 Organization Chart for Alpha Electronics Division

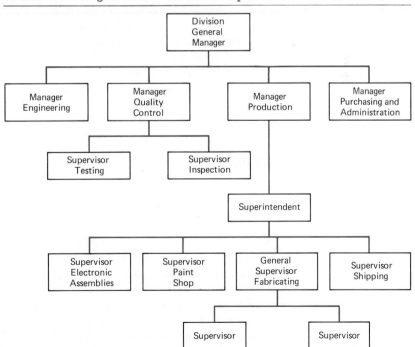

and the number of late shipments inched upward. Fred gave these developments much thought and especially so during a business trip to England and Sweden. There he came across several plants where industrial processes had been redesigned with *some* degree of success. Performance had increased in several units, and many supervisors and workers who had participated in the redesign programs had expressed better feelings regarding their work situations and organizations. Fred was generally impressed with the results.

When Fred got back to his plant he called the Director of Personnel at corporate headquarters.

Fred: Charlie, this is Fred—just got back from our European trip last week.

Charlie: How did it go?

Fred: Great! That's one of the things I would like to talk to you about. When our industrial group visited Sweden, they took us into Volvo and some of the power plants—talked about the redesign of jobs—pretty impressive stuff. Got some possibilities for us?

Charlie: Honestly, Fred, I don't know. There are a lot of variables in these situations.

Fred: My thinking was that maybe we should look into it. When we got together last month for the executive meeting my "figures" didn't look so good—and they haven't been getting any better.

Charlie: Fred, I know what you mean. That plant survey we took for you—motivation job satisfaction—seemed to indicate that maybe there are some things to look at. [See Exhibit 14.9.]

Fred: For sure! When you showed me the results from the general company study taken two years ago and how our guys stack up now— well, I guess it's time we did something.

Charlie: What do you want to do?

Fred: How about stopping by next week and taking a closer look at this job-enrichment stuff? OK?

Charlie: OK.

Questions

1. What kind of company is Industrial Computer Systems, Inc.? What is its business? Has it been successful? Is it run formally or informally? How is it organized?

2. Describe the nature of Alpha Divisions' organization and work activities. Name and classify your assumptions.

3. Assume you are a new General Manager coming into an organization such as the Alpha Division. You are interested in *both* performance and individual job-related satisfaction or morale. *Without* the benefit of inside information or surveys of one kind or another, what would occur to you regarding job-redesign or job-enrichment possibilities? Name and clarify your assumptions.

Exhibit 14-9 Summary of Employee Attitude Survey Alpha
Electronics Division (1976–1978)

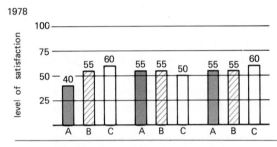

A, composite of economic and security factors.
B, composite of social and responsibility factors and reaction to supervision.
C, composite of job factors, personal challenge, accomplishments.

4. Consider the two summary job descriptions (see Exhibits 14-10a and 10-b) and identical information for the Paint Room Supervisor and for the Circuit Card Stacker. What would be your preliminary assessments (on the five factors) for job-enrichment possibilities? Name and justify your assumptions. Use Exhibit 14-9 for your analysis.

Exhibit 14-10a Job Description: Circuit Card Stacker

Reports to: Supervisor, Electronic Assemblies
Supervises: None

General Responsibilities

Is responsible for requesting firm inventory, circuit cards that are used in making subassemblies and assemblies. Stacks needed circuit cards at correct work stations and draws more of these from inventory as they may be needed for production during the shift.

Exhibit 14-10b Job Description: Supervisor, Paint Shop

Reports to: Production Superintendent
Supervises: Paint sprayers (3)
              Lettering and stencil person (1)
              Inspector (1)

General Responsibilities

Supervises the spraying and lettering of various housing panel boards and decorative parts used in installations of the industrial computer lines. Makes sure that all painted parts meet color and various layout specifications and are produced on time. Carries out tasks as assigned by the Production Superintendent. Is expected to work in cooperative way with other production supervisors and staff members in Quality Control, Purchasing, and Engineering.

---

5. You are a consultant with Quality of Work Life, a group organized to carry out job-enrichment and job-design studies. As part of your preliminary work at the Alpha Electronics Division, you examined the record of employee attitudes regarding various work-related factors (see Exhibit 14-9). What would be your initial interpretations? How would their interpretations be connected to company problems they have reported?

References

Alber, Antone, and Melvin Blumberg, "Team vs Individual Approaches to Job Enrichment Programs," *Personnel,* **58**(1) (January-February 1981): 63–75.

Argyris, Chris, *Management and Organization Development.* New York: McGraw-Hill (1971).

Blake, Robert, and Jane Mouton, *Corporate Excellence Diagnosis.* Austin, Tex.: Scientific Methods (1968).

Burack, Elmer H., and Robert D. Smith, *Personnel Management: A Human Resource Systems Approach.* New York: John Wiley (1982).

Davis, Louis, and F. Taylor, *Job Design.* 2nd ed., Pacific Palisades, Ca.: Goodyear Publishing (1978).

DeGreen, Kenyon, *Sociotechnical Systems: Factors in Analysis, Design and Management.* Englewood Cliffs, N.J.: Prentice-Hall (1973).

Ford, Robert N., "Job Enrichment Lessons from AT&T," *Harvard Business Review,* **51** (January-February 1973): 96–106.

Ganster, Daniel, "Individual Differences and Task Design: A Laboratory Experiment," *Organizational Behavior and Human Performance,* **26**(1) (August 1980): 131–148.

Glaser, Edward M., "State-of-the-Art Questions About Quality of Worklife," *Personnel,* **53**(3) (May-June 1976): 39–47.

Hackman, J. Richard, "The Design of Work in the 1980's," *Organizational Dynamics,* **7** (Summer 1978): 3–17.

Hackman, J. Richard, Greg Oldham, Robert Janson, and Kenneth Purdy, "A New Strategy for Job Enrichment," *California Management Review,* **17** (Summer 1975): 57–71.

Herzberg, Frederick, Bernard Mausner, and Barbara Snyderman, *The Motivation to Work.* New York: John Wiley (1959).

Herzberg, Frederick, and Alex Zautra, "Orthodox Job Enrichment: Measuring True Quality in Job Satisfaction," *Personnel,* **53**(5) (September-October 1976): 54–68.

Jamieson, David, "Training and OD: Crossing Disciplines," *Training and Development Journal,* **35**(4) (April 1981): 12–17.

Katz, Daniel and Basil S. Georgopolous, "Organizations in a Changing World," *Journal of Applied Behavioral Science,* **7**(3) (May–June 1971); 342–370.

Kiggundu, Moses, "An Empirical Test of Theory of Job Design Using Multiple Job Ratings," *Human Relations,* **33**(5) (May 1980): 339–351.

Likert, Rensis, *The Human Organization.* New York: McGraw-Hill (1967).

Marrow, Alfred, David Bowers, and Stanley Seashore, *Management By Participation.* New York: Harper and Row (1967).

McGregor, Douglas, *The Human Side of Enterprise.* New York: McGraw-Hill (1960).

Oldham, Greg R., J. Richard Hackman, and Jon L. Pierce, "Conditions Under Which Employees Respond Positively to Enriched Work," *Journal of Applied Psychology,* **61** (August 1976): 395–403.

Orpen, Christopher, "Effect of Flexible Working Hours on Employee Satisfaction and Performance: A Field Experiment," *Journal of Applied Psychology,* **66**(1) (February 1981): 113–115.

O'Toole, James, ed. *Work and the Quality of Life: Resource Papers for Work in America.* Cambridge, Mass.: The MIT Press (1974).

Peterson, Richard B., "Swedish Experiments in Job Reform," *Business Horizons,* **19** (June 1976): 13–22.

Pierce, Jon L. "Job Design in Perspective," *The Personnel Administrator,* **25**(12) (December 1980): 67–74.

Poza, Ernesto J., and M. Lynne Markus, "Success Story: The Team Approach to Work Restructuring," *Organizational Dynamics,* **8** (Winter 1980): 3–25.

Rainey, Glenn, and Lawrence Wolf, "Flex-Time: Short-term Benefits; Long-term?" *Public Administration Review,* **41**(1) (January-February 1981): 52–63.

Ronen, Simcha, and Sophia Primps, "The Impact of Flexitime on Performance and Attitudes in 25 Public Agencies," *Public Personnel Management,* **9**(3) (1980): 201–207.

Schein, Edgar, *Organizational Psychology.* Englewood Cliffs, N.J.: Prentice-Hall (1965).

Shea, Gregory, "Work Design Committees—The Wave of the Future," *Journal of Applied Management,* **4**(2) (March-April 1979): 6–11.

Terkel, Studs, *Working: People Talk About What They Do All Day and How They Feel About What They Do.* New York: Pantheon Books (1974).

Walters, Roy, "How to Increase the Productivity of Bank Employees," *Bank Marketing,* **13**(1) (March 1981): 24–25.

Walton, Richard E., "Work Innovations at Topeka: After Six Years," *Journal of Applied Behavioral Science,* **13** (July-August-September 1977): 422–433.

White, J. Kenneth, "Individual Differences and the Job Quality—Worker Response Relationship: Review, Integration, and Comments," *Academy of Management Review,* **3** (April 1978): 267–280.

CHAPTER 15

CAREER PLANNING

KEY QUESTIONS ADDRESSED IN CHAPTER	1. What are the "what," "why," and "how" of career planning for the individual?
	2. How can the idea of life spaces and a novel view of organizational structure help people to gain insight into their career needs and performances?
	3. What is the career-stage model? How can you use this to establish career strategies for yourself?
	4. How does organization career management differ from individual career planning?

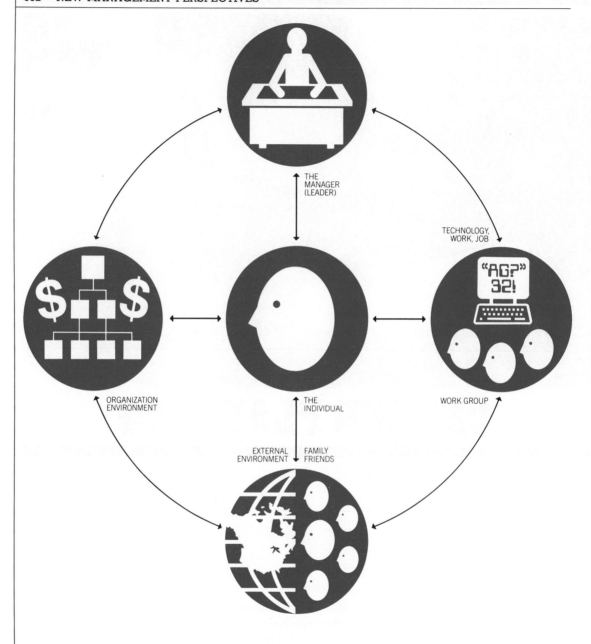

Work-life spaces: The individual viewpoint

If a man does not keep pace with his companions, perhaps it is because he hears a different drummer. Let him step to the music which he hears.

Henry David Thoreau

THE CHAPTER IN BRIEF

The What

Career management brings the organization's human resource needs and programs for achieving these together with the career needs and concerns of individual organization members. **Organization career management** focuses on the needs of the organization and the demand for its products and services. The organization is concerned with increasing efficiency and profits and ensuring its own continuance. Since organization members are largely responsible for the success or failure of an organization in meeting its needs and achieving its goals, organizational resources must be channeled into the development of personnel, that is, developing individual talent, productivity, cooperation, and so on. **Individual career planning,** on the other hand, concentrates on the fulfillment of individual needs, values, abilities, and interests within a career–life context. The individual wants a career that provides interesting work, monetary payoffs, a positive social climate, and a sense of self-satisfaction. The nature of each of these requirements varies, of course, with the individual. For one person, a positive social climate is an atmosphere where co-workers wear blue jeans, have flexible work hours, and address each other on a first-name basis. Others prefer a more formal and structured work setting that is fast paced and high pressured. The main point here is that an individual wants a career that is personally satisfying and meets his or her particular preferences.

The Why

The necessity for effective career management has intensified in recent years owing to large-scale social changes and a staggering array of legislation. These trends have had a dramatic impact on the world of work and careers. Women are entering the work force in large numbers. The changing composition of the work force has created new problems for men, women, and organizations, which must be dealt with effectively. The government has become increasingly involved with such issues as Equal Employment Opportunity, retirement age, restrictions on retirement funds, and reports on the status of "targeted" (certain minority or ethnic, for example) groups. Organizations have to meet new standards and sometimes have to enact certain procedures or curtail currently existing ones. For example, entrance tests for police officers in a major city had to be changed when it was disclosed that they were culturally biased and discriminated against the hiring of certain ethnic groups.

Even as technology continues to develop at a breakneck pace, there is a growing dependence by organizations on people for performance—and a growing dominance of service, as opposed to manufacturing, activities. Organizations cannot run effectively and efficiently unless they are well managed, and good management must entail career development within the organization.

The How: Career Management and the Life-Space Model

Earlier chapters describe the concept of life spaces, and this concept is relevant to how organization managers think about career issues as these affect the individual. The life space of the individual is influenced by, and interacts with, the life spaces of the group, work, organization, and external environment. Organizational career management must consider that an individual's sense of career progress is dependent upon the ideas and influence of friends and associates (*group*); the opportunities emerging "outside"; the new pressures or threats from the external environment or from inside the organization itself; and the challenge or demands imposed by the individual's work.

Where individuals are now and where they will be in the future must also be considered. A person who moves from an executive secretarial position to a job as office supervisor will face many new problems, and will require different skills and greater development in managerial practices.

Organizational career management also needs to focus on the sources of opportunity or change in the external environment that affect career thinking. New laws, for instance, may require an asbestos factory to improve its safety standards or a city hospital to hire more nonwhite doctors.

An organization often has many rules, policies, and regulations that must be adjusted to promote career programs. Training sessions must be instituted to keep employees abreast of problems and issues within the organization and events outside of the organization. Career counseling can also help meet the needs of organization members in dealing with problems, looking to improve their performance, or trying to guide their careers.

The way employees are supervised or treated by management has a major impact on how they feel about themselves and how they will perform. If managers are seen as supportive and concerned with individual development, then their subordinates will frequently react in kind. Intimidation or excessive criticism by a supervisor may actually reduce performance and increase turnover.

As suggested in Chapter 14, work in general can be more self-fulfilling. Whenever possible, therefore, managers should develop the conditions within which workers who desire it, can obtain a greater sense of accomplishment and challenge from their work as well as appropriate monetary returns.

The life-space concept suggests a broad perspective for the manager. It assists in understanding of what an organization consists, the types of influences within the organization that affect individual members, and ways to satisfy company needs and personal objectives.

There is another view of organizational functions and activities that, along with the life-space idea, can prove quite useful in career

Exhibit 15-1 Individual Career Mobility: Organization Perspective

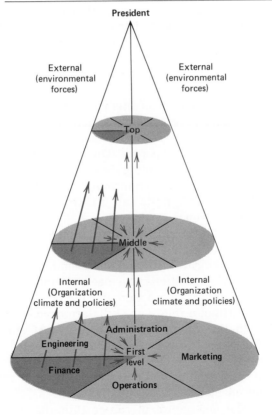

Source: Based on Edgar H. Schein's model in *Career Dynamics: Matching Individual and Organizational Needs.* Reading, Mass.: Addison-Wesley (1978).

thinking and planning for the individual and manager. Edgar H. **Schein** of MIT has looked at organizations in **three dimensions** (career model of mobility). Career thinking of necessity involves the movements between units and between levels (promotion) of an organization (see Exhibit 15-1). Options also exist for movement within functions such as marketing or making cross-functional moves. Naturally, the career mobility of people must also take into account options individuals may exercise for leaving one employer and going to another.

Schein's model provides us with a novel way to view an organization by depicting some of the key mobility patterns. First, the exhibit shows that an organization, its activities, and members are affected by *both* external and internal developments and trends. Second, the *layers* reflect the successively higher levels of authority. Thus, one aspect of a career path is the fact that promotion carries one higher into the organization. The vertical stem represents upward movement as well as the career path favored in a particular organization for upper movement. For example, this might be through finance, administration, or any of the activities shown in Exhibit 15-1. The point is that a particular route usually turns out to be a favored one because of the owner's philosophy or simply because of the nature of the organization.

A third feature of this model is the fact that at any given *level* one's career progress may be *within* a functional area (for example, operations or marketing) or across functional lines—where policy, skills, and practice permit. Thus, for the purposes of individual career planning, understanding how the promotion paths work, the influence of organizational politics, and the possibilities for progress within or across units can greatly assist one in making intelligent career decisions.

Finally, the skills required by the organization change as people move up to higher levels in the organization. At entry or first-line levels technical skills tend to predominate. As one advances to higher managerial positions the need to understand the big picture increases; this requires a greater use of conceptual and administrative skills. Human-relations skills are needed at all managerial levels, but their form varies considerably. At supervisory levels, people skills often involve relatively large numbers of people in a group context and individually. At higher managerial levels, many one-to-one relationships and much more variety characterize interpersonal relationships.

The emergence of career thinking and organizational career management cannot be attributed to any single event or activity (see Burack and Mathys, 1980; Burack and Smith, 1982). A remarkable group of occurrences have all come together to bring about this situation. There are three areas of development that collectively provide a kind of **"critical mass,"** or the necessary preconditions for this era of career interest. They are: (1) concepts, (2) methods, and (3) change.

BACKGROUND

Concepts

Structure of Occupations

A new way of looking at *occupations* has emerged in which an occupation is viewed as a structure made up of various *sets of skills, abilities,* and *activities*. Many of the skills and knowledge learned in one work setting can be applied to another work setting. Jobs are therefore no longer seen as isolated entities but as interrelated working activities, in which the transference of previously acquired and developed abilities is possible. For example, many of the managerial skills that a person might develop while working as an assistant manager in a grocery store can be adapted and transferred to a management position in a department store. Correspondingly, some purchasing specialists develop skills found useful in various production-planning positions. Evidence also suggests that certain leadership qualities, organizational abilities, and communication skills are transferable from one occupation to another. All of this suggests that occupational mobility is *greater* than many individuals realize.

Systems Thinking

Systems thinking is another new way of thinking about organizations, their structures, processes, activities, and people and the relationship between these. For example, the introduction of a new planning procedure in department K may affect the skills of people in department K as well as the procedures and human skills in departments Y and Z.

Adult Education

In the past adult education seemed to be only for those few who took it upon themselves to take classes at a local college, church, or community center or to read on their own. Now the need has grown to assess the various types of career-related learning that take place over the person's whole lifetime. This is an approach in which adults are seen as largely determining their own needs and priorities. These, in turn, seem to orient them in making career choices, which will provide self-satisfaction and will increase opportunities for learning. For ex-

Learning is a life long process.

ample, the participation of adults in "management development" programs has exploded since 1970. Numerous new programs have been introduced. Participants are selecting programs from a wide assortment of possibilities including internal organization offerings, institutes, work shops, self-study courses, and, of course, formal school offerings.

Situational Thinking

As we mentioned in the first chapter, situational thinking recognizes that much managerial thinking and analysis is *contingency oriented*. The nature of the situation that is being dealt with determines the type of approach chosen. This kind of thinking has in many circles replaced analyses that try to handle all types of situations with one particular management approach. From a career viewpoint this suggests that a variety of experiences is likely to enable a manager to better deal with situations in a rapidly changing world.

Methods

In this time of massive changes a variety of methodological changes have arisen, which affect the present career climate. New approaches to work have been developed and previously known methods have been modified.

Work–Job Analysis

This area is concerned with the study of work and jobs, the determination of how best to do a job, and the development of written work procedures and descriptions of responsibilities (*position description*) for the job holder. Taylor's scientific management and Weber's bureaucratic model represent major pioneering efforts in viewing individual and networks of jobs. What has taken place here is a revolution in how jobs are looked at and what qualifications are required to perform them well.

In the past the view of work was often affected by racial prejudice or longstanding assumptions about "men's work" and "women's work." Also, many work analysts, personnel people in organizations, and industrial psychologists thought that education, personality traits, and other personal features were good indicators of ability to perform on the job. Scientific advances in the work field, aided by new legal regulations, especially laws related to Equal Employment Opportunity (EEO), have shattered these assumptions and myths. Now we take an approach aimed at what the job holder must accomplish to be successful. In other words, we focus on the *desired end behaviors* (rather than traits) for a particular job.

Let us look at an example to see how past and modern practices differ in this regard. In the past people who were physically large were considered good job prospects for some supervisory jobs because they possessed traits that were thought to indicate personal strength, which was thought to be an important basis for leadership. Now the emphasis is on the appropriate execution of jobs, tasks, and responsibilities: "A person who performs satisfactorily must be able to *do* 'such and such.' " New and powerful techniques have been developed that cut across the entire organization and leave Taylorism and more traditional techniques far behind in this regard.

Assessment of Potential

New advances have been made in assessing individuals, their potential for skill development, and the application of these skills to jobs within the organization in which they are employed. These assessments are concerned with evaluating learning and skill capacity and the ability to perform specialized or supervisory functions. Improvements in the assessment of potential stem mainly from a better understanding of what supervisors and managers do. As a result, better worker–job matches can be made.

Performance Appraisals and Standards

Performance appraisals use performance *standards* in judging how well a worker performs his or her job. The technique is meant to be systematic. The standards provide specific measures of performance. Sketchy, impressionistic appraisals are avoided. Particular work tasks and responsibilities are broken down into components, and each component is evaluated according to objective quality standards. For example, "excellent" typing performance might be described as: "works at the rate of 70 or more words per minute for a typical cross section of work and with no more than x errors."

To make appraisals effective for career purposes managers need to tell workers "where they stand." This feedback should be done early and often and emphasize the positive rather than the negative.

Self-Assessment

Recently there has been an increase in the creation of self-study materials designed to help people explore career directions. These materials contain useful career information as well as self-tests for assessing skills and career interests and aiding career planning. The fundamental assumption underlying career self-study materials is that *career directions and choices* must be an individual responsibility. The individual becomes increasingly *self-directed* as he or she gains knowledge and experience and a sense of his or her personal work style and preferences.

Change

There are four areas of change that have helped lead the way to the current state of management practices and human resource concerns: (1) the individual, (2) the organization, (3) the environment, and (4) the government.

Change from the Viewpoint of the Individual

The large and fast influx of women into the work force has changed our understanding of women's roles and our perception of the work world. Women today make up approximately 50 percent of the labor force.

In the 1979 California case of *Marvin* vs *Marvin* involving actor Lee Marvin and Michelle Marvin (they were living together but not married; she changed her name legally), the judge awarded Michelle $104,000 "for rehabilitation purposes to re-educate herself and to learn new, employable skills" (*Newsweek,* 1979). The theory behind this court decision is that women, like men, are capable of supporting themselves economically and, possibly, expected to be given the proper education—and training. Furthermore, women are now considered a major component of the work force.

Legally, for the most part, women are on equal footing with men in the work force. They must be given the same opportunities as men with equivalent qualifications and must receive equal pay for equal work. A new pay issue is that of equal pay for comparable or equivalent work. What is being contested here is that it is unfair that so-called traditional women's positions like secretarial or nursing positions are on a lower pay scale than "comparable" male positions (*Newsweek*, 1979). For example, a skilled executive secretary may contribute more to her company than a company custodian, yet she is likely to earn less simply because "secretaries have always been paid less" (*Newsweek*, 1979). This stance was upheld in a New Jersey court action against Westinghouse Electric Corporation when the judge ruled that "allegations and proof of unequal but comparable work" do not violate Federal law (*Newsweek*, 1979). Various forces are likely to continue redefining equality.

There is still much resistance against liberation of the modern woman. Many women do not receive pay commensurate with their responsibilities and achievements. Others may not be given the kind of respect they deserve by fellow workers. Still others suffer from identity crises centering around leaving the home and competing in the male-dominated work world. Some women are still sexually ha-

Office workers *Dolly Parton, Lily Tomlin* and *Jane Fonda* tell their chauvinist boss *Dabney Coleman* how they think the office should be run.

rassed by their employers and asked to do "favors" if they want to stay employed or be promoted.

Job mobility has become increasingly valued in recent years. People feel more inclined to change jobs or locations in order to advance their careers. Sometimes the motivation is more money, a new set of surroundings, added prestige, or an attempt to learn something new or satisfy a newly developed interest. Job mobility also seems to be more glamorous than it was in the past when it was often associated with instability and failure.

Another change is that many people seem to feel that a job should provide more than just economic returns. Some will forego increased pay for more satisfying work or a better social atmosphere. There are others who prefer to work shorter hours so that they will have the opportunity to partake in activities outside of work, even if this involves a substantial salary cut.

Whereas in the past many minorites and ethnic groups felt that they were being held back from succeeding in the work world, gradually, growing numbers are beginning to think they can make it too, even though the going may be tough at times.

Finally, the high cost of living has created greater economic demands upon the individual. When inflation hovers in double-digit figures, a salary that provided a comfortable living 10 years ago may not even make ends meet today. To compensate for these economic pressures many people have had to take on extra jobs or work longer hours. With rising costs and a desire for the "good life" immediately, a dual-career family becomes more of a necessity than an option.

Change from the Viewpoint of the Organization

Organizations have become increasingly complex. Technology continues to advance at an ever-growing pace. Computers make it possible to accumulate and manipulate vast amounts of information at split-second speeds, to run complicated machinery, and to perform complex tasks. Technology creates new jobs and replaces old ones. It simplifies as it complicates and requires growing degrees of specialization and reeducation, both of which have career implications. Workers, managers, and specialists must be kept abreast of the rapid changes if they are to be prevented from becoming ineffective or obsolete. Lifelong learning is rapidly becoming a way of life for organization members—and few remain untouched by this need.

Change from the Viewpoint of the Environment

As environmental developments contribute to turbulence and change, organizations are impelled to cope with these conditions with better planning and management. This means developing new flexi-

GREAT PERSON PROFILE

Joan Ganz Cooney (1929–   )

Joan Ganz Cooney was born and raised in Phoenix, Arizona. After receiving her B.A. from the University of Arizona she became a reporter for the *Arizona Republic*. She later moved to New York where she became a network publicist. In 1962 she became a producer of public affairs documentaries for Channel 13, the Public Broadcasting station in New York. Her career was to take a new direction at a dinner party in her home in 1966 when the idea of exploring the potential of television as a preschool educator was discussed with several influential people, including a vice-president of the Carnegie Foundation. The next day Carnegie asked Cooney to conduct a study on the feasibility of educating young children through the medium of television. She not only found the idea intriguing but also viewed it as an *advancement* in her *career:* a way of gaining more influence over the new projects she accepted.

Her report was enthusiastically received by both government and foundations. The idea slowly evolved and in 1967, with the support of the Carnegie Foundation, the Ford Foundation, and the United States Office of Education, she founded the Children's Television Workshop (CTW), a not-for-profit organization whose creations include "Sesame Street," "The Electric Company," and "3-2-1 Contact."

Cooney had an idea for bringing about improvements. But she struggled with complicated business concepts and had to learn them fast. For this reason she surrounded herself with capable people. Soon after Sesame Street was introduced in 1969 it became immensely successful. Big Bird, Bert, Ernie, and the Cookie Monster were "buddies" to millions of preschoolers. With the help of these Muppet characters Cooney was able to start a products business—toys, games, books, and records—that put CTW on a firmer footing, making it largely free of government or foundation support.

Today the Children's Television Workshop is a multimillion dollar business. Cooney attributes much of its success to "getting the breaks" as well as being able to perform once given the chance. Although she is highly successful, her career is not an unusual example of how people find their place in life while seeking some career goal or advancement opportunity.

bility to meet the requirements of constant shifts and uncertainties. Organization members must learn to work more effectively through cooperation, coordinated action, and increased participation.

Growing social, political, and economic trends affect the organization's career thinking. The increasing educational and income level of the average worker means that he or she will have new needs to meet, interests to satisfy, and values to fulfill. More people are feeling "the good life" is within their grasp and that they are entitled to it. Organizations are challenged to help bring about these possibilities.

Change from the Viewpoint of the Government

The government has become increasingly involved in the affairs of organizations, for instance, in **Equal Employment standards** preventing discrimination by race, creed, color, or sex. New regulations in health and safety reduce the chances of injury and illness on the job. Government regulations also affect minimum wages, pension policies, retirement age, and working conditions.

The When of Career Management

Career management is a recent development that largely coincides with the passage of equal employment legislation and the enactment of various related acts and executive orders. The "big push" on basic employment and training came in the 1960s. The major thrust for careers, training, and Equal Employment was not felt until the early-to-mid-1970s, and the "full throttle" was not experienced until the end of the decade.

Is There a Common Ground for Individual Career Planning and Organizational Career Management?

Individual career planning centers on the life goals of the individual, whereas organizational career management is concerned with the needs of the organization. Shall the two approaches ever meet?

The possibilities for a *common meeting ground* arise from the fact that the individual becomes the basis for the organization to achieve its needs. In turn, the individual has much to gain from organizational affiliation. If the organization is to operate effectively certain needs, interests, and goals of individual members must be fulfilled. Disgruntled workers can be lazy, uncooperative, ineffective, and unproductive. They may even sabotage organization operations. Clearly, neither side gains from this type of result. The common meeting ground is solidly established when the individual can realistically see how many of his career values can be achieved through affiliation and continued employment with an organization. This can be realized, of course, only if the individual understands his career-related values and goals as well as the opportunities for realizing these within an organization.

YOU, YOUR CAREER, AND THE WORK WORLD

Who Am I? Where Am I going?

Socrates, the famous philosopher of ancient Greece with a habit of asking pointed questions, can be credited with defining "step one" in the career planning process: "know thyself." Before you can begin to develop a career that is "right" for you, you must have a good grasp of just who you are. So the first step of career planning is to understand what are your talents, abilities, skills, interests, needs, values, and potential. You have to ask yourself what you want out of life, out of your career? What do you value or want to accomplish? What are your work style and preferences? Once you begin to come up with answers to these questions you have taken a giant step forward, perhaps one of the most important steps in planning your career.

Goals and "Baselines": A Career Game

The "career game" requires a sense of direction—where you are going and how you will get there. The "where" depends on your set of goals. Career goals should reflect your needs, values, interests, and abilities. They are desired ends, aims that you want to achieve like helping others, making a million dollars (preferably before age 30), or reaching the top of a "classy" company like IBM. One thing that ought to be stressed, however, is that good goals are realistic, manageable, and obtainable.* For most people the last two examples of goals represent fantasies rather than realistically obtainable objectives. Even the first example of a goal is not a good one, since it is too general. We should try to state our goals as *specifically* as we can. A better version of "helping others" would be: "To help people with their medical needs" (for instance, as a doctor or nurse) or "with their monetary needs" (as a business consultant, accountant, or lawyer). A goal can be reached by taking any one of a number of *paths*. Often one path may be more practical or efficient than another. Sometimes several *path steps* need to be taken to reach a goal. Becoming a department manager may require working in a department for a certain amount of time, taking a special management course, getting good performance ratings, and successfully completing an interview with the store director. Certain path steps may be *dependent* on others. You might not be able to take the management training

*For additional ideas see Elmer H. Burack, Maryann Albrecht, and Helene Seitler, *Growing—A Woman's Guide to Career Satisfaction.* Belmont, Ca: Lifetime Learning Press (1980).

course until you have worked in the department for a specified period.

You need to establish **baselines** to determine how far, fast, and well you have progressed in pursuing your goals. Sometimes it is necessary to keep a written record of the advances you have made, so that you can see just how far you have come, how far you have to go, and the time frame in which you are operating. A written record can provide you with satisfaction about your progress and can encourage you to stick to a firmer timetable. Timing often affects career opportunities: more time usually means more opportunities.

Time–Career Life Lines

Since career choices and events are played out over time, it is useful to connect up the series of important events in your career. This series forms your *time–career life line*. The **time line** consists of three elements: time, events, and connections. Time–career life lines help to identify important events in your career, especially those that lead to improvements in your skills and abilities and thereby lead to career progress. The next exhibit suggests how you might "map" your **career lifeline** (Exhibit 15-2). Notice that the high school years include important events—joining a debate team and the first summer job. The jobs held by the individual are also shown. Importantly, the jobs are shown as well as the approximate time of each activity. As a result of this plot it is possible to establish a baseline to judge progress concerning your career and life goals.

Search: Exploring Possibilities

There are a number of ways to discover the kind of career you are interested in pursuing. One way is to speak with people who are working in a field in which you might have an interest. For example, if you are interested in architecture you could speak, on the phone or in person, with students who are studying architecture as well as with beginning or established architects. By speaking with a number of people in various stages of career development or in different areas of architecture, you will be able to gain an overall perspective of the field. You might ask about the kinds of things architects do, what they like and dislike about being architects or students, what their interests and daily lives are like, salary ranges, work hours, and so forth. You can obtain some of the best information about a field from those in it—as long as you talk to a variety of people.

A second way to explore career possibilities is through school. If you think you might be interested in a certain field, take a couple of courses in it. Try to find a job in the field, or a related field. The combination of learning and experience will give you a good idea whether a particular career direction is for you.

Exhibit 15-2 Time–Career Life Line

o Start high school

   o Join debate team

      o First summer job

         o Start college

           o Receive B.A.

              o Start job as salesperson at Atlas Automotive Supplies

                 o Promoted to assistant manager

                   o Quit job, begin new job

| 15 | 20 | 25 | 30 | 35 |

Age

Another way to examine your career alternatives is to use the library to gain information about career areas and opportunities. There are a number of good books on career planning that have been published recently, for example, *What Color Is Your Parachute?* by Richard Bolles. Visiting companies that you might be interested in working for is also an effective means. You could speak with people in the personnel department or might even talk to supervisors or other employees. The *Directory of Occupational Titles* published by the United States Government lists thousands of jobs and the types of skills they require. Finally, it is an excellent idea to make use of the career counseling and placement office at your college. It can usually provide you with the latest information about careers and job opportunities and may help you find employment. Many counseling offices have computer-assisted programs or tapes that help in the search process. They also would be aware of career seminars or forums, many of which are free, that could be attended. In addition, they will help you examine your interests, skills, talents, and goals through a variety of tests—often given as a free service by the college.

Career Paths and Your Stage in the Career–Life Cycle

Erik Erikson (1963), the noted psychologist, observed that every person passes through eight stages in the course of his or her lifetime, and these stages make up an important part of what he called the individual's **life cycle** (see Exhibit 15-3). In each stage the individual is confronted with a particular developmental task and must work through this stage before fully passing on to the next stage. Each stage is also preceded by a preparation period as individuals prepare

(Copyright © Field Enterprises, Inc., 1979.)

themselves for the next stage. The stages are usually determined by age. People within a particular age range tend to experience similar anxieties and problems or to undergo similar forms of thinking, activity, or development. For example, in Erikson's adolescent stage, approximately 15 to 25 years old, the main task is establishing a sense of ego identity. It is a time for seeking social acceptance and searching for meaning, values, mentors, and a sense of self. Donald Super, a well-known figure in career circles, and his associates (1970) point out that there are also **career stages** that closely correspond with Erikson's life stages. For example, during adolescence a person starts to explore his or her interests and occupational opportunities. This stage marks the beginning of the person's job search.

Your age, career development, and preferences are parts of a broader career fabric. Since each life–career stage is characterized by various typical experiences, you can learn to anticipate the kinds of issues and concerns with which you will have to deal. This foresight will enable you to better cope with situations, to plan ahead in dealing with anticipated problems, and to realize that the anxieties and problems you are experiencing are not strange or peculiar in most cases. *Passages* by Gail Sheehy (1976) is excellent reading in the area of life and career stages.

One Step at a Time—But with a Plan in Mind

There are many distractions that can steer you off your **career path,** such as a bad job experience, faulty information, or a personal crisis. Developing a realistic career plan with *alternative paths* is necessary for meeting change and uncertainty. If something does not work out as you expected you will not be lost, because you will have created options and contingency paths for yourself. Career planning will enable you to foresee future opportunities and to keep options open. You will also be able to minimize chances for failure or unnecessary problems and anxiety. Of course, you are not able to plan too far ahead, because you will have to meet changes in the environment and in your values and abilities. Shifts in the economy may cause you to

Exhibit 15-3 Erikson's Life Stages and Super's Career Stages

Leave Family 16–22	Reaching Out 23–28	Questions 29–34	Explosion at Midlife 35–43	Stability 44–50	Acceptance, Mellowing 51 on
• Break family hold	• Search for identity	• Some wavering of assurance	• Time going by	• Stable time	• Avoid emotional issues
• Influence of group beliefs	• Reach out for other	• What is life?	• Death will come	• Seek out old friends, values	• Shorter(er) run orientation
• Brittle friendships	• Acquire mentor	• Seek acceptance	• Unstable		• Little concern for past
	• Seek worldliness	• Incompat-ible drives	• Question values		• Less concern for future
		• Seek order and stability	• Time for change?		• Come to accept things
		• Sense of mobility	• Mentor for young person?		
		• Marital bliss may decrease			

Source: Based on the work of Roger Gould (UCLA), Dan Levenson (Yale), and George Valliant (Harvard) and *Time* "New Light in Adult Life Cycles" (April 28, 1975). From Elmer H. Burack and Nicholas Mathys, *Career Management in Organizations: A Practical Human Resource Planning Approach.* Lake Forest, Ill.: Brace-Park (1980).

change your economic priorities. Or a new job experience may open up unexplored avenues or bring to light hidden talents or interests. A large part of career planning is *planning for change.*

Point of No Return?

A **career** is a sequence of work and life experiences, some good and some not so good. Both types will occur but the important thing is that something can be learned from each. You should recognize that a particular career decision is not for all time. Many career decisions will be made in your lifetime. If a decision does not work out as planned, you should not feel eternally doomed. If you are flexible and build contingencies into your career plans, you probably can try a new path. Remember, it is worthwhile to take the time to search out alternatives because making a career choice means committing your time and your resources. The more time and energy you invest in a career path, the more difficult it becomes to switch paths if things are not working out—so choose wisely.

GREAT PERSON PROFILE

Cyrus Rowlett Smith (1899–   )

Cyrus Rowlett Smith was born in Minerva, Texas as the second of seven children. He had to help support the family when their father left them. From the age of nine he held a number of odd jobs, ranging from cotton picker to bank teller, none of which proved of lasting interest to him. In 1920 he moved to Austin, where he attended the University of Texas and pursued a nondegree seeking program for students without a high school diploma. Among the courses he took was accounting, and in 1924 he took a job with Peat, Marwick, Mitchell & Co. When one of his clients gained control of Texas Air Transport, Inc., he asked Smith to help him run it. As a favor to the client Smith agreed to try it for a year. To his surprise, he liked it.

Having explored different professions in vastly different fields, C. R. Smith had arrived at something that intrigued him, and the future of commercial aviation was a great challenge. In the excitement following Lindbergh's flight to Paris, Aviation Corporation was formed—absorbing Texas Air Transport along with several other companies. By 1934 it had evolved into American Airlines with C. R. Smith as its president.

His willingness to reevaluate his work situation and take on something new is typical of the *exploratory career stage* that most people experience in their careers. The reward was a career spanning the major developments in commercial aviation, until his retirement in 1974. He was among the pioneers who made commercial air travel commonplace in the United States.

Turning Failures into Successes

As we mentioned, things do not always work out as expected or planned. That is why it is important to develop alternative paths or strategies, that is, *contingency approaches*. Everyone encounters failure at one point or another. You must learn to profit from your mistakes and to move on. Failure can teach you to recognize the circumstances that lead to failure. This knowledge will enable you to minimize future failures and to create future successes. Failures also tell you something about yourself, the kinds of things you like and do not like and can and cannot do. You have to take action to see to it that you do not repeat your mistakes or failures. It is not enough to recognize a difficulty unless you do something about it. Sometimes it is just a matter of spending more time searching before jumping into an activity or job.

ORGANIZATION CAREER MANAGEMENT

Connecting Business Planning and People Planning

In the past much of the business planning done by managers and specialists considered almost exclusively economic or marketing factors. Relatively little attention was paid to human resources and how people fit into organizational plans. Now firmer bonds are being built between organizational plans and people plans. This often leads to the growth of programs for the development of human resources.

Basis of a Career-Planning System

Organizational career management joins business planning with human resource plans to achieve business goals and then, thoughtfully connects the individual into this complex system. Exhibit 15-4 summarizes the key features of a **career-planning system** that joins the indicated activities. The *what's done* side of the exhibit shows the basic activities, people, and outcomes that become part of a workable career-planning system. Clearly, the *who does it* indicates that many different officials, managers, and specialists must be joined together in good fashion if the individual activities and outcomes are to become actual occurrences. Virtually the entire organization must be joined together in a well-organized way. From the individual's viewpoint these "basics" include places and people that he or she can turn to in pursuing a career. They also indicate things you can be looking for in considering an employer.

Information and Communication Are Musts for Career Activity

Career planning and thinking, much like other organizational processes, build on information and communication. Information is needed about job opportunities and requirements. It must then be communicated to all employees so that they will have an "equal opportunity" for new positions. The wide dissemination of information also ensures that all qualified people will come to the attention of management. Finally, employees must also be given the chance to communicate their preferences and interests. These may be communicated informally through conversations with a supervisor, or, more formally, through written forms or interviews.

Exhibit 15-4 Basics of a Career Planning System

What's Done?	Who Does It?
Business Planning	
Managers and specialists monitor environment for opportunity, threat, trends change	Planners
	Officers
Needs, possibilities and alternatives are identified	Heads of functional units
Organization strengths and weaknesses are taken into account	(e.g., marketing, finance)
Decision making on future directions	Managers
Organization: Human Resource Planning	
Define future organizational structure	Personnel
Determine types of managers, specialists, and employees that will be needed	planners
Determine how many will be needed	
Determine when? where?	
Information for data system	
Organization Career Management	
Who is to fit into future programs	Personnel managers
Training and development programs	Personnel planners
Counseling	Career counselors
Succession plans for officers and senior managers	Line managers
Communication of job opportunities	Job analysts
Defining recruiting and entry-level job requirements	
Putting Programs into Effect	
Recruiting	Recruiters
Training	Training and
Development	development specialists; line managers

Where Do Line Managers Fit in?

Line managers or supervisors play the greatest role in career matters because they regularly interact with their unit members. The power and relationships of the line supervisor with his or her unit members must be preserved rather than being eroded by staff specialists. Inappropriate staff intervention or interference often causes problems like undercutting the supervisor–employee relationship.

Too often students tend to seek what they perceive as secure jobs in government or specialized staff areas rather than take on the added responsibility, stress, and challenge of line-management positions. This has contributed to the high overhead and lower productivity that is common in much of United States industry today. What is needed is a return to line management's bottom-line responsibility as long as that responsibility includes the career development of people. To do this, line managers need to have access to accurate, relevant information, and they require personal skills (especially in communications) and training.

Blending Organizational and Individual Plans

Individual career plans must be adequately addressed by the organization. The individual has to learn to satisfy career goals within an organizational context. The blending of organizational and individual planning takes place at various points in time: when recruiting the person, when entering a training or development program, when consulting (counseling with a supervisor), and when planning a career program. The needs of the organization and the individual change with time. The proper blend must therefore be reassessed periodically. The "fit" or compatibility is not always perfect. It is usually a matter of achieving a compromise or approximate fit. For example, an organization may need a person to begin training for sales supervision. You may desire to make your next move to supervision in customer relations. Yet, you may see the available opportunity as a reasonable one and go after it.

Programming Plans and Equal Employment Opportunity (EEO)

Equal Employment Opportunity creates a framework for an organization's career thinking and approaches. Of course, it calls for nondiscrimination in recruiting, hiring, and treatment of prospective employees. However, the proper implementation requires the availability of career counseling and the establishment of *career ladders* or the workable *connections between jobs*. These career ladders represent traditional lines within units as well as those uncovered through newer job-study techniques—which "cut across" traditional departmental lines. A career ladder enables an organizational member to progress within the organization's hierarchy in a number of ways. In the past, movement within the organization was fairly limited to a single sequence of progression. Now, opportunities are available for many types of movement both horizontally and vertically, as shown in Exhibit 15-5.

Individuals move up organizational career ladders. The scope of career possibilities and opportunities is greatly affected by organizational policy and the imagination with which officials and managers approach career planning. For the career ladders illustrated in Exhibit 15-5, much freedom exists for people to pursue careers in sales,

Exhibit 15-5 Organizational Career Ladder

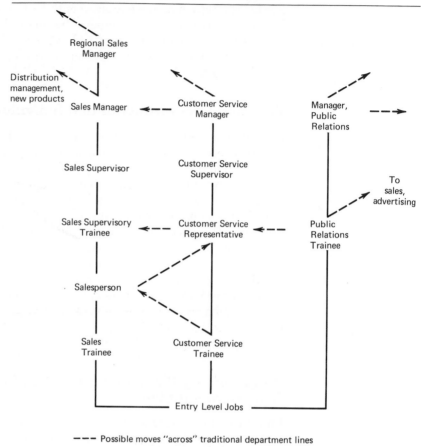

Regional Sales
Manager

Distribution
management,
new products

Sales Manager   Customer Service
Manager

Manager,
Public
Relations

Sales Supervisor   Customer Service
Supervisor

To
sales,
advertising

Sales Supervisory
Trainee   Customer Service
Representative   Public
Relations
Trainee

Salesperson

Sales
Trainee   Customer Service
Trainee

Entry Level Jobs

--- Possible moves "across" traditional department lines

Source: Based on Elmer Burack and Nicholas Mathys, *Organization Career Management: A Practical Human Resource Planning Approach.* Lake Forest, Ill.: Brace-Park Press (1980).

customer service, public relations, advertising, and other areas. For example, the career path for the individual in Exhibit 15-6 shows that in the period from 1974 to 1982 the person was able to move across many different departments. In fact, in about 1980, the person was training for Sales Supervision, but qualified for a job as Customer Service Supervisor that came about because of an unexpected resignation. Also, the person listed is considering a future in Sales Management or Customer Service. Clearly this person is moving up as he or she gains managerial skills, furthers formal education, and is prepared to undertake additional education and responsibility.

Exhibit 15-6 Individual Career Paths

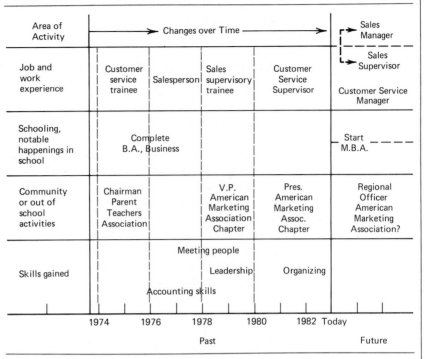

Area of Activity	Changes over Time →				Sales Manager / Sales Supervisor
Job and work experience	Customer service trainee	Salesperson	Sales supervisory trainee	Customer Service Supervisor	Customer Service Manager
Schooling, notable happenings in school	Complete B.A., Business				Start M.B.A.
Community or out of school activities	Chairman Parent Teachers Association		V.P. American Marketing Association Chapter	Pres. American Marketing Assoc. Chapter	Regional Officer American Marketing Association?
Skills gained		Accounting skills	Meeting people Leadership	Organizing	

	1974	1976	1978	1980	1982 Today	
		Past				Future

Organizational Career Ladders and Individual Career Paths

Exhibit 15-5, showing organizational career ladders, indicates what a specific company was able to do in "opening up" career opportunities for its members and new recruits. In past years only traditional paths of movement existed. Now it is possible for employees to move between various departments and functions. Now employees are given a chance to build skills for new jobs despite the fact that a job title might not seem wholly related to their job objectives. Obviously, job titles mean little in career thinking and discussions. Work must be examined closely in terms of its fundamental job elements in order to develop workable career ladders.

Exhibit 15-6 shows how an individual's career-planning analysis can be carried out. Shown in this exhibit is the job–career life line of the type previously described. This person has gone through sales training, selling, supervision of sales training, and customer service. Notice that this person finished a B.A. degree while working. At the same time he or she was quite active in the community as well as professionally. From this broad background, he or she gained much valuable experience. For the future, this person is considering two different routes—one, back in sales supervision; and the other, further advances in customer services.

Supervisory and Managerial Needs and Abilities

In the past, the attainment of a given employment level was often emphasized as a means of determining a person's preparation for a managerial or supervisory position. Jobs were frequently described in terms of general managerial functions like planning, organizing, developing, or directing. Now the emphasis has shifted to developing sets of factors that are related to work and can be used to describe many different jobs at a variety of levels, that is, **end-job behaviors.** The focus is on the *things people actually do in a job* and on *what makes for successful performance* of a job. These factors and descriptions are often organized under general categories of performance skills, as in the following: organization and planning; problem analysis; ability to commit company resources; leadership; decision making; relationships with people; written communication; oral communication; creativity; innovation; tolerance for stress; adaptability, flexibility; manual and sensory abilities, dexterity; and numerical, clerical skills. Each category contains anywhere from one to eight items. One job may be described as needing as many as 100 different skills or abilities for successful performance. An understanding of these skills and abilities enables intelligent career preparation because people get a much more specific and exact idea of what is involved in a particular job. It also permits more precise training to meet individual job requirements. For example, a recent community college graduate may decide that he or she is interested in becoming a computer programmer. This individual might find out that there are 50 different skills that he or she must master to be a competent programmer. He or she can receive proper training in those areas where improvement is needed or to make up for lack of experience. Once the individual has mastered the 50 skills, he or she is qualified to apply for a position as a programmer.

Supervisory Selection: Bases for Qualification

The first point to recognize is that what managers and supervisors do varies widely between companies. Even within a single company, the same job title may involve significantly different responsibilities owing to location, clientele, philosophy of local management, or special problems. Arkie's Clothing Store, for example, has several outlets in the Chicago area. The sales manager working at a branch store in downtown Chicago will have different responsibilities and problems and will require different skills from a sales manager working in a branch store in the suburbs.

In the past, supervisors were selected on the basis of periodic performance ratings as trainees or as employees in lower-level jobs, and by direct recruiting for these positions. Now individuals selected may have to meet established levels of performance in the following areas:

Technical skills.

- Merchandising methods.
- Price lines.
- Discounting.
- Operation of sales terminals.
- Interpretation of inventory figures.
- Window layout arrangements.
- Training of new employees.
- Restocking, orders.
- Other.

Administrative skills.

- Organization of store office.
- Processing of credit.
- Scheduling employees.
- Relations with regional office.
- Hiring needed replacements.
- Coordinating sales and inventory.
- Other.

Human relations skills.

- Effective orientation of new people.
- Disciplining.
- Motivating poor sales performers.
- Handling customer complaints.
- Dealing with personal problems of employees.
- Other.

This list is only suggestive—the actual checklist for the training for store supervisory personnel has some 100 different skills or behaviors expected of a store supervisor. Supervisors are carefully trained against these sets of skill objectives. For each skill, a group of *benchmarks* is established so that it is possible to determine how well the skill is being performed.

AND NOW BACK TO YOU

Points of Entry into Supervision and Management

Those interested in having a career in management or supervision have a number of points of entry. One way is through a cooperative education program. Many colleges and universities offer degrees in which the student is able to combine academic course work with field experiences in the work world. In these programs course credit is given to students for working in jobs that supplement their class studies. Thus, a student majoring in business management might be placed as a management trainee at a local retail store. He or she would acquire valuable work experience with which to strengthen his or her practical education in business management. At the same time, the student would receive academic credit or pay for his or her efforts. Students at schools that do not have cooperative programs can still find part-time jobs. It is not a good idea to wait until graduation to gain your first work experiences. The more work- and management-related experiences that you can gain while still in school, the better equipped you will be for finding a good job when you finish. Many companies have recruiting, hiring or supervisory trainee programs. In these programs the trainee is groomed for a management position. Programs concentrate on the development of managerial skills and a familiarity with the operation of various departments within the company.

Your Best Shot

You want to maximize your chances of finding a good job that meets your needs, values, and interests. Finding a job is not too difficult— finding one really suited to you takes more time. Your success in getting a "good" job is not only affected by your job qualifications, but how you present yourself. Employers *are* influenced by such things as your appearance, clothing, and manners. If you walk into an interview right out of a baseball game, with grass-stained jeans and a torn sweatshirt, and treat the interviewer discourteously, do not be too surprised if you are not hired. You should prepare a neat, well-organized resumé containing your educational background, work experiences, and skills. Make use of any "contacts" or "leads" you have. You should not feel funny about doing this, since it is a common practice in the business world. Check newspaper ads and your campus career planning and placement office. You will undoubtedly have to set up and attend many interviews. If an interview does not work out successfully, try to determine what went wrong and how you can improve your performance next time. In being an interviewee, you

Community college merchandising student gets practical experience in a work-study program.

are trying to "sell yourself." It is a good idea to have one of your friends interview you to give you practice answering questions as well as feedback about how you can improve your presentation.

A Job Is What You Make of It

Even a "good" job will only be as good as *you* make it. You will be given certain responsibilities and will be required to perform a variety of tasks. You can put forth the bare minimum and just "get by," or you can put in effort to make the job work for you. You have certain talents and interests that, if you use a little ingenuity, can be incorporated into your job to make it more personally satisfying. That may involve using your creativity, making a special effort to get to know your co-workers, or contributing a little something extra. You have to take an active stance to make your job work for you and better meet your needs.

Knowing When to Bail Out

Like everything in life, not all jobs are successes. Sometimes a job does not meet your career needs and it is time to "bail out." As we said earlier, building in contingency plans and alternate paths is an important aspect of career planning. When one path does not work out, you are not left stranded. Knowing when to bail out of a job or career is difficult to define. In many ways, it is a very subjective matter. Unhappiness, excessive anxiety, and boredom are usually indicators that something is wrong. Sometimes these conditions can be changed by talking with your supervisor and making the appropriate changes. Sometimes they have to be weathered through in the short run because the long-term benefits will be satisfying to you. Sometimes they indicate that you have chosen a job or career that does not meet your needs, interests, and goals or is incompatible with your talents, skills, and abilities. You have to assess the situation and reassess your career values and plans to determine the proper course of action. Sometimes "bailing out" means finding a new job within the same career direction. Sometimes it means finding a new career direction. Some hard thinking and feedback from your supervisor, co-workers, a counselor, or friends are necessary.

Strictly for Women

Women should realize that the work world is not yet free of prejudices and "hang-ups." Many men, especially older men, still think that "a woman's place is in the home." Many who have accepted women into the work force still feel that women's work positions should be "lower" than those of men. Some are threatened by female authority, and others are just plain "male chauvinists." Society has yet to achieve a state of "people liberation." At times, certain women, in an attempt to prove themselves or to offset the attitudes of male colleagues who have underestimated their talents, will be excessively assertive and aggressive. This position often serves to increase tensions and support prejudices. It is rather difficult to deal with because it is usually a defensive reaction. Sometimes, however, it may be the *only* way to overcome obstacles.

The Real World: Race, Creed, Color

It goes without saying that our society has not achieved equality of race, creed, and color, even though these rights are guaranteed by our Constitution. Prejudice still exists, and it is not absent from the world of work. Though nondiscrimination in work is the law of the land, many employees continue to practice discrimination in their hiring and promotion procedures and in their treatment of employees. Discriminating practices and biased behavior should be brought to the attention of offenders and talked out. Sometimes this may not be sufficient. Infringements should be reported to management or even to the appropriate government agency.

Coping

If you are having trouble or encountering problems, do not keep them to yourself and "add wood to the fire." It is usually a good idea to talk out your problems with friends or peers. Perhaps they can give you suggestions on how to cope with a situation. In talking things over you will gain a clearer picture of the situation in which you are involved. You may also find that it is not as unusual or strange a circumstance as you thought. Others may be experiencing similar problems and frustrations. Perhaps you should approach your boss and tell him how you feel. He may be able to help you work things out. Getting the support and feedback of others will enable you to better cope with your career and your life.

SUMMARY

Career management is a two-sided process: individual career planning and organizational career management. The individual needs to view his or her whole working life as the unfolding of a career. Through careful assessment of personal needs, interests, values, skills, abilities, and talents, and the gaining of adequate career-related information, the individual can determine specific, realistic, manageable goals for himself or herself. In turn, these provide a basis for developing career paths and contingency plans to obtain those goals. The individual is primarily responsible for the direction of his or her career. As he or she gains knowledge, experience, and a sense of his or her own work style and preferences he or she will become increasingly self-directed.

The organization needs to be concerned with the careers of its members in order to ensure that the needs and goals of the organization are fulfilled, namely, increased efficiency and continued growth. The organization develops recruiting, training, and development programs in order to maximize the satisfaction of human resource requirements. These, in turn, further the achievement of organizational goals. The growing numbers of women and minorities entering the work force, coupled with shifting political, economic, and government trends, have all contributed to changes in the way individuals see their careers and the way in which organizations deal with their members. Managers can learn to cope more effectively with the needs of their employees or associates when they begin to consider the different life spaces influencing individual actions and performances. In turn, individuals need to understand the workings and ladders of career progress in their organizations. Individuals and organizations must achieve a mutual accommodation of what is desired, needed, and available.

Questions for Study and Discussion

1. What are the two sides of career management? What is the focus of each?

2. Give a few examples of how new legislation has intensified the need for career management.

3. What is a *critical mass?* How does this concept apply to careers today?

4. Explain the "structure" concept of looking at occupations.

5. Explain the new concept of adult education.

6. How do past and modern practices differ in terms of being qualified for a particular job?

7. What is the fundamental assumption of individual career planning and career self-study materials?

8. What are some career changes that have taken place from the viewpoint of the individual?

9. What is the common ground for individual and organizational career management?

10. Describe how the life-space concept can be applied to organizational career management.

11. What are the basic elements of individual career planning?

12. What are the main qualities of wisely chosen career goals?

13. What is a life cycle? What are its implications?

14. What kinds of people and activities are involved in organization human resource planning? In organization career management?

15. How does communications fit into career activity?

16. What are career ladders? How have they changed?

17. How has the description of managerial or supervisory function changed?

18. What are some points of entry into supervision and management?

19. Make a career–life line for yourself.

20. Develop your own career plan.

21. What do you consider basic requirements of temperament for a successful line manager?

CASE: J.B. STORES

J.B. Stores was a national chain of general merchandise stores handling goods such as inexpensive clothing, housewares, automotive supplies, garden items, and household drugs. In a 10-year period, this company tripled its number of stores and was selling through more than 500 outlets.

The store chain was more than 20 years old, but for a long time had grown at a very slow pace. About 12 years ago, the President and founder had been on a routine field trip and met a sudden death in a car accident. The Board of Directors felt that a major leadership vacuum had been created and that it should be filled as rapidly as possible. But all felt that the person selected must be able to guide them aggressively to achieve the potential they felt existed for their business.

An extensive job search was undertaken through the usual channels. The company also informed its many suppliers of its need. The person finally selected for the Presidency was Mary Beth Kennedy, a Vice President for a large advertising firm. Kennedy's firm was thoroughly familiar with the merchandising–retail business, and she herself had been an account executive for J.B. Stores. She also had about eight years of retail experience with another very large retail chain similar to the Sears, Roebuck Company. The amazing part of the whole series of events was the fact that Mary Beth was only 35 years old when offered the Presidency—it was solid recognition for a remarkable career. She graduated college at 21 years of age with a good, but not unusual, academic record. After college, Mary Beth went to work for a large, national retail firm and remained with them for eight years. She loved the work and eventually became the manager of one or their large stores. After a few years, she decided to leave and take a crack at her own business.

Mary chose the field of advertising, because of her creative flair and her ability to deal with people and interpret the needs of clients. She ran her own business quite successfully for more than three years, when she was "spotted" by the senior officer of a national advertising firm. She received a salary offer with fringes and partnership participation, a deal "she could not refuse." When she was offered the Presidency of J.B. Stores, the advertising firm felt it appropriate to "step aside" so that she could further pursue her career.

A Period of Great Growth

Mary Beth Kennedy completely immersed herself in the activities and problems of the store chain. Her aggressive merchandising policies and creative advertising and promotion ideas sparked highly profitable growth. At the same time she initiated an aggressive new store program that resulted in several new outlets being opened every month, over a four-year period. Mary Beth was deeply immersed in the plans and programs needed to support the rapid expansion of J.B. Stores. Yet, as the chain started to reach the 500 mark, she experienced a growing feeling that some important elements in the picture were not coming together. For several years, the senior managers had tried, with increasing difficulty, to find or develop enough capable people for store management, not to mention the many floor and department supervisors also required. A case in point was the planned opening of three new stores in the Atlanta, Georgia area. Store location, construction, and initial inventory stock had been planned well. Also, the local advertising and promotion program was carefully laid out and contained the same elements that had been so successful elsewhere. However, only one of the three people chosen for store managers was available for the two-week preopening, training period. The other two had left the company. In addition, the supervisory nucleus to be drawn in from other stores was incomplete, and supervisors were "unavailable" in several of the key, high-traffic departments.There were some similar problems with local personnel plans. It had been their intention to draw and train some of the supervisors from people hired locally. This was only partially successful for a variety of reasons. Some of the people hired, though talented, had a fear of supervisory responsibilities and turned down the opportunity. In other situations, local labor conditions were tight, and it was hard to attract talented people that could be trained for supervisor.

What's Going On?

The President asked Fred Jenkins, Vice President of Personnel, to stop by Mary Beth's office so that they could review and discuss the store management situation. Fred and Mary Beth reviewed the developments of the last two years in great detail, since most of their managerial problems had surfaced during this period. In the course of the discussion, Mary Beth remarked to Fred: "I've heard an awful lot lately about employees and their *careers* . . . but not enough of them seem to be making their careers with us. How are we going to get on top of this?"

Questions

A. Mary Beth Kennedy—Person:
   1. Draw a time–career life line for Mary Beth Kennedy.
   2. What personal factors seemed to account for her success?
   3. Did Mary Beth have a career plan?
   4. Where was she in her career life cycle?
B. Mary Beth Kennedy—President:
   5. What was the "store management" problem?
   6. What business and other factors brought about the situation?
   7. What do you see as the general managerial responsibility and functions for the following?
      (a) Department supervisor in a J.B. store.
      (b) Store manager in a J.B. store.
      (c) Regional manager for a group of stores.
   8. What type of people planning should have been taking place? Why was there such a shortage of managerial talent?
   9. What should the role be of store supervisors and managers in

training and developing people? What resources and abilities do they need?

10. Propose a career management program for J.B. Stores. Describe briefly how it might work.

Optional assignment: Take the role of Fred Jenkins. Prepare a preliminary managerial report for the President. Use the following format. Under each main heading are some topics that could be covered.

I. Background of Situation

What's been happening generally in the economy.
Events in J.B. Stores, its growth, current needs.
General problems.
Purpose of report ("to summarize briefly the situation regarding the managerial situation and to set out a preliminary action program for improvement").
Key assumptions.

II. Analysis

Growth of organization.
Managerial and supervisory needs.
Business planning and people needs.
The need for career management.
The training and development of supervisors and managers.
Future needs.

III. Preliminary Proposal

Policy.
System.
Programs.
Potential problems.
Discussion.

References

Beam, Henry, "A Framework for Personal Development," *Human Resource Management,* **19**(2) (Summer 1980): 2–8.

Burack, Elmer, Maryann Albrecht, and Helene Seitler, *Growing—A Woman's Guide to a Successful Career.* Belmont, Ca.: Lifetime Learning Press (1980).

Burack, Elmer, and Nicholas Mathys, "Career Ladders, Pathing and Planning: Some Neglected Basics," *Human Resource Management,* **18**(2) (Summer 1979): 2–8.

————, *Organization Career Management.* Lake Forest, Ill.: Brace-Park Press (1980).

Burack, Elmer H., and Robert D. Smith, *Personnel Management: A Human Resource Systems Approach.* New York: John Wiley (1982), especially Chapter 18.

Dalton, Gene W., Paul H. Thompson, and Raymond L. Price, "The Four Stages of Professional Careers—A New Look at Performance by Professionals," *Organizational Dynamics*, **6** (Summer 1977): 19–42.

Erikson, Erik H., *Childhood and Society*. 2nd ed. New York: Norton (1963).

Ference, Thomas P., James A. F. Stoner, and E. Kirby Warren, "Managing the Career Plateau," *Academy of Management Review*, **2** (October 1977): 602–612.

Hall, Douglas T., *Careers in Organizations*. Pacific Palisades, Cal.: Goodyear Publishing Co. (1976).

Hall, Francine S., and Douglas T. Hall, "Dual Careers—How do Couples and Companies Cope with the Problems?" *Organizational Dynamics*, **6** (Spring 1978): 57–77.

Kaye, Beverly L., "How Can You Help Employees Formulate Their Career Goals?" *Personnel Journal*, **59**(5) (May 1980): 368–372, 402.

Kosnik, Thomas J., "The Young Manager—Aiming for the 'Right' Company: Choosing from Among Job Offers," *S.A.M. Advanced Management Journal*, **44** (Spring 1979): 44–54.

Leach, John, "The Career Planning Process," *Personnel Journal*, **60**(4) (April 1981): 283–287.

"Legal Battle of the Sexes," *Newsweek* **11** (April 30, 1979): 68–75.

Luthans, Fred, David Lyman, and Diane L. Lockwood, "An Individual Management Development Approach," *Human Resource Management*, **17**(3) (Fall 1978): 1–5.

Morgan, Marilyn A., Douglas T. Hall, and Alison Martier, "Career Development Strategies in Industry—Where Are We and Where Should We Be?" *Personnel*, **56** (March-April 1979): 13–30.

Schalders, William N., "Developing an In-House Career Planning Workshop," *The Personnel Administrator*, **25**(10) (October 1980): 45–46.

Schein, Edgar H., *Career Dynamics: Matching Individual and Organizational Needs*. Reading, Mass.: Addison-Wesley (1978).

Sheehy, Gail, *Passages*. New York: E.P. Dutton (1976).

Super, Donald, and Martin Bohr, Jr., *Occupational Psychology*. Belmont, Ca.: Wadsworth (1970).

"Teaching Women How to Manage Their Careers," *Business Week*, **28** (May 1979): 150ff.

Walker, James W., "Does Career Planning Rock the Boat?" *Human Resource Management*, **17**(1) (Spring 1978): 2–7.

———, "Let's Get Realistic About Career Paths," *Human Resource Management*, **15**(3) (Fall 1976): 2–7.

Walter, Verne, "Self-Motivated Personal Career Planning: A Breakthrough in Human Resource Management," *Personnel Journal*, **55** (March 1976): 112–115ff.

GLOSSARY

Acceptance theory of leadership (authority). A theory associated with Barnard which suggests that a subordinate's decision to accept a superior's order is the ultimate source of authority.

Achievement-motive. Refers to work motivation induced by a person's need or desire to achieve.

Activities. Time-consuming parts of work processes, denoted by arrows in procedural or network diagrams.

Assessment center. A systematic technique used to evaluate employees through exercises such as simulation, interviews, and group exercises in order to aid in the selection of future managers.

Authority. (1) (Fayol) "A combination of official (derived from one's position) and personal (combining intelligence, experience, moral worth, past service, etc.) factors." (2) The official right and power to make decisions affecting the behavior of subordinates, including the right to give orders and demand obedience, that is, the right to direct others. (3) Power to influence or command thought, opinion, or behavior.

Autocratic. Used here regarding a managerial style in which one person possesses the key organizational (decision-making) power.

Automation. Automatically controlled operation of a process or a system by mechanical or electronic devices that take the place of humans.

Functional authority. The right or power inherent in a position to issue instructions or to approve actions of persons in positions not reporting directly to the person holding such authority.

Line authority. The kind of authority where a superior has direct supervision over a person.

Staff authority. The nature of the staff relationship is advisory; therefore, the authority vested in staff positions stems from experience, expertise, and function.

Behavior modification. A motivational concept which holds that behavior that is positively reinforced is likely to be repeated in the future and is superior to behavior that is negatively reinforced.

Board of directors. A group of people usually selected by shareholders in a company and required by law to monitor the actions of officers administering the company.

Bounded rationality. Decision-making conditions such that limited information forces the manager to identify and analyze only some of the alternatives available and then to select, from these, an alternative that he or she predicts will yield a satisfactory return to the organization.

Brainstorming. A method for developing new ideas and/or solutions to a problem in which a group of people is encouraged to submit (propose) as many ideas as possible, regardless of how far-fetched. The most feasible idea is then chosen and adapted.

Break-even analysis. A planning and decision-making tool that indicates among other results, the level of operations required for total revenue to equal total cost.

Budget. (1) A plan listing all the expenditures and income expected during a given future period for an individual or an organization. (2) A statement of plans and expected results expressed in numerical terms (a "numberized" program).

Bureaucracy. A formal organization structure that emphasizes a rational, carefully developed system of specializing and coordinating work, adherence to fixed rules, and a hierarchy of authority. The concept and its development is that of Max Weber.

Career. A life-work activity for which one is trained or a sequence of work and life experiences; or, more broadly, a satisfying human experience; a major result of one's work; a life activity.

Career ladder. A "ladder" in which the successive steps symbolize the different levels in one's career.

Career path. The road leading from the first level of a career to the last (and presumably highest), through stages of work, individual development, learning experiences, and promotion.

Career planning (individual). Decisions involved in career choices—the planning of one's life work and fulfillment of individual needs, values, abilities, and interests within a career life context.

Career planning system. A system in which organizational career management joins business planning with human resource plans to achieve business goals, and then, thoughtfully connects the individual into this complex system.

Career stages. The broad segments of a working career, such as early-, mid- and late career. Each stage often reflects various types of characteristic problems, issues, and personal development.

Carrying costs. The direct costs of keeping inventory on hand.

Change. The process of transforming an entity from one state to another, to modify or make radically different. Often the result of social, technical, political, or economic trends.

Change agent. Consultant or company member used as a facilitator or catalyst in administering or facilitating. May also be a formal role as part of organization development.

Change management. The skillful administering of a change process or program to help the organization cope with a changing environment and new challenges.

Chain of command. The communications and order-giving chain of superior-subordinate relationships in an organization.

Centralization. The act or process of concentrating power and authority, higher up or at the top of the organization. May also be used in a geographic sense as in the concentration of facilities.

Certainty. Decision-making conditions that are predictable or (essentially) unchanging.

Climate. Environmental conditions characterizing a group or an organization. The latter may encompass rules, policies, and the reward system of the organization.

Coach/coaching technique. A widely used management development technique in which ef-

fective managers develop new managers by one on one teaching.

Cognition. The act or process of knowing, including both awareness and judgment.

Cohesiveness. The degree to which group members act uniformly, present a united front, or as a single unit (rather than as individuals) in the pursuit of group objectives.

Colleague management. A highly participative management style, often among a group of individuals considered to be peers, that is based on professional affiliation, business and organization skills, experience, education, or potential contribution to an organization's welfare.

Committee. A group of individuals established by an organization who are officially empowered to consider issues affecting the organization, or to function in a certain capacity, that is, to deal with a specific issue.

Communication. The interactive process of exchanging information.

Communication network. A system of organized channels of communication often formally established in the organization. For those informally established, see "Grapevine."

Concept. An image or abstract idea conceived in the mind.

Concurrent control. Control that takes place simultaneously with the work being performed.

Conformity. A measure of individual adherence to group norms as a result of perceived group pressure or commonly shared ideas.

Conglomerate. Corporations with large, diversified holdings that have been acquired through a series of business transactions. There need be no relationship among the businesses acquired. (A widely diversified company.)

Consensus. General agreement.

Consideration. Continuous and careful thought, taking various factors into account. In a leadership context, the term is one of two styles thought to be used by leaders. In this context, it refers to empathy, sensitive treatment, and essentially people-oriented management.

Contingency approach. A concept that recognizes the differences in people and the specifics of a situation such that the appropriate leadership style, organizational design, or market strategy depends on the unique circumstances and features of the particular situation (facing the organization or the manager).

Contingency model of leadership. A theory formulated by Fiedler suggesting that the most effective style of leadership chosen depends on the particular situation and takes into account the nature of work, the power of the supervisor and leader-group relationships.

Contingency planning. The process of developing a set of alternative plans to fit a variety of possible future conditions.

Contingency oriented. See "Contingency approach."

Control. The function of assuring the effective performance of the organizational system by establishing standards of performance and then comparing those standards to actual performance, taking corrective action if necessary.

Corrective action. Activity aimed at bringing organizational performance back to a standard or desired level (after a deviation from desired results).

Coordination. Achieving harmony of individual effort (with work, customer needs, etc.) toward the accomplishment of organization, department, or group purposes and objectives.

Creativity/creative thinking. "The mental activity in a problem-stating/problem-solving situation where artistic or technical inventions are the result" (William Gordon). The activity typically leads to new associations between existing concepts and ideas or quite new ideas and/or approaches.

Critical incidents method. An approach to job analysis that focuses on direct, objective acts or what individuals must do to satisfy job and organizational requirements, rather than on indirect measures like personality assessment tests.

Critical path method. A technique for scheduling and/or cost control that employs a network that reflects all of the events and activities to be accomplished in a project, and their critical interrelationships. The critical path is that sequence of activities through the network requiring the least time, start to finish.

Culture. Behavior patterns and values of (a) social group(s).

Cybernetics. The field of theory behind self-regulating logical processes.

Decentralization. (1) (of authority). The tendency to disperse decision-making authority in an organization structure. (2) (of performance). Dispersion or distribution of functions and powers from a central authority to regional and local authorities. See the definition for centralization for a more rounded view of the concept. The geographic dispersal of operations in an enterprise.

Decision making. The process of evaluating and deciding on a given or alternative course of action.

Decision theory. An analysis of management activities and functions that concentrates on *rational decision making* as the core of the management task in which a set of general concepts and techniques aid the decision maker in choosing between alternatives.

Delegation of authority. The vesting, by a supervisor, of decision-making discretion in a subordinate. The determination of results expected from a subordinate, the assignment of tasks, delegation of authority for accomplishing these tasks, and the nature of responsibility for the accomplishment are part of this act.

Delphi-method (technique). A group forecasting and decision-making technique in which the members respond to questionnaires asking for their expert judgments on a particular topic. The process is carried out as a series of decision stages. Members benefit from the responses of other panelists but do not interact directly with each other. (Also called "jury of executive opinions.")

Department. A distinct area, division, or branch of an enterprise over which a manager has authority for the performance of specified activities and results.

Departmentalization/departmentation (by function). The grouping of activities in accordance with a characteristic or common function such as engineering, credit, production, or X-ray.

Design. An underlying scheme that governs the functioning of an organization or system.

Dictionary of occupational titles (DOT). A classification of more than 20,000 jobs, which provides information about them for employment and statistical purposes.

Differentiation. The tendency for a system to become more specialized in its structure and behavior patterns. This is accomplished by dividing the organization into areas of specialization or subsystems so that each of the subsystems can better adapt to its part of the total external environment and deal with it more effectively.

Discipline. Control gained by enforcing obedience or order, that is, an orderly or prescribed pattern of conduct or behavior.

Division of work. (Fayol) "The specialization of tasks necessary to achieve efficiency in the use of labor."

Division of labor. The principle of dividing a job into all of its component operations, and having each operation (or a small number of operations) performed separately by one worker.

Drive. A force resulting from tension and leading to personal action or an attempt to carry out a particular activity (part of the motivational process).

Dual careers. Two professions pursued simultaneously.

Economic Order Quantity (EOQ). The quantity of raw materials, parts, products, or supplies that should be purchased to minimize total inventory costs.

Effective. The quality or state of being operative, producing a decided, decisive, or desired effect.

Efficiency. Operation as measured by a comparison of output with cost or what was obtained for the energy, resources or time committed.

Element. (of work) A combination of two or more micromotions, usually thought of as a more or less complete entity, such as picking up, transporting, and positioning an item.

Environment. The aggregate of social and cultural conditions affecting the existence of an organization.

Equal Employment Opportunity (EEO). Legislation prohibiting discrimination on the basis of race, color, creed, sex or national origin when hiring people for employment.

Events. Denoted by circles in network diagrams, these represent completion of work.

Exchange. Reciprocal giving and receiving.

Executive. In business, a loosely used term for a manager; one who makes decisions and sees that they are carried out.

Expectancy theory approach. This approach to work assumes that several work or career options are available to a person and that each individual has the capacity to make a conscious choice among alternatives relative to valued goals or objectives.

Expectancy theory of motivation. A motivation theory proposing that people make conscious choices of activity based on their expectations about the future and a sense of valued goals or objectives.

Expected value. The numerical value of an outcome that results when multiplying (alternative) costs or gains with assigned probabilities.

External system. The work or behavioral patterns exhibited by organization members, prescribed by rules or regulations. Also see "Internal system" for the other aspect of this concept. The work supporting this idea is that of Georges Homans.

Extrinsic rewards. "Tangible" rewards such as increased pay, promotion, or improved working conditions.

Factoring. The process of taking responsibility for collecting accounts receivable, and for customers' credit.

Facilitator. A kind of change agent to communicate and implement change.

Feedback. The return of information or data on results so that future performance can be improved based on past activity or results.

Force field analysis. An analytic attempt to sketch the social and psychological forces affecting members of a work group, and to determine their likely direction of change. This theory is attributed to Kurt Lewin.

Forecasting. Anticipating future business conditions and the state of the economy on the basis of various assumptions and statistics that describe past and current conditions.

Formal group. A collection of individuals formed by management or the organization and charged with specific functional responsibility.

Formal organization. The managerially specified structure of relationships and related procedures that are used to manage organizational activities.

Franchise. (1) An exclusive right granted by a government to an individual or firm, to perform a service or activity of a public nature. (2) **Dealer franchise.** A continuing relationship between a manufacturer or specialist in a service and a retailer, in which the former supplies the latter with manufacturing and/or marketing techniques, a brand image, and other expertise for a price: for example, McDonald's.

Function. (1) Professional or official position. (2) The action for which a person or thing or unit is specially fitted or used.

Functional authority. An individual who has the responsibility and rights to give orders involving a particular area of work activity in one's own department as well as other units.

Gantt-chart. A graphic means of planning work related activities and the time required for them. Also may be used for control by facilitating the comparison of actual performance with a predetermined standard.

Goal/objective. The end toward which effort is directed. The end points of planning toward which activity is aimed. Purposes of an organization, including service objectives, profit objectives, and social objectives.

Grapevine. An informal communications network that arises spontaneously without managerial sanction.

Grass roots. The expression used when referring to the lower level of a society or an organization, as distinguished from the higher levels of power and leadership.

Hawthorne Studies. Studies undertaken by industrial researchers under the direction of Elton Mayo between 1927 and 1932 at the Hawthorne (Illinois) facility of the Western Electric Company. These studies led to an emphasis on the social and behavioral aspects of managing workers.

Hearing. The process of *perceiving* sound.

Human relations. The relations between the individual members of the organization. This term is also used with reference to a school of thought in management science that focuses on the relationship and interaction between superiors and subordinates.

Hygiene approach to motivation. Psychologist Frederick Herzberg's theory that certain human needs motivate and others merely cause dissatisfaction if they are not met. The latter class of needs is made up of "maintenance" or "hygiene" factors. In a work situation these factors are salary, company policy and administration, quality of supervision, working conditions, interpersonal relations, status, and job security.

In-basket exercises. A simple simulation in which the trainee is presented with a number of letters and memos requiring judgment as to appropriate actions within a specified time limit.

Industrial dynamics. A simulation approach to planning and control in which flows of information, materials, personnel, capital equipment, and money are viewed as an interacting system that influences performance, enterprise growth, fluctuation, and decline.

Industrial Revolution. The period of economic change from the late eighteenth century to the mid-nineteenth century, during which the economies of many western countries, until then based on craft and agriculture, became industrialized, following inventions such as the steam engine and the cotton gin.

Informal group. A collection of individuals that arises as a natural outgrowth of human interaction, developing without conscious managerial effort. People are held together by commonly shared values, problems, interests, and the like.

Informal leader. A "natural" leadership figure arising spontaneously from a group of organization members, without formal appointment or management actions.

Informal organization. Joint activities and relationships, specific among individuals, often built on social needs and arising from and "supplementing" the formal organization structure.

Initiator. Used in the text as a person instructed or adept in a special field. Synonymous with change agent.

Inputs. The materials, information, and other items that a system acquires (imports) from its environment, for example, raw materials for a manufacturer.

Integration/vertical. The expansion of a business through the acquisition of more divisions or other firms engaged in earlier or later stages of processing of a directly related product or service.

Integration/horizontal. The expansion of a business through the acquisition of related distribution capabilities or directly related processing capabilities that are essentially the same as those already possessed.

Interaction. Mutual/reciprocal action or influence (as in communications).

Interdependence. The mutual dependence of one person, unit, or department on another.

Internal system. Behavioral patterns emerging from the formal "external system" that are often informal in nature.

Intrinsic reward. Warm personal feelings or a sense of achievement resulting from one's performance, accomplishments, or successes.

Inventory turnover. A comparison of sales to average inventory levels over a specified period of time as an indicator of the effectiveness of inventory control.

Job. The set of all work tasks that must be performed by a worker.

Job analysis. Detailed study of a job to identify key work elements and to determine an efficient basis for the conduct of work.

Job descriptions. Listing of key job responsibilities or work-related functions to achieve success. Also, often includes reporting relationships and job highlights.

Job enlargement. Expanding job content with the intention of making it less specialized and more interesting—usually adding more, similar tasks.

Job enrichment. Making jobs more meaningful and challenging to the individual employee by adding responsibility and autonomy.

Job rotation. A technique designed to increase the employee's experience by shifting him or her periodically from one job to another.

Job satisfaction. The response or attitude of a person toward different dimensions of his or her work. Jobs are thought to have perhaps four or five different features, *each* of which may affect a person's sense of satisfaction.

Job specifications. A listing of the qualifications necessary to perform different jobs.

Leadership. The art or process of influencing people so that they will strive (willingly) toward the achievement of organizational or group goals.

Leadership continuum. The concept advanced by Tannenbaum and Schmidt in which leadership is viewed as involving a variety of styles that range from highly boss-centered to highly subordinate-centered, depending on situations and personalities.

Leadership behavior. Leadership style, that is, the manner in which a manager acts in his or her role as a leader.

Leadership styles. Various descriptive profiles have been developed such as: (1) *Autocratic:* absolute leadership to one person, with unlimited power and authority. (2) *Consultative:* a style in which a leader takes the opinions of others into account by deliberating with them before making a decision. (3) *Group:* cooperative leadership, that is, leadership authority shared among group members.

Leadership/trait studies. See "Trait approach to leadership."

Leading. Performing the act of leadership.

Learning curve. Graphic representations of improving performance on the part of the individual workers as they learn to do specific tasks.

Liaison (unit). Organizational unit with responsibility for coordinating the activities of two or more units of the organization.

Life cycle. A series of stages through which an individual group or system passes during its lifetime that are thought to reflect characteristic human development issues and experiences. Also, see "Career stages."

Life space model. A model that identifies the major components of a manager's environment. These components are the internal climate or environment of the organization, the environment external to the organization, the technological work environment, and the work groups and individuals with whom the manager must deal or supervise. The model focuses on the manager's relationships to those elements in his or her environment that lead to a unified system of managing respective portions of the work world.

Line position. Line positions are those that have *direct* responsibility for accomplishing the objectives of the enterprise.

Linear programming. A mathematical technique used to determine an optimal or best solution for an objective given multiple resources and subject to stated restraints.

Long-range planning. Planning for a rather extended period of time in the future, often three or more years, to foresee the fulfillment of commitments being made today; attempting to take into account the future impact of today's decisions.

Maintenance (hygiene) factors. See "Hygiene approach to motivation."

Management. The job of planning, organizing, and controlling any enterprise or functional unit and to achieve certain stated objectives.

Management by Objectives (MBO). A planning technique in which a subordinate and immediate superior jointly establish goals for the subordinate. The goals are used to motivate, develop, control, and evaluate the subordinate's performance.

Management development. The process of individual growth for the full utilization of one's managerial capabilities.

Management Information System (M.I.S.). A system that collects data on internal operations and the external environment and transforms the data into information that is presented or available to managers in *usable* and relevant form.

Management science. Often associated with managerial analyses and decision making based on statistical or mathematical models, and the use of the computer. In general, systematic approaches to the management area.

Managerial grid. A specific technique of analyzing leadership styles whereby leaders are classified on a grid with two dimensions—concern for people and concern for production. This technique is based on leadership research done at Ohio State University.

Managers. Those who undertake the task and functions of managing, at any level, in any kind of enterprise.

Man-Machine system. A semiautomated system in which the worker still has significant personal influence on the quality and quantity of output. Generally, a term to emphasize the combination of human and technical elements accounting for performance.

Market-share. An often used benchmark in measuring company performance referring to the percentage share of the total (industry) market served by one particular firm.

Mass production. Usually involves production in high quantity/volume using numerous machines and controls, and carefully organized to achieve high level performance.

Matrix structure. An organizational structure in which both vertical authority relationships and "horizontal" work relationships coexist and have been made a permanent part of the organization structure. Additionally, the makeup of the work relationships or group members will vary depending on the projects or tasks to be performed.

Maximizing. Behavior in which the manager selects from all possible alternatives the "best" alternative yielding maximum returns (to the organization).

Mechanistic organization. An organization characterized by a rigid division of roles into functional specialties. Duties and responsibilities are well defined, and the decisions tend to be made at upper levels of the hierarchy.

Mentor. A (more) experienced individual who provides guidance and assistance to a newcomer in an organization.

Micromotion.   The smallest work activities, involving elementary movements such as reaching, grasping, positioning, or releasing an object.

Mission or purpose.   The *basic function* or task of an enterprise or agency or any department of it.

Mobility.   The capability of individuals moving or being moved to different departments, functional units, or organizations.

Model.   A simplified representation of an actual system that provides understanding a more complex situation or relationship.

Motivation.   (1) A need or desire causing a person to act. (2) A concept that refers to the direction, strength, and persistence of an individual's behavior.

Motivators.   Forces that induce individuals to act or perform; forces that influence human behavior. Also, used in a specialized way by Frederick Herzberg to denote satisfier factors.

Need hierarchy.   A widely used classification of human needs with five levels arranged in a hierarchy ranging from physiological needs to self-actualization needs. Developed by Abraham Maslow.

Network analysis techniques.   The term used to describe project planning methods involving sequential and multiple relationships. Two well-known approaches are CPM and PERT.

Nonprogrammed.   Usually referring to decisions in situations for which there is no predetermined method of dealing with them.

Nonroutine decision.   Decisions dealing with unstructured, nonrecurring problems, without a predetermined method of resolution.

Norm.   A generally agreed on standard of behavior or level of performance to which group members are expected to adhere or strive.

Objective.   Something toward which effort is directed, an aim or end of action (see goal). In this book, used in a way to suggest an intermediate point toward securing a goal.

Obsolescence.   Here used to describe employees who are becoming less functional in their work because of a lack of updated skills and knowledge to maintain effective performance.

Open system.   A system that interacts with or is exposed to its external environment.

Operations research.   Application of the scientific method and research techniques to the solution of organizational, logistical, and many other types of problems.

Optimizing.   Choosing the best option among alternatives to achieve maximum efficiency, either with minimal cost or maximum output value.

Office of the president.   Part of the colleague management approach, often consisting of (a number of) people who share the responsibilities of the firm's senior person and who seek consensus on important issues, or when faced with complex problems or situations.

Order costs.   The clerical and administrative costs necessary to place an order.

Organic organization.   Roles and job structure are loosely defined. Emphasis is on flexibility, person-to-person relations, and adaptability to change. (Examples are R & D laboratories, think tanks, etc.)

Organization career management.   Focuses on the needs of the organization and the demand for its products and services, brought together with career needs and concerns of individual organization members.

Organization (structure).   A concept used in a variety of ways such as (1) a system or pattern of any set of relationships in any kind of undertaking; (2) an enterprise; (3) cooperation of two or more persons; (4) all behavior of all participants in a group; and (5) the intentional structure of roles in a formally organized enterprise.

Organization development.   A planned effort to increase the organization's effectiveness and health through probing into its problems and adopting new techniques involving primarily its human resources. Also, studies of and attempts to improve, group effectiveness in organizations.

Organizational renewal.   Revitalization of the organization's ability to achieve its goals and cope with the environment.

Organizing.   The managerial activity involved in creating a formal structure of tasks, authority and relationships.

Outputs.   Materials, information, or other

items resulting from an enterprise's or system's activity—and furnished to its clientele or to other units.

Parkinson's law. A contention that work expands to fill available time, resulting in organizations that grow in size regardless of workload.

Participation. Usually refers to a leadership style in which the leader consults with subordinates, involving them in the decision-making process.

Path-goal theory of leadership. A leadership theory that views the leader's function as clarifying the subordinate's paths to work-goal attainment and increasing their opportunities for personal satisfaction.

Payoff table. A table in which different alternatives are combined with different states of nature, each assigned an appropriate probability, and with which it is possible to forecast the payoff or expected value of alternative decisions under different conditions.

Performance appraisal. Control designed to measure how effectively an individual has performed based on predetermined performance standards.

Personal power. The ability to influence the behavior of others stemming usually from the strength of an individual's personality.

Personnel Classification System. A system classifying employees by criteria such as skills, security, experience, and wage level.

Personnel Department. The functional unit of an organization formally assigned responsibilities for personnel activities.

PERT Program Evaluation and Review Technique (see "Network analysis" and "Critical path method").

Physiological needs. The basic needs for sustaining human life resulting from food, water, clothing, shelter, sleep, and sexual satisfaction.

Planning. Activities designed to define goals and determine methods by which to achieve them—inherently oriented to the future.

Planning process. A rational approach to accomplishing an objective and evaluating alternatives in the light of goals sought.

Policy. A basic statement that serves as a guide for administrative action. Policies are more general in nature than rules and procedures.

Power. The ability to influence the behavior of others based on personal qualities, authority, or political considerations.

Power motive. Refers to motivation induced by a desire to be in charge of, control, and/or direct other individuals.

Principles. Fundamental truths, or what are believed to be truths at a given time, explaining the relationships between two or more sets of variables, usually an independent variable and a dependent variable; principles may be descriptive, explaining what will happen, or prescriptive (or normative), indicating what a person should do. In the latter case, principles reflect a scale of values, such as efficiency, and therefore imply value judgments.

Principles of Management. Fundamental truths, or what are believed to be truths in the field of management science, as listed by Henri Fayol.

Precontrol/Preventative Control. Control that occurs *before* work is performed, that is, designing the work so as to minimize the need for direct supervision.

Proactive planning. Planning that seeks to take advantage of anticipated opportunities in the future.

Probability. A measure of likelihood of occurrence supported by strong, but not conclusive evidence.

Procedure. Chronological sequence of required actions detailing the exact manner in which an activity must be accomplished.

Process. A series of actions or operations leading to an end; a continuous operation or treatment, especially in manufacture.

Production. The use of technology to make goods (available) for human wants; the creation of utility.

Productions management/operations management. The management or administration of the physical production process. More generally, operations management deals with the planning, control, and administration of virtually any work process.

Profit. The surplus of sales dollars over expense dollars.

Program. A complex of policies, procedures, rules, task assignments, steps to be taken, resources to be employed, and other elements necessary to carry out a given course of action to achieve an objective, and normally supported by capital and operating budgets.

Programmed. Used here when describing predetermined responses to given or routine situations.

Project (planned). Undertaking of specific plan or design: for example, a definitely formulated piece of research, or a task/problem engaged in by someone.

Project management. The management of special tasks (projects) that cannot be easily handled by routine procedures and traditional organization structures, and for which a temporary group or task force is formed. Individual's requirement to satisfy or meet a sense of fulfillment in regards to acceptance, esteem, recognition, achievement, independence, and the like. Also, the needs to be fulfilled beyond one's physiological needs.

Quality of Work Life (QWL). A movement in recent management thought that seeks to improve the social and psychological dimensions of work and thus to improve the results of working for both the organization and the individual. Work redesign, more self-determination by work groups, and participation in managerial decision making are common aspects of QWL.

Reactive planning. Response to events that occur reflecting lack of anticipation or preplanning.

Reporting relationships. The formal structure of an organization, or the formal authority linkages and the network of superior-subordinate relationships in the organization.

Responsibility. The obligation or understanding of a job holder as to their duties, activities, and functions.

Return on investment (ROI). A measure of corporate financial success that is computed by dividing annual profits by capital or equity value.

Risk. (decision making) Conditions under which the possibility of loss or injury prevail. Also, in decision theory, indicates situations where some degree of uncertainty exists; therefore, probabilities of occurrence are (can be) assigned.

Role. The behavior or set of activities expected of a particular individual.

Routine decision. Decisions dealing with recurring problems, to which standard procedures apply.

Rule. A statement prescribing specific action to be taken for a given situation and permitting little or no discretion on the part of the manager.

Satisfaction. The contentment experienced when a want or need is met.

Satisfiers (Herzberg). Factors related to the job's content or task, mentioned when workers interviewed in Herzberg's study spoke of satisfaction with their work. Also, see "Hygiene factors" for the other aspect of this concept.

Service departments. Activities or units that support the line activities of an organization. The support of activities is provided by groups of specialists who facilitate such things as coordination, control, and administration.

Satisficing. Making a decision that is adequate to get the task done—recognizes that time or economic limitations do not permit an optimal response to be developed.

Scalar chain. Chain (of command arranged like a ladder) of hierarchical levels or authority relationships in an organization.

Schein's "Three Dimensions." A model of individual career mobility, taking into account the movements within and between units and authority levels.

Scientific management. Turn of the century (c. 1900) management studies that became known as "scientific management." Frederick W. Taylor was the central figure in this growing body of systematic management studies. It aimed to increase employee productivity through the systematic analysis of work, resulting in "one best way" to perform a task.

Sentiments. Attitudes or thoughts toward another prompted by personal feelings.

Share of market. (See "Market-share.")

Simulation. A model that represents the operations of a real system by describing the behavior of individual components of the system and the effects of their interaction. Decisions, and their possible outcomes, may be simulated for purposes of study without affecting the real system.

Single-use plans. Plans developed to meet a unique one of a kind situation.

Situational analysis. Similar to contingency management and employed when one recognizes differences in situations: an approach emphasizing that there can be no "one best way."

Situational approach to leadership. Leadership approaches that are based on the particulars of a given event, activity, or the like, confronting the person.

Social responsibility. The expectation that organizations should act in the public interest and contribute to the solution of social and ecological problems.

Socio-technical system. A system viewed as an interconnection of physical, technological and social elements in an organization.

Span of control. Refers to the (limited) number of persons a manager can supervise, that is, the number of subordinates reporting to a given manager. Also, may imply the number that can be dealt with effectively.

Specialization. The recognition that various aspects of work, due to growing complexity, require expertise of a particular type. Thus, craft skills as found in metal working operations, and in past decades, formal education, became increasingly associated with the knowledge base of "specialists."

Staff. Groups, the primary responsibility of which, is to support line activities, assist in organizational administration and provide advice or counsel as needed.

Staff authority. (See "Authority.")

Staff position. (See "Staff.")

Standard time. Represents the amount of time it takes for the average worker to complete a task under representative work conditions and at a normal work pace.

Standards of performance. The level of activity that serves as a target or model for evaluating work, unit, or organizational effort. (They are "benchmarks" determining the adequacy of organizational performance.)

Standing plan. Objectives, policies, and other plans which are continuous, and are designed to handle routine situations.

States of nature. Used here to describe characteristics of the external environment, some of which may be beyond the control of the decision maker.

Status. The standing or prestige of a person or group compared with other persons or groups.

Strategic planning. The process of determining how a business should make the best possible use (assignments) of its resources in the future, and specifically focused on the achievement of particular corporate goals and objectives.

Strategy. Program of action and deployment of resources to attain specific objectives or goals.

Structure. Interdependent parts or functions in a definite pattern of organization.

Suboptimization. Operating at a less-than-optimal level.

Supervisors. Like "Managers," but ordinarily refers to representatives of management at the lowest level, or first line, of managing.

System. (1) An interacting or interdependent group of items forming a unified whole. (2) A set of components that are related in the accomplishment of some purpose.

Systems approach to management. A school of thought emphasizing a series of steps of systematic thinking and analysis in the process of managerial function, planning, and problem solution.

Systems theory. A school of thought recognizing the organization as one element acting interdependently with a number of other elements in the external environment as well as itself being comprised of a number of interactive subsystems.

Tactic. Action plans by which strategies are executed.

Task. The combination of two or more elements into a complete activity.

Task force. A team of individuals responsible for coordinating a study or other efforts involving a number of organizational units. Also, see project group.

Technology. The body of knowledge concerned

with applying science to the production of goods and services or work systems generally.

Technological forecasting. Forecasting the future technologies that may affect the operations of an enterprise.

Tension. A condition and/or personal feeling brought about by the lack of fulfillment of individual needs (part of the motivational process).

Theory. A systematic grouping of interrelated principles and concepts that reflects sufficient understanding of a subject area to permit prediction of results when various changes or modifications occur affecting the subject area.

Theory X-Theory Y. Two schools of management thought, theory X being the technically oriented scientific approach, and theory Y emphasizing the social structure promulgated by human relations advocates. Work attributed to Douglas McGregor.

Think tank. Research and development group, originally formed by companies and the government to improve the creative process in organizations.

Time and motion study. Type of analysis made by the followers of Frederick Taylor and his scientific management school of thought to determine what a fair day's work really was, and to find the one best way of doing any given job. Techniques involve study of elemental work units and time measurements.

Trait approach to leadership. The approach that studies leadership by identifying physical, mental, and personality aspects of the person.

Unity of command. A precept holding that employees should receive orders from one superior only.

Uncertainty. State of (decision-making) conditions under which something is not certain or cannot be relied on to occur. In decision theory, "uncertainty" reflects a situation in which ordinary probabilities (as in "risk" conditions) can't be assigned.

Valence. A term used in the expectancy theory of motivation to denote the degree of importance of an outcome to an individual.

Validity. The state of being supported by objective truth or generally accepted authority—to have a conclusion correctly derived from premises.

Value. A person's innermost idea of an ideal or highly desired mode of behavior or personal conduct. Generally related to the type of person he or she wants to be, and the life he or she wants to lead.

Venture structure. A project management structure designed to foster innovation and creativity within organizations, usually by establishing a venture unit within an existing department and supplying it with the necessary resources and authority.

Venture teams. Groups consisting of individuals appointed by managers to study the feasibility and advisability of engaging in certain activities.

Vroom-Yetton leadership model. Theory of leadership that clarifies the conditions under which subordinates should participate in decision making, and to what extent. Also, a development approach to improving the leadership performance of individuals.

Wage incentives. Individual pay that is related to the quantity produced. Also, the extra payments for production above a predetermined standard.

Work design. Defined as the function of specifying the work activities of an individual or group in an organizational setting.

Zero-based budgeting. A budgeting technique requiring managers to justify their entire budget request in detail.

Zone of indifference. A category of subordinate attitudes toward authority in which certain orders are accepted without question.

PHOTO CREDITS

Chapter 1   Chapter Opener: Daniel S. Brody/Stock Boston. Page 11: New York Public Library. Page 16: Courtesy Ford Motor Company. Page 19: Elyse Rieder Courtesy of American Management Association. Page 21: Samuel C. Williams Library of Stevens Institute of Technology, Hoboken, New Jersey. Page 29: Courtesy of Xerox. Page 31: Courtesy of Holiday Inn, Inc. Page 34: Courtesy of New York Automobile Show.

Chapter 2   Chapter Opener: Louis Goldman/Photo Researchers. Page 48: Culver Pictures. Page 54: Courtesy of Professor Ronald Greenwood. Page 62: Ellis Herwig/Stock Boston. Page 64: L. Merrim/Monkmeyer. Page 67: Courtesy General Motors Corp. Page 70: Joel Gordon. Page 72: Courtesy of Bechtel Corp. Page 75: Courtesy of Bell Labs.

Chapter 3   Chapter Opener: Tom Hollyman/Photo Researchers. Page 88: Courtesy of A.T. & T. Company. Page 90: Dan Miller/Woodfin Camp. Page 97: Gabor Demjen/Stock Boston. Page 100: Joel Gordon. Page 105: Courtesy of NCR Corp. Page 110 bottom: Mark Antman.

Chapter 4   Chapter Opener: Christopher Morrow/Stock Boston. Page 124: Owen Franken/Stock Boston. Page 126: Courtesy of RCA Corp. Page 129: Courtesy of MortonNorwich. Page 134: Courtesy of Sears, Roebuck and Company.

Chapter 5   Chapter Opener: Gus Boyd/Photo Researchers. Page 163: Courtesy of Joyce E. Colon/Westinghouse Electric Corp. Page 166: Courtesy of George S. Moore. Page 175: Peter Angelo Simon/Photo Researchers. Page 177: Eiji Miyazawa/Black Star.

Chapter 6   Chapter Opener: Georg Gerster/Photo Researchers. Page 196: Library of Congress. Page 204: M. E. Warren/Photo Researchers. Page 205: Courtesy of Bell Labs. Page 214: Stephen L. Feldman/Photo Researchers. Page 216: Courtesy of Kaiser Industries.

Chapter 7   Chapter Opener: Nicholas Sapieha/Stock Boston. Page 234: Peter Menzel/Stock, Boston. Page 237: The Free Library of Philadelphia. Page 246: Christopher Morrow/Stock Boston. Page 249: Courtesy of Carnegie Corporation of New York.

Chapter 8   Chapter Opener: Ira Berger/Woodfin Camp. Page 270: Joel Gordon. Page 272: Courtesy Proctor & Gamble. Page 275: Rocky Weldon/ Leo de Wys. Page 280: Peter Southwick/Stock Boston.

Chapter 9   Chapter Opener: Bruce Roberts/Rapho-Photo Researchers. Page 309: Robert Houser/Photo Researchers. Page 310: Bruce Roberts/Photo Researchers. Page 312 top: Courtesy of Ford Motor Co. Page 312 bottom: Fabian Bachrach, Courtesy of General Motors Corp. Page 317: Courtesy of IBM.

Chapter 10   Chapter Opener: Mark Antman. Page 348: Ken Karp. Page 349: Cary Wolinsky/Stock Boston. Page 354: Rhoda Sidney/Monkmeyer. Page 358: Eiji Miyazwa/Blackstar.

Chapter 11   Chapter Opener: Ken Robert Buck/Stock Boston. Page 381: Robert George Gaylord/Black Star. Page 388: Courtesy of William Blackie. Page 391: Burk Uzzle/Magnum.

Chapter 12   Chapter Opener: Will McIntyre/Photo Researchers. Page 412: Courtesy of McDonnell Douglas Corp. Page 415: Jean Pierre Laffont/Sygma. Page 416: Ken Karp. Page 427: Courtesy of K mart Corp. Page 436: Peter Southwick/Stock Boston.

Chapter 13   Chapter Opener: Ken Karp. Page 452: James Foote. Page 456: Henry Ford Museum, The Edison Institute. Page 460: State Historical Society of Wisconsin. Page 463: Jerry Berndt/Stock Boston.

Chapter 14   Chapter Opener: Michael Hayman/Stock Boston. Page 490: Yale University Art Gallery, Gift of George Hoadley. Page 504: Courtesy of SAAB-Scania of America, Inc. Page 510: Ellis Herwig/Stock Boston. Page 519: Marvin E. Newman/Woodfin Camp.

Chapter 15   Chapter Opener: Joel Gordon. Page 538: U.S. Postal Service. Page 543: Photo by Karsh of Ottawa. Courtesy of Children's Television Workshop. Page 550: Courtesy of American Airlines. Page 559: Ed Hof/The Picture Cube.

INDEX